PEOPLE OF THE COVENANT

An Introduction to the Old Testament

HENRY JACKSON FLANDERS, Jr.
BAYLOR UNIVERSITY

ROBERT WILSON CRAPPS
FURMAN UNIVERSITY

DAVID ANTHONY SMITH
FURMAN UNIVERSITY

SECOND EDITION

JOHN WILEY & SONS
New York   Chichester   Brisbane   Toronto

ISBN 0 471 07011-4

Library of Congress Catalog Card Number: 74–190205

PRINTED IN THE UNITED STATES OF AMERICA

10 9 8 7

TO OUR STUDENTS
Our reason for being teachers

Preface

This textbook for the introductory course in the study of the Old Testament intends to give the beginning student a reliable foundation in Old Testament study. Assuming little previous preparation by the student, it is designed to be used in conjunction with primary biblical materials. Scripture passages appropriate to the subject under discussion are provided for each section.

People of the Covenant surveys the history of Israel, beginning with Genesis as the theological prelude to the history of a people of faith, and carrying Israel's story to the century preceding the Christian era. Our approach is interpretative. Using the Old Testament as a basis, archaeological, literary, and theological contributions are utilized to give a clear over-all picture of Old Testament history. Throughout, Israel's story is placed in its Ancient Near Eastern setting but is interpreted as distinct because of its profound religious dimension.

As a body of literature considered authoritative by a large segment of the modern religious community, the Old Testament has quickened the realization that much of our Western life and culture has Near Eastern roots. Both Jewish and Christian scholarship increasingly recognizes the significance of the moral, ethical, and religious message of the Old Testament for our time. During the past decade this scholarship has produced a body of research that is incorporated, where relevant, throughout the text. Ample attention is given to the treatment of the prophets and Wisdom writings and we have endeavored to clarify the development of postexilic Judaism.

In addition to scripture assignments, teaching aids include illustrations, chronological charts within and at the end of the

v

book, maps, glossary, annotated bibliographies at the end of each chapter, and a general bibliography.

The scripture quotations in this volume are from the *Revised Standard Version of the Bible*, copyrighted 1946 and 1952 by the Division of Christian Education, National Council of Churches, and used by permission. Usually "Yahweh" has been inserted for "the LORD." Quotations from J. B. Pritchard, *Ancient Near Eastern Texts*, are used with the permission of Princeton University Press.

Obviously the selection and arrangement of materials and comparative emphases remain the responsibility of the authors. However, our work could not have gone forward without continuing suggestions and support from faculty and administration colleagues and encouragement from our families. For this we are deeply grateful.

HENRY JACKSON FLANDERS, JR.
ROBERT WILSON CRAPPS
DAVID ANTHONY SMITH

Waco, Texas
Greenville, S.C.
November, 1972

Contents

CK SEA

A R M E N I A

CASPIAN
SEA

T I G R I S

M E S O

HARAN

S Y R I A

NINEVEH

MEDIA

P O T A M I A

NUZI

E U P H R A T E S

MARI

R I V E R

R I V E R

A R A B I A N

BABYLON

B A B Y L O N I A

DESERT

E NEAR EAST

PERSIAN
GULF

0   50   100   200

PEOPLE OF THE COVENANT

An Introduction to the Old Testament

1

Setting the Stage

THE OLD TESTAMENT INTERPRETATION OF HISTORY

The Old Testament is a collection of literature from ancient Israel. This literature took shape over a period of more than a thousand years and contains numerous different literary types and styles. Although diversity and complexity are present throughout, the whole of Old Testament literature has in common an orientation toward history and a deep religious faith. This literature's primary concern is to interpret the workings of God within the events of Israel's history. Through its pages run the scientific, theological, and psychological ideas of the day, but the elaboration of these is not its focus of attention. The Old Testament centers upon the action of God in the affairs of men as they react to him and seek to interpret the meaning of his action for life and faith. Even though it deals extensively with the affairs of Israel in history, it is a history book only in the sense that history is the context in which the acts of God are described.

The Israelite Understanding of History

The Old Testament is first and foremost a presentation and interpretation of the acts of God. Its writers looked at events as men of faith; they wrote as men of faith. For them the essence of history was the revelation of God, and as a consequence, their understanding of history was colored by their understanding of God. God played a prommient role in the life of the Israelites,

3

and it was natural for him to do so, because history is the arena of his activity.

Thus, in the Old Testament, history and faith are inextricably combined. On the one hand, God's continual action in the things which happened to the nation shaped her self-consciousness. Every remembered event in Israel's history molded the theological thought of the people—their understanding of themselves in relation to their God. On the other hand, the peculiarly molded mind of Israel, with its orientation toward God, caused the memory of that history to be constructed in a particular way. Israel's religious mind was ever active in selecting, arranging, interpreting, and revitalizing the historical memories so that they finally took the form in which we now have them. Thus, both event and religious interpretation of event were incorporated in the Hebrew understanding of history. This theological orientation in no way negates the historical value of the Old Testament historical narratives. It does mean, however, that the record is the product of theological selection and interpretation. While the facts of the events remain just as real, they may be clothed in extraordinary forms. The forms are the vehicle and the vehicle does not negate the fact it carries. History so written sometimes makes factual summary most difficult, if not impossible. Such history at times obscures distinctions between historical data and later meanings attached to those data, but these distinctions are not always necessary to the understanding of religious truth contained in the writing.

The Crucial Moment

The merging of history and faith in Old Testament literature is typified in the way that two prominent events are treated. These events are the Exodus from Egypt and the establishment of the covenant with God at Sinai. Together they form the crucial moment in Israelite history. Deliverance from Egypt is the mighty act of God by which he emphatically demonstrates his peculiar concern for Israel. All which preceded this moment is interpreted in its light. It gives meaning to everything which follows. Both Israel's conception of God and her awareness of her own destiny can be traced to that time when God delivered her from bondage in Egypt and made her his own people at Sinai by entering into covenant with her.

Survey of the History of Israel

The Old Testament begins with a theological prologue to the history of Israel. Genesis 1–11 sets the stage for all which follows, poignantly portraying mankind as sinful and in need of forgiveness and assistance from God. Against this backdrop the Old Testament drama is to be viewed and interpreted. The history of Israel is the record of the particular people through whom God worked to make his forgiveness and assistance available to all peoples. This record begins with the patriarchal ancestors of Israel who moved from Haran in Mesopotamia into Canaan sometime after 2000 B.C. In Canaan they lived as nomads in the central hill country. During a time of famine, they moved into Egypt where adequate food was available. Settling there, they found favor with the Egyptians and prospered. Eventually, however, they were enslaved by the Egyptian pharaoh and their life became burdensome.

  I. Patriarchal period, c. 2000–1700. (Genesis 12–50)
 II. Period of national formation, c. 1700–1000. (Exodus, Numbers, Joshua, Judges)
    A. Sojourn in Egypt, c. 1700–1300
    B. Exodus from Egypt, c. 1280
    C. Conquest of Canaan, c. 1250–1200
    D. Amphictyony, c. 1200–1020
III. Monarchy, 1020–587. (Samuel; Kings, Chronicles)
    A. United Monarchy, 1020–922
    B. Divided Monarchy,
      1. Israel, 922–722/21
      2. Judah, 922–587
IV. Exile in Babylon, 597–538.
 V. Restoration and Reconstruction, 538–63. (Ezra, Nehemiah)
    A. Under the Persians, 538–332
    B. Under the Greeks, 332–167
    C. Independence, 167–63

Figure 1–1. Outline of Old Testament history. The biblical books in parentheses are the narrative sources for the periods with which they are listed.

During the reign of Ramses II (1290–1224), the Israelites escaped from Egypt under the leadership of Moses. They spent a generation in desert wanderings. Most important among the events of this period was the religious experience they had at Sinai, the holy mountain of God, by which they were forged into a religious unity—the people of Yahweh, the name by which God was particularly known by the Israelites.

Around the middle of the thirteenth century B.C., Joshua succeeded Moses as leader of the Israelite tribes and led them into Canaan. There, joined by some kindred tribes who had not gone down into Egypt, Joshua and the people won a series of signal victories over the Canaanites and made the land their own. At the conclusion of this conquest Joshua loosely organized the Israelites into an amphictyony, or religious confederacy, of twelve tribes. The unifying factor was the worship of the same God, Yahweh, at a central sanctuary. This religio-political organization served adequately for more than two centuries. During this time, Israel was busy securing her hold upon Canaan. Increasing pressure from enemies made necessary a more efficient political organization.

A monarchy was established with Saul as king, and under his successor, David, it blossomed into an empire. This empire, however, was short-lived. It began to decline during the reign of Solomon, David's son and successor. Immediately after Solomon's death (922 B.C.) the empire was divided into two kingdoms, Israel in the north and Judah in the south. These kingdoms, greatly weakened by the division, became pawns of the great empires of the Ancient Near East. Their destinies were largely determined by the international affairs of Egypt, Assyria, and Babylon. The northern kingdom lasted only until 722/721 B.C., when it was overrun by Assyria and many of its inhabitants were scattered across the East. Soon thereafter the southern kingdom became a vassal of Assyria and remained so until 612 B.C. when the Assyrian empire fell before the rising power of Babylon. Then Babylon became the oppressor of Judah. In 587 B.C. Nebuchadnezzar, king of Babylon, destroyed Jerusalem, the capital of Judah, and carried the major portion of the Judean people to Babylon as captives. However, Babylon soon lost her world supremacy to the Persian empire (539 B.C.), under whose benevolent rule the exiles of Judah were allowed to return home. Under the leadership of Sheshbazzar, Zerubbabel, Ezra, and Nehemiah the returned exiles rebuilt Jerusalem and restructured their way of life.

Sources for Israelite History

The ancients did not write histories. They kept chronicles and preserved traditions, even elaborated on certain outstanding events; but they left nothing like ordered historical and interpretive accounts of their past. Even a people like Israel for whom history was particularly important had little interest in history writing as a critical analytical literary method. Nothing existed anywhere in the ancient world like the kind of historical records and analyses we know in modern history texts or in portrayals like Bruce Catton's works on the American Civil War. Undoubtedly the ancient world had skilled chroniclers and occasionally able interpreters of isolated events. One of the earliest and ablest of the latter was the Israelite who recorded with brilliance the dramatic and tragic events of David's affair with Bathsheba and the disintegration of his family and court (II Samuel 9–20; I Kings 1, 2). This historian (and this writer is worthy of the name) and his work was an isolated phenomenon in Israel. Any attempt therefore to reconstruct the history of ancient Israel must recognize at the outset that the sources available are not the sort with which a modern research historian customarily works.

The Old Testament Narratives. The single most important source for the history of Israel is the Old Testament. Extensive historical narratives within the Old Testament preserve the traditions of Israel's beginnings, her settlement and life in Canaan (Palestine), and her exile from and return to that land. Traditions of the patriarchs; traditions of exodus and conquest; traditions of the monarchy, exile, and restoration provide the biblical narration of the nation's past and her destiny as Yahweh's people. All of these materials constitute Israel's memory of events in her experience which were pregnant with religious meaning. While this kind of memory does not shape history in a formal scientific sense, it offers data of greater value. To some extent the history of Israel may be reconstructed from these materials, but more significantly they provide insight into the life and faith of a believing community.

The historical narratives in the Old Testament, for the most part, are not firsthand contemporary records comparable to those found in the inscriptions and records of other ancient peoples. Instead they are religious works which have gone through a long history of compiling, editing, and copying. These include traditions of Israel's origins, a history of Israel in the land of Canaan, and a priestly overview of all Israelite history.

1. *Traditions of Israel's Origins.* Fortunately two complementary collections of material about the origins of the Israelite community of faith have been preserved in the Old Testament. Each in its own way is a compilation of earlier traditional material of varied character and form and of diverse origin and purpose. The authors who shaped these collections should not, however, be thought of as mere compilers or editors. Their works are brilliant theological expositions of Israel's origins and the meaning of Israel's faith.

a. *The Yahwistic Tradition.* The earliest interpretation of Israel's origins was written in the southern kingdom of Judah sometime around the tenth century B.C. [1] It is often called "Yahwistic" because of a decided preference which its author shows for the divine name Yahweh, the peculiarly Israelite personal name of God. This work is of epic proportions and combines Israelite traditions from the creation of the world to the conquest of the land of Canaan. Drawing from the reservoir of oral tradition, the Yahwist (as the author is usually designated) constructed a literary masterwork. Writing as a man of faith and as a member of the Israelite covenant community, he chose as his starting point the historical moment of the Exodus, the moment when the Hebrew people enslaved in Egypt became the people of Yahweh. He then expanded the account of the Exodus by including materials dealing with the Sinai covenant and the conquest of Canaan. Moving backward from this point, he brought together stories about the patriarchs—Abraham, Isaac, and Jacob —unifying them around the theme of the promise made to Abra-

---

[1] The sequence of these histories is more firmly established than the precise dates assigned to them.

ham. He then added the stories of primeval history—those early stories which show God's concern, not for Israel alone, but for the entire race of man. In all of this he wanted to express Israel's faith in Yahweh, whose acts of redemption had been manifested in Israel's history.

  b. *The Elohistic Tradition.* A second tradition covering the same span of time, with the exception of the stories of primeval history, was written about a century later in the northern kingdom of Israel. Its author, who is called "the Elohist" because of his use of the divine name Elohim (the common Semitic name for God), gave expression to the covenant faith as it was embodied in the North. This history preserves the traditions of the ancient tribal confederacy and centers around the themes of the promise to the patriarchs, the Exodus from Egypt, the wandering in the wilderness, and the conquest of Canaan. To a large extent it is based upon the Yahwistic account, with which the Elohistic writer seems to have been familiar and which he may have used as a source. Overall, however, it seems to lack both the theological breadth and depth and the literary artistry of its Yahwistic predecessor. Perhaps this is because the Elohist tradition is only partially preserved and serves for the most part to supplement the better preserved Yahwistic materials.

Soon after the fall of the northern kingdom in 722/721 B.C., Judean editors combined the Yahwistic and Elohistic traditions into a literary unit. They naturally gave preference to the southern version and often bound the two accounts together inseparably. As a consequence, the Elohistic tradition is only fragmentarily preserved. The combined Yahwistic and Elohistic material is found in Genesis, Exodus, and Numbers.

  2. *A History of Israel in the Land of Canaan.* A more extensive history was written in the sixth century during, or just after, the Babylonian exile. It is a monumental record of Israel from Moses to the exile and includes the books of Deuteronomy, Joshua, Judges, I and II Samuel, and I and II Kings. Following a well-thought-out plan and a unified theological perspective, it presents a description of "Israel in her land" from the viewpoint of the theology of history found in the book of Deuteronomy: obedience to Yahweh leads to welfare and peace; disobedience

to Yahweh leads to hardship and defeat. This "philosophy" colored the author's approach to the history of his people and determined the materials to be included in his account. This Deuteronomic history is, therefore, like the Yahwistic and Elohistic traditions, a subjective interpretation written from the viewpoint of a man of faith.

3. *The Priestly Overview of all Israel's History.* A priestly group led in the restoration of the Israelite community after the return from Babylonian exile. Among other things they produced an extensive representation of Israel's history. It is embodied in two works, a Priestly stratum within the books of Genesis through Numbers and a unified retelling of Israel's story in the books of Chronicles-Ezra-Nehemiah. The material in Genesis through Numbers is primarily concerned with Israel's religious institutions but also preserves variant forms of some of the traditions used by the Yahwist and Elohist. The period from creation to Moses is divided into four successive eras, as if God's revelation followed a prearranged systematic plan. The first of these eras extends from the creation to the flood, the second from the flood to Abraham, the third from Abraham to Moses. The fourth era encompasses Moses and the Sinai legislation. In this framework the priestly history sets the origin and development of the Israelite cultic legislation. Much of the material out of which this history is constructed is quite ancient and was taken from the temple archives which the priests had saved when the temple was destroyed.

Using their own document as a framework, the priestly writers edited a unified history from creation to the conquest in which they incorporated the previously combined Yahwistic and Elohistic accounts. The result is the combined tradition found in Genesis, Exodus, Leviticus, and Numbers. These materials were soon united with Deuteronomy and with secular and cultic legal codes to form the Book of Law (Torah). This collection is often designated by the term Pentateuch.

The second of the priestly histories, Chronicles-Ezra-Nehemiah, begins with Moses and retells the story of the Israelite people down to the time of the restoration of the nation following the Babylonian exile. For the early part of this period it roughly parallels the narratives in Samuel and Kings, upon which it de-

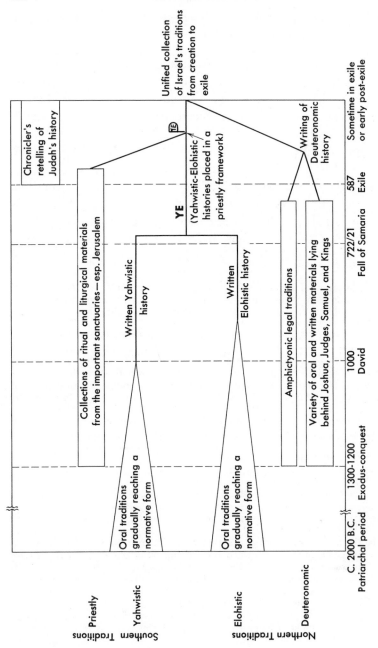

Figure 1–2. The development of Israel's historical and legal traditions.

pends for source material. For the postexilic age it draws upon the memoirs of Nehemiah and Ezra.[2]

Archaeological Discoveries. Another important source of information about ancient Israel is the vast amount of material brought to light by archaeology. Exploration and excavation in the Near East have made available to biblical scholars a wealth of information about the world in which Israel lived and the ancient empires and peoples with whom the Israelites had contact. Each year this knowledge increases as more questions are answered by the penetration of pick and trowel. This information, however, is much more specific about surrounding nations than it is about Israel herself. From cuneiform [3] texts on clay tablets, from monumental inscriptions in Syria, Mesopotamia, and Asia-Minor-Armenia, and from hieroglyphic [4] representations on

[2] The publication of Julius Wellhausen's *Prolegomena To The History of Israel* in 1885 established an approach to the materials in the Pentateuch which became standard for biblical scholarship. Wellhausen maintained that these books were the combination of four documents labeled J for Yahwist, E for Elohist, D for Deuteronomist, and P for Priestly. Wellhausen held that the sequence of the documents was unquestionably from earliest to latest (JEDP) and that they reflected the evolutionary development of the faith and culture of Israel. Upon the earlier traditions it "recorded" J imposed the faith and customs of Israel at the time of its writing about 980 B.C. E did the same. D was the prophetic distillation of ethics and religion, while P presupposed the fully developed cultus of the postexile.

This hypothesis, regnant in scholarship for over half a century, has been greatly modified by more recent studies. Although the Wellhausen sequence is accepted as established, his evolutionary presuppositions have been largely rejected. It is now understood that each "document" is the compilation of oral traditions which can be traced far back of their time of writing. Thus, they reflect the circumstances of both the period they describe and the time in which they were finally edited. A full and able discussion of this development is found in C. R. North, "Pentateuchal Criticism," in *The Old Testament and Modern Study*, H. H. Rowley, ed., 48–83.

[3] Cuneiform was the wedge-shaped method of writing used for many ancient Semitic languages. The reading of cuneiform inscriptions of the Mesopotamian area is largely due to the work of Sir Henry Rawlinson in deciphering the famed Behistun Rock, an inscription carved on the side of a mountain in the Zagros range. This inscription, dating to the time of Darius I (522–486), is a trilingual recounting of the military exploits of the Persian king. Beginning his work in A.D. 1835, Rawlinson painstakingly copied and deciphered the inscription, thereby unlocking the secrets of Babylonian cuneiform literature.

[4] Hieroglyphics was the picture method of writing used by the ancient Egyptians. The decipherment of Egyptian hieroglyphics was made possible by the discovery in A.D. 1798 of the Rosetta Stone, a slab of black granite found in the Nile Delta by members of a Napoleonic expedition. Like the Behistun Rock, the Rosetta Stone was covered with a trilingual inscription. The latter included the old hieroglyphic, an ordinary Egyptian script, and Greek. Starting with the Greek, a French scholar, Champollion, began deciphering the hieroglyphic and by A.D. 1822 was able to announce that he could read the language of ancient Egypt.

Egyptian temples, government buildings, tombs, and papyrus scrolls, come contemporary records from ancient Assyria, Babylon, Hatti, Egypt, and elsewhere. These include royal inscriptions, temple records, business documents, private correspondence, and religious texts. Of particular importance are inscriptional materials of many types which reflect the movement of peoples throughout the Near Eastern world and the chronicles of various states which give extensive information about their national and international affairs. Without materials like these the affairs of Israel's ancient neighbors would be relatively unknown. With them the histories of Egypt, Assyria, and Babylon can be extensively reconstructed. Comparable materials from ancient Israel, for the most part, have not been found.

The civilizations of the Ancient Near East have also been illuminated by vast amounts of non-inscriptional materials. Articles of everyday use, objects of art, public and private buildings, and even entire cities have been uncovered. The Old Testament world at large is, therefore, well illustrated and in some cases is far better known than some more recent historical periods.

P lestinian archaeology [5] has recovered the daily life of Israelites. It has uncovered cities, revealing homes, pottery, tools, fortifications, means of storing food and water, and innumerable other details about life and customs. The time when certain Palestinian cities were attacked and destroyed has been determined, and occasionally the fate of their inhabitants has been graphically revealed. The building and commercial enterprises of David, Solomon, and other important kings of Israel and Judah have been illustrated. However, few specific inscriptions from Israelite kings have been found [6] and almost no private inscriptional material has yet come to light. There is an agricultural calendar from Gezer, some inscribed jar seals from various Palestinian cities, and some military correspondence from Lachish. Archaeology in Palestine thus has painted a vivid background of Israelite history, but unfortunately it has not filled in many gaps in the story.

[5] For details of Palestinian archaeology see: W. F. Albright, *The Archaeology of Palestine;* G. E. Wright, *Biblical Archaeology;* L. H. Grollenberg, *Atlas of The Bible;* and the journals *The Biblical Archaeologist* and *Bulletin of The American Schools of Oriental Research.*

[6] The names of some Israelite kings have been found on ostraca and similar objects, but lengthy inscriptions are almost entirely unknown.

Specific References to Israel from Ancient Near Eastern Records. Archaeological discoveries from outside Palestine have furnished important specific information about Israel. Inscriptions and records from Egypt, Assyria, Babylon, and elsewhere occasionally mention contacts which these nations made with one of the Hebrew kingdoms. The Egyptian pharaoh Merneptah (1224–1216) mentions Israel in a stele erected in his fifth year. According to the annals of Shalmanezer III of Assyria, Ahab of Israel contributed 200 chariots and 10,000 men to a coalition which fought against Assyria in 853 B.C. Jehu of Israel is pictured on the Black Obelisk of Shalmaneser III in the only known representation of an Israelite monarch. Another Assyrian ruler, Sargon II (722–705), described the destruction of Samaria which brought to an end the kingdom of Israel in 722/721 B.C. His successor Sennacherib (705–681) described an attack upon Judah by which the Judean king Hezekiah was "shut up like a caged bird within Jerusalem." In his chronicles Nebuchadnezzar of Babylon gives details about his attack on Jerusalem, which in 587 B.C. brought to an end the southern kingdom of Judah. These and similar references from extra-biblical sources have provided welcome supplements to the biblical narratives themselves. Such references are not without problems, however, because it is frequently difficult to correlate them with information in the biblical narratives.

When these biblical and nonbiblical materials are supplemented by the exciting diverse non-narrative literature which grew out of various periods in Israel's history, a comprehensive picture of Israel's life and faith emerges. Prophetic oracles, apocalyptic visions, and wisdom poems cannot always be easily placed in their proper historical context; however, when they can be accurately located, our understanding of that period of Israel's history is enriched. Further the historical background aids the interpretation of the prophetic oracle, wisdom saying, or apocalyptic vision.

Literature in the History of Israel

Old Testament literature includes large blocks of material which relate Israel's history, but hymns sung in worship, laws for cult and state, oracles or sermons from prophets, and didactic poems and short stories are also part of her holy writings. Whatever their literary type, however, Hebrew scriptures ought to be approached within their proper historical context. The relationship of the literature to Israel's history may be previewed thus:

I. Patriarchal period, 2000–1700. No literary activity can be traced to this period. Oral, tribal, ancestral traditions were shaped and circulated.

II. Period of national formation, 1700–1000. Continuation of the oral tradition and, late in the period, the beginning of literary collection: Song of Deborah (Judges 5); Song of Miriam (Exodus 15:21); liturgical confession (Deuteronomy 26:5–11); and early legal and cultic traditions (Exodus 20:1–17).

III. United Monarchy, c. 1020–922. Collection of tribal traditions which were later expanded and edited into great epic traditions of the history of all Israel; expansion of legal and cultic traditions. Toward the end of this period the first epic of Israel's beginnings (the Yahwistic tradition), was edited in Judah; traditions from David's reign, particularly the court history in II Samuel 9–20 and I Kings 1–2; beginning of wisdom literature; continuing expansion of legal and cultic traditions.

IV. Divided Monarchy: Israel and Judah coexisting, 922–722. Second epic of Israel's beginning (the Elohistic tradition); earliest prophetic narratives (Elijah and Elisha materials); early historical materials from Israel and Judah; continued development of legal and cultic material.

V. Divided Monarchy: Judah alone, 722–587. Collection of prophetic oracles of Amos, Hosea, Micah, Isaiah, Jeremiah (not all of these books but major portions thereof; each book contains some later additions, some contain considerable later additions); earliest form of Deuteronomy and the Deuteronomic history of Israel in her land (Joshua-II Kings); continued growth of legal and cultic materials.

VI. Exile, 597–538. Ezekiel, Deutero-Isaiah (chs. 40–66); Priestly tradition of Israel's origins; collection of Psalms; elaboration of wisdom materials; Lamentations.

VII. Post Exile, 538–63. Late prophetic writings; apocalyptic literature in Daniel; Ruth and Esther; Job and Ecclesiastes; Chronicler's history work.

INTERPRETATION OF OLD TESTAMENT LITERATURE

Literary Historical Interpretation

The Old Testament's theological concern for history as the arena of God's activity, or Heilsgeschichte (salvation history), makes imperative a concern for the historical setting of Old Testament literature for one who studies it. Critical scholarship (in the sense of careful analytical investigation) tries, therefore, to discover, so far as is possible, the identity of the author, the time and place of origin, and the sources used for each major section of the Old Testament. These things are not as self-evident for ancient literature as one might assume and traditions about them are frequently misleading. For example, the idea that all of Genesis through Deuteronomy was written by Moses early in Israel's history overlooks the complex historical background of rich and diverse literature which actually developed over nearly a millennium of changing Israelite history. Careful study of the Torah has called in question the tradition, but has illuminated in a way that tradition never could, the real historical background in which Israel's early traditions and her legal and cultic systems developed. This kind of study of Old Testament literature is called literary criticism and proceeds by analysis of vocabulary, style, content, and historical allusions. Besides date and authorship, literary criticism is concerned with internal structure of a section or book. Is it a unity? If not, what is the nature of any additions and what are the stages by which the work has developed to its present form? This kind of analysis is not just a matter of historical curiosity. Rather, it grows out of the fundamental concern to take seriously the literature's concern for history and to discover something of the historical unfolding of Israel's life and faith. The discussions of the various sections of Old Testament literature to follow will use this methodology in such a way that its significant contributions will become increasingly apparent.

Literary criticism, however, is only one way to recover the context in life, the actual historical situation, of various sections of the Old Testament literature. Many parts of the Old Testament are already editorial gatherings of material of diverse origin and purpose, and consequently are literary products only in a secondary or redactional sense; literary criticism cannot alone restore the original setting and purpose of a given unit. Individual passages must be carefully analyzed to determine their setting and the form of their presentation. This analysis of form brings the student closest to a passage's context and purpose.

Study of Literary Types

The Old Testament is filled with fascinating literary diversity. Recognition of this variety enriches one's enjoyment and understanding of this significantly rewarding collection of religious literature. One discovers that scripture is not necessarily dull and prosaic—although some of it may well be—but exciting and stimulating literary fare. Religiously this is quite important because theologically important ideas cannot grasp the heart unless their expression grasps the mind. An awareness of various literary types in the Old Testament makes reading scripture more enjoyable and stimulating. Further such knowledge clarifies the origins, development, use, and meaning of any given section of Israelite religious writings.

Form Criticism. Literature grows out of or is applied to specific situations. Thus the interpreter of a text must ask: "Who is speaking?" "Who is listening?" "What is the prevailing mood of the situation?" "What effect is sought?" These are questions raised by literary criticism about large units of material. Form criticism asks them about more limited sections and goes even further. "What literary type is involved?" "What is the nature and history of this type of literature and for what purpose is it regularly used?" At the same time one must ask: "What other texts apply to this or similar situations?" "How do these texts relate to one another?" "What do they together tell us about the kind of situation to which they relate?" One writer sums this up by saying, "no biblical text can be adequately understood without a consideration of the setting in life of its literary type . . . no way of life in ancient Israel . . . can be exhaustively detailed without a thorough study of all literary types relating to it." [7] Therefore, analysis of literary forms in which Israel expressed her traditions and beliefs pushes study behind the "documents" of the Old Testament to the formative influences and sources of the literature. In addition, study of literary form has shown how closely Old Testament literature was bound up with the life of the Israelite people. It was not literature "for the sake of art" but literature "for the sake of life."

[7] Klaus Koch, *The Growth of the Biblical Tradition,* p. 33.

Varieties of Literary Types and Their Importance for Old Testament Interpretation. The basic types are poetry and prose. Variations in each category are numerous, but selected examples of each will illustrate their character, content, and style. A simple systematic classification of poetry and prose types gives some sense of the richness of Israelite literature.[8]

1. *Poetry.* In Israel poetry as a literary type is probably older than prose. It was characteristic of early peoples who ascribed special power and effectiveness to fixed formula with rhythmic wording and sound. Poetry in Israel often retains the power of an utterance objectively directed to change a situation. For example, the formula of priestly benediction in Numbers 6:24–26 undoubtedly intended to create the ends about which it speaks:

> The Lord bless you and keep you:
> The Lord make his face to shine upon
>   you and be gracious to you:
> The Lord lift up his countenance upon
>   you and give you peace.

as did the commissioning of a prophet in Jeremiah 1:9–10:

> Behold, I have put my words in your mouth.
> See, I have set you this day over nations and
>   over kingdoms,
> to pluck up and to break down,
> to destroy and to overthrow,
> to build and to plant.

Most Old Testament poetry has advanced beyond this stage of "set words" to be applied in certain life situations, but it has its roots in that sort of dynamic attempt to deal with reality.

Out of these roots Israel developed an extensive poetic literature. A sharp line between poetry and prose cannot be drawn everywhere in the Old Testament. Nonetheless certain characteristics of Hebrew poetry are distinguishable. Clearly rhythmic arrangement was typical. Hebrew songs were sung to the accompaniment of music and dancing. Unfortunately the old tradition of rhythm was lost and cannot be reconstructed, but apparently

---

[8] This procedure is followed in the form-critical sections of the introductions of Eissfeldt, Weiser, and with modifications Sellin-Fohrer. Klaus Koch, *The Growth of the Biblical Tradition*, pp. 25–26, points out some of the disadvantages of this kind of classification. These disadvantages, however, are not significant for a beginning study of the Old Testament.

rhythm was a matter of stress or emphasis based on significant words and the thought structure of the poetic line. A more certain feature of Hebrew poetry was the regular use of verses with two parts or lines which have a definite relationship to each other. In some cases the relationship is a direct parallelism [9] in thought between the first and second members.

> The earth is Yahweh's and the fulness thereof.
> the world and those that dwell therein. (Psalm 24:1)

Or there can be an antithesis between the ideas expressed in the two lines, so that the antithesis of the second line sharpens the emphasis of the first.

> Yahweh knows the way of the righteous,
> but the way of the wicked will perish. (Psalm 1:6)

Often the second line merely continues or completes the idea of the first.

> I have set my king
> on Zion, my holy hill. (Psalm 2:6)[10]

These basic forms appear in both simple and complex arrangements. The best way to understand the rich variety of Old Testament poetry is to read it. The following classification gives examples of the more important types of poetry.[11]

Sayings: Sayings represent attempts on occasions of almost every kind to express thoughts with solemnity, richness of expression, or exhilaration not common to everyday speech. Their range is extensive.
1. Sayings from the life of an individual: Psalm 127:3, Genesis 35:17, Isaiah 9:5, Psalm 2:7, Genesis 2:23, Genesis 24:60, Ruth 4:11, Hosea 2:4, Job 1:21.
2. Sayings from the life of the community: II Samuel 15:10, I Samuel 10:24, II Samuel 14:4, Exodus 17:16, Numbers 10: 35–36, II Samuel 10:12, I Kings 5:17, Genesis 9:6, Deuteronomy 25:9.

[9] Thus the term *Parallelismus membrorum* which is applied to this characteristic of Hebrew poetry. It is not fully appropriate but is regularly used.

[10] Under the designation *Parallelismus membrorum*, the first of these examples is called "synonymous parallelism," the second "antithetical parallelism," and the third, which is not really a parallelism at all, "formal" or "synthetic" parallelism.

[11] The classification is based on that in Otto Eissfeldt, *The Old Testament: an Introduction.*

3. Cultic sayings:
   a. Divine sayings (sayings where the speaker is under-
     stood to be Yahweh, although the spokesman is
     known to be a priest or prophet): Exodus 33:19,
     Exodus 22:28, Leviticus 11:44–45.
   b. Priestly sayings: Numbers 6:24–26, Zechariah 2:17.
4. Prophetic sayings: here are included most oracles of
   the prophets, many of which are adaptations or utiliza-
   tions of other literary forms. Typical examples are:
   Jeremiah 2:1–3, 5–13, Amos 2:6–11, 4:1–3, 5:2–5.
5. Wisdom sayings:
   a. Proverbs: Jeremiah 23:28, I Kings 20:11, Jeremiah
     21:29, Proverbs 13:3, Isaiah 10:15.
   b. Riddles: Judges 14:14, 18.
   c. Wisdom sayings, practical wisdom for living: Prov-
     erbs 10.

Songs: Israel loved singing and its literature is filled with songs.
Most of these are cultic, but some secular songs are also
preserved.
1. Secular songs: Numbers 21:17–18, Song of Solomon, II
   Samuel 1:19–27, 3:33–34.
2. Cultic songs:
   a. Hymns: Psalms 8, 29, 47, 65, 87, 100, 105, 150.
   b. Communal Laments: Psalms 44, 74, 79, 80, 85, 123.
   c. Individual Laments: Psalms 3–7, 12, 25, 28, 140.
   d. Songs of Thanksgiving: Psalms 67, 124, 30, 32, 41.
   e. Songs associated with the life of the king: Psalms
     2, 18, 20, 45, 72, 110.
   f. Wisdom Songs: Psalms 1, 37, 49, 73, 91.

2. *Prose.* In the present form the stylistic characteristics of
Old Testament prose is frequently the result of transmission and
editing. Generally, however, in prose narrative the language
moves forward passionately from word to word and action to
action. Numerous short sentences are linked together by *and*
with the effect of moving swiftly to a sudden conclusion. Other
peculiarities of prose are determined to a large extent by the
literary type. A wide variety of prose forms was used in Israelite
literature. These can be classified into four comprehensive
groups: speeches, records, laws, and narratives. Like Israelite
poetry, Israelite prose can be appreciated best by examination of
some typical examples.

Speeches: Speeches include sermons and prayers which also represent immediate contact between speaker and person
or persons addressed.

        1. Speeches: Joshua 24, I Samuel 12, I Kings 2:1–9, Judges 9:7–20, II Kings 18:19–25, 28–35.

        2. Sermons: Deuteronomy 3:18–22, 7:1–26, Ezekiel 20.

        3. Prayers: Judges 16:28, I Kings 3:6–9, Judges 10:10.

Records: Relatively few Israelite records have been preserved. Those available are particularly interesting.

        1. Contracts: Genesis 21:22–32, 31:44–54, I Kings 5:16–23.

        2. Lists: Genesis 10, I Chronicles 1–9, II Samuel 8:16–18, Exodus 35:21–29.

Laws: The Old Testament contains laws regulating every aspect of Israel's life: Exodus 21:2–22, Deuteronomy 15:12–18.

Narratives: [12] 1. Narratives with poetic non-literal character: These narratives represent the popular comment on what has happened, kept alive by oral tradition. Examples include: Genesis 2:4b–4:26, Genesis 11, Genesis 25:1–6 and 16:4–14, Genesis 25:21–26, Exodus 4:24–26.

        2. Historical narratives: Judges 9, II Samuel 9–20, I Kings 1–2.

        3. Novella or short stories of particular persons in historical setting: Genesis 37, 39–48, 50, Ruth and Jonah.

DEVELOPMENT AND PRESERVATION OF OLD TESTAMENT LITERATURE

In a sense the study of Old Testament literature is an adventure in faith. Both poetic and prose forms were developed and preserved among a people who understood themselves as a faith community and judged their literature to be religiously valuable to their faith and worship. Works were preserved by pious men who considered it a part of their religious obligation. In history, through the lives of leaders, and by means of religious institutions, Israel claimed the power of God in the selection and preservation of materials of high value and lasting merit. The very existence of the Old Testament is a fact of significant theological value. Insofar as contemporary Jewish and Christian communities continue to see God active in the transmission of the literature through centuries of trial and conflict, they share the faith of ancient Israel.

---

[12] All narrative types originate in storytelling.

Origins

Much of the prose and poetry of the Old Testament was handed down in fragments from generation to generation by word of mouth or in written form. Certain types of the literature went through a long stage of oral tradition, being transmitted from father to son to grandson with a great degree of accuracy. Only gradually was it gathered into larger collections. In this way the ancient traditions were preserved, passed on, and collected in the period before Israel became literary minded.

Writing played a fairly insignificant role in the ancient world and was confined, for the most part, to specialists. Ancient peoples "learned by heart" the traditions which were meaningful to them and trained their memory to be extraordinarily retentive. Those skilled in memory were signally honored.

The scribe who learns his text by heart escapes the enemy, is honored in his own land. In the congregation of the learned where my name is constantly spoken I will open his ears.[13]

Israel shared with her neighbors this ability to learn by heart. In the period before the Israelite monarchy the great religious traditions of Israel were preserved and shaped in the human memory. They were recited by poets and singers at religious festivals, social gatherings, or other public occasions.

As we read the literature of the Old Testament, therefore, we do well to remind ourselves constantly that its stories were made to be told, its psalms to be sung, its oracles to be spoken with authority, its laws to be the memoranda of the authorities in a court of appeals.[14]

Early Collections. Inevitably various units of tradition must have been written down and copies of them treasured as religious possessions of tribal and local communities. So, for example, certain tribes treasured the traditions about Abraham while others preserved the Jacob stories.

Units of tradition were woven into cycles of stories stamped with peculiar emphases and experiences of Israel's various tribes. These tribal traditions, recited at annual religious ceremonies,

---

[13] Quoted in Eduard Nielsen, *Oral Tradition*, p. 19. Persons in the Near East have retained this skill. Some Arabs can recite the entire Koran without mistake, even though they can neither read nor write.

[14] H. W. Robinson, *The Old Testament: Its Making and Meaning*, p. 21.

were gradually welded into great Israelite "sagas." Among them were sagas on the patriarchs, the deliverance from Egypt, the wandering in the wilderness, the giving of the law of Sinai, and the conquest of Canaan. Such traditions became shaped by liturgical usage and reached a fairly uniform oral form prior to the rise of the monarchy under Saul and David.

To facilitate transmission, material was gathered around small "memory units" which shared a characteristic style and form.[15] These individual "memory units" came out of living situations. They were associated with some act or event, historic or cultic. Gradually the meaning of the event took concrete form of expression within the "memory unit." Deuteronomy 26:5–10, for instance, is an early credal confession around which an extended tradition was built.[16] Its confession of Yahweh as director of Israel's ancestors became the basis for an elaborate narrative of national origins. By this slow process of historical refinement Israel found means for expressing her covenant faith. Superficial items were eliminated; the important was emphasized; the precise word was selected. Some stories which probably circulated among other peoples were transformed into vehicles to express Israel's faith in God. When literary activity began to flourish in Israel during the days of the monarchy, there was a great reservoir of material, both oral and written, from which a writer could draw. And this deposit gradually became larger.

Collections of materials of similar nature were continually being made and existing collections were being expanded. Just as a great historical tradition was gathered around the small credo of Deuteronomy 26:5–10, so were collections of laws, songs, prophetic utterances, and wisdom materials made by individuals or groups who were particularly interested in each of these types of literature. The legal minds in Israel expanded the basic codes of law into the extensive legal corpus now found in the Old Testament. Around a basic code of law (that of Moses) judges, scribes, and legal-minded priests gathered an ever increasing amount of legal material. They brought the law code up to date and adapted it to meet changing historical, social, and

---

[15] The formal characteristics are: a monotonous but smooth-flowing style, recurrent expressions, a certain rhythm and euphony.
[16] See below, pp. 146 f., 441–442.

economic circumstances. Ancient and modern laws often stood side by side in the same code. Since Moses was looked upon as the "great lawgiver" and laws enacted by Moses lay at the root of the developed code of Israel, the entire legal corpus came to be called Mosaic law. Just as all United States law can be called constitutional because it is in the spirit of the Constitution (although some of it obviously arose long after the Constitution was written), so all of Israel's law, both early and late, could be called Mosaic because it was written in the spirit and in the tradition of Moses.

In a similar way the temple prophets and singers grouped the psalms for use in the worship life of Israel. In these collections, it was intended to supply what was necessary for every form of worship. The psalter, therefore, like the law code contains material from almost every period of Israel's history and presents a cross section of her religious life. The same thing happened with the prophetic works. Israel's great prophets were more speakers than writers and, as a consequence, some did not put into written form the books which bear their names. Their oracles were recorded by followers and later collected into books including biographical information about the prophets.

Israel's wisemen both grouped wisdom sayings current in the nation and then expanded these collections by including material from the wisdom literature of other people of the ancient world. Wisdom literature flourished in Egypt and Mesopotamia as well as in Israel, and the Old Testament recognizes the international flavor of wisdom. Included in the book of Proverbs are collections attributed to Agur and Lemuel, both of whom were Arabs; and certain sections of the book reflect the Egyptian wisdom book of Amenemope,[17] as well as the wisdom sayings in the Mesopotamian story of Ahikar.[18]

Thus the literature of Israel began to take shape as men brought together materials of enduring theological value. As the collections were being made the community of faith was gradually moving to the acceptance of this literature as the inspired "word of Yahweh."

---

[17] A collection of proverbs and precepts dating between the tenth and sixth centuries B.C. Cf. J. B. Pritchard, *Ancient Near Eastern Texts*, pp. 421 ff.

[18] A collection of Aramaic proverbs from the end of the Assyrian Empire.

Canonization

As one or another of these collections came to be of particular importance to the worship life of a segment of the people of Israel it would be looked upon as authoritative and binding. In it, the people recognized the authentic voice of religious authority speaking to them. In other words, they regarded it as scripture. The technical term used to describe collections so regarded is "canon," and the process by which collections came to be looked upon as authentic is called "canonization." The word "canon" is a transliteration of a Greek word which in turn is to be traced to an old Babylonian word meaning "reed." Since the reed was one of man's earliest measuring instruments, the word "canon" came to designate a "measuring rod" and, finally, "that which regulates, rules, or serves as a norm or pattern for other things." It is in this sense that it was applied to scripture. Materials were looked upon as authoritative, as scriptural, when they met a certain standard—i.e., when they proved themselves, in one way or another, to be the authentic voice of religious authority speaking to men.

The canonization of the Old Testament was a long and somewhat complicated process. It had its beginnings in the attempt of various groups of the Israelite people to decide which among the religious writings existing in their community were those in which they could clearly recognize the voice of God. The process of canonization was, therefore, something different from the process of collection since there is ample evidence of the collection and use of religious writings which never became part of any scriptural canon. In general, the effort to safeguard the community from some external or internal threat to its religious life led to the approval of certain writings to the exclusion of others. Undoubtedly, the Old Testament as we now have it was only a small part of Hebrew literature extant in pre-Christian times. Numerous books now lost are quoted or otherwise embodied within the canonical books.[19] Also, it is clear that the Old Testament of Protestantism is the limited collection of Palestinian Judaism. The Septuagint, the Greek Old Testament of the Jews of Alex-

---

[19] For example, the Book of Jasher (Joshua 10:13, II Samuel 1:18), the Book of the Wars of Yahweh (Numbers 21:14), the Book of the Acts of Solomon (I Kings 11:41), Chronicles of the Kings of Judah (I Kings 14:29), Chronicles of the Kings of Israel (I Kings 14:19), and others.

andria in Egypt, contains many other books, some of which are accepted as canonical by the Roman Catholic Church.

Time was an essential factor in turning inspired religious writings into canonical authories. Few books were canonized until long after they had been written. Other standards by which books or collections were measured as canonical can no longer be ascertained. It is certain, however, that the decision to include or exclude a book was not made upon the basis of literary merit. Religious usage seems to have been the primary criterion. The books included were those which had found their place in the cultic life of the people and which were, therefore, of religious importance.[20] It is probable that the great majority of Old Testament books were received through common consent and were "informally" accepted into a canon long before any council made formal decisions.

The first clear evidence of a document being given "official" status is found in II Kings 22:3 ff. In 621 B.C., during the political and religious reform of Josiah of Judah, a book of the law was discovered during some reparations in the temple. The reading of the book caused much consternation resulting in further reforms and a solemn covenant by both king and people to live by the words of the newfound law. For them this lawbook became authoritative because they acknowledged that it contained the authentic voice of religious authority. In effect, it was canonized. The law code so regarded is substantially the code of Deuteronomy. During the centuries that followed, canonization proceeded along the lines of three divisions of the Old Testament.

The Canonization of the Torah. In 587 B.C. Judah was overrun by Babylon, Jerusalem was destroyed, and the elite of the land were carried as captives to Babylon. During their exile the religious leaders of the Jews carefully preserved and studied the surviving literature. After the Babylonians fell to the Persians, Jewish captives were permitted to return to Judah. Sometime around 428 B.C. the priest Ezra arrived in Jerusalem with a book of Law (Torah) which was quickly accepted as authoritative by the Jewish community in and around the capital.[21] It seems

---

[20] See Gunnar Östborn, *Cult and Canon: A Study in the Canonization of the Old Testament,* for a discussion of this problem.

[21] Ezra 7:10, 25 f.; Nehemiah 8.

likely that this lawbook was roughly equivalent to the first five books of our Old Testament, which the Jews call the Torah. The entire Law was accepted either upon this occasion or soon thereafter, because the Samaritans (who finally and decisively separated themselves from the Jews sometime between 400 and 200 B.C.) accepted the Torah and only the Torah as their scripture. It is not probable that they would have accepted it from the Jews after the schism, nor would they have welcomed a comparatively recent Jewish innovation in the period of tension which preceded the breach. It can be assumed, therefore, that the Torah was already accepted as authoritative before the separation of Jews and Samaritans.

The Canonization of the Prophets. The next major body of material to be recognized as authoritative was the prophetic literature. In the Hebrew scriptures the prophetic literature is divided into two sections, the Former Prophets and the Latter Prophets. The collection of Former Prophets includes Joshua, Judges, I and II Samuel, and I and II Kings. These books are placed in the prophetic collection both because they reflect the ideas of the prophetic group (who were thought by some to have been their authors) and because prophets play a significant role within them. The Latter Prophets include Isaiah, Jeremiah, Ezekiel, and the Book of the Twelve (Hosea, Joel, Amos, Obadiah, Jonah, Micah, Nahum, Habakkuk, Zephaniah, Haggai, Zechariah, Malachi).

The authority of the prophetic works developed after the exile. Since the prophets had interpreted the approaching disaster as Yahweh's judgment upon the nation, the exile gave their messages the confirmation of history. When postexilic prophetism fell into disrepute and began to die out the writings of the prophets of old became objects of serious study. Hence, they were being raised to a status approaching that of Torah.

The first clear evidence of existence of a prophetic collection comes from the second century B.C. The non-canonical book, The Wisdom of ben Sirach, alludes to the books of Joshua, Judges, Samuel, Kings, Isaiah, Jeremiah, Ezekiel, and the "Twelve Prophets." Presumably ben Sirach knew a collection of the prophets. When a grandson of ben Sirach translated his grandfather's work from Hebrew into Greek in 132 B.C., he added a prologue in which he spoke of "the law, and the prophets and others that have followed in their steps," and "the law itself, the prophecies, and the rest of the books." These expressions indicate both that the prophetic collection had already achieved a status comparable with that of the Torah and that the third section of the Canon was beginning to take shape.

The Canonization of the Writings. The third division of the Hebrew scriptures was being canonized by New Testament times. Luke 24:44 speaks of "the law of Moses, and the prophets, and the psalms," while in Matthew 23:35 "from the blood of innocent Abel to the blood of Zechariah" means from Genesis to Chronicles —the entire range of Old Testament scripture. The third division of the Hebrew canon includes Psalms, Proverbs, Job, Song of Solomon, Ruth, Lamentations, Ecclesiastes, Esther, Daniel, Ezra-Nehemiah, and Chronicles. It was called *The Writings* and achieved canonical status around the turn of the first century A.D.

The Fixation of the Canon at the "Synod" of Jamnia (A.D. 90–100). Jewish controversies with Christians, who accepted the authority of writings not found in the Hebrew collections, made a final step imperative. A group of Jewish scholars met at Jamnia in Palestine in A.D. 90–100 to attempt to limit the number of books regarded as authoritative. The decisions of the Jamnia rabbis were at best semiofficial and were not universally accepted and our information about their deliberations is inadequate. Evidently, however, the final setting of the Canon occurred for Palestinian Judaism about this time as the result of a definite narrowing of the range of books included in synagogue collections.

The Alexandria Collection. While the Palestinian Jews were completing their canon of scripture, a similar phenomenon was occurring at Alexandria in Egypt. The Jews there had translated the Old Testament into Greek. For these Alexandrian Jews, the Torah seems to have been the only portion given authority. However, they included in their collection the Prophets and Writings, as well as certain works not accepted by the Palestinian Jews. No single manuscript tradition of this collection exists. This makes it difficult to determine the extent of their collections, particularly since it seems to have varied from community to community. Certain works not in the final Palestinian collection were taken over by the early church (many were used by New Testament writers) and passed from Greek into the Latin Bible.

The Law (Torah)	The Prophets (Nebiim)	The Writings (Kethubim)
Genesis	Former:	Psalms
Exodus	Joshua	Proverbs
Leviticus	Judges	Job
Numbers	Samuel	Song of Solomon
Deuteronomy	Kings	Ruth
	Latter:	Lamentations
	Isaiah	Ecclesiastes
	Jeremiah	Esther
	Ezekiel	Daniel
	Book of the Twelve	Ezra-Nehemiah
		Chronicles

Figure 1–3.   The Hebrew Canon.

Although included in the Canon of the Roman Catholic Church, they were rejected by Luther and other reformers who accepted only those books included in the Palestinian collection.

The Apocrypha and Pseudepigrapha [22] pg 525

The books included in the Alexandrian collection but excluded from the canon of the Hebrew scriptures are called the Apocrypha. The Roman Catholic Church accords them [23] equal authority with the books of the Jamnia canon, but Protestant Christianity rejects them as scripture. Their historical importance, however, is recognized in Protestant circles since they illuminate a crucial period of Jewish and Christian history—200 B.C. to A.D. 100.[24] Some also contain impressive religious and theological materials. The books of the Apocrypha were originally written in Greek,

[22] "Apocrypha" comes from a Greek word meaning "hidden" and "pseudepigrapha" means "false title." Neither word is descriptive of the contents of the collections.

[23] The Roman Church prefers to call these works "deuterocanonical," rather than "apocryphal."

[24] These dates are approximate since the problem of dating apocryphal books is a complex one.

Hebrew, or Aramaic, although they survive only in Greek, Latin, or Syriac.

The term Pseudepigrapha applies to certain Jewish writings of the period 200 B.C. to A.D. 200 found in neither the Old Testament nor the Apocrypha. For a time these writings were popular in certain branches of the early Christian church.

I Maccabees	Baruch, including Epistle of Jeremy
II Maccabees	Susanna
I Esdras	Bel and the Dragon
II Esdras	The Rest of Esther
Wisdom of Jesus ben Sirach or	Prayer of Manasses
Ecclesiasticus	Song of the Three Holy Children
Judith	Book of Wisdom
Tobit	or Wisdom of Solomon

Figure 1—4. The Old Testament Apocrypha.

There is no established collection of the Pseudepigrapha, and modern editors of these ancient works have various arrangements of the materials. Among the more noted pseudepigraphical writings are Enoch, Psalms of Solomon, Testament of the Twelve Patriarchs, and Assumption of Moses. Like books of the Apocrypha, those of the Pseudepigrapha are of primary value for a period for which light is always welcome.

The Old Testament Text

The language in which most of the Old Testament was originally written is Hebrew. For a small part of it, however, Aramaic was used. The Aramaic sections include Genesis 31:47, Jeremiah 10:11, Ezra 4:8–6:18, 7:12–26, and Daniel 2:4–7:28. Like most other Semitic languages, Hebrew and Aramaic are written from right to left. All twenty-two letters of their alphabet are consonants and all ancient Old Testament manuscripts were written without vowels or punctuation.

Old Testament books were originally written on scrolls, made of leather, called parchment, or papyrus, a kind of "paper" made from the stem of a fibrous Egyptian plant.[25] In the third and fourth centuries A.D. the book or codex form appeared. This for-

---

[25] The only example of scrolls from Old Testament times are of leather, but it seems certain that papyrus scrolls were also used in old Israel.

mat, with its ease of reference and capacity for enlargement through the addition of pages, soon replaced the awkward scroll for most purposes.[26] Manuscripts, both in scroll and book (codex) form, were manually reproduced by two methods. Either a scribe copied by sight a manuscript which he had before him or a reader would read a manuscript to a number of scribes who would record what they heard. The latter method produced more scrolls in a shorter time, but the former was more accurate. Both methods had weaknesses, and, consequently, a number of errors crept into a text during the process of transmission.

These scribal mistakes are usually divided into four types: errors of the ear, errors of the eye, intentional alterations, and textual inclusions of marginal notations. Errors of the ear occurred when manuscripts were being reproduced by dictation and the scribes failed to distinguish between words which sounded alike but had different meanings or between letters with a similar sound.[27] Errors of the eye occurred when the manuscripts were being copied by sight and the scribe misread the text or failed to note his place accurately. Thus he might inadvertently repeat a letter, word, line, or paragraph, or omit a letter, word, line, or paragraph.[28] Intentional alterations were less frequent, but they did occur.[29] These have been observed in passages which a scribe found theologically offensive or which he thought contained a grammatical or structural mistake or where he felt he could clarify the reader's understanding. Occasionally the copyist found in the margin of the scroll notations which he believed belonged in the text. These he included in his reproduction of the text.[30]

Realizing that such mistakes did occur, Jewish scribes devised

---

[26] The synagogue continued to use the scroll for copies of the Torah.

[27] The best illustration of this type of error is the well-known verse from Psalm 100: "It is he who made us and not we ourselves." The word here translated "not" is the Hebrew lo'. Another Hebrew word lo would have the same sound and makes better sense in the verse. "It is he who made us and we belong to him."

[28] In I Samuel 14:41 an entire line was omitted in the Hebrew text. Compare the KJV which is based on the Hebrew text and the RSV which has supplied the missing line from the Septuagint.

[29] Israelites bearing the name of the Canaanite deity Baal were sometimes given a variant name in which the baal element was changed to bosheth. Cf. II Samuel 2:8 with I Chronicles 8:33; 9:39.

[30] In Genesis 10:14 a marginal gloss, "whence came the Philistines," has been incorporated in the text, but in the wrong place, thus revealing its marginal origin. The Philistines came from Caphtor, not Casluhim.

elaborate schemes to safeguard the text. As a rule, new manuscripts were corrected against the original from which they had been copied. In addition, an extensive system of checks and counterchecks was established to determine the accuracy of every new manuscript.

Two groups of Jewish scholars were largely instrumental in copying and safeguarding the manuscripts. They were the Sopherim—"Men of the Book"—and their successors, the Masoretes—"Men of the Masora." The Sopherim had their beginning sometime in the fourth century B.C. and continued their work until the early Christian era. They copied manuscripts, marked doubtful passages, added marginal notes giving alternate readings which they thought were more correct than those in the body of the text, and divided the manuscripts into sentences and sections for liturgical usage. The Masoretes continued and elaborated this project. They collected and catalogued errors found in the text, noted every unique form, and counted the letters of the individual books. All of this information they gathered and placed in the margins of manuscripts, thus surrounding the text with a protective hedge, which they called the *masora*.

In addition the Masoretes in the seventh to ninth centuries A.D. added vowels and accents to the texts. This was perhaps their greatest contribution since thereby they preserved the sound of the Hebrew language. By New Testament times, Hebrew had been replaced by Aramaic as the spoken language of the Palestinian Jewish people. Hebrew scriptures continued to be used in the synagogues, but they had to be translated into Aramaic before the people could understand them. Thus, by the seventh century A.D. Hebrew had become a book language. Since the written language used only consonants, the sound of the language was in danger of being forgotten. The Masoretes, who knew the sound of the language from memory, devised a system of vowels, which they inserted in the consonantal texts.

The work of the Sopherim and the Masoretes gradually produced a somewhat standardized text which was looked upon as authoritative. During the tenth century A.D. two main families of Masoretes flourished in Palestine, that of ben Asher and that of ben Naphtali. The texts produced by these two families were quite similar, although they differed in certain details. There is every indication that one tradition was utilized by both families. For a time the two texts were rivals, but in the twelfth century A.D. that of ben Asher was accepted as standard. This codex was prepared by ben Buja'a and later was given vowels by ben Asher in A.D. 1008. It is the oldest extant manuscript of the entire Old Testament and is the basis for modern editions of the Hebrew text.

Figure 1–5. Portion of an early tenth century A.D. Hebrew manuscript opened to Leviticus 5:18–6:5. The notations around the three columns are the masora. The vowel points and accents are above and below the letters of the text. (Source: Trustees of British Museum.)

Since the copyists faithfully destroyed old, worn-out manuscripts from which they had made new copies, it was by accident
that any ancient copies were preserved. Until recent years, the
only Hebrew manuscripts predating A.D. 1008 were: a codex of
the Prophets written in A.D. 895, a codex of the Torah dated A.D.
820 and 850, a collection of sixth century A.D. miscellany from a
synagogue storeroom in Cairo, and two collections in Russia about
which little is known.

Since 1947, however, a large number of manuscripts have been
discovered in a series of caves on the western plateau above the
Dead Sea.[31] These have brought to light a wealth of Old Testament materials. Among the new-found scrolls, all of which date
from the first or second century B.C., are portions (often only
scraps) from every book of the Old Testament except Esther.
Relatively complete scrolls of Isaiah, Leviticus, and Psalms have
been found, along with sizable portions of a number of other
books.

Versions

Ancient Versions. To meet the religious needs of various communities of Jews and Christians, the Old Testament was from
time to time translated into other languages: Aramaic, Greek,
Syriac, Latin, and others.

1. *The Aramaic.* When Hebrew ceased to be spoken by the
Jews in the postexilic period, Aramaic became the common
language. Hebrew Scriptures continued to be read in the synagogues, but the reading was accompanied by an oral Aramaic
paraphrase for the understanding of the people. Gradually these
paraphrases were standardized. They were called "targums," and
were more free explanations of the Hebrew text than literal translations. Early in the Christian era these were put into writing.
The most important of the targums are the Targum of Onkelos
(the Torah) and the Targum of Jonathan (the Prophets).

2. *The Greeks.* Translations into Greek were the earliest and

[31] The literature on the Dead Sea Scrolls is voluminous and continues to grow.
Good summaries may be found in the following and their bibliographies are in-
valuable for further study: Millar Burrows, *The Dead Sea Scrolls,* 1955, and *More
Light on The Dead Sea Scrolls,* 1958; Josef Milik, *Ten Years of Discovery in the
Wilderness of Judaea,* 1959; and Frank Cross, *The Ancient Library of Qumran
and Modern Biblical Study,* 1961.

most significant translations. They are commonly known as the Septuagint ("the Seventy") because of the tradition that seventy-two men translated them. For sake of brevity, the Greek translations are often referred to simply as the LXX. The ancient and legendary Letter of Aristeas claimed that the Septuagint was an official project of the Greek government of Egypt around 200 B.C. According to this letter seventy-two learned Jews, brought from Palestine to Alexandria and isolated on an island in the harbor, completed their task in seventy-two days. They were supposed to have worked in pairs and to have produced thirty-six copies of the Old Testament at the identical moment and without variation in the Greek. This story is pure fantasy. Actually, the Septuagint was produced to meet the needs of the Jewish population of Egypt whose language was no longer Hebrew, but Greek. There is not actually a single Septuagint, but a collection of translations, whose producers varied greatly in practice and ability, knowledge of Hebrew, and style.[32] The work of translation took place over a long period of years. The Torah was translated around 250 B.C., but the translation of the remaining books was not completed until the first century A.D. As mentioned above, a wider range of books was permitted in the Septuagint than in the Palestinian canon. The Bible of the early Christians was these Greek translations and most Old Testament quotations found in the New Testament came from them. The Septuagint had a great influence upon the Latin versions and upon modern English translations.[33] Other Greek versions are also known, but they are not comparable in importance to the Septuagint.

3. *The Syriac.* When Christianity spread into the interior of Syria in the late first or early second century A.D., the Old Testament was translated into Syriac. This version probably was carried by the first Christian missionaries to India and China.

4. *The Latin.* There were two Latin translations of significance. Around the end of the second century A.D. a series of Latin translations of various Old Testament books began to circulate in the Latin speaking churches of North Africa. These

[32] See Ernst Würthwein, *The Text of the Old Testament,* pp. 36–37.
[33] The names of many of the Old Testament books in our Bible came from the LXX, e.g., Genesis, Exodus, Deuteronomy.

early translations are generally called the *Old Latin Version*. Their roughness and disunity made them unsatisfactory, and in A.D. 382 Pope Damasus commissioned Jerome to produce an official revision. At first he labored at revising the Old Latin on the basis of the Septuagint. Later, however, he resorted to the Hebrew. His translation, called the *Vulgate*, was, therefore, based on the Hebrew, the Old Latin, and the Septuagint. It met with considerable opposition when it appeared, but by the seventh century it had become the Bible of the Roman Catholic Church and is still regarded as such.

These various manuscripts in Hebrew and other languages reflect a variety of text forms. That is, there are variations, some major, most minor, in their preservation of any given passage. Obviously it is expedient for the understanding of the Old Testament for scholarship to study the variant text readings to try to determine the correct or "original" reading. The wide selection of manuscripts available makes this a difficult but rewarding task. This task constitutes a science in its own right, called Textual Criticism, which has added greatly to our understanding of the Hebrew scriptures.

The English Bible. The first complete translation of the Bible into English was made by the followers of John Wyclif, "the father of English prose, the morning star of the Reformation, and the flower of Oxford scholarship," who demanded that the Bible be made available to Englishmen in their mother tongue. This translation was completed around A.D. 1382 and was based on the Vulgate.

The first translation based on the original languages was produced around 1525 by William Tyndale. The first printed edition of the Bible in English, the Coverdale Version, appeared in 1535. These were followed by the Great Bible (1539), the Geneva Bible (1560), and the Bishops' Bible (1568).

In 1611 a group of translators commissioned by King James I completed a work of seven years and gave the English speaking world:

The Holy Bible: Containing the Old Testament and the New: Newly translated out of the Original tongues: and with the former translations diligently compared and revised by his Majestie's special Commandment.

Immediately it replaced the Bishops' Bible, and after fifty years or so it replaced the Geneva Bible in popular use. For three and a half centuries the King James Version has remained the accepted Bible of English-speaking Protestantism.

The discovery after 1611 of a great number of ancient biblical manuscripts made desirable further translations utilizing these materials. The first of these were the English Revised Version of 1885 and the American Revised Version of 1901. These translations, while more accurate than the King James, do not equal its superlative literary character. Another step in translation was taken in 1952 with the publication of the widely accepted Revised Standard Version, and more recently The New English Bible has appeared.

In the endless process of translation and transmission the religious traditions of ancient Israel are continually made alive in the contemporary community of faith.

GEOGRAPHY OF THE ANCIENT NEAR EAST

To understand history, some knowledge of geography is essential, for history and culture grow on the field of geography, or, to use another figure, geography is the field on which the game of history is played. To understand Israel, then, one must know something of the physical characteristics of the Near East. Since the destiny of Israel was profoundly affected by the place Palestine occupied in the total geographic picture of the Near East, our concern must encompass Mesopotamia, Asia Minor-Armenia, Arabia, and Egypt, as well as Palestine-Syria.

The "strange new world" of the Old Testament is a little world of great contrasts. It contains fertile river valleys and vast desert wastes, rugged barren mountain slopes and inviting upland enclaves. It reaches to the heights in Armenia and plunges to the depths in the Dead Sea. This area was the matrix of mankind, with its lower mountain slopes, oases and river valleys forming the cradle of civilization. Within it the great states of the ancient world were located, and out of its deserts and down from its mountains periodically came human floods which brought an end to one cultural epoch and the beginning of another.

Life was not easy in the Ancient Near East. Inhabitants constantly had to face challenges hurled at them by the geographical conditions of their land. For some, the terror was drought and famine; for others, flood and destruction; for others, the constant ordeal of eking out a living in areas where nature herself seemed opposed to survival.

The Fertile Crescent

The Old Testament world is commonly called the Fertile Crescent. This appellation, first used by James H. Breasted, the famous Egyptologist, is adequate only if one remembers that the region's fertility is not to be judged by normal standards, but in contrast to the barren mountainous or desert areas on its perimeters. The Fertile Crescent includes the Nile River valley and delta, the Palestinian-Syrian coastal plans, and the alluvial plains of the Tigris and Euphrates rivers.

As stated, this fertile area is surrounded by unpromising terrain. In Egypt the desert crowds the river bed. Its advance is halted only by the annual overflow of the Nile. Along the northern and eastern edges of the Asiatic segment of the Crescent, a series of mountain ranges and plateaus forms a semicircle. In Palestine, the fertile areas are broken by low but rugged hills which run from north to south through the center of the land.

Desert forms the inner perimeter of the Asiatic portion of the Crescent. This vast interior is partially uninhabitable desert and partially semi-wasteland capable of supporting only sparse nomadic life. In the wasteland, winter provides rain enough for pasture, and the nomad is free to roam with his flocks. In summer, however, life is restricted to areas close around the oases. The true desert area, not blessed by winter rains, is always inhospitable to man and is virtually impenetrable.

Egypt

Since the sixth century B.C., Egypt has been called "the gift of the Nile." The inhabited area is basically an unusually narrow oasis made by the river. The Blue Nile and the White Nile, whose sources lie in the interior of the African continent, merge and flow some nineteen hundred miles northward to the sea.

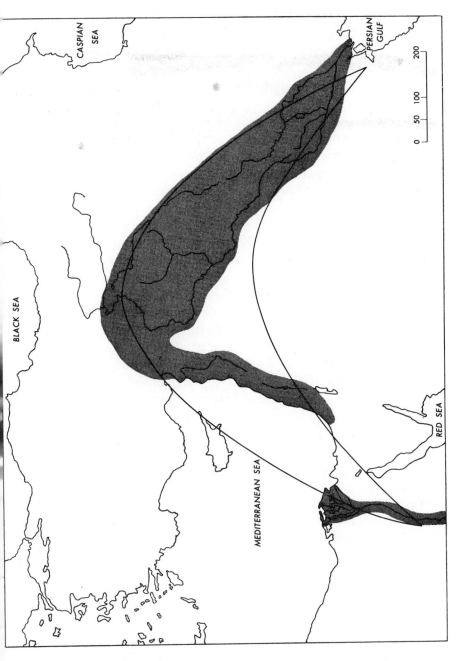

Figure 1–6. The Fertile Crescent.

For the last 750 miles, below six stretches of treacherous rapids or cataracts, the river traverses the territory of ancient Egypt. For the greater part of this distance the river flows through a valley with limestone cliffs close on both sides. This narrow trough was known as Upper Egypt. At ancient Memphis, near modern Cairo, the Nile spreads out into a delta forming a large fertile triangle crossed by many streams through which the river flows to the sea. This delta area constituted Lower Egypt. During the earliest times, Upper and Lower Egypt composed two separate and independent "kingdoms." For all practical purposes, however, Egyptian history opens with the time of their union.[34]

To all Egypt the annual inundation of the Nile brought life-giving fertility and moisture. Even today, there is no measurable rainfall in Upper Egypt. In Lower Egypt it varies from eight inches at Alexandria to one inch at Cairo. It is no wonder that the ancient Egyptian looked to the Nile as a god. The water began to rise early in July, reached its peak in October, and began to recede early in November. Seed was planted in the still-moist refertilized soil and in the spring, if the floods were good enough, there could be a harvest great enough for Egypt to serve as the granary for the ancient world. Egypt was so dependent upon the Nile that the balance between prosperity and disaster was quite delicate. The seven years of plenty and the seven years of famine known from the Joseph stories "was no fantasy for Egypt; it was always a threatening possibility." [35]

The Egyptians have been constantly faced with the necessity of preserving and utilizing the water of their river so that the soil's fertility would last more than just a few months. They early developed an extensive system of irrigation and spent a great deal of time and labor in bringing water from the river to cultivated fields. Indeed, Egypt was a land "watered by the feet" of those who walked the treadmills of the ever-moving water wheels which lifted the precious water to the levels of irrigation canals by which it was lowered to the fields.

[34] Around 3100 B.C. a ruling family from Upper Egypt united the two parts of the land and started a series of dynasties which lasted about three thousand years. Tradition assigns the leading role in this effort to Menes, who is pictured wearing a crown which combines the symbols of both Upper and Lower Egypt.

[35] John A. Wilson, *The Burden of Egypt*, p. 10.

The Nile Valley has been accurately called "a tube, loosely sealed against important outside contact." [36] On the west and east lay vast stretches of desert, through which no enemy could move with force. In the northeast the Sinai region was less forbidding, but still furnished a formidable barrier to any would-be aggressor. To the north lay the treacherous waters of the Mediterranean Sea. In the south were the cataracts of the Nile and vast stretches of inhospitable land. Shut up inside this tube, isolated from the remainder of the world and protected from his enemies, the ancient Egyptian focused his attention upon himself. His land was the land. His people were the people. This great sense of national pride produced an accompanying stability of government. Apart from occasional moments when inner weakness and turmoil enabled Asiatics to invade and gain control over Egypt, the management of the country was in the hands of native Egyptian rulers. As a consequence, the civilization of ancient Egypt retained the same characteristics for more than twenty centuries, and the main outlines of its history are easy to follow.

Altogether, the comparative regularity of the Nile, the security against outsiders, the regularity of the sun, and the stability of his government gave the Egyptian a sense of "essential optimism about his career in this world and the next." [37] He could rely upon both his world and his gods, who acted neither capriciously nor arbitrarily. His was an ordered world.

Mesopotamia

Mesopotamia means "the land between the rivers," and literally designates the area which lies between the Tigris and Euphrates rivers. Generally, however, it refers to the entire area through which these two rivers run. Mountainous and hilly where the rivers rise in the north and northwest, the terrain of Mesopotamia gradually levels into a great alluvial plain. In the north there is enough rain for agriculture, and abundant grazing land provides a paradise for nomadic herdsmen. The ancient alluvial plain in the south, now barren and desolate, was formed by the gentle slope of terrain from the Euphrates, which is slightly higher in elevation than the Tigris. Like Egypt, therefore, south-

[36] *Ibid.*, p. 11.
[37] *Ibid.*, p. 13.

ern Mesopotamia was made fertile by the waters of her rivers. Yet, the Tigris and Euphrates were more capricious than the Nile. Their floods were sporadic and often highly destructive.

Unlike Egypt, Mesopotamia was exposed on every side to outside influences and invasion. From time to time marauding tribes descended from the mountains in the north and east and from the endless steppes in the west. Sweeping everything before them, they laid waste the land and brought to sudden end the culture of centuries. Occasionally they did bring new blood and vitality to a dying era and helped to birth a new civilization out of the dying agony of its predecessor.

Northwestern Mesopotamia was the land of Israel's origins. The homeland of her patriarchal forebears was the area around Haran, an Amorite center located on a northern tributary of the Euphrates river. From here Abraham began his journey to the land of promise; to Haran he sent for a wife for his son Isaac; here his grandson Jacob sojourned among Amorite kinsmen and found wives and fortune.

Mesopotamia was also home for the great empires which influenced Israel's life and thought and which, on occasion, posed serious threats to her security. The early cultures of Sumer and Akkad left their imprints upon all the ancient world. So did the later kingdoms of both the Amorites, centered in Mari and Babylon, and the great Mittani or Hurrians, in which Amorite culture merged with that of the Indo-Aryans. Assyria centered in the highlands of Upper Mesopotamia and Babylon radiated fabled splendor and power from her great city in the southern alluvial plain. Israel's destiny was inseparably bound to the desires and fortunes of these powerful states.

Asia Minor—Armenia

All of Asia Minor and Armenia was mountainous and suffered from inadequate rainfall. Here, as elsewhere in the Ancient Near East, irrigation was necessary if there were to be strong states. The peoples who lived here were of hardy mountain stock and were excellent fighters. Under proper conditions they established organized states second to none in the Fertile Crescent. In the second millennium B.C., Asia Minor was the home of the Hittites, an empire so powerful that it fought on even terms with Egypt at a time of Egypt's greatness. In the first part of the first millennium B.C., an energetic people known as the Urartu established a strong Armenian kingdom which nearly brought Assyria to her knees in the eighth century.

Palestine—Syria [38]

The focus of the entire Near East lay along the Mediterranean seaboard in the area known as Palestine–Syria. In this area Israel lived as a nation literally at the crossroads of the world. She served as the land bridge between the continents of Asia and Africa. All the major land and sea routes converged on the tiny kingdom. No wonder that ancient Israel thought of Shechem as the navel of the earth and that medieval geographers called Jerusalem the center of the world.

Geographically, then, Palestine was the point of contact between the great Asiatic and Egyptian empires. The fate and destiny of its peoples were largely determined by international relations between these two centers of world power. More often than not Palestine was within the sphere of influence of one or another of these empires. Only when Egypt and the Asian states were weak did Israel attain any real international stature. When Egypt, Assyria, or Babylon began to fade, Israel could blossom, but never for long and seldom to full flower before she was overshadowed by one of her stronger neighbors.

Syria. The northern part of the land bridge between Asia and Egypt was known as Syria. This area was dominated by two groups, the Phoenicians and the Arameans, both of racial stock similar to Israel. The Phoenicians, who lived along the coast, turned their eyes to the sea and became a great seafaring people. They were never a part of Israel, although upon occasion important trade agreements bound the two peoples together. In the inland part of Syria was the Aramean kingdom of Damascus, often a foe of Israelite states to the south.

---

[38] The description of Palestine–Syria was taken for the most part from the following: George Adam Smith, *The Historical Geography of the Holy Land;* Denis Baly, *The Geography of the Bible;* and G. E. Wright and Floyd V. Filson, *The Westminster Historical Atlas to the Bible.*

Palestine. This land derived its name from the Philistines, who settled along its southern coast in the twelfth century B.C. First, the locale became known as Philistia and later the Greek form of the term, Palestine, came to be used for the entire region. An even older name used in the Old Testament for the area was Canaan. This name originally meant "land of the purple" and probably had reference to the manufacture of purple dye from the murex shellfish found along the coast.

Palestine is divided into four geographical zones.

1. *Coastal Plain.* The western-most of these divisions is a maritime plain which extends the entire length of the land, broken only at the point where the Carmel mountain range juts into the sea. This coastal area is subdivided into three plains—Acre in the north, Sharon in the center, and Philistia in the south.

The Plain of Acre extends some 25 miles north from Mount Carmel and is from five to eight miles in width. It did not play an important part in Old Testament history, and it is doubtful that it ever really belonged to Israel,[39] being instead the possession of the Phoenician kingdom of Tyre.

The Plain of Sharon lies between Carmel and Joppa. It is about 50 miles long and 10 miles wide. In the north it is largely wild wasteland and marsh. The hills along its eastern boundary are well watered and drain onto the plain, forming wide marshes. In the rainy seasons, the region is impassable. In ancient times the southern part of Sharon was covered by an impenetrable oak forest. This explains why Israel never settled in the region, even though it was the only section of the coast over which they had effective control. They thought of Sharon as "something extraordinary, rather exotic and outside their normal experience."[40]

South of Sharon's marshes and forests the character of the plain changes greatly. The land gradually rises to form gentle ranges up to 300 feet high. In ancient times, this area, known as the Plain of Philistia, was open country nearly all arable. It was dotted with grain fields and olive orchards.[41] The only difficulty to agriculture was the drifting sand which created a "formidable barrier" along the entire coast, often extending beyond two miles inland.

[39] Baly, *The Geography of the Bible,* p. 130.
[40] Baly, *The Geography of the Bible,* p. 136; cf. Isaiah 65:10; 33:9; 35:2.
[41] Judges 15:5.

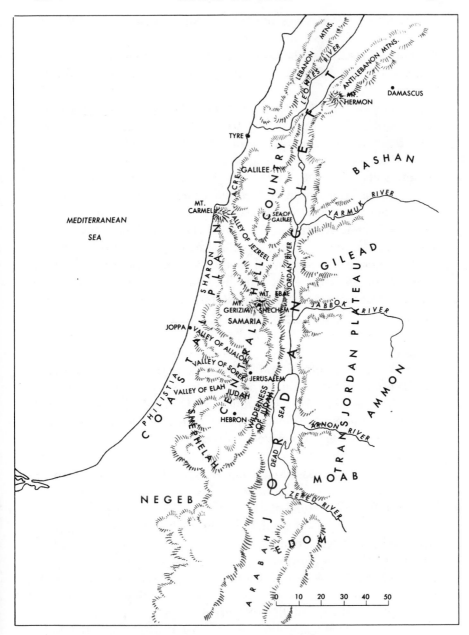

Figure 1–7. Topography of Palestine.

The Coastal Plain was never a center of Israelite strength in Old Testament times. The nation never had effective control over any part of it, except the untenantable Plain of Sharon. The chief centers of Israel's population and interest lay in the Central Hill Country.

2. *Central Hill Country.* An almost continuous range of rugged rocky hills forms the "backbone" of western Palestine. It begins in the Lebanon range in Syria and extends to the desert country in the extreme south of Palestine. Its entire length is broken solely by the Valley of Jezreel, which separates the Galilean hills from those of Samaria. The range is high only in Syria, where it rises to about 6000 feet. The highest point in Palestine is near Hebron in the south where the hills extend 3370 feet above sea level. The lack of height in the central hill country, however, is more than offset by the steep and rugged character of the terrain. Although this range of hills is broken at only one place, for purposes of description it may be divided into three sections: Galilee, Samaria, and Judah.

Northern Galilee is a rugged plateau with windswept slopes which in ancient times were probably heavily forested. This area was sparsely settled and inconsequential in Israelite history since it often was not actually Israelite territory. Lower or southern Galilee is less hilly and much of its land is arable. Two level plains, one north of Nazareth and the other northwest of the Sea of Galilee, were intensively cultivated.

South of Galilee the central range is cut by a series of plains which offers easy passage from the coast to the Jordan River valley. The name by which this pass was best known was the Valley of Jezreel (later known by the Greek name, Esdraelon). This fertile area was of strategic military importance in ancient times and was often a decisive battle ground. Within this valley almost every major power in the Near East fought at least one battle. Of the many cities located there, Megiddo was the most important because it guarded the pass connecting the southern coastal plain with the Valley of Jezreel.

At the geographical center of western Palestine are the hills of Samaria. From a watershed which averages 2000 feet in elevation, these rocky and sterile hills descend toward the Plain of Sharon, dotted by olive groves and fields. On the east the hills drop more sharply to the Jordan Valley. Viewed from a distance these hills give the impression of a single mountain massif. The two most conspicuous peaks are Ebal and Gerizim, which are in the heart of the district. They were significant militarily. Since the main road met near them, control of their slopes meant control of the country. Also they had great religious significance for Israel. Between them the people gathered at the end of the war of conquest to ratify a covenant with Yahweh. Scattered throughout this mountainous region are numerous plains, meadows, and spacious vales, which create a sense of openness. The abundance of good land in these areas made Samaria a fair place in which to live. It was firmly under Israel's control throughout most of her pre-exilic history.

South of Samaria lay the mountain fastness of Judah. Its heights form an upland plateau bordered on the west by a series of low rolling foothills and on the east by the bleak and fearsome "Wilderness of Judah," which drops off sharply to the Dead Sea. The plateau itself was moorland forested in ancient times with small trees. A prevailing impression was of stone:

The torrent-beds, the paths that are no better, the heaps and heaps of stones gathered from the fields, the fields as stony still, the moors strewn with boulders, the obtrusive scalps and ribs of the hills.[42]

In the brief rainy season grain in the fields would hide the multitude of stones and short-lived grass and flowers would clothe the naked hillsides, but soon the grass withered and the flowers faded.[43]

Less than half of Judah was cultivatable; the remainder was desolate wilderness. Springs or pools were found only at Gibeon, Jerusalem, Bethlehem and Hebron. There were no streams and even in the rainy season only a few rills. However, the area was well-guarded and easy to defend. On the east were the steep ascent from the Jordan and the stern barrier of the Dead Sea. The western approaches to Judah were protected by hills of the Shephelah and a great uplifted fold of rock. The northern and southern sectors had less effective natural defenses. The north in particular, afforded easy access to the plateau from either side. Nevertheless for the most part the people of Judah's heartland were insulated in a mountain stronghold. The terrain between

[42] G. A. Smith, *The Historical Geography of the Holy Land*, p. 307.
[43] Isaiah 40:7.

this upland plateau and the Jordan cleft was tortuous in the extreme. Perhaps no landscape on the face of the earth was less inviting than this "Wilderness of Judah." The barren slope plunged chaotically to the depths below. Here there were no

Figure 1–8. The rugged and barren terrain of the "Wilderness of Judah." (Source: Paul Popper, Ltd.)

cities of habitation, but the rugged terrain gave refuge to both monks and outcasts who shunned the towns.

Judah's western frontier was better favored. It was a region of low rolling hills separated from the plateau by a series of valleys which ran north and south. The Israelites called this territory the Shephelah or "lowlands." It was a thickly settled and fertile zone, rich in grain, vineyards, and olive groves. The area was important to Judah as a protective frontier. Unless it was in their control, the hill country was left exposed. The conquest of the Shephelah was a necessary preliminary to any conquest of the highlands.[44]

[44] Cf. Joshua 10 and the campaigns of Sennacherib of Assyria and Nebuchadnezzar of Babylon. See Pritchard, *Ancient Near Eastern Texts*, 287–288, and II Kings 18:13–19:37; 24:1–25:26.

The narrow division between the Judean highlands and the Shephelah was marked by a line of fortified towns guarding the natural valleys across the region. The most important of these valleys were Aijalon, the primary route up into Judea from the plain; Sorek, which branched into three approaches to Jerusalem; and Elah, famous as the place where David killed Goliath. In the south the Judean hills dropped abruptly into a broken plains area known in Old Testament times as the Negeb. This area was a sparsely settled desert wilderness cut by countless dry valleys and dotted with sand dunes. There is little rainfall in the Negeb and it is constantly swept by winds, hot and sand-laden in the summer, but cold and cutting in the winter. Here lay several of the wildernesses which are mentioned in the Old Testament.[45]

3. *The Jordan Cleft.* A great geological rift splits Palestine as if some giant of old had smitten the land with a battle axe, leaving gaping wounds. The cleft extends through Syria where it divided the Lebanon from the Anti-Lebanon range; it continues through Palestine as the Jordan River valley, and farther south it forms the Arabah, Gulf of Aqaba, and Red Sea.

The Jordan River rises on the western slopes of Mount Hermon in the Anti-Lebanon range. For a while the river runs above the level of the sea, but soon reaches sea level near Lake Huleh.[46] Thence it drops rapidly to the Sea of Galilee, approximately 685 feet below sea level. The "sea" is a beautiful fresh water lake surrounded on almost every side by hills descending gently to the shore. Leaving the Sea of Galiliee, the river twists its tortuous way down, down to the Dead Sea which is 1290 feet below the Mediterranean. The Jordan Valley north and south of the Sea of Galilee was intensively cultivated during ancient times and its small tributary streams supplied networks of irrigation chanels. Farther south, however, the valley was less inviting. The river ran through a narrow, jungle-like depression wherein roamed all kinds of wild animals. This southern portion of the valley largely was uninhabited except where major tributaries entered the Jordan from the east end at Jericho, where a great spring flourished. Although shallow enough for fording at a number of places, the

---

[45] Cf. I Samuel 23:15, 24; 24:1; II Chronicles 20:16; Numbers 13:3, 21.

[46] The modern state of Israel rechanneled the waters of this lake so that it no longer exists.

Figure 1–9. The Sea of Galilee with gently sloping hills in the background. (Source: Trans World Airlines.)

Jordan was a natural barrier to communication between east and west Palestine. Hence, the Transjordan area was never as completely under the control of the Israelite nation as the territory on the western side of the river.

The Jordan empties into the Dead Sea. This body of water has no outlet and as a consequence has about 25 per cent salt content. Fish entering the sea from the river die in a matter of minutes. In ancient times the Dead Sea did not extend as far south as it

Figure 1–10. "The Jungle of the Jordan" showing the river's wandering course through the Jordan Cleft. (Source: Paul Popper, Ltd.)

does today. It ended opposite the peninsula presently extending from its eastern shore. The area around the sea was, and is, most desolate. On the east and the west are forbidding heights and in summer the heat is oppressive. Add to this the deadness of the sea and the area is almost ominous. Below the Dead Sea the great rift continues in a dry river bed known in the Old Testament as the Arabah, an area similar in nature to the Negeb region to the west.

4. *Transjordan Plateau.* Four streams, the Yarmuk, the Jabbok, the Arnon, and the Zered, flow into the Jordan and divide Transjordan into five areas. North of the Yarmuk was the land of Bashan, a fertile area where agriculture was restricted only by inadequate rainfall. Nevertheless, the area was noted for its extensive grain production. Between the Yarmuk and the Jabbok was Gilead, a well-watered area capable of supporting a large population. In Old Testament times Gilead was more directly associated with Israel than any other area east of the Jordan River. The kingdom of Ammon was located between the Jabbok and Arnon rivers and was periodically controlled by the Israelite kingdoms west of the Jordan. South of the Arnon's deep valley lay the kingdom of Moab, a high and level plateau to which the Israelites rarely laid claim. The southernmost section of Transjordan, the area below the Zered, was Edom, a strong kingdom which controlled the desert trade as well as the copper and iron deposits found along the border of the Arabah.

Thus, the land of Canaan is seen as an area of diversity and fragmentation. In the mountains of this region the Israelites spent most of their history. The hardships of a history tied so intimately to an austere land contributed to their understanding of themselves as the people of God and with this perspective they interpreted their destiny.

SUGGESTED READINGS

Israelite Understanding of History

ALT, ALBRECHT, *Essays on Old Testament History and Religion,* tr. R. A. Wilson (Doubleday, 1967).

BARR, JAMES, *Old and New In Interpretation* (Harper & Row, 1966).

BRIGHT, JOHN, *The Kingdom of God* (Abingdon, 1953). One of the better theological interpretations of Israel's history.

KRAUS, H. J., *The People of God in the Old Testament* (Lutterworth, 1958). Excellent interpretive sketch of the history of Israel as a dialogue.

NAPIER, B. DAVIE, *From Faith to Faith* (Harper & Row, 1955).

NORTH, C. R., *The Old Testament Interpretation of History* (Epworth, 1946).

RENDTORFF, ROLF, *God's History* (Westminster, 1969).

WRIGHT, G. ERNEST, *God Who Acts* (Regnery, 1952). Monograph representing a point of departure for Old Testament theology.

Old Testament Text, Versions, and Canon

BARCLAY, WILLIAM, *The Making of the Bible* (Abingdon, 1961). Includes both Old and New Testament. Brief, but helpful.

FILSON, FLOYD V., *Which Books Belong in the Bible?* (Westminster, 1957).

KENYON, FREDERIC, *Our Bible and the Ancient Manuscripts* (Harper & Row, 5th ed. rev., 1958).

ROBERTS, B. J., *The Old Testament Text and Versions* (University of Wales Press, 1951).

WÜRTHWEIN, ERNST, *The Text of the Old Testament* (Basil Blackwell, 1957). Fullscale technical treatment.

Geography of Ancient Near East

AHARONI, YOHANAN, and AUI-YONAH, M., *The Macmillan Bible Atlas* (Macmillan, 1968).

AHARONI, YOHANAN, *The Land of the Bible* (Westminster, 1967).

BALY, DENIS, *The Geography of the Bible* (Lutterworth, 1957).

MAY, HERBERT G., *Oxford Bible Atlas* (Oxford University Press, 1964).

SMITH, GEORGE ADAM, *The Historical Geography of the Holy Land* (Geo. H. Doran, 1902). Dated, but still classic.

Interpreting the Old Testament: Form and Literary Criticism

HARRELSON, WALTER, *Interpreting the Old Testament* (Holt, Rinehart and Winston, 1964), pp. 28–40.

KOCH, KLAUS, *The Growth of the Biblical Tradition* (Charles Scribner's Sons, 1969).

NIELSEN, EDWARD, *Oral Tradition* (S.C.M. Press, 1954).

VON RAD, GERHARD, *The Problems of the Hexateuch and Other Essays* (McGraw-Hill, 1966).

The Meaning of The Old Testament

BRIGHT, JOHN, *The Authority of the Old Testament* (Abingdon, 1967).

DE DIETRICH, SUZANNE, *The Witnessing Community* (Westminster, 1958).

LYS, DANIEL, *The Meaning of the Old Testament* (Abingdon, 1967).

ROWLEY, H. H., *The Faith of Israel* (S. C. M. Press, 1956).

SMART, JAMES, *The Interpretation of Scripture* (Westminster, 1961).

WESTERMANN, CLAUS, ed., *Essays on Old Testament Hermeneutics* (John Knox, 1964).

WRIGHT, G. ERNEST and FULLER, REGINALD H., *The Book of the Acts of God* (Doubleday, 1957).

2

In the Beginning

The first book in the Old Testament is appropriately named *Genesis*, beginning. Although Palestinian rabbis had called the book *bereshith*, which is the opening word of the Hebrew Bible and means "in beginning," the Greek word *genesis* was used as the superscription for the book in the Septuagint. Subsequently, the word was carried over into the Vulgate and thence into English versions.

In Genesis the Israelite community expresses her faith in God as creator of the universe and of the people of Israel. Belief that the creative power of Yahweh was exercised in nature when he created the universe and in history when he created Israel is evident in the structure of the book.

I. Israel's Primeval Traditions. Chapters 1–11
1. The Traditions of the Creation of the World. 1:1–2:4a and 2:4b–24
2. The Tradition of the Fall. Chapters 3 and 4
3. The Traditions of the Flood. Chapters 5–9
4. The Table of Nations. Chapter 10
5. The Tradition of the Tower of Babel and the Confusion of Languages. Chapter 11
II. Israel's Patriarchal Traditions: the Beginning of the Creation of Israel. Chapters 12–50
1. The Abraham Traditions. 12:1–25:19
2. The Isaac Traditions. 25:19–26:34
3. The Jacob-Esau Traditions. Chapters 27–36
4. The Traditions of Jacob's Family, largely the story of Joseph. Chapters 37–50

This story of beginnings was self-consciously formulated by the people of Israel who, looking back from things as they were to things as they were theologically understood to have been, interpreted ancient traditions about their tribal ancestors and the early age of mankind. Throughout Genesis two realities are emphasized: the sin of man and the grace of God. The primeval traditions in chapters 1–11 tell of God as creator and of man's creaturehood and sinfulness. The Patriarchal traditions in chapters 12–50 tell of the beginnings of God's redemptive activity. Clearly these materials were formulated and edited by Israel with a theological perspective: the primary character is Yahweh, the God of Israel; the primary concern is neither scientific nor historical, but religious.

The setting of the primeval traditions is the time before Abraham, the one eventually claimed as ancestor of all the various tribes who after the exodus and conquest composed the community of Israel. These traditions provide the theological introduction to the history of Israel. Their basic purpose is to give a picture of man as a creature in rebellion against his creator and, therefore, in need of redemption.

The primeval traditions represent the attempt by men of faith to answer fundamental questions about existence and meaning. Like all men they were concerned to know who they were and how they were related both to the world and to ultimate reality. They answered these questions in terms of their encounter with Yahweh as savior and ruler over their lives. They believed, therefore, that Yahweh is the creator, that man is significantly responsible to him for his own life in the world. But they knew existentially that man is a sinner in rebellion against his creator and that human culture is, in a sense, the consequence of egotistic denial of the sovereignty of God. Typically as illustrative, rather than literally as historical, the primeval traditions wrestle with ever-present realities by telling the stories set in the time before Abraham.

Although the materials of Genesis 1–11 come from different locales and from different periods, they present together the beginnings of mankind from the point of view of the Exodus faith, i.e., faith in Yahweh as a redeeming and creating God. The believing Israelites describe in theological terms the rebellious nature of man which made the redemptive activity of God necessary. In developing this theme they used available materials from all over the Ancient Near East, but they always imposed upon them the conception of God derived from the Exodus deliverance—God who revealed himself as merciful and loving by his redemptive action in Israel's history. The resultant account provides a religious orientation for men in the world and a rationale for understanding the nature and meaning of life.

THE TRADITIONS OF THE CREATION OF THE WORLD (GENESIS 1 AND 2)

Israel's Creation Faith

Israel's faith in Yahweh was not based exclusively or primarily upon his creative activity, but upon his work of redemption. The nation had come to know him, not by speculation about the world and how it came into being, but through historical experience. Her encounter with him had been direct at the Exodus and in the wilderness of Sinai. Creation faith was, therefore, only a corollary to historical faith. Accepting Yahweh as lord and controller of history, it was only a step to the belief in him as the majestic creator of the world and all that it contains.

> Have you not known? Have you not heard?
> Yahweh is the everlasting God,
>   the creator of the ends of the earth.
> He does not faint or grow weary,
>   his understanding is unsearchable.
> He gives power to the faint,
>   and to him who has not might he
>   increases strength. (Isaiah 40:28–29)
> . . . .
> Thus says Yahweh,
>   who created the heavens
>   (he is God!)
>   who formed the earth and made it
>   (he established it;
>   he did not create it a chaos,
>   he formed it to be inhabited!):
> "I am Yahweh, and there is no other." (Isaiah 45:18)

The God of Israel was creator and sustainer of creation. He had not withdrawn from creation to let it proceed on its own laws and regulations. He continued to be active in his world.

> O Yahweh, how manifold are thy works!
> In wisdom hast thou made them all;
> the earth is full of thy creatures . . .
>
> . . . .
> These all look to thee,
> to give them their food in due season.
>
> When thou givest to them, they gather it up;
> when thou openest thy hand,
> they are filled with good things.
>
> When thou hidest thy face, they are dismayed;
> when thou takest away their breath,
> they die and return to their dust.
>
> When thou sendest forth my breath,
> they are created;
> and thou renewest the face of the ground.
>
> Psalm 104:24, 27–30)

Israelite memory contained two extensive creation stories which were utilized by the editors of the Torah to express this mature faith in Yahweh as creator. The older tradition, Genesis 2:4b–25, transmitted orally for an indefinite time, was incorporated into the Yahwistic history of Israel in the tenth century B.C. The companion piece, Genesis 1:1–2:4b, was given its form by the exilic compilers of the Priestly history in the fifth century. Since it shows traces of an earlier less sophisticated form, it likewise preserves preexilic ideas of creation.

The Yahwistic Creation Story: Genesis 2:4b–25

The Yahwistic creation story is a beautiful, yet simple, idyll. The human race is personified as a man, 'adam (the Hebrew word means "mankind"). Yahweh is described in anthropomorphic terms, i.e., he is pictured as a man. He stooped in the dust and out of it molded [1] a man ('adam) into whose nostrils he breathed his own lifegiving breath.[2] He planted a garden and placed man within it. Working in the garden, he grew all kinds of trees. He walked with the man in the garden and they conversed with one another. When the man found no companion among the beasts which had been fashioned, Yahweh put him to

[1] The word used describes the work of a potter molding the pliable clay with his hands.
[2] The Yahwistic equivalent of the Priestly "in the image of God." Cf. Genesis 1:26, 27 and below, pp. 65–66.

sleep and, performing surgery upon him, made woman. Of course, this does not mean that the ancient Israelites literally conceived of God working with his hands or possessing a body like a man's. The language is figurative description. With such language finite beings attempt to describe the infinite. Even the most sophisticated theological and philosophical language about God is anthropomorphic, because all language is of human creation and God is not. There is no reason, therefore, to assume that story language like that of the Yahwist is theologically less expressive than more sophisticated and less concrete theological and philosophical talk. What is crucial for either is communication, and the Yahwist's story was heard and understood in old Israel.

The viewpoint of this early account is that of a Palestinian peasant. The man is the tiller of the soil and the garden is a fruitful place in a dry wilderness. Rain is the source of life in this oasis and the chaos outside the garden is a waterless waste. The story obviously has as its background the land of Canaan, which the Israelites looked upon as a good land blessed by Yahweh and flowing with milk and honey. Notice how skillfully the Yahwist has related man to the physical environment best known to his (the Yahwist's) contemporaries. Man was created to live in their kind of world. The good earth of Canaan is the stage for his life and he will farm its soil. Human existence is creaturely existence and in a real sense the world is man's intended place. But man is not just a product of nature, he is animated by the breath of Yahweh. In this simple picture the Yahwist portrays something of the majesty of human existence. Man is a creature of Yahweh upon whom he depends and to whom he is ultimately responsible, not only for life but for meaning and joy.

The order of creation in the Yahwistic account is: man, the garden, trees, animals, and woman. The account begins and concludes with the creation of mankind, male and female, the focus of concern in the Yahwistic story. Man was created before plants and animals and creation was not complete until woman was created to be his companion. With the bestowal of the divine breath man became a living being,[3] different from all other crea-

---

[3] The Hebrew is *nephesh hayah*, "living breathing thing."

tures. The garden, plants and animals were created for man's use. Clearly the Yahwist tradition is more concerned with creation of man than with creation of the world, although the latter is extremely important to him also. In a profound way this tradition has depicted the reality of man's human existence. He is made from the ground and the earth is his abode.[4] That is, he is a creature and is mortal. But man is not simply a product of nature; he is a creature of Yahweh, the source of his life. He exists for Yahweh and is dependent upon him. Yet, because Yahweh is graciously disposed toward him, man is a partner in creation. He approves and names every living creature, thus sharing to a degree in the creative act. In Semitic culture only one who has authority and power could bestow a name on anything.

Man was placed in 'eden "to till it and to keep it." The Yahwist locates the garden in Eden to the east. Such a geographical description is purposefully cryptic because the story is not concerned to locate geographically the primeval paradise. The Hebrew word 'eden is possibly symbolic. It means "delight" or "enchantment" and the Israelites may have thought of the garden of Eden as a "delightful garden" or a "park of enchantment." Some, however, suggest that the word 'eden may be related to the Babylonian word, edinu, meaning "plain" or "desert," indicating that the garden was planted in a plain or like an oasis in the desert. It is also possible that Eden is intended only as a proper name, a place name. In any case its location on a map is not intended.

The figurative description of the garden is equally unconcerned with geographical location. A river flowed through Eden and, after leaving the garden, divided to become four rivers. In the world known to ancient Israel, rivers were the great source of fertility; agriculture and civilization flourished only in the great river valleys. The picture, therefore, is of a great life-giving river of such magnitude that even after leaving the garden it still supplies four large streams. The writer's concern is with the sustaining abundance of man's original world.[5]

[4] In Hebrew the words "man" and "ground" come from the same root: the verse, therefore, contains a play on words: "Then Yahweh God formed 'adam from the dust of 'adamah."

[5] For defense of a geographical description, see E. A. Speiser, "Genesis," in The Anchor Bible, I, 19–20.

The cartographic descriptions of the story roughly resemble a skeleton map of the earth's surface as the Babylonians conceived it. They depict the earth as centering in Babylon around which are certain towns and canals with the entire area encircled by the ocean. Finally, at the extreme outside of their maps are the most distant regions indicated by triangles.[6]

The similarity between Hebrew and Babylonian cartography reflects more a common world view than any direct dependence

Figure 2–1. This sixth century B.C. clay tablet illustrates the campaigns of Sargon of Akkad (c. 2300 B.C.), but is in effect a world map. Compare the reproduction of the map in Figure 2–2. (Source: Trustees of the British Museum.)

[6] Cf. Georges Contenau, *Everyday Life in Babylon and Assyria*, pp. 225–226; and Emil Kraeling, *Bible Atlas*, p. 43.

of one upon the other. Certainly the Babylonian world view does not clarify the geography in the Genesis narrative. Any efforts to resolve the descriptions of the story are futile, because the Genesis tradition was not burdened with geographical concerns. Rather it says figuratively that "even the blessings of nature are ultimately derived from the grace of God in the creation."[7] The tradition as developed in Israel had theological rather than historical meaning. The lifegiving powers of the great rivers known to Israel and the cultures which developed along them were attributed to their origin in the river that flowed out of Eden. Later Israel replaced the "lost" Eden as the center of the world with Jerusalem, where Yahweh dwelt in the temple on Mt. Zion. The sacred city was, therefore, the creative center from which life-giving powers extended into the chaos of the ungodly world of other nations, and at the end of history would become in some sense a new Eden.[8]

Man was placed in the garden paradise to dress it and keep it. He was to work there. Paradise included honest and satisfying physical and productive activity. The ritual curse on work in 3:17–19 considers work which is only burdensome toil as evil but not work itself. To work was man's created destiny. If Yahweh worked as creator, why should man not work as creature?

Man's paradise was not complete, however, without companionship. Yahweh worked with man to find a suitable companion for him among the animals. At no point is the Yahwist's tradition more anthropomorphic than here. In an almost humorous way he depicts both God and man seeking an animal mate for man as if neither knew that only a creature of man's own kind would be a satisfactory companion. Here at the beginning of the Old Testament we become aware of a sense of humor which, more often than is realized, characterizes biblical literature. Man's hunger for fellowship was unsatisfied by animals, and woman was created. A deep sleep fell upon the man, so that the secret of Yahweh's miraculous act might remain concealed from him, and Yahweh made a woman from a part of man's body. The

[7] Alan Richardson, *Genesis I–XI*, p. 65.
[8] For a picture of a life-giving river which flowed from the altar of Yahweh in Jerusalem, see Ezekiel 47.

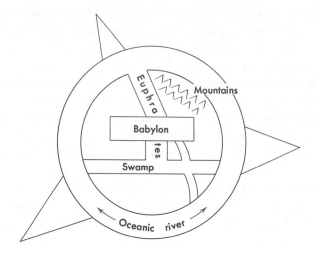

Figure 2–2.   Ancient Babylonian world map.

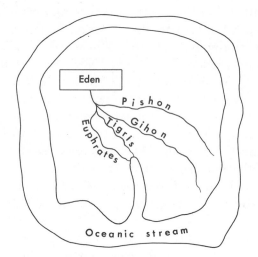

Figure 2–3.   Genesis world map.

inextricable union of male and female is epitomized in the creation of woman from the man's rib.

> Then the man said,
>   "This at last is bone of my bones
> and flesh of my flesh:
> She shall be called Woman (Hebrew *'isha*),
> because she was taken out of Man (Hebrew *'ish*).   (2:23)

The woman was formed out of the man's side. Hence woman's place is at the side of man, ready at all times to be a "help" to her husband. The man is to cherish and defend his wife as part of his own being without whom he is incomplete. So, although centering on the activity of God as creator, the Yahwist's story includes an additional emphasis on the nature of the meaningful relationship between man and woman. Jesus later referred to the concluding verses of this account to illustrate the principle of relationship between marriage and creation.[9]

The Priestly Creation Liturgy: Genesis 1:1-2:4a

The Old Testament opens with a majestically simple declaration of Israel's creation faith.

> In the beginning God
> created the heavens and the earth. (Genesis 1:1)

The Priestly narrative of creation which begins with these words was shaped distinctly and unmistakably by the character and mind of Israel. Although it is heavily dependent upon Ancient Near Eastern creation traditions the emphasis upon Yahweh's creative word and, therefore, his absolute sovereignty over and independence of nature is characteristically Israelite. Although written in final form long after the Yahwistic story of Genesis 2, it appropriately introduces Israel's scripture because it is a mature statement of the community's belief about God's relationship with the world and about the nature of man as a creature of God.

In structure the Priestly account is prose, but in intention and character the tradition is poetical, with poetic power excelled by few passages in the Hebrew scriptures. Genesis 1 clarions the events of creation in rhythms and refrains which reflect the cultic celebration of Yahweh as creator. The world is the scene of the glorious majesty of God. Everything in the universe reflects his glory by performing its ordained service "after its kind." In Genesis 1 God is presented differently from the anthropomorphic picture of the Yahwistic story. With creative words God calls into being everything that is. He speaks and that which was not comes to be. Israel believed that the divinely spoken word was forceful and filled with power. When God said, "Let there be

9 Matthew 19:4–6; Mark 10:5–9.

light," *there was light.* For Israel the word of Yahweh always accomplished its purpose and what it accomplished was good. Here in the Genesis account we confront the concept of the creative word for the first time, already in a theologically developed form.[10]

Does this chapter teach *creatio ex nihilo,* "creation out of nothing"? Although not explicitly stated, something very near that is implied. The Hebrew word for "create" (*bara'*) is used only of God and implies something completely beyond human imitation or comprehension. An absolute beginning is intended in Genesis 1:1, and at that beginning God was present to utter the creative word. The real intent and purpose is to say that whenever beginning occurred, God was there to begin it and is therefore worthy of praise and worship because he is lord over the world.

In the Priestly account, creation is divided into six orderly periods, each represented as lasting one twenty-four hour day.[11] On the first day, light was created; on the second, the firmament of heaven; the third, dry land by separation from water and then vegetation; the fourth, heavenly bodies; the fifth, fish and fowl; the sixth, animals and man—male and female together. On the seventh day, God rested from his work, i.e., the Sabbath was created. Here the observance of the Sabbath gains the sanction of the Priestly writer who looked upon it as a day of rest and rejoicing in the goodness of God. The view of creation as a process not completed in six twenty-four hour days is a late, post-biblical scientific concept which could not possibly have been known to the ancient Israelites among whom this tradition developed. Consequently the faith statements of this chapter should not be placed in conflict with ideas about the origin of the universe offered by modern science. This "liturgy" celebrates creator and creation rather than describes them. By refusing to describe them it avoids circumscribing and confining those realities whose full dimensions are ultimately beyond us. Science is not as innocent at this point.

[10] The idea of the creative power of the divine word is familiar outside Israel in both Egyptian and Babylonian theology. In neither place, however, is it given fundamental significance as here.

[11] This is the normal meaning of "It was evening and it was morning."

The dark, formless, empty chaos was turned into a world of godly order and design by successive exclamations of the divine word. Each thing created had its divinely ordained purpose and each was subordinate to Yahweh. One strange feature present in the story seems intentional. Light was created before the light bodies. Of course, the ancients knew the sun as the source of light. They were so much aware of the importance of the sun and, mistakenly, the moon, as sources of life and light that they made them objects of worship—gods in their own right. The express purpose of the Priestly writer is to contradict such beliefs. He declares light to be independent of the sun and moon and describes the heavenly bodies as mere instruments in the hands of Yahweh, the only true God.[12]

For the priestly tradition the creation of all else was but prelude to the creation of man ('adam), an act in which Yahweh participates more intimately and intensively than all other works of creation. Yahweh makes mankind in his image and after his likeness. In detail the perspective of the Priestly writer differs from that of the Yahwist. The Yahwist personifies the human species in a pair of individuals, a man and a woman to whom are given symbolic names. The man is called Adam, "mankind"; the woman Eve (Hebrew havvah), which means "life" or "living." The Priestly writer, however, describes the creation of a race. The climax of creation is 'adam, here used collectively to mean "mankind." *Same on page 57*

> So God created man ('adam) in his own
> image, in the image of God he created
> him; male and female he created them. (1:27)

Man enjoys distinction from all other created things. More important, however, is the emphasis upon man's unique relation to the Creator. The same idea is expressed in one of the Psalms:

> Know that the Lord is God!
> It is he that made us, and we are his;
> we are his people, and the sheep of his pasture. (100:3)

Man is essentially a creature of God and owes his existence to the Creator. Like all else he is created, but he is not at one with the rest of creation. Man shares the natural limitations of creature-

[12] See Psalm 8:3; 19:6.

hood, but also he may rise above creation. Man shares certain characteristics with the animals. Like the animals he is mortal,[13] but he differs from them because he has the capacity to respond to and communicate with God. He is a responsible creature to stand beneath his Creator, aware that he is in his presence and under his judgment. Man who does not see himself as of creaturehood, but not creature; of God, but not a god, is in some sense less than man. This Hebrew understanding of the dignity of man's creation was expressed later in Psalm 8:5–6:

> Thou hast made him (man) little less than God,
>   and dost crown him with glory and honor.
> Thou hast given him dominion over the works of
>   thy hands;
>   thou hast put all things under his feet.

Further, the concept of creation in the image and likeness of God included man's dominion. He is the created being to whom all else is committed by the Creator who commands man to

> Be fruitful and multiply,
>   and fill the earth and subdue it;
>   and have dominion . . . (1:28)

The mandate is for man to come to terms with the universe, to investigate its secrets, and to serve as its master under the overarching sovereignty of God. However, man is to remember "that he is lord over creation and ruler of nature not in his own right or to work his own will; he is God's vice-regent, charged with the working of God's will, responsible to God for his stewardship." [14]

Here the biblical idea of creation implicitly judges the abuse of nature. The Yahwist describes man as *keeper* of the garden, and the Priestly emphasis upon man's dominion must be understood in the context of man's responsible management of a creation whose maker, sustainer and owner is God.

The Priestly liturgy affirms the goodness of creation with a seven-fold refrain, "God saw that it was good." [15] This expression marked each work as one corresponding with God's intention, "perfect, as far as its nature required and permitted, complete,

---

[13] Cf. Psalm 49:12.

[14] Richardson, *Genesis I–XI*, p. 55.

[15] The formula is present after each work of creation except the second (The LXX, however, has it here as well).

and the object of the Creator's approving regard and satisfaction." [16] Israel, not an ascetic people, enjoyed the full richness of a good creation.

> Thou dost cause the grass to grow for the cattle,
>   and plants for man to cultivate,
> that he may bring forth food from the earth,
>   and wine to gladden the heart of man,
>   oil to make his face shine,
>   and bread to strengthen man's heart.
> . . . .
> When thou openest thy hand,
>   they are filled with good things. (Psalm 104:14–15, 28b)

The Relationship of the Yahwistic and Priestly Stories to One Another

Obviously two different traditions about creation have been preserved by the editors of Genesis in the Yahwistic and Priestly creation stories. The two stories have distinct styles and vocabularies. They use different words for God (*Yahweh* in the Yawistic account; *Elohim* in the Priestly version), and the descriptions of the Creator and creation vary. The most conspicuous contrast is in the fundamental structure of the stories.

Priestly	*Yahwistic*
Earth's original state a watery chaos.	Earth's original state a waterless waste.
The work of creation divided into six separate operations, each assigned to one day.	No time reference.
The order of creation—	The order of creation—
(a) light	(a) man formed from the dust
(b) firmament	(b) the garden
(c) land, separation of earth from sky, vegetation	(c) trees
(d) heavenly bodies	(d) animals
(e) birds and fishes	(e) woman, created out of man.
(f) animals and man, male and female together.	

Nevertheless, the traditions express similar theological perception about the nature of God and the created order and of man's relationship to the created order and of his place in the world.

[16] Driver, *The Book of Genesis,* p. 5.

Thus, the two stories complement one another to express adequately Israel's creation faith and her understanding of the essential nature of man as a creature of God. In preserving them both Israel was doubtless aware of their differences. She was more concerned that together they express a perspective toward the relationship of natural reality and ultimate being that transcends any and all attempts to speak of the creation in literal and historical terms.

The Relationship of the Biblical Stories to the Creation Myths of the Ancient Near East

Behind the stories of creation in Genesis 1 and 2 is the cosmology (view of the world) typical of the whole Old Testament and the ancient Semitic world.[17] One could not expect such a view to correspond to modern scientific conceptions of the universe. As seen below, the Hebrew divided his universe into three levels, all clearly stated in the familiar words of the Second Commandment:

> You shall not make yourself a graven image,
> or any likeness of anything that is in
> *heaven above,*
> or that is in the
> *earth beneath,*
> or that is in the
> *water under the earth.* (Exodus 20:4) [18]

The flat, circular earth occupied the center of the world. Over it stretched a solid dome, the firmament of Genesis 1 (literally "a beaten out place"), which firmly rested on the mountains around the edge of the earth. Inside the dome the sun, moon, and stars moved in their proper courses, as if on tracks. Above the dome were the "waters above the firmament," originally part of the primeval ocean before it was divided at the creation of the world.[19] Instead of flooding the earth these waters supplied rain, snow, and hail when God opened the proper "windows of heaven." [20] Above the heavenly waters were the chambers of

---

[17] Similar cosmologies are found in the myths and traditions of other primitive peoples. See for comparison Charles Long, *Alpha: The Myths of Creation.*
[18] Italics inserted.
[19] Cf. Genesis 1:6, 7; Job 38:8–11; Psalm 104:6–9.
[20] Job 38:22–30.

God himself.[21]   Beneath the earth was the Great Deep, a mighty ocean where all earthly waters had their source.[22]   The earth rested secure on great pillars sunk deep in the subterranean waters.   Within this lower region was *Sheol,* the gloomy abode of the dead.

Other ancient peoples had conceptions of their world and its creation similar to those of the Israelites.   Egypt conceived of the earth as a flat platter with a corrugated rim.[23]   The bottom of the platter was the alluvial plain of Egypt; the rim was the mountainous foreign lands.[24]   The platter of existence floated in abysmal waters called *Nun.*   Out of primordial *Nun* life first issued and still from it the sun rose daily.   *Nun* fed the Nile and consequently sustained life.   Above the earth was the sky, an inverted pan defining the outer limits of the universe.   The underworld, the counterpart of the sky, bounded the limits below.

The Egyptian explained creation as related to the inundation of the Nile.   Annually he witnessed the recreation which came as the fertile mud appeared out of the waters of the receding Nile.   Reason told him that what he saw every year must also have happened at the beginning.   The world came into being as order was established out of the chaos of the primeval *Nun.*   From the waters arose a hillock with a self-created god, Atum, squatting upon it.   After the waters of the abyss had receded, Atum continued creation by naming the parts of his body, and with each name called a pair of gods into being.[25]   The gods so produced were the god of air and the goddess of moisture, the god of earth and the goddess of sky.   Out of earth and sky came the creatures which populate the universe.

√ The most famous extra-biblical story of creation is the Babylonian epic of creation, *Enuma Elish.*   Recited on the fourth day

[21] Psalm 104:3; 29:10.

[22] Genesis 7:11; Psalm 104:10.

[23] A fuller discussion of Egyptian cosmology may be found in J. Wilson's article on "Egypt" in Frankfort, *et al., The Intellectual Adventure of Ancient Man,* pp. 29–121.

[24] The Egyptian hieroglyphs for "Egypt" and for "foreign lands" convey the same idea.

[25] Another version of the tradition records that Atum spat these lesser gods out of his mouth; still another indicates that they were the result of self-pollution—an attempt to overcome the problem of generation by a god alone without a goddess.

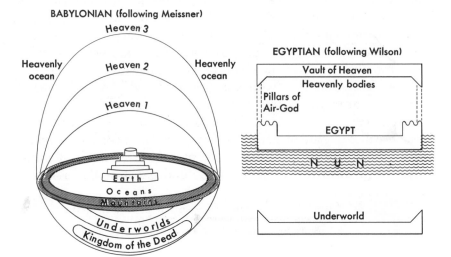

Figure 2–4. Ancient conceptions of the universe.

Sources:

S. H. Hooke, *In the Beginning*, p. 20.

B. Meissner, *Babylonien und Assyrien*, Vol. II. Used by permission of Carl Winter Universtitäsverlag.

Adapted from *The Intellectual Adventure of Ancient Man* by H. and H. A. Frankfort, John A. Wilson, Thorkild Jacobson and William A. Irwin by permission of The University of Chicago Press.

of the Babylonian New Year's Festival, *Enuma Elish* is a story of the birth of the gods and the creation of man in a well-ordered universe.[26] It begins with a picture of the earliest period of primordial time when only the divine couple, Apsu (the fresh water) and Tiamat (the salt water), was existent.

> When on high the heaven had not been named,
> Firm ground below had not been called by name,
> Naught but primordial Apsu, their begetter,
> And Mummu-Tiamat, she who bore them all,
> Their waters commingling as a single body.

Eventually, many gods sprang from the first pair and finally rebelled against their authority. Apsu was slain by Ea, and Tiamat in revenge launched a well-planned attack on the younger gods. Marduk, son of Ea and principal god of the city of Babylon, was made champion of the younger gods and entered into mortal combat with Tiamat. After a titanic struggle Marduk triumphed, killed Tiamat, and from her body made the heavens and the earth:

> He split her like a shellfish into two parts:
> Half of her he set up and ceiled it as sky,
> Pulled down the bar and posted guards.
> He bade them to allow not her waters to escape.
> He crossed the heavens and surveyed the regions.
> He squared Apsu's quarter, the abode of Nudimmud,
> As the lord measured the dimensions of Apsu.
> The Great Abode, its likeness, he fixed as Esharra,
> The Great Abode, Esharra, which he made as the firmament.

Thus, order was established out of chaos and heaven and earth were created. Thereafter, Marduk decided to make mankind workmen for the gods.

> Blood I will mass and cause bones to be.
> I will establish a savage, "man" shall be his name.
> Verily, savage-man I will create.
> He shall be charged with the service of the gods
> That they might be at ease!

A god who had aided Tiamat in her battle with Marduk was used as material for the creation of man.

There are many similarities among these ancient accounts of creation. In all the stories the cosmology is that which was typi-

[26] For a full text of the story see J. B. Pritchard, *Ancient Near Eastern Texts*, pp. 60–72.

cal of early culture. Hebrew, Egyptian, and Babylonian accounts describe the establishment of order and meaning through a victory over primordial chaos. The Priestly and Babylonian accounts even follow essentially the same order.

Enuma Elish	*Genesis 1*
1. Primordial water chaos—Apsu and Tiamat enveloped in darkness	1. Earth is formless, and void and the chaotic deep (*Tehom*) enveloped in darkness
2. Appearance of Marduk, "Sun of the heavens"	2. The creation of light
3. Marduk overcomes chaos in titanic battle with Tiamat and fashions the sky from one half of her body	3. The firmament of the heavens is created
4. Earth is formed	4. Waters gathered together and dry land appears
5. Constellations are established	5. Light bodies are created
6. Man is made (as an afterthought) to serve the gods	6. Man is created in God's image to have dominion over all of creation
7. The gods hold a banquet	7. God rests on the seventh day

Evidently, the Israelite community within which Genesis 1–2 found expression was familiar with both Babylonian and Egyptian creation narratives. In the form of her story and the world view reflected in it, Israel differed little from her contemporaries.

However, Israel's expression of her creation faith far surpasses the traditions of creation present elsewhere in her world. The genius of the Israelite creation story is a theological genius. In her conception of the character of the creator God she is unique. In contrast to the grossly polytheistic struggle of *Enuma Elish*, Genesis describes the creative activity of one, sovereign God who with a word establishes order out of chaos. Israel's faith was that he through whom the world came into being was one, Yahweh the sole omnipotent God, creator and redeemer of Israel. Yahweh, who had called Israel into being, had also spoken the world into existence. Marduk and others to whom the role of creator had been assigned were nonentities, wholly unworthy of comparison with Yahweh. In the Genesis accounts other deities of the ancient

world, the heavenly bodies, are stripped of their divine prerogatives becoming mere instruments in the hand of Yahweh used in
delineating day and night.

Behind *Enuma Elish* and other creation stories from the Ancient Near East was the thought of a personal, chaotic force constantly seeking to undo the work of the gods. The Old Testament
occasionally reflects this thought.[27] Elsewhere in the Old Testament traditions defeat of chaos is expressed as the conquering of
the primordial sea (Psalm 104:9; 148:6) and as a terrible battle
fought by Yahweh against a dragon called Rahab or Leviathan
(Psalm 74:13 f.; Job 26:12 f.; Isaiah 27:1, 51:9 f.). But always
chaos is inferior to Yahweh and powerless before him. Like the
heavenly bodies, chaos is an instrument in Yahweh's hand.

The Genesis view of man as the climax of creation, made in
the image and likeness of God, is further evidence of the theological superiority of Israelite creation faith. Man was made to have
dominion over the world and to enjoy fellowship with its creator,[28] not to be a servant in the household of the gods doing work
they were reluctant to do for themselves. Placed in a good world
man was intended to lead a good life, enjoying the blessings
bestowed upon him by a gracious God. He lives in a good world
brought into existence by the sovereign power of the only God
—known as a God of redeeming love—in whose hands it constantly
remained. The earth stands firmly upon its pillars, the mountains are steady and chaotic waters do not return to cover the
land. Day follows night and season follows season as Yahweh
intends. Man, therefore, is secure because God protects the
world against chaos. In other words man lives in a world whose
existence and meaning is derived from God and he is safe. For
this he is constantly thankful.[29] This is Israel's creation faith!

Although far removed from modern scientific descriptions (it
is closer to the medieval than the contemporary view), this
Israelite model of the universe illustrates belief in the God-main-
tained order of the world—a belief profound enough to be heeded

[27] Isaiah 27:1; Job 38:8–11; Jeremiah 4:23 f.
[28] The Westminster Confession includes the arresting statement, "The chief end
of man is to glorify God and enjoy him forever."
[29] Cf. Psalms 24:2; 104:5, 9; 136:6; Genesis 8:22; Psalm 74:16 f.

by both ancient and modern scientific man. ⌈In fact, science of all ages has grown out of an understanding of nature as orderly and rational. In this sense scientific achievement has its roots in the ancient Israelite faith in an ordered universe.⌋

THE TRADITION OF THE FALL: REBELLION AND VIOLENCE (GENESIS 3 AND 4)

The Yahwistic story of creation left mankind (Adam and Eve) in Eden's garden of paradise. The reality of life, however, is not Eden and man does not live in an environment of paradise. Genesis 3 and 4 give the Yahwist's explanation of what happened to "good" creation. Contrary to divine intention, the "good" creation is corrupted by man's "evil" distortion of the purpose of God. Man rebels against the sovereignty of his creator and violence among men results. Elements of the story originally may have been etiological explanations [30] of why snakes crawl, why pain accompanies childbirth, and why thistles infest the earth. The Yahwist, however, used this material for a purpose far more profound than to answer questions about origins.

The story is not only descriptive of what *was;* it depicts what *is.* Here is the account of, not only what happened to Adam, but also what characterizes the experience of all *'adam.*[31] Created in the image of God, man is a creature of two-dimensional responsibility, one vertical and the other horizontal. He is responsible to God and to his fellow man. In the act of sin, however, man acts irresponsibly in both dimensions. Genesis 3 tells of his irresponsibility toward God; Genesis 4 of his irresponsibility toward his fellow man.

Man as creature is always in the terrible position of both knowing his creaturely limitations and imagining what it would be like to be without these limitations. Man the creature can imagine that he is absolute, i.e., that he is god. Out of this insecure ambiguity rises an attitude of rebellion and pride that is destructive to the nature of man as God created him. Biblical theology calls this rebellion sin.

[30] An etiological explanation is one which seeks to account for the origin of a thing or condition. It answers the elementary questions, "Where did this come from?" and "Why is this so?"

[31] See above, pp. 57, 65–66.

Rebellion: Genesis 3

The Yahwistic writer described the sinful nature of man by telling a story. Traditionally in theology this has come to be known as the story of man's fall; it is better understood as rebellion. In the midst of the garden there were two trees doubtless familiar and meaningful images from the lore of eastern culture: the "tree of life" symbolizing man's unbroken communion with God, and the "tree of the knowledge of good and evil" representing those prerogatives which belong to God. Adam and Eve were forbidden on punishment of death to eat of the fruit of the "tree of knowledge of good and evil."

With exceptional dramatic gift for storytelling the Yahwist describes the disturbance of the peace of Eden when Eve yielded to the subtle temptations of a serpent which had persuaded her that the tree was good for food, a delight to behold, and a source

Figure 2–5. A cylinder seal from c. 2000 B.C. and its impression showing a man and woman seated at a sacred tree, a common motif in Ancient Near Eastern art. (Source: Trustees of British Museum.)

of wisdom. The serpent represents that which is wise but mysterious and wily, a force of dangerous evil. Before such enticement the couple is defenseless. First Eve and then Adam eat of the fruit, yielding to the anticipation that they would become like God. In essence they are attempting to escape creaturehood. The knowledge gained, however, proved to be quite different from that which the tempter had promised. Immediately they become aware of sin and guilt and find that their fellowship with God has been destroyed. Upon hearing God in the garden they seek to conceal themselves from his sight, but find his gaze inescapable. They are confronted by God with their sin and judgment is passed upon them. In telling this story the writer again is concerned more with the existential reality of man than with the primeval and historical origins of sinfulness. The theological judgment of the Old Testament is that the story of the rebellion of Adam and Eve is the story of every human being.

First, the serpent is cursed. Punishment came to the serpent because, as the tempter, it represented the element out of which sin arose. Man had to recognize in the tempter's punishment how God's curse rests upon all evil. It was doomed to be a grovelling creature all of its life, living in irreconcilable enmity with man.

> I will put enmity between you and the woman, and between your seed and her seed; he shall bruise your head, and you shall bruise his heel. (3:15)

This verse is known as the *Protoevangelium* or "first gospel" because it reflects an ultimate victory over sin. The verse describes the perpetual conflict which man wages with evil demonic power and implies that final victory will belong to man. Hence, early in biblical literature is expressed an idea which will reach its maximum development in the New Testament conception of the ultimate redemption of the human race by Christ's victory over sin and death.

Second, the woman is sentenced to pain in childbirth. To the Hebrew the bearing of children was woman's greatest joy, a means for fulfilling her destiny. Now her greatest joy is to be marred by pain. Third, for man work is to be burdensome and accompanied by disappointments and vexations. In creation work was not a curse,[32] it becomes a curse to man because of sin. His days would be filled with toil and toil is irksome. Thus, two of the harsh and cruel realities of the world are described as direct results of sin. God intended neither that woman suffer as she brought children into the world, nor that thorns and thistles of the ground turn man's work into a burden. But man corrupted God's creation and had to live with it.

This story concludes with dramatic emphasis that Eden is closed to reentry. Man is expelled from the garden and no longer has access to the tree of life. His sin has alienated him from

---

[32] Genesis 2:8 and 15.

God. "Paradise is irreparably lost; what is left for man is a life of trouble in the shadow of a crushing riddle, a life entangled in an unbounded and completely hopeless struggle with the power of evil and in the end unavoidably subject to the majesty of death." [33] Cherubim and "a flaming sword which turned every way" guarded the tree of life. A *cherub* (plural *cherubim*), a winged sphinx with a human head, familiar throughout the Ancient Near East, represents in the Old Testament the majestic presence of God. Thus God's decree of expulsion from paradise was enforced by his power and majesty. The earthly garden of innocence, purity, and ideal happiness could not be reentered by man.[34] Now man's only hope for immortality rested in God. His sole hope for renewed access to a tree of life was that God himself would act to remove the barriers.[35] The Yahwistic story does not state this explicitly, but it is the clear implication of the whole Old Testament.

The Yahwist is convinced that even in judgment God reveals concern for his creatures. Woman continues to bear children, though in pain; man does reap a harvest from the earth, but with toil. When man stands guilty and ashamed before God, God respects him in his shame and clothes him with his own hand. And, driven from the garden, he still can abide in the presence of God, who continuously seeks to restore the fellowship broken by man's sin. Man is judged by God but not finally rejected.

Violence: Genesis 4

The story of Cain and Abel presents another aspect of sin. Man who rebels against God proceeds to act in wanton violence against his fellow man. After his thwarted attempt to become like God, Adam's (i.e., man's) life continues in a world of violence, not of paradise.

In some early form the story of Genesis 4 may have been an explanation of the continued animosity between the farmer and

---

[33] Gerhard von Rad, *Genesis*, p. 98.

[34] Driver, *The Book of Genesis*, p. 51.

[35] A number of Ancient Near Eastern stories deal with the themes of the loss of paradise, the loss of immortality, and the reality of death. The more important of these are the "The Story of Adapa" and the "Gilgamesh Epic," both of which can be found in Pritchard, *Ancient Near Eastern Texts*, pp. 72–99, 101–103.

the nomad,[36] but this was not the purpose in the mind of the Yahwist. His intention was to show how things went foul as the result of man's rebellion against his creator and to show how foul they went. Adam's disobedience was followed by his son's outburst of self-will, pride, and jealousy culminating in a total renunciation of human ties and affection.[37] Brother murdered brother. In bringing these two stories together the Yahwist has fashioned a penetrating judgment of both man and society.

Cain and Abel, the older and younger sons of Adam and Eve, each offers his best as a sacrifice to Yahweh. Cain, a farmer, offers the produce of the ground. Abel, a shepherd, brings the firstlings of his flock. Yahweh accepts the sacrifice of Abel and rejects that of Cain. Why Abel's sacrifice is accepted or Cain's is rejected, the story does not bother to tell.[38] Certainly the kind of sacrifice has nothing to do with acceptance or rejection. The central purpose of the story, however, is concerned with murder, not sacrifice. Rejection of Cain's sacrifice presents the circumstances within which his jealous anger arises. Jealousy grows into raging hatred and Cain kills Abel. Like Adam and Eve, Cain immediately hears the disturbing voice of Yahweh, "Where is Abel, your brother?" Refusal to be his brother's keeper is his instrument of rebellion against Yahweh, as well as the logical second step in man's rejection of his creaturehood. Cain is condemned to a life of wandering in the "land of wandering" (Nod). Lest he be freely slain without protection of a clan, he was marked as being under protection—an evidence of divine grace. No less than the story of Adam and Eve this is the account of every man. The Yahwist condemns all inhumanity, not just an ancient murderer.

The Israelite Understanding of Man as a Sinner

Genesis 3 and 4 describe the reality of man's existence in the world. Created in the image of God, man was to have dominion over the earth and all that it contained. But he was to be Yahweh's representative. Man's dominion was to be exercised

---

[36] Cf. The Sumerian story, "Dumuzi and Enkimdu: the Dispute Between the Shepherd-God and the Farmer-God," in *Ancient Near Eastern Texts*, pp. 41–42.

[37] Driver, *The Book of Genesis*, p. 62.

[38] Because a man's sacrifice is acceptable only as he is acceptable, we might speculate that the attitude of Cain was wrong.

under the overarching sovereignty of the Creator. The Creator not the creature, was supreme. However, the creature is "to image" the Creator. The image of God means for man "a relationship with, and dependence upon, the one for whom he is only the representative." [39] In and from this relationship with God, man is to reflect God's nature within that world over which he, man, has dominion. Therefore, man must "maintain his relationship with God, he must remember that he is only an ambassador and his dominion over creation will be effective only in proportion as that relationship becomes more real." [40]

As a creature responsible to God, man also has responsibility to his fellow man. He is created to live in community. He is commanded to "be fruitful and multiply and fill the earth." God intends that Cain be his brother's keeper, the object of his concern and his love. Under God and in conformity with his righteous will, man is to live in true community with his fellow man.

Genesis 3 and 4, however, recognize that the reality of life is quite different from the ideal of Eden. In retrospect these chapters endeavor to explain the discrepancy between life as it is and life as it ought to be. The stories found in Genesis 3 and 4 are interpretations of man's sinfulness, his rejection of his responsibility to both God and his fellow man. The attempt of Adam and Eve to be like God was a distortion of the dignity and holiness of their creation. Because they were created in the image of God, they were able to rebel against him. Made above the animals and below God, Adam and Eve became enamoured, even intoxicated, with the idea that they could be God. They rebelliously denied their responsibility as God's representatives. The desire to be free from God caused them to reject the limitations set upon their creatureliness (symbolized in the tree of the knowledge of good and evil). They repudiated God in favor of their own powers and desires.[41] The tragedy of man's life is that he wants to go his own way, to assert himself, and to free himself from obedience to God's law. He is proud and wants equality with God. In effect, he wishes to be God. This was the sin

[39] Edmund Jacob, *Theology of the Old Testament*, p. 171.
[40] *Ibid.*
[41] Davie Napier, *From Faith to Faith*, pp. 41 f.

committed by Adam and Eve. It is the sin of every man and is the reason he lives outside the garden. A theologian summarizes the fall of man:

It is revolt, it is creature's departure from the attitude which is the only possible attitude for him, it is the creature's becoming Creator, it is the destruction of creatureliness. It is defection, it is the fall from being held in creatureliness. This defection is a continual falling, a plunging into bottomless depths, a being relinquished, a withdrawal ever farther and deeper. And in all this it is not simply a moral lapse but the destruction of creation by the creature. The Fall affects the whole of the created world which is henceforth plundered of its creatureliness as it crashes blindly into infinite space, like a meteor which has torn away from its nucleus. [42]

The sequel to self-assertion and rebellion against God is irresponsibility toward man. Chapter 4 narrates how sin gains control over a man. Sin not only brings alienation from God, but also corrupts human relationships. In short, man lives in a broken community. Cain's question, "Am I my brother's keeper?" reflects this brokenness of community. Man's world is filled with murder, strife, hatred, and war; and men are not their brother's keepers. Brother murders brother. With the vertical line of responsibility broken, the horizontal line likewise disintegrates. Such a broken community, according to the Yahwist, is not the intention of God. It is the direct result of sin. It is sin!

The Yahwist, then, gives voice to the Israelite position regarding the nature of sin. The essence of sin is man's self-centered denial of his distinctive endowment. Made a creature, he wants to be equal to his Creator. Sin is grounded in a pride which both rebels against God and manifests a self-love which violates the rights and privileges of one's neighbor.

Both of these stories judge man's sin. God's awful presence cannot be avoided. Adam cannot escape the God who searches for him. Cain inevitably is confronted by his responsibility to his brother. Both Adam's flagrant disobedience of God and Cain's violence against his brother bring God's judgment. The condemning power of these stories is only fully realized, however, when it is understood that they describe existential realities, not just historical realities. They condemn the sin of every man by powerfully representing the inevitable consequences of any and every man's rejection of God and his fellowman, whether it be

[42] Dietrich Bonhoeffer, *Creation and Fall,* p. 77.

man at the beginning of history or man in the present or in the future.

However, the judgment is not vindictive. God's basic concern is redemption of man as a sinner. The redemptive motif begun here continues throughout the remainder of Genesis 1–11 and is the basis for God's work through the nation Israel.

In concluding the story of Cain, the Yahwist describes the origins of civilization and, at the same time, passes judgment on culture. The first city was built by Cain, a murderer. Civilization began under the mark of Cain alienated from God, but an object of his concern and grace. In such an environment sin intensified. Lamech boasted of his foul deeds:

> I have slain a man for wounding me,
>   a young man for striking me.
> If Cain is avenged sevenfold,
>   truly Lamech seventy-sevenfold. (4:23b–24)[43]

Life was cheap and vengeance gave way to endless vindictive retaliation. Of course this judgment of culture should not be pressed too far. In fact, it betrays the peasant or nomadic background of its origin. On the other hand, no one who has lived in the midst of a developed but cruel and inhuman society would deny that the consequences of impersonal society are infinitely dangerous.

THE TRADITION OF JUDGMENT (GENESIS 5–8:20; 9:18–28; 11)

The Genesis story of man in sin moves from climax to climax. Rebellion and violence are followed by wantonness and the race is all but destroyed by flood. Finally, from the Tower of Babel man declares himself independent of the God he feels he no longer needs. Consequently, he is portrayed as scattered abroad over the face of the earth—lost man in a world without meaning. This picture of man in his sin and under God's judgment is painted in Genesis 5–11.

From Adam to Noah: Genealogies

Before telling the flood story, Genesis bridges a wide historical gap with two genealogies. The first of these, 4:25–26, belongs to

---

[43] "Seventy-sevenfold" is the Hebrew equivalent of our "to the nth degree."

the Yahwistic tradition and traces the lineage of Israel through Seth, appointed by Yahweh to replace the rejected Cain. Here the Old Testament begins to distinguish between Israel, the true people of God, and other nations. Cain and his descendants are cast aside and the true heritage is traced through Seth. This brief passage is the first of Yahweh's "beginnings again." Seth was in a sense a new creation, a fresh and new beginning. The Yahwist is convinced that while man may rebel against God, God never absolutely rejects man. There is a sense in which all men are rebels, but always rebels with whom God would begin anew. Sinful humanity for the Yahwist, and for biblical faith in general, is ever and again potentially redeemed humanity and the people of God.

The second genealogy is Priestly and with ten traditional generations spans a vast temporal gap between the creation and the flood. Each individual in this catalogue lived an extraordinarily long life. The total time spanned was 1656 years in the Hebrew text, 1307 years in the Samaritan Pentateuch, and 2242 years in the Septuagint. The variance in the total figure indicates that there were more than one tradition about the ages of these men. Like other ancient peoples Israel told of a time when men lived to fabulous age. The ancient Sumerians, for example, had a tradition which calculated the time span between creation and the flood as 241,200 years.[44] A later form of the same tradition [45] gives the astounding total of 432,000 years for the combined length of reign of the ten kings who ruled between the creation and the flood. While the total in the Genesis list is not as large, a similar purpose is achieved. Both traditions express the belief that an exceedingly long period elapsed between the creation and the flood.

Besides preserving a variant account of a common ancient tradition the insertion of this section into the narratives of Genesis 1–11 is used to indicate that mankind had populated the earth and as he multiplied sinfulness increased. This point is emphasized by mention of Enoch, who "walked with God," as the

[44] See Pritchard, *Ancient Near Eastern Texts*, pp. 264–266.
[45] That of Berossos, a priest of Marduk at Babylon in the third century B.C.

singular exemplary figure during dark days when mankind was filling the earth with wickedness.[46]

The Flood

One of the strangest stories in the entire Old Testament introduces the story of the flood. ⌊"Sons of God" (semidivine beings from the heavenly court) married "daughters of men" and spawned a race of giants (Hebrew, "fallen ones"). In preserving this bizarre tradition Genesis emphasizes the increasing moral depravity of the world [47] and prepares its readers for the deluge to follow. The compiler of this material placed this old fragmentary narrative in a rich theological context and used it to suggest that man's simple and purposeful rebellion against the creator is compounded by inexplicable evil influences upon him. Man's rebellion was cosmic in scope, affecting the whole creation.[48] This idea could not have been better expressed than by the story of the union of corrupt semidivine beings with human flesh.

> Yahweh saw that the wickedness of man was great in the earth, and that every imagination of the thoughts of his heart was only evil continually. And Yahweh was sorry that he had made man on the earth, and it grieved him to his heart. So Yahweh said, "I will blot out man whom I have created from the face of the ground. . . ." (6:5–7a)

Corruption had seized the whole mind and purpose of mankind. It was complete and continuous. Such flagrant wantonness could not go unpunished.

The story of the flood is the Genesis explanation of the punitive action of God made necessary by the gross evil of mankind. Here also the Genesis theologians used for their theological purposes a tradition common to their culture. Behind the biblical story lay

[46] The reference in Genesis 5:24 does not necessarily imply that Enoch escaped death.

[47] Cf. Napier, *From Faith to Faith*, p. 48. Theoditus, Chrysostom, Jerome, Augustine, Calvin, *et al.*, interpret the "sons of God" in Genesis 6:1 f. to refer to the pious portion of the human race, especially the descendants of Seth, who stand over against "the daughters of men," that is, the descendants of the evil Cain. Whether or not the Genesis writer had this in mind, he used the story to dramatize the evil of mankind which provoked God to action. The title "sons of God" is also used in Job 1:6, Psalm 89:6, and Daniel 3:25, but not in contrast with "daughters of men."

[48] Cf. Romans 8:20–22.

a tradition common to the ancient world of a severe inundation of unforgettable proportions. The Genesis account preserves two versions of the tradition, originally separate but now interwoven. One version belongs to the Yahwistic stratum of materials, the other to the Priestly.

The Genesis story of the flood is simple, but pointed. Discontented with the wickedness of his creation, Yahweh decreed its destruction. Only the righteous Noah found favor in the eyes of Yahweh. He and his family were saved from destruction and became instruments for the salvation of other living creatures. An enormous ship was built and animals were taken into it. When Noah and his family had entered the ark, the deluge began. Waters covered "all the high mountains under the whole heaven" until "every living thing that was upon the face of the earth" died.

But Yahweh remembered Noah and made a great wind to blow, causing the waters to subside. The ark came to rest on Mt. Ararat and after testing the water level by loosing several birds, Noah and his family disembarked. Their initial action was to build an altar and offer sacrifice to Yahweh. Thus, by God's grace, mankind, represented by Noah, was delivered from destruction to begin anew.

A flood was also given a prominent place in the *Gilgamesh Epic,* an ancient Mesopotamian tale which deals with the quest for immortality. Gilgamesh was a legendary ruler of the city state of Uruk on the lower Euphrates. After the death of his closest friend, he began a search for the secret of immortality. In his quest he learned that one man, Utnapishtim, had been able to escape the common fate of mankind. After a long search Gilgamesh found Utnapishtim, who told the following story about the secret of his immortality.[49]

> I will reveal to thee, Gilgamesh, a hidden matter
> And a secret of the gods will I tell thee:
> Shurippak—a city which thou knowest,
> And which on Euphrates bank is situate—
> That city was ancient, as were the gods
> within it,
> When their heart led the great gods to produce
> the flood.

[49] The following quotations are from James B. Pritchard, *Ancient Near Eastern Texts,* pp. 93–97. The Pritchard volume contains the full text of the epic, pp. 72–99.

Figure 2–6. The eleventh tablet of the Assyrian version of the Gilgamesh Epic recording the Babylonian account of the flood. The Epic dates from the late third millennium B.C. This tablet comes from seventh century Nineveh. (Source: Trustees of British Museum.)

The gods intended to destroy all mankind, but one of them, Ea, warned Utnapishtim to heed the following advice:

> Man of Shuruppak, son of Ubar-Tutu,
> Tear down this house, build a ship!
> Give up possessions, seek thou life.
> Forswear worldly goods and keep the soul
>   alive!
> Aboard the ship take thou the seed of all living
>   things.

Utnapishtim was not to warn his neighbors of the coming deluge. In fact, he was to use deception, if necessary, to keep the plan of the gods from them. The ship was built and loaded and then the flood came. From the ship Utnapishtim watched the storm reach such savage proportions that the gods themselves were frightened and regretted that they had decreed the flood.

. . . shrinking back, they ascended to the
    heaven of Anu.
The gods cowered like dogs crouched against
    the outer wall.
Ishtar cried out like a woman in travail,
The sweet-voiced mistress of the gods moans
    aloud:
"The olden days are alas turned to clay,
Because I bespoke evil in the Assembly of the gods."

The deluge lasted six days and nights, but on the seventh day the storm subsided. Stillness set in and all mankind had returned to clay. The ship came to a halt on Mt. Nasir and Utnapishtim tried to find out if the waters were subsiding.

I sent forth and set free a dove.
The dove went forth, but came back;
Since no resting-place for it was visible, she
    turned round.
Then I sent forth and set free a swallow.
The swallow went forth, but came back;
Since no resting-place for it was visible, she
    turned round.
Then I sent forth and set free a raven.
The raven went forth and, seeing that the waters
    had diminished,
He eats, circles, caws, and turns not round.
Then I let out all to the four winds
    and offered a sacrifice.
. . . .
The gods smelled the savor,
The gods smelled the sweet savor,
The gods crowded like flies about the sacrificer.

After the gods held a council, one of them went aboard the ship, touched the foreheads of Utnapishtim and his wife, and blessed them thus:

Hitherto Utnapishtim has been but human.
Henceforth Utnapishtim and his wife shall be like
    unto us gods.

The similarity between this story and the Genesis account of the flood is obvious. Both are based upon some known flood of impressive proportion. No physical evidence for a flood of the proportions demanded by both Genesis and the *Gilgamesh Epic* exists. Such a flood would have been worldwide—covering everything. The Mesopotamian Valley, however, more than once was flooded by its great rivers. One of these cataclysms may have been accompanied by destruction on such a scale that it became the theme of an ancient tradition which lies behind both of these writings.[50]

The religious meaning of Genesis 6–9 transcends the question about the historical nature of the flood. The religious concepts underlying the Israelite account are strikingly different from those found in the *Gilgamesh Epic*. According to Genesis Yahweh sent the flood as an act of righteous retribution upon a morally depraved race; in the *Gilgamesh Epic* destruction was indiscriminate—the just and the unjust alike were blotted out. In Genesis the disclosure of the coming flood was made by Yahweh himself in full accord with his own will and purposes and mankind was granted time to repent and avert destruction; in the *Gilgamesh Epic*, however, the disclosure was made on the sly by Ea contrary to the intentions of the other gods. Again, in Genesis, Yahweh was in complete control of the natural elements—he was not surprised by the flood or its severity; but in the *Gilgamesh Epic* the storm got out of control and the gods fled to the highest part of heaven and cowered like dogs. Finally, the picture of gods so dependent upon Utnapishtim's sacrifice that they hover about him like flies was totally foreign to the Israelite conception of Yahweh, who exists independent of all of creation.

The theological superiority of the Israelite story is most clearly seen in its use by the writers of Genesis. Here is presented the biblical view of a corrupt human race in which the righteous are few. In the awfulness of his judgment Yahweh destroys the wicked, but in the wonder of his mercy he delivers the righteous and the race.[51] To the Genesis writers this redemptive concern reflected in the flood story provides the rationale for Yahweh's selection of Israel to be his people. Since the flood was unsuccessful in resolving the sin problem (evidenced by the sin of Noah), Yahweh elected a people and entered into covenant with them to the end of redemption.

The Yahwistic version of the flood story closes with the story

[50] Cf. André Parrot, *The Flood and Noah's Ark*, pp. 51–2; John Bright, "Has Archaeology Found Evidence of the Flood?" in *The Biblical Archaeologist Reader*, pp. 32–40; Alexander Heidel, *The Gilgamesh Epic and Old Testament Parallels*, second edition.

[51] Richardson, *Genesis I–XI*, p. 97.

of Noah's disgrace in nakedness and drunkenness (perhaps a parallel to "the fall" of Adam and Eve). However, the real focus of the story is Canaan, Noah's grandson and the ancestor of the Canaanites whose licentious religion was always a threat to the purity of Israel's worship. The story serves as a polemic against the drunken sexual excesses of the Canaanite cult. Noah, the righteous hero of the flood, succumbed to the new powers of culture available to him. Consequently, he pronounced a terrible curse on the Canaanite way of life, represented by a person. Thus later Israel could justify the enslavement and annihilation of the peoples of Canaan.[52]

The Tower of Babel

The Yahwist concluded the primeval history with the story of the tower of Babel. Its use is perhaps a selfconscious repetition

Figure 2–7. The ruins of the ziggurat of ancient Ur, built c. 2100 B.C. The terraces of this multicolored temple-tower were planted with trees. A similar arrangement at Babylon may have created the impression of "hanging gardens." (Source: Trustees of British Museum.)

[52] Cf. Joshua 1–12 and pp. 191–192 below.

of the theme of judgment already expressed in the story of the flood. In ancient times Sumerian settlers in the land of Shinar (Babylon) organized themselves into powerful cities and erected sacred towers, or *ziggurats*. The most famous of these towers was at Babylon [53] and was called *Etemenanki*, "House of the foundation of heaven and earth." The original mythological motif is clear. The ziggurat is a sacred mountain where heaven and earth meet and those who live around it are secure because they have access to the gods. The sacred mountain in a sense allows them to participate in the life of the gods and, therefore, to live in a meaningful world. The Yahwist has transformed these motifs into a story which illustrates Israel's understanding of man's place in the universe. Mankind, ambitious to achieve unity, decides to build a city and a tower. Presuming to effect his own security, mankind puts ultimate trust in his own power and efforts, even to the extent of attempting to scale heaven—as if God did not exist. God crushes these puny efforts by destroying the city and the tower and by confusing the language of mankind. Although this explained for Israel the origin of languages, the central emphasis of the story was man's collective exaltation of himself over against God. His self-asserting rebellion against the Creator, his refusal to be a creature, was for the Israelites the cause of mankind's broken community.

In the tower of Babel story, then, is focused the basic themes of Genesis 1–11. Mankind is pictured in characteristic rebellion against his creatureliness. Such antagonism results in both broken community and the judgment of Yahweh. Punishment comes as the effort of Yahweh to reclaim. In spite of confusion, communities continue to exist.

THE BEGINNING OF COVENANT: GENESIS 8:20–9:17; 10; 11:10–32

Through Noah God is decribed as starting over. The life of mankind was not extinguished, but was given a new beginning.

[53] The Akkadian name for Babylon was *Bab-ilu* or *Babel* which means "the gate of God." It seems certain, then, that the Israelites had Babylon in mind when they told this story. The etymology of the word given in Genesis, typical of the popular etymologies found throughout the Old Testament, plays upon the sounds of words and connects *Babel* with the Hebrew *balal*, which means "to confound" or "to mix."

Creation was restored and the original command to mankind was reinstituted:

> While the earth remains, seedtime and harvest,
> cold and heat, summer and winter, day and
> night, shall not cease.
>
> And God blessed Noah and his sons, and said
> to them, "Be fruitful and multiply, and fill the
> earth. The fear of you and the dread of you
> shall be upon every beast of the earth . . .
> Every moving thing that lives shall be food for
> you; and as I gave you the green plants, I
> give you everything." (8:22–9:3)

An emphasis upon covenant, therefore, stands alongside the themes of judgment (flood and tower of Babel) which climax the primeval traditions of creation and rebellion. The flood marked the ending of one epoch and the beginning of another and, according to the Israelite theologian compilers of these materials, God's word to the new epoch is a word of blessing and grace. In spite of profound disturbance mankind may know in the continuity of life itself that Yahweh has not withdrawn. God has not retreated in the face of rebellion and has not abandoned his sovereign claim over all creatures. Noah and his family are alive and with them God makes covenant promising his presence and requiring of them the responsible allegiance originally demanded by the act of creation. The Creator covenants with the creatures and promises his constant care and protection without which life could not continue.

> "Behold, I establish my covenant with you and your
> descendants after you,
> and with every living creature that is with you,
> the birds, the cattle, and every beast of the earth
> with you, as many as came out of the ark.
> I establish my covenant with you, that never again
> shall all flesh be cut off by the waters of a flood,
> and never again shall there be a flood to destroy
> the earth."
> And God said, "This is the sign of the covenant which
> I make between me and you and every living creature
> that is with you, for all future generations:
> I set my bow in the cloud, and it shall be a sign
> of the covenant between me and the earth.
> When I bring clouds over the earth and the bow
> is seen in the clouds,

> I will remember my covenant which is between me and
> you and every living creature of all flesh;
> and the waters shall never again become a flood to
> destroy all flesh." (9:9–15)

Chaos may have threatened in the flood, but the bow of the covenant symbolizes the guarantee that chaos will not prevail. God is sovereign even over the rebellion of man. This sovereignty will be exercised not only in judgment but also in redemption.

The idea of covenant, found here for the first time in the Old Testament, is fundamental to an understanding of the entire Bible; covenant follows covenant. The zenith of covenant development was reached in the time of Moses when the peoples he had led out of Egypt entered into covenant with Yahweh and were constituted as the "people of God." From Moses' time, the covenant became the basis for Israel's national life. Centuries later, the prophet Jeremiah [54] expressed hope for the future restoration of a destroyed and exiled nation in terms of a new covenant. This hope Jesus declared to be fulfilled in his life and death: "This is my blood of the new covenant which is poured out for many." [55] With the concept of covenant the primeval traditions move into the world of the nations.

The Nations and Abraham

Genesis 10 provides a transition between primeval history and Israel's specific development by setting the world stage with an array of peoples and nations. The Hebrew narrators trace all races of man to the three sons of Noah. Although not a scientific ethnology, the genealogy is an attempt to give rational explanation of the phenomena of race, language, and the dispersion of peoples.[56] The persons mentioned are eponymous; that is, they represent peoples or countries. Ham, Shem, and Japheth, Noah's three sons, were represented as the eponymous ancestors of all nationalities known at the time the Hebrew traditions were taking shape. The arrangement is based upon geographical proximity, not racial kinship. The Hamites were the peoples of South Arabia, the Canaanites of Syria-Palestine, and those peoples be-

---

[54] See Jeremiah 31:31–34.
[55] Mark 14:24.
[56] Napier, *From Faith to Faith*, p. 58.

longing to the Egyptian sphere of influence—the Egyptians, Cushites, and other North Africans. The Japhethites occupied Armenia, much of Asia Minor, Greece, and the Mediterranean isles. The descendants of Shem, later called "Semites," comprised virtually all the rest of the peoples of western Asia: the Assyrians, Aramaeans, Israelites, and Arabs.

One point often overlooked in study of this passage is that, in spite of the brokenness of community, a unity of mankind prevails. God in his purposes embraces all nations as objects of his concern. His interest in Israel has no meaning, therefore, apart from Israel's role as the instrument by means of which redemption is made available to all peoples.

The genealogy of Genesis 11:10–32 brings the primeval history to a close by focusing attention upon one people chosen by God to be the agent of his purposes for all mankind. The line of Shem gradually narrows to the family of Terah, father of Abram, who sired the covenant people and thus became a blessing to all mankind.

In their sketch of primeval history the biblical writers have prepared the way for the history of the redemptive activity of God. The realistic pessimism of the description of the tragedy of human existence deepened as the narrative moved from the rebellion of Adam and Eve to the frustrated attempts at self-redemption at the Tower of Babel. Mankind was alienated from God. But Genesis 1–11 is just the prologue; there follows the story of reconciliation.

SUGGESTED READINGS

Genesis

DRIVER, S. R., *The Book of Genesis* (Methuen, 1904). Old but still helpful.

ELLIOTT, RALPH, *The Message of Genesis* (Broadman, 1961).

FINEGAN, JACK, *In the Beginning* (Harper & Row, 1962). Homiletical in tone.

VON RAD, GERHARD, *Genesis* (Westminster, 1961). Best commentary in English, theologically challenging.

RICHARDSON, ALAN, *Genesis I–XI* (S.C.M. Press, 1953). Fine brief commentary.

SPEISER, E. A., *Genesis*, Anchor Bible (Doubleday, 1964).

Archaeology and Background

GASTER, T. H., *Myth, Legend, and Custom in the Old Testament* (Harper & Row, 1969).

HEIDEL, ALEXANDER, *The Gilgamesh Epic and Old Testament Parallels* (University of Chicago Press, 1949).

HOOKE, S. H., *In the Beginning* (Clarendon, 1947).

PARROT, ANDRÉ, *The Flood and Noah's Ark* (S.C.M. Press, 1955), and *The Tower of Babel* (1955). Short readable summaries.

PRITCHARD, J. B., *Ancient Near Eastern Texts* (Princeton University Press, 1955). Contains the creation and flood stories of the Ancient Near East.

Creation

ANDERSON, BERNHARD W., *Creation Versus Chaos* (Association, 1967).

GILKEY, LANGDON B., *Maker of Heaven and Earth* (Doubleday, 1959).

LONG, CHARLES H., *Alpha: The Myths of Creation* (G. Braziller, 1963).

3

The Patriarchs

The formative period in Israelite history was the era which encompassed both the Exodus and the conquest of Canaan. To Israelite historians, however, these events were fulfillment of promises made to their patriarchal ancestors, Abraham, Isaac, and Jacob. They believed that in his dealing with these men Yahweh began his activity of redemption, an activity which reached a climax in the deliverance from Egypt and the entrance into the land of promise. The patriarchal period, then, was the time of Israel's origins, or of her prehistory. The patriarchal narratives in Genesis 12–50 are virtually the only sources of information about this prehistory, and these are by no means documents contemporaneous with the events which they relate. They are, however, documents of highest theological importance.

THE DEVELOPMENT OF ISRAEL'S PATRIARCHAL TRADITIONS

The patriarchal stories are the traditions of the people of faith handed down from generation to generation in various clans which later made up the nation of Israel. The interpretation of these traditions which follows makes it clear that their present form was influenced by the Exodus-Sinai event which for Israel was instructive about all history. In fact the present Genesis narratives present an epic of Israel's origin unified around the theme of covenant promise. Three versions of this epic are found in the Yahwistic, Elohistic and Priestly histories of Israel. Even though the final shaping of the patriarchal traditions was separated by centuries from the events they describe, the epic form authentically reflects the conditions and customs of the ancient world between 2000 and 1500 B.C. There can be little doubt that it reflects the activities and movements of those wandering Arameans who were the fathers of Israel.[1]

Originally, however, the patriarchal stories were clan traditions, not traditions of Israel as an entity. They represented the particular "histories" of important tribal groups which, after the Exodus, formed in Canaan the twelve tribe confederacy of Israel. They were independently gathered around the memory of the various patriarchal figures (Abraham, Isaac, Jacob). Some of them were remembered in cultic celebration of the clan god or "god of the fathers." Others explained tribal customs and names (etiological stories). Others vindicated territorial claims by explaining how the tribe occupied the area it held. Still others related to sacred places and moments and appear to be attempts to explain a particular tribe's sense of the sacred in its midst. In fact, however, these originally separated traditions belonged together, because, no matter how diverse had been the pre-exodus-covenant-conquest experience of the people of the tribal confederacy of Israel, faith in Yahweh led them to believe that they shared in common his leadership in bringing them together.

One other characteristic of the patriarchal stories should be carefully noted. Abraham, Isaac, and Jacob were not solitary individuals. They were chiefs of sizable clans [2] and the simple stories about them conceal complex clan movements. "In them the individual blends with the group, and his doings reflect those of the group." [3] In Israelite thought the individual was important only to the extent that he was participant in the activity of the larger group of which he was a member.[4] He always looked on himself as a part of a larger whole—the nation, the clan, or the family. Therefore, narratives which seemingly describe the action of an individual often actually depict the action of the group of which the individual is a member. As a consequence, whether a certain narrative presents an interesting event in the life of its

[1] Deuteronomy 26:5.
[2] Bright, *A History of Israel*, p. 83.
[3] *Ibid.*
[4] Cf. A. R. Johnson, *The Vitality of the Individual in Ancient Israel*.

hero or portrays an interlude from the life of the clan of which he is the head cannot always be determined. When reading these narratives, therefore, it is well to remember that the historical reality reflected may be far more complex than the story would seem to indicate.[5]

THE WORLD OF THE PATRIARCHS

The patriarchal traditions are set in the first part of the second millenium B.C. (2000–1500). By the time Abraham made his journey from Haran in Mesopotamia to Canaan great civilizations had already risen, prospered, and decayed. In fact, the world of the patriarchs was both old and confused. Established states were either being overthrown or experiencing cataclysmic dynastic changes. New peoples were entering the areas of civilization from the mountains and the deserts. They conquered their less barbaric neighbors only to be conquered in turn by their victims' culture.

The first identifiable people to settle permanently in Mesopotamia were the Sumerians, who established a series of city-states around 3000 B.C. Sometime around 2500 B.C. a group of Semitic people overran the Sumerian city-states and in the twenty-fourth century Sargon of Akkad established the first real empire in history. Less than a century later, a coalition of peoples from the Zagros mountains north of Akkad destroyed this Semitic empire and paved the way for a resurgence of Sumerian culture, which came to flower in the famous Third Dynasty of Ur (2060–1950). This resurrected glory, however, was short-lived and soon disappeared before onslaughts of peoples from several points of the compass. Important among these were the Elamites from the region southeast of Mesopotamia and the Hurrians (Old Testament "Horites"), who came in ever increasing numbers from the mountains northeast of Mesopotamia. The Hurrians finally attained their greatest prominence in the central Mesopotamian kingdom of Mitanni during the fifteenth and fourteenth centuries. Clearly the history of Mesopotamia during the first part of the second millennium B.C. was characterized by instability.[6]

[5] Bright, *A History of Israel,* p. 83.

[6] A comprehensive analysis of Mesopotamian history may be found in R. T. O'Callaghan's, *Aram Naharaim.*

Egypt, however, enjoyed stability during the patriarchal age. Protected by natural defenses, she experienced the most prosperous period of her history. During a large part of this era, Canaan was within the Egyptian sphere of influence and the Canaanite residents were free to enter and leave Egypt almost at will.

The Amorite Invasions ✓

The most striking movement of the age (and by far the most important for an understanding of Israel's origins) was the invasion of the whole Fertile Crescent by a wave of Semitic [7] peoples from Arabia. These people moved "on toward the sea, like the mighty Euphrates itself, at times checked in its course but finally engulfing all before it." [8] Periodically, they gathered in larger hordes and raided the sown land. Pressing out from the desert upon the fringes of civilization, they made their appearance in Mesopotamia, Syria, and Palestine. This nomadic pressure, which reached its zenith around 2000 B.C., caused a progressive depopulation of Canaan [9] which by 1900 B.C. was in the hands of seminomadic tribes.[10] In Transjordan the movement terminated sedentary life for more than six hundred years and the land east of the Jordan river became range country for seminomadic invaders.

From 2000 B.C. the Amorites or "Westerners," as these Semitic people were called, became more interested in settling down than in making fresh raids through the countryside. A Mesopotamian hymn to the god of the west reflects this transition in the life of these peoples. First, the hymn declares:

> For the Amorite the weapon is his companion—he
> knows no submission.
> He eats uncooked meat,
> Through his whole life he does not possess a house,
> His dead companion he does not bury.

[7] People belonging to the same racial group as the Israelites and in this case a group of Amorites, some of whom were the precursors of Israel. In the Old Testament Semites are generally the descendants of Shem.

[8] R. T. O'Callaghan, *Aram Naharaim*, p. 18.

[9] Such cities as Ai were destroyed.

[10] The Egyptian "execration texts" came from the twentieth and the nineteenth centuries. Comparison of the texts from the two centuries illustrates the progressive depopulation of Canaan.

Then, it marks gradual adaptation to sedentary life:

> Now Martu possesses a house . . .
> Now Martu possesses grain.[11]

During the two hundred years after 2000 B.C., practically every new dynasty of local princes throughout Mesopotamia was of Amorite origin and, shortly after 1800 B.C., two powerful Amorite states were established: one in Mari on the upper Euphrates and another at Babylon farther to the south. In Palestine and Syria a rapid recovery occurred as the seminomads began to settle down around 1900 B.C. Many new towns appeared, especially along the coastal plain and in the Jezreel and Jordan valleys, where city-state organizations developed, but large areas, particularly in the central mountains, remained sparsely settled.[12]

The migration of Israel's earliest ancestors was a part of this great Amorite movement. Although the biblical tradition cites Ur in Chaldea (Babylonia) as the birthplace of Abraham,[13] it clearly indicates that the area which he and the other patriarchs regarded as their homeland was the vicinity of Haran in northwestern Mesopotamia.[14] This land between the Tigris and Euphrates rivers in their upper courses was a center of Amorite activity precisely at the time the patriarchs are reckoned to have been there. In addition, the described mode of life of the patriarchs is almost identical with the type of nomadism characteristic of the Amorites.

A vivid and trustworthy impression of the appearance of one group of these nomadic Amorites has been preserved. It is a scene from a large painting in the tomb of Khumhotep, an Egyptian noble who lived around 1900 B.C.[15] Called the "best representation from antiquity of Asiatics, probably Amorites of the time of Abraham," [16] it portrays the family of a chieftain named Absha entering Egypt. The men are bearded and wear many-

[11] Quoted by Phillip K. Hitti, *History of Syria*, p. 66.
[12] Cf. the later series of execration texts mentioned above.
[13] Genesis 11:26 ff.
[14] Genesis 11:31; 12:4; 28:10.
[15] Color reproductions of this painting may be found on the jacket of E. W. Heaton's book, *Every Day Life in Old Testament Times*, and in *The Jewish People, Past and Present*, I, 37.
[16] G. E. Wright and Floyd V. Filson, *The Westminster Historical Atlas to the Bible*, p. 23.

colored tunics or kilts apparently of wool. The women are clothed in tunics very similar to those of the men; in their hair they have what appear to be ribbons. Some of the men wear sandals, while the women and children wear soft leather shoes. Two of the men carry water bags of skin slung over their shoulders. The males are armed with bows, javelins, and throw sticks. One man carries an ax, while another appears to be playing an eight-stringed lyre. Two pairs of bellows in the scene may indicate that there were metal workers in the entourage. Asses are the beasts of burden; one carries a load of implements, another a pack on which two children are riding.

The nomadism of these Amorites was essentially different from that of the familiar Arab bedouin of the past three thousand years. Whereas the Arabs have been camel nomads, the Amorites were ass nomads who were totally dependent upon pasturage for their herds of cattle, sheep, goats, and asses. Since such animals needed water at least every other day, the Amorites could not live in any part of the true desert except in late winter and early spring. During the larger part of the year, they were obliged to live near oases, on the outskirts of settlements, or in the hill country of Palestine, Syria, and Mesopotamia. The difference in culture between settled Semites and nomadic Semites, who thus lived side by side, could not have been appreciable. The step from nomadic life to that of sedentary culture was not an impossible one and many Amorites adapted to the more civilized environment and became people of the soil.

Arameans and Habiru

A later wave of migrations throughout Mesopotamia occurred between 1500 and 1000 B.C. when Aramean peoples invaded every corner of the Fertile Crescent, absorbing antecedent elements as they passed from a nomadic to a settled way of life. They established their earliest states in northwestern Mesopotamia, so that their movement seems to have been a late wave of the Amorite westward expansion. They eventually settled among the Amorite population already in Syria and Palestine and established there a number of small states—Zobah, Damascus, Hamath, Edom, and Moab. Among these Arameans were some of the people referred to as Habiru, who played a major role in the disturbances which shook Canaan in the fifteenth and fourteenth centuries.

During the second quarter of the fourteenth century, Egypt was occupied with problems of internal dissension and rebellion. Her control over Canaan was relaxed and from north to south attempts were made to throw off Egyptian rule. Revolt followed on the heels of revolt and general disorder prevailed. Playing a major role in these disturbances was a nondescript group of people called Habiru,[17] who seemed willing to fight on any and every side. Again and again they are mentioned in letters sent from Canaanite princes to Egyptian overlords. This body of correspondence, filled with unanswered pleas for help, was uncovered at Tell el-Amarna in Egypt and has been the source of valuable information concerning Canaanite affairs during this period. However, it does not identify the Habiru.

The Habiru and Hebrew are startlingly similar and it seems probable that there is an etymological relationship between the words. However, this does not mean that "Habiru" and "Hebrew" [18] are synonymous. The term "Habiru" is of much wider application than is "Hebrew" and was used for over two millennia to refer to a people of various ethnic backgrounds scattered throughout the Ancient Near East. A people so widespread temporally and geographically are not easily to be equated with Israel's ancestors. Yet, the possibility of some relationship between the two cannot be ruled out.

Careful study of the texts in which Habiru are mentioned [19] indicates that the term is semi-derogatory and loosely means "foreigners." It is applied to an ubiquitous group of folk who were, for the most part, of foreign extraction (from the point of view of the writers of the texts) and who were generally considered inferior by those among whom they settled. Their manner of life varied from place to place as they adapted themselves to the prevailing conditions of their locales. Some were nomads; others took root and settled down. Some were slaves or long-term servants; others were free men. Some attained rank and

---

[17] Two thorough studies of these people are found in Moshe Greenberg, *The Hab/piru*, 1955, and Jean Bottéro, *Le Problème des Habiru A La 4ᵉ Rencontre Assyreologique Internationale*, 1954.

[18] The first biblical use of "Hebrew" is in Genesis 14:13.

[19] They are mentioned in texts from Cappadocia, Larsa, Mari, Elam, Alalak, Nuzi, Boghazkoi, Canaan, Egypt, Ras Shamra, and Babylon.

status in their communities, although these were exceptions to the rule. Some formed raiding parties and lived off the spoils of their warfare; some fought as mercenaries in the armies of other peoples. Some lost their identity by absorption into neighboring cultures; others preserved their own traditions. Clearly, then, any blanket identification of Habiru and Hebrew goes beyond the evidence. However, it does seem probable that certain of the elements which later made up the twelve-tribe Israelite confederacy were Habiru. The Hebrews did belong to that class of people which their contemporaries designated as Habiru.

Archaeological and historical research has provided a well-lighted picture of the second millennium B.C. Consequently a great deal is known about the type of people the patriarchs were, whence they came, how they lived, and how they were related to great nations of ancient times.[20] Excavations at important centers of Amorite culture have supplied vast amounts of valuable material. Mari and Babylon on the Euphrates, capital of strong Amorite states, have revealed the high stage of civilization achieved by peoples akin to Israel's ancestors. Documents from Nuzi, a city of the Hurrians, who pushed into Northern Mesopotamia during the sixteenth and fifteenth century and took over much of the earlier Amorite culture, illuminate some previously difficult biblical passages and indicate that patriarchal legal and social customs were consistent with normal Amorite practices of their day.

Egypt too has supplied information of value for our understanding of Israel's early history. Besides the tomb painting from around 1900 B.C. already described in detail, there are some intriguing curse texts which supply information about the political situation in Canaan at the time the patriarchs were living there as nomads. These "execration texts" were curses against Egypt's enemies written on figurines or bowls. These were ceremoniously broken to put the curse into effect. The earliest group, dating from the twentieth century B.C., indicates that Canaanite life of the period was nomadic or seminomadic. They mention only two cities in Canaan, Jerusalem and Ashkelon. A second group of

[20] See W. F. Albright, *From the Stone Age to Christianity*, pp. 162–168, 236–243. Also R. de Vaux, "Les patriarches Hébreux et les découvertes modernes," *Revue Biblique*, 53 (1946), 321–348; 56 (1949), 5–36, and H. H. Rowley, "Recent Discoveries and the Patriarchal Age" in *The Servant of the Lord and Other Essays*, pp. 271–305.

texts, coming from the nineteenth century, mentions many cities and their kings. Clearly, Amorite nomads of Canaan had begun to settle down and build city-states. Especially enlightening among the Egyptian materials is the *Tale of Sinuhe*,[21] which describes an exiled Egyptian's life in Canaan and provides an interesting first-hand account of the nomadic way of life.

Excavations in Palestine are progressively uncovering the second millennium levels of old Canaanite cities, thus bringing to light the culture of the patriarchal period. In addition Nelson Glueck's extensive explorations [22] in the Negeb have authenticated the biblical picture of patriarchal wanderings in that arid area. In all these discoveries no objective evidence about any one of the Israelite patriarchs has been found, but their world has been greatly illuminated.

THE PATRIARCHAL TRADITIONS (GENESIS 12–50)

The patriarchal traditions related the religious and legal claims of the Israelite tribal confederacy of later times to a sacred past when Yahweh made himself known to men whose descendants became the community of Israel. The patriarchs are designated as recipients of revelations of promise and covenant (Gen. 12:2; 15:12–21; 17:1–14; 26:1–5; 28:10–17), as religious founders, and as charismatic leaders of their tribes. The purpose of the traditions, therefore, is not to recount history, but to show that the coming together of certain tribal groups to form the covenant community of Israel was not accidental but the fulfillment of the intent of God.

The Abraham Traditions (Genesis 12–26)

The Abraham traditions focus upon his settlement in Canaan, the later home of the community of Israel. He came there from Haran in northwestern Mesopotamia, the primary homeland of Israel's ancestors. The patriarch's migration from Haran to Canaan, though not delineated in the Old Testament, must have followed established trade or caravan trails used by Amorite no-

---

[21] See Pritchard, *Ancient Near Eastern Texts*, pp. 18–22.

[22] Three articles on Nelson Glueck's work in the Negeb have been reprinted in *The Biblical Archaeologist Reader*, I, 1–21.

mads. From Haran to Damascus in Syria there were two possible routes: (1) across the Euphrates at Carchemish and then down the main highway through Hamath and Kadesh to Damascus, (2) from Haran to Tadmor, an oasis city, and thence to Damascus. From time immemorial these two trade routes carried travelers and merchandise from the Euphrates to Phoenician seaports on the Mediterranean and the distant Nile lands. Amorite nomads undoubtedly used both of these trails. From Damascus Abraham probably followed the central pathway into Canaan. This route crossed the Jordan south of Lake Huleh and then proceeded down the central highway. In Canaan Abraham traveled throughout the central highlands and down into the Negeb. He stopped at Shechem, Bethel, Hebron, and Beersheba. These cities were in relatively unsettled country well suited for the wanderings of nomadic clans. The biblical picture of patriarchal migration, therefore, is one of Amorite nomads or merchants moving about in unsettled areas attempting to avoid strong states and areas of heavy population.

Promise and Covenant. The biblical writer, however, did not see the migrations of Abraham merely as part of a widespread movement of peoples. His journey had purpose and direction. For the covenant community of faith the emigration of their patriarchal ancestors was neither an aimless nomadic quest for pasture land, nor a money-seeking venture of merchant princes, but a movement from promise toward fulfillment. Abraham journeyed from Haran to Canaan in obedience to a command of Yahweh, who had singled him out as an instrument through whom all mankind would be blessed.

Now Yahweh said to Abram, "Go from your country and your kindred and your father's house to the land that I will show you. And I will make of you a great nation, and I will bess you, and make your name great, so that you will be a blessing. I will bless those who bless you, and him who curses you I will curse; and by you all the families of the earth will be blessed." [23]

To demonstrate the religious nature of the journey, the tradition emphasizes that Abraham built altars and worshipped Yahweh regularly along his nomadic wanderings. Nor was the patriarch's wandering here and there, to and fro in Canaan understood as

[23] Genesis 12:1–3.

the casual drifting of the typical nomad. He was a man of faith performing the purposeful ritual within which Yahweh's promise to him was objectified.[24] Erection of an altar was a guarantee of the presence of God, and, therefore, to a degree the founding of a world—a cosmos in which meaning and identity could be secured. The land promised to Abraham was Canaan, but it was land of promise only because of the divine presence there which Abraham acknowledged by worship. Thus, Abraham, in symbol, if not in fact, made the land of Canaan his land and assured its possession by his descendants.

The stories about Lot offer a vivid contrast. Lot entered Canaan with Abraham and lived there with him in the presence of Yahweh. But when he went his own way at an offer by Abraham of any place he would have, he in effect moved from cosmos into chaos because he went away from the presence of Yahweh. Security was with Abraham; to go any other place was to abandon safety and forfeit opportunity. The tradition makes all of this clear in the dramatic depiction of the catastrophic fate of Sodom and Gomorrah and the tragic deterioration of Lot who ends up in a cave bearing incestuous sons by his own daughters. The tradition extends the portrayal as an etiological revelation that the sons are destined not to be recipients of Yahweh's promises to Abraham but ancestors of the Moabites and Ammonites, peoples historically hostile to the ways and ambitions of Israel. Lot, though part of the ancestral tradition, was not remembered as contributing to the covenant community.

The later community which shaped the traditions of Israel's origins clearly saw their own covenant relationship with Yahweh as grounded in covenant between Yahweh and Abraham. (Covenants were solemn religious contracts in the ancient world. They were ritually sealed and curses were pronounced against all violators of their requirements.) Some placed obligations upon all parties involved while others between overlords and subject peoples were unilateral. Specific requirements were placed upon the subject peoples, but no obligations were imposed upon or accepted by the overlord. (Covenants between Yahweh and Israel were of this latter kind. For Israel the primary covenant was the

[24] Genesis 13:14b–17.

Figure 3–1.   Judean hills. In this area Abraham, the nomadic shepherd, wandered. (Source: Israel Office of Information.)

covenant with Moses and all Israel at Mt. Sinai after the Exodus deliverance (Exodus 19–20:20). That covenant formed Israel both as a community and as the people of Yahweh, i.e., as "the people of the covenant," and, as the interpreters of Israel's prehistory point out, fulfilled the covenant promises made to Abraham. Thus both the Elohistic and the Priestly historians preserve traditions of a covenant made with the patriarch. In fact, as noted previously, this promise covenant is the theme around which the patriarchal traditions are unified as both "history" and theological confession. The Elohist's story begins, for example, with the account of covenant in Genesis 15, in some way understood as the beginnings of God's action with Israel. The Priestly tradition is concerned to show that Yahweh's covenant with Abraham had "already established the abiding relationship between God and people." [25] The emphasis upon Yahweh as maker and keeper of covenant, therefore, influenced both the content and the organization of the traditions of Israel's origins. This is more dramatically true of the Exodus traditions which will be discussed later.

1. THE ELOHIST COVENANT. The Elohist presents the covenant as God's pledge of faithfulness. It is a unilateral contract, but Yahweh, not Abraham, binds himself to the covenant. Abraham made preparation for an ancient ritual of covenant making. According to the custom, animals would be slain and divided; then all parties entering into covenant would pass into the sacred place between the parts thereby taking upon themselves the stipulated responsibilities (cf. Jeremiah 34:18). In the Elohist story, however, Abraham watches an eerie scene in which "a smoking firepot and a flaming torch passed between these pieces." This must mean that Yahweh himself took the place of the subject people and bound himself to his promise to Abraham. Yahweh pledged his faithfulness. Also implied is the idea that what was to be done through Abraham was Yahweh's activity—an activity in which he permitted Abraham and his descendants to participate.

2. THE PRIESTLY COVENANT. The Priestly tradition, which is scarcely represented elsewhere in the present form of the patriarchal stories, goes beyond the Elohist in emphasizing the covenant with Abraham (Genesis 17 and 23). For the Priestly writers Yahweh's relationship to Israel was established by the covenant with Abraham, not by the Sinai covenant. The Priestly history does not even contain the account of the Sinai covenant which is central for the Yahwist and the Elohist. With direct and concise language the priestly writer spells out the significance of Israel's relationship with God in terms of covenant made with Abraham.

The covenant is with Abraham and his descendants forever and will bring them blessings of prominence and possession of the land of Canaan. The patriarch's name would be changed as a sign of the new relation between him and God. Essentially, this implied that Abraham was a new creation and that he was bound to God who had authority over him. So it must always

[25] Walter Harrelson, *Interpreting the Old Testament*, p. 65.

be for Israel. (The seal of the covenant, therefore, was circumcision [26] as the physical sign that Israelites were exclusively Yahweh's possession.) Circumcision itself, however, did not establish covenant, but was only symbol of the acceptance of covenant established by the grace of Yahweh. Yahweh's pledge of faithfulness to Abraham is symbolized in the promise of a child and descendant who is the eponymous ancestor of Israel. Thus all Israel participates in the promise made to Abraham. Finally, the priestly writer uses the ancient account of the patriarch's purchase of a burial cave for his wife and himself to show that Abraham and Sarah would share in the land of promise if only in death. What the patriarchs claimed as promise, the covenant community of Israel later enjoyed as the good gift of Yahweh. Although it represents a later age and perspective than the Elohistic account in chapter 15, the priestly covenant with Abraham is of great theological significance.

Response to Covenant. (Abraham, the recipient of the promise and a participant in the covenant, did not always act as a man of faith. The covenant was secure, not in Abraham's, but in Yahweh's faithfulness.) In a series of stories, some of which are distinctly unflattering, Abraham is described as all but denying the validity of both promise and covenant. When famine struck Canaan, Abraham moved into Egypt, as was the custom of nomads of southern Canaan. Since Canaan was within the Egyptian sphere of influence, the border could be crossed with the customary permission of Egyptian frontier guards. When the Egyptian Pharaoh saw Abraham's wife and desired her, Abraham claimed that Sarah was his sister and allowed her to be taken into Pharaoh's house. In seeking to save himself, Abraham almost surrendered the promise. In Pharaoh's harem Sarah could bear no sons to Abraham and without sons he could not become the father of a great nation. Yahweh, however, intervened and returned Sarah to Abraham, and at Pharaoh's request they returned to Canaan.

The covenant with Abraham included the promise of "descendants that cannot be numbered for multitude." But without

---

[26] Circumcision was practiced by most ancient peoples, except the Philistines. Its use in Egypt dates to the fourth millennium B.C.

a son, Abraham's only heir was Eliezer of Damascus, his chief steward.[27] That the promise could be fulfilled through his household slave was impossible. Abraham whose name had been changed to "father of a multitude" was childless. This made the covenant unrealizable. (Unfulfilled longing for a son of covenant caused the patriarch to take things into his own hands.)

Now Sarai, Abram's wife, bore him no children. She had an Egyptian maid whose name was Hagar; and Sarai said to Abram, "Behold now, Yahweh has prevented me from bearing children; go in to my maid; it may be that I shall obtain children by her." And Abram hearkened to the voice of Sarai. So, after Abram had dwelt ten years in the land of Canaan, Sarai, Abram's wife, took Hagar the Egyptian her maid, and gave her to Abram her husband as a wife. And he went in to Hagar, and she conceived. . . . (Genesis 16:1–4a)

The presence of Ishmael, the son born to Hagar, in the household of Abraham led to contention. To Sarah he was a constant reminder of her childlessness and failure as a Hebrew wife. To Hagar the child was a source of personal pride and contempt for Sarah. Finally after Sarah had given birth to a son, Abraham allowed Sarah to drive Hagar and Ishmael away. Hagar, however, was assured by the promise of Yahweh to make her child the father of a great nation.[28] He was to become "a wild ass of a man," and be remembered in both Israelite and Moslem tradition as the father of the powerful bedouin tribes of Arabia. Like Lot he is depicted as belonging to the ancestral but not to the covenant tradition.

The true heir to the covenant was Isaac, the miraculous child of Abraham and Sarah's old age. When all hope for a son was gone, Yahweh demanded faith and promised Abraham (now one hundred years of age) that Sarah (now ninety) would bear his heir. The Yahwist's account of this announcement to the elderly couple is a classic of story telling.[29] Three travelers stopped at Abraham's tent in the heat of the day and the gracious patriarch, with characteristic nomad hospitality, invited them to remain for a meal which Sarah quickly prepared. While the men were eating, one of them, the representative of Yahweh, told Abraham that he would return that way the following year and at that

[27] Genesis 15:2.
[28] Cf. Genesis 16:7–14; 21:8–14.
[29] Genesis 18:1–15.

time Sarah would have a son. Neither Abraham nor Sarah could believe such a thing and Sarah, who after the way of women was eavesdropping on the men's conversation, laughed aloud at such a preposterous promise. With Yahweh, however, all things were possible and Sarah bore Isaac,[30] the son of the promise, the heir through whom Abraham became a blessing to many nations. With stories like these the Israelites remembered their ancestors as men of doubt but also of covenant faith.

The theme of covenant promise, however, is most forcefully expressed in the story of the sacrifice of Isaac. Yahweh said to Abraham:

Take your son, your only son Isaac, whom you love and go to the land of Moriah, and offer him there as a burnt offering upon one of the mountains of which I shall tell you. (Genesis 22:2)

This was the crucial moment in the story of the patriarch for he was asked to sacrifice the only concrete evidence that the promise made to him (and also to those who preserved the tradition) could be fulfilled.[31] The ancient narrative tells with stark dramatic simplicity how Abraham obeyed and journeyed with Isaac to Mt. Moriah. Each step of this journey was a fresh martyrdom,[32] and he was able to continue only because he dared to believe that God would not require both Isaac and the death of the promise,[33] although he was willing to sacrifice both if Yahweh required. When the moment of sacrifice came, Abraham's knife was raised and ready to plunge, but God intervened to provide a substitute, a goat caught by its horns in the brush.

This story, full of excitement and suspense, is an excellent example of the way in which Israel gave theological meaning to her history. In preserving the sagas of her ancestors the patriarchs, she did not merely chronicle events and catalogue characters; she gave to them the flavor of vibrant life, vital and full, and filled their stories with evidences of her living faith.

From this account on, the story of Abraham blends with that of Isaac. Other events in Abraham's life are mentioned; Sarah

---

[30] The name "Isaac" is formed from a verb meaning "to laugh."
[31] Cf. Davie Napier, *From Faith to Faith*, pp. 69–70, and von Rad, *Genesis*, p. 239.
[32] Franz Delitzsch, *A New Commentary on Genesis*, II, 87.
[33] Genesis 22:5 and 8.

died and was buried in the family tomb,[34] Abraham married again and had additional sons,[35] died in good old age full of years and was gathered to his people.[36] The traditions about the patriarchs upon which the Yahwistic and Elohistic narratives are based obviously included more details than were necessary for the theological purposes of Israelite faith. These items, however, were only incidental to the main emphasis of patriarchal history which is not the detailed record of events in individual lives, but the story of a promise made to the faithful by Yahweh, God of Israel.

√ The Isaac and Jacob Traditions (Genesis 24–36)

The narrative continues with the traditions about Isaac to whom the promise was repeated and those about Jacob, who was the father of the Israelite tribes. Behind the simply told narratives about Isaac and Jacob lay the continuation of the rather complicated process by which those people who later came to make up the nation of Israel first entered Canaan from their original homeland in northwest Mesopotamia.

Isaac. Isaac appears in the Old Testament as a transitional figure between the two more imposing personalities of Abraham and Jacob. Since he was the measure of neither of these men, most of his story is fused with the traditions concerning them. Isaac is primarily known either as the son of Abraham in the Moriah experience or as the father of twins who fought for the patriarchal inheritance. However, the meager materials preserved about him do reflect movements of importance for an understanding of Israel's historical traditions.

There is, for example, the story of the search for a suitable wife for Isaac. Abraham sent his servant Eliezer to Haran to search for a wife for his son of inheritance.[37] Clearly the tradition knew Haran as the real homeland of Israel's ancestors. Evidently, Israel's patriarchal forebears were considered strangers in Canaan—aliens in a foreign land. The return of the servant from Haran with the fair Rebekah probably reflects one of a series of migrations which increased the "Israelite" population in Canaan.

[34] Genesis 23.
[35] Genesis 25:1–6.
[36] Genesis 25:7–8.
[37] Genesis 24.

The Isaac narratives further reveal that the clan of Abraham continued for some time a shepherd way of life and only gradually made Canaan its settled residence. The transition from nomadism to settled culture was replete with problems and tension. Isaac lived for a time near Gerar, a city on the southern coastal plain, and spent the last part of his life in constant conflict with those whose territory he was attempting to settle. The record of a struggle over watering places between the shepherds of the Isaac clan and those of the cities illustrates continuing conflict between the nomads and the city dwellers.[38] The rather humorous story about the quarrel over Isaac's wells is a profound portrayal of the hardships faced by Israel's forebears as they sought to find living room in a land where they were aliens and strangers. The contest ended in a standoff. After making a covenant of mutual non-aggression with Abimelech of Gerar, Isaac moved to Beersheba in the Negeb. However, the struggle continued with Isaac's successors as increasing numbers of "Israelites to be" made their way into Canaan.

Jacob. The stories about Jacob may be grouped into three major cycles: the first is connected with Esau, the second with Laban, and the third with the city of Shechem in central Palestine. The portrayal of Jacob in these traditions reflects the relationship of the Palestinian ancestors of Israel with the surrounding peoples.

1. JACOB AND ESAU. The Jacob-Esau cycle portrays both the bitter struggle between two men and the intense rivalry between two nations of which these men are representative. Jacob and Esau are the twin sons of Isaac, but they are more than individuals. They are also the eponymous ancestors of peoples who bear their names. The old stories out of which the Jacob tradition is shaped apparently championed clever Jacob over stupid Esau as an expression of popular Israelite sentiment against Edom. Jacob is Israel; Esau is Edom. After Israel became a nation and settled in Palestine, she lived in proximity to the people of Edom who ranged from the Arabah to the southernmost portion of the Transjordan Plateau. The bitter rivalry which existed between the

---

[38] Genesis 26:17–33. The names given some of these wells, Esek ("contention") and Sitnah ("quarrel"), reflect the bitter nature of the struggle.

two nations was intensified by the fact that they were of kindred stock and culture. The Genesis story traces the origin of this conflict to the sibling rivalry between the sons of Isaac. The outcome of the rivalry was Israel's explanation of her supremacy over Edom.[39] As Jacob supplanted Esau as the son of inheritance, so Israel overshadowed Edom as the nation of covenant privilege.

And Isaac prayed to Yahweh for his wife, because she was barren; and Yahweh granted his prayer, and Rebekah his wife conceived. The children struggled together within her; and she said, "If it is thus, why do I live?" So she went to inquire of Yahweh. And Yahweh said to her,
"Two nations are in your womb,
and two peoples born of you shall be divided;
the one shall be stronger than the other,
the elder shall serve the younger." (Genesis 25:21–23)

The contrast between the two men is painted with bold strokes. Esau was a man of the fields and the favorite son of Isaac. Generous, earthy, and full of the enjoyment of life, he was governed by the impulses and desires of the moment with little sensitivity to the deeper levels of life. Jacob was fair of skin and reserved in disposition. He had little heart for the outdoors and early became the favorite of his mother. Subtle and scheming, Jacob clutched at every advantage to improve his station. He, though selfish, looked toward the future. On the surface, Esau presented the better prospect for continuing the covenant. However, the ambition and perseverance of Jacob reveal character deeper than that of Esau and, when purged of personal and selfish aims, more suitable for the purposes of Yahweh.[40]

Although Esau was the first-born and thereby claimant to the birthright, Jacob gained supremacy over his older brother by buying (at an opportune moment) Esau's birthright.[41] Further, with the cunning help of Rebekah, Jacob tricked Isaac into giving him the blessing which the old man intended to give Esau.[42] The latter course of action was necessary to secure the inheritance

[39] This supremacy over Edom was gained during the days of David and maintained thereafter in periods of Israelite strength.

[40] This comparison of the two men is based upon that of S. R. Driver, *The Book of Genesis*, p. 249. Israel's national characteristics are reflected in Jacob and no doubt those of Edom in Esau.

[41] Genesis 25:29–34. The transference of inheritance from one brother to another was a fairly common practice of the day. For example, the Nuzi tablets report an incident in which a brother sold his inheritance for three sheep.

[42] Genesis 27.

for Jacob, because in patriarchal culture the father's blessing was regarded as a legally binding will and testament. Once given it could not be revoked. Therefore, Isaac, although deceived, could not change the blessing he had given Jacob.

. . . I have blessed him? yes, and he shall be blessed. (Genesis 27:33b)

Esau, dissatisfied with the lesser blessing which he had received and angry at his brother who had twice supplanted [43] him, sought to kill Jacob. The young deceiver had to flee for his life.

✓2. JACOB AND LABAN. At this point the Jacob-Esau cycle is interrupted by the story of Jacob and Laban. This story, which earlier circulated independent of other Jacob material, entertainingly describes the fortunes of the self-exiled Jacob in the Mesopotamian homeland of his forefathers. As with his father and grandfather, Jacob's basic ties were to the region of Haran, and thence he went on the pretext of securing a wife. The story of his struggles there with Laban represent the relationship of Israel and the Aramean peoples of Syria and the upper Euphrates valley.

The heart of this tradition is the theologically important emphasis upon Jacob as recipient of the covenant promise. Forced to flee from the anger of Esau, Jacob set out for the patriarchal homeland. At a stopping place on the journey Yahweh appeared to him in a dream and identified himself as the God of Abraham and the God of Isaac. Then he made the same promise to Jacob that he had made earlier to Abraham and Isaac.

The land on which you lie I will give to you and to your descendants; and your descendants shall be like the dust of the earth . . . and by you and your descendants shall all the families of the earth bless themselves. Behold, I am with you and will keep you wherever you go, and will bring you back to this land. . . . (Genesis 28:13–15)

When he awoke, Jacob called the name of that place Bethel, "house of God."

In the experience of Jacob at Bethel the clan of Jacob is identified with the heritage of Abraham. Originally independent traditions of clan ancestors are thus bound together by the repetition of the patriarchal promise. God promised to bless the group

[43] The name Jacob is a play upon this verb.

coming into Canaan with Abraham. The promise is repeated to the migrants coming from Haran to Canaan in the days of Isaac. At Bethel those sharing in the eventual return of Jacob from Haran are identified with the same patriarchal promise. Later the matured and unified people of Israel looked back upon their checkered and diverse history with the assurance that they had all been led toward Canaan by the same God.

In the Haran area Jacob lived with his uncle Laban, the brother of Rebekah. The stories of the relationship between these men further illustrate Jacob's shrewdness. Understandably, these must have been favorite and often-repeated tales among the Israelites. The victory in the first encounter went to Laban, who tricked Jacob into marrying his elder daughter Leah as well as the younger daughter Rachel with whom the young man was in love. In the end, however, it was Jacob who again "supplanted." His wives bore him many sons and his business brought him great wealth. After many years in Haran, Jacob was a rich and successful man, largely at the expense of his relatives. Jacob's prosperity led Laban's sons to lament,

Jacob has taken all that was our father's; and from what was our father's he has gained all this wealth. (Genesis 31:16) [44]

The religious confrontation at Bethel did little to change Jacob. In Haran he remained the same man of intrigue who had taken his brother's birthright and blessing. When he realized that "Laban did not regard him with favor as before," Jacob decided to return to Canaan and his kindred.

✓ 3. JACOB AND ESAU AGAIN. The climax of the tradition about Jacob is reached in the story of the night encounter at the ford of the Jabbok.[45] This is essentially an account of Jacob's religious transformation. In an indescribable way, Jacob wrestled with an angel of Yahweh, with Yahweh, and with himself. Although the details are obscure, the results of the encounter are clearly manifest. Jacob had the novel experience of meeting one who was

[44] S. H. Hooke, *In the Beginning,* p. 102, states that behind Jacob's adventures in Haran lies historical tradition concerning both the movements of Israel's Aramean ancestors and relations of a group already settled in Canaan to another group of the same stock living in the vicinity of Haran.
[45] Genesis 32:22–32.

Figure 3–2. The Jabbok River, on the bank of which Jacob "contended with Yahweh." (Source: Luc. H. Grollenberg.)

more than a match for him. He lost. And he came out of the experience as a new man. Thus, Jacob's stolen blessing became legitimate and the promise at Bethel confirmed.[46] He became Israel, the "perserverer with God," [47] a figure through whom Yahweh could continue his redemptive activity. The name "Israel," also given to Jacob in Genesis 35:10, is here interpreted freely and contrary to its linguistic meaning. The word "Israel" means either "may El rule" from *sarah* or "El is righteous" from *yashar*. The meaning "may El rule" seems particularly appropriate for a people whose political ideal was always theocracy.

The emphasis placed upon the story of the encounter at the Jabbok ford in the theologically oriented narrative of Genesis all but overshadows the originally more important story of the reconciliation of Jacob and Esau. The account of the meeting is filled with emotion and pathos as brothers confront one another

---

[46] Elliger as cited in von Rad, *Genesis*, p. 318.
[47] A thorough study of the name Israel is found in G. A. Danell, *Studies in the Name Israel in the Old Testament*.

—the wronged ready to forgive and the transgressor seeking forgiveness.

Esau ran to meet him, and embraced him, and fell on his neck and kissed him, and they wept. (Genesis 33:4)

The story, told with obvious sympathy for Esau, closes with the brothers' realistic decision to part again, each to go his own way. Esau returned to Seir in the Negeb and Jacob journeyed to Shechem in the central hills of Canaan. Thus again is reflected the historical circumstances of Israel and Edom. Though they were kindred peoples, they were not destined to live together.

✓ 4. JACOB AND SHECHEM. The third cycle of Jacob stories is primarily concerned with the settlement of Israel's ancestors in the area around Shechem,[48] as newly arrived peoples established themselves in central Canaan. While these stories doubtless associate Jacob with Shechem, they more clearly describe the settlement of some of Jacob's descendants (i.e., Jacob tribes) in that area. The homeward migration of Jacob and those associated with him may be identified with movement of Aramean peoples from Mesopotamia to Canaan during the fifteenth and fourteenth centuries B.C. The Canaanite prince of Shechem, a certain Labayu, entered into covenant with Habiru who lived nearby and gave them grazing rights to the land around his city. The general picture of the third cycle of Jacob stories fits this situation quite well and it might be harmonized with the Habiru activity. Sometime early in the fourteenth century, invading Israelite tribes (Habiru) entered the hill country around Shechem and made a covenant with the inhabitants of that city.[49] Two of these tribes broke the covenantal agreement and attacked Shechem. Then they were driven from the area by the Shechemites.[50] Other Israelite tribes remained in the land and carried on a continuous struggle with Canaanite princes who sought to drive them from the hill country. Gradually some of them gained such a strong foothold in this area that they remained there while their kindred tribes journeyed to Egypt and subsequently participated in those events which constituted the foundation of the Israelite nation.

[48] Cf. Genesis 33:18–20; 34; 35.
[49] Cf. Genesis 34.
[50] Cf. Genesis 35:5, 6.

Traditions of the Family of Jacob (Genesis 37–50)

Genesis 37:2a reveals the source of the Joseph stories as well as traditions about other sons of Jacob, "This is the history of the family of Jacob." The dramatically powerful and theologically significant stories about Joseph dominate this source, which nevertheless contains interesting materials about the tribal groups which later by covenant with Yahweh became Israel. Perhaps the Shechem materials (Genesis 33:18–34:31) came from this source.

The Sons of Jacob. In his description of Jacob's family the Yahwist depicts the complex origins of the tribes which formed later Israel. Jacob had thirteen children, twelve sons and one daughter. Six of Jacob's sons were by his wife Leah; two by Leah's slave Zilpah; two by his second wife Rachel; and two more by Rachel's slave Bilhah. These clearly represent twelve principal tribes (the sons) and one lesser tribe (the daughter). In the period prior to the Exodus the historic twelve-tribe structure of Israel was taking embryonic form. Their distribution as sons of wives or slaves reflects a national awareness of unequal degrees of kinship.[51] The clans of which the future Israel was composed, clearly cognizant of their varying backgrounds, also recognized a strong bond which brought them together. The common bond was the religious heritage of promise and covenant represented in the traditions about Jacob, grandson of Abraham. This was their heritage although their histories were not the same. They were in reality a "mixed multitude" bound together as recipients of the promise.

The complex nature of the process by which the various tribes entered Canaan and the historical relationships between them is such that precise analysis is impossible. However, the biblical narrative indicates that the relationships were somewhat as follows. There were two principal groups of tribes, one represented

[51] Martin Noth claims that the twelve tribe confederation "only became a final and enduring reality in Palestine" (*The History of Israel*, p. 53; see also, pp. 53–84). John Bright, on the other hand, argues that since the feelings of kinship do not reflect the position of the tribes in Canaan, they "must stem from a tribal prehistory before the final settlement. . . ." (*A History of Israel*, p. 142; see also, *Early Israel in Recent History Writing*, pp. 37–40).

as Jacob's sons by Leah, the other by Jacob's sons by Rachel. The Leah group included Reuben, Simeon, Levi, Judah, Issachar, and Zebulon. These tribes formed a six-tribe confederacy located around Hebron in southern Canaan.[52] According to the Old Testament tradition the concubine clans of Gad and Asher (Jacob's children by Leah's handmaid) were closely associated with the Leah clans. This relationship, however, must have belonged to the period before the post-Exodus migration to Canaan because, insofar as their history can be traced from the Old Testament narratives, there is no basis for associating the two groups with one another.[53]

The other important group of tribes was composed of Joseph and Benjamin, the sons of Rachel. This group probably formed the nucleus of a second tribal confederacy centering in Shechem in central Canaan. With them are associated the loosely related concubine tribes of Dan and Naphtali. By the time of the Israelite conquest of Canaan, these tribes had been united with the southern group to become a twelve-tribe confederacy of all Israel.

The apparent fluctuation in constituency makes it difficult to determine the precise composition of Israel's tribal confederacy even during the post-conquest period. It is clear that the number "twelve" remained constant, almost sacrosanct, but the component members were not always the same. For example, when the tribe of Levi ceased to be a secular clan and became priests, the tribe of Joseph was divided into the tribes of Ephraim and Manasseh, named after Joseph's sons. In addition, some Old Testament passages refer to a tribe of Machir [54] and a tribe of Gilead.[55] The stabilization of the twelve-tribe confederacy, however, was early and once stabilized it never changed. This is evidenced by the fact that Reuben, which early lost significance, and Simeon, which was absorbed into Judah, continued to be reckoned in the tribal lists.

All of this, confusing though it is to student and scholar alike, represents the biblical narrator's attempt to show both the unity and diversity out of which Israel emerged as a nation.

[52] Martin Noth, *The History of Israel*, p. 89.
[53] John Bright, *Early Israel in Recent History Writing*, pp. 115 ff.
[54] Judges 5:14; Numbers 32:39 f.; Joshua 13:24–31.
[55] Judges 5:17; 11:1.

Joseph: The Sojourn in Egypt. The final series of stories in the prelude to Israel's history focuses upon Jacob's favorite son, Joseph, whose fortunes in Egypt mirror the experiences of all the Israelites who sojourned in that land. (According to Israel's own understanding of her history, the nation had its beginning in Egypt. The Exodus was the determining event in her self-understanding.) While her ancestors were enslaved by the Egyptians, Yahweh looked upon them with favor, chose them to be his own people, and acted to set them free. The story of Joseph is Israel's explanation of how they came to be in Egypt.

The story is told with exceptional skill.[56] In fact, the plot is almost flawlessly executed, moving from beginning to climax to resolution with no real deviation from its main theme. Joseph, Jacob's favorite but spoiled son, lost favor with his brothers by his proud and haughty ways. As a consequence his brothers used the first opportunity to rid themselves of the irksome nuisance. They sold him to slave traders who took him to Egypt where he became the property of the captain of Pharaoh's guard. Unwilling to yield to the seductive advances of his master's wife, he was falsely accused of improper behavior and thrown into prison.[57] God did not abandon him, however, and soon Joseph found favor with the jailer. Having correctly interpreted the dreams of two fellow prisoners, both former servants of Pharaoh, Joseph was summoned to practice his art for the ruler, who was himself troubled by a series of ominous dreams. Joseph interpreted them to the Pharaoh's satisfaction as signs of a terrible forthcoming famine which would destroy Egypt if the proper preparations were not made. Since the famine would be preceded by seven years of extraordinary abundance, Joseph encouraged the Pharaoh to store up for the hard days which would follow. The Pharaoh consequently appointed him a chief minister of Egypt. In this position Joseph, during the seven years of plenty, stored an abundance of food for the famine years. When the famine came, Egypt alone was ready and men from all countries came to

[56] S. R. Driver has pointed out that it combines the elements which Aristotle regarded as essential to a good drama: the "reversal" (of the intended effect of an action into its direct opposite) and the "recognition." Cf. *The Book of Genesis,* pp. 319 f.

[57] Cf. Genesis 38. The comparison of this portion of the Joseph story with the Egyptian "Story of the Two Brothers," in which the same motif appears, has long been discussed. The Egyptian story may be found in Pritchard, *Ancient Near Eastern Texts,* pp. 23–25.

buy from her granaries. By all of this the Israelite storyteller stresses the obvious benefit which falls to a people in whose midst dwells an Israelite who has Yahweh's favor.

Among the visiting buyers were the brothers who many years before had sold Joseph into slavery. Although forced by necessity to stand before their brother, they did not recognize him and he did not use the advantage of his position to take revenge upon them. However, he did put them to a private test to determine whether or not they had changed through the years. When he found that they had cared well for both their father and their younger brother Benjamin, he disclosed himself and nobly forgave them. Joseph, with fairness, acknowledged that he too had changed with the years.

The brothers returned home and reported to Jacob that Joseph was still alive. They persuaded the aged patriarch to take up residence in Egypt where Joseph had made provision for them. They were settled in an area called the land of Goshen, located in the northeast section of the Nile Delta near a fertile valley (the present Wadi Tumilat) linking the Nile with the Bitter Lakes region.

Although the Egyptian coloring of the Joseph story is thorough and was doubtlessly provided by those who knew Egypt well, its historical material is vague. For example, no mention is made of either the city to which Joseph was brought or the name of the Pharaoh for whom he served as prime minister. Such details were essentially unimportant to the Israelite narrators who were foremostly concerned with Yahweh, who directed the career of Joseph. Yahweh, not Joseph, is the hero of the story, and the fundamental theme is Yahweh's providential guidance of his people even during their settlement in Egypt. Throughout the intricacies of the drama, Joseph was viewed as having been destined by Yahweh to become a chief minister of Egypt in order to save that land from famine and thereby save his own people from starvation. His indeed was the story of one who was able to say:

As for you, you meant evil against me; but God meant it for good, to bring it about that many people should be kept alive, as they are today.[58]

Again the emphasis is upon the covenant faithfulness of Yahweh.

[58] Genesis 50:20; cf. 45:5–7.

The Religion of the Patriarchs

(The narratives of Genesis do not furnish adequate information for an exact description of patriarchal religion.) However, certain discernible features throw light upon the manner in which the cults of the various clans were later subsumed under that of Yahweh.[59] In traditions which took their final form within the Israelite community of faith, it is not surprising that the God of the patriarchs is often called Yahweh.[60] Historically, however, Yahwism began with Moses.[61] Therefore, while it may have been Yahweh who appeared to the patriarchs, they had not really known him by that name [62] and they did not yet know the fullness which the revelation of Mosaic days would provide. However, the actuality of the patriarchal cults, the extent of their devotion, and the continuity between their worship and that of Mosaic days is more than an anachronistic projection backwards of the faith of later Israel.

(Each patriarch freely chose his own form of worship of God and entrusted the care of his clan to God known in this particular manner. Although the patriarchs worshipped God under various names—El Shaddai [63] (God the Mountain One), El 'Elyon [64] (God Most High), El 'Olam [65] (God of Eternity), El Roi [66] (God the Seer), and El Bethel [67] (God of Bethel)—there was always a close personal tie between the clan father and his God. God was the patron deity of the clan and was given names illustrative of that fact; i.e., the God of Abraham,[68] the Kinsman (Fear) of Isaac,[69] and the Mighty One of Jacob.[70] (This close personal relationship between the deity and clan is the distinguishing mark of patriarchal religion.) There was "a keen sense of kinship between clan

[59] The definitive work on patriarchal religion is Albrecht Alt, "The God of the Fathers" in Essays on Old Testament History and Religion, pp. 3–86.

[60] The Yahwistic stories of the patriarchs regularly use this term as the name of the patriarchal deity.

[61] Cf. Exodus 3 and 6.

[62] Exodus 6:3.

[63] Exodus 6:3; Genesis 17:1.

[64] Genesis 14:18–24.

[65] Genesis 21:33.

[66] Genesis 16:13.

[67] Genesis 31:13; 37:7.

[68] Genesis 28:13; 31:42.

[69] Genesis 31:42, 53.

[70] Genesis 49:24.

and deity: the God was the unseen head of the house; its members the members of his family." [71] The clans entered into covenant relationship with their God. These covenants included an element of promise, primarily of land and descendants. If the clan remained loyal to their deity, he would give them those things they most ardently desired—land upon which to live and offspring to provide continuity to the clan.

One other fact is clear. The ancestors of Israel worshipped God under the name El, a designation no doubt adopted after their migration to Canaan, since El was the name of the chief god of the Canaanite pantheon. Names like El Shaddai, El 'Elyon, El 'Olam, and El Roi, "attest belief in a God who is most high, enduring in power, and who watches over the affairs of his people." [72]

The worship of the patriarchal clans was filled with simple dignity. At its center was the ritual sacrifice presided over, not by an official priesthood, but by the patriarch himself. Images, elaborate cultus, and orgiastic excesses like those typical of the cults of Canaan had little place in patriarchal religion. In fact, such practices were distasteful to the nomadic forebears of Israel. Each clan had shrines or places of worship associated with its eponymous ancestor. Those places where the patriarchs had experienced the presence of God became shrines at which their descendants worshipped God. Thus, in later tradition Hebron and Beersheba were particularly associated with Abraham, Beersheba with Isaac, and Bethel and Shechem with Jacob. These religious sanctuaries probably were the centers around which patriarchal traditions both developed and were remembered and preserved.

Most likely within the various clans the patron God was worshipped to the practical exclusion of other gods. This does not mean that the patriarchal religion was monotheistic. Out of this type of religion, however, monotheism would ultimately grow, since later Israel could say with honesty that the patriarchs had worshipped Yahweh and he had directed their movement to Canaan.

[71] John Bright, A History of Israel, p. 90.
[72] Ibid.

THE HISTORY OF THE PERIOD OF THE SOJOURN

Israelite clans sojourned in Egypt for approximately four hundred years, from about 1700 to 1300 B.C. This does not mean that all of Israel's ancestors were in Egypt throughout this period. Indeed they were not. Some came and went at will; others never left Canaan. The Jacob-Shechem stories reflect migrations from Mesopotamia of some of Israel's ancestors precisely during this period when others of them were in Egypt.[73] During this time momentous changes occurred in both Egypt and Canaan. While the biblical narratives only hint at some of these, they were nevertheless of vital importance to the development of the history of Israel.

The Hyksos Occupation of Egypt and Canaan

The great wave of Amorite invasions with which we have associated the major patriarchal migrations to Canaan was followed by another series of population movements. Both Canaan and Egypt were invaded by an array of Asiatic peoples whom the Egyptians named Hyksos, "rulers of foreign lands." The Hyksos swept into Egypt during a time of political weakness and instability. Aided by advanced weapons, the war chariot and the laminated bow, they overthrew the native Egyptian dynasty around 1710 B.C. and hastened to build a great empire of their own which included Canaan and southern Syria. Their area of absolute control in Egypt was limited to the northern half, so with wisdom they established their capital in the Nile Delta at Avaris. Upper Egypt, paying tribute to the Hyksos kings, still enjoyed considerable autonomy. The invaders, while few in numbers compared to the native Egyptians, probably remained a feudal ruling class. After overrunning the country and crushing all resistance, they appear to have withdrawn to the delta from where they ruled the land.

The Hyksos dominated Egypt and Canaan for a century and a half before an Egyptian revolution in 1570 B.C. headed by Ahmose I brought their regime to an end. Avaris was captured and the Hyksos fled to Canaan pursued with vengeance by Egyptian

[73] See above, pp. 111–118.

forces. Several Palestinian cities, Shechem among them, were destroyed as the Egyptians sought to recover their former Asiatic empire.

[The stories of Joseph's experiences in Egypt and the subsequent settlement there of Jacob's family can be linked with the Hyksos domination.)From time immemorial the seminomads of Canaan had turned to Egypt in time of drought. Egyptian officials allowed bedouins from stricken areas to enter Egypt and live in the delta. An Egyptian frontier officer in about 1350 B.C. wrote the Pharaoh that such a group "who knew not how they should live, have come begging a home in the domain of Pharaoh . . . *after the manner of your fathers' father since the beginning. . . .*" [74] Such migrations would have been particularly common during the time of Hyksos control of the delta of Egypt. No doubt, the migration of Jacob and his people represented "one trickle in the flood which submerged Egypt." [75]

According to the biblical narratives, the Israelite settlement in Goshen was near Pharaoh's court.[76] Before the Hyksos invasion the Egyptian capital had been at Thebes in Upper Egypt, over three hundred and fifty miles from the land of Goshen. The Hyksos capital at Avaris was in the very area where the Israelites were reported to have lived. When the Hyksos were expelled, Avaris was destroyed and the capital was returned to Thebes, where it remained until after 1300 B.C. The Hyksos period, when Egypt was under Semitic rule, was also the time when conditions were propitious for the rise of a Semite like Joseph to the position of prime minister in Pharaoh's court. The probability, therefore, is that Israel's ancestors entered Egypt sometime during the period of Hyksos' domination.

Egyptian Revival Under the Eighteenth Dynasty

The new dynasty (the eighteenth according to the reckoning of the third century B.C. Egyptian historian, Manetho) established

[74] See G. E. Wright, *Biblical Archaeology*, p. 56. Emphasis added.
[75] L. H. Grollenberg, *Atlas of the Bible*, p. 40. Many of the names associated with the Hyksos are Semitic, lending some support to the hypothesis that some ancestors of the Israelites may have been associated with the Hyksos. H. H. Rowley, however, argues that Joseph went into Egypt in the Amarna Age. See his *From Joseph to Joshua*, pp. 110 ff. His argument is worthy of consideration.
[76] Genesis 46:28 ff.

by Ahmose was ambitious, aggressive, and able. Under its leadership Egypt's strength was recovered and her empire was restored. Egypt once again ruled the East. Ahmose's immediate successors, all named Amenhotep or Thutmose, were men of energy and ability who sought to extend the frontiers of Egypt as deep into Asia as possible. Their armies were strong and by the time of Thutmose III (1490–1435), Egypt's empire stretched northward through Canaan and Syria to the mouth of the Orontes river. Swiftly Egypt had been brought to the zenith of her power.

This period of dominance lasted until early in the fourteenth century when, during the long and peaceful reign of Amenhotep III, signs of impending trouble began to manifest themselves. When the erratic Amenhotep IV came to the throne, a calamity of major proportion arose.

Israel	Egypt
1. Sojourn in Egypt, c. 1700–1300 Israel's movement into Egypt began c. 1700 and additional migrations occurred throughout the period	1710 Hyksos domination of Egypt 1570 18th Dynasty, Independence won by Ahmose I 1570–1546 Egyptian strength at a peak Thutmose III 1490–1435 Religious revolution, unrest, weakness in Amarna period
Oppression of the Hebrews	Amenhotep IV 1370–1353 1310 19th Dynasty, Building and Strength Establishment of Delta capital
2. Exodus from Egypt, c. 1280 Moses	Seti I 1308–1290 Ramses II 1290–1224
3. Conquest of Canaan, c. 1250–1200 Joshua	1200 20th Dynasty Ramses III 1175–1144
4. Amphictyony, c. 1200–1020 Struggle with Canaanites, c. 1100 Philistines dominated southern Canaan by time of Saul	Defeat of sea peoples resulting in settlement of Philistines in Canaan 1065 End of Egyptian Empire

Figure 3–3. Backgrounds of national formation, c. 1700–1020.

The Age of Akhnaton (Amarna Age)

The ninth king of the Eighteenth Dynasty, Amenhotep IV (1370–1353) was a man of deep religious feeling. Coming to the throne after the long and peaceful reign of his father Amen-hotep III, he began a revolution which shook Egypt to her foundations. He was a proponent of the cult of Aton (the Solar Disk), whom he declared to be the sole god and in whose honor he changed his name to Akhnaton (Splendor of Aton). Open conflict developed between this heretical king and the powerful Theban priests of Amon, the high god of Egypt. As a result Akhnaton withdrew to a new capital city which had been built to his order. He named the city Akhetaton (Place of the Effective-Glory of the Aton).[77]

The Aton cult was too refined for the masses and never gained a popular following. In fact, the innovation was opposed by both the established priesthood and the majority of conservative Egyptians. In time, Egypt was shaken by such internal dissension that it was impossible to hold the empire together and it began to crumble away. Conditions became especially chaotic in Canaan where prince after prince pleaded in vain with the Pharaoh to concern himself with this Asiatic province and send them aid.[78]

Akhnaton himself was tragically affected by the chaotic conditions which prevailed in his land. He broke with his queen and perhaps with the Aton religion. Following a series of unsuccessful attempts to restore order and return to the old way of life, he died or was assassinated. His successors were two sons-in-law,[79] neither of whom was a particularly effective ruler. With them the once great Eighteenth Dynasty came to a dismal end. Thus it was that the first known religion of monotheistic [80] character brought dissension to its land, ruin to its founder, and death to many of its adherents.

Restoration of Order

Standing in the gap between the Eighteenth Dynasty and the Nineteenth was Haremhab, once faithful general of Akhnaton

[77] The modern name for this site is Tell el-Amarna.

[78] This correspondence was found at Tell el-Amarna and supplies a dramatic picture of conditions in Canaan in the mid-fourteenth century B.C.

[79] One of these sons-in-law was Tutankhamen, whose splendid tomb was discovered unplundered and intact in 1922. The riches which accompanied this relatively unimportant man in his death reveal the great splendor of ancient Egypt.

[80] The religion of Akhnaton was not pure monotheism since the Pharaoh himself was still regarded as a god and the status of other gods was never clarified. Cf. Wilson, *The Burden of Egypt*, pp. 221–228. Any relationship between the supposed monotheism of Akhnaton and the fully developed monotheism of later Israel goes far beyond the evidence.

and now the savior of Egypt. This forceful and able man purged Egypt of the Aton heresy and its destructive side effects and inaugurated at the close of the fourteenth century B.C. Egypt's final period of greatness.

Through these momentous years the Israelites continued to live in the Goshen area of the delta. Their lot probably changed somewhat when the Hyksos were expelled, but since the delta remained largely occupied by Semitic peoples, they and others like them must have preferred to remain where they were rather than cast their lot with the defeated Hyksos. They may have dwelt almost unnoticed in the territory which had been assigned to them, following their old ways of life, drawing their livelihood from their flocks. The biblical narratives silently pass over this period. The silence has been explained by the fact that "nothing occurred in which the people recognized the special providence of God, or which led to a significant enrichment of the spiritual heritage of Israel." [81]

Eventually the Israelites were enslaved by the pharaohs and forced to work on royal building projects. As Egyptian slaves they were only one small group among the many foreigners who were Egypt's workmen. But as people of the promise, they were destined for deliverance, not by some unexpected benevolence of the pharaoh, but by an act of Yahweh, their God.

SUGGESTED READINGS

The Patriarchal World

ALBRIGHT, W. F., *From the Stone Age to Christianity* (2nd ed., Johns Hopkins, 1946). A classic work from a leading scholar.

FINEGAN, JACK, *Light from the Ancient Past* (2nd ed., Princeton University Press, 1959). Historical and archaeological study of the civilizations of the ancient world.

FRANKFORT, HENRI, *The Birth of Civilization in the Near East* (Indiana University Press, 1954).

GLUECK, NELSON, *Rivers in the Desert: A History of the Negeb* (Farrar, Straus and Giroux, 1959).

HUNT, IGNATIUS, *The World of the Patriarchs* (Prentice-Hall, 1967).

MEEK, T. J., *Hebrew Origins* (Rev. ed., Harper & Row 1950).

MOSCATI, SABATINO, *Ancient Semitic Civilizations* (Putnam, 1958) and *Face of the Ancient Orient* (Putnam). The latter is available in paperback edition.

[81] Grollenberg, *Atlas of the Bible,* p. 41.

PFEIFFER, C. F., *The Patriarchal Age* (Baker, 1961). Conservative summary study.

The Patriarchs of Israel in Their Background

FREEDMAN, DAVID NOEL, and CAMPBELL, EDWARD F., eds. *The Biblical Archaeologist Reader*, II and III (Doubleday, Anchor Books, 1964 and 1970) Relevant articles.

GLUECK, NELSON, "The Age of Abraham in the Negeb," *The Biblical Archaeologist*, XVIII (1955), 2–9.

GORDON, C. H., "Biblical Customs and the Nuzu Tablets," *The Biblical Archaeologist*, III (1940), 1–12.

HOLT, JOHN MARSHALL, *The Patriarchs of Israel* (Vanderbilt University Press, 1964).

ROWLEY, H. H., "Recent Discoveries and the Patriarchal Age," *The Servant of the Lord and Other Essays* (Lutterworth, 1952).

4

The Exodus and the Sinai Covenant

The book of Exodus unfolds a drama central to the understanding of the entire history of Israel. The drama was Yahweh's action in the emancipation of his people from Egyptian slavery. Israel's belief that the Exodus events were the activity of redemption gave meaning and value to all which the nation remembered. To Israel it was the crux of history in a way similar to the event of the Incarnation to Christianity. (All that preceded and all that followed were interpreted against the background of what God did for his people on that occasion.) The nation's theology developed out of what was made known about God in this signal event. The Exodus was *the* mighty act of Yahweh.

THE DEVELOPMENT OF ISRAEL'S HISTORICAL TRADITIONS: THE EXODUS, THE WILDERNESS, AND THE COVENANT TRADITIONS

Israel's memory and interpretation of her origins is primarily preserved in the epic histories of the Yahwist and the Elohist and in the more narrowly selective Priestly history. In these works diverse traditions of originally separate tribal and clan groups have been theologically brought together and unified around the themes of *covenant promise to the patriarchs; exodus from Egypt and covenant at Sinai; wandering in the wilderness;* and *entrance into the promised land.* Even before the work of the epic historians, these themes had already emerged as significant foci for recollection and celebration of salvation-history and appropriate stories had been related to them for cultic use. The Yahwist and Elohist then shaped the themes and associated traditions into a grand salvation history of the whole covenant community of developed Israel. Tribal and clan traditions thus became all-Israel traditions and tribal ancestral heroes became ancestors and heroes of the Israelite nation.

The History of Israel's Origins: Genesis–Numbers

The Yahwist and Elohist histories eventually included primeval traditions (as in Genesis 1–11) and in their original forms must have included traditions about the conquest of Canaan. Legal and cultic materials were also added as appropriate to an understanding of the religious character of the historical narrative. They thus represented comprehensive narratives of Israelite origins from creation to the settlement in Canaan. As they exist now in the Old Testament, they are combined into one history which terminates with the wilderness narratives and with Israel prepared to enter Canaan. Their account of the conquest is only fragmentarily preserved in the early chapters of Joshua. This truncation is the indirect result of the combination of the Deuteronomic historian's [1] *History of Israel in the Land of Canaan* (Joshua–Kings) with the epic histories of Israel's origins. The introduction of the former was for all practical purposes the conclusion of the latter. In the combination of the two histories the conquest traditions are preserved only in their Deuteronomic form.

Old Testament scholarship, therefore, debates about three combinations of the Old Testament books in which these histories are preserved:

1. Some consider the basic units to be Genesis–Deuteronomy, the traditional Jewish Torah (Law) designated as Pentateuch (the five writings) by modern scholarship, and Joshua–Kings, the traditional Former Prophets of Judaism.
2. Some trace the Yahwistic and Elohistic strata through Joshua and beyond and designate Genesis–Joshua as Hexateuch.
3. Some accept the truncated form of the history of Israel's origins,

[1] See below, pp. 180–187.

Genesis–Numbers and designate it as Tetrateuch and consider Deuteronomy–Kings as the Deuteronomic history.

Because the Deuteronomic history seems to be of one fabric, the third combination of materials is accepted here. The histories of Israel's origins extend in their present forms through Numbers. Deuteronomy introduces and gives the theological presuppositions of the history of Israel in Canaan and extends through Kings.

The Book of Exodus and the Exodus-Sinai Covenant Traditions

The book of Exodus must, therefore, be understood as a part of the larger epic-like collection of Israel's historical and legal traditions beginning with the stories about Abraham (the primeval materials were added as prologue) and continuing through the time of wilderness wandering and conquest of Canaan. That Exodus exists now as a separate and named entity is due to the simple fact that the great literary history of Israel's origins had to be apportioned between five separate scrolls, each of which was named for convenience of reference. There is no meaningful break between Genesis and Exodus. The materials in Exodus relate to the Genesis traditions as fulfillment of promise and to those that follow by ordering Israelite life and worship.

  I. Traditions of the Exodus. 1:1–15:21
     A. Moses. 1:1–7:7
     B. Signs and wonders. 7:8–10:29
     C. Passover and exodus. 11:1–13:16
     D. Miracle at the sea. 13:17–14:31
     E. Praise to Yahweh for deliverance. 15:1–21
 II. Wilderness Traditions. 15:22–18:27
III. Covenant Traditions. 19:1–24:11
     A. Theophany on Sinai and the Decalogue. 19:1–20:21
     B. The Book of the Covenant. 20:22–23:33
     C. The Covenant. 24:1–11
 IV. Covenant Cultic Legislation. 24:12–31:17
  V. Miscellaneous. 31:18–40:38

The events in Exodus are the heart of Israel's historical tradition. *Yahweh brought up Israel out of the land of Egypt* was always a fundamental expression of Israelite faith. The covenant community believed that in the Exodus-Covenant events "Yahweh had by a decisive act demonstrated for Israel that he was at work

in history and at the same time clearly took Israel to himself." [2]
Perhaps, therefore, the title given Exodus in the Hebrew text,
"These are the names," is a more appropriate designation than
the more familiar "Exodus" applied by the Septuagint. The Hebrew title is taken from the book's opening words:

> These are the names of the sons of Israel who came to Egypt.

More than just a narrative about the "way out" of Egypt, Exodus
is a confession of faith about the origins of Israel.

Exodus and Covenant as Central Themes

The interrelated themes of Exodus and Covenant fill the book
of Exodus and form the heart of the narratives of Israel's origins
and of all Israelite faith. Exodus and covenant are the essence
of salvation history. The Exodus and covenant traditions are inseparably intertwined in Israelite theological and cultic attempts
at national understanding. The dramatic narratives of the Exodus are climaxed in the covenant. Israel was delivered from
Egypt to enter into covenant with Yahweh at Sinai. The covenant traditions are always the traditions of the delivered people.
The fundamental unity of the two themes is clearly expressed in
the religious confession with which the covenant ceremony opens.

> I am Yahweh your God, who brought you out of the land of Egypt, out of
> the house of bondage. (Exodus 20:2)

Together, therefore, the themes of Exodus and covenant represent the inseparable union of Yahweh's revelation of his nature
in his saving acts in history and his revelation of his will in covenant. The two themes and the stories associated with them were
brought together by the Israelite community at worship as the
basic Israelite confession of faith.[3]

THE EXODUS (EXODUS 1–15:21)

The Date of the Exodus

While the Old Testament narratives speak eloquently of the
significance of the Exodus, they say almost nothing about when

---

[2] Martin Noth, *Exodus*, p. 10.
[3] So essentially Arthur Weiser as against Gerhard von Rad and Martin Noth.

it happened. No specific dates are given and even the Egyptian Pharaohs who play a large part in the story go unnamed. But these omissions are not without reason. The biblical historian so focused his attention upon Yahweh, the chief character in the redemptive drama, that he scrupulously avoided distracting details about the Egyptian opponent.

Egyptian records make no mention of the Israelite story. The escape of a relatively small number of Semitic slaves from Pharaoh's land would occasion no official comment. In addition, any mention of it would have been an acknowledgment of defeat for the god-incarnate Pharaoh of Egypt and this was an impossible consideration.

However, evidence both within and without the Old Testament suggests a tentative date for the events which became so important for Israel's theological self-understanding. It is fairly certain that the Exodus took place in the first half of the thirteenth century, since conditions in Egypt, Transjordan, and Canaan during this period fit well into the picture of the biblical account. Exodus 1:11 states that the Israelites labored at Ramses and Pithom. To have done so, they had to be in Egypt in the reign of Seti I (1308–1290) or Ramses II (1290–1224), the Pharaohs who built these cities. Prior to the time of these rulers, there had been few if any building projects in the delta area of Egypt where the Israelites lived. In addition, the events of the first few chapters of Exodus imply that the Egyptian court was nearby. The Egyptian court was in the delta in the time of Seti I and Ramses II. The latter actually made the city of Ramses his capital.

The course of events subsequent to the Exodus also point toward the first half of the thirteenth century for the departure from Egypt. When the Israelites entered the Transjordan region on their way to Canaan, they were forced to detour around Edom and Moab because they found there strong nations which refused them passage. Archaeological explorations indicate that there was no sedentary occupation of this area between the nineteenth and thirteenth centuries B.C.[4] Moreover, archaeological evidence indicates a conquest of Canaan late in the thirteenth century. Since Israel's arrival there occurred about a generation

---

[4] See Nelson Glueck, "Explorations in Eastern Palestine," in *The Annals of The American Schools of Oriental Research*, 1933–34, 1945–49. A popular presentation of Glueck's explorations is in his, *The Other Side of Jordan*.

after the Exodus, the Exodus must be placed early in the same century. In addition, there is an Egyptian inscription from the fourth year of Merneptah (1224–1216), the successor of Ramses II, which describes an Egyptian campaign into Palestine. Among the peoples mentioned as having been encountered on the expedition are the Israelites. This would indicate that they had entered Canaan prior to 1220 B.C.

Admittedly the picture is complex and historians differ in assessing the evidence presented by archaeology and the biblical account. The weight of evidence, however, seems to indicate the situation in Egypt during the time of Seti I and Ramses II as the background for the narratives in the first part of Exodus. In all probability, therefore, Seti was the Pharaoh of the oppression [5] and Ramses the Pharaoh of the Exodus.[6]

Moses

When the energetic Egyptian ruler Seti I began his building projects in the delta of the Nile, he found in the Asiatics who had settled there a ready source of labor. The eyes of Egypt were turned to the future, not to the past. The Hyksos rulers under whom Semites like Joseph had been given prominent positions had been driven from the land centuries before, the glory of the pre-Amarna age was ancient history, and the era of the heretic Akhnaton could not too soon be erased from memory. The virile and energetic second king of a new dynasty, who was beginning to re-establish Egypt's Asiatic empire, was concerned with the nation's new frontiers. Therefore, he had little interest in Semitic peoples living in his land, except as they could be made to serve his ends. Thus he made them slaves and engaged them in his building projects. Thereby he was able to accomplish two objectives: he added to his labor supply and rendered difficult any incipient rebellion on the part of these foreigners.

In this context the Exodus tradition focuses upon Moses as a Semitic slave who by the intervention of Yahweh rises to political and theological greatness and upon the escape of "Israelite" slaves from Egypt as the redemptive act of Yahweh. From the outset

[5] Exodus 1:9 ff.
[6] Exodus 2:23.

the drama is presented as a struggle between Yahweh and Pharaoh. The Pharaoh made the lot of Israel exceedingly hard. But even under oppression they maintained their spirit and prospered. Their behavior began to inspire awe among the Egyptians. There was something "eerie and unnerving about this people." [7] As an extreme resort the Pharaoh ordered their growth curbed by the destruction of their sons. All male babies were to be slain at birth.

The stories of a child who escaped Egyptian executioners when he was found in a basket in the Nile by Pharaoh's own daughter, who grew up in the palace, [8] and who was trained in the traditions of his people by his Israelite mother are too familiar to need retelling. But even in these tales about his early life, Moses is not the central figure. Essentially the stories are not about Moses, but about Yahweh. The writers see the words and deeds of God revealed in the birth and infancy of Moses, as evidence of redemptive concern for his people. At a time when Israel had neither strength nor hope, God acted to deliver her. Moses was to be his agent of intervention in the decisive moment of Israel's history. [9]

The story of God's preparation of Moses centers in a period of exile in Midian. The exile was occasioned by Moses' action on a day when he could no longer stand idly by and watch the oppression of his people. [10] When he saw an Egyptian beating an Israelite to death, he displayed some of the basic characteristics which would distinguish him throughout his career. With reckless but courageous audacity, he gave expression to violent anger called forth by a passionate sense of justice, and killed the Egyptian. [11] Thus he sacrificed his own security by identifying with his people. The story of God's redemptive action is made more dramatic by the account of Moses' exile and preparation for the difficult task to face him in the years to come.

The place of exile was the land of Midian. Midian proper was

---

[7] J. Coert Rylaarsdam, "The Book of Exodus" in *The Interpreter's Bible*, I, 855.

[8] A similar story about Sargon I occurs in Akkadian literature. See Pritchard, *Ancient Near Eastern Texts*, p. 119.

[9] Cf. von Rad, *Moses*, pp. 7–9.

[10] Exodus 2:11 ff.

[11] These traits of Moses are delineated by Rylaarsdam, "The Book of Exodus," in *The Interpreter's Bible*, I, 862.

east of the Gulf of Aqabah in northwestern Arabia, but portions of the Sinai Peninsula may also have been called the land of Midian. In this latter area Moses found refuge among Kenite kinsmen and here experienced the seminomad existence characteristic of the life of the ancient patriarchs of Israel. In a profound sense "Moses came back to his forefathers by way of his flight . . . A man of the enslaved nation, but the only one not enslaved together with them, had returned to the free and keen air of his forebears." [12]

Seated at a well (the definite center of a clan or tribe), he met the daughters of the old Kenite priest Jethro. They were attempting to water the flocks which they were tending when other shepherds drove them away. Moses came to their rescue and, when the girls told their father of this gracious act, the kindly priest demanded that Moses abide with them. Moses found the fellowship of the home to his liking and became part of it by marrying Zipporah, one of Jethro's daughters.

Revelation at Sinai. The narrative of Moses in Midian depicts a nomadic shepherd wandering far and wide seeking pasture and water for his flock. Thus Moses entered to greater depth into the customary way of life of his ancestors Abraham, Isaac, and Jacob. In the course of his wanderings he came one day to the "mountain of God." Probably this site had been so called since ancient times, because mysterious phenomena which occurred upon it gave rise to the belief that gods resided there. At this place, whose sacred character he recognized, Moses had an encounter with deity.

The dramatic presentation of the encounter emphasizes the significant meaning of the experience for Moses. Upon the mountain a bush burned without being consumed. When Moses turned aside to examine the unusual sight, a voice from within the flame called his name and he knew that he was in the presence of the sacred. Curiosity about the bush was lost in a sense of holy presence. Complete attention focused upon that awesome voice which identified itself:

I am the God of your father, the God of Abraham, the God of Isaac, and the God of Jacob. (Exodus 3:6)

[12] Martin Buber, *Moses*, p. 38.

This was no alien deity "discovered" by Moses on the mountain; [13] it was the God of his fathers who had sought him out, and before his presence Moses hid his face. This was also the God of those who told the story and who believed that Yahweh in seeking Moses sought them and in redeeming the Israelite slaves he acted also for them.

Through this theophany Moses became intently aware of God's purpose to deliver the enslaved Israelites from Egypt, and surrendered to an overwhelming assignment in the historical drama. Moses was to return to Pharaoh and lead his kinsmen to freedom. Moses' initial protest,

Who am I that I should go to Pharaoh, and bring the sons of Israel out of Egypt? (Exodus 3:11)

was dismissed by God's assurance,

I will be with you; and this shall be the sign for you, that I have sent you: when you have brought forth the people out of Egypt, you shall serve God upon this mountain. (Exodus 3:12)

God's reply thus changed the question. It was not a matter of "Who is Moses?" but "Who is God?" and "What does he intend?" The adequacy of the prophet was dependent upon the adequacy of God, who had both commissioned him and promised to accompany him. The success of the venture was not dependent upon Moses' resources, but was guaranteed by the God who now commissioned him to the task. Since this was God's project, God was at the center of it—Moses was only an instrument in his hands. Further this sense of the presence of Yahweh represents a fundamental affirmation of Israelite faith. The genius of Israel was never her own worth or accomplishments, but her sense of and response to the creative and redemptive presence of Yahweh.

"Yahweh" Is His Name. The revelation to Moses on the holy mountain contained an additional element. The Elohist presents it as response to a practical question about authority raised by Moses. How should he convince the Israelites that God had actually spoken to him? To go to his kinsmen in Egypt and tell them of his experience at the mountain, he would have to know God's name. To be believed, this new revelation must be accom-

[13] Buber, *Moses,* p. 44.

panied by a new name. Also, and more important, Moses wanted to know the mystery of the divine nature, the secret of the being of this God. In Semitic thought the character or identity of a being, human or divine, was expressed in his name. Much more than a combination of letters used to distinguish one being from another, a name represented the total being of the one who bore it. To know a name was to know the essential self or identity of a person. The answer which God gave to Moses then, was at once both cryptic and satisfactory, both concealing and revealing his true nature. He said, "*I am who I am.* Say this to the people of Israel, '*I am* has sent me to you.'" (Exodus 3:14) The exact meaning of this phrase is ambiguous, perhaps intentionally so. The fullness of the mystery of God is not to be known through his name. "*I am who I am*" could also be translated, "*I am because I am*" or "*I will be what I will be*" or with slight alteration "*I cause to be what is.*" Whatever the exact meaning of the name, in knowing it Moses is given confidence. At the same time he should understand that God never gives himself away to be known and controlled. The name of God does not provide the one who knows it with power over God.

There must be significance in the fact that here is the only place in the Old Testament in which the first person form of the divine name is used. Elsewhere it is always in the third person. God could indeed speak of himself as *I cause to be* or *I am;* Israel, however, could only say *he causes to be* or *he is.* In both cases the Hebrew verb involved is "h-y-h." When vocalized, the third person form "Y-H-W-H" [14] becomes "Yahweh," the peculiarly Israelite name for God.

However, the divine reply did not end with this veiled and intentionally ambiguous revelation of his name. The secret of his being was not to be discovered in his name alone, or even primarily, but rather in what he was about to do. Yahweh was to be known, not in static being, but in the redemptive confrontation of his people. The question "Who is God?" would be answered in time through events about to take place.

Go and gather the elders of Israel together, and say to them, "Yahweh, the God of your fathers, the God of Abraham, of Isaac, and of Jacob, has ap-

---

[14] The tetragrammaton YHWH appears first without vowels. Vowels were not added to the Hebrew text until the days of the Masoretes.

peared to me, saying, 'I have observed you and what has been done to you in Egypt; and I promise that I will bring you up out of the affliction of Egypt, to the land of the Canaanites, the Hittites, the Amorites, the Periz-zites, the Hivites, and the Jebusites, a land flowing with milk and honey.' " (Exodus 3:16–17)

The ultimate question for Israel, therefore, was not just "Who is God?" but also "What has God done?" In presenting Yahweh, the Old Testament does not focus upon the philosophical nature of his being, but upon the redemptive quality of his activity.

Further, the God who here revealed a new name also identified himself with the God of Abraham, the God of Isaac, and the God of Jacob.[15] The new name is evidence of both new revelation and additional understanding of the same God who had directed the fortunes of Israel's forefathers. Under this new name, Yah-weh, he was about to make himself known to the enslaved Isra-elites, whose cries he had heard and whose cause he would champion. The might of El Shaddai, "God the Mountain One" of the patriarchs, would be revealed in an act of redemption.

Thus, prepared by his experience in the wilderness of Midian and fortified with the assurance that his was the cause of God, Moses was ready to return to Egypt.

The Mighty Act of Yahweh

The Contest with Pharaoh. The narrative concerning Moses' encounter with the Pharaoh [16] is charged with dramatic suspense from beginning to end. Step by step, episode by episode the ac-count unfolds with sustained interest the vacillating contest until Yahweh through Moses becomes victor over the powers of Egypt. Returning to Egypt Moses risked everything. The Israelites had to be persuaded that Yahweh had appeared to him and would act to deliver them. They had to be led to faith.

Then Moses and Aaron went and gathered together all the elders of the people of Israel. And Aaron spoke all the words which Yahweh had spoken to Moses, and did the signs in the sight of the people. And the peo-ple believed; and when they heard that Yahweh had visited the people of Israel and that he had seen their affliction, they bowed their heads and worshiped. (Exodus 4:29–31)

[15] Exodus 3:15.

[16] "Pharaoh" is a title of the sovereigns of ancient Egypt, not the name of a specific ruler.

In confrontation with Yahweh the Israelites' attention was turned toward a sovereign superior to the Pharaoh. Now issue could be drawn with Pharaoh. The Israelites requested permission to worship Yahweh in the wilderness.

Pharaoh interpreted the request as evidence of both idle time on the part of the slaves and labor agitation on the part of Moses.

Figure 4–1. An unbaked brick of Egyptian clay and straw, imprinted with the name and title of Ramses II (1290–1224), Pharaoh of the Exodus. (Source: Trustees of British Museum.)

He reacted by increasing the work load of the slaves. While demanding the same quota of brick, he no longer permitted them to use the straw which made the clay easy to handle. This reprisal was so effective that the Israelite foremen accused Moses and Aaron of making the life of the people more difficult. Moses in turn protested to Yahweh. Thus, the Old Testament heightens the drama by magnifying the obstacle to Yahweh's victory. In the face of the obstacles the people and Moses wavered; Yahweh's hand remained firm and his deliverance sure.

With increasing tension the narrative indicates that the initial efforts of Moses and Aaron before Pharaoh proved abortive. A magical act of turning a rod into a serpent was duplicated by the Egyptian magicians. Although some hint of victory was preserved in the devouring of the Egyptian serpents by those of Aaron, the intended transformation of Pharaoh's will did not result. Rather, Moses and Aaron were insufficient to win a contest with the Egyptians. The struggle was essentially between the Pharaoh and the God of Israel; only sovereign Yahweh himself was capable of overpowering the exalted ruler of Egypt.

With artistic appropriateness the battle between Yahweh and Pharaoh is set on the banks of the Nile, where the Egyptian gods should have been supreme. With preliminary skirmishes indecisive, a series of ten major engagements are listed in Exodus as coming in successive order. None of the sources mentions all ten plagues. The Yahwist describes eight; the Elohist, five; and the Priestly writer, five. Only the reddening of the Nile and the death of the first-born are reported by all three. The plagues of flies and the diseased cattle are exclusive to the Yahwist; lice and boils are found only in the Priestly source. The total of ten is probably the idealization of a tradition that many divine signs and wonders happened in Egypt. The first two plagues were matched by the Egyptian magicians, but the others were openly acknowledged by the magicians themselves to have been by "the finger of God" and beyond their competitive powers.

Seven of the ten plagues could be related to phenomena associated with the annual rise of the Nile. A reddening of the Nile is caused by minute organic life when the river nears its crest in August. Great numbers of frogs prevail in the autumn, usually in September. G. E. Wright notes that plagues would occur more often were it not for the ibis, "a bird which feeds upon vermin and frees the country of them." [17] The decomposing

---

[17] Wright, *Biblical Archaeology*, p. 54.

dead frogs suggest lice and flies, followed in turn by pestilence suffered by cattle and people. Thunderstorms, although not common, occasionally do great damage in the region, as have plagues of locusts. The *Khamsin,* a hot wind in the springtime, resembles the dust or sandstorm in the "darkness to be felt." [18]

The way in which the book of Exodus relates the plagues to the purpose of Yahweh illustrates the Hebrew understanding of miracle. It is erroneous to transpose to the mind of the Hebrew the twentieth century thought pattern which confines miracle only to the realm of the supernatural. In the Old Testament miracle refers to the marvel of Yahweh's power available for the cause of his people. Since both nature and history are the domain of Yahweh's behavior, miracle does not imply the breaking of natural law. Miracle is Yahweh's continual working in the history of his people apprehended by faith.

Behold, I make a covenant. Before all your people I will *do marvels,* such as have not been wrought in all the earth or in any nation; and all the people among whom you are shall see the work of Yahweh; for it is a terrible thing which I will do with you. (Exodus 34:10. Emphasis added.)

With this orientation the mind of faith could see in even ordinary events the hand of Yahweh. Faith's interpretation could lift such events out of the realm of the common place and see them as the redemptive deeds of Yahweh. Indeed, faith itself is the fundamental miracle.

The Old Testament relates miracles especially to those periods of crisis when Israel was intently aware of God's action in her behalf. Such times were the Exodus, the period of the dawn of the prophetic movement, the age of intense conflict with Canaanite religion, and the Babylonian exile. In all events the mark of the miracle was not its "miraculous" character, but its revelation of Yahweh, who wondrously and intently worked with his people.[19]

That the plagues had some natural counterparts, then, was of little consequence to the mind which recalled and interpreted the occurrences. The relation of the plagues to natural event made them no less marvelous to the believer. Yahweh was still in them accomplishing his ends. Yahweh was Lord! In his sovereignty

---

[18] Exodus 10:21.
[19] Jacob, *Theology of the Old Testament,* pp. 223–226.

he accomplished the deliverance of his people from a tyrant who refused to surrender them willingly and from divine powers which were powerless before him. Israel always emphasized Yahweh's direct association with their emancipation. So marvelous was their deliverance that they never concealed the fact that they had once been slaves, a thought most offensive to others. Neither the powerful Pharaoh nor all of Egypt's splendid array of gods was able to restrain the power of Israel's God. Yahweh prevailed over all forces arrayed against him.

The Old Testament narrative skillfully accents the drama by stressing that Pharaoh resisted Yahweh's superiority. Although awed by the first nine plagues, he stubbornly refused to release the slaves. Pharaoh's subjection was achieved in the tenth plague, the death of the first-born children of the Egyptians, including the son of Pharaoh. The Egyptians were so distressed that they immediately sought to placate the God of Israel. They equipped the former slaves with silver, gold, and clothing; they gave them numerous flocks and herds, and asked them to leave.

Passover. Passover commemorated the Exodus. Indeed the Exodus traditions, as noted already, were shaped and passed on in the context of this important festival. Celebration of Passover called to mind the passing-over from Egypt into Canaan. The feast's symbolism and story recalled the ominous last night in Egypt, visit of the angel of death, and the crossing of the Sea of Reeds. The Feast of Unleavened Bread and the dedication of the first-born were observed with Passover. Each contributed unique dimensions to a comprehensive recollection of the Exodus event. Feasts like Passover and Unleavened Bread were much older in Israel than the time of the Exodus, going back to earliest nomadic days when they were nature rites. The formal structure of the older feasts was preserved, but the meaning for the covenant community was now different. Yahweh's act of deliverance overshadowed whatever natural fertility significance the festivals once had. Whereas the focus might once have been creation, it was now redemption. Together the festivals reenacted the experience of deliverance from Egypt.

And you shall tell your son on that day, 'It is because of what Yahweh did for me when I came out of Egypt.' And it shall be to you as a sign on

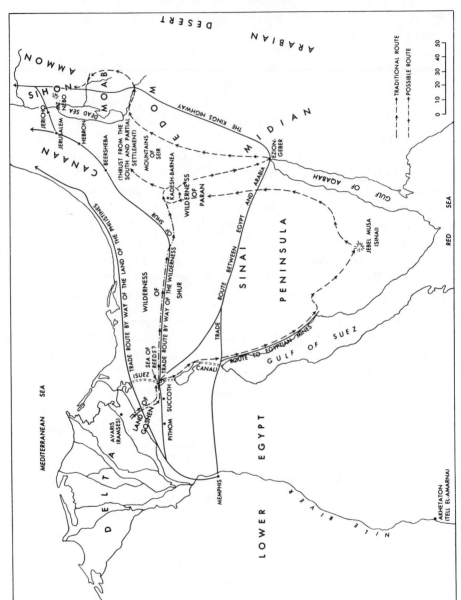

Figure 4-2. Route of Exodus.

your hand and as a memorial between your eyes, that the law of Yahweh may be in your mouth; for with a strong hand Yahweh has brought you out of Egypt. You shall therefore keep this ordinance at its appointed time from year to year. (Exodus 13:8–10)

One of the ironies of the days following the Exodus was the ease with which the Israelites forgot. On occasions Moses had difficulty holding them to any semblance of faith. Although many momentous events were experienced, discernment of Yahweh's work within these events was clearer later than at the time of their occurrence. Most men are able to evaluate happenings in their lives as significant only in retrospect.

The Miracle at the Sea. Yahweh's supremacy is clearly demonstrated by the biblical historian in the story of the plagues. The victory was God's and by that victory he gained the release of the people he now claimed for himself. Regularly, however, when Israel celebrated the Exodus, the first thought was of the wonder at the Sea.

> In the sight of their fathers he wrought marvels
>   in the land of Egypt, in the fields of Zoan.
> He divided the sea and let them pass through it,
>   and made the waters stand like a heap. (Psalm 78:12–13)

Naturally, therefore, the narrative builds up to the peak of the miraculous crossing of the Sea of Reeds.

From the general vicinity of Ramses, the fleeing slaves began to move southeastward, probably following the usual road to Succoth. From Succoth the regular caravan route to southern Canaan ran northeastward along the Mediterranean coast. However, the Israelites moved to the south of the usual route into the wilderness of the Sinai Peninsula. Pharaoh, having changed his mind about allowing them to leave Egypt, sent chariots in pursuit of the fleeing slaves. By the time Pharaoh's army caught up with them, the Israelites had arrived at the marshy strip extending sixty-five miles between the northern tip of the Gulf of Suez and the Mediterranean Sea. Seemingly, the Israelites were trapped between the marsh before them and chariots approaching from the rear. Again as he had done in the plagues, Yahweh intervened to rescue his people. The Israelites passed safely through the "sea of reeds" [20] or papyrus lake (*yam suph* is literally trans-

[20] Exodus 14:21b.

lated "sea of reeds," but was rendered "the Red Sea" in the Septuagint), but in the same body of water the chariots of the Pharaoh bogged down and were destroyed. Again Yahweh had been victor in overpowering the enemy of his people. He continued to deliver the Israelites step by step.

After crossing the Sea of Reeds, Israel paused to celebrate and joined in a song of deliverance. Miriam, sister of Aaron and Moses, took a tambourine and, while accompanied by music and dancing, sang a hymn to Yahweh. This event inspired one of the earliest couplets of Hebrew poetry:

> Sing to Yahweh, for he has triumphed gloriously;
> the horse and his rider he has thrown into the sea!   (Exodus 15:21)[21]

The Exodus, then, had lasting meaning because "Yahweh had acted." He acted for Israel, upon Israel, and through Israel, and by means of this activity Yahweh singularly disclosed himself. Confronted by this revelation and grateful for their deliverance, the Israelites responded in obedience and worship. Their deep religious gratitude is reflected in an affirmation spoken when they approached Yahweh with the first fruits of their harvest:

> A wandering Aramean was my father; and he went down into Egypt and sojourned there, few in number; and there he became a nation, great, mighty, and populous. And the Egyptians treated us harshly, and afflicted us, and laid upon us hard bondage. Then we cried to Yahweh the God of our Fathers, and Yahweh heard our voice, and saw our affliction, our toil, and our oppression; and Yahweh brought us out of Egypt with a mighty hand and an outstretched arm, with great terror, with signs and wonders; and he brought us into this place and gave us this land, a land flowing with milk and honey. And behold, now I bring the first of the fruit of the ground, which thou, O Yahweh, hast given me. (Deuteronomy 26:5-10)

For Israel Yahweh was never a withdrawn observer. He was continuously identified with his people. From the call of Moses in the "burning bush" onward, step by step, the character of Yahweh was revealed through his actions. His relationships with Israel in the Exodus disclosed his identification with the subjugated, oppressed, dispirited, and those without advocate. Superior to other gods and master of the elements, he worked within the course of history in particular moments and circumstances.

But Yahweh was more than a participant in events. He was in

---

21 The longer poem contained in 15:1-18 is a later Israelite expansion of this early couplet.

absolute control—sovereign over all. Whatever occurred was traceable to him in one way or another. Barrenness, leprosy, flood or drought, victory or defeat in battle, the "hardening of the heart," or whatever, owed its existence to Yahweh. He was within and working through all things.[22]

In the centuries following their emancipation, the Israelites looked back upon the Exodus and conquest as Yahweh's doing. He was operative in the entire event and associated with its every particular. Even at such a point as the accentuation of the drama by Pharaoh's hostility and opposition, Yahweh was considered responsible for his "hardening."[23] Although Moses and Aaron were attendants, Yahweh gave birth to the nation. No moment in all the nation's history was to be compared to that moment and this mighty act of Yahweh was his thundering proclamation of concern for his people. The Babylonian Talmud emphasized the meaning of the event: "In every generation a man is bound to regard himself as though he personally had gone forth from Egypt."[24]

THE WILDERNESS (EXODUS 15:22–18:27)

From the Sea of Reeds the fugitives moved eastward. Instead of moving northward by the most direct route to Canaan from the Egyptian borders, they turned eastward, avoiding the frontier fortifications and the heavily guarded commercial and military highway. "God did not lead them by the way of the land of the Philistines, although that was near."[25]

---

[22] The early Hebrew believed implicitly and concretely in Yahweh as sovereign. The logic of a good God causing evil was not a question to him. Later, when the nation came under the influence of neo-Babylonian and Persian thought, patterns of dualism in thinking about good and evil became evident.

[23] Exodus 8:15, 32; 9:12; et al.

[24] I. Epstein, ed., The Babylonian Talmud, Seder Mo'ed, Pasahim (The Soncino Press), p. 595. Even in modern Judaism the Exodus remains the most indicative events in history. The historical novel by Leon Uris, Exodus, concludes with this commemoration: "This night is different because we celebrate the most important moment in the history of our people. On this night we celebrate their going forth in triumph from slavery into freedom."

[25] Exodus 13:17. To be sure, the Philistines did not reside in the land to the southeast of Canaan at the time of the Israelite Exodus. But, since the name "Philistine" was inseparable from that land at a later period, the writer could refer to it anachronistically by its popular name. In a similar way today, one refers to early New York without using the name New Amsterdam.

The band of migrants included "a mixed multitude," [26] indicating that other than descendants of Jacob were in the company. Later in Canaan the mixed company would be joined by others of kindred origins. The number involved in the migration is difficult to state. The reference in Exodus 12:37 to six hundred thousand males of fighting age is incompatible with several features of the story. This number of warriors indicates that the total population would have been two and a half million. Pharaoh sent only six hundred chariot men to pursue them, [27] hardly enough men to overcome a force a thousand times their number. Two midwives were enough to serve the entire colony. [28] Further, when they approached Canaan, they were too few to engage the inhabitants in battle. [29] These facts indicate that six hundred thousand men is too large. Perhaps six hundred families would be a more nearly correct estimate. [30]

The memory of victory at the Sea of Reeds gave confidence to the Israelites as they faced the wilderness sojourn. Their adequate deity was in control.

And Yahweh went before them by day in a pillar of a cloud to lead them along the way, and by night in a pillar of fire to give them light, that they might travel by day and by night; the pillar of cloud by day and the pillar of fire by night did not depart from before the people. (Exodus 13:21–22)

Fire as a symbol for deity was not new to the Israelite. In the covenant established with Abraham, Yahweh's participation had been dramatized as a "smoking fire pot and a flaming torch" passing between two parts of the sacrifices. [31] In the Exodus tradition fire characterizes Yahweh's providential guidance and care of his people. Further, Moses was considered God's personal representative. As he had been "a god" to Pharaoh, [32] so he symbolized Yahweh to these freemen. As they followed Moses or as they trailed the smoking firebrand through the wilderness, they followed Yahweh.

[26] Exodus 12:38.
[27] Exodus 14:7.
[28] Exodus 1:15–20.
[29] Cf. Exodus 23:29 ff.
[30] Some scholars explain the high figure by suggesting that the Hebrew term *'eleph*, translated "thousand," should be translated as "family" or "fighting unit." Others suggest that a later census figure has been read into the earlier story.
[31] Genesis 15:17.
[32] Exodus 3:16; 7:1.

The enthusiasm generated by the experience at the Sea of Reeds rapidly dissipated as the travelers faced the desert of Etham, or Shur ("well") and the rigors of wilderness life. Food and water were seldom adequate. Dangers surrounded them and enemies opposed their advance. Argument, strife, and discontent broke out on many occasions. The water of Marah was bitter and the people protested. The unleavened bread became tasteless, and the assembly demanded meat. They voiced their discontent against both Moses and Yahweh. Complaining became so exaggerated that they even longed to return to bondage in Egypt, where at least they "sat by the fleshpots and ate bread to the full." [33] Skillfully the traditions mirror the continuing faithlessness of Israel in their account of wilderness complaints. Every Israelite ought to have seen himself in these traditions.

Israel's faithlessness is set in vivid contrast to the faithfulness of Yahweh. Throughout the ordeal he adequately provided for the needs of his congregation. Manna, a honey-like substance deposited by scale insects which suck plant sap for nitrogen and discharge superfluous quantities,[34] was collected. The sweetness of the manna, still called *mun* by the Arabs, provided them with necessary sugar. Flocks of quail were easily caught in the evenings. Water was provided by crushing hard-surfaced limestone rocks to release water from springs underneath. Victory against the Amalekites was gained because the people took heart at the sight of Moses, Yahweh's leader. When Moses' arm was out of sight, the skirmish went against Israel; when his arm and staff were in view, they revived and repelled the forces of Amalek. Moses' aides, Aaron and Hur, compensated for his fatigue by holding up his arms.

Although the timing of Yahweh's assistance sometimes disappointed the people, he never failed them. Through Moses he led them safely and intact to the mount called Sinai. The experiences of these traveling days were remembered through song, story, and festival intended always to remind Israel who they were and to whom they belonged.

[33] Exodus 16:3.
[34] Cf. F. S. Bodenheimer's discussion of "The Manna of Sinai" in *The Biblical Archaeologist Reader*, I, 76–80.

THE COVENANT (EXODUS 19:1–24:11)

The destination Moses had in mind from the beginning of the immigration was Sinai,[35] the mountain on which Yahweh had first appeared to him. From this place supremely holy to him, he had set forth alone many months before on the fantastic mission of emancipation. Now successful, he returned to the point of his departure to further encounter with Yahweh.

Location of Sinai

Since the sixth century A.D., tradition has located Sinai in a range on the southern tip of the Sinai peninsula, identifying it with a mountain now called Jebel Musa. The famous monastery of St. Catherine is located at its foot. With this mountain in mind, it has been assumed that the Israelites travelled from Egypt down the west coast of the peninsula and that the oases and sites mentioned in the Exodus account were along this route.

Exploration has been of little help in locating either Sinai or the oases, but a number of reasons call the traditional view to question. First, in the scriptural account there is no mention that the pilgrims encountered Egyptians at any point along the trail. This is somewhat surprising if they travelled southward along the eastern shores of the present Gulf of Suez. Along this route they would have passed Egyptian mines heavily guarded by troops. It is doubtful that the Egyptian troops would have allowed them to pass uncontested. Again, the peninsula of Sinai is about two hundred and fifty miles long from the Mediterranean to the southern tip. This line of flight would certainly have been out of the way which led to Canaan. Further, Kadesh, a site that repeatedly occurs in the biblical story dealing with the wilderness period, was located in the Negeb, far north of the traditional Sinai. In the general area of Kadesh are springs sufficient to support several thousand migrants. Also, some poetic expressions [36] designated Seir and Paran as the point of origin of Israel's religion. These and other reasons have led many con-

---

[35] Sinai is used in the Yahwistic and Priestly histories; Horeb is used in the Elohistic and Deuteronomic histories.

[36] E.g., Deuteronomy 33:2; Judges 5:4, 5; Habakkuk 3:3.

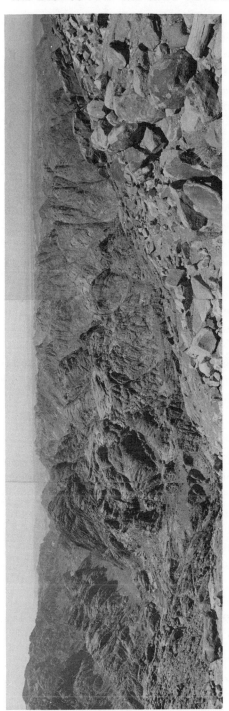

Figure 4-3. Panorama of the Sinai range taken from Jebel Musa, the traditional Mt. Sinai. (Source: University of Michigan Museum.)

temporary scholars to lean toward a location for Sinai somewhere in the Mount Seir range, the general area round Kadesh.

The traditional Jebel Musa site, however, will not be readily surrendered. A foremost archaeologist, G. Ernest Wright, holds that a few of the stations along the route to Jebel Musa can be identified with some degree of probability and finds it

extremely difficult to understand why the early church would have located the sacred spot in the most inaccessible and dangerous area imaginable for pilgrims, especially at a time when the tendency was to do just the opposite, unless the tradition was so old and firmly fixed that no debate was permitted about it.[37]

Whatever the location of Sinai, Moses was doubling back over an area which he had traveled while shepherding the flocks of Jethro. In bringing the company of Israel to a site which had abiding religious meaning for him personally, he led them through an area which he had already explored, searching out adequate water holes and suitable camp grounds.

Sinai was the point where Israel began her move toward maturity as a nation. The safe passage through the Sea of Reeds gave Israel her birth by water. At Sinai she was nurtured and disciplined into adolescence with awakening religious and social structure. What followed these experiences grew out of them as the man grows out of the boy.

The Kenite Background of Mosaic Yahwism

At Sinai the tribes which had left Egypt were joined by Kenite groups. Tradition preserves memory of this by the story of Moses' reunion with his wife and sons and his Kenite father-in-law. Jethro rejoiced in the accomplishments of Yahweh and advised Moses. As a direct result of Jethro's advice, a simple judicial system was established. Jethro suggested the appointment of able men to settle small matters; hard cases were still brought before Moses. As the priestly and prophetic leader of Israel, Moses continued to inquire of Yahweh and promulgate new decisions. The application of these to specific cases was the task of subordinate judges. This story may relate early Israelite legal procedures to the practices of their patriarchal ancestors whose life-style

---

[37] Wright, *Biblical Archaeology*, p. 64.

was similar to that of Kenites. Through Moses, though, justice is related to Yahweh. As supreme judge Moses was the human instrument through whom Yahweh's will was mediated as law. The law which governed Israel, therefore, was divine law.

Jethro's acknowledgment of Yahweh and the ready way Moses accepted his advice raise the question of possible relationship between the Yahwism of Moses and the presumed Yahwism of his Kenite in-laws.[38] Indeed when Moses and Jethro were reunited at Sinai, Jethro offered a sacrifice to Yahweh,[39] an indication that Yahweh was God of the Kenites and Jethro was his priest. In later years the Kenites were champions of Yahweh worship and loyal supporters of Israel. It is possible, therefore, that Yahweh worship entered Israel with the encouragement of Jethro. The period in history when the Elohist and Priestly writers introduce "Yahweh" in connection with the Sinai experience offers some support to the idea that the name, at least, came to Israel from the Kenites. In describing Moses' experience at Sinai the Priestly writer states directly, "I am Yahweh. I appeared to Abraham, to Isaac, and to Jacob as God Almighty, but by my name Yahweh I did not make myself known to them." [40] Further, the Elohist uses "Elohim" as the divine name until after Moses had his "burning bush" experience.[41] Only the Yahwist author uses "Yahweh" as far back as Genesis 4. All of this makes the Kenite hypothesis attractive, but it is not accepted by all scholars [42] and should be considered at most a tentative hypothesis.

Even if Moses did learn the name Yahweh from his Kenite in-laws, the religion he established in Israel was something other than the religion of the Kenites. During the days of his deep and disturbing religious experience, Moses came to a decisive moment when he represented Yahweh before Israel. "Whatever Yahweh may have meant to the Kenites, he meant something other

[38] The most able presentation of this "Kenite" hypothesis is in H. H. Rowley, *From Joseph to Joshua,* pp. 148 ff. See also K. Budde, *Religion of Israel to the Exile,* Chapter 1.

[39] Exodus 18:12.

[40] Exodus 6:2, 3.

[41] Exodus 3.

[42] For example, Yehezkel Kaufman, *The Religion of Israel,* pp. 242–244, and Martin Buber, *The Prophetic Faith,* pp. 24–30.

to Israel." [43] The God of Israel surpassed the god of the Kenites. The true character of Yahweh was not found in his name alone, but in Israel's experience of his redemptive work with his people. Israel came to understand the redeeming power and care of Yahweh in the exodus experience. Throughout the succeeding centuries he was Yahweh, "who delivered us from bondage in Egypt." What Yahweh worship became in Israel completely overshadowed whatever earlier history it may have had. For Israel the foundations of religion were laid in the experiences of the exodus and the covenant.

Election, Covenant, and Law

Growth from the infancy of initial surrender to the maturity of a fully-committed people of covenant came only with great agony for Israel. The Exodus and wilderness experience pointed toward and was epitomized at Sinai. Here at the foot of the holy mountain the real covenant promised to Abraham was established. At Sinai the Israelites held their constitutional assembly, formulated the essential ethical premises of the covenant, and clarified the nature of their community. In short, Israel voluntarily became the people of Yahweh, who had brought her from Egypt.

Election. For Israelite faith, therefore, the covenant at Sinai in reality brought to a climax the selective activity of God which Israel traced back to the call of Abraham. In her patriarchal ancestors Israel believed she had been chosen to be Yahweh's peculiar people through whom he would bless all mankind.

> But you, Israel, my servant,
> Jacob, whom I have chosen,
> the offspring of Abraham, my friend;
> You whom I took from the ends of the earth,
>   and called from its farthest corners,
> saying to you, "You are my servant,
>   I have chosen you and not cast you off."   (Isaiah 41:8–9)

The elected people delivered from bondage in the Exodus saw their consecration established in covenant with Yahweh. Thus faith made the wonders of the Exodus the fulfillment of promises made to Abraham, Isaac, and Jacob.

[43] H. H. Rowley, *The Rediscovery of the Old Testament*, p. 122.

It is because Yahweh loves you, and is keeping the oath which he swore to your fathers, that Yahweh has brought you out with a mighty hand, and redeemed you from the house of bondage, from the hand of Pharaoh King of Egypt. (Deuteronomy 7:8)

This sense of election lay at the heart of Israel's self-understanding. She existed only because Yahweh had chosen her from among the nations and had redeemed her from Egyptian bondage. In herself she was nothing, but through elective grace she became the people of Yahweh. This relationship was expressed in later literature by the figures of Yahweh's wife (Hosea 2:19–20; Jeremiah 2:1–7; Ezekiel 16 and 23), his first-born son (Exodus 4:22), and his inheritance (Exodus 34:9; I Samuel 10:1; Psalm 28:9). She had no inherent greatness which caused Yahweh to choose her; her greatness lay only in the fact that Yahweh had chosen her.[44] Both existence and worth were owed to the redemptive activity of a sovereign God, who made her his people.

Israel often forgot that Yahweh had chosen her for service, and not for privilege. Her only privilege was to serve Yahweh. She had been singled out, not to receive a blessing, but to be one, and failure to do so would necessitate her rejection.

Covenant. The covenant expressed at Sinai is the foundation bond between Yahweh and his people. To the patriarchs Yahweh had promised his blessing and from them entreated faithfulness. Now to the children of Abraham, Yahweh had undeniably and forthrightly demonstrated his faithfulness by bringing them out of Egypt. In the Sinai commitment the people were responding to Yahweh's initiative action by forming a covenant community. In affirmation of the covenant, Israel as a theocratic nation began to take definitive shape.

The form of the Sinai covenant resembled the suzerainty treaties of the ancient Hittites.[45] Contracts between the Suzerain, or Great King, and his vassals typically began with a preamble stating the name and title of the king. Following the preamble, a prologue recounted the king's benevolences which placed his vassals in a state of continual obligation. Stipulations being imposed upon the vassals composed the body of the treaty. Yahweh

[44] H. H. Rowley, *The Biblical Doctrine of Election*, p. 19.
[45] See G. E. Mendenhall, *Law and Covenant in Israel and the Ancient Near East.*

of Israel's covenant is her great king and more. The atmosphere of Sinai indicates a clear distinction between the people and their God. By acts of purification the people had prepared themselves to come into the presence of Yahweh. Smoke, noise, quakings like a volcanic eruption accompanied by an earthquake, symbolize holiness and revelation. This was no covenant between equals. The holy Yahweh rightly demanded obedience. If Israel were to be his people, they had to take upon themselves the sacred obligations of covenant. As his people they had to respond to his redemptive activity by pledging obedience to his covenant and law.

You have seen what I did to the Egyptians, and how I bore you on eagles' wings and brought you to myself. Now therefore, if you will obey my voice and keep my covenant, you shall be my own possession among all peoples; for all the earth is mine, and you shall be to me a kingdom of priests, and a holy nation. (Exodus 19:4-5)

The essence of Yahweh's covenant demands upon Israel is found in the Ten Commandments or, as the Hebrews called them, "The Ten Words." The Ten Commandments, or Decalogue, are the basic statements of Mosaic law. Although various presentations occur in Exodus 34 (a ritual decalogue) and Deuteronomy 5, their first and most popular listing is in Exodus 20:

I am Yahweh your God, who brought you out of the land of Egypt, out of the house of bondage.

1. You shall have no other gods before me.
2. You shall not make yourself a graven image.
3. You shall not take the name of Yahweh your God in vain.
4. Remember the Sabbath day, to keep it holy.
5. Honor your father and your mother.
6. You shall not kill.
7. You shall not commit adultery.
8. You shall not steal.
9. You shall not bear false witness against your neighbor.
10. You shall not covet.

In the Decalogue Yahweh as a God of holiness made ethical claim upon his chosen people. The covenant relationship was grounded in obedience to Yahweh through ethical behavior. The first four commandments clarify specific obligations of the covenanter toward Yahweh. The last six deal with his responsibility toward his fellow man.[46] These two "legs" of concern in Israel's earliest ethical formulations are typical of biblical religion throughout. To Israel and to Jesus the bilateral obligation of man to love God with all his being and to love neighbor as oneself remained the summary of the law.[47]

Clearly, then, the covenant bound the chosen people to Yahweh in a solemn relationship of obligation and obedience. It was not a commercial bargain, but rather Israel's pledge of loyalty to one who had first chosen and saved her. The covenant was based on what Yahweh had already done. No obligation was placed on Yahweh, who had already pledged himself to Israel. The initiative in the covenant was Yahweh's and Israel had the opportunity of accepting or rejecting his overture. She was free to choose whether or not she would be Yahweh's people. If she accepted the covenant, she bound herself by its demands. If she repudiated the demands of covenant, she in reality denied Yahweh and would no longer be his people. If Israel were not obedient to the divine will which ruled her, no real covenant relationship could exist. But since those bound by covenant were ruled by a common will, its establishment created a community of aim and purpose.

Since obedience and loyalty to Yahweh could not automatically pass from father to son, the covenant had to be renewed by each generation. Successive covenant renewals, however, were not complete beginnings again. Every generation inherited the religious traditions and blessings which imposed covenantal claims upon it. Consequently, they were under solemn moral obligation to renew the covenant. Not to renew would be apostasy.

History demonstrated the failure of Israel to keep the covenant and much of her later literature centers around Yahweh's attempts to win her back and renew his claim for her loyalty. Continually Israel's story was one of judgment and salvation. Yahweh stood always ready to abide by the covenant as Israel turned from her evil ways, renewed her vows, and became Yahweh's servant.

[46] Man's disregard of these responsibilities is vividly portrayed in Genesis 3 and 4.

[47] Deuteronomy 6:5 and Leviticus 19:18 are the Old Testament passages quoted by Jesus in his famous summary of the law. Cf. Luke 10:25–28.

Law. The covenant furnished the setting for both the common and the cultic law of Israel. Law and covenant were inseparably intertwined. Keeping of the law was man's covenant obligation. Every member of the community was a covenant person and no part of their activity was exempt from covenant obligation. The nature of this responsibility was clarified by Israel in the Covenant Code, a succinct ethical elaboration of the Decalogue found in Exodus 20:22–23:33. The covenant code is an application of the fundamental principles of the Ten Commandments to specific matters of daily conduct. Each commandment is the comprehensive foundation for the building of a fitting superstructure of specific legislation. For example, the commandment, "You shall not kill," embraces the principle of basic respect for human life. The covenant code seeks to make the principle practical by distinguishing situations in which a life is taken.[48]

Whereas the Ten Commandments probably came from Moses himself, the covenant code most likely represents an accumulation of laws coming from later periods in Israel's history. Certainly parts of the covenant code suggest a later, more settled life of the people. Included in its instruction is legislation on altars, sacrifices, slaves, capital and non-capital crimes, property rights, social morals, the Sabbath, and feasts. The code closes with Yahweh's exhortation that Israel remain obedient.

The Israelite covenant code is young among ancient codes of law. The codes of Ur-Nammu (c. 2060 B.C.), Eshnunna (c. 2000 B.C.), Lipit Ishtar (nineteenth century B.C.), Hammurabi (c. 1700 B.C.), the Assyrian code from the time of Tiglath-pileser I (twelfth century B.C.) are all older than the covenant code of Israel.[49] These codes, like that of Israel, ascribe their origin to the deity worshipped by the people among whom they were formulated. Indirect ties, very likely, existed between the biblical codes and their Ancient Near Eastern counterparts. Israel must have utilized this common legal heritage, but no example of direct borrowing can be demonstrated. And certainly the religious concerns of the extra-biblical codes are not so pronounced as those of Israel's law.

---

[48] Cf. Exodus 21:12–15.

[49] Cf. Pritchard, *Archaeology and the Old Testament*, pp. 206–227. Translations of these codes may be found in Pritchard, *Ancient Near Eastern Texts.*

Figure 4–4. The stele of Hammurabi inscribed with 282 laws. The scene crowning the eight foot stele shows the Babylonian king Hammurabi receiving the symbols of authority from the sun god Shamash. (Source: Louvre. Photograph by Archives Photographiques-Paris.)

A distinctive of the Israelite code is to be found in the particular form given to its basic laws. In the Torah two general types of law are found: conditional (or case) law, and absolute or apodictic law. Conditional law had a characteristic formula: "If – – – – happens, then – – – – will be the legal consequence." This type law was found everywhere in the ancient world and was typical of all the ancient codes. Absolute law, on the other hand, was more characteristically Israelite and expressed unconditional covenant demands. There were no "ifs" about it. It was absolute and was stated in categorical language. The best examples of absolute law in the Old Testament are, of course, the individual commandments of the Decalogue.[50] Further examples are found in Deuteronomy 27 where curses are pronounced upon twelve types of violators of the covenant.

For Israel all law was rooted in the grace of God and was conceived as a special revelation, an expression of Yahweh's will. It was a Yahweh-given source of justice and security, binding on community and individual alike. While the covenant law had been given to the community as a whole, it singled out the individual and addressed him directly with the divine "Thou shalt . . . . ." As a result life in Israel assumed a meaning and dignity unknown elsewhere in the ancient world.[51]

COVENANT CULTIC LEGISLATION (EXODUS 24:12–40:38; LEVITICUS 1–5, 23)

A religion may be understood on the basis of its teachings, the behavior of its adherents, and the symbols used in its worship. The Decalogue expresses succinctly the foundational ethic of Israel's faith. The Covenant Code is concerned with justice in the practical application of this ethic in the daily behavior of the Israelite. Levitical law, so called because the Levites were the designated priests, defines the ritual practice of the worshipping community.

Like her judicial covenant code, Israel's ceremonial legislation emerged over a period of several centuries, not attaining the form described in the final chapters of Exodus and the book of Leviticus[52] until the time of the Priestly writing in the sixth century B.C. However, the Israelites looked to Moses as the founder of their cult and consequently related to him the ritual practice of the wilderness days and all which they included in their ceremonial law down to the days of the exile. Worship inevitably draws upon a cultic heritage and utilizes meaningful elements from the past; but at its best worship is also characterized by

[50] Albrecht Alt, "The Origins of Israelite Law," in *Essays on Old Testament History and Religion*, pp. 103–171.

[51] See Wright, *The Old Testament Against Its Environment*, pp. 58–59.

[52] The Hebrews designated the book, "Yahweh called," after words in the opening verse.

spontaneity and relevance. Israel in coming before God both repeated what was old and did new things. Therefore, the presentation of Israel's worship which follows should not be taken as exhaustive or even as typical of Israelite worship at any given moment of her history. Rather, it is suggestive of certain fundamental emphases.

Symbols of the Sacred

Worship is approach into the presence of and response to *the sacred*. Israel believed profoundly in the sacred presence of Yahweh, the holy one, and found her assurance and her responsibilities in the sense of his *being with* them. The presence of Yahweh was symbolized to them through the ark and the tabernacle and temple.

The Ark. The ark, called "the ark of Yahweh," "the ark of the covenant with Yahweh," or "the ark of the testimony," was an oblong wooden box, three and three-fourths by two and one-fourth feet, either open or closed at the top. To the outer four corners near its top four rings were attached through which two shafts were passed, one on either side. Thus, the ark could be carried by two priests, one before and one behind, with the shafts resting on their shoulders. This apparatus was the portable throne for Yahweh. Two cherubim [53] were positioned on the top of the ark, as symbolic guardians of his presence.

The ark symbolized the immanence of Yahweh. The holy deity, who could not be represented by a physical image, was symbolized as present with his people. He was not remote and disinterested, but near and involved. As the ark was with Israel, so Yahweh remained at hand. An ancient song pertaining to the ark reminded the people that the ark indicated the presence of deity.

And whenever the ark set out, Moses said, "Arise, O Yahweh, and let thy enemies be scattered; and let them that hate thee flee before thee." And when it rested, he said, "Return, O Yahweh, to the ten thousand thousands of Israel." (Numbers 10:35–36)

The ability of Yahweh to be with his people anywhere they might go was symbolized by the prohibition against removing the carry-

[53] Two-winged creatures with the body of an animal and the head of a man.

ing poles from the ark.[54] Wherever Israel was, there Yahweh would be also.

The ark first served as a religious symbol in the life of Israel during her wilderness days and continued to play an important role in her life during the time of the monarchy, when from David's time on it was housed in the Jerusalem sanctuary. However, its influence seems to have waned as the nation abandoned nomadic life. By the time of the destruction of Solomon's temple in 587 B.C., the ark was lost from Israel's history.

The Tabernacle and Temples. The ark was kept in a "tent of meeting" or tabernacle.[55] The tabernacle was a movable "dwelling" where Yahweh met his people. It belonged to the wilderness period, although its description probably is an elaboration of later times. As Israel passed to the more settled conditions of post-nomadic days, the mobile sanctuary became less and less meaningful. It may have been destroyed by the Philistines during the late years of the amphictyony since David had to build a temporary housing when he brought the ark to Jerusalem.[56] The tabernacle was ultimately replaced by the more elaborate and imposing temple of Solomon.

The architecture of the tabernacle focused on the presence of Yahweh who symbolically dwelled in the Holy of Holies, the innermost part of the sanctuary. This symbolism continued that of the ark—conveying the immanence of the transcendent deity. Yahweh is present in the midst of Israel and moves with them wherever they go.[57]

During the Israelite monarchy, the tabernacle was replaced as a symbol of Yahweh's presence by permanent sanctuaries at Jerusalem in Judah and at Dan and Bethel, the cultic centers of Israel. The Israelites, however, did not restrict Yahweh's habitation to

---

[54] Exodus 25:15.

[55] A helpful discussion of the tabernacle may be found in Frank M. Cross, Jr., "The Priestly Tabernacle" in *The Biblical Archaeologist Reader*, I, 201–228.

[56] Cf. II Samuel 6:17.

[57] Joseph, *Antiquities*, III, vi, 4, considered the entire sacred area to portray the earth (the court), heaven (the Holy Place), and the innermost heaven (the Holy of Holies), as interpreted from the Solomonic statement on the dedication of the temple: "But will God indeed dwell on the earth? Behold, heaven and the highest heaven cannot contain thee; how much less this house which I have built!" (I Kings 8:27). However, this is late and far removed from the wilderness experience.

any of these sanctuaries. He dwelled among them as a creative and redeeming presence, but did not dwell in the sanctuaries as a man "lives" in one place or another. Yahweh's otherness was preserved along with his approachableness.

Ordering of Time: Sacred Days and Seasons

Worship in Israel was not restricted to any certain days. Burnt offerings were presented at the sanctuary daily,[58] and the individual worshipper could present a thank offering or gift offering upon any occasion he saw fit.[59] There were particular times, however, at which the Israelites felt "drawn to approach the deity with peculiar earnestness of supplication or thanksgiving." [60] Certain days and periods were set apart from all the rest by their holiness. These were the festival days, the fast days, and days of commemorative significance.

Annual Feasts. Three annual feasts are prescribed in the liturgical calendar in Exodus 23.

Three times in the year you shall keep a feast to me. You shall eat the feast of unleavened bread; as I command you, you shall eat unleavened bread for seven days at the appointed time in the month of Abib, for in it you came out of Egypt. None shall appear before me emptyhanded. You shall keep the feast of harvest, of the first fruits of your labor, of what you sow in the field. You shall keep the feast of ingathering at the end of the year, when you gather in from the field the fruit of your labor. Three times in the year shall all your males appear before the LORD GOD. (Exodus 23:14–17).

The three annual feasts were Passover-Unleavened Bread (*Pesach-Mazzoth*), the Feast of Weeks or Firstfruits (*Shabhuoth*), and the Feast of Ingathering or Tabernacles (*Sukkoth*). All three were originally connected with the agricultural year. As practiced by the nations surrounding Israel, they were recognitions of the manifestations of divine power in nature or, even more, recognitions of the divine powers of nature itself. Behind the major festivals of the pagan world lay the conception of sympathetic magic. By imitative action men thought they could become identified with powers of nature and thus make the

---

[58] II Kings 16:15.
[59] Leviticus 7:11–15.
[60] H. Wheeler Robinson, *Religious Ideas of the Old Testament*, p. 137.

powers do what they wanted. In Israel there was nothing of this sort in the official festivals of Yahwism.

Two of the three major feasts of Israel early became anniversaries of events in which Yahweh's power had been manifested. In them the great events of Israel's history were actualized, i.e., brought to life in actual experience of the worshippers. This does not mean that history repeated itself, but that the basic historical facts of religion were experienced as real as if the worshipper were himself present and taking part in them. In the festival he relived the redemption of Yahweh which had been revealed in historical events.

The Passover-Unleavened Bread festival [61] was interpreted as a reenactment of the experience of deliverance from Egypt.

> And you shall tell your son on that day, "It is because of what Yahweh did for me when I came out of Egypt." And it shall be to you as a sign on your hand and as a memorial between your eyes, that the law of Yahweh may be in your mouth; for with a strong hand Yahweh has brought you out of Egypt. You shall therefore keep this ordinance at its appointed time from year to year. (Exodus 13:8-10)

Passover itself was a one-day feast, but it came to be so closely associated with the seven day festival of Unleavened Bread which immediately followed that it became the exalted initiatory day of an eight-day celebration. It was celebrated in the month of Nisan. As a whole this festival was a meaningful recreation of that momentous night when the angel of death "passed over" the dwellings of the Israelites and Yahweh delivered them from bondage. This feast came to enjoy preeminence among the annual celebrations. Its drama, along with its warm ritual, kept alive the memory of Yahweh's supreme act on behalf of his people. In later centuries it came to have great significance for the Christian community, since during its celebration Jesus as the Lamb of God was crucified and later resurrected. Through these events Christians also celebrate Yahweh as redeemer.

The Feast of Weeks (also called Pentecost, since it was observed fifty days from the sheaf waving ceremony which opened the Feast of Unleavened Bread) was celebrated in the month of Siwan at the completion of the barley harvest. It remained an agricultural festival throughout Old Testament times. As an

[61] Leviticus 23:5-8.

agricultural feast, however, it was not a quasi-magical celebration intended to insure the fertility of the soil in the year to come. As we have noted already, this aspect of nature worship common in surrounding cultures played no part in Israelite worship. In the Feast of Weeks Israel expressed her gratitude to Yahweh for the abundance of good things which he had poured out upon them. In later Judaism the festival was made an anniversary of the giving of the law at Sinai.

Israel celebrated the redemptive activity of Yahweh also at the Feast of Ingathering.[62] During this festival the Israelites lived in booths for seven days, rekindling the memory that Yahweh made the people dwell in booths when he brought them out of the land of Egypt.[63] This festival was the great day of thanksgiving, when the fruits of the year had been gathered, especially the harvest of the vineyards. It was also the time of the celebration of the New Year's Festival—a moment when, according to many scholars, Israel renewed the covenant of Sinai, reminding themselves of Yahweh's goodness to them and their responsibilities to him. This festival was celebrated in the fall, usually in the month of Tishri.

Israelite Months	*Julian Months*
Nisan or Abib (Passover-Unleavened Bread)	March–April
Iyyar or Ziw	April–May
Siwan (Weeks or Pentecost)	May–June
Tammuz	June–July
Av	July–August
Elul	August–September
Tishri or Ethanim (Ingathering or Tabernacles)	September–October
Marheshwan or Bul	October–November
Kislew	November–December
Tebeth	December–January
Shebat	January–February
Adhar (repeated on leap years)	February–March

Nisan was the first month with regard to the computation of Passover. For all other purposes the year began in the Fall, on the first day of Tishri.

Figure 4–5. The Israelite calendar.

[62] Leviticus 23:33–44.
[63] Leviticus 23:43.

Fast Days. The Israelite ecclesiastical year also included one scheduled fast day, the Day of Atonement (Yom Kippur), observed on the tenth day of Tishri. Its central concern was the atonement made for the sin of the nation. Consequently, it had no commemorative significance. In early Israel it was likely observed from time to time, but it was only with the postexilic concern for sin and its removal that this day was given a fixed place in the liturgical calendar. Elaborate rituals were undergone to make atonement for the high priest (who officiated at the ceremonies of this day), his family, and all the people of Israel. Then the sins of the community were symbolically laid upon a goat which was led into the wilderness, representing sins' removal.

Days of Commemorative Significance. Two times were set apart in Israel as times of commemorative significance. They were the weekly Sabbaths and New Year's Day as a time of covenant renewal.

The Sabbath [64] was observed from earliest times in Israel as a special day of religious, historical and moral meaning. Exodus 20:11 gives a theological explanation for Sabbath observance by describing it as a memorial of Yahweh's rest at the completion of creation.[65]

For in six days Yahweh made heaven and earth, the sea and all that is in them, and rested on the seventh day; therefore Yahweh blessed the seventh day and hallowed it.

A historical explanation of the Sabbath is found in Deuteronomy where the concern is with the meaning of the day for Israel.

You shall remember that you were a servant in the land of Egypt, and Yahweh your God brought you out thence with a mighty hand and an outstretched arm; therefore Yahweh your God commanded you to keep the sabbath day. (Deuteronomy 5:15)

A third interpretation, in reality a corollary to the other two, is also found in Deuteronomy. The Sabbath is to be observed for humanitarian reasons:

The seventh day is a sabbath to Yahweh your God; in it you shall not do any work, you, or your son, or your daughter, or your manservant, or your

[64] Leviticus 23:1–4.
[65] Cf. Genesis 2:1–3.

maidservant . . . that your manservant and your maidservant may rest as well as you. (Deuteronomy 5:14)

In Israel, therefore, the Sabbath was a day of profound religious and social significance.

The way in which the Sabbath was observed changed through the years. Throughout, however, it was a day of rejoicing in Yahweh. On this day Israelites rested from customary pursuits and celebrated Yahweh as creator. The restrictive laws which characterized Sabbath observance in the Judaism of the New Testament had not come into existence in Old Testament times and, for the most part, the Sabbath was a day of joy and gladness.

The New Year was ushered in for Israel by a fall harvest festival and was a time of exceptional religious importance. For all primitive societies the New Year was a time of renewal when man at worship participated in the moment of creation and guaranteed the transformation, cleansing, and renewal of their natural and social world. New Years was this and more for ancient Israel—more because Israel at New Years celebrated not only natural creation but her own redemptive creation in exodus and covenant. For Israel the fall harvest festival of Tabernacles which ushered in the New Year was primarily a time of covenant renewal.

Two features dominated Israel's fall festival of renewal. The first was the appearance of Yahweh at the sanctuary and a celebration of his presence (see Psalms 18, 50, 68, 77, 97). The present Lord was portrayed as creator, conqueror of his and Israel's enemies, and judge of the nations. During the monarchy these characteristics were attributed to Yahweh as king (see Psalms 47, 93, 95–99).[66] The second dominant feature was the ceremonial presentation of the divine law (Deuteronomy 27). The requirements of the present Lord were proclaimed in the form of curse ritual. Those who disobeyed Yahweh's law would be judged by that law and by Israel.

In response to the presence of Yahweh, ceremonially represented, and in obedience to his law Israel pledged herself to the deity in covenant allegiance. All of this is reminiscent of Yah-

---

[66] The emphases of these Psalms now have distinctive characteristics from the monarchical period. Nevertheless, they reflect motifs more primitive in Israel than the times of Saul and David.

weh's appearance at Sinai and the revelation of the law of the covenant. The New Year then began with covenant renewal when the community committed itself to be the people of Yahweh, people of the covenant.

The Response to the Sacred: Worship

Sacrifice, Prayer, Psalms. The most obvious means by which the Israelites worshipped Yahweh was sacrifice. The Priestly writers have written in great detail about the sacrificial rites, how they were to be performed, how the cultus was organized, the proper animals to be sacrificed, etc. Nowhere, however, have they presented a theology of sacrifice.[67] Although exactly what sacrifice meant to the worshipper is difficult to determine, essentially it must have represented Israel's attempt to respond to the holiness of Yahweh. There seem to have been three fundamental purposes for offering sacrifice: (1) to make a gift to Yahweh, (2) to enhance communion with Yahweh, (3) to atone for sin. No one of these ideas explains all the sacrifices and their ritual. Primitive notions may have sometimes been blended with refined religious feeling, and prescribed sacrificial customs were often followed, not because they were filled with theological meaning, but simply because they belonged to immemorial tradition. In either event, sacrifice remained the expression of Israel's response to Yahweh.

Here we have one of the clearest influences of cultural environment upon Israel. The form of Israel's sacrifices, for the most part, cannot be distinguished from that of her neighbors. However, the central purposes of sacrifices in Israelite usage were distinctly different. For most of the ancient world sacrifices were regarded as essential for the well-being of the deities; they needed them. This was never true in Israel. The sacrificial system in Priestly theology was Yahweh's revelation, his gift to Israel. As such it was the "prescribed form of worship, of praise, thanksgiving, communion, and especially of atonement for sin," which he accepted when performed in the proper manner and with the proper attitude.[68] Sacrifice, then, was the divinely given traditional mode for expressing religious sentiments. As such, it contained the three

[67] Wright, *The Old Testament Against Its Environment*, p. 102.
[68] *Ibid.*, p. 104.

basic purposes for offering sacrifice. It was primarily a gift to Yahweh, at times a gift which resulted in communion and at other times a gift to atone for sin.

In Israel sacrifice was valid when properly performed with the proper spirit. Not sacrifice itself, but obedience in life mediated blessing and renewal to man. The ritual was potent only when accompanied by genuine penitence and submission. On the other hand, penitence and submission alone were not enough in the cases where sacrifice was prescribed. The faithful act of offering a sacrifice was essential. The Israelite could not save himself, either by penitence or sacrifice. It was Yahweh's divine power which reached down to save him in the moment when he offered himself with his sacrifice.[69]

The Old Testament describes several types of sacrifice which are expressions of Israel's ritual approach to Yahweh. The Burnt Offering [70] was an animal sacrifice in which a whole animal was burned on the altar as "a pleasing odor to Yahweh." Before sacrificing the animal the offerer placed his hand on its head to identify himself with it, thus symbolizing his own full consecration to Yahweh in praise and love. The Peace Offering [71] was the most common type of sacrifice. An expression of thanks for deliverance, it was consummated by a covenant meal in which the worshippers had fellowship with one another and with Yahweh. The blood, fat parts, and internal organs of the sacrificial animal (symbolizing its life) were burned upon the altar to Yahweh. The remainder of the animal was eaten by the worshippers who thus felt that they were guests at Yahweh's table, or better, that he was a guest at theirs. The Sin Offering [72] and the Guilt Offering [73] were sacrifices made for unintentional or inadvertent violations against the holiness of Yahweh. Deliberate sin was not covered by the sacrificial system at all. It is a mistake, therefore, to suppose that Israel made light of sin, imagining that it could be counteracted by sacrifice.[74] In the sin and guilt sacrifices

---

[69] The substance of the paragraph comes from H. H. Rowley, *The Rediscovery of the Old Testament*, pp. 161–183.

[70] Leviticus 1:1–17 and 6:8–13.

[71] Leviticus 3:1–17 and 7:11–21.

[72] Leviticus 4:1–5:13 and 6:24–30.

[73] Leviticus 5:14–6:7 and 7:1–10.

[74] Nathaniel Micklem, "The Book of Leviticus" in *The Interpreter's Bible*, II, 24.

there was an emphasis upon the blood in which was the life of the sacrificed animal. This release of life was the necessary condition for forgiveness of sin but only as it symbolized the dedication and renewal of the worshipper's own life.

The Tribute or Gift Offering [75] was a cereal offering which normally accompanied a burnt offering, or a peace offering. Cereal was offered cooked without incense or uncooked with incense. Thus it was presented as a sweet savor to Yahweh, a "memorial" which represented the offering of the worshipper himself. As he presented his cereal offering, the Israelite gave himself to Yahweh.

Many other kinds of sacrifices were offered in ancient Israel; however, sacrifice was not the only means of worship. There were also the private communion of prayer and the liturgical participation in song. These occupied a more definite place in worship in the later history of Israel than they did in the early days, but they played some role from the very beginning. Many of the Psalms were sung in connection with the worship and many others were originally private prayers of individual worshippers which were found to be expressive of the feelings of many and were therefore adopted as prayers for public use.

The Priesthood.   Priests were mediators through whom Israel approached Yahweh. They were especially set apart to represent the people before Yahweh and to minister his demands. The priests instructed the people in "the way" (Torah) of Yahweh and tried to help them make proper response to his will. When sacrifices were offered, more often than not the priests made them.

Their influence in directing the course of Israel's history is immeasurable. No other group wielded a comparable influence. They were primarily responsible for conserving the cherished religious traditions of the nation. They provided the materials which ultimately comprised a large part of the Torah. Even though they were involved in institutional forms which could easily become devoid of significant religious content and often received scathing denunciations from the prophets, they played a vital role in the development and preservation of Israel's faith.

Instructions in the ritual responsibilities of the priesthood

[75] Leviticus 2:1–16 and 6:14–23.

comprise a major segment of the Priestly writing, especially that which has been preserved in the book of Leviticus and portions of the book of Numbers. Here are described the cultic practices which arose between the time of the Exodus and the final compilation of the Priestly writing in the sixth century B.C.

The personnel of the priesthood, as well as the details of its function, varied from time to time. In the patriarchal period the natural head of a family or clan provided priestly functions, as Abraham did when he constructed altars and offered sacrifices. Evidently before the appointment of a special class of priests at Sinai, some Israelites were already serving in the role,[76] probably following the example of early Egyptian associates. However, the tradition of an ordained, constituted priesthood is related to the tradition of the consecration of Aaron and his sons to the order. The exact requirements for the priesthood were not always rigidly applied, since various types served in this capacity.[77]

The Significance of the Cultus

The cultus is to be appreciated for what it represented to Israel. The ceremonials of the people were their art forms of worship and, as such, embodied the basic religious values of the worshipping community, even when the worshippers were insensitive to these spiritual values. The modern person may discount the crude and unsophisticated nature of many of these early cultic patterns, but he must acknowledge the real meaning which they had for those to whom they were given.

The total impact of the cultus was the holiness of Yahweh. When the Israelite spoke of worship, he used words expressive of his attitude toward such a God. He "presented himself" before the Holy One; he "bowed down" in his presence; he entered into his service. Yahweh, the awe-inspiring, unapproachable God of Israel, could be approached in acceptable worship. Acceptable worship and life is defined in Leviticus 17–26, the Code of Holiness. Even as Yahweh is holy, Israel must be a holy people:

You shall be holy to me; for I Yahweh am holy, and have separated you from the peoples, that you should be mine.   (Leviticus 20:26)

[76] Cf. Exodus 19:22.
[77] Thus the book of Leviticus discusses priestly matters, the responsibility of Levi.

To Israel, then, the cultus expressed their "set-apartness" to the holy Yahweh. In ceremonial practice they maintained their covenant responsibilities to the *sacred* who had selected them.

Israelite worship reflects a number of motifs. The memory of momentous events recalled the might of Yahweh and his works. The sense of sin and personal responsibility for it was expressed in drastic action for cleansing. Contrition and confession were epitomized in tangible petitions for Yahweh's forgiveness. There was joy and thanksgiving because of the goodness of Yahweh who had been gracious to them in history and through nature. Israel's worship, therefore, celebrated Yahweh as the redeemer and sustainer of those whom he had chosen to be his people at the time of the Exodus. Consequently, while the cultus of Israel was often far from pure and sometimes abused, rightly conceived and used, it was an effective means of worshipping God.

SUGGESTED READINGS

Exodus

HERBERT, GABRIEL, *When Israel Came Out of Egypt* (S.C.M. Press, 1961). A summary of the problems of the exodus.

MEEK, T. J., *Hebrew Origins* (Rev. ed., Harper & Row, 1950).

NOTH, MARTIN, *Exodus* (Westminster, 1962).

——, *Leviticus* (Westminster, 1965).

PYTHIAN-ADAMS, W. J., *The Call of Israel* (Oxford University Press, 1934).

ROWLEY, H. H., *From Joseph to Joshua* (The British Academy, 1950). Highly competent technical analysis of the problems of the exodus-conquest.

RYLAARSDAM, J. C., "Exodus" in *Interperter's Bible*, I.

TOOMBS, LAWRENCE, *Nation Making* (Abingdon, 1962). An introductory guide to Exodus, Numbers, Joshua, Judges.

WRIGHT, G. ERNEST, "Route of Exodus," *The Interpreter's Dictionary of the Bible*, II (Abingdon, 1962).

Moses

BUBER, MARTIN, *Moses: The Revelation and the Covenant* (Harper & Row, 1958).

VON RAD, GERHARD, *Moses* (Lutterworth, 1960).

Two exceptional studies, both available in paperback edition. The latter is particularly helpful to the beginning student.

Egypt

BREASTED, JAMES HENRY, A History of Egypt from the Earliest Times to the Persian Conquest (2nd ed., 1927).

KEES, HERMANN, Ancient Egypt: A Cultural Topography (University of Chicago Press, 1962).

STEINDORFF, GEORGE, and SEELE, K. C., When Egypt Ruled the East (University of Chicago Press, 1957).

WILSON, J. A., The Burden of Egypt (University of Chicago Press, 1951). An interpretative history.

Worship

DE VAUX, ROLAND, Studies in Old Testament Sacrifice (University of Wales Press, 1964).

HARRELSON, WALTER, From Fertility Cult to Worship (Anchor Books, Doubleday, 1970).

———, "Worship in Early Israel" (Biblical Research, III, 1958), 1–14.

HERBERT, A. S., Worship in Ancient Israel (Lutterworth, 1959).

KRAUS, HANS-JOACHIM, Worship in Israel (John Knox, 1966).

RINGGREN, HELMER, Sacrifice in the Bible (Association, 1962).

ROWLEY, H. H., "The Meaning of Sacrifice in the Old Testament," BJRL, XXXIII (1950–51), 74–110.

ROWLEY, H. H., Worship in Ancient Israel: Its Forms and Meaning (Fortress, 1967).

Also

ALT, ALBRECHT, "The Origins of Hebrew Law," Essays on Old Testament History and Religion, tr. R. A. Wilson (Doubleday, 1967).

DAVIDMAN, JOY, Smoke on the Mountain (Westminster, 1953). Homiletical on Ten Commandments.

MENDENHALL, G. E., Law and Covenant in Israel and the Ancient Near East (Biblical Colloquium, 1955).

NEWMAN, MURRAY LEE, JR., The People of the Covenant: A Study of Israel from Moses to the Monarchy (Abingdon, 1962).

ROWLEY, H. H., The Biblical Doctrine of Election (Lutterworth, 1950).

STAMM, J. J., and ANDREW, M. E., The Ten Commandments in Recent Research, Studies in Biblical Theology, series 2, No. 2 (Alex R. Allenson, 1967).

TRUEBLOOD, ELTON, Foundations for Reconstruction (Harper & Row, 1946). Homiletical on Ten Commandments.

5

Conquest and Amphictyony

From Sinai the people of Yahweh moved toward Canaan. The dramatic act of Yahweh begun in the deliverance of his elect people from Egyptian bondage was consummated in their settlement there. Emancipated and equipped with the core of a religious code, they conquered a land in which to develop patterns of loyalty. In the long process of conquering Canaan and forming a simple organized life, Israel struggled for economic and political identity. Her problems were many, strange, and tedious and often caused her to forget the basic religious dimension of her struggles. When she failed to encounter the new influences of Canaan under the controlling conditions of the covenant, she was not actually the people of Yahweh. The account of Israel in her land preserved in Joshua-Kings is essentially a serious theological attempt to understand Israel's life and destiny in terms of her failure to respond to Yahweh in faith. Israel's failure to be fully Yahweh's people was, however, already sensed by the Yahwistic and Elohistic historians in their emphasis on Israel in the wilderness.

IN THE WILDERNESS (NUMBERS 11–14, 20–24, 27)

The Book of Numbers

Events transpiring in the wilderness around Kadesh-barnea prior to the beginning of the conquest of Canaan under Joshua are recorded in the book of Numbers. Here are related the vicissitudes of the newly constituted people of Yahweh in their agonizing early development. The Hebrew title of the book, "In the Wilderness," is more appropriate than the Septuagint based designation, "Numbers," since the latter refers only to the opening account of a census of Israel.

Numbers lacks the coherency and proportion of other Old Testament writings and is difficult to outline or summarize. There are three major narratives sections, into which are incorporated various legal materials similar to those found in Exodus and Leviticus.

I. Preparations for Departure from Sinai. 1:1–10:10
II. Journey to Kadesh and Attack on South Canaan. 10:11–21:13
III. Journey from Kadesh through Transjordan. 21:14–36:13

Much of the cultic legislation is of value only as an interesting cross section of cultic history.

All through the book of Numbers the national and individual unfaithfulness of Israel is set in contrast with Yahweh's holiness. The people are portrayed in weakness and rebellion. Moses, Aaron, Miriam, and other religious leaders shamefully stumbled. In spite of human unreliability, Yahweh remained steadfast. He continued to deal with his own in the slow, sometimes imperceptible, realization of his will. Numbers is, therefore, the story of a holy God contending with a rebellious, yet fragile people, who remain the people of promise solely because of Yahweh's holiness.

From Sinai to Transjordan

From Sinai Israel moved north toward Canaan. The narrative represents this as a time of bitter complaining and dissatisfaction. The people tired of the manna, and the quail which Yahweh provided made them sick. Members of Moses' family, Miriam and Aaron, attacked Moses for marrying a Cushite [1] woman. Miriam, a prophetess,[2] raising the louder protest, felt that Moses' action had jeopardized his unique position as mediator between Yahweh and the people. It may be, however, that all that was

---

[1] From either Ethiopia (II Chronicles 14:9 ff.; Habakkuk 3:7) or northern Arabia or east of Babylon.
[2] Exodus 15:20.

demonstrated here was her jealousy of Moses' status. Miriam became leprous,[3] interpreted as Yahweh's defense of Moses. Moses magnanimously interceded for her and she recovered. Events like these forbode evil days to come for a people of such faltering and uncertain character.

The most forceful presentation of Israel's weakness and lack of faith, however, is the story of the "spies from Kadesh" (Numbers 13, 14). When the Israelites arrived at Kadesh, spies were sent into Canaan. They were to find out about the land's productivity, the strength of its cities, the nature of its inhabitants and to gather data important to prospective settlers. They reported the fruitfulness of the land, the strength of the people, and the fortifications of the cities.[4] They mentioned the Amalekites, nomads ranging to the south of Judah; the Hittites, a people of greatness in Asia Minor during the second millennium B.C. who still exercised influence in Canaan; the Jebusites, a small but formidable tribe around Jerusalem; and the Amorites, Semitic peoples residing largely in the low hills of the south and southwest. Only two spies, Joshua and Caleb, encouraged immediate advance against Canaan. In a way this was saying that only two out of ten believed in God, and so it always seemed to be in Israel. The others disagreed. Emphasizing the strength of the city fortifications and the size of the people, they referred to some of Canaan's inhabitants as "nephilim," or giants.[5] The high thick walls of some Canaanite cities had left an exaggerated impression upon the nomad mind. The spies may even have revised their report about its productivity, since one account records that they did not believe Canaan capable of sustaining a large population. Numbers 13:23–27 records a favorable report on Canaan, "it flows with milk and honey," while Numbers 13:32 unfavorably reports that "the land through which we have gone, to spy it out, is a land that devours its inhabitants." Faced with the pessimistic report of the ten spies, the Israelites were on the verge of returning to Egypt. When Joshua and Caleb suggested that they could conquer Canaan by the power of Yahweh, they were stoned. This display of faithless ingratitude angered Yahweh, who was ready to disinherit his people and begin again with the descend-

[3] In the Old Testament many skin diseases besides true leprosy were designated by the general term translated leprosy.
[4] Numbers 13:27–28.
[5] Cf. Genesis 6:4.

ants of Moses and Aaron. In words strikingly reminiscent of the promises made to the patriarchs, Moses is described as father of a great nation:

How long will this people despise me? And how long will they not believe in me, in spite of all the signs which I have wrought among them? I will strike them with pestilence and disinherit them, and *I will make of you a nation greater and mightier than they.*[6]

Nowhere else is Moses better depicted as a representative and leader of his people than in this story. He interceded on Israel's behalf and Yahweh substituted a generation's stalemate for the immediate execution of the people. None of the rebellious generation, except Joshua and Caleb, were permitted to enter Canaan. The remainder were doomed to wander in the wilderness until they died. Rebellion, even when forgiven through prophetic intercession, has serious consequences.

When the spies who had made an unfavorable report about Israel's chances of success against Canaan died in a plague, the people immediately reversed their decision. Against the advice of Moses they attacked the Canaanites at Hormah [7] without divine sanction (Moses and the Ark remained back at camp). They had little chance for success. The Canaanites drove the majority of the tribes back into the southern Negeb. Portions of Judah and Simeon, however, probably remained in the area around Hormah living as nomads.[8] This story explains the later presence in this area of tribal groups sympathetic with Israelites who were settling in other parts of Canaan.

The group which fell back from Hormah returned to the area around Kadesh where they continued to wander for a generation. The Numbers account of this experience makes it a punishment for faithlessness, but the delay was much more than this. The years thus spent were years of consolidation. A generation grew up which had not been in Egypt. In the face of the arduous conquest, they would not be tempted to return to Egypt. A new leader who was not associated with the complaints of the wilderness period would replace Moses. Yahweh was uniting and disciplining his people for the task which lay before them.

[6] Numbers 14:11–12; emphasis added.
[7] Numbers 14:44–45 and 21:1–3; Cf. Judges 1:16–17.
[8] Cf. Numbers 21:1–3 and Judges 1:16–17.

Since the Israelite tribes had been unable to enter Canaan from the south, their leaders decided to move into Transjordan before again attempting to enter Canaan proper. The king of Edom was asked for permission to pass through his land on the old "kings highway," the link between Syria and the rich copper deposits in the Arabah. The request, however, was denied, illustrating long-standing enmity between Israel and her kinsmen, the Edomites. Denied the easy route through Edomite territory, Israel moved eastward along Edom's northern border and thence northward into Transjordan.

On this journey occurred a number of events which cannot be located or dated with accuracy. They simply belong to the nation's memory of the wilderness wandering. Miriam died and was buried at Kadesh. A plague of serpents was averted by the making of a bronze image. Moses "sinned" by striking a rock to obtain water,[9] rather than speaking to it as instructed. He and Aaron were denied entrance into the Promised Land. Aaron died and was buried on Mt. Hor (somewhere south of the Dead Sea).[10] Eleazer became his successor by donning the priestly robes. The report of all these events emphasizes Yahweh's faithfulness to provide. Both the people and their leaders continually demonstrated faithlessness and unworthiness of what Yahweh had done for them. Only the Holy Yahweh remained faithful.

The Conquest of Transjordan

The Israelites travelled along the western edge of Edom and then turned eastward along the northern border. Moab was also bypassed along her eastern side until the river Arnon was reached. At this point the Amorite kingdom of Sihon stood in Israel's path. When passage through his land was denied, Sihon was engaged in battle at Jahaz and the Israelites defeated him.[11] This victory gave them territory from the Arnon to the Jabbok rivers.

The territory north of the Jabbok belonged to the kingdom of Bashan, whose king was Og. At Edrei, the capital of Bashan, Israel again was successful in battle and Transjordan became hers

---

[9] Numbers 20:2–13.

[10] Cf. Numbers 20:22 ff. The phrase "gathered unto his people" suggests an Israelite belief in some mode of existence in Sheol.

[11] Numbers 21:21 ff.

—with the exception, of course, of Edom and Moab. Israel was on the march and the land of promise lay ahead.

Balaam.[12] Before continuing the story of conquest, Numbers presents an intriguing story accentuating Yahweh's protection of Israel and the security the nation enjoyed under his sovereignty. The story told in both poetry and prose [13] emphasizes the foolishness of attempting to interfere with the will of Yahweh. Even an honest prophet of foreign origin could not ally himself with the enemies of Yahweh's people.

Balak, king of Moab, greatly concerned with the victories won by the Israelites, summoned Balaam,[14] an eastern diviner or *baru* of signal reputation. Balaam was a typical diviner, possessing the powers believed by the ancients to be latent with prophets. He was brought from Pethor, a town on the upper Euphrates, to curse the invading Israelites so that Balak might be successful against them in battle. Balaam is portrayed as a true prophet who, although greatly tempted by exalted status and wealth, could not proclaim other than an oracle from God. He was not an Israelite, but is presented as one who answered to Yahweh, whether in Pethor or Moab.

The story of Balaam and his ass must have been popular with the Israelites, who surely must have been amused by the prophet whose powers of discernment were inferior to those of his beast of burden. The ass was an animal respected by the Semites and perhaps was worshipped in an early period. Some even believed that it was among those animals possessing powers of clairvoyance.

In the Balaam story, we have a meaningful theme set in the terminology, theology, and type of literature suited both to the times and to its hearers. Yahweh bends everything toward the realization of his will. The man who aligns himself against Yahweh commits folly. Security is found only in doing Yahweh's bidding. Defeat is the prognosis for those opposed to Yahweh and his people.

---

[12] Numbers 22–24.

[13] The poetry sections seem to be of an earlier date than the prose.

[14] "Balaam" is to be distinguished from "Baalim," a number of local Canaanite deities.

Moses' Death. When the conquest of the Transjordan was near completion, Moses stood in the "land of Moab" and delivered his farewell address to Israel. Soon thereafter on Mt. Nebo, he died. His body was buried, but the thrust of his life is yet far from the grave. The name of Moses is found in any list of those who have most influenced the history of man. Besides his gift of the Decalogue to mankind, his influence on the Torah, his role as an emancipator, and his contribution to the establishment of the only theocracy of sizable proportion to continue for any length of time, three of the major living religions (Judaism, Islam, and Christianity) are to be directly or indirectly traced to him. Men of such long shadows rarely pass across the world scene.

Joshua, one of the two spies who had encouraged the taking of Canaan, was chosen as Moses' successor.[15] Israel's new leader was battle trained and an able warrior. He had possibly assisted Moses in the highly successful campaign against the Midianites which concluded the conquest of the Transjordan.[16] As he took the helm, he readied preparations for the conquest of Canaan itself. The tribes of Reuben and Gad and one-half of Manasseh were assigned territory in Transjordan with the understanding that they would settle there only after assisting in the conquest of Canaan. Thus, with Transjordan under control and a new leader in command, Israel stood poised to enter the land of promise.

THE DEVELOPMENT OF ISRAEL'S DEUTERONOMIC TRADITIONS (DEUTERONOMY 1–34)

The Book of Deuteronomy

The book of Deuteronomy stands between the book of Numbers, which recounts the conquest of the Transjordan, and the book of Joshua, which describes the taking of Canaan. Literally it serves as a conclusion to the Torah and as an introduction to the Deuteronomic history work (Deuteronomy-II Kings), to which it gives direction and theological perspective. As with

---

[15] Numbers 27:12–23.
[16] Numbers 31.

the other books of the Torah, this scroll was known in Israel by its opening words, "these are the words" or "the words." The Septuagint translators rendered a phrase, "a copy of this law," in 8:18 and 17:18, as *deuteronomion*, "second (or repeated) law," and this term became the title of the book.

Deuteronomy is essentially a résumé of Israel's religion posited within a sermonic framework. It is an expansion of Mosaic law code arranged so that its public proclamation might be effective.

I. First Address. 1:1–4:40
  A. Historical review. 1:1–3:29
  B. Appeal for faithful obedience. 4:1–40
II. Second Address. Chapters 5–28
  A. Law and its meaning. Chapters 5–26
  B. Curses of disobedience. Chapter 27
  C. Blessings of obedience and curses of disobedience. Chapter 28
III. Third Address: Exhortation to Renew Covenant. Chapters 29–30
IV. Concluding Things about Moses. Chapters 31–34

The first sermon [17] is a recounting of the acts of Yahweh, closing with an exhortation to obedience and absolute fidelity. Infidelity and disobedience will result in the dissipation of the nation.

The second sermon [18] is the longest and forms the core of the book. It is a presentation of Yahweh's law. The first part of the discourse (chapters 5–11) begins by citing the Decalogue and continues with an elaboration upon the first commandment. It sets forth the fundamental principles which undergird all particular legislation. Disobedience is an invitation to catastrophe and the wilderness experience corroborates the fact. The second part of the discourse (chapters 12–28) contains the laws themselves. The code relates to all phases of Israelite life—civil, moral, ceremonial. It closes with an appeal for obedience with its promised reward as opposed to the curse found in disobedience. Chapter twenty-seven seems to be an interpolation dealing with the preparation for a covenant ceremony at Shechem, perhaps observed at the end of the conquest.

The third sermon [19] exhorts Israel to keep the covenant and

---

[17] Deuteronomy 1:6–4:40.
[18] Deuteronomy 5:1–28:68.
[19] Deuteronomy 29:30.

presents the alternatives of life or death to the covenant community. The blessings and curses of chapter 28 are the ceremonial expression of these alternatives. The choice belongs to the nation and repentance is an ever-present recourse for apostasy.

There follow additional words of encouragement and exhortation and Moses' parting blessing upon the individual tribes. The book closes with the account of Moses' death and an evaluation of his work as a great prophet.

The structure of the book fits well with the liturgical progression of the ceremony of covenant making.[20] Perhaps, therefore, Deuteronomy is an expanded commentary on the Sinai experience formulated as three sermons attributed to Moses. Thus the laws of Deuteronomy are dependent upon the Covenant Code,[21] although they represent a later development within the community. The law code upon which the Deuteronomic sermons are based was compiled at the religious shrines of Shechem and Shiloh organized in the days following the conquest of Canaan. At these central sanctuaries, which became bonds of unity for the Israelite tribes for over one hundred and fifty years, a ceremony of covenant renewal was held each new year. The high point was the reading and acceptance of the law of Yahweh. The homiletical presentation of law in Deuteronomy seems to have grown out of the law read on these occasions. To this corpus of ancient cultic tradition were added later refinements and interpretations until Deuteronomy made a later appearance in its present form. As it now stands in the canon, Deuteronomy is "a finished, mature, beautifully proportioned and theologically clear work." [22] Its audience includes those widely separated from the wilderness and conquest experiences. As Moses addressed those who stood across the Jordan from the land of promise, so the book proclaims without equivocation that throughout her history Israel remained the object of Yahweh's election and salvation.[23] In this sense the book is a profound theology of the Exodus.

Although Deuteronomy reaches superlative moral heights, it

---

[20] G. E. Wright, "Cult and History," *Interpretation*, XVI (1962), 10.

[21] Exodus 20:23–23:19. Deuteronomy should be studied along with other legal codes in the Old Testament: the Holiness Code (Leviticus 17–26) and the Priestly Code (Leviticus 1–7; 11–15).

[22] Gerhard von Rad, *Studies in Deuteronomy*, p. 37.

[23] *Ibid.*, pp. 70 ff.

also advocates ruthless treatment of the enemies of Israel and worshippers of other gods. The *cherem* (ban) called for the sacrifice of all enemies and their property as an offering to Yahweh, either by death or redirection into his service. Further, Deuteronomy reduces the problems of suffering and adversity to a simple equation—pain and penalty to the disobedient; pleasure and prosperity to the obedient. In spite of these liabilities, however, the book links Israel with her founding days and admonishes her to the best of the covenant faith. It proclaims the message of the redeeming God, who established a covenant with the people whom he had emancipated from slavery. He is Yahweh, who cannot be fully symbolized by substance. He loved Israel when she had not merited it and ever remained faithful to his commitments to her. She is to respond by a loving obedience in the acknowledgment that her security is found in him alone. She is his people and must demonstrate his nature through her conduct. This calls for integrity and justice. As his people, she has a destiny assured by her faithfulness to Yahweh. Apart from this Israel has no future, only death.

It is not surprising that the code of Deuteronomy played an important role at times in later Israelite history when proclamation of the law was highly desirable. In the midst of a political and religious reform during the reign of King Josiah (640–609) of Judah, a law book, probably Deuteronomy, was found in the temple. It was read publicly and became the basis for national religious revival.

Deuteronomy was a favorite of the New Testament writers. Jesus replied to his wilderness temptation [24] by quoting from three places in the book; and for the first part of his answer concerning the first and great commandment,[25] he cited the Deuteronomic version of the first commandment in the Decalogue. His teachings in the Sermon on the Mount may have had in mind Deuteronomy 18:13. Altogether more than eighty quotations from Deuteronomy occur in the New Testament. The reasons for this attraction to the book are obvious. Here is found an exalted summary of the religion of Israel. Like few other portions of the Old Testament, it soars beyond the expected and

[24] Matthew 4.
[25] Matthew 22:37.

grasps the concern of Yahweh for his people and calls for their response in love.

The Deuteronomic History

Deuteronomy introduces an extensive collection of literature dealing with Israel's life in the land of Canaan. This collection is four Old Testament books: Joshua, which describes the conquest of Canaan and the division of its territory among the twelve Israelite tribes; Judges, which deals with the life of the early Israelite amphictyony or tribal confederacy and the defense of the land; Samuel, which continues the account of the confederacy, depicts the struggle with the Philistines and in the Saul-David narratives describes the establishment of the Davidic monarchy; and Kings, which continues the story of the monarchy down to the disaster of Babylonian exile in 587 B.C.

Before analyzing these books individually it must be decided whether they are four individual and independent works or a large block of material forming an ideological and literary unit. At first glance the corpus appears to be made up of four separate works: Joshua, Judges, Samuel, Kings. They are patently so divided in the canon of the Old Testament. Closer examination, however, reveals that throughout the corpus there are materials of diverse types and origins (hero tales, tribal traditions, royal records, prophetic traditions, popular stories, etc.) which cannot be delineated by the fourfold Old Testament structure. Actually, the canonical divisions are both artificial and arbitrary. Between Joshua and Judges no real division exists. Judges opens with materials which largely parallel the content of Joshua 1–11 and, unlike the rest of Judges, deals with the conquest, not the defense of the land. The books of Judges and Samuel are joined by two links: first, the man Samuel for whom the latter book is named appears as the last of the judges and, second, the appendices to Judges in chapters 17–21 prepare for the emergence of the monarchy by their repeated mention of disasters which occurred *before Israel had a king.* Finally, I Kings 1–2 forms a direct sequel to II Samuel 13–20 so that a break between the books of Samuel and Kings separates material that belongs together. Equally supportive for the unity of all these materials is the pervading presence of editorial influences reminiscent of the book of Deuteronomy. In fact these editorial sections tie the originally divergent materials together. The conclusion, therefore, is that the books of Joshua, Judges, Samuel, and Kings in their present form comprise a literary unit.)

There are two major opinions concerning the manner in which these materials are united. (One claims that the unity is the result of an editorial interweaving of source strata. According to this analysis the early source strata (Yahwistic and Elohistic) of the Pentateuch or Hexateuch can be traced through the books of Judges and Samuel and even into Kings. For the period of Israel's life in Canaan these strata were edited from the perspective of the book of Deuteronomy and were bound together with Deuteronomic additions. The weakness of this analysis is that no attempt to assign the materials in Judges-Kings to narrative strata has ever been very successful.

(More probable, but not without its own problems, is the suggestion that the books from Deuteronomy through Kings form a single historical work. The author of this history worked in Judah during the exile and combined into a single unit originally independent materials, *i.e.*, the aforementioned hero tales, tribal traditions, royal records, etc. His own contribution was editorial and expository, reflecting always his particular interpretation of the disastrous course of Israel's life in Canaan.)

Strongly favoring this analysis is that it provides a reasonable explanation both for the gathering together of the various materials preserved in Joshua-Kings and for the obvious Deuteronomic tone pervading them all. There are, however, some objections. One is the argument that from section to section there are differences of editorial perspective. (For example, Judges reflects a cyclic interpretation of history with the constantly repeated sequence of apostasy-punishment-repentance-deliverance, while Kings presents "a course of history that leads downward in a straight line to destruction." [26] Again, the book of Samuel shows almost no evidence of Deuteronomic influence. Nevertheless, the idea of a Deuteronomic historian who intentionally set out to provide an interpretation of Israel's road to tragedy best accounts

---

[26] Georg Fohrer, *Introduction to the Old Testament,* p. 194.

for the form and tone of the books Joshua-Kings. That these materials were originally prefaced by the book of Deuteronomy also makes sense, since that work lays the theological groundwork for the interpretation of history which follows. It has already been observed that Deuteronomy had at one time existed independent of the other strata of the Torah and was later combined with them. Conceivably it was at some time separated from the larger Deuteronomic history and added to Genesis-Numbers, perhaps without an intention that the following history be considered a separate and different work. Neither Torah nor Deuteronomic history is complete without the other. Separated, the former has no conclusion and the latter no beginning. In effect, if not by original intention, Deuteronomy successfully ties the two together.

The following interpretation of Joshua-Kings assumes their place in a Deuteronomic history work. The discussion of each section will indicate how the Deuteronomic historian used his sources to further his theological purpose. First there must be a clear brief statement of that purpose. Only with an understanding of the perspective of faith from which these materials were brought together can one properly evaluate the Deuteronomist's contribution to Old Testament theology and history. For him the old narrative materials were inadequate interpretations of what really took place between Yahweh and Israel. He wrote at a time "when the saving history over Israel was at a standstill and when . . . the question which had to be answered was, how had all this come about and how could it have been possible for Yahweh to reject his people?" [27] Therefore, he tried to supply the reader with special theological guidance which would aid in understanding Israel's history and destiny. He was strongly influenced by the materials in Deuteronomy which set forth certain theological ideals for the people of the covenant in times of crisis. Now in another and climactic crisis the Deuteronomic historian applied some of these ideals to his interpretation of Israel's history. In this sense his work is preaching. It should be noted, however, that the Deuteronomic historian was not slavishly bound

[27] Gerhard von Rad, *Old Testament Theology*, I, p. 342.

to all of the Deuteronomic ideas. Some of its emphases did not capture his imagination and he had theological perceptions of his own which colored his account in Joshua-Kings.

Above all he was convinced that it was the sin of Israel that had brought her to tragic end. This sin was the rejection of Yahweh for the gods of Canaan. Israel had had to choose between worship of the Lord of History and the Baal nature cults. Unwisely and to her shame and sorrow, she had chosen the latter. Thus, as von Rad has succinctly summed it up, the work of the Deuteronomist is "a comprehensive confession of Israel's guilt." [28] He writes, therefore, of Yahweh's *judgment word* in Israel's history, exercised again and again in a measured way but finally and all but irreversibly in the catastrophe of national destruction and exile. At the same time, however, he wrote of Yahweh's word of promise. For him this was not so much the promise to the patriarchal ancestors as it was the promise or covenant with David. This was a promise of salvation. The judges saved Israel from chaos, but not permanently. Kings had had the potential of being Yahweh's representative to bring his people to the full and good life, but none, not even David, actualized that potential. The possibilities of the covenant had repeatedly gone unrealized.

Promise and salvation, however, were still offered. They must be grasped by the faithful. Even though the Deuteronomist was preoccupied with Israel's guilt, he offered his history as a kind of national confession and hinted throughout that forgiveness was available and redemption possible. By implication he anticipated the ideal one who would come to Israel to serve "his people as deliverer not merely on one occasion alone," [29] who would be king and would do all that the nation had failed to do. Thus he interpreted Israel's history as guilt and judgment within which was offered messianic promise. Admittedly the latter was only an undercurrent and was never prominently exploited. To a people in chaos, and its exile was chaos, the word of salvation came as a whisper or a still small voice. It was so in the Deuteronomic history.

[28] *Ibid.*, p. 337.
[29] *Ibid.*, p. 329.

CONQUEST (JOSHUA 1–12)

The Deuteronomic history opens with an account of the conquest of Canaan as an act of Yahweh's faithfulness to his patriarchal and covenant promises. By doing so it anticipates its judgment upon Israel for failure to be Yahweh's people in the land he had given them.

Inhabitants of Canaan

"Canaan" probably first meant "land of the purple." This title referred to the dye industries for which the area was noted. The coloring was derived from a shellfish or *murex mollusca*, widely found along the Palestinian coast. The Greeks later called the area Phoenicia from a Greek word also meaning "purple."

When used for a people, "Canaanite" seems to have been a term covering a mixture of people living in the area between Gaza and Hamath, a territory including both Palestine and a part of Syria. The first of these peoples may have migrated into the land from the Arabian Desert. By 3000 B.C. cities such as Jebus (Jerusalem), Megiddo, Byblos, Ai, Jericho, Gezer, Hamath, and Beth-shan had been established. Some of these cities yield evidence of occupation hundreds to several thousand years before this date.

The people of Canaan distinguished themselves by several cultural achievements. If they were not responsible for the invention of the alphabet, they were responsible for its improvement and dissemination across the Mediterranean world. Most of the western world uses alphabets based upon the Canaanite or Phoenician. As prominent seafaring people, they laced together in a loose fashion of communication the diverse corners of the Mediterranean. Consequently, they were themselves edified by these contacts. Whether by caravan or by ship, they were in the path of the movements and ideas of the world. Their architecture, musical instruments, ceramics, and early use of copper and iron established them as an advanced people for the age.

At the time of the conquest the Israelites appraised accurately that "the people who dwell in the land are strong and the cities are fortified and very large." [30] Had the Canaanites become uni-

---

[30] Numbers 13:28.

fied, the history of the Near East might have been written quite differently. However, this never happened. The terrain of Canaan was rugged and natural elements tended to separate the people. Instead of consolidating their strength into a great nation, they narrowly crystallized their life around city or town centers. They developed city-states like those of the Greeks. A city with its neighboring countryside considered itself a unit for purposes of government and defense. Each had its own king and administered its own affairs. Occasionally two or more would ally themselves to meet a common enemy,[31] but most often each went its own way. Most of these city-states were in the desirable lowlands and the plains which were more suitable for agriculture and grazing. Only a few, such as Jebus, Hebron, Luz, and Shechem were in the highlands or mountains where the water supply was meager.

From 2000 to 1200 B.C. Canaan was largely under the influence of Egypt. She looked to Egypt during the Hyksos mastery of the Nile. After the native Egyptians expelled the Hyksos and regained control of their land, Canaan was considered a part of the Egyptian empire for about two hundred years. Outposts were established at fortified cities such as Gezer and Beth-shan, and Egyptian vassals controlled some cities. During the Amarna period, Egyptian influence on the region was only nominal. Since Akhnaton was primarily interested in his experiments with religion, his leadership in administering the affairs of state was uncertain. Consequently, vassals, city kings, and Egyptian officials did largely as they pleased. We have already noted that some of Israel's ancestors were among the Habiru who took advantage of this situation to gain a foothold in the land of Canaan. Settling down around Shechem, they waited for the proper time to assert themselves more strongly.

Other peoples also resided in the land of Canaan. The *Amorites* were kinsmen of Israel's patriarchal ancestors who moved into Canaan in the same series of immigration as Abraham, Isaac, and Jacob. Unlike their Israelite counterparts, however, they quickly settled down and established city-states of their own. The *Hittites*, remnants of outposts of the Hittite empire of cen-

[31] Joshua 10:12.

tral Asia Minor, settled in isolated pockets here and there in Canaan. The *Jebusites* were those Canaanites who lived at the city of Jebus and the *Horites* were Hurrians, whose point of origin was Mitanni in northern Mesopotamia. Some Horites may have resided in Edom or Seir.

Consequently, when Israel came to Canaan, she found a land populated with many diverse groups, among whom were peoples kindred to her ancestors. In the process of conquest and settlement among these peoples Israel absorbed many of them. Thus, when Israel entered Canaan, she came into a territory where she had previously-established ties and allegiances. For a long while Hebrews or Amorites of one description or another had been entering the land. Although they had been to varying degrees the "outs" and had not crashed the Canaanite structure, they were there and were related to Israel. When Joshua and his company moved in, these peoples were ready to identify with Israel and help overthrow the land.[32]

The Book of Joshua

Israel's tradition of the conquest appears in the book of Joshua which opens the second division of the Hebrew canon, but it cannot be arbitrarily separated from the Torah. The promise of land to the patriarchs was realized in the conquest. Joshua has certain affinities with the Yahwistic, Elohistic, and Priestly histories, but it actually belongs to the Deuteronomic tradition. Deuteronomy's reiteration of the law sums up Torah and leads into the story of the fulfillment of promise. Joshua describes the first phase of the fulfillment by telling of the conquest, allocation, and settlement of Canaan, the land promised to Israel's father Abraham. The period covered is about 1250–1200 B.C. Since Joshua is the primary character of the conquest, the book bears his name. The work may be broadly outlined:

    I. The Conquest of Canaan. 1:1–12:24
        A. Crossing the Jordan. 1:1–5:15
        B. Campaign into central Canaan. 6:1–10:27
        C. Campaign into southern Canaan. 10:28–43

---

[32] This doubtlessly casts some light on the question of why Joshua was able to take central Canaan without effort following the fall of Jericho and Ai-Bethel.

The book of Joshua presents a problem to any morally sensitive reader. Brutality and savage conquest is not only condoned, but also sanctioned as the will of Yahweh (cf. 6:16–21). The book portrays war as an instrument of deity in the hands of elect people. All who oppose them do so at the risk of their lives, including the infant and the woman.

Such obvious inhumanity must be understood in the light of a wartime psychology. Whatever the side or the century, man often enters battle feeling that he is on the side of God or gods or the "right." Such a general philosophy both promotes the idea that whatever he does is in some fashion an act of God and rationalizes a multitude of sins as vindicated by the cause. In this context modern man can understand, but not excuse, the early Israelite, for at this point the twentieth century A.D. is not so far separated from the thirteenth B.C.

The book of Joshua demanded that the inhabitants of Canaan be *cherem*, usually translated "utterly destroyed," but probably better translated "placed under the ban" or "devoted" in the sense of an offering to God. Since Yahweh was the protagonist and the real victor in battles, Israel felt that spoils belonged to him. The *cherem* indicated this ownership and recognized Yahweh's prerogative to do with the booty as he wished. Therefore, the Israelites considered the accomplishment of the *cherem* as a religious act to be performed with complete faithfulness and devotion.[33] Sometimes "utter destruction" was enforced as sacrifice to God. At other times the enemy was simply enlisted in the service of Yahweh.

Joshua's sanction of cruelty as the will of God illustrates the

---

[33] Violators were punished summarily, as Achan and his family in the campaign against Bethel-Ai. Even in peace time an Israelite city which practiced idolatry might be placed under the *cherem*. See Deuteronomy 13:12–18.

limited perspective which even a religious community might have at any given moment. Throughout the Old Testament some men perceive Yahweh with greater clarity than their contemporaries, but most are caught up in the thought forms which are a part of their culture. Some even revert to more primitive outlooks. A graph of religious understanding during the Old Testament period would be irregular, but generally upward. Israel could openly and honestly reflect on days when she served Yahweh unworthily because of her confidence that Yahweh did not wait for the nation to deserve him. She well understood that the God of Israel was not small, capricious, and slow; it was Israel who moved tardily and unsteadily toward maturity of both faith and understanding.

The brutality of the conquest, then, was more the result of Israel's limited grasp of the nature of Yahweh than of Yahweh's purpose. Although the savagery of Israel cannot be excused, it can be understood as an act of faith and obedience. Hopefully later generations would behold greater light, but the shutters of understanding are always conditioned by the environment. God remains the same; man changes as God's revelation breaks forth upon him.

The Joshua Account of the Conquest

The book of Joshua (chapters 1–12) presents a generalized theological interpretation of Israel's conquest of Canaan. A cursory reading of its materials leaves the impression that all the land fell into Israelite hands under Joshua and all her prominent enemies were resoundingly defeated or otherwise immobilized. Archaeological and historical discoveries reveal a longer and more complicated story quite difficult to correlate with the Joshua narrative. Some sites of the ancient Canaanite cities disclose several levelings during the thirteenth century. Other cities appear to have been destroyed both before and after Joshua, but not during his time. Also, some cities and areas of Canaan were not occupied by Israelites until after the monarchy was established. Real possession of the land appears to have been an extensive and drawn out affair and much was acquired by alliances and slow assimilation with the earlier inhabitants of Canaan

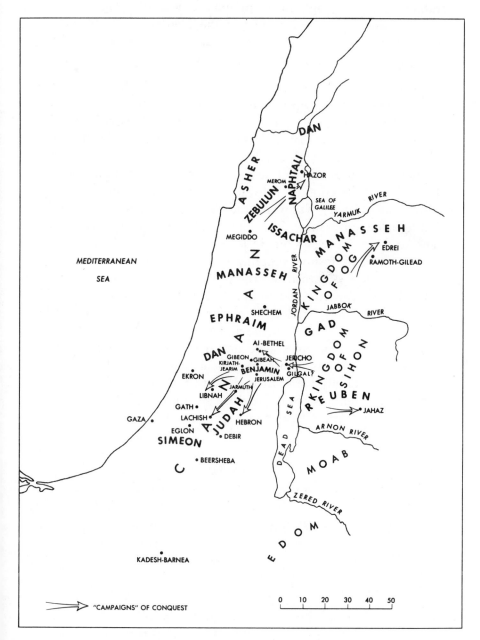

Figure 5–1.   Conquest and settlement.

rather than by a single major military expedition. The idealized
account of the book of Joshua is the Deuteronomic historian's
presentation of old conquest traditions edited to show that faithful Israel shares in the victories of Yahweh.

Holy War. The Joshua story is a narrative of a holy war. The
entire account points up the Hebrew undersanding of a sovereign
God working for the people with whom he was in covenant. The
army was called the *'Am Yahweh* ("the people of Yahweh") and
was under strict sacral regulations. The warriors were "holy."
Preparations for battle included elaborate cultic acts to insure that
the will and direction of Yahweh were known and obeyed. Victories won in such a war were credited to Yahweh and the spoil of
battle belonged to him. The capture of Canaan was a sacral act.
The land was Yahweh's gift to Israel.[34]

The book of Joshua simplifies the conquest into a threefold
campaign: first, a thrust into the central highlands; second, overpowering an Amorite league of cities to the south; third, a skirmish with a confederation of northern kings. The entire story
is told with a dramatic flair to emphasize Yahweh's role. Prior to
crossing the Jordan, spies were sent over into the city of Jericho.
A prostitute named Rahab gave them sanctuary and, in return,
she and her family were assured protection on the day of siege
when her neighbors would perish. By means of the reconnais-
sance Joshua learned that the Canaanites, although protected behind heavy walls, were greatly afraid. The crossing of the Jordan
was miraculously accomplished with priests in the lead carrying
the Ark of the Covenant. Clearly Israel saw the event as a work
of Yahweh. As he had been with Moses at the Sea of Reeds, he
was with Joshua in the crossing of the Jordan. Landslides have
at times blocked the Jordan and may have enabled the Israelites
to cross. Whether by natural or unnatural intervention, the cause
belonged to Yahweh and all the earth yielded to him. This religious confidence of Israel is preserved throughout her sacred literature. In Judges 5 Deborah sings of Joshua's time:

> Yahweh, when thou didst go forth from Seir,
>   When thou didst march from the region of Edom,
>   the earth trembled . . .

[34] Cf. Joshua 1:2, 11; 10:14, 42; etc.

and Psalm 114 declares:

> When Israel went forth from Egypt,
> the house of Jacob from a people of strange language,
> Judah became his sanctuary,
> Israel his dominion.
> The sea looked and fled,
> Jordan turned back.
> The mountains skipped like rams,
> the hills like lambs.

The flow of the Jordan's waters, like all nature, is subject to Yahweh in whose hand is the destiny of his covenant people.

West of the Jordan Joshua set up a memorial of stones from the river bed.[35] In preparation for the holy war the males who had come out of the wilderness generation were circumcised.[36] Those who had received an Egyptian style circumcision were probably recircumcised with flint knives in the same fashion as Moses. Engagement in holy war required participation in several rituals and adherence to numerous regulations. In Yahweh's war all participants must demonstrate their singular commitment to Yahweh's leadership. The tradition of the rites performed at Gilgal and of the memorial erected there almost certainly reflects some cultic act celebrated at the Gilgal shrine during the amphictyony. At Gilgal Israel began to live off the land of Canaan and made it a base camp for the military campaigns against the Canaanite city-states.

Thrust into the Central Highlands. The Joshua narrative of conquest depicts three highly successful military operations. First, Jericho was overrun and a thrust was made into the central highlands at Ai. Since archaeological excavations reveal that major cities at the site of Jericho were destroyed around 1600 B.C. and not rebuilt well after the time of Joshua,[37] it is presumed that the forces met here were from a fortress on the mound at the time, not a city. Such as they were, the defenses and numbers on the hill would have appeared awesome to the Israelites. The siege of Jericho is pictured as a ritual

---

[35] Joshua 4:8–10, 19–24.

[36] The idea that their reproach before Yahweh was thus "rolled away" (Gilgal) was given as explanation for the name of the site.

[37] Kathleen Kenyon has written extensively on her excavations at Jericho. Many of her articles appear in the *Palestine Exploration Quarterly*.

Figure 5–2. Excavation at site of ancient Canaanite city, Jericho. Extensive diggings indicate that here is the oldest town in Palestine yet discovered. (Source: Jordan Tourist Department.)

act. The priests and their sacerdotal functions were integal to the entire affair. Soldiers, as a consequence of their purifications, became "holy men" for the duration of the engagement. The order of march to Jericho was a vanguard, seven priests blowing ram's horns, the ark and a rear guard. The religious nature of the endeavor is evident in every way. This was more a cultic procession than a march to war. Even the sound of the ram's horns may have symbolized the voice of Yahweh.[38] Six days of marching in silence were followed by a seventh day on which six trips around the city were followed by a seventh on which the signal was given by the rams' horns and the people burst forth in shouting. The walls of the city were leveled and the entire city, as *cherem*, was sacrificed to Yahweh. Included in the destruction was every living thing: men and women, young and old, and even the animals. The single exception was the harlot Rahab, who had collaborated with Israel, her family and property. The riches of the city, silver, gold, and vessels of bronze and iron, were placed in a treasury for Yahweh; then the city was burned. It is quite possible that later at Gilgal or Shechem a cultic procession like that described in Joshua 6 was combined with a ceremonial crossing of the Jordan into a great celebration of conquest victory.[39] Later Israel may have merged the actual fight at Jericho with this ceremonial celebration to produce the idealized picture presented in the book of Joshua.

Equally problematic is the tradition about defeat and victory at Ai. Ai means "ruin" and is a manifestly inappropriate name for a city. Archaeological evidence, in fact, reveals that Ai was destroyed about 2200 B.C., and was not reoccupied until Iron Age I when a small village was established there.[40] Martin Noth suggests that the tradition of the fighting at Ai is an etiological legend explaining the impressive ruins which already by the time of the Israelite monarchy were commonly called *ha 'ai* "the ruin." [41] W. F. Albright, however, holds that Ai referred to in Joshua is Bethel, a city hardly a mile and a half

38 Cf. Numbers 10:10.

39 Hans-Joachim Kraus, "Gilgal: Ein Beitrag zur Kultusgeschichte Israels," *Vetus Testamentum*, I (1951), 181–199.

40 Cf. Joseph A. Callaway, "New Evidence on the Conquest of 'Ai," *Journal of Biblical Literature*, LXXXVII (1968), 312–320.

41 Martin Noth, *The History of Israel*, p. 149, n. 2.

away from the Ai ruins. When the city on the site of Ai was destroyed in 2200 B.C., its inhabitants moved a short distance away and built Bethel. This Bethel was destroyed about 1250 B.C., approximately the time that Joshua was attacking Canaan. The Joshua account, therefore, would refer to an attack on Bethel, not Ai.[42] Recently in light of new excavations at Ai, Joseph A. Callaway has suggested that the biblical tradition of the conquest of Ai and of other areas in Canaan is an elaboration of "minor scale raids on small villages," like Iron Age I village at Ai. Further, he argues that the conquest was mainly achieved by political integration with the Iron Age I inhabitants of Canaan.[43] This, however, would have been after the generally accepted time of Joshua.

Albright's analysis is the most widely held view today and we follow it here. The problems, however, are many and cannot be easily solved. Their dimension could be enlarged with other data, but enough has been cited to make it obvious that Israel's settlement in Canaan was not so simply or directly accomplished as the Joshua narrative would imply.

Whatever happened at Ai, the biblical account is of holy war and the issue is *cherem*. The initial defeat at Ai-Bethel was blamed on a violation of Jericho's *cherem* by one of the Israelites named Achan. Since he had violated the rules of the holy war, all Israel was disqualified from victory. Once Achan and all of his family had been killed by stoning, however, the army was considered cleansed. On the second assault, by use of ambush, the city was taken as *cherem* and the Israelites moved away as victors. The *cherem* of Ai-Bethel thus became the substitute for that of Jericho which had been negated by the sin of Achan.

The account of Israel's initial thrust into Canaan is throughout more concerned to emphasize Yahweh's sovereignty over Israel and the Canaanites than to describe precisely actual details of battles. This concern to show that Israel's settlement in Canaan is fundamentally a cultic achievement accounts for the insertion of a covenant ceremony at this point in the narrative. This was as crucial to Israel's success as the initial victories. The setting

---

[42] W. F. Albright, "'Ai and Beth-aven," *Annual of The American School of Oriental Research*, IV (1924), pp. 141–149. The Judges 1 account of the conquest mentions an attack on Bethel, but none on Ai, a seeming confirmation of the above analysis.

[43] Callaway, *op. cit.*, pp. 315–320. This theory deserves careful consideration.

of the covenant is Shechem where kindred people who had already settled in central Canaan were incorporated into the community of Israel.

The story of the covenant with a league of Gibeonite cities serves the same purpose. These cities by deception entered into covenant with Israel. Clearly the book of Joshua indicates that even the deception of Israel's enemies was turned to the advantage of the covenant people. Yahweh's victory could not be turned aside. Cities of the league became Israel's allies and therefore under protection of the holy war. Leaders in the deception became "hewers of wood" and "drawers of water"; that is, slaves to the cause of Yahweh.

Defeat of Southern League. Joshua continues by reporting dramatic victories in southern Canaan. Royal Canaanite cities in the south were alarmed and under the leadership of Adonizedek, king of Jebus, attacked Gibeon. Joined with Jebus in this Amorite coalition were the cities of Hebron, Jarmuth, Lachish, and Eglon. Jebus and Hebron were in the hills; the others in the Shephelah. Treaty bound Joshua to the defense of the Gibeonites and it was to his strategic advantage. From Gilgal the Israelites moved into the Jordan Valley and routed the coalition. The Amorites retreated down the only route of escape, the valley of Aijalon or Beth-horon pass. As they fled, Joshua's guerrilla tactics tore their armies to shreds. The kings hid themselves in a cave at Makkedah until they were found and killed. Victorious in the field campaign, Joshua then moved to lay siege to their cities. Libnah, and then in succession, Lachish, Eglon, Hebron, and Debir or Kirjath-sepher fell to him. Several of these battle sites have been excavated and archaeologists have noted destructions during the general period of Israelite conquest, but the biblical material obviously compacts into a brief period struggles which may have lasted a decade or more.

Conquest in the North. The third phase of the military conquest, according to the book of Joshua, is against a group of northern kings who allied themselves under Jabin, king of Hazor. Hazor was the largest city of the region and likely one of the largest cities of Palestine. Earlier it had been an exceptionally strong fortress. but by Joshua's time it had been already reduced to a shadow of its former strength. Joshua met the coalition at its rallying place near the Waters of Merom and defeated them in battle. Then he attacked Hazor and again the *cherem* was observed; Hazor was totally destroyed.

Since the Joshua account of conquest is the idealized narrative of a holy war, it should not be considered a self-contained version of Israel's struggle to possess the promised land. That struggle began with the patriarchal migrations to Canaan and continued through the years of the sojourn in Egypt as certain people later incorporated into the Covenant community of Israel settled here and there in Canaan, particularly in the area around Shechem. Moreover, the conquest did not end with the campaigns of Joshua, decisive though they might have been. Even after this main phase of the struggle was over and the territory had been allotted among the tribes, each of them had to consolidate itself in its area. Moab, Ammon, and Edom were not subdued and Canaanite opposition remained until the monarchy. In struggle against these forces some of the Israelite tribes were almost lost to history.[44] Nevertheless, the issue as a whole was settled by Joshua's victories, which assured the fulfillment of the promise to Abraham. The land of Canaan was now in the hands of his heirs. Although the period of conquest was a long one and centers of important opposition remained in the valleys and elsewhere, Israel understood Yahweh's promise to have been fulfilled with the fall of Hazor. Yahweh had been true to his promise as the people had been faithful to his lordship.

So closes a chapter begun with Abraham. A second Moses brought fulfillment to the nation's enduring hopes and dreams. As an Israelite read the story of his people's origins in search for their identity, the book of Joshua must have provided exhilarating reading. At this point in the story he could only exult in the thought that Israel's faith had brought her far and Yahweh had taken a no-people and made her a "nation" with a land she could call her own.

Holy Land and Covenant People

The book of Joshua makes clear that it was Yahweh's holy war, as led by a second Moses named Joshua, which acquired the land

---

[44] Cf. Judges 1 and its picture of individual tribal warfare against Canaanites.

of Canaan in fulfillment of Yahweh's promises [45] to the patriarchs, including blessings, descendants, a new relationship with Yahweh, and the land of Canaan. The patriarchs had lived as strangers in the land of promise which was not their land.[46] Only in the burial cave had they found a place which really belonged to them.[47] But during the time of Joshua the promise was fulfilled; Yahweh gave the land to Israel. This truth underlies the Israelite idea that the conquest was a holy war. In battle Yahweh fought for Israel, driving her enemies from the land. The land which was won was his gift to Israel, and evidence of his mercy, grace, and sovereignty. The conquest was interpreted as a sacral act by which the promise to the patriarchs became a reality.

Alongside this concept, however, Israel held to another idea which was just as important to them. A widespread tradition emphasized that the land of Canaan was still Yahweh's land,[48] or his heritage.[49] The tension between these ideas was supremely important for the life and worship of Israel. They could never look upon the land as totally their possession. Although it had been given them at the conquest, it remained Yahweh's land, and accordingly, remained the Land of Promise.

Since Canaan continued to be Yahweh's heritage, Israel interpreted her role to be proving herself worthy of dwelling in Yahweh's land. If she were to enjoy a long and happy possession of the land, she had to obey Yahweh's law.[50] Canaan's virtual paradise, tended by Yahweh, would be Israel's only so long as she was faithful to her covenant obligations. If Israel failed to live by his law, Yahweh would absent himself from the land and the paradise would turn to chaos.

To keep the land holy Israel had to be particularly careful to avoid defilement by the sins characteristic of the Canaanites.[51]

---

[45] Blessings: Genesis 2:1–3; descendants: Genesis 13:14–16; relationship: Genesis 17:4–8; Canaan: Genesis 12:7.

[46] Gerhard von Rad, "Verheissenes Land und Jahwes Land im Hexateuch," *Zeitschrift des Deutschen Palästine-Vereins*, LXVI (1943), is an able presentation of the whole idea here under discussion.

[47] Genesis 23; 25:7–10; 50:13.

[48] Leviticus 25:23; Joshua 22:19; Jeremiah 2:7; 16:18.

[49] I Samuel 26:19; II Samuel 14:16; Jeremiah 50:11; Psalms 68:9; 79:1.

[50] Leviticus 26:3–12.

[51] Leviticus 18:25–29; 20:22–24; Deuteronomy 21:22 ff.

She had to abstain from the offensive fertility customs of these people lest she, like them, defile the land and be driven from it. In her later history the nation did defile Yahweh's land and made his heritage an abomination. In the presence of such corruption the eighth century prophets warned Israel that such unfaithfulness would result in her expulsion from Canaan to die in an "unclean" land.[52] The prophet Ezekiel in Babylonian exile envisioned Yahweh himself being driven from Jerusalem because of abominations practiced there.[53] To abide in Yahweh's land, his heritage, Israel had to be holy, because the land was holy.

Such thinking about the land also influenced Israel's legal code. Laws pertaining to first-fruits,[54] the tithe,[55] and gleaning[56] were closely tied to the idea that the people lived as strangers and sojourners in Yahweh's land. The first of the harvest was brought to the sanctuary as an offering because the people considered themselves serfs or tenants on the property of their God. Similarly, the tithe was an instrument for sharing the bounty of the land with the priests, the sojourners, the orphans, and widows. Sheaves were to be left in the fields for the poor to gather. In these ways the Israelites, themselves sojourners and strangers in a holy land, shared with the less fortunate among them. In doing so they brought blessings upon themselves and the land in which they lived.

AMPHICTYONY (JOSHUA 23, 24; JUDGES 1–16)

Covenant Renewal and Amphictyonic Organization

Joshua 23–24 brings the book of Joshua to its expected theological climax. Memory of a ceremony of covenant renewal at Shechem in which there was participation by all the tribes or their representatives was basic to Israel's organization into a twelve-tribe amphictyony. The term *amphictyony* is derived from Greek usage denoting a religious confederacy united around

---

[52] Amos 7:17; Hosea 9:3.
[53] Ezekiel 10.
[54] Exodus 23:19; 34:26; Leviticus 19:23; 23:10; Deuteronomy 26:1.
[55] Leviticus 27:30; Deuteronomy 14:22 ff.
[56] Leviticus 19:9–10.

worship at a central sanctuary. It is used here to designate a league of tribes formed around a common religious commitment. Although there is some anachronism in this usage, it accurately describes the nature of Israel's unity during these days.[57] The biblical account of the conquest states that the tribes which came out of Egypt with Moses and entered Canaan under Joshua came to the region of Shechem and there reestablished relations with kindred groups which had previously settled in that area. About the same time, Hebrew elements in the south (portions of Judah and kindred tribes) also joined the group which had entered under Joshua. Thus the book of Joshua claims that those who had long been in the land and the newcomers led by Joshua joined in a common effort to seize the land and make it their own. The covenant faith of the Joshua tribes is suggested as an important factor in their success. The bond of unity, loosely established at the time of their opposition to the common enemy, must have been more firmly established at the conclusion of the conquest when the tribes gathered at Shechem and entered into a covenant relationship with one another and, what is more important, with Yahweh.

The tribes which assembled at Joshua's command must not have been a completely homogeneous unit. Although they were kindred peoples, they had entered Canaan at different times and under different circumstances. For the most part, a common cause under the same God against a common foe was the only bond that held them all together. Unless that bond was formalized, there was the danger that it would be forgotten as, with the passing of time, strong military and political forms developed. The book of Joshua states that, just as she had done in the holy war of conquest, Israel presented herself before Yahweh at Shechem and pledged her allegiance to him.[58] This provided them henceforth with a common bond no longer limited to warfare against a common enemy, but involving united participation in all of the saving deeds of the covenant God.

The ceremony of amphictyonic organization took the form of a ritual of covenant making. The ceremony recorded in Joshua

---

[57] See Martin Noth, *Das System der Zwölf Stämme Israels.*

[58] The verb "to present oneself" used here is the same verb used in Joshua 1–12 of the assembling of troops for battle.

24 was one in which the covenant was renewed.[59] The original covenant had been made at Sinai; the Shechem covenant was the Sinai one renewed and extended to include tribes not present when the original covenant was ratified. After the people were assembled at Shechem, a résumé of Yahweh's redemptive acts in the form of an ancient confession of faith was presented to them. Challenge to decision and response and the actual ceremony of covenant making followed.

Three groups presented themselves before Yahweh at Shechem: (1) those tribal elements which had not been in Egypt and were not worshippers of Yahweh, at least not of Yahweh as the covenant God, but who recognized their relation to the tribes which had been led into Canaan by Joshua,[60] (2) those who were more fully identified with Canaanite culture and religion,[61] (3) those tribes which had entered Canaan with Joshua and who were descended from those who had been at Sinai.[62] Those in the first group, presently worshippers of the patriarchal deities, were summoned to acknowledge Yahweh as Lord and to receive the story of his dealings with the tribes which had left Egypt as their own story of faith. They were asked to recognize that the God of Abraham was the same God who had delivered Israel from Egypt and who had given them the good land of Canaan. The second group was challenged to abandon Canaanite religion in favor of the Yahwistic covenant faith. Obviously, by this time various Canaanite elements had joined Israel, and it was imperative that they be made aware of the obligation and responsibilities which this union placed upon them. If they were to share in the deeds of the covenant God, they must also share in his worship. Also, worship of the deities of a land implied submission to the people of that land; therefore, all allegiance to the gods of Canaan had to be forsaken in favor of allegiance to Yahweh to whom in reality the land belonged. The third group, those led out of Egypt by Moses and into Canaan by Joshua, reaffirmed their allegiance to the God who had delivered them from Egypt, protected them in the wilderness, and given them a new land. They also were to recognize that all

[59] Walter Harrelson, "Worship in Early Israel," *Biblical Research,* III (1958), 1–14.
[60] Joshua 24:2, 15.
[61] Joshua 24:15.
[62] Joshua 24:5–9.

Figure 5–3. Looking westward through the pass of Shechem with Mt. Gerizim on the left and Mt. Ebal on the right. Here at the end of the conquest Joshua led Israel in a ceremony renewing the covenant of Sinai. For generations Shechem remained an Israelite amphictyonic center. (Source: Willem Van de Poll. Photograph by Monkmeyer Photo Service.)

the tribes presenting themselves before Yahweh at Shechem were the recipients of the patriarchal promise.

Thus the entity "Israel" emerged from the mass of kindred Habiru who had for centuries been entering into Canaan. The people of Yahweh were those joined together by a common religious tie. They were identified by their covenantal relationship with Yahweh and consequently began their life in the land of promise as a religious confederacy or amphictyony in which Yahweh was their king.

Life in the Amphictyony

In number Israel's amphictyony of twelve tribes resembled those of other peoples. There are numerous examples of federations of either twelve or six tribes.[63] Possibly the number originally related to monthly or bimonthly service at a central shrine. The number twelve became sacrosanct for Israel, even when the existence of twelve Israelite tribes was not a historical reality. Although some tribes faded from the historical scene while some prominent subtribes made their appearance, Israel all the while preserved the tradition of twelve tribes descended from Jacob's sons.

The Political Responsibilities of the Amphictyony. The amphictyony supplied Israel with a loosely knit political structure. The central human figure (Yahweh was actual head) was "the judge of Israel." [64] The man who held this office was responsible for the preservation and interpretation of the divine law to which Israel was subject. This law had been promulgated at the ceremony by which the amphictyony had been organized and was regularly proclaimed anew at covenant renewal. Its main concern was to preserve intact Israel's relationship to Yahweh and to prevent disturbance of this relationship by unlawful acts.[65]

[63] Twelve Aramean tribes, Genesis 22:20–24; Ishmaelite, Genesis 25:8–16; Edomite, Genesis 36:10–14; and the famous Greek amphictyonies like the Delphic League.

[64] Samuel is the only one about whom we have detailed information. These are not to be confused with the military heroes of the day who were also called judges. See Martin Noth, "Das Amt des 'Richters Israels,'" in *Festschrift für Alfred Bertholet*, pp. 404 ff.

[65] Noth, *The History of Israel*, p. 103.

This rule by Yahweh's law separated Israel from other peoples. She took particular care to see that the statutes of this divine law were carried out; and the punishment of the transgressor, by force of arms if necessary, was an important part of amphictyonic life.

Associated with "the judge of Israel" were tribal representatives sent to the amphictyonic center by the individual tribes. Cooperating with "the judge," these men were responsible for the political and religious leadership of the confederacy. Among their responsibilities were proclamation of the holy war (in face of major crises), establishment and maintenance of cities of refuge, and the settlement of boundary disputes. Certain economic and social matters were also left in their hands. They regulated commerce and the slave trade and acted on other matters too difficult to be dealt with at the local tribal level.

Israel's constitution as a tribal entity in the form of a twelve-tribe amphictyonic society was significant for the whole course of her subsequent history. Politically, amphictyony gave her a type of national life that lasted for around two hundred years. This commitment provided a unity that enabled a people who had not known sedentary existence since departing from Egypt to adjust to the soil, weather, and terrain for survival and prosperity. Through "trial and error" they learned from their neighbors to build cities marked by advancement in tastes, technological skill, and productivity. Later the kingship, which replaced amphictyonic organization, was possible only because in confederacy the tribes had already been rather loosely, but significantly, united as one people under one God, Yahweh, with "the judge" as the symbol of unity.

Amphictyonic Worship and Struggles with Canaanite Religion. Since the confederacy of Israelite tribes was essentially a religious organization, the center of amphictyonic life and its unifying bond was the central sanctuary at which the tribes worshipped Yahweh. The amphictyonic center remained at Shechem for a while, but for a much longer time it was located at Shiloh, where the Ark and the Tabernacle provided a sacred center. Religious life at the sanctuary was built around three annual feasts: the

Feast of Passover–Unleavened Bread, the Feast of Weeks, and the Feast of Tabernacles.[66] These ancient festivals celebrated Yahweh's acts in behalf of his people. The most important of these during amphictyonic days was the Feast of Tabernacles when there was a ceremony of covenant renewal.[67] The decisive meaning of this ceremony was the reaffirmation of allegiance to Yahweh. The recitation of Yahweh's deeds of salvation was a part of the observance which brought the history of Israel to life. Sacred history was re-enacted, relived, and made equally binding upon every generation in which it was presented. This is clear in the Deuteronomic introduction to the Decalogue:

Yahweh our God made a covenant with us in Horeb. Not with our fathers did Yahweh make this covenant, but with us, who are all of us here alive this day. (Deuteronomy 5:2–3)

These sacral festivities accentuated the uniqueness of Israel's God. He was the God who had chosen them, delivered them, and watched over them in majestic and memorable fashion until he guided them into possession of the land. They worshipped him as sovereign and sought to obey his bidding. He was king over their theocratic nation and, since theirs was a covenant relationship, his demands had to be met for the covenant to be maintained.

Covenant renewal, however, was not adequate guard against apostasy. Throughout this period the true worship of Yahweh struggled for preservation. The major threat was syncretism with native Canaanite religions. In recent years a great deal about Canaanite religions has been learned from the Ras Shamra cultic texts. These tablets were discovered in 1929 at the site of an old Canaanite city named Ugarit on the coast of northern Syria. They are dated roughly during or before the middle of the fourteenth century B.C. These discoveries show that Canaanite religion centered in fertility cults. A pantheon of deities was headed by a rather inactive chief god name El, "the King, Father of Years." El's female counterpart was named Asherah, symbolized by a wooden pole. Active under El was the male stormgod, Baal (Lord), who was praised as the creator of man. Baal was god of

[66] See pp. 163–168.
[67] Cf. Deuteronomy 31:9–13.

Figure 5–4. A "baal of lightning" from Ras Shamra, dated to the first half of the second millennium. This fertility deity towers over a smaller figure, either a lesser deity or a subject of the god. (Source: Louvre. Photograph by Archives Photographiques-Paris.)

both the elements and fertility. He was portrayed as a bull and represented by a standing stone (*massebah*). His female counterpart was his companion sister, Anath, who was revered as a goddess of war, bloodthirsty and passionately sexual.

The religion emphasized a myth which was re-enacted annually by its devotees. The drama rehearsed a death and resurrection of Baal. The myth's re-enactment was believed to continue the rhythmic cycle of nature. Hereby man sought both to control the order of nature and to be associated with his deity. Among the practices of the worshippers were orgiastic rituals involving sex in several forms, including religious prostitution and homo-sexuality. By means of "sympathetic magic" they attempted to induce fertility. Many types of images related to the worship were believed to possess magic powers of fertility.

These religious forces in Canaan, all related to their new man-ner of life as agriculturalists, held a threatening attraction to the Israelites. Many of these recent settlers, no doubt, saw no serious violation of Yahweh worship in paying due respect to an ancient god of the land. Thus many Israelites named their children for Baal and frequented the Baal shrines. They did not think of forsaking Yahweh; they only added the fertility practices of the native farmers. The struggle for pure religion continued long into the period of the monarchy. Although in time Yahweh, a "jealous" God, won out, the contest was long and the ordeal of purging sometimes approached catastrophe. The strength of Israel's amphictyonic bond largely accounts for the survival of her faith during this period.

Amphictyony was a transitional age for the Israelites. Yah-weh had been their God from Egyptian servitude to settlement in the land of Canaan. He had been victorious in battle and adequate to their needs as a people on the move. But now a new day faced them with an altogether different way of life. How was Yahweh related to agricultural and pastoral existence? Changes in theological concepts were called for by their new status as "landed" people. Theological questions, however, were inseparably bound to practical questions of when to plow, plant, weed, and harvest. Countless lessons had to be learned if Israel was to be as successful in the field as she had been as nomads and holy warriors. Skills had to be acquired from their enemies, the Canaanites and others who had lived long on the soil. In an age when deities were aligned with the cycles of the seasons and other elements basic to agriculture, the Israelites faced an almost impossible assignment of separating Canaanite farming tech-niques from Canaanite religion. The Deuteronomic writer em-phasizes repeatedly the infidelity of the Israelite tribes to Yahweh in favor of the pagan deities. But the primary relationship be-tween Yahweh and his people during this most difficult era was kept alive. The preserved memory of Yahweh's acts during the age centers in the heroics of military "judges" who opportunely appear to deliver Yahweh's people from oppressors.

THE JUDGES AND THE BOOK OF JUDGES

The book of Judges is a theological interpretation of Israel's history during the days of amphictyony. The Deuteronomic historian recounts the heroism of various local military leaders to emphasize Yahweh as the deliverer of Israel during times of her distress. The deeds of the judges are told through the literary device of a cycle which reflects the Deuteronomist's understanding of Israel's judgment as based on her infidelity to Yahweh and Israel's blessing as based on Yahweh's faithfulness. The cycle: the people fall away from Yahweh (apostasy); Yahweh permits her enemies to fall upon her (oppression); under oppression the people repent and call upon Yahweh (repentance); and Yahweh calls out a leader and delivers her (deliverance). Then the cycle would begin again.

The book of Judges has the following structure:

I. Conquests by various Israelite tribes. 1:1–36
II. Introduction to the stories of the Judges. 2:1–3:6
   A. Death of Joshua and the rise of a post-conquest generation. 2:1–10
   B. Israel's cycle of apostasy, oppression, divine deliverance. 2:11–16
   C. Israel's unrepentance and her peril before her enemies. 2:17–3:6
III. The Age of Judges. 3:7–16:31
   A. Othniel *vs.* Cushan-Tishathaim. 3:7–11
   B. Ehud *vs.* the Moabites. 3:12–30
   C. Shamgar *vs.* the Philistines. 3:31
   D. Deborah and Barak *vs.* the Canaanites. 4:1–5:31
   E. Gideon *vs.* the Midianites. 6:1–8:35
     (Story of Abimelech, son of Gideon. 9:1–57)
     (Tola and Jair. 10:1–5)
   F. Jephthah *vs.* the Ammonites. 10:6–11:40
     (Jealousy of the Ephraimites. 12:1–7)
     (Ibzan, Elon and Abdon. 12:8–15)
   G. Samson *vs.* the Philistines. 13:1–16:31
IV. Appendices. 17:1–21:25
   A. Micah and the relocation of the Danites. 17:1–18:31
   B. A Levite and the Benjaminites of Gibeah. 19:1–21:25

The length of time covered by Judges and the amphictyony must be determined by data found outside the book. If it is assumed that each judge followed on the heels of his predecessor, the period covers four hundred and ten years. However, the judges were largely local and some were contemporary. The time of the judges probably lasted through most of the two centuries just prior to the days of the monarchy; that is, from about 1200 to 1020 B.C.

The Shophet

The name "judge," as used for these temporary leaders in the period covered by the book of Judges, is something of a misnomer. The term designates in contemporary English "one who decides" or "one who renders a verdict." However, the Hebrew term *shophet*, which is translated "judge," means "deliverer" or "one who sets things right" or even "one who rules."

Although not elected, the *shophetim* of Israel were both civil and military rulers over those who acknowledged their leadership. They ought not be confused with "the judge of Israel," who was leader of the entire amphictyony. Their status was temporary and not subject to inheritance. They acquired and held their position by virtue of the fact that "the spirit of Yahweh was upon them"; that is, they were charismatics. Apparently the prestige and following of a local judge might grow as he was proven to possess extraordinary powers, attributable to Yahweh. Thus, occasionally, a judge might lead a coalition of two or more tribes. Twelve of these judges are mentioned in the book of Judges, but six of them remain only names.

Accounts of the feats and foibles of the judges provide some of the best examples of storytelling in Hebrew literature and some of the stories appear to have been relatively unchanged by their incorporation into the large saga of the Deuteronomic historian. The basic format of the stories, although with numerous variations in detail, is: dire oppression by a non-Israelite foe; a commoner from one of the tribes is endowed with the spirit of Yahweh; the commoner with his new charisma manifests himself to Israel summoning one or more tribes into Yahweh's battle and Yahweh delivers the Israelites from their oppression. The final proof of the judge's charisma is Yahweh's act of victory in battle.

The book of Judges makes clear the limitations of the conquest under Joshua. Considerable amounts of land had not been placed into the hands of Israelites and all peoples outside the amphictyonic commitment had not been subjugated or rendered impotent. The era was one of great strain and tension. Israel was largely restricted to the mountains of Canaan. Her enemies controlled the plains. In spite of amphictyonic ties she was fragmented according to tribes and divided by natural boundaries of river and mountains. Consequently, she was weak and poor and often fell prey to her cultured and better equipped neighbors. Many towns experienced destruction and some of them more than once. The non-Israelite inhabitants of Canaan evidently capitalized upon the disorganized structure of Israel and used her largely at will to their own advantage and profit. These oppressors were strong enough to overpower a single tribe. Only the appearance of judges at crucial times saved Israel from total collapse and loss of identity during this period.

Deborah and Barak

The story of Deborah and Barak is one of the most intriguing traditions in the book and illustrates the ancient character of materials which form the book of Judges. Judges 4 and 5 present two versions of the same story; chapter 4 in prose, chapter 5 in poetry. The setting is the area surrounding the Plain of Esdraelon. The occasion was a revival of great strength by the Canaanites from their resounding defeat at Hazor by Joshua. The leaders of the Canaanites were Jabin, king of Hazor, and Sisera, commander of the military forces.

Deborah was both a prophetess and a judge in Ephraim at a place between Ramah and Bethel when she summoned Barak from Kedesh-naphtali. She challenged Barak to lead an army of Yahweh against the Canaanites. Assured of her support, he accepted the mission. In the prose account, ten thousand men from Zebulun and Naphtali assembled at Kedesh in response to his call; in the poem, men from Ephraim, Benjamin, Issachar and Machir

(a portion of Manasseh) were also involved. All of the responding tribes were located in the north and bordered the plain which
had been ruled by the Canaanites.

The important battle occurred on the Plain of Esdraelon about
1125 B.C. and was decisive. A torrential storm assisted the Israelites by overflowing the banks of the river Kishon and rendering
the nine hundred formidable iron chariots of the Canaanites useless in the mud. The Israelites closed in afoot and overwhelmed
their enemies. Although Israel did not control Esdraelon following the battle, she did have free access through the strategic area
and the tribes on both sides of the plain were brought into closer
relationships.

In the prose section the account closes with a story introducing
another heroine. Sisera escaped the battle and fled for sanctuary
at the tent of Heber the Kenite. Alone at the tent Heber's wife
Jael received Sisera, gave him milk to drink, and hid him under
a rug. Instead of standing guard as instructed, she took a hammer
and drove a tent peg through his temple while he rested from
his weariness. The poetic account differs in details, but Jael's
heroic killing of Sisera is preserved.

Deborah's song of victory in chapter 5, dated about 1100 B.C.,
is one of the oldest poems in the Old Testament. The song praises
the victory at Esdraelon as a mighty act of Yahweh over his
enemies, the Canaanites. It praises and blesses all who responded
to the call to holy war and scornfully rebukes those tribes refusing
out of self-interest to join in Yahweh's battle. The little village of
Meroz is even cursed for its failure to provide some requested
service. Yahweh is poetically portrayed as coming on the clouds
from Mount Sinai and Edom to deliver his people. The kinship
of this mode of representation of Yahweh to Canaanite-Phoenician
imagery, as well as other stylistic elements in the poem, convey
the influence of the cultural environment into which Israel had
moved.[68]

By means of the poem Israel had fixed in her memory the great
day when,

> From heaven fought the stars,
> from their courses they fought against Sisera.

[68] W. F. Albright, "The Song of Deborah in the Light of Archaeology," *Bulletin of The American School of Oriental Research,* 62 (1936), 26–31.

> The torrent Kishon swept them away,
> the onrushing torrent, the torrent Kishon.
> March on, my soul with might.   (5:20–21)

and the hope,

> So punish all thine enemies,
>   O Lord!
> But thy friends be like the sun
>   as he rises in his might.   (5:31)

Two stories of unknown origin are appended to the book of Judges (chapters 17–21), probably included here merely because they are about two of the tribes, Dan and Benjamin. The first story (17–18) relates the migration of a portion of Dan from central to northern Canaan. Presumably the Philistines had taken over most of their original land and forced them to move. The story tells of a Levite out-for-hire who accepts employment as family priest for Micah an Ephraimite only to be persuaded by the migrating Danites to become their priest. Together with the Danites, he stole Micah's valuable religious images and later placed them in a shrine at Dan. The story probably was preserved to account for a shrine at Dan prior to Jeroboam I's action in establishing one in the tenth century B.C.

The second appendix (19–21) centers on the tribe of Benjamin. It is an example of intertribal friction, and even skirmish war, which often blotted the religious confession of tribal unity.[69] The story may have been preserved by Judeans to blacken Saul's reputation and tarnish the fame of the Benjaminites as fearless warriors.

The story concerns a wandering Levite who was dishonored by men of Gibeah, the Benjaminite town which was to be Saul's first capital. Men of Israel were assembled at Mizpah to hear the Levite's complaint. The assembly demanded unsuccessfully that the wrongdoers of Gibeah be surrendered for violation of the amphictyonic covenant. War ensued, Benjaminite men were practically wiped out, and a ban against marriage to Benjaminites was introduced. The story ends with an ingenious plan to preserve the tribe by providing virgins from Jabesh-gilead for men of Benjamin. The tribe survives, not by their own ability, but by the patronage of other Israelites.

[69] Cf. also Judges 12:1–6.

Theology of Judges

The book of Judges offers little description of high religion, but it does reflect colorfully aspects of Israelite life during the age of amphictyony. Hostility between Israel and neighboring tribes and the open friction among Israelite tribes themselves is clearly pictured. Temporary charismatic leaders, not always admirable, dominate the scene and, in so far as possible, are interpreted as instruments of Yahweh's providence.

In the way he uses the materials in Judges the Deuteronomic historian at times seems to be critic of certain features of the time of the amphictyony, but for him these are illustrative of the relationships between Yahweh and Israel in any age. The faithlessness of Israel is repeatedly set alongside the faithfulness of Yahweh. Fidelity to Yahweh appears only in crises. The amphictyonic center is not a pillar of strength. The priesthood is hardly applauded. Even some of the heroes appear in caricature. A depraved son of Gideon murdered seventy brothers in a fool's try at kingship. Jephthah offered human sacrifice to Yahweh in the person of his own daughter, extraordinary in Hebrew history. Samson, mighty in muscle and wild in animal appetites, is stupidly vulnerable to betrayal and re-betrayal by Philistine women. Generally the deliverers show little or no knowledge of Moses' teachings or the religious traditions of Israel.

Yet the book is not completely without religious value. Although the leaders are presented as military heroes, their imperfections are not praised. The book seems to say, "This is the best that Yahweh had to work with during this time." Yahweh, even through weak judges, remains covenant God, who directs the affairs of his people in troubled days. The book closes with the words, "In those days there was no king in Israel; every man did what was right in his own eyes" (21:25). Although this appears to praise monarchy by condemning amphictyony, the Deuteronomist also records the failure of the kings to bring Yahweh's people to the full and good life. He understood that neither judge nor king, but only Yahweh himself, could be Israel's hope.

The obscurity of religious leadership and the attractiveness of many features of Canaanite religion make it little short of amazing that Hebrew religion could survive during the amphictyony.

However, threatened as it was, the worship of Yahweh did survive and was preserved until a better day.

The Coming of the Philistines

During the early part of Israel's amphictyony, the Philistines appeared on the soil of Canaan. So influential were these people that they gave the land its name for centuries to come. They were one of many "sea peoples" who moved out of the Aegean Sea and settled along the eastern shores of the Mediterranean from Ugarit in the north to Ashkelon in the southwest of Canaan. Some of these "sea peoples" attacked Egypt as early as Merneptah and were driven back at great cost. Soon after 1200 B.C., they pressed to the borders of Egypt again and were repelled by Ramses III (1175–1144) in a great sea and land battle. Thwarted in their attempt to enter Egypt, they occupied the coast of Canaan.

The Philistines settled in five major cities along the southern coastal plain: Gaza, Ashkelon, Ashdod, Ekron, and Gath. Each city, with its surrounding area, was ruled over by a "lord." Since there were close fraternal ties between the lords, the people were sufficiently united to constitute a major threat to the Israelites. Their appearance at the beginning of the Iron Age in Canaan, coupled with the fact that they had an almost monopolistic control over the iron coming into the land, made them a formidable enemy. Iron weapons gave them an advantage over their neighbors which was not to be broken until Israel came into free use of the metal. This strong group along with other "sea peoples" was responsible for crushing the hopes of the Egyptians under Ramses III to establish an empire across the East. Egypt's last hope for renewed empire glory was exploded and she faded into the shadows of other empires.

After their occupation of the coastal plain, the Philistines largely adapted themselves to Canaanite culture, language and religion. They grew in prowess and influence and gradually began to dominate Israel. It is significant that no judge came forward in Israel to deliver them from Philistine oppression. Samson's personal grudge fight against them was singularly unsuccessful from the point of view of Israel's desire for independence. They were not delivered by Samson. They could recite the stories of his exploits around their camp fires, but the harsh reality was that they were totally dominated by the hated peoples from the sea. The amphictyonic structure was not adequate to deal with a threat of such dimensions, so the tribes turned toward centralized political control. Religious syncretism may have weakened the amphictyonic tie, but the political pressure of the Philistines really brought the old order of confederacy into question.

SUGGESTED READINGS

Background

BRIGHT, JOHN, *Early Israel in Recent History Writing* (S.C.M. Press, 1956). An analysis of various approaches to the early history of Israel.

KAUFMANN, YEHEZKEL, *The Biblical Account of the Conquest of Palestine* (Magnes, 1953). A constructive study of the conquest and settlement.

MEEK, T. J., *Hebrew Origins*. (Rev. ed., Harper & Row, 1950).

NOTH, MARTIN, *The History of Israel* (A. and C. Black, 1960), pp. 68–84.

RUST, ERIC C., *Judges, Ruth, and Samuel* (John Knox, 1961). Brief readable commentary for laymen.

WRIGHT, G. ERNEST, *The Old Testament Against Its Environment* (S.C.M. Press, 1950). Interpretative study of Israel's faith against its Ancient Near Eastern background.

Archaeology

ALBRIGHT, W. F., *Archaeology and the Religion of Israel* (2nd ed., Johns Hopkins, 1946).

BURNEY, C. F., *Israel's Settlement in Canaan* (Oxford University Press, 1919).

KENYON, KATHLEEN, *Digging Up Jericho* (Ernest Benn, 1957).

Deuteronomy

CUNLIFF-JONES, H., *Deuteronomy*, Torch Bible Commentaries (S.C.M. Press, 1951).

VON RAD, GERHARD, *Studies in Deuteronomy* (Regnery, 1953). A brilliant description of the Deuteronomic theology of history.

———, *Deuteronomy* (Westminster, 1966).

WATTS, JOHN D. W., "Deuteronomy" in *The Broadman Bible Commentary*, II.

WELCH, A. C., *The Code of Deuteronomy* (James Clark, 1924).

WRIGHT, G. ERNEST, "Deuteronomy" in *Interpreter's Bible*, II.

Joshua

BRIGHT, JOHN, "Joshua" in *Interpreter's Bible*, II.
MORTON, WILLIAM H., "Joshua" in *The Broadman Bible Commentary*, II.

Judges

DALGISH, EDWARD R., "Judges" in *The Broadman Bible Commentary*, II.
MYERS, JACOB M., "Judges" in *Interpreter's Bible*, II.

Numbers

OWENS, JOHN J., in *The Broadman Bible Commentary*, II.

Covenant and Law

WRIGHT, G. ERNEST, and FREEDMAN, DAVID N., *The Biblical Archaeologist Reader*, I (Doubleday Anchor Books, 1961). Relevant articles.

6

The United Kingdom

The story of the institution of monarchy in Israel is contained in the books of Samuel and Kings. The separation of these books from one another in modern Bibles is very artificial since both are integral parts of the Deuteronomic history. The division occurred for ease of handling of the ancient Hebrew scrolls. When the Hebrew text was translated into Greek, vowels were added nearly doubling the size of the volume, so the book of Samuel and the book of Kings were each divided into two scrolls.[1]

BACKGROUND FOR THE MONARCHY (I SAMUEL 1–7)

The Book of Samuel

The book of Samuel spans the period from the end of the amphictyony to the closing days in the life of David. Although concerned primarily with events in the lives of Saul and David, the book carries the name Samuel. The singular religious leader Samuel formed the major link between the judges and the kings, anointed the first two monarchs of Israel, and was responsible for the royal lineage passing from the tribe of Benjamin to the tribe of Judah. His genius influenced the entire period and, therefore, the book bears his name.

---

[1] The book of Ruth, found between Judges and Samuel in most Bibles, belongs among the Writings, the third division of Hebrew scripture. Although the setting for Ruth is the period of the amphictyony, the book was written centuries later.

The book of Samuel may be outlined according to the predominance and interplay of its principal characters:

I. Samuel. I Samuel 1–6
    A. Eli and Samuel. 1–3
    B. The history of the ark. 4–6
II. Samuel and Saul. I Samuel 7–15
    A. Samuel the judge. Chapter 7
    B. Selection and anointing of Saul. 8–10
    C. Wars and disbeliefs of Saul. 11–15
III. Saul and David. I Samuel 16–II Samuel 1
    A. Anointing and rise of David. I Samuel 16–18
    B. Saul's hostility to David. I Samuel 19–20
    C. David as fugitive from Saul. I Samuel 21–26
    D. Saul's defeat and death by Philistines. I Samuel 27–31
    E. David's lament at death of Saul and Jonathan. II Samuel 1
IV. David, king at Hebron. II Samuel 2–4
V. David, king at Jerusalem. II Samuel 5–20
    A. Defeat of Philistines and return of the ark. II Samuel 5–6
    B. Other victories. II Samuel 7–8
    C. Hospitality to Mephibosheth. II Samuel 9
    D. War with Ammonites. II Samuel 10
    E. Bathsheba and Nathan's rebuke. II Samuel 11–12
    F. Absalom stories. II Samuel 13–19
    G. Revolt of Sheba. II Samuel 20
VI. Appendices. II Samuel 21–24

Samuel, Saul and David are the chief characters in the Samuel story which unfolds Israel's change from a tribal confederacy with loose, inadequate ties to a strong, centralized government under a monarch. Samuel was the last of the judges of Israel; Saul, both king and judge, but definitely neither; and David, the established monarch. Thus, in recounting the transition from amphictyony to monarchy, the book of Samuel describes Israel's move from charismatic to dynastic leadership, Samuel representing the former and David the latter.

The narratives in the book of Samuel are not all of a piece. Repetitions, opposing accounts, stories telescoped together, narratives in tension with one another—all indicate the loose compilation of heterogeneous literary traditions. A number of ancient sources are discernible: (1) the narrative concerning the ark, (2) the story of Saul's rise, (3) the story of David's rise, (4) the story of David's reign. All of these narratives originated in the immediate context of their contents, the time of Saul and David. In the strongly nationalistic and historically conscious period after David's reign these traditions were brought together into a specific account of the course of events from the Philistine troubles to the establishment of the Davidic state. Generally this history was a popular endorsement of the new political structure. The events leading to the selection of a king are viewed charitably and the coronation of Saul is presented as a divine act to deliver Israel from her enemies.

Later this history was overlaid with supplementary narrative material about Samuel and Saul representing a distinctly different view of the events. This material represents a prophetic attempt to come to grips with the early history of the monarchy and its significance for later Israelite history and faith. Written after Israel had experienced oppression at the hands of degenerate rulers, it presents the dark side of the monarchy. Here Israel's king was appointed as Yahweh's compromise with the insistent demands of the people. Samuel as a prophet expressed the concern that the nation would forsake Yahweh in relying on the monarchy. This view of Israel's history emphasizes the conflict between earthly power established by power politics and divine power available through faith in Yahweh. The Deuteronomic historian took these materials about the early monarchy and fitted them into the scheme of the Deuteronomic history work. For him, the kings of Israel generally failed to realize the purpose of the covenant, both in themselves and in their leadership of the elect people, that they be in character and religion the people of Yahweh to the world.

The dual source of the book of Samuel, then, reflect the bilateral judgment of history upon the monarchy of Israel. As long as the centralized organization preserved the religious emphasis of the amphictyony, it was a blessing; when the strength of the political structure replaced dependence upon Yahweh, it was a curse. For example, the initial success of the monarchy under the regency of David was a blessing; the long stage of degeneracy under religiously insensitive leaders was a curse. Samuel's fear that the people of Israel would forsake their first love for Yahweh in dependence upon the monarchy did become an actuality. He and religious leaders after him had the responsibility to remind the nation of her basic religious calling. When the monarch operated charismatically under Yahweh, a great era followed. But when Yahweh was not sovereign over his vice-regent, the regime was profane. Inclinations to such profanity were continual temptations to Israel. Her hours of greatest abomination were those when she was only nominally the nation of Yahweh. Religious leaders, therefore, became perpetual prodders of the conscience of the nation, reminding her that she belonged to Yahweh in fact as well as in name.

Breakdown of Amphictyony

As generations passed and the Israelite tribes were forced to meet enemy after enemy either individually or two or more tribes in consort, the inadequacy of the amphictyonic organization to meet all circumstances became apparent. On at least one occasion during the amphictyony an experiment in monarchy was attempted which in itself was an acknowledgement of the confederation's weaknesses. Abimelech, son of the hero-judge Gideon by a Shechemite concubine, capitalized on his father's reputation and secured for himself the crown which had been refused earlier by his father. He established his capital at Shechem, revered as the place where Joshua led the people to renew the covenant. Although his Shechemite ties through his mother increased his local support, the experiment was short-lived. A people's revolt dissolved the temporary monarchy and the event amounted to little more than a prediction of things to come.[2] Although this early attempt failed, Israel could not long withstand a change from the loosely knit amphictyony.

The Philistines provided the sequence of events which finally led to the establishment of the monarchy. Their growth in prowess and their demand for additional territory was directly responsible for the amphictyony's collapse. Israelite armies of the loose and decentralized confederation had dealt heroically with numerous prior emergencies, but militarily they were no match for the efficient machine of the Philistines. Conflict between Israel and Philistia was grounded in cultural divergence of long standing. Living along the maritime plain the Philistines

2 Judges 8:22–9:27.

had a cosmopolitan outlook from their commercial contacts with other peoples; Israel was isolated in the hills. The Philistines worked and fought with iron tools and weapons; Israel had only flint and soft copper. The Philistines had a monopoly on the available iron and carefully withheld the technique of its production from Israel.[3] Even the ceramics of Israel were inferior. Culturally, the Philistines far surpassed their inland neighbor. Hence, political dominance of the Philistines during the days prior to the monarchy was only one of many aspects of Philistine supremacy over the less accomplished Israelites.

For some years after their arrival in Canaan, the Philistines were confined to the maritime plain. However, as they increased in numbers and power, they began to move inland and Israelite tribal groups along the border felt their pressure. The stress of the situation is preserved in the Judges story of the Philistine forced migration of a sizable portion of the tribe of Dan to a new land in the north of Canaan. Although Israel had other enemies, none compared to the Philistines. Only when a leader arose who could break the power of Philistia would the fortunes of Israel improve. To the Israelites such a leader would have to be a king. To the Deuteronomist, the amphictyony was the ideal form of government for Israel and the move to a monarch was rebellion against Yahweh who had never failed to meet Israelite needs in a crisis.

The Philistine crisis reached a critical stage when the amphictyonic center at Shiloh fell. The Deuteronomic story focuses in Eli, the leading priest and "judge of Israel," and his two sons. Eli was faithful, but Hophni and Phinehas were selfish and corrupt men who used the sanctuary and its sacrificial system for personal gain and sensual gratification. The Philistines won a signal victory at Aphek (or Ebenezer), near the Philistine coastal domain.[4] Prior to battle, Eli had brought the Ark of the Covenant to the camp of Israel to the joy of the Israelites and the intimidation of the Philistines. The Israelites nevertheless were defeated; Hophni and Phinehas were killed. The Ark, symbol

---

[3] The first datable iron agricultural implement discovered in Israel by archaeologists is a plowpoint coming from Saul's capital, Gibeah. Cf. G. E. Wright, *Biblical Archaeology*, p. 120.

[4] I Samuel 4. Quite likely this event occurred between 1050 and 1030 B.C.

of Yahweh's presence and Israelite unity, was captured. In one swift stroke the Israelites sustained both military collapse and spiritual demoralization. Receiving the report of the disaster, Eli fell, broke his neck, and died. The morale of Israel was dramatically epitomized by the name given to the child of Phinehas born at the time of the defeat. His dying mother named the infant "Ichabod" meaning "no glory." The evaluation of the narrator is succinct:

The glory has departed from Israel; for the ark of God has been captured (I Samuel 4:22).

Archaeological evidence indicates that the Philistines followed their victory at Aphek with a march on Shiloh. The ecclesiastical capital of Israel was burned to the ground. The captured Ark of the Covenant made a plaguing round of the Philistine cities before it was finally returned to Kirjath-jearim in Israel. Notice how the ancient tradition of the Ark plays up the malevolent presence of the sacred by emphasizing that plague followed it through Philistine country and Philistine gods were powerless in its presence.[5] The Philistines saw to it, however, that the ark was not freed to become a unifying symbol for Israel. With the sanctuary at Shiloh gone and the ark out of the public eye, the amphictyonic order was shattered. Important to the Deuteronomist was the loss of the sanctuary at which Yahweh was to be worshipped. Although all appeared hopeless at Shiloh's fall, Israel actually stood on the threshold of a new day. The catastrophe forced Israel to reexamine religious values which had been preserved in the old amphictyonic order. The national destiny as wrought and sustained by Yahweh had to be clarified. Obviously with Shiloh in ruins and the Philistines crouching at the door something had to be done. Political and theological change was necessary for Israel's survival. With Israel in dire straits Samuel became the maker of an age.

As the man who stood in the breach between the old and the new, Samuel occupied an ambiguous role, appearing as judge, priest, and prophet. His multiplicity of roles may be explained by a conflation of sources. Even so, the combination of these several functions make Samuel unique in Israel's memory. He

[5] I Samuel 5:2–5.

served as "the judge of Israel," frequenting the important shrines of Bethel, Gilgal, and Mizpah.[6] At times he resembled the charismatic military judges, leading Israel into battle against the Philistines. Certainly he performed priestly functions in anointing kings and blessing troops. As spokesman for Yahweh he preached as a prophet. Even as the diverse roles of judge, priest, and prophet merged in him, so the hopes for a new day of unity and identity centered in him. What Moses had been to the Exodus, what Joshua had been to the conquest, that Samuel was to the monarchy.

SAMUEL AND SAUL (I SAMUEL 7–31)

Selection and Anointing of Saul

There are problems associated with the determination of the actual history of the transition to monarchy. Materials are scarce. Perhaps this may be attributed to the Deuteronomist's lack of sources. He obviously possessed more traditions about monarchy than about the amphictyony. On the monarchy he weaves together independent cycles of stories about Samuel, Saul and David. His concerns are primarily theological and prophetic. He stresses the judgment of Yahweh on all the kings for their failure to realize the covenant promise and blessings. He measures all kings against his ideal sovereign David, whom he presents not as perfect but as embodying the noblest of all expressions of kingship under the sovereignty of Yahweh. The Deuteronomist is vitally concerned with the worship of Yahweh at a single sanctuary because in his judgment the centralization of Yahweh worship at one shrine was essential in the choice by the people of Yahweh over the Baals of Canaan.

The book of Samuel portrays the nation faced with disaster asking Samuel to anoint a king for them. The establishment of a monarchy seemed the only hope for survival. A king would provide the authoritarian leadership necessary in a crisis situation. A strong centralized government would surpass the city-state system of the Philistines, and, while it might not immediately turn the tide, the tribal leaders hoped for ultimate victory.

[6] I Samuel 7:15–17.

With such aspirations for success the leaders demanded that Samuel select a king.

The book of Samuel presents the selection and anointing of Israel's first king, Saul, from two points of view. The early pro-monarchy tradition [7] makes Saul the central figure and the favored of Yahweh, while the late antimonarchy tradition [8] glorifies Samuel and describes Saul as rejected by Yahweh. The two perspectives provide a much more adequate portrayal of both Saul and Samuel than could be derived from only one point of view. One relates the story of the tall handsome Benjaminite, the son of Kish, coming to the residence of the seer, Samuel, seeking infor-fation about some lost asses of his father. Samuel, authorized by Yahweh to anoint a prince for Israel, secretly performed the rite. A subsequent successful campaign by a united Israel against the Ammonites satisfactorily demonstrated that the spirit of the Yahweh was upon him. Consequently all Israel together recognized Saul as Yahweh's anointed sovereign and at Gilgal publicly installed him as king.

In the other tradition Samuel rebelled at the idea of kingship and reluctantly anointed Saul after insistent demands by the people for a king. In effect these demands were tantamount to rejection of Yahweh as well as Samuel and his sons, judges of some success, in order to gain a king "like all the nations." Samuel interpreted the desire of the people as apostasy. Traditionally the tribes had been held together by their amphictyonic commitments to Yahweh; now they were seeking unity through political structure. To Samuel the two were antithetical. Only at the command of Yahweh did Samuel yield.

Hearken to the voice of the people in all that they say to you; for they have not rejected you, but they have rejected me from being king over them. (I Samuel 8:7)

After a severe warning to Israel about what she could expect from a king,[9] Samuel cast lots which fell upon Saul and, at Mizpah, Saul was proclaimed king of Israel.

These dual perspectives may well reflect the selective process

[7] I Samuel 9:1–10; 11; 13:3b–15.
[8] I Samuel 7:3–8:22; 10:17–27; 12.
[9] I Samuel 8:10–18. The present wording of this warning is clearly Deuteronomic.

whereby Saul became the fully recognized ruler over Israel. During the period of transition from the loosely organized tribal confederacy to the more stabilized monarchy, a certain amount of vacillation must have occurred. Through several convocations the tribal units gradually came to agree upon their new way of life. Entwined in all the events was Samuel, whose emotions must have been ambivalent due to the degree of his personal involvement. Clearly he was being asked to take a secondary role. Throughout Saul's reign, Samuel must have found himself strangely torn between support of and opposition to the whole idea of the monarchy. One can wonder if Saul's outcome would have been different had he enjoyed the enthusiastic support of the religious leader of Israel.

On the other hand, Samuel's attitude of general suspicion of the monarchy served Israel creatively during the crisis period. Samuel's fear that Israel would forsake Yahweh in her dependence upon a king was based on reality. When Saul began to violate the covenant commitment, Samuel's role became clearer. At signs of depravity in the monarchy, Samuel's voice again became a cry of Yahweh's judgment on the disgraces of corruption. Herein was Samuel's primary role in Israel's history. He was Yahweh's agent for preserving Israel's basic covenant identity when the nation as tribal groups moved from amphictyony to monarchy. To the Deuteronomist, Samuel's judgment of Saul pointed up the demands of one anointed as Yahweh's king: that out of a personal closeness to Yahweh he lead the people in the way of faithful and obedient adherence to the covenant. That meant one like David.

Saul as King

Saul's story in the book of Samuel focuses on his selection as king, his early demonstrations of Yahweh's victorious power, and his slow deterioration. Most of the remaining information is embedded within the David saga, the real heart of the Deuteronomic account of the early monarchy. Saul's story is a sad one of brilliance diminishing toward darkness, of the awful journey from God-anointed to God-forsaken, of glory departed. For the Deuteronomist, Saul is a prime example of the folly of turning away from Yahweh.

Saul began his reign in approximately 1020 B.C. as a judge of charismatic endowments. Samuel recognized the young man as one on whom rested the spirit of Yahweh. Anointing by Samuel was official religious endorsement of Saul. However, popular acceptance by the people was also necessary to make him king. A convocation in which Samuel openly declared his support won considerable following for Saul, but what really thrust him into the public eye was a military campaign waged against the Ammonites.

The town of Jabesh-Gilead in Transjordan had been attacked by the Ammonites, who demanded the right eye of all inhabitants as the terms of surrender. Jabesh-Gilead appealed to the newly-anointed Saul for help and "the spirit of God came mightily upon Saul." [10] He killed one of the oxen with which he was plowing, cut it into twelve pieces and sent the parts to the twelve tribes, threatening to act similarly with any tribe which failed to join in a holy war to relieve Jabesh-Gilead. The response was unanimous and the military effort decisively victorious. At Gilgal, following this victory, the people gave Saul their enthusiastic endorsement. He became king in fact. As a bonus he gained the unfailing devotion of Jabesh-Gilead.

Although bearing some similarity to that of Edom and Moab,[11] the early kingship in Israel was unique in form. In some ways, it attempted to give a permanent structure to charismatic judgeship. Saul came to the kingship primarily as a charismatic warrior and continued as Yahweh's designated leader because of the perennial Philistine threat. Installed as king at the amphictyonic center at Gilgal, Saul made no discernible change in the nature of the tribal organization, so far as we can tell. In short, his reign was marked by no clear break with the old order of Israel.

The pomp, splendor, and ornateness often associated with eastern rulers were absent from the reign of Saul. He established no royal court. A large part of the army came from his own tribe of Benjamin and headquarters were retained at his hometown, Gibeah. Saul had no harem, levied no regular taxes, conscripted no troops. What could be called his palace was more like a rustic fortress than the luxurious dwelling of an eastern monarch. Located on a prominent hill about three miles north of Jerusalem,

[10] I Samuel 11:6.
[11] Martin Noth, *The History of Israel*, p. 171.

Figure 6–1. The ruins of Saul's massive palace-fortress at Gibeah. (Source: G. Ernest Wright.)

the Gibeah residence was strongly fortified by a double wall, the outer one about seven feet thick. At each corner was a protective tower. The overall dimensions were at least 169 by 114 feet. Indeed this palace-fortress was formidable and adequate, but without splendor.[12] The unadorned exterior of the building and its ordinary contents reflect the simplicity of the life of Israel's first monarch. Saul remained more akin to his judge predecessors than to wealthy and cosmopolitan potentates.

Saul's Early Success. Like the judges before him, Saul was a warrior. With a simple and primitive understanding of the ways of Yahweh, he did what he could do best—he waged holy war for Yahweh. On the battlefield the king performed brilliantly during the early part of his reign. By military exploits he maintained the allegiance of all the tribes, which was in itself an innovation. The personal magnetism of Saul caught the imagination of his

[12] For a full description of the palace see Wright, *Biblical Archaeology*, pp. 121 f.

soldiers so that they followed him with pride. Thus, he laid a foundational *esprit de corps* which was to live after him and be utilized by his more glamorous and better-endowed successor.

Saul's most thrilling military success was against the Philistines.[13] He had gathered a sizable army of three thousand men, a portion of which he placed under the command of his son, Jonathan. The Israelites were successful in a preliminary skirmish against a garrison of the Philistines. When the Philistines amassed a mighty force for a retaliatory attack and when Samuel did not appear to reassure Israel of victory, the frightened Israelites fled to out-of-way places for sanctuary. Suddenly Saul found himself at Gilgal with no more than six hundred men to meet the awaited Philistine onslaught. Only an heroic maneuver by Jonathan at Michmash saved the day for Israel. Stating, "Nothing can hinder Yahweh from saving by many or by few," Jonathan recklessly plunged into the Philistine camp, creating chaos. Saul and his army attacked and the Philistines were routed. Although this major victory did not destroy the enemy, the Philistine threat was temporarily abated. Their garrisons were driven from the central mountain country and Saul and the Israelites enjoyed greater freedom of movement in their own territory.

The victory over the Philistines almost cost Jonathan his life. The *cherem* of the holy war had been in effect for the campaign. Further, Saul had proclaimed all food taboo during the day of battle. Jonathan, not aware of his father's prohibition ate some honey and Saul ordered his execution for violating the vow. Only the intervention of the people, who pleaded that the victory was proof of Yahweh's presence, saved Jonathan from being sacrificed, even as Jephthah's daughter during the period of the judges. This narrative gives every evidence of authenticity.

The defeat of the Philistines was followed by other victorious campaigns.[14] Victories over the Moabites, Edomites, and the Aramean kingdoms of Zobah are mentioned with elaboration in the biblical account. The Amalekites, who from their home in the desert around Kadesh had continued to harass the Israelites, were subdued. So decisive was the victory over the Amalekites that they passed off the stage of the Israelite drama. Assisting

13 I Samuel 13:1–14:46.
14 I Samuel 14:47–15:9.

Saul in these campaigns were his sons and his cousin, Abner, the powerful captain of the king's army.

Saul Without Samuel

We have already noted that Saul and the monarchy had little more than nominal support from Samuel. Two stories probably belonging to the supplementary tradition reflect a negative evaluation of Saul. In these events Samuel withdrew what support and encouragement he had given to the king. During the Philistine campaign, Samuel failed to arrive at Gilgal in time to bless the army for the holy battle. Saul assumed the priestly function and offered sacrifices. This action was interpreted by Samuel as presumption and the seer announced that Saul's house would not continue to rule over Israel. Compare this event with II Samuel 6. When David assumed the priestly function, he was praised by the writer. Sacerdotal and secular functions evidently had not been clearly defined at this point in Israel's history. The judgment against Saul reflects the antimonarchial bias of some of the materials out of which the Deuteronomist weaves his tale. In a way the theme of the Saul stories is a question, "Is Saul the man after God's heart?" The answer both in the ancient materials and in the Deuteronomic use of them is, "No, unfortunately, he is not." [15]

The Deuteronomist reports a second event even more decisive in the rejection of Saul by both Samuel and later history. This occurred following the campaign against the Amalekites. In victory Saul violated the *cherem* by sparing Agag, the Amalekite king, and saving the best of the spoils. Saul's explanation was that these had been preserved for a special sacrifice at Gilgal. Samuel's Deuteronomic reply shows the completeness of Saul's condemnation.

> Behold, to obey is better than sacrifice,
>   and to hearken than the fat of rams.
> . . . .
> Because you have rejected the word of Yahweh,
>   he has also rejected you from being king. (I Samuel 15:22–23)

Samuel personally slaughtered Agag by cutting him to pieces. In this forceful and gruesome story the historian shows how Saul

---

[15] Cf. Hans Wilhelm Hertzberg, *I and II Samuel*, pp. 118 and 123.

had begun to follow a personal, rather than a Yahweh-centered, policy. Saul, the political and military leader, is condemned for aspiring to the religious authority of Samuel. In the revised theocracy, this was unacceptable. Consequently, Saul had to go. Samuel the kingmaker is pictured as Samuel the king-breaker. The action of the prophet in this cast must be understood, if not appreciated, in terms of primitive behavior. Nevertheless, one cannot help but feel for Saul and against Samuel and raise question about the conception of God as one who unfeelingly seeks the death of his enemies.

Saul without Samuel became increasingly tragic. From the death of Agag to the end of his life, he perceptibly disintegrated. Certainly, the fact that Saul fared so poorly without Samuel to lean on is testimony to his inadequacy for the kingship. His plight was intensified by the maneuvering of the aging Samuel, who not only withdrew his support, but also probably arranged for the next king to move into place. A better equipped man might have withstood the pressure of the situation, but not Saul. He became depressed to moroseness. Physically every inch a man, he often acted like a child, fleeing from the small and even the imaginary. His commands were obeyed without question, yet he could not command his own emotions. Without Samuel, Saul was a man without Yahweh. Without a sense of divine destiny, he trembled before shadows.

Separated from Samuel, Saul's problems continued and multiplied and mounted. The Philistines refused to let up in their attacks. The tribes still retained too much autonomy and independence—a weaker man could hardly have held them together. Samuel was against Saul and his charisma was departing from him. Mental depression tormented him. Jealousies were beginning to assume unnatural proportions. And, not the least of the factors, a man named David appeared.

Having removed his endorsement from one king, Samuel selected another. The narrative describing this has striking similarities to the story of the anointing of Saul [16] and is told with exceptional sense of drama. Under the pretext of offering sacrifices in the village, he came to Bethlehem in Judah to the house

[16] I Samuel 16:1–13.

of Jesse. During the oblations required as preparation for sacrifice, each of the members of the family came before Samuel. Finally David, the youngest son, was brought in from the fields and, to the surprise of his family, was selected as Saul's successor. David, in contrast to Saul, was not selected because of his physical stature. Samuel was restrained from anointing the more imposing Eliab, the elder brother, by the words of Yahweh,

Do not look on his appearance or on the height of his stature . . . for Yahweh sees not as man sees; man looks on the outward appearance, but Yahweh looks on the heart. (I Samuel 16:7)

Samuel anointed the handsome, ruddy lad and the spirit of Yahweh came upon David. Unknown to Saul, his successor had been chosen and now moved toward his own destiny.

Saul and David

The decline of Saul's influence and the rise of David to the place of popular acclaim are parts of the same story. In the Deuteronomic account,[17] obviously colored by the bias of later evaluation, the lives of Saul and David are interwoven. Saul lived out a dreary existence as a rejected man—abandoned by Samuel and forsaken by Yahweh to struggle with the isolation of his own confusion. Compounding Saul's travail was the growing popularity of a young national hero who ironically came to the public eye through the palace of Saul.

Two stories of David's introduction to Saul are preserved. One reports his selection as the king's musician and armorbearer. His music stilled the rage of the agitated, depressed king, and in this role he won the early royal affection and favor. The other account reports that David came to the attention of Saul through the well-known Goliath incident. After the shepherd lad had met successfully the taunting challenge of the giant Philistine, killing him with his own sword, Saul inquired about the hero's name.[18]

Both accounts reflect a pleasant relationship between Saul and

---

[17] I Samuel 16:14–31:13.

[18] II Samuel 21:19 credits Elhanan with Goliath's death and I Chronicles 10:5, obviously trying to reconcile the two traditions, says that Elhanan killed Goliath's brother. The interpretation that Elhanan and David refer to the same man, David being simply a throne name, is improbable. See Bright, *A History of Israel,* p. 172.

David at the outset of their acquaintance. David became a part of palace life and enjoyed the favor of the king. Mutual devotion developed between David and Jonathan. Although David's popularity and later his marriage into the royal family made him a logical and formidable threat to whatever aspirations Jonathan might have had to the throne, the two remained steadfast friends.[19]

David's early days in Saul's palace were also a period of growing popularity with the masses. His military prowess not only won him rapid promotion in the army and the loyalty of soldiers who fought under him, but also captured the imagination of the public. Soon women in the streets, welcoming home the soldiers, chanted,

> Saul has slain his thousands,
> and David his ten thousands. (I Samuel 18:7)

David's success and popularity bred uneasiness and distrust in the distorted mind of the rejected Saul. The troubled king, already personally on the defensive because of his separation from Samuel and his fear that the charisma had also departed, saw in David the aspirant to the throne. Possibly rumors of David's anointing ran through the palace. Apprehension mounted to jealousy and jealousy to a fear which culminated in Saul's decision to kill the young upstart commander in his army.

Erratically Saul attempted numerous measures either to mar David's heroic image or to kill him. Once, Saul reneged on his promise to give his daughter Merab as wife to the slayer of Goliath.[20] Again, when he discovered that his younger daughter Michal was in love with David, he maneuvered the situation hoping for David's death. Through his intermediaries Saul set the price for marriage to his daughter as one hundred Philistine foreskins. David brought two hundred foreskins and Michal became his wife. Another royal plan was aborted.

An early attempt to slay David with a spear as he played for the depressed Saul was the temperamental action of an agitated king, but eventually the efforts of Saul became cool and calculated attempts to kill an opponent. Jonathan and his servants

[19] Cf. I Samuel 20:42.
[20] I Samuel 17:25.

were instructed to slay David. A group of soldiers was sent to arrest David at his residence, but Michal delayed the pursuers and her husband escaped. All of Saul's plans met with failure.

As a consequence of the numerous attempts by Saul to rid himself of his young opponent, David was forced to flee the palace. In spite of several efforts by Jonathan to reconcile the two, Saul's hostility was too deep for David to remain in Gibeah without endangering his life. Therefore, David left the palace and spent the next several years as a fugitive from the king. During these years, however, David never wavered from his profound respect for Saul, Yahweh's anointed king.

David first sought sanctuary with the religious leaders. He came to Samuel in Ramah and was delivered from the pursuing Saul only when the king was caught up in the religious fervor of a band of ecstatic prophets. David fled to Nob where he received assistance from a group of priests led by Ahimelech. He was given the holy bread and the sword of Goliath, which had evidently been brought to Nob as a religious relic. Saul continued his pursuit and David had to leave for Philistia. For assisting David, eighty-five priests of Nob, including Ahimelech, were ruthlessly murdered. Saul's Israelite warriors would not lay sword to the priests, so an Edomite mercenary, Doeg, did the work of execution. Of the priests only Abiathar, a son of Ahimelech, managed to survive the bloody purge and escape to David's camp.

From Nob David fled to Gath and sought refuge there with the Philistine king Achish. However, the Philistines became suspicious and the outlaw escaped Gath only by feigning madness. He returned to the hill country of Judah and made his hideout near the cave of Adullam in the Shephelah region southwest of Bethlehem.[21] There David became the leader of an "outlaw" band as debtors, fugitives, and political malcontents joined him. Abiathar, a priest of Nob, joined the group. Like the outlaws of the early American West who moved from one hideout to another to elude arrest, these men of Israel with prices on their head ranged across the wilderness. The group was organized around David and maintained itself by selling protection to

---

[21] I Samuel 22:3, 4 suggests that David took his parents to Moab for protective custody.

Figure 6–2. The austere, desert mountains of Judah where David ranged with his outlaw band. (Source: Paul Popper, Ltd.)

wealthy men along the borders of Judah. A characteristic story of this period which reveals something of David's power in Judah is about the ill-natured Nabal,[22] a Calebite, who insult-

22 I Samuel 25.

ingly refused to return a favor from David. Only a secretive large gift by Nabal's beautiful wife, Abigail, diverted the impulsive wrath of the outlaws. David's eventual marriage to Abigail made all the property of Nabal the possession of his band.

During this period of exile, David established an ambiguous relationship with the Philistines. On occasions he attacked them in the interest of Israelite groups.[23] At other times the Philistines knew David as the enemy of Saul and, therefore, their friend. When David found himself driven into Philistine territory, he shrewdly played both ends to accomplish his own purposes. He struck the Philistines when the opportunity came, but often sided with these neighbors of Judah against common enemies. Finally David became weary of both the mobile existence of his large band of outcast warriors with their families and the continual role of fugitive from Saul. He took his company to Achish of Gath. The Philistine king accepted David as a vassal and gave him the village of Ziklag, whence David's brigands made strategic raids against Israel's enemies in the Negeb region. David so distributed the spoils of the raids between Achish and the clans of Judah that both thought he was on their side. Thus, David befriended the Philistines and maintained his reputation of loyalty to his own people.[24]

Throughout the outlaw days David was hounded by Saul. Sometimes bounty hunters such as the Ziphites [25] sought to sell out the outlaw chieftain. However, each effort of the king ended in failure. Saul's energies were so divided between campaigns against the Philistines and attempts to capture David that he was able to achieve neither objective. On at least two occasions, at Engedi [26] and in the wilderness of Ziph,[27] David, who was already anointed as Saul's successor, had opportunity to slay Saul, but displayed magnanimity toward his pursuer. For a period Saul seemed to be touched, but his distorted mind never allowed any permanent reconciliation to be established.

The resolution of the controversy between David and Saul came with dramatic suddenness on the plain of Esdraelon at

23 I Samuel 23:1–13.
24 I Samuel 27.
25 I Samuel 23:14–24.
26 I Samuel 24.
27 I Samuel 26.

Mount Gilboa. Here the Philistines marshalled for attack upon the Israelite forces. David and his men were among the army of the Philistines and might have been in the battle against their own people but for Philistine fears that the Bethlehemite might defect to his kinsmen. David's force was released to return to Ziklag.

On the eve of the battle Saul was a pitiable sight. A story is preserved which conveys the depths of the king's depravities and despondence. The tragic and deluded king made every effort to find some religious reassurance of victory. Dreams, oracles, and the prophets failed him. Finally, he resorted to a measure exceptional for an Israelite, particularly a king. Magic was forbidden by law and, although Israelites were tempted to consult with the dead like their neighbors, necromancy and mediums were specifically forbidden by Saul himself. Out of desperation Saul disguised himself, sought out a witch at Endor and had her summon the dead Samuel. The medium reminded Saul of his rejection by Yahweh and predicted defeat for Israel and death for Saul and his sons. The king was left in nocturnal anguish to face the enemy with little more than his courage. This story more than any other negatively evaluates Saul.

The battle was decisive in favor of the Philistines. Saul and three of his sons, Jonathan, Abinadab, and Malchishua,[28] died. The Philistines found the corpses, cut off Saul's head, displayed his armor in a temple of Ashtaroth, and hanged the bodies of the royal family on the walls of Bethshan. Friends from Jabesh-Gilead, which Saul had delivered early in his reign, took the bodies from Bethshan and buried them at Jabesh. Israel's first king had come to an inglorious end.

Israel's losses at Gilboa were devastating and demoralizing. Her king and most of her choicest fighting men were killed. Once again Israel was in dire straits. The Philistines were in power over the heart of western Canaan. But a better day was about to dawn under the leadership of David.

THE REIGN OF DAVID (II SAMUEL)

The outstanding figure in Israel's monarchy, united or divided, was David. Prepared through the providence of a devout up-

[28] I Samuel 31:2; cf. 14:49 where a son named Ishri is listed but no Abinadab.

bringing, indoctrinated in palace life at the court of Saul, and disciplined by the rigors of outlaw existence in the rugged terrain of Judah, he came to the kingdom at an opportune time. No strong empire was on the international scene. Egypt was no longer a threat, the Hittite empire had been destroyed, and Assyria had not yet become a mature power. Saul had borne the weight of a clumsy and shifting amphictyony and softened the fall of outmoded political formats. The time was ripe for the establishment of a more stabilized political organization. The building of the sturdy and respected state of Israel was primarily the work of one man—David.

The regal career of David falls into three distinct periods. For two years after the death of Saul he reigned in Hebron over the tribe of Judah alone.[29] Then he ruled in Hebron for an additional five and a half years over all of Israel. The most extensive period of his reign came after the transfer of the capital to Jerusalem, where for thirty-three years David remained in control.[30] During this period of approximately forty years, Israel became a recognized power among the states of the Near East.

King of Judah

After Gilboa Israel's experiment with monarchy appeared to have ended in failure. The venture had begun well with the cautious sanction of Samuel. Saul's initial forays against the Philistines had been successful. Trouble began with Samuel's early disenchantment with the anointed king and ended with Israel's devastating defeat at Gilboa. Now the Philistines controlled interior western Palestine. At this point the story turns directly to David, the outlaw fugitive from Saul who was Yahweh's anointed successor to the throne.

Circumstances were peculiarly propitious for the rise of David, and he was patiently willing to avail himself of the opportunities. For one thing, David was on quasi-friendly terms with the Philistines. They considered him the enemy of the house of Saul and were willing to give him support in order to keep the Israelites divided in loyalty. Most certainly it was with Philistine consent

---

[29] Cf. II Samuel 2:10.
[30] See II Samuel 5:5.

that David became ruler in Hebron. However, David carefully avoided so identifying himself with Philistia that he alienated his own people. Never during his associations with the Philistines had he engaged in battle against Israel. Throughout his outlaw experience he played successfully the dual role of ally of the Philistines and loyal adherent to Israelite traditions.

Further, the people of Judah supported David because he was Judean. As a native of Bethlehem he was a hero of their tribe. This natural tie binding David to Judah had been enhanced during the months when he and his band had protected the outlying areas of Judah from the marauding neighbors.[31] Hence the natural affinities of Judah were toward one of their kind who had established himself as a seasoned military campaigner. The tribe of Judah had always been one of the strongest tribes of Israel, but she had largely gone her own way and her relationship with the other tribes during the amphictyony appear to have been rather casual. Therefore, independently, she acclaimed David as king of Hebron. The action not only commenced the reign of Israel's most illustrious monarch, but also gave Judah "an enduring political form. A state of Judah emerged as a separate entity," [32] prefacing competitive animosity which would eventually divide the monarchy.

Undoubtedly, David gained support by his attitude toward the house of Saul. His behavior was motivated, not so much by the desire to maneuver the followers of Saul into his camp as by genuine appreciation for "Yahweh's anointed" and personal feelings of warmth toward the family, especially Jonathan. The passionate lament over Saul and Jonathan in II Samuel 1:19–27 reflects in haunting beauty the sincere emotion of David in grief.[33]

> Thy glory, O Israel, is slain upon thy high places!
> How are the mighty fallen!
> Tell it not in Gath,
>   publish it not in the streets of Ashkelon;

[31] The story of Nabal, as described above, is a characteristic illustration of David's protective insurance.

[32] Bright, A History of Israel, p. 175.

[33] G. W. Anderson, A Critical Introduction to the Old Testament, pp. 80–81, states that this passage in itself is sufficient to establish David's reputation as a poet of rare power.

lest the daughters of the Philistines rejoice,
    lest the daughters of the uncircumcised exult.

Ye mountains of Gilboa,
    let there be no dew or rain upon you,
    nor upsurging of the deep!
For there the shield of the mighty was defiled,
    the shield of Saul, not anointed with oil.

From the blood of the slain,
    from the fat of the mighty,
the bow of Jonathan turned not back,
    and the sword of Saul returned not empty.

Saul and Jonathan, beloved and lovely!
    In life and in death they were not divided;
they were swifter than eagles,
    they were stronger than lions.

Ye daughters of Israel, weep over Saul,
    who clothed you daintily in scarlet,
    who put ornaments of gold upon your apparel.

How are the mighty fallen
    in the midst of the battle!

Jonathan lies slain upon thy high places.
    I am distressed for you, my brother Jonathan;
very pleasant have you been to me;
    your love to me was wonderful,
    passing the love of women.

How are the mighty fallen,
    and the weapons of war perished!

David brought swift retribution to one who brought the news of
Saul's death [34] and sent a message of gratitude to those of Jabesh-
Gilead who had given decent burial to Saul and his sons.[35] Certainly these deeds won the sympathetic ear of many who had followed Saul.

David's wise policy toward Saul's house is seen further in his
attitude toward the civil struggle which developed soon after his
accession at Hebron. A surviving son of Saul, Ishbosheth,[36] with
the help of Abner, captain of Israel's army, claimed the crown.

---

[34] II Samuel 1:2–16; 4:10.
[35] II Samuel 2:4–7.
[36] Called "Eshbaal" in I Chronicles 8:33.

At best Abner's monarch was a pretender. Since dynastic rule was not accepted in Israel, Ishbosheth could claim little loyalty as Saul's son. Further, he did not have military force either to expel the Philistines or to challenge David. One gets the impression that Ishbosheth was a weak pawn in the maneuvering hands of the ambitious Abner, who was primarily looking after his own interests.

David's policy in this situation was to wait it out. Skirmishes between David's band and the forces of Abner occurred, but the resolution of conflict came through a quarrel between Ishbosheth and Abner over the possession of one of Saul's concubines. The rift resulted in Abner's offer to transfer his allegiance to David. Abner came to Hebron with a large group of supporters and David welcomed them with amnesty. The prospect of a second military leader was considered a major threat by Joab, David's commander, and he took the first opportunity to murder his rival.[37] Soon thereafter two officers of Ishbosheth assassinated the son of Saul and came to David seeking reward. Joab was publicly reprimanded for killing Abner and the two officers executed for the murder of Ishbosheth, but David's grief at the passing of the opposition must not have been very deep. With brevity and lack of emotion David lamented Abner:

> Should Abner die as a fool dies?
> Your hands were not bound,
>   your feet were not fettered;
> as one falls before the wicked
>   you have fallen. (II Samuel 3:33–34)

King of All Israel

From the outset of the Hebron reign the loyalty of all Israel began gradually to shift to David. At the death of Ishbosheth, a landslide of acclaim came to David.

So all the elders of Israel came to the king at Hebron; and King David made a covenant with them at Hebron before Yahweh, and they anointed David king over Israel. (II Samuel 5:3)

Like the judges and Saul before him, David was made king primarily because of his gifts, *i.e.*, he was a charismatic leader;

[37] II Samuel 3:22–39.

Yahweh's spirit rested upon him. After he had been made king over all Israel, David confronted two major problems. Externally, the perennial Philistine threat still plagued Israel and, internally, the northern and southern clans of Israel remained divided in spirit. To the former and overt problem David gave his immediate attention.

The Philistines naturally recognized the acclamation of David as a resurgence of united Israel and set forth to counteract it by destroying the ambitious nation. The details of the resultant conflict as fragmentarily presented in II Samuel 5:17–25 are not clear. Possibly the exploits recorded in Chapters 21 and 22 belong to these Philistine campaigns.[38] In fact, no thorough account of the Philistines' defeat has been preserved. They were apparently overcome by a series of fierce engagements. Never again were they a serious threat to Israel. The Philistine control over iron was broken and the introduction of its common use among the Israelites brought economic revolution to the country. David was free to give attention to the consolidation of the state.

By charismatic gifts and his generous attitude toward the house of Saul, David had already won considerable support throughout Israel. Now with the Philistines subdued, he took perhaps the most important political and religious step of his reign. In order to eliminate an impression that his reign was no more than an expansion of his reign of Judah, he moved the capital to Jerusalem, a Jebusite city in the territory of Benjamin associated with neither Judah nor the northern tribes.

By the time of David, Jerusalem was already an old city. The site had been occupied as early at 3000 B.C. and was actually called "Jerusalem" as early as 1900 B.C. Joshua had been unable to take it from the Jebusites in the conquest of Canaan, and heretofore Jerusalem had neither political nor religious connotations to Israel. Using his personal troops rather than levied forces, David captured the city and made it his private holding, the "city of David." Israelites began to flock to the new capital and gradually it became the center of Israelite life.

The astute David was keenly aware of the importance of the religious ties which had bound the diverse tribal groups in the

<hr/>

[38] H. W. Robinson, *The History of Israel*, p. 62. Note especially the bringing of water from the well of Bethlehem.

now-departing amphictyonic order. Accordingly, he moved to preserve these unifying feelings by making his new capital the center of Israelite cult. He transferred the Ark of the Covenant from Kirjath-jearim to Jerusalem. A tent was erected for housing the Ark, and, amidst pageantry and rejoicing in which David

Figure 6–3. Modern Jerusalem showing the Kidron Valley on the right. The rectangular area encloses the Moslem Mosque of the Rock, believed to have been the site of Solomon's temple. The ancient "city of David" lay south of the rectangular area, overlooking Kidron. (Source: Arab Information Center.)

openly participated, the religious symbol of Israel was transferred to its new home. Henceforth Jerusalem, previously without Israelite religious associations, would become the religious capital of Israel and remain so, with some interruptions, even to this day. It was actually the "city of David" and would be ruled over by his dynasty until 587 B.C. Both its religious and political significance were enormous.

A large portion of the reign of David was spent in extending the borders of Israel to encompass all of Palestine and in consolidating an area which could be called home by the nation. After Jerusalem, other city-states of Palestine became vassals of David with little or no resistance. For the first time "Israel," formerly denoting a tribal confederacy whose members occupied only parts of Palestine, now designated a geographical unit encompassing the whole of the land of promise.

Since David reigned at a time when the Hittites were weak and both Assyria and Egypt were concerned with problems elsewhere, his foes were the small neighboring states and he was able to extend the boundaries of his state by conquest. Ammon, Edom, and Moab were overrun as David pushed the boundaries of Israel to their greatest extremity. Philistia was shut up in a coastal cage and the friendship of Phoenicia was maintained through alliance with Hiram of Tyre.

The sweeping military success of David was made possible largely by his personal army, composed of professional soldiers assembled during his outlaw days rather than men levied from the Israelite tribes. Foreign mercenaries, expecially Philistines,[39] made up a sizable part of the army. Deeds of outstanding courage seem to have been rewarded with a place in the king's special honor guard, a legion of merit known as "The Thirty."[40] The exploits of this fighting force largely accounted for Israel's becoming during the time of David the most powerful of the small states between Mesopotamia and Egypt. This was the golden age of Israel's political glory.

Court History of David's Reign

The "Court History of David" (II Samuel 9–20 and I Kings 1–2) provides not only the most important materials concerning David's rule but is also one of the superb pieces of historical narrative preserved from the ancient world.[41] It suggests an eyewitness as its author, perhaps someone in the royal court of David who continued through the early years of the reign of Solomon. The narrative is realistic, presenting life as it is lived in conversa-

[39] "Cherethites and Pelethites" refer to "Cretans and Philistines." According to II Samuel 15:18, six hundred warriors from the Philistine city of Gath followed David.

[40] Cf. II Samuel 23:13, 24.

[41] Another outstanding example of Ancient Near Eastern historiography is the narrative of David's rise: I Samuel 16:14–II Samuel 5 and II Samuel 8:1–15.

tions and episodes, but at the same time skillfully framed so as to
sustain drama for its readers.

Although David spent the early part of his reign conquering
all of Israel's major opponents, the latter part of his rule was not
characterized by peace. Within both his family and the state
tensions erupted into open bitterness and revolt. The "Court History" gives as much attention to these difficulties as to earlier
successes. Deeds of ignominy are reported with utter frankness.
The beginning of these was David's sin with Bathsheba, the wife
of one of David's special honor guard.

The incident with Bathsheba occurred during the Ammonite
war while Uriah the Hittite, Bathsheba's husband, was with the
army in Transjordan. David yielded to lust, appropriated Bathsheba as his own, and soon learned that she was to bear his child.
Afraid of being found out, the king attempted to cover his deed
by having Uriah returned from the battlefront. When Uriah refused to violate his soldier's ban by visiting his wife, David
"arranged" for the brave warrior's death in battle and married
Bathsheba.

The Old Testament condemns David's sin with the same clarity that it praises his deeds of valor. Nathan, the prophet of
Yahweh, to the king's face portrayed him as one who had stolen
the "one little ewe lamb" owned by a poor man.[42] The prophet's
ingenious use of an imaginary court case so struck David that he
immediately accepted responsibility for the deed and in remorse
confessed his sin to Yahweh. Although his confession brought a
sense of Yahweh's forgiveness, David was unable to escape the
results of his folly. He became an over-indulgent parent who
thoroughly spoiled his sons [43] and a pampering husband who
could not resist the desires of his wife.[44] The uneasiness of David's family life, coupled with the people's ambiguous ideas about
how his successor was to be chosen, contributed to restlessness in
the kingdom during the closing years of his reign.

The most tragic consequence of all was the rebellion of Absalom, David's son by an Aramean princess. David's oldest son
and possible claimant to the throne, Amnon, seduced Tamar, the

[42] II Samuel 12.
[43] See I Kings 1:6.
[44] See I Kings 1:15 ff.

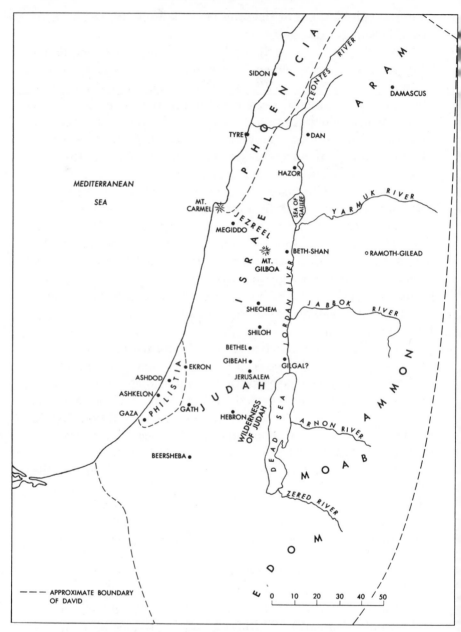

Figure 6–4. Kingdom of David and Solomon.

sister of Absalom. After two years in which Amnon went unpunished, Absalom coolly murdered his half-brother and fled. After three years in exile, Absalom was allowed to return to Jerusalem and after two additional years he was finally restored to the good graces of his father. However, he secretly plotted the overthrow of government. Gradually winning the ear of many with various grievances against the throne, Absalom was finally proclaimed king in, of all places, Hebron! He obviously hoped thereby to insure Judah's support for his policies. The insurrectionists marched upon Jerusalem and David had to flee the city. David's personal army remained loyal; forces were recouped and the rebellion quelled. Absalom, to the deep grief of his father, was slain by Joab. The elders of Judah, fearful of possible retribution for their rebellious actions, reluctantly approached David for reconciliation. David accepted them into his camp and even promised that the rebel general, Amasa, would replace Joab as captain of the army. Peace was brought to this quarter, but rebellion broke out in another.

A group from the northern tribes, embittered by David's kind treatment of the Judeans who had joined in Absalom's rebellion, were led in revolt by Sheba of Benjamin. Joab, with David looking the other way, killed Amasa and again assumed uncontested command of David's professional army. The brief rebellion was then put down as rapidly as it had begun. Sheba was assassinated and David was again without opposition.

David's Contribution to Israel

In spite of his domestic troubles and the political disturbances during the last years of his reign, David stands with Abraham and Moses as a major determiner of the direction of Old Testament history. Building upon the transitional accomplishments of Saul, David firmly established monarchy as a pattern for Israel's government. He overcame the military opponents of Israel, extended her boundaries to embrace all of Palestine, and created in the minds of divergent peoples some sense of national identity. Apparently David governed directly with no prime minister and few cabinet officials of real authority. In his own person David symbolized political unity.

Moreover, David ably preserved a fundamental religious identity in both his personal and national commitments. David greatly loved Yahweh and this influenced all his actions. Jerusalem became both the political and religious capital of the land and in a sense David served as both king and priest. Many loyalties previously centered in Samuel passed to David when the aged seer died.

In time the personal weakness of David became less important to the people and much of their theology and national hopes became centered in their great hero. In the Deuteronomic tradition David became the primary figure for accomplishing God's purpose in history. He was remembered as one selected by Yahweh to administer "justice and equity to all his people." [45] So definite was this selection that not only David, but also his dynasty, was established in Jerusalem where a theology of "covenant with David" developed. David himself was remembered as saying:

> Yea, does not my house stand so with God?
> For he has made with me an everlasting
>   covenant,
>   ordered in all things and secure. (II Samuel 23:5)

This unbreakable covenant with the Davidic house forced the Sinai covenant into the background in the Davidic state until the late seventh century B.C., when a rediscovery of Mosaic Torah once again placed before Israel her obligation to serve the covenant of Yahweh. Historic and prophetic traditions originating in the south reflect the supremacy of the bond with David. Neither the Yahwistic history nor the Judean prophets, Isaiah and Micah, emphasize the Sinai event. Isaiah, in particular, makes much of the covenant with David and its promise of Jerusalem's inviolability. Thus David's covenant and David's city became central to subsequent religion, literature and even the later messianic hope.

The Davidic tradition, therefore, gave the nation ruled by his dynasty political stability for over three hundred years. Furthermore, the idea of a covenant with David became the source of Israel's later dreams of restoration from the travail of Babylonian exile, and furnished a vehicle for prophetic messianic expectations.

---

[45] II Samuel 8:15. See chapter 7.

SOLOMON (I KINGS 1–11)[46]

With David, Solomon shared the desire to make Israel a grand and glorious nation. Against the backdrop of extended boundaries and increasing national prowess Solomon envisioned a land of oriental opulence. Israel's splendor among the nations became a consuming passion of the newly anointed ruler. But, unlike his father, Solomon's desire was tempered neither by sensitivity to the thoughts and feelings of the common man of Israel nor by consideration of religious values cherished by the people. Whereas David had known the plight of economic survival in rugged Palestine, his son knew only the prosperity of the palace. Whereas the reign of David had been prefaced by the rigors surrounding the Hebron rule, Solomon was "born in purple." David's victories over Israel's enemies meant that Solomon was spared the hard discipline of battle. Peace had arrived and Solomon's dream could be nurtured. All that the son knew first-hand of the battlefield had been learned during the Absalom rebellion. Here the victory of David may have been so resounding as to remove any of Solomon's suspicions regarding his right to be absolute despot and make the people his obedient subjects. Undoubtedly, his background had marked influence on the character of Solomon's rule. Most important of all, Solomon was a lesser man than David.

Solomon's Accession

The account of Solomon's accession to the throne is part of the Court History of David and justifies Solomon's claim to the throne by depicting him as victorious among David's sons in a long and unsavory struggle for succession. The accession of Solomon to the throne was more the result of palace intrigue than charismatic selection or inheritance. As David neared death and his strong grasp on the kingdom loosened, two parties within the palace began to vie for control. One party was led by Joab, long David's strong-arm man, and Abiathar, the priest who had been David's

[46] The books of Chronicles give an account of the period of the monarchy which in many ways parallels that in Kings. However, since the Chronicles account dwells upon the history of Judah and mentions Israel only incidentally, only the account in Kings is listed here as primary source material. David's reign is covered in I Chronicles, Solomon's in II Chronicles 1–9.

counsel since the days of Adullam. These, seemingly without any protest from the king, supported Adonijah, the logical successor by the rule of primogeniture.

A second party was organized by Nathan, the prophet involved in the Bathsheba event. He had the support of Bathsheba in winning David's favor for her son Solomon. One can only surmise what part David's sense of guilt may have played in leading him to accede to Bathsheba's request. Probably Solomon received support more because he was the son of David's most influential wife than because of the young man's personal equipment for the kingship.

With an announced decision of his father, Solomon was publicly proclaimed "ruler over Israel and over Judah." [47] Soon after the death of David, he secured his rule in forceful and drastic fashion. His major opponent Adonijah was executed, Abiathar was deposed from his priesthood, and Joab was slain even as he clung to the horns of the altar. "So the kingdom was established in the hand of Solomon." [48] The faction with the power to enforce its rule won the contest. David's support carried some weight, but the cheering of the populace was only *ex post facto* approval of that which had been done by force. The day of selecting a king of Israel on the basis of charismatic gifts was over, and Samuel must have moved a little in his grave.

Accomplishments of Solomon's Reign

Solomon's reign is reported in the first eleven chapters of Kings and can be outlined as follows:

I. David places Solomon on the throne of Israel. I Kings 1–2
II. Solomon's reign. I Kings 3–11
    A. His reputation for both wisdom and splendor. I Kings 3–4
    B. His construction and dedication of the temple. I Kings 5–8
    C. His heights and subsequent decline. I Kings 9–11

With the kingdom rid of internal opposition early in his reign, Solomon was able to accomplish his dream to bring glory to the kingdom. There was little or no challenge from outside the borders of Palestine. Egypt was too weak to interfere. The fall

[47] I Kings 1:38–40; cf. vs. 35.
[48] I Kings 2:46.

of the Hittite kingdom had left Asia Minor without a strong power. Syria was not yet a major threat, although the action of Rezon in having himself proclaimed king in Damascus [49] might well have been taken as an ominous sign.

The only political force of any consequence on the scene at the accession of Solomon was Phoenicia. The new king took immediate steps to continue his father's treaty arrangements with this neighbor to the northwest. Hiram, king of the Phoenician city of Tyre, became Solomon's primary accessory in accomplishing the material advancement of Israel. Phoenicia provided both skilled craftsmen and unskilled labor for Solomon's construction projects. The maritime skills of these seafaring people also enabled Solomon to extend his commercial activities through Phoenician ports, and Phoenician sailors assisted his merchant fleet which sailed to the south and east from the Israelite port at Ezion-geber on the Gulf of Aqabah. With the direct help of these neighbors Israel's natural resources were tapped for the first time as building materials and as export commodities. In every possible way Solomon used agreements with Phoenicia to Israel's advantage.

Although the international situation offered little overt threat, Solomon "modernized" his army. While he never fought a major campaign, he maintained a strong fighting force including fourteen hundred war chariots and twelve thousand horsemen.[50] Archaeological excavations at Megiddo reveal vast installations for stabling horses in one of several "chariot and horse cities." In addition, Solomon built many fortifications for the defense of the land.

The most remarkable accomplishment of Solomon's reign was his ambitious construction program. Undoubtedly, the Deuteronomic historian considered the temple to be the most significant contribution made by Solomon. Three full chapters are given to the description of the building and furnishings of the magnificent structure.

The temple combined the splendor of Phoenician achitecture [51] with traditional symbols of Hebrew worship. An outward vesti-

[49] I Kings 11:23–25.
[50] I Kings 10:26.
[51] See Wright, *Biblical Archaeology*, pp. 136–140.

Figure 6–5. The ruins of Solomon's stables at Megiddo where c. 450 horses were quartered. The vertical pillars served as roof supports and hitching posts. Two mangers are seen in the center of the picture. (Source: Courtesy of the Oriental Institute, University of Chicago.)

bule was entered through large ornate doors standing between two bronze pillars. The main sanctuary held the sacred furniture: the golden candlesticks, the table of shewbread, and the altar of incense. The Holy of Holies was reached by a flight of stairs leading up from the main sanctuary. In this cube was Yahweh's throne, the Ark of the Covenant. The temple, therefore, represented Yahweh's presence. Although patterned by Phoenician architects following Phoenician design, the temple and its cult remained thoroughly Yahwistic.[52]

The temple was splendidly ornate, making ample use of copper and Lebanon cedar, but it was probably no more elaborate than other of Solomon's buildings. The king's palace built near

[52] For a good brief discussion of the temple, and its role in Israelite life, see G. E. Wright, "The Temple in Palestine and Syria," in *The Biblical Archaeologist Reader*, I, 169–184.

Figure 6–6. Sketch of Solomon's temple based on the Howland-Garber reconstruction. (Source: Paul Leslie Garber, Agnes Scott College. Sketch by Gladys Futral.)

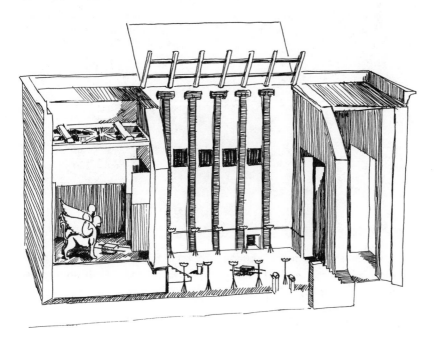

Figure 6–7. Cutaway of Figure 6–6.

the temple must have been costly, since it required thirteen years to be built, as compared to seven years for the construction of the temple.[53] The palace complex, fronted by the massive cedar pil-

[53] David had accumulated some of the materials for the temple.

lars cut from the forests of Lebanon, served as treasury, armory, and courtroom, as well as residence for the regal harem.

Solomon's construction at Ezion-geber on the Gulf of Aqabah represented a remarkable innovation in Israel's history. Manned with Phoenician sailors and Israelite novices, ships sailed from the seaport of Ezion-geber on commercial voyages which took more than a year. These voyages brought the far ports of the East into easy access of Israel through the Red Sea. Imports must have included gold, silver, ivory, and jewels of other lands, as well as tales of distant peoples spun by returning sailors.

Figure 6–8. Cedars of Lebanon. From the forests of Lebanon Solomon received timbers for his building enterprises. (Source: Arab Information Center.)

The extensive internal development of Israel by Solomon was made possible by his emphasis on the expansion of lucrative trade arrangements. One of Solomon's main points of genius was demonstrated in far-reaching and mutually beneficial trade agreements with the neighbors of Israel. The interchange between

Solomon and Phoenicia has already been noted. A continuing alliance with Hiram put Israel indirectly in contact with many points of Phoenician westward maritime expansion—Sicily, Cyprus, Sardinia, North Africa, Spain.

Trade in horses and chariots provided another significant aspect of Solomon's commercial activity.

Solomon's import of horses was from Egypt and Kue . . . A chariot could be imported from Egypt for six hundred shekels of silver, and a horse for a hundred and fifty; and so through the king's traders they were exported to all the kings of the Hittites and the kings of Syria. (II Kings 10:28–29) [54]

Evidently Solomon seized the opportunity to serve as middle-man in a lucrative exchange of horses and chariots. Strategically located between Egypt and the kings of the north, his "agency" became the only avenue of exchange for these important implements of warfare.

This extensive commercial activity brought much wealth to the coffers of Israel. Undoubtedly, Solomon became wealthy. The material prosperity which marked the kingdom during his reign was possible largely because of wealth accumulated through trade.

Although the major area of growth during Solomon's day was material, there were also significant literary and cultural achievements. Literature flourished. Writings of the period reflect the continuing interests of Israel in her historical heritage. The Court History of David, one of the major resources for the writing of II Samuel 9–20 and I Kings 1–2, came from Solomon's reign, as did the Yahwist's great epic of Israel's beginnings.[55]

Wisdom literature [56] also flourished. A later tradition attributing the book of Proverbs to Solomon is undoubtedly an overgeneralization, but the wisdom tradition of which the book is representative was certainly in the making. The Kings' account describes Solomon as one who "uttered three thousand proverbs and his songs were a thousand and five" (I Kings 4:32). He spoke wisdom through the channel of the fable and some of his sayings may be incorporated in the postexilic book, but his primary support of wisdom was probably more through his patron-

[54] "Kue" was most likely Cilicia in Asia Minor.
[55] See above, pp. 8–9, 57–58, 74–78.
[56] See pp. 472–485.

age of scribes than personal production of literature. This connection, nonetheless, illustrates the cultural sophistication of Solomon's reign.

Weaknesses

The reign of Solomon was a period of peace and prosperity
during which Israel reached the zenith of her material splendor.
Jesus' reference to "Solomon in all his glory" was certainly justified by the circumstances. Yet the achievements of the period
were not without their price. Many persons of Palestine shared
the achievement and wealth of Solomon, but to the vast majority
the glory itself became a burden. Solomon became an ostenta-
tious monarch concerned only with his own grandeur and pomp
to the exclusion of consideration for the long-term welfare of his
people. Early the people began to simmer in unrest.

The ambitious projects of Solomon could not be financed from
local resources and a major portion of the bill was paid by income
from commercial enterprises. However, taxation was also a part
of the plan to pay the toll. Solomon organized the land into
twelve districts, each supervised by an officer. Divisions were
made irrespective of old tribal lines and Canaanites were also
included in the assessment. Each division was to supply a
month's provisions for the king; and, if the list in I Kings 4:22 ff.
is not exaggerated, this was quite an order. Undoubtedly such
a program of taxation became a heavy burden to the common
man. Beyond the revenues involved, this new administrative
division weakened tribal sovereignty, incorporated Canaanites
into the system of the state, and consolidated power in the hands
of the king.

The burden was increased by Solomon's practice of recruiting
labor battalions to assist with building projects. Both foreigners [57]
and native Israelites [58] were included. One month of every three
was to be given in the service of the king. This hated labor
force, or corvée, included about thirty thousand native Israelites
working in Lebanon. Another one hundred and fifty thousand
were engaged in work at home as burden-bearers and quarry

[57] I Kings 9:15–22.
[58] I Kings 5:13 f.

men. These numbers did not include the officers who supervised the work.

Consequently, Solomon burned the taxation candle at both ends. Not only did the amount of taxation become heavier and heavier, but also the productive ability of the masses was decreased as large segments of the populace were forced into the corvée. For many, therefore, material progress became not so much a source of pride in the prosperity of their land as a striking symbol of the extensive sacrifice extracted from them to humor the insatiable desires of a pompous king.

The growing unrest of the masses over the undue pressure of taxation was also encouraged by the lax religious behavior of the king. As contacts with outside peoples became commonplace, Solomon became more cosmopolitan in his outlook. The Old Testament cites the expansion of the king's harem as the most obvious example of his liberal attitude toward extra-Israelite culture, including foreign religions. The historian laments that Solomon had "seven hundred wives, princesses, and three hundred concubines." [59]

Such a harem was not just an indication of Solomon's pleasure and sensual desire. Marriages were contracted for political purposes. Political treaty sealed with marriage was Solomon's stratagem to secure the boundaries of Israel and maintain friendship with neighboring peoples. The importance of such alliances is seen in his marriage with the daughter of Pharaoh [60] by which he received one of the most important city-states of southern Palestine, Gezer,[61] the gateway to the pass leading from Joppa to Jerusalem. Other marriages were contracted with the Moabites, Ammonites, Edomites, Phoenicians, and Hittites.

Solomon permitted the worship of his wives' deities. Hard by Jerusalem and the sanctuary of Yahweh, shrines to foreign deities were constructed. Solomon's toleration of outside religions was more than Yahwistic religious leadership could endure. His "wives had turned away his heart after other gods, and his heart was not wholly true to Yahweh his God, as was the heart of David" (I Kings 11:4). Solomon's religious tolerance had con-

[59] I Kings 11:3.
[60] I Kings 3:1 f.
[61] I Kings 9:16.

taminated the pure faith of Israel by allowing the encroachments of outside faiths. The religious leadership of Israel must have remembered the admonition of Samuel that the selection of a king carried the inherent danger of forgetting their dependence upon God.[62]

Thus, the reign of Solomon is a study in dramatic contrasts. Unquestionably the peak of material prosperity was achieved. With boundaries solidified, important communications with neighboring peoples consummated in exchange of cultural ideas. Natural resources were developed on an extensive scale. This internal development may account partially for the tradition which looked upon Solomon with great favor. However, the significant material achievements of the king were made at enormous sacrifice by the common man. Immediate luxuries had been bought at the price of lasting prosperity. Enamoured with dreams of splendor, Solomon designed fiscal policies with only one end— producing enough income to pay the bill. More often than not, these policies operated to the detriment of long-range fiscal growth for the nation.

Here then was a king who had lost touch with his people. He was not only insensitive to the needs of those who made up his nation, but he was also callous to national religious ideals. Amphictyonic relationship had been replaced by oppressive administrative organization. Israel's king had in Solomon become more an eastern potentate than Yahweh's vice-regent, symbol of the community's covenant commitment. Israel was now a long way from Shechem. Although Solomon was able to maintain tight control on the kingdom during his lifetime, beneath the placid surface a storm was brewing. The death of the king became the occasion for the eruption of this unrest.

SUGGESTED READINGS

Background

JOHNSON, A. R., *Sacral Kingship in Ancient Israel* (University of Wales Press, 1955). An interpretation of the cultic role of the kings of Judah.

---

[62] Cf. I Samuel 8:6 ff.; Deuteronomy 17:14 ff.

WELCH, A. C., *Kings and Prophets of Israel* (Lutterworth, 1952). Selected studies.

Note references to general history works in basic resources list.

The Book of Samuel

CAIRD, GEORGE B., "1 and 2 Samuel" in *Interpreter's Bible*, II.

HERTZBERG, HANS WILHELM, *I & II Samuel* (Westminster, 1964).

PHILBRECK, BEN F., JR., "1–2 Samuel" in *The Broadman Bible Commentary*, III.

The Court History of David's Reign

VON RAD, GERHARD, *Old Testament Theology* (Harper & Row, 1962), I, 312 ff.

7

The Divided Kingdom: Israel

The Old Testament contains two sources on the period of the divided monarchy. The primary account is the part of the Deuteronomic history work [1] found in the single book of Kings, which is presently divided into two books. The author wrote from the exilic period, after the fall of Jerusalem in 587 B.C., and is concerned with the apostasy of Yahweh's covenant people which occasioned the devastation of the Temple city and the deportations of Israelites to foreign soils. He utilized the available chronicles of the kings of both Israel and Judah in the formulation of his interpretative narration of the era. For him the division of kingdom was itself evidence of the rebellious will of the covenant people, if not a direct act of punitive judgment by Yahweh. He relies on several sources for data on the kings of the two kingdoms, but adds an evaluation of the reigns of the kings based primarily on their comparison to the ideal sovereign David, and whether or not the Jerusalem Temple was the single acceptable place to worship.

Using the records of the two kingdoms, he weaves them together, following a definite pattern in presenting the kings of both nations. [2] The introduction for each of the kings of Israel includes (1) the dating of the king's reign in terms of the reigning king of Judah, (2) the name of the capital from which he reigned, (3) the duration of the reign, and (4) a brief and condemning characterization of the king (except for Shallum, who

[1] For discussion of the large Deuteronomic history work, see above, pp. 184–187.
[2] Cf. *The Interpreter's Bible*, III, 8–10.

reigned only one month). Four items also appear in the introductions of the kings of Judah: (1) the date of accession in terms of who is king of Israel, (2) age at which the king came to the throne, (3) the name of the queen mother, and (4) a brief comparison of each king with David. The recounting of the kings moves from Judah to Israel and back again until the northern kingdom has disappeared from the scene.

The book of Kings may be outlined as follows:

I. Solomon's selection by David and reign. I Kings 1–11 [3]
II. The two kingdoms of Israel and Judah. I Kings 12–II Kings 17
    A. Jeroboam of Israel and Rehoboam of Judah. I Kings 12–14
    B. Early wars between the two states. I Kings 15–16
    C. Elijah and Ahab. I Kings 17:1–22:40
    D. Elisha stories. I Kings 22:41–II Kings 8:29
    E. Jehu's revolt and massacre. II Kings 9–10
      (Against house of Ahab and worshippers of Baal)
    F. Narratives of the two kingdoms to the fall of Israel. II Kings 11–17
III. The kingdom of Judah to her fall. II Kings 18–25

The second source belongs to the priestly tradition and is part of a large literary unit including the books of Chronicles, Ezra, and Nehemiah. These works are generally referred to as the Chronicler's History and, when taken together, survey the whole period of Israelite history [4] from Genesis through the reforms of Ezra and Nehemiah. The priestly chronicler emphasizes the religious life of Judah. Overall the work can be outlined:

I. Genealogical survey from Adam to Saul. I Chronicles 1–9
II. The monarchy (Saul, David, and Solomon). I Chronicles 10–II Chronicles 9
III. From the division of the kingdom through the Exile. I Chronicles 10–36
IV. Return from Exile and restoration of the temple. Ezra 1–6
V. The work of Ezra. Ezra 7–10
VI. Rebuilding Jerusalem's wall. Nehemiah 1–7
VII. Reading the Book of Law under Ezra and further reforms. Nehemiah 8–13.

Since he wrote a considerable time after Samaria's fall, the Chronicler was unconcerned with the northern kingdom. Writ-

---

[3] For discussion of materials under this heading, see above, pp. 251–260.
[4] For an introductory discussion of this work, see Hugh Anderson, *Historians of Israel* (2) in Abingdon's Bible Guides.

ing out of the background of the postexilic period, he sought to support the priestly faith of the restored nation. To accomplish this particular religious bias the writer included and excluded items at his discretion. For example, his primary interest in David was as a religious leader. Military accomplishments are mentioned, but only incidental to the picture of the religious patriot who built Jerusalem as the holy shrine and whose line was continued by covenant of Yahweh. David's outlaw career and his behavior with Bathsheba have no place in the Chronicler's account.

Sometimes the Chronicler quoted his Samuel-Kings source word-for-word. Again, he altered details to illustrate his point, as when he described Satan's provoking David to number Israel.[5] On other occasions, he added to the Samuel-Kings story events taken from other sources. Both Chronicles and Ezra-Nehemiah are the result of this process of adding and editing, subtracting and modifying—all for the purpose of supporting the Hebrew faith of the postexilic period.

Because of this bias, the Chronicler's account must be supplemented by and set over against other history of the same period. For this reason, the Deuteronomic source will be given primary consideration in this chapter with Chronicles serving as an additional or auxiliary source.

THE REVOLT AND ESTABLISHMENT OF ISRAEL
(I KINGS 12:1–16:20) [6]

The death of Solomon brought Old Testament history to a critical point. Distrust of the royal house had been poured into the caldron of unrest until it began to seethe during the closing days of Solomon's reign. Opposition began to take definite structure before the death of the king. Reflecting the attitude of religious leaders, Ahijah, a prophet of Shiloh, confronted Jeroboam, one of Solomon's construction foremen in Ephraim, with the idea of revolt.[7] Jeroboam was told directly by Ahijah that he would become king of Israel.[8] What began as a private an-

[5] I Chronicles 21:1.
[6] Also II Chronicles 10:1–19.
[7] I Kings 11:27 f.
[8] I Kings 11:37.

nouncement soon became the subject of household conversation. Solomon heard the rumor and Jeroboam not only was forced "to resign," but suddenly found himself fleeing the anger of the king. He found refuge with the pharaoh of Egypt, Shishak, who was anxious to make friends with anyone of prominence in Israel. Even though Solomon rid the country of Jeroboam and squelched an early uprising, the seeds of discontent continued to grow and at Solomon's death bore fruit. The kingdom established by David had begun to disintegrate internally during the last days of Solomon. Evidence of the monarch's waning strength was the beginning of disturbance on Israel's borders. Although open warfare was averted, Edom in the south and significant areas of Syria in the north were lost to Israel. A prophet of the times might easily have read in the external and internal affairs of Israel the approaching disaster.

Reopening Old Conflicts

The uneasy state of affairs during the last years of Solomon was aided and abetted by long standing conflicts which were brought to the surface by rumblings of discontent. Traditional and geographic divergence within and among various tribal groups was brought to the surface immediately by the rumblings. Only by "personal courage and shrewd policy" [9] had David been able to win the affection of the people and amalgamate these tribal groups into a nation. The nation was not yet far enough from these competitive feelings to avoid their resurgence. Emerging in a struggle for supremacy were the tribes of Ephraim and Judah. Both had long enjoyed some supremacy among the tribes. The memory of Israel gave the Joseph tribes a role over other northern tribes and counted Ephraim greater than Manasseh. The status of the Joseph tribes was projected back to the day when Joseph dreamed of his superiority over his brothers and openly boasted of his dreams. Further, in a fascinating account of patriachal blessing Jacob gave first regard to Ephraim in spite of the fact that Manasseh was the older of Joseph's sons. The words of the patriarch reveal the later status achieved by Ephraim:

[9] H. W. Robinson, *History of Israel*, p. 70.

[Manasseh] "shall become a people, and he also shall be great; nevertheless his younger brother shall be greater than he, and his descendants shall become a multitude of nations." . . . Thus he put Ephraim before Manasseh. (Genesis 48:19–20)

The literary records of tribal origins also give Judah a place of importance among the tribes. Genesis 49 contains a series of blessings upon all the tribes and the sayings about Judah are extravagantly laudatory.[10] It is a young lion, conqueror of enemies, and therefore honored by the other tribes. Again the words depict a station achieved by Judah in the nation's history:

The scepter shall not depart from Judah,
    nor the ruler's staff from between his feet,
Until he comes to whom it belongs;
    and to him shall be the obedience of the peoples. (Genesis 49:10)

The emergence of both Judah and Ephraim as tribes of supremacy encouraged an individualistic spirit which is revealed in the biblical record. After Gideon's sweeping conquest of the Midianites in the time of the judges, Ephraim complained that she had not been called to the battlefield to share the victory. Slightly later during the leadership of Jephthah, the tribe again protested that she had not been called to champion the cause of Israel. Judah had reflected an independent spirit in the days of early settlement in Canaan. Before the tribes led by Joshua entered Canaan from the Transjordan, a major segment of Judah had come into the land from the south. Around Hebron she had formed an amphictyonic structure of her own prior to the creation of the twelve-tribe amphictyony at Shechem. Separately Judah had acclaimed David king and later supported the Absalom rebellion. Both Ephraim and Judah had long backgrounds independent of one another and were accustomed to action independent of each other. The duality of even David's kingdom is attested when Solomon is selected as king "over Israel *and* over Judah." (I Kings 1:38–40)

The dominance of Judah and Ephraim inevitably led to antagonism between the two. This was a major factor in the split of the kingdom. Solomon may have even unknowingly encouraged the rift by preferential treatment of Judah. It has already been noted that his administrative districts for taxation did not coin-

10 See Gerhard von Rad's discussion in his *Genesis*, pp. 406–423.

cide with old tribal boundaries. The listing of divisions in I Kings 4 suggests that Judah may have been given special considerations. If this were the case, the jealousy of other tribal factions was aroused, making them antagonistic to Solomon's successor. Thus at the death of Solomon the cleavage among the tribes became acute.

The individuality of both Judah and Ephraim was encouraged by the geography of Palestine. No feature of Palestine's topography was more outstanding than the central ridge of mountains which ran the length of the land and occupied the larger part of the area between the Jordan and the Mediterranean. This rugged terrain was better suited to local than to strong, centralized government.

Judah was isolated in the heart of the mountain heights. Between Jerusalem and Jericho is an area so rugged that it has become proverbial. To Judah's east was the Dead Sea, which separated her from Reuben and Gad. With the Mediterranean to the west and the wilderness of the Negeb to the south Judah was almost an island to herself. Geography tended to wall it in from caravan routes passing outside its borders. By way of contrast, the terrain of the Joseph tribes to the north was exposed to trade lines which connected Damascus, as a hub, with other points in the Near East. The roads running along the Mediterranean coasts turned eastward through the plain of Esdraelon, which served as the only important pass through the mountains of western Palestine. Whereas Judah remained largely isolated from outside contact and influence, the northern Joseph tribes were largely open to cosmopolitan influences. Thus, geography contributed to the rift which had been developing between north and south for a long while.

Not among the least important of the factors contributing to the disruption of the kingdom was the desire of many religious leaders to reactivate the old amphictyonic traditions. Ahijah, the prophet who prompted Jeroboam, stood unquestionably in the tradition which favored Samuel over Saul when he encouraged Jeroboam to act in response to Yahweh's will.[11] For Ahijah, the claim of the Davidic house to rule in perpetuity was not the guide

---

[11] I Kings 11:29–39.

in the selection of the new king. Covenant with Yahweh at Sinai had precedence over covenant with the house of David. Therefore, the restoration of the idealistic amphictyonic policy of selection by charismatic gift was attempted. This action indicates that part of the religious leadership still stood in the tradition of Samuel, who saw in kingship a violation of Yahweh's covenant with his people. Therefore, they reacted against one who had introduced forms of worship against the will of Yahweh. David, a man of simple and direct communion with God, could be endured, but the cold and worldly Solomon was an affront to their religious sensitivity. The Deuteronomic historian repeatedly makes clear Yahweh's judgment against Solomon for corruption of Yahwism. To officially condone and encourage the worship of deities other than Yahweh was abhorent to all devout Yahwists. The deep dissatisfaction of responsible religious leaders with the monarchy as typified by Solomon led them to press for a return to the amphictyony and charismatic leadership.

The Revolt (922 B.C.)

Any successor to Solomon, therefore, was in trouble from the outset. David with all his personal resources, charismatic and otherwise, had made a serious attempt to weld the diverse and incongruous parts of the kingdom, but Solomon followed with neither the popular personal magnetism, the religious commitment, nor the political astuteness of his father. The policies of David designed to bind the tribes together were abandoned by Solomon and a serious disruption was threatening at his death. Perhaps a man sensitive to the fires that caused the caldron to seethe could have avoided an open revolt. But Solomon's son was not that man.

On Solomon's death in 922 B.C., his son Rehoboam was immediately accepted as king by the tribes of the south, Judah and Benjamin. Strong supporters of the Davidic house, they were willing to accept Rehoboam by right of dynasty. Among the northern tribes, however, other forces were at work. Many desired to return to the ways of the old amphictyony in which individual tribes enjoyed a large amount of independence and freedom. They were not so closely tied to the house of David that they felt bound to one of his lineage. Also historic tradition dating from the ascension of David himself to the throne of all Israel required that the northern tribes ratify the kingship.[12] Anointing by a prophet of Yahweh was an important step in the selection of a new king. Since Ahijah was a recognized prophet, his earlier anointing of Jeroboam could not be disregarded merely because Jeroboam had been politically exiled in Egypt. (The northern tribes, therefore, appear to have reserved judgment on accepting Rehoboam until they had opportunity to question him. At Shechem, the sacred place of covenant renewal, the tribes assembled to make decision on Solomon's successor.)

When Rehoboam arrived at Shechem, the seething caldron spilled over. Jeroboam I, recalled from political exile in Egypt, led the delegation of northern tribes to approach the incoming monarch with a direct request for relaxation of the heavy burdens of Solomon in return for allegiance. The older advisors of Rehoboam suggested that he take advantage of this opportunity to gain support by making concessions, but the young men who had grown up with Rehoboam and likely envisioned a more splendid state than Solomon's advised that this was the time to assert authority. Rehoboam declared:

My little finger is thicker than my father's loins. And now, whereas my father laid upon you a heavy yoke, I will add to your yoke. My father chastised you with whips, but I will chastise you with scorpions. (I Kings 12:10b–11)

The response of the northern tribes was immediate.

What portion have we in David? We have no inheritance in the son of Jesse. To your tents, O Israel! Look now to your own house, David. (I Kings 12:16)

Their decision was final. The north wanted nothing to do with a continuation of the policies of Solomon. Jeroboam offered a hope of reform and return to religious and divine leadership as in the amphictyony. When Adoram, Rehoboam's labor captain, began to designate the hated corvée, the people killed him. Fearing for his own life, Rehoboam retreated to Jerusalem and Jeroboam was proclaimed king of the north. Rehoboam's first inclination was to enlist an army to force the rebellious north into

---

[12] II Samuel 5:1–3; I Kings 12:1.

subjection, but the intervention of the prophet Shemaiah, coupled with a possible threat from Jeroboam's old friend Shishak, saved possible civil war and extensive bloodshed.

Lines between north and south were now clearly drawn. The northern boundary of the tribe of Benjamin, about ten miles north of Jerusalem, became the dividing point. The major portion of Benjamin remained loyal to the house of David and joined Judah to form a political entity which bore the name of its major tribal group, "Judah." [13] The remainder of the tribes retained the name, "Israel." Following the revolt the latter group of tribes struggled unsuccessfully to recapture the ideal of charismatic rule, while the southern tribes strengthened the rule of David's dynasty. Thus, north and south went their separate ways. Although the prophets continued to think of Yahweh's people as an essential whole, the political unity so arduously achieved and difficultly maintained under Saul, David, and Solomon was gone forever.

Israel and Judah Compared

Following the division, the Deuteronomic historian tells the story of both Israel and Judah, but he is prejudiced in favor of Judah. His major concerns are the Jerusalem temple, the line of David, and the role of the prophets of Yahweh, whether in Israel or Judah. Purity of Yahwism is at the heart of his evaluation of the era of the divided kingdom.

The historian's concern is not to give a complete résumé of the histories of either Judah or Israel. In fact, he forthrightly refers the reader to sources for more information about the kings whose reigns he has sketched. The non-extant "Chronicles of the Kings of Israel" and "Chronicles of the Kings of Judah" provided a more extensive coverage of the history than that found in Kings. The Deuteronomic writer, however, recounts history to demonstrate a central conviction: infidelity to Yahweh brings destruction to both Israel and Judah. This premise had special application to Israel. Her rebellious rejection of the Yahweh cult which centered in the Jerusalem temple was the epitome of infidelity. Jeroboam was the prime culprit, and no Israelite king after him received the wholehearted endorsement of the historian. A re-

[13] The tribe of Simeon had been absorbed into Judah sometime during the period of the judges, if not before.

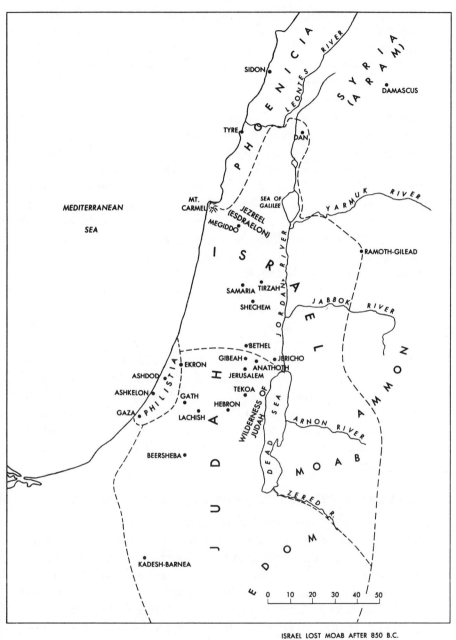

ISRAEL LOST MOAB AFTER 850 B.C.

JUDAH LOST EDOM AFTER 850 B.C.

Figure 7–1.   Kingdoms of Israel and Judah.

curring condemnation of each king knelled the doom of Israel: "He did what was evil in the sight of Yahweh, and walked in the way of Jeroboam and in his sin which he made Israel to sin." [14]

The revolt was a strange paradox in Israel's history. On the one hand, many religious leaders of the north fervently desired to revitalize the old amphictyonic order within which they believed the covenant relationship was given noblest expression. On the other hand, the historian, writing with conviction regarding the centralization of worship in Jerusalem, condemned the action of the northern tribes as heretical. Of course, what he denounced was not the amphictyonic ideal, but the rejection of Jerusalem worship. He believed that if the amphictyonic design were to be preserved, it would be preserved in Jerusalem. He praised or condemned kings of Judah according to their support of centralized worship in Jerusalem, a practice given impetus by David. Thus, the book of Kings provides a rationale for tracing Israel's religious heritage through the tribe of David, i.e., through Judah.

The northern kingdom continued for approximately two centuries after the death of Solomon before it was destroyed in 722/21 B.C. by the rising power of Assyria. Judah existed almost twice as long before she fell to the Babylonians in the early part of the sixth century B.C. Even after Jerusalem's destruction in 587 B.C., the history of Yahweh's people continued in a remnant of Judah. We shall, therefore, trace the course of Israel's development and then return to the revolt of 922 B.C. to consider Judah's story.

Jeroboam I (922–901 B.C.) and Beginning of Decline

The reign of Jeroboam I illustrates for the Deuteronomic historian the conspicuous idolatry which in his judgment characterized Israel (now designating only the northern tribes) throughout her history. "Jeroboam, the son of Nebat, who made Israel to sin" became an infamous epithet which not only condemned Jeroboam, but also emphasized Israel's continual apostasy.

When Jeroboam returned from Egypt and was proclaimed king of Israel, he immediately selected a strong center for his

14 Cf. I Kings 15:30,34.

Near Eastern Power of Influence in Palestine		Israel		Judah	
EGYPT					
918–Shishak invaded Judah		Jeroboam I	922–901	922–915	Rehoboam
				915–913	Abijah
SYRIA		Nadab	901–900	913–873	Asa
Benhadad I	c. 880–842	Baasha	900–877		
		Elah	877–876		
		Zimri	876		
		Tibni *	876–?		
		Omri *	876–869	873–849	Jehoshaphat
(853–Battle of Karkar)		Ahab	869–850		
		Ahaziah	850–849		
Hazael	c. 842–806	Jehoram	849–842	849–842	Jeroham or Joram
				842	Ahaziah
		Jehu	842–815	842–837	Athaliah
		Jehoahaz	815–801	837–800	Joash or Jehoash
		Joash	801–786	800–783	Amaziah
		Jeroboam II	786–746	783–742	Uzziah *
Rezon	c. 740–732	Zechariah	746–745	750–735	Jotham *
(732–Fall of Damascus to Assyria)		Shallum	745		
		Menahem	745–736		
ASSYRIA		Pekahiah	736–735		
Tiglath-pileser	745–727	Pekah	735–732	735–715	Ahaz
		Hoshea	732–722		
Shalmaneser V	727–722				
Sargon II	722–705				
(722/1–Fall of Samaria)		* Note a period of co-regency.			

Figure 7–2.   Israel, 922–722 B.C.

rule.   Shechem was the natural choice.   It had been the locale of the amphictyonic covenant renewal.   Solomon had used the site as the seat of one of his prefectures [15] and thereby made it a hub of administrative activity.   Consequently, Jeroboam "built" Shechem; that is, he fortified the city.   Evidence of this construction has been unearthed in recent excavations.[16]

Other building projects were undertaken by Israel's first king. Since Shechem, even with additional fortifications, was not a strong defensive location, Penuel was also fortified.   This town dominated the eastern road from the Jordan Valley and conse-

[15] Cf. Emil Kraeling, Bible Atlas, p. 213.

[16] See G. E. Wright, "Shechem: The Archaeology of the City" in The Biblical Archaeologist, XX (January, 1957), pp. 19–32. Also James F. Ross and Lawrence E. Toombs, "Three Campaigns at Biblical Shechem," Archaeology, XIV (September, 1961), pp. 171–179.

quently served as an outpost for the defense of Shechem. Tirzah was selected for the palace residence and remained the home of royalty until the days of Omri.

A more religiously significant action of Jeroboam was erection of shrines for worship of Yahweh at Dan and Bethel. The division of the kingdom had left Israel without the primary religious symbols of their faith: the temple and the Jerusalem priesthood. To allow Israelites to return to Jerusalem for religious observances was to risk their allegiance to the north. Jeroboam's solution was to construct sanctuaries at Dan in the northern part of Israel and at Bethel in the south. These centers were nearer than Jerusalem and more convenient to the Israelites. Golden calves at each site were the primary cult objects. Also, new priests (volunteers from the tribes) were provided to replace Levites who had migrated to Jerusalem at the time of the separation.

Some reasonable questions arise at this point. What was the meaning of the golden calves? Was this direct apostasy on the part of Jeroboam? Did Jeroboam intend to replace Yahweh worship with some native cultic practice? The answer to these questions is probably negative. In fact Jeroboam, himself designated to the throne by God's prophet, was a thorough Yahwist. He gave his sons names which depicted loyalty to Yahweh. Shrines at Dan and Bethel were for worship of Yahweh and not pagan deities. In the judgment of the historian Jeroboam is condemned not because he built idols to false gods, but because he established Israel's worship outside Jerusalem. To the historian this evidenced the folly of the revolt and Jeroboam had provided this primary symbol of Israel's apostasy.

The form of Jeroboam's cultic symbols may have been influenced by the practice of neighboring peoples who often represented their gods (visible or invisible) as standing or riding on animals.[17] For example, the storm god of Syria was pictured as riding upon a bull-calf. Like the cherubim in Solomon's temple, the golden calves were symbolic of the presence of the invisible Yahweh.

The uncritical masses, perhaps, could not make clear distinctions between calves as symbols and calves as objects of worship.

---

[17] See Wright, *Biblical Archaeology*, pp. 147–148.

Consequently, further syncretism with native Canaanite practice, which used bulls in the worship of El and Baal, was encouraged by the unfortunate introduction of the calf symbol. To this syncretism the later Israelite reformers reacted violently. Their condemnation of the "sin of Jeroboam" may account for the story about Aaron's golden calves. The account, set in the Mosaic era, served as a polemic against the shrines at Bethel and Dan.

Throughout the reign of Jeroboam intermittent conflict with Judah continued. Although it was largely subdued, there were some sporadic outbreaks of open violence. Such an outbreak occurred when Abijah was king of Judah. While the Kings account gives little importance to Abijah's victory, the book of Chronicles glamorizes it as one from which Jeroboam was unable to recover.

Following the reign of Jeroboam I, Israel struggled continuously. Internally, the stability of the crown became less and less sure. For a quarter of a century, there were abbreviated reigns, assassinations, and bloody attempts at the throne. Not a single king was able to maintain charismatic leadership. Not until the army commander Omri (876–869) led a successful revolt and placed himself on the throne did Israel experience any measure of stability. Externally, Israel remained at odds with Judah. Had not Shishak devastated Judah financially and crippled her militarily during Rehoboam's reign, Judah undoubtedly would have given Israel more trouble than she did. One of Judah's major interferences was the purchase of the Syrian King Benhadad's assistance in halting fortification of Ramah on Judah's border. This introduction of Syrian intervention in Israel-Judah affairs was portentous of greater Syrian intrusion to come.

FROM ZENITH TO NADIR: OMRI TO COLLAPSE OF NATION (I KINGS 16:21–II KINGS 17:24) [18]

Israel could not have endured much longer the instability of her first fifty years. The time of David and Solomon was past and men of their stature were not soon to be found, if ever. The complexion of the near eastern political scene had greatly changed and real return to charismatic rule was impossible. The loose

[18] Compare II Chronicles 18, 22–25.

structure of the amphictyony was ill-suited to survive the pressures of growing military threat from many points in the eastern world. In fact, by the second quarter of the ninth century the northern and eastern borders of Israel were shrinking with the encroachments of Benhadad of Syria. Also, after a two-hundred year nap Assyria was arousing from her slumber. Ashur-nasir-pal II, whose name was almost synonymous with brutality, was reaching Assyrian fingers of conquest into Upper Mesopotamia with longing eyes cast toward the Mediterranean. Egypt, though still dormant in strength, was always ready to use the Palestinian area as a buffer against the Asian powers.

If Israel were to survive in the power struggles of the east, the conflict between amphictyonic ideal and dynastic continuity had to be resolved. The man who was able to bring a measure of stability to Israel's throne in such a situation was Omri. He established a dynasty lasting for three generations and structured administrative policy which restored something of Israel's power and prosperity.

Omri (876–869 B.C.)

The Deuteronomic historian dismisses the rule of Omri with a brief discussion of eight verses,[19] evidently considering the reign of Omri to have contributed little to the religious history of Israel. With the conventional format Omri is condemned as provoking Yahweh to anger by following the ways of Jeroboam, who caused Israel to sin; that is, he did not destroy the shrines at Bethel and Dan and restore proper respect for the Jerusalem sanctuary. Nevertheless, Omri was undoubtedly a king of superior ability. His reign was comparatively brief and much of it was spent in securing the throne from his competitor, Tibni. But he restored so much stability to Israel's throne that long after his death, the Assyrians referred to Israel as "the land of the house of Omri."

Soon after the struggle with Tibni had been won, Omri began to exercise a foreign policy resembling that of David and Solomon. His objective was to establish strong relationships with neighbors around him. His plan extended to both Phoenicia and Judah.

[19] I Kings 16:21–28.

An alliance with Phoenicia was sealed by the marriage of Omri's son, Ahab, to Jezebel, the royal princess of Tyre. Although this alliance was to bear undesirable fruit in the religious history of Israel, its immediate result was valuable both politically and commercially. Phoenicia, long a prosperous and faithful ally, provided additional strength to Israel in confronting the rising threats of Syria and Assyria in the east. Further, Phoenician trade with the now-established posts of North Africa was at its peak. The alliance provided once again, as in the days of Solomon, expanded trade relations which brought considerable wealth to Israel's treasury. There may even have been an effort to rebuild the old and profitable port of Ezion-geber in the south.[20]

Even though lines of demarcation were now so well settled that reunification was practically impossible, Omri advocated cooperative endeavors between Judah and Israel. This desire was later implemented by the marriage of Athaliah, the daughter of Ahab (or his sister),[21] to Jehoram, a Judean prince.

Omri also had military success. An inscription on a Moabite monument, the Moabite Stone, suggests a successful campaign in Transjordan by which Moab was subjected. This inscription from Mesha, king of Moab contemporary with Ahab, states that ". . . Omri, king of Israel, he humbled Moab many years . . . Omri had occupied the land of Medeba, and (Israel) had dwelt there in his time . . ."[22] The Kings account elaborates that Mesha of Moab "had to deliver annually to the king of Israel a hundred thousand lambs, and the wool of a hundred thousand rams."[23] This is only one illustration of the strength with which Omri expanded the influence of Israel.

The primary monument to Omri's successful administration was his transfer of the capital to Samaria. Although Shechem was the natural capital of the north because of its amphictyonic associations, the town could not be easily defended. Even be-

[20] I Kings 22:48.
[21] II Kings 8:18; II Chronicles 21:6 list Athaliah as the daughter of Ahab; II Kings 8:26 and II Chronicles 22:2 have her as the daughter of Omri (R.S.V. granddaughter). The birth of her son around 864 B.C. indicates that she was not the daughter of Ahab and Jezebel, who had themselves been married only ten years at the time. She may have been a daughter of Ahab by another and earlier wife than Jezebel.
[22] Pritchard, *Ancient Near Eastern Texts*, p. 320.
[23] II Kings 3:4.

Figure 7–3. The Moabite Stone, discovered at Dibon in Transjordan, describes the victory of Mesha, the Moabite king, over Israel after the death of Ahab. The inscription also refers to Moab's earlier subjection to Omri. (Source: Louvre. Photograph by Archives Photographiques-Paris.)

fore the days of Omri, Tirzah had been utilized as capital by some of the minor kings of Israel. Now Omri chose a new city which was more aligned with his affinities toward Phoenicia. Lying seven miles northwest of Shechem, it was the gateway to the commanding plain of Esdraelon and consequently to Phoenicia. The strategic significance of the city is confirmed by the extensive use of the site during the Greek and Roman periods. Its location on the summit of a gently-sloping hill made it almost impregnable to standard tactical assault. Three walls around the hill begun by Omri and completed by Ahab provided a formidable defense against outside invaders. A century later mighty Assyria could capture the capital only after extended siege.[24] Samaria remained the capital throughout the duration of Israel's history. Like Jerusalem it became a hub of life in Palestine but to the later prophets the name of the town became a symbol of the sin and idolatry of the northern kingdom. As a place of "strength, fertility and beauty combined," however, its equal in all Palestine would be difficult to find.[25]

Undoubtedly the strength brought to Israel's throne by Omri prolonged her life and restored something of the splendor of Solomon's reign. But also like the time of Solomon, this day of Omri's prosperity was accompanied by an internal moral deterioration later to be denounced vehemently by Amos and Hosea.

Ahab (869–850 B.C.)

Policies begun by his father were largely continued by Ahab. The fortification of Samaria was completed and adornments of elaborate ivory work were added to her buildings. The "pool of Samaria" [26] may have been built by him. He also built at Megiddo and in Transjordan.[27] The procedure of friendly arrangements with neighboring nations was continued. Jezebel assured Phoenicia's friendship and the course of events during the early days of Ahab's reign indicates his willingness to be friendly to both Judah and Syria.

The very complicated relationship between Israel and Syria is not easily reconstructed. The Kings narrative [28] is unclear and contemporary records are of little help in determining the se-

[24] Although the hill of Samaria was greatly disturbed by Greek and Roman builders, it has been extensively excavated. Here George A. Reisner and Clarence S. Fisher, working in 1908–1910, developed their now famous stratigraphical method of digging. Instead of cutting trenches across the mound, they excavated small areas, carefully recording all findings so as to be able to reconstruct on paper the entire site. This procedure has contributed greatly to the gigantic strides taken by archaeology during the last half century.

[25] Edward Robinson, *Biblical Researches in Palestine*, II (1941), pp. 307–309 as quoted in Wright, *Biblical Archaeology*, p. 151.

[26] I Kings 22:38.

[27] Cf. Wright, *Biblical Archaeology*, p. 153.

[28] I Kings 20.

quence of events. Evidently a struggle existed between Ben-hadad, the Syrian king, and Ahab which lasted many years. Initially Samaria was attacked by Benhadad who won a nominal victory. Benhadad conducted a second campaign on the plain of Esdraelon, since Israel's god was considered "a god of the hills." Here a resounding Israelite victory culminated with Ben-hadad, rope about his neck, bowed before Ahab pleading for mercy. Ahab was surprisingly lenient and spared the Syrian's life. The only indemnity demanded was restoration of certain border cities and a covenant of alliance. Since mercy was un-expected from a victor dealing with the vanquished, how can Ahab's action be reconciled to the usual contemporary practice?

Leniency from one so long antagonized by Benhadad is evi-dence of the political astuteness and farsightedness of Ahab. For two or three centuries the power of Assyria had become more and more evident. Since Assyria's early westward movements around the turn of the eleventh century (Tiglath-pileser I), her imperialistic designs had become increasingly feared by Phoeni-cia, Syria, and Israel. The brutal Ashur-nasir-pal II (883–859) had renewed the Assyrian drive toward the Mediterranean and his successor, Shalmaneser III (859–824), actually reached for the whole of the Fertile Crescent. Undoubtedly this mounting threat of Assyrian might influenced Ahab to act kindly toward Benhadad. Half a friend with military strength was better than none in such days.

The annals of the conquests of Shalmaneser [29] provide ade-quate and reliable information about the struggle between As-syria and the smaller and weaker states near the Mediterranean. Benhadad of Syria organized a coalition of resistance composed of twelve kings of the Syria-Palestine region. "Ahab the Israelite," was one of three key leaders of the coalition. Ahab contributed a major force of ten thousand foot soldiers and two thousand chariots. Battle was joined in the vicinity of Karkar on the Orontes. Shalmaneser claimed an overwhelming victory, but if there were a victory, it was not complete enough to allow Shal-maneser either to take Damascus or to march into the territory of Israel.

[29] Cf. Pritchard, *Ancient Near Eastern Texts,* pp. 276–277.

Biblical data do not mention the battle of Karkar. However, the fact that the annals of Shalmaneser date the battle precisely in the sixth year of his reign (853 B.C.) makes this a pivotal event for Old Testament chronology. Since the battle of Karkar can be placed with some degree of accuracy in the reign of Ahab, it provides a point of reference for calculating surrounding events.

That the victory of Shalmaneser was not as overwhelming as he claimed is witnessed by the breakup of the Israelite-Syrian coalition soon thereafter. Evidently both Benhadad and Ahab felt Assyria was no longer an eminent threat. Soon there was a resurgence of conflict between these two. This time the focus of contention was the city Ramoth in Gilead. Again looking for increased numerical strength against the Syrians, Ahab accomplished a coalition with Jehoshaphat of Judah. In contrast with their omission of Karkar, biblical historians give extended attention to the campaign for Ramoth-gilead. In the account [30] Micaiah, the true prophet of Yahweh, braved a threat of opposition by "4000 false prophets" and portrayed approaching disaster for Israel. In spite of his efforts to "confuse the oracle," Ahab lost his life in the struggle for Ramoth-gilead.

According to the Deuteronomist, the reign of Ahab provided the setting for one of the major tests for Yahwism in the northern kingdom. The king's Phoenician wife Jezebel was an ardent missionary for her native deity Baal Melkart and also a strong believer in the absolute powers of a king. She was so very successful that had it not been for the heroic intervention of the Yahwistic prophets, Micaiah, Elijah and Elisha, the nation would have been won over to a Phoenician expression of Canaanite fertility, and kingship in Israel would have lost its Yahwistic commitment and ethical foundation.

The two sons of Ahab to succeed him on the throne were in their father's ignoble tradition and the prophet Elisha took the initiative to end the dynasty. For years Israel and Syria had been dissipating their strength by perpetual conflict with each other over Ramoth-gilead, instead of allying themselves with one another to resist the growing threat of Assyria, as they had done at Karkar. Elisha both lent encouragement to the Syrian Hazael to

[30] I Kings 22.

usurp the throne of Syria and commissioned the anointing of an Israelite army captain named Jehu as king. The army backed the newly anointed, and a revolution was on. A blood purge destroyed the house of Ahab and Jehu founded a new dynasty.

The Jehu Dynasty

For all its religious overtones the revolution led by Jehu was a political disaster. It is true that he established a dynasty of some stability. Jehu (842–815) ruled Israel for twenty-seven years and four kings of his house extended his dynasty over Israel for almost a hundred years. Jehu's dynasty was the longest lived in Israel's history. And yet, Israel was set on a course leading to political and religious disaster.

For one thing, the enstrengthening alliance and friendship with Phoenicia that had prevailed since the days of David was now forever broken. The profitable exchange through the ports of her sea-faring neighbor was lost to Israel. Also, the reprisals of Jehu had damaging repercussions in Judah. Whereas the Omrides had fostered friendly relations with Judah, Jehu's purge included Ahaziah of Judah, who was also of the house of Omri. This action extended the revolution against the Omrides in Israel to the royal house of Judah and widened the chasm separating the two kingdoms.

Further, whatever had remained of western coalition against Assyria was obliterated. Rather than unite with his neighbors to resist the growing power of Assyria, Jehu chose the way of concession. Soon after the revolution, Assyria under the aggressive Shalmaneser III began moving westward again toward the Mediterranean. Instead of rallying to the support of Israel's only buffer against Assyria, as Ahab had done at Karkar, Jehu purchased his own protection from Shalmaneser with tribute. The black obelisk of Shalmaneser depicts the scene of Jehu's humiliation. He is portrayed as prostrate before Shalmaneser, forehead to the ground, acknowledging the sovereignty of Assyria. This expedient compromise led Hazael of Syria to take devastating retaliation on Jehu. When Shalmaneser had returned to Assyria, Hazael launched a campaign against Israel which not only "threshed Gilead with threshing sledges of iron," [31] but also brought Israel very near the point of extermination.

[31] Amos 1:3.

Figure 7-4. The black obelisk of Shalmaneser III of Assyria recording the military achievements of the first thirty-one years of his reign. (Source: Courtesy of the Oriental Institute, University of Chicago.)

Thus, Jehu, who lived by the sword, died by the sword. His reign by military strength ended a failure. Israel was brought to humiliating extremity. Jehu was weakly succeeded by his son Jehoahaz (815–801), and all during these years "the anger of Yahweh was kindled against Israel" (II Kings 13:3). Israel's military strength was reduced to a mere fifty horsemen, ten chariots, and ten thousand footmen.[32] Thus, during the last quarter

[32] II Kings 13:7.

Figure 7–5. Close up of panel showing "Jehu, son of Omri" bowed before Shalmaneser and his Assyrian attendants. This is the only contemporary representation of an Israelite king. Jehu brought tribute of "silver, gold, a golden bowl, a golden vase with pointed bottom, golden tumblers, golden buckets, tin, a staff for a king. . . ." (Source: Trustees of the British Museum.)

of the ninth century, Israel was reduced to the status of a dependency of Syria.

Israel's circumstances, however, were dramatically changed during the days of the next two kings of the Jehu dynasty. Joash (801–786) and Jeroboam II (786–746). The occasion for this reversal was another of the frequent resurgences of Assyria which abruptly broke the ascendancy of Syria. Just prior to the reign of Joash a campaign by Assyria crushed Damascus (in 802) and threatened Israel. Internal dissensions, however, prohibited Assyria's further move westward and once again Israel enjoyed peace because of the weakness of her neighbors. Joash took advantage of the occasion to recoup Israel's strength.

The stellar gem in the Jehu dynasty, however, was Jeroboam II. Although the Kings narrative discloses little about the events of his reign, he evidently was a leader of great importance. Contemporary to Jeroboam's reign was the rule of Uzziah (Azariah) in Judah. Both men were capable rulers and under their leadership the territories of Israel and Judah were extended "from the entrance of Hamath as far as the Sea of the Arabah," (II Kings

14:25) the limits of the old Davidic kingdom. Geographical expansion was accompanied by tremendous and sudden internal prosperity. With both Syria and Assyria preoccupied with difficulties, control of the great trade routes fell once again to Israel. In a span of a quarter century Jeroboam II was able to bring a nation tottering on the brink of abysmal destruction to the verge of glory unknown since the days of Solomon. Excavations at Samaria have brought to light ostraca from this period reflecting an extensive fiscal organization which surely brought wealth into the coffers of Jeroboam II.[33]

Decay and Downfall

The social consequences of this sudden prosperity, however, were destructive. Empty rituals, drunkenness, violation of the poor, and temple prostitution were characteristic of the growing internal decay rapidly eclipsing the abbreviated external prosperity achieved by Jeroboam. Two prophets, Amos and Hosea, sought courageously and forthrightly to correct the moral and religious course Israel had taken, but the prophetic word of Yahweh went unheard essentially and the nation's moral decadence worsened. Jeroboam's death was followed by twenty-four years of continued degeneration of the social structure and instability of leadership which, along with the reviving potency of Assyria, spelled certain disaster for the people of the northern kingdom.

In the decade following Jeroboam's death, Israel had five kings, none of whom could provide able leadership for the nation. Zechariah (746–745) had been in power only six months when he was assassinated by Shallum (745). After only a month's rule the latter was liquidated by Menahem (745–736), who maintained his control by paying tribute to Assyria. Menahem was followed by his son Pekahiah (736–735), who was promptly eliminated by one of his military officers Pekah (735–732). Such anarchy and instability, coupled with the internal sickness decried by the prophets, made Israel's resistance to Assyria only nominal. Destruction of the nation was at hand. "Her ship of state, leaking at every seam, without compass or competent helmsmen and with its crew demoralized, was sinking." [34]

[33] Wright, *Biblical Archaeology,* p. 158.
[34] Bright, *A History of Israel,* p. 254.

The major political factor in the downfall of the northern kingdom was the restoration of Assyrian power. No name of this era is comparable to that of Tiglath-pileser III (designated in the biblical account as Pul), who came to the Assyrian throne about the time of Jeroboam II's death around 746 B.C. Tiglath-pileser was an extremely capable and energetic ruler. After securing the Assyrian neighborhood, he directed his ambitions toward the west. While Syria and Egypt were his primary targets, Israel's strategiç position as the bridge of the Fertile Crescent made her involvement a foregone conclusion. Tiglath-pileser was exceedingly successful in his westward march and soon was receiving tribute from most of the states of Syria and northern Palestine. In 732 B.C. Damascus fell to him and Israel's buffer was gone. Now she stood naked and exposed to the direct onslaughts of Pul.

Tiglath-pileser's control of the west persisted until his death in 727 B.C. Hoshea (732–722), who followed Pekah to Israel's throne, took Pul's death as a signal for revolt. Hoshea refused to pay tribute to the new Assyrian monarch, Shalmaneser V, who consequently moved against Israel. Samaria did manage to withstand a three-year siege, thus validating Omri's choice of the city as an easily defendable capital. However, Shalmaneser's successor, Sargon II, was able to destroy both the city and nation in 722/21 B.C.

Instead of the usual procedure of exacting tribute and demanding allegiance, Sargon deported and dispersed many of the Israelites across his vast domain. According to Assyrian records twenty-seven thousand, two hundred and ninety Israelites were resettled beyond Mesopotamia. These deportees were replaced by displaced people from other areas of the Assyrian empire. The amalgamation of these imports with the remaining natives resulted in a half-breed folk referred to in the New Testament as Samaritans. As far as the Deuteronomist was concerned, the tribes of the north were lost to the elect nation of Israel. The prophets would plead for a re-identification of the north with the "new Israel," but the fall of Samaria marked for the Deuteronomist the natural end for a revolt born and bred in the spirit of apostasy.

The march toward destruction, presaged by the prophets Amos and Hosea, moved forward as though no recourse for escape had been presented. Without repentance or return to covenant fidelity, Israel as a nation was doomed. Outside the covenant they were not Yahweh's people and he was not their God. Yahweh had "sent her away with a decree of divorce." [35] A covenant broken was no longer a covenant. Having turned from Yahweh to the world, they were now of that which they chose. Still there was hope for her return and salvation, but for the moment only Judah remained to face, as had her sister, the choice between covenant fidelity or a destiny similar to Israel's.

ORIGINS OF PROPHECY IN ISRAEL

Prophecy came into prominence in Israel during the period of the monarchy. This was at a fairly advanced stage in ancient Israel's faith and worship. Prophecy represented both a challenge to and a confirmation of age-old sacral institutions of law and cult. The prophetic movement in Israel developed into something distinctively Israelite when men like Amos or Isaiah spoke "the word of Yahweh" to communities confronted with critical situations, but its origins were dependent upon the traditions of Israel's neighbors, especially those in Canaan.

Prophecy in the Ancient Near East

Prophetic figures of many types were found throughout the Mediterranean world. Sacred texts from Mesopotamia mention an important class of divinatory priests [36] whose function was the pronouncement of oracular words from the deity. By divination of various omens [37] they discovered and proclaimed the divine answer to perplexing questions. Their oracles were considered

---

[35] Jeremiah 3:8.

[36] The Akkadian word is *baru*, "to behold," and refers to ritual divination. Cf. Alfred Haldar, *Associations of Cult Prophets Among the Ancient Semites* for a good study of the pre-Israel prophetic groups.

[37] Among the many kinds of omens the following were most common: observation of oil and water in a cup, observation of entrails of sacrificial animals (especially the liver), observation of celestial phenomena (astrology), birth omens, physiognomical omens, observation of the flight of birds, interpretation of dreams of others, dream visions experienced by the priests themselves.

the "message of the gods," and were recorded as "omen texts" to be consulted any time that a similar omen should occur.

Working alongside these divinatory priests was another group characterized by ecstatic trance.[38] Their function was to receive oracles through a trance state in which their minds had gone forth to be replaced by the breath (spirit) of God. The trance was induced by raving frenzy and oracles spoken from this ecstatic state were considered the very word of the deity. These divinatory ecstatics were organized into prophetic guilds, the members of which were called "sons." Such prophetic bands were not unlike bands of ecstatic prophets found in Israel in the closing days of the amphictyony.

Texts from Mari, the great Amorite city of the second millennium B.C., speak of the "man of Dagan" who was a messenger with a specific divine commission to fulfill. He appeared "unasked and unbidden with a definite divine charge." As proof of his prophetic authority he introduced himself with the words, "The God Dagan has sent me." The similarity to the Old Testament description of the prophets of Israel is unmistakable and cannot be accidental. Some roots, then, of Israelite prophecy go back to the Amorite heritage from which Israel sprang.[39]

Prophetic guilds also operated in Canaan. In fact, ecstatic prophecy is more characteristic of Canaanite religion than of any other. The Egyptian Wen-Amon's account of his travels is especially illuminating. In describing his adventures in the Canaanite city of Byblos he said,

While he (the prince of Byblos) was making offering to his gods, the god seized one of his youths and made him possessed. . . . And while the possessed youth was having his frenzy on this night, I had already found a ship headed for Egypt and had loaded everything I had into it.[40]

That this type of ecstasy was also characteristic of the prophets of Baal we know from the Old Testament itself, where their orgiastic frenzy is well attested.[41]

---

[38] Akkadian *mahhu*, "to rave," or Sumerian *uddu*, "to go forth." The reference clearly is to ecstasy.

[39] A thorough analysis of the relationship between the prophets of Mari and those of Israel and the meaning of this relationship for our understanding of the Old Testament may be found in Martin Noth, "History and the Word of God in the Old Testament," *Bulletin of the John Rylands Library*, XXXII (1950), pp. 194–206.

[40] Pritchard, *Ancient Near Eastern Texts*, p. 26.

[41] I Kings 18:28–29.

The earliest prophets of Israel bear a striking resemblance to all of these divinatory and ecstatic religious functionaries, and the first bands of them encountered in the books of Samuel can hardly be distinguished from their Near Eastern counterparts. Quite probably, therefore, the Israelite prophetic movement is their adaptation of a religious office common to their world. Doubtless Israel had been acquainted with "prophets" even before they were formed as a people or a nation, i.e., in the pre-Exodus-Conquest experiences of their forefathers. The settlement in Canaan brought them into intimate contact with a prophetic movement of a flamboyant type. Thus exposed to the ecstasy and prophesying of their Canaanite neighbors, some of the Israelites themselves began to, as the Old Testament puts it, "play the prophet."

Prophetic Terminology

Several words are used in the Old Testament to describe the prophet. The most important of these are *ro'eh*, "seer"; *hozeh*, "seer" or "visionary"; and *nab'i*, "spokesman." The first two of these words reflect the divinatory side of Israelite prophecy and are often used in a verbal form in introductions to prophetic oracles. The book of Amos opens, "The words of Amos, who was among the shepherds of Tekoa, which he saw (*hozeh*) . . ." [42] The books of Nahum and Obadiah are described as visions (*hazon* from *hozeh*) of the prophet. [43] The precise meaning of these two words should not be overstressed, however, since they are roughly synonymous with the more widely used and more inclusive term *nab'i*.

The word *nab'i* is the most important of the prophetic words, but its precise meaning cannot be etymologically determined. [44] Among the many suggestions which have been made, the most attractive trace the word to an Akkadian root *nabu*, "to announce," "to call." If the word is taken in the active sense, the prophet (*nab'i*) is "one who announces" or, if the form is taken as passive, "one who has been called." It does not stretch the facts too far to say that in a real sense both are true. The prophets of Israel

[42] Amos 1:1.
[43] Nahum 1:1 and Obadiah 1:1.
[44] A good resume of the literature on the word *nab'i* is found in H. H. Rowley, "Old Testament Prophecy and Recent Study," in *The Servant of the Lord and Other Essays on the Old Testament*, pp. 96 ff.

were "called" of Yahweh to "announce" his word. The clearest illustration of what the Old Testament means by *nab'i* is found in Exodus 7:1.

And Yahweh said to Moses, "See, I make you as God to Pharaoh; and Aaron your brother shall be your *nab'i* (spokesman)."

Beginnings of the Prophetic Movement in Israel

Among the Israelites Yahweh had always had "spokesmen" who interpreted history in terms of the divine will and who saw Israel as a people peculiarly responsible to the sovereign God. Not, however, until the crisis days of the ending amphictyony does the Old Testament mention prophetic bands similar to those of Canaan and the rest of the Ancient Near East. The spirit of Yahweh which had rested upon the judges in times of trouble, empowering them to defeat the enemies of his people, now came to rest upon the prophets filling them with the irrepressible word of Yahweh. I Samuel 9 and 10 presents a vivid picture of Samuel as a seer or diviner who was associated with a group of roving ecstatics. Saul, the young Israelite king-to-be, seeking information about the lost asses of his father, came to Samuel, an old and respected diviner who upon payment of a price would consult the oracle of Yahweh. After supplying information about the whereabouts of the lost animals, Samuel went further and arranged for Saul to meet a band of ecstatic prophets who roamed in the vicinity. Saul did as instructed and encountered a strange group "playing the prophet" to the accompaniment of harp, tambourine, flute, and lyre. Clearly these were ecstatics. When Saul met the prophetic band, "the spirit of Yahweh came mightily upon him, and he prophesied among them." [45] Infected by the ecstasy of this strange group, Saul himself became ecstatic and played the *nab'i*.

Later in the story Samuel is associated directly with the ecstatic bands. Always, however, Samuel, as the man of Yahweh, stands above the group. We are told that he was a man held in honor because "all that he says comes true." [46] This indeed was one of the tests of true prophecy in later Israelite tradition. [47] In Samuel,

[45] I Samuel 10:10.
[46] I Samuel 9:6.
[47] Cf. Deuteronomy 18:21–22.

then, there is the merger of two functions, divination and ecstasy, both to obtain a word (oracle) from God. Also we see in Samuel the beginnings of Israelite prophecy as it transcended the milieu which gave it birth. The prophetic movement in Israel, at least as represented by the prophets at its spiritual center, appears as a radical and enhancing transformation and refinement of Ancient Near Eastern prophetism. The Israelite called by Yahweh to be his spokesman confronted his people with a message of ethical and moral integrity unmatched in the ancient world. Like his Near Eastern counterparts, he at times was a diviner. He might even (and often did) obtain his "word from Yahweh" in an ecstatic trance, but the content of his message set him apart. The Israelite prophets were distinguished from those of other cultures because they stood in the council of Yahweh whom they believed to be righteous, holy, and sovereign.

The Prophetic Consciousness [48]

Conspicuous in the Samuel accounts of the beginnings of Israelite prophecy is the role played by the spirit of Yahweh. The ecstatics there began to play the *nab'i* when "the spirit of God came mightily upon them." The same is true of the later classical prophets, although the latter more often spoke of possession by God's word than possession by his spirit. What sort of phenomenon was this spirit possession? It was the Israelite equivalent of the ecstatic experience of the prophets in the remainder of the ancient world and more.

In the wilderness of Sinai the "spirit of Yahweh" filled the artisans who designed and made the ornamentation for the tabernacle.[49] By the power of the "spirit" which came upon them the military judges defeated the enemies of the people of Yahweh.[50] When the "spirit of Yahweh" came mightily upon Samson, he killed Philistines and took their property to pay a bet.[51] "In the

---

[48] The writers are dependent upon the work of A. R. Johnson for much of the material in this section. Cf. *The Cultic Prophet in Ancient Israel; The One and the Many in the Israelite Conception of God;* and *The Vitality of the Individual in the Thought of Ancient Israel.*

[49] Exodus 35:30–35.

[50] Judges 3:10; 11:29.

[51] Judges 14:19.

spirit" he slew the Philistine host with the jawbone of an ass.[52] And, as we have seen, the "spirit of Yahweh" fell upon the ecstatics in Samuel's day and caused them to play the *nab'i*. This invasive power of presence, then, performed a variety of tasks in the course of the Old Testament narrative, coming upon men and inspiring them to the extraordinary. In a more refined way the great prophets of Israel felt themselves captured by the divine spirit and in them the spirit of Yahweh did its noblest work.

In what sense were the prophets aware of this divine presence? Doubtless both ecstasy and divination were media of revelation, but they were by no means the only ways by which Yahweh was known by his servants. Visions or dreams, and ordinary events and sights became instruments which reminded a prophet of the divine will for a particular moment or situation. The very diversity of prophetic personalities and backgrounds indicates that no one means would sufficiently explain their inspiration. Amos was an indignant herdsman; Hosea, husband of an unfaithful wife; Isaiah, a man of station in Jerusalem; Jeremiah, a descendant of a line of outcast priests; Ezekiel, a priest in exile. All, however, were men in communication with Yahweh.

The prophet was first and foremost a man caught by Yahweh, whatever the means. In fact, he was one into whom the very personality of God had been extended. When the prophet spoke, it was as if, or was, Yahweh who spoke. In the symbolic acts of the prophets it was Yahweh who acted. The totality of the prophetic being was lifted up into the "spirit of Yahweh" and Yahweh's personality was extended into him so that he became an instrument of the divine will.

Israelites believed that man was a center of vital power and his personality extended beyond the body into all that he has and even beyond that. It could be imparted to others. The spoken word was for them an objective thing carrying with it the personality of the person who uttered it. Thus, both blessing and curse had potent power and, once uttered, could not be changed —words could not be retracted until they accomplished their purpose—the one cursed was cursed, the one blessed was blessed. Remember Isaac's word to Esau when he discovered that he

---

[52] Judges 15:14, 15.

mistakenly had given Jacob the blessing intended for the older Esau.

> Who was it then that hunted game and brought it to me, and I ate it all before you came and I have blessed him? . . . *yes, and he shall be blessed.* (Genesis 27:33)[53]

In a similar way one's personality extended into one's name. As long, therefore, as the name continued, the personality remained. Hence, the birth of a male heir who would preserve the family name created excitement.[54] The personality also extended into one's household and even into one's servants.

In a higher sense this also was true of Yahweh. Even more than man he is a center of vitality which can be extended into the world of his creation. He was present in his name. When his name was uttered, Yahweh presented himself in the midst of his people. In this light the familiar Priestly benediction takes on new depths of meaning.

> Yahweh bless you and keep you:
> Yahweh make his face to shine upon you,
>   and be gracious to you:
> Yahweh lift up his countenance upon
>   you, and give you peace.
> *So shall they put my name upon the people of*
> *Israel, and I will bless them.* (Numbers 6:24–27) [55]

More important for an understanding of prophecy is the extension of the divine personality through Yahweh's spirit and word. Through his spirit he was with men, his personality entered into them making them his men. The prophetic ideal was to be in accord with the spirit of Yahweh which had entered into his spokesman.

> Create in me a clean heart, O God,
>   and put a new and right spirit within me.
> Cast me not away from thy presence,
>   and take not thy holy Spirit from me.
> Restore to me the joy of thy salvation,
>   and uphold me with a willing spirit. (Psalm 51:10–12)

When the prophet was in accord with the spirit of Yahweh, he was the temporary extension of Yahweh's personality. Though

---

53 Emphasis added.
54 Deuteronomy 25:5 ff.
55 Emphasis added.

the *nab'i* remained himself. Yahweh had taken the human personality up into himself. Yahweh's spirit had entered into him
transforming him into a *man of God.* When he spoke, he spoke
the words of Yahweh. Something of God was present in the
prophetic word and extended into history not to return until it
accomplished its purpose.[56] The word was uttered and the situation changed—made different by the word which was in some
sense creative of the event about which it was spoken.

Israel's prophets were not merely frenzied ecstatics, like some
of their Ancient Near Eastern counterparts. Although for some
of them ecstasy did occur, their certainty that they were commissioned by Yahweh did not rest on ecstatic experiences, but on
the conviction that they had received Yahweh's clear intelligible
word, filled with moral and religious content.[57] The prophet, in
Israel, was one who had a sense of audition and vocation. He was
a prophet because he had stood in the presence of Yahweh and
could do no other than speak.

Such an assurance was a personal thing. There was no objective way to prove the experience. The true prophets of Israel
were, consequently, faced again and again with the soul-rending
question as to the validity of their prophetic word—a question
forced upon them by the presence in Israel of other prophets
whose messages did not coincide with those proclaimed by the
true prophets. These other prophets also claimed the presence
of Yahweh's spirit. How then could an Amos or Jeremiah be certain that he was right and those who disagreed with him wrong?
How did they know that their message came from Yahweh and
was not merely the projection of their own views and desires?

They could judge some prophets false because they were men
of immoral life whose messages corresponded to their character.
They were professionals who prophesied for hire and consequently
spoke what their employers wanted to hear. This caused them
to be dishonest in their use of prophetic revelation. They lacked
originality, mimicked genuine prophetic oracles, and passed off
lying dreams as real prophetic visions.[58]

---

[56] Isaiah 55:10–11.

[57] Sigmund Mowinckel, "Ecstatic Experience and Rational Elaboration in Old
Testament Prophecy," *Acta Orientalia*, XIII (1935), p. 287, as quoted by O. Eissfeldt in "The Prophetic Literature," *Old Testament and Modern Study*, p. 140.

[58] These criticisms were delineated by John Skinner, *Prophecy and Religion*,
pp. 191–194.

The true prophet was not validated, however, simply through judgment upon his opponents. His message could be distinguished as genuine in and of itself. Certainly the true prophet spoke not for hire, but because of an impulse to speak independent of, and often contrary to, his own volition. He felt a compulsion to utter words which were as "fire in his bones." The power of the prophet's word came from Yahweh. The prophetic oracle had a rational content consistent with Yahweh's will as known in history and could thus stand the test of time. What the true prophet said had moral worth and immediate relevance, although often contrary to what his audience wanted to hear. Consequently, in the last analysis the real proof of the prophet's message lay deep in the prophetic personality. He *knew* he was a true prophet standing in personal relation to Yahweh. This immediate consciousness of having the mind of Yahweh was the ultimate secret of prophetic inspiration. H. H. Rowley has summed it up well:

What is really vital is the relation of the prophet and his word to God. The prophet who is properly so called was a man who knew God in the immediacy of experience, who felt an inescapable constraint to utter what he was profoundly convinced was the word of God, and whose word was at bottom a revelation of the nature of God no less than of His will, who saw the life of men in the light of his vision of God, and who saw the inevitable issue of that life, who therefore declared that issue and pleaded with man to avoid it by cleansing and renewing their lives. He was a true prophet in the measure of his experience of God, and the measure of his experience was the measure of his receptiveness and of his response to it.[59]

Prophecy Before the Classical Period

The classical period of Israelite prophecy began in the eighth century B.C. with the ministries of Amos and Hosea. Already before this there were *nebi 'im* like Samuel whose activity contributed to the later full development of prophetic faith. These early prophets were not of a single type, and generalities about them would be misleading. In fact, the prophetic movement was never a singular homogeneous movement apart from the conviction characteristic of every true prophet that he spoke Yahweh's word in his own particular context. Consequently,

[59] H. H. Rowley, "The Nature of Prophecy in the Light of Recent Study," in *The Servant of the Lord and Other Essays on the Old Testament*, p. 128.

rather than trace any specific lines of prophetic development, it
seems better to discuss some significant early prophets.

Gad and Nathan in the Reign of David. Two prophetic figures
appear in the traditions about David. Gad is a seer who acts as a
herald and minister of the will of Yahweh supplying the king
with oracular words from the deity. He also rebuked the king
for action which he thought inappropriate. Nothing else about
Gad is told. Nathan, however, is distinctly represented as divinatory prophet and court politician. He is influential in the intrigue through which Solomon's succession to the throne was
achieved and participated in Solomon's coronation. He was not,
however, in the strictest sense a court functionary—at least, he
does not appear as such in the court lists of David or Solomon (II
Sam. 8:15–18; I Kings 4:1–6). Nathan was active in religious
matters and influenced to some degree the construction of the
Jerusalem temple. Of greater importance, however, for the later
character of prophecy is the fact that he applied moral sanctions to
the king when with typical prophetic utterance he judged David
with the parable of the ewe lamb. This belongs to that grand
tradition of prophecy that leads through Elijah to the classical
prophets.

Micaiah ben Imlah. That prophets were not typically spokesmen for the court or the establishment is further illustrated in the
story of Micaiah ben Imlah. This prophet, as already noted,
predicted tragedy for Ahab at Ramoth-gilead and provides an
interesting insight into the nature of prophetism in the early
divided monarchy. During the reign of Ahab, a staff of "official"
prophets had been maintained about the court at court expense.
Jezebel maintained a force of prophets of her own, estimated by
the historian as four hundred and fifty. These corps functioned
as formal consultants to the king and queen. The gregarious nature of the ecstatics simply enhanced this function.

Micaiah and his contemporary Elijah stood in marked contrast
to these official prophets. They stood alone and spoke upon the
impulse of their own experience with Yahweh. Micaiah, in opposition to both the desires of the king and the views of the
majority of the prophets, presented the word of Yahweh as he
understood it. His message did not support the throne; it spelled

out doom and disaster. Micaiah, then, stood outside of the ranks of official prophetism. For the first time prophet of woe stood opposed to prophet of weal, expressing both an idea and an attitude which would characterize prophecy for the next several centuries. Prophetic independence of the throne was established so that oracles of denunciation were often directed toward the throne. In prophetic thought following Micaiah and Elijah the maintenance of the monarchy was unnecessary to the preservation of the best of Israelite faith.

Baal vs. Yahweh: The Work of Elijah. The prophetic sections incorporated in I Kings, chapters 17–19 and 21,[60] mirror Israel's religion as interpreted by Micaiah and his prophetic contemporaries. The narratives about Elijah are not homogeneous and are complicated but their details bear the stamp of history and individuality. The picture painted is one of struggle between the native fertility faith of Canaan and the historic Yahweh faith of Israel. In the portrayal Jezebel is a heroine championing the cause of the Baalim and Elijah is the hero of Yahweh. The historical background is the reign of Ahab.

The contract marriage which brought the Tyrian princess Jezebel to Israel as the wife of Ahab may have been a wise political move, but it threatened disaster for Israel's religion. Jezebel, a devotee of the Phoenician Baal Melkart, became queen with a consuming passion to make her god the god of Israel. The Canaanite fertility religion, of which the worship of Melkart was only one expression,[61] had been a major threat to Yahweh worship since Israel's arrival in Canaan. But now this particular type of cult had an ardent missionary. Ahab, following the earlier pattern of Solomon, constructed a temple of Baal in Samaria for Jezebel's benefit.[62] Jezebel, apparently with the king's sanction, began an enthusiastic effort to make Melkart the only god of Israel. Against her missionary measures stood the masses' traditional allegiance to Yahweh. Consequently, Jezebel created a

[60] The Septuagint reflects the unity of these chapters by placing Chapter 21 immediately after Chapter 19.

[61] Excavations at Ras Shamra in northern Syria have uncovered numerous Canaanite religious texts. From these we have learned a great deal about the fertility religion of the Baalim. See above, pp. 207–211.

[62] I Kings 16:32.

conflict between the two rival state cults, each of which tended
to be mutually exclusive of the other.

The ardor with which Jezebel promoted Baalism was met with
an equally vigorous assertion of Yahwism. The champion of Yahweh in this situation was Elijah, the Tishbite. Elijah appears in
the narrative as a man of enormous powers: unapproachable, unpredictable, often hated but ever faithful to Yahweh, and always
someone to be reckoned with. At a time when Jezebel and the
cause of Baal were evidently winning the struggle for supremacy,[63] this prophet sought to show Baal to be no god at all. He
attempted to rally the decadent forces of prophetism in allegiance
to the historic faith. Although he was little concerned with the
Jerusalem sanctuary and undisturbed by the shrines of Jeroboam,[64]
his Yahwism was in the tradition of Moses. He came from Gilead
east of Jordan where Yahwism would have preserved its isolation
from other cults more than was the case west of the river, where
more and more it associated with the cult of Baal. Elijah was,
therefore, horrified at the syncretism which he encountered in
Israel. He proclaimed that Yahweh would have no other gods
before him, and the people of Israel could no longer go halting
between two opinions. Like Samuel he interpreted the state as
the enemy of Yahweh when it incorporated compromise at any
level. Jezebel, as perpetrator of the compromise, was an anathema
to Yahweh. It is no wonder that Elijah desired little to win
friends or influence the palace. The only solution evident to him
was a holy war and the purging of the land.

The struggle between the two exclusive faiths was epitomized
in the contest on Mt. Carmel, conducted in an area where Baal
supposedly had the upper hand—fertility. The question to be
answered was, "Who controls the productivity of the land—Baal
or Yahweh?" A famine had devastated the country. Even the
king was forced to scour the land for snitches of water and patches
of grass to keep the animals alive. The cause of the drought was
clear to the prophet. Ahab had forsaken the commandments of
Yahweh by following the Baalim. Here was the source of the
problem and here would be found its solution. Elijah challenged

---

[63] I Kings 18:4 f.

[64] He built an altar on Mt. Carmel apparently independent of both cultic systems; cf. I Kings 18:30.

the host of Baal prophets to gather on Mt. Carmel where Yahweh
or Baal would resolve the struggle.

The Mt. Carmel contest is described in one of the most dramatic of Old Testament episodes.[65] The prophets of Baal were
typical ecstatics who arduously performed their frenzied ritual to
induce action by Baal. Elijah taunted the ecstatics that their
god must be relieving himself or napping or musing. Then, when
the ecstatics had failed, Elijah went quietly into his ritual. An
altar to Yahweh, previously torn down, was restored. Sacrifice
was prepared. The breaking of the drought was symbolized by
pouring water on the altar until trenches around it were filled. In
response to Elijah's prayer, the "fire of Yahweh fell," consuming
the sacrifice, even lapping the water from the trenches. The
prophets of Baal were slain. The drought was broken. Yahweh
was vindicated; he controlled the elements; he was Israel's God.

Jezebel reacted by determining to kill Elijah, as she had other
prophets of Yahweh.[66] Fearing for his life, Elijah fled to the
sacred mountain of Horeb (Sinai). After experiencing the traditional manifestations of Yahweh's revelation in earthquake, wind,
and fire, there came in an awesome stillness the reassurance that
the cause of Yahweh would prevail. The house of Ahab would
be overthrown and Yahweh's faithful would be preserved.

Jezebel's effort to establish Baal worship was only one point of
concern to Elijah. Perhaps of equal importance was Jezebel's
conception of the role of king. She viewed the king in typical
oriental fashion as an absolute despot. To her, he ruled with un-
limited privilege with his subjects as pawns to his desires. Jezebel's interpretation of the monarchy and Elijah's reaction to it are
reflected in the story of Naboth's vineyard.[67]

Naboth, a peasant farmer, refused to surrender his land to the
king under any circumstances. To Naboth the land was not his
to sell. It had been passed down within his family as a sacred
trust from Yahweh. Although unbecomingly sulking in despair,
Ahab evidently accepted Naboth's right of refusal. But not Jeze-

[65] I Kings 18:17–40. The account as it presently appears probably weaves together two ancient stories, one embodying acts to bring about an end to the
drought and another describing the production of fire as evidence of Yahweh's
supremacy.

[66] I Kings 18:4, 13; 19:10, 14.

[67] I Kings 21.

bel. The king was king with rights to take what he wanted. If Ahab wanted the land, it belonged to him. Since Ahab would not assert himself, the queen manipulated the "courts of justice" to have Naboth condemned for treason and blasphemy and then executed.

Elijah's reaction was again immediate and forthright. Confronting Ahab in the vineyard, he called the stoning of Naboth a murder demanding blood revenge. Since no kinsmen of Naboth remained, Yahweh himself would see that justice was done. Jezebel had triggered an explosion which would eventually destroy Ahab's house.

If the action of Micaiah provided a transitional moment in the history of prophecy, the work of Elijah was a day of prelude. Traditional Mosaic faith with an exclusive God intimately concerned for the covenant community was his consuming passion. As Yahweh's spokesman, he firmly opposed a monarchy which tried either overtly to introduce a foreign cult or covertly to usurp the role of Yahweh. Energetically he proclaimed a covenant Yahweh who both contests with Baal on Mt. Carmel and champions the cause of the underprivileged in social relationships. This dual proclamation of Yahweh's sovereignty and Israel's ethical responsibility provides a fitting prelude to the prophets who followed him.

Elijah rallied forces of discontent in Israel which were to erupt into open revolution in the years just after his death. Although the prophet himself was a lonely and isolated individual, his passion for pure Yahwism had found many sympathizers among the religiously sensitive Israelites. Many of the prophetic bands were no longer tolerant of the Melkart cults and vast segments of the populace had been offended by Queen Jezebel's concern for the "divine rights" of the king. With such people the message of Elijah had found a sympathetic ear.

Elisha. The coming of Elisha provided an aggressive leader who could make practical the ideals of his prophetic predecessor. In many ways Elisha was very different from Elijah. Whereas Elijah operated alone, Elisha worked in close harmony with the schools of prophets. Elijah sneered at the court, but Elisha had friends within the palace. Yet, the two men shared a common interpretation of the destiny of Israel. Both were intensely patriotic to the amphictyonic tradition and forthrightly criticized the royal household for its disloyalty to the Yahweh covenant. Out of the discontent aroused by the message of Elijah, Elisha precipitated a holy war which consummated in the destruction of the dynasty of Omri.

Elisha is known through a series of stories (II Kings 6–8) which portray an aspect of his work which was remembered by popular tradition. Nowhere else in the Old Testament are so many miracles crowded into so small a space. This makes it somewhat difficult to reconstruct the historical events associated with the prophet. For example, elsewhere in the Old Testament miracle occurs to arouse awe for Yahweh and to compel devotion to him. In the Elisha cycle, however, miracles as a floating axhead,[68] the tearing of cursing boys by bears,[69] and the purifying of pottage [70] are seemingly related to enhance the man himself. Yet, out of this corpus of stories, a man with a mission emerges. This is essentially because these stories do not so much enhance Elisha as they express "sheer delight . . . at the repeated and astonishing proofs of the prophet's charisma." [71]

Elisha must not be understood, primarily, however, as a charismatic miracle worker, but as one of a withdrawn and unusual company of people called *beni hanabi'im,* "sons of the prophets." These people were probably poor and without status, but they represented "pure uncontaminated Yahwism and its divine law" [72] and were important for its survival and the character it would attain among the classical prophets.

The ministry of Elisha relates to the period following the death of Ahab about 850 b.c. and was probably confined to the reigns of Jehoram (849–842) and his successor, Jehu (842–815). During this period the prophet was the man behind the scenes of the political drama. He played a significant role in the unfolding circumstances relating to the fall of the Omrides. This may seem surprising work for one whose background was the "sons of the prophets," but it was not since this group never ceased to be in-

68 II Kings 6:1–7.
69 II Kings 2:23–25.
70 II Kings 4:38–41.
71 Gerhard von Rad, *Old Testament Theology,* II, 27.
72 *Ibid.,* p. 28.

terested in Israel's public life. Elisha was more than an interesting hero about whom gathered fascinating tales. The zealous
character of the devout community to which he belonged left
him with a consummate passion for purging Israel of the evil house
of Ahab. Unwilling simply to let time take its course, he became
an active agent in maneuvering the political means to the end of
accomplishing his religious purpose. The tool in his hand was a
captain in Israel's army, Jehu.

The backdrop for the overthrow of the Omri dynasty was
the long-lived struggle between Syria and Israel for the prize
of Ramoth-gilead. Hazael, with the undisguised encouragement
of Elisha,[73] had murdered his predecessor and usurped the throne
of Syria. Jehoram of Israel interpreted this as an opportune time
to recover Ramoth-gilead and, with the aid of Ahaziah of Judah,
sought to do so. The tide of the initial battle went against Israel;
Jehoram was wounded and retired to Jezreel to recover. Jehu,
the army captain, was left in charge of the campaign for Ramoth-
gilead.

The moment for Elisha's action had arrived. He commissioned
a prophet to go to Ramoth-gilead and anoint Jehu as king. The
army backed the newly anointed, and a revolution was on. A
blood purge of the house of Ahab followed, related in all of its
gory details in II Kings 9. Following Jehu's hurried chariot ride
from Ramoth-gilead to Jezreel, the blood of the Omrides flowed
freely until "Jehu slew all that remained of the house of Ahab in
Jezreel, and all his great men, and his familiar friends, and his
priests, until he left him none remaining."[74] Jehoram was killed
and his corpse thrown into the vineyard of Naboth—with dramatic
fitness illustrating that the blood-revenge law had been satisfied.
The hated Jezebel was thrown from an open window and igno-
miniously trampled. The orgy of reprisals extended even to the
worshippers of Baal.[75] Even a century later Hosea recalled with
horror the bloody overthrow of the Omrides. Although the Kings'
writer praised the revolutionist, Hosea proclaimed Yahweh's
judgment, "I will punish the house of Jehu for the blood of Jezreel" (Hosea 1:4).

[73] Cf. II Kings 8:7–15.
[74] II Kings 10:11.
[75] II Kings 10:18–27.

It is ethically impossible to defend the bloody horror of Jehu's purge. Even by ancient laws of blood revenge typical in Israel, his measures were too extreme and brutal. Undoubtedly Jehu felt that he was furthering the cause of Yahwism in Israel. Not only did he have the support of the Yahweh prophet Elisha, but he also had the prophet Jehonadab as an ally in revolt. This son of Rechab [76] opposed the cultural development of Israel and, as a descendant of the Kenites, piously advocated a conservative interpretation of Israel's faith. Jehonadab evidently saw in the revolution an opportunity to express his zealous opposition to the agrarian culture of Israel and was all too anxious to support Jehu. How disillusioned he must have been in the later developments of the Jehu dynasty!

Elisha's ways led to excess and abuse but were clearly intended to convince Israel that Yahweh was with them as he had been with Israel in holy wars of old. This sense of Yahweh's devastating presence was shortly inherited by prophets who turned it to a revolution of morality and ethics, not of politics and blood. The mature superiority of the latter is clear in Amos and Hosea.

⌄THE FIRST OF THE CLASSICAL PROPHETS

The prosperity, expansion, and national confidence of Jeroboam II's reign in the eighth century B.C. were accompanied by widespread religious enthusiasm. The festivals were popular and the sanctuaries of the northern kingdom were thronged. Yahweh's great deeds were remembered and his covenant was renewed as a guarantee of Yahweh's protection of the nation in the years to come.

However, the religion, though flourishing, was decadent. Ethical obligation was almost completely forgotten as covenant came to be considered fulfilled by elaborate ritual and lavish support of the national shrines. The essence of Israel's religion was lost and replaced by the ceremonial means intended to keep it alive. Sacrifice, ritual, even prayer ceased to be means to an end and became ends in themselves. Yahweh was personally unknown to those who ceremonially worshipped him the most.

---

[76] Those with similar ideas in later times were known as Rechabites, named after the illustrious opponent of things cultural.

Yahwism in a pure form was no longer maintained. Numerous local shrines became openly pagan as the Canaanite fertility cult was practiced everywhere. Baal had become as important a deity as Yahweh. Yahweh worship which laid stern ethical and moral requirements upon its followers was losing to the sensual excesses of Baal worship which appealed to the base instincts of the average Israelite. Some Samaria ostraca indicate that almost as many Israelites had names compounded with Baal as with Yahweh. Yahwism so diluted had no hopes for maintaining the covenant law. The priests were part of the system and would not speak out against it, and no effective rebuke came from the cultic and court prophets. The syncretism so abhorant to Elijah had spread to an extent which even he might not have feared.

The distinctive social structure of Israel based on covenant brotherhood had completely lost its character. A class of newly rich had arisen and exploitation of the poor was commonplace. In every way Israel had ceased to be a covenant people. Basic covenant law had no meaning to them and the faith of Mosaic days was neglected. Yahweh was not God to them, but a talisman to be kept against possible days of trouble. In the peaceful interim the baals were gods enough for Israel. In light of such circumstances Yahweh's voice had to be heard and Amos and Hosea became his spokesmen.

Amos

> You only have I known
>   of all the families of the earth;
> therefore I will punish you
>   for all your iniquities. (Amos 3:2)

In this incisive judgment upon the covenant people, the prophet Amos thundered forth "in a moment, the explosion and discharge of the full storm of prophecy." [77] All that we know about the man who uttered this short oracle are the few facts given in the book called by his name, and it is more concerned with the "words of Yahweh" which he spoke than with biographical details of his life. He was a herdsman or sheepmaster from Tekoa, a Judean village lying a few miles south of Jerusalem in the rugged wilderness of

---

[77] George Adam Smith, *The Book of the Twelve Prophets*, I, p. 145.

Judah. The severity of life in this barren region contributed to the simplicity and devastating power with which he proclaimed the word of Yahweh.

Amos was not, however, merely a rustic shepherd. He probably owned his own flocks, and in addition grew sycamore fruit. Of course, he was not wealthy—he cared for his own flock, perhaps sold his own wool, and tended his sycamore trees—but he was a man of some substance. He knew much about conditions throughout Israel and Judah and was aware of what was going on in other countries. He may have traveled widely as a wool merchant. Certainly in this capacity he visited Israelite trade fairs at Bethel and other shrine cities. While there he broke forth in the fury of prophetic anger against the injustices so characteristic of the prosperous but decadent state of Israel.

The Word of Yahweh. When Amaziah, priest at Bethel, demanded that Amos cease prophesying and leave Israel, the prophet insisted that he did not belong to the popular bands which prophesied for pay and, therefore, was not obligated to heed priestly commands. He was responsible only to Yahweh and spoke only because Yahweh compelled him to speak. Thus, he was a prophet by divine calling, not a professional representative of the state religion.[78]

In a series of autobiographical visions Amos portrayed the temporal and psychological developments leading to his becoming a prophet. An examination of these visions provides a point of departure for understanding other oracles contained in his book. The basis of each of the visions is an event or situation visible to everyone. For the prophet, however, these situations became media of divine revelation. The first vision occurred in early spring.

Thus Yahweh God showed me: behold, he was forming locusts in the beginning of the shooting up of the latter growth; and lo, it was the latter growth after the king's mowings. When they had finished eating the grass of the land, I said,
"O Yahweh God, forgive, I beseech thee!
How can Jacob stand?
He is so small!"
Yahweh repented concerning this; "It shall not be," said Yahweh. (7:1–3)

[78] Amos 7:10–17.

Locust plague, the dread of the agriculturalists, devastated the Tekoa region, devouring the second crop so that there was no hope for recovery. This meant trouble for all and perhaps even disaster, but for Amos it was a sign that Yahweh was determined to call Israel to account for her sins and punish her in his wrath. Amos' plaintive prayer, however, was heard and Yahweh changed his mind.

But soon a different and more terrible vision indicative of Yahweh's impending judgment appeared to the Tekoan herdsman.

Thus Yahweh God showed me: behold, Yahweh God was calling for a judgment by fire, and it devoured the great deep and was eating up the land. (7:4)

Was this the searing of the earth by drought, or the scorched earth policy of invading Assyrian troops? It mattered not, because either would be symbolic of the wrathful judgment of a God angry because of Israel's gross sinfulness. As before, the disaster was forestalled by the prayer of Amos.

> O Yahweh God, cease, I beseech thee!
> How can Jacob stand?
> He is so small! (7:5)

In these prayers for his people Amos became a prophet.[79]

Later at Bethel other visions clearly revealed to Amos the true condition of Israel, a sinful nation deserving of Yahweh's judgment.

He showed me: behold, Yahweh was standing beside a wall built with a plumb line, with a plumb line in his hand. And Yahweh said to me, "Amos, what do you see?" And I said, "A plumb line." Then Yahweh said, "Behold, I am setting a plumb line in the midst of my people Israel; I will never again pass by them; the high places of Isaac shall be made desolate, and the sanctuaries of Israel shall be laid waste, and I will rise against the house of Jeroboam with the sword." (7:7–9)

Like a wall out of plumb, Israel did not deserve to stand. For Amos the wall under construction had become Israel and the workman with the plumb line, Yahweh.

Swiftly the visions moved to a climax as a basket of summer fruit (*qayits*) by word association became a sign that the end

---

[79] Gustav Hölscher, *Die Propheten,* p. 195.

(*qets*) was at hand. Then the last and most terrible vision convinced Amos that he must take up his prophetic work.

I saw Yahweh standing beside the altar, and he said:
> "Smite the capitals until the thresholds
> shake,
> and shatter them on the heads of all the
> people;
> and what are left of them I will slay
> with the sword;
> not one of them shall flee away,
> not one of them shall escape." (9:1)

Yahweh was to be found at his accustomed place, but not to bless, redeem, or forgive. Sacrifices would not be received; prayers would not be heard. He stood by the altar in judgment, with the sword of Israel's doom in hand. Aware of this and compelled by the God whose call he had heard, Amos began to prophesy.

The Prophecies of Amos. The book of Amos may be concisely outlined as follows:

Editorial Introduction. 1:1–2.
I. Oracles against the nations and Israel. 1:3–2:16.
II. Oracles of doom. 3:1–6:14.
III. Visions of the end. 7:1–9; 8:1–3; 9:1–4.
IV. Amos and Amaziah. 7:10–17.
V. More oracles of doom. 8:4–14; 9:5–8.
Epilogue: Hope for eventual restoration. 9:11–15.

The book contains some fairly extended sermons delivered on single occasions, plus shorter oracles from other occasions. Most of them came from Amos himself and were remembered and recorded by his followers. Certain of the oracles, however, may have been added by later editors of the prophetic literature. Fragments of a hymn are found in 4:13, 5:8–9, and 9:5–6, which complement the speeches to which they are connected. Although its precise origin cannot be determined, this hymn may be from the Jerusalem cultus. The oracle in 9:11–12 about the restoration of Judah and Jerusalem could hardly be from Amos since it presupposes the Babylonian exile. The concluding oracle of restoration, however, belongs to the popular eschatological expectation of the eighth century. Its hope for the triumph of Yaweh's purpose in the future is not incompatible with Amos' view that the end for Israel was imminent.

The Motto of the Book. When Amos began to speak Yahweh's words which had come to him,[80] Israel's doom was already close at hand. The inevitable punishment was already in progress and could not be turned back.

> Yahweh roars from Zion,
>   and utters his voice from Jerusalem;
> the pastures of the shepherds mourn,
>   and the top of Carmel withers. (1:2)

Yahweh was moving upon his land to devastate a sinful people. There would be no escape since even the fertile Carmel range upon which the rains most often fell was to wither in the blast of war.

Yahweh, God of the Nations. In an electrifying series of oracles Amos portrayed a world in moral chaos. Its nations were guilty before a sovereign God. There was no loyalty or honor among the peoples. Not only the covenant people, but all mankind stood under Yahweh's righteous judgment. Israel and her neighbors had disobeyed a law which all men, because they are men, must acknowledge, a law "which was bound up with the very constitution of this world." [81]

Using the imprecatory oracular form common to the cult of his day, Amos pronounced judgments upon enemy peoples in the name of Israel's God. Syria, Philistia, Phoenicia, Edom, Ammon, and Moab in turn were damned "for three transgressions, and for four." Of these denunciations his listeners approved. Then the prophet turned his wrathful words upon Judah, and still his listeners approved. That nation, although kin to Israel, was guilty like the rest. The final and most severe castigation of all, however, was reserved for Israel, who had been unfaithful to her covenant responsibilities. That nation with a sacred history behind her was guilty of social injustice and cruelty. In the face of Yahweh's gracious action and the warnings of the past Israel was ungrateful. She oppressed the poor and weak. She permitted ruthless and cruel power to crush the rights of the needy

---

[80] 1:1 "words . . . which he saw."
[81] Adam C. Welch, *Kings and Prophets of Israel,* pp. 125–6.

in the rampaging corruption of both secular and religious life. Upon such a people judgment had to come and Amos was its herald.

> "Flight shall perish from the swift,
>   and the strong shall not retain his strength,
>   nor shall the mighty save his life;
> he who handles the bow shall not stand
>   and he who is swift of foot shall not save
>   himself,
>   nor shall he who rides the horse save his
>   life;
> and he who is stout of heart among the mighty
>   shall flee away naked in that day,"
>   says Yahweh. (2:14–16)

Monotheism. Amos, then, clearly believed that Yahweh was sovereign in judgment over the foreign nations. Indeed, he was concerned for all peoples and kingdoms far and near in every dimension of their activity.

> "Are you not like the Ethiopians to me,
>   O people of Israel?" says Yahweh.
> "Did I not bring up Israel from the land
>   of Egypt,
> and the Philistines from Caphtor and the
>   Syrians from Kir? (9:7)

Yahweh was sovereign too in nature's realm. He withheld the rain or sent it as he pleased (4:7). At his command the great seas would dry up and the lands be burned with drought (7:4). Blight and pestilence were instruments of his purpose (4:9–10). In all his world Yahweh alone was God.

This was practical monotheism born, not of speculation, but of religious faith which saw history as the great arena of divine activity. In the preaching of Amos thoughts begun with Abraham and Moses took explicit form as Israel's Yahweh was described as God of all men.

Election, Privilege, and Service. Although Amos believed Yahweh to be God of all nations, he recognized a special relationship between Yahweh and Israel—a relationship of Yahweh's own making, not of Israel's choosing. In stating this the prophet echoed the popular nationalistic theology of his day, "You only have I known of all the families of the earth." But his conclusion was not the expected word of assurance, "Therefore I will forgive your sins and bless you." Instead he said, "Therefore, I will punish you for all your iniquities" (3:2). Thus the prophet exploded the popular, easy, superficial optimism of the official priests and prophets. To know Yahweh was a deadly serious thing. To be his choice covenant nation meant great responsibility. Israel had been elected for service and, when she entered into covenant with Yahweh, she bound herself to him with cords of responsibility. She could cast aside those bonds, but not with impunity. Rebellion against Yahweh was a capital offense. Because she was his chosen people, Yahweh would punish Israel all the more severely.

The Death of a Nation. In poignant lamentation Amos depicted Israel as a nation already as good as dead.

> "Fallen, no more to rise,
>   is the virgin Israel;
> forsaken on her land,
>   with none to raise her up."
> . . . .
> Therefore, thus says Yahweh, the God of
>   hosts, the Lord:
> "In all the squares there shall be wailing;
>   and in all the streets they shall say,
>   'Alas! alas!'
> . . . .
> for I will pass through the midst of you,"
>   says Yahweh. (5:2, 16–17)

But even though the prophet was sure of doom's certainty, he still called them to repentance. As their "covenant conscience" he pled with Israel to turn to Yahweh from their evil ways. "Seek Yahweh and live." "Seek good and not evil, that you may live." If Israel would turn to Yahweh, he might yet turn aside the devastation. But Israel had to seek him in truth and justice, not by a false pretentious cult which merely added to the enormity of the people's corruption.

Anything less than true righteousness would not suffice and Israel had forgotten how to do right.[82] History's lessons had gone unheeded as again and again Israel ignored the signs of Yahweh's dissatisfaction. Famine and drought, blight and pestilence, and finally war had been sent upon the land, yet Israel did not return

[82] Amos 3:10.

unto him.[83] Therefore, Israel was doomed to meet Yahweh on
the great and terrible "Day of Yahweh." In popular theology
this day was the future's day of blessing. But Amos saw no
blessing for a sinful degenerate people. To wish for the Day of
Yahweh was to wish for woe, for that day would be devastation.

> It is darkness, and not light;
>   as if a man fled from a lion,
>   and a bear met him;
> or went into the house and leaned with
>   his hand against the wall,
>   and a serpent bit him.
> Is not the day of Yahweh darkness, and
>   not light,
>   and gloom with no brightness in it? (5:18b–20)

With this bitter humor Amos spoke of the doom about to befall
a nation already dying.

Escape from Divine Wrath.   Amos, incensed as he was by the
gross injustice and oppression of callous and recalcitrant Israel,
held some hope that from the maelstrom of Yahweh's vengeful
wrath some could escape or be rescued. Not everyone was evil
and surely some deserved mercy. A remnant would be saved
and perhaps the prophet hoped that with them Yahweh could
begin again to shape a covenant people. This remnant, however,
would be small and saved from the very depths of death itself.

Thus says Yahweh: "As the shepherd rescues from the mouth of the lion two
legs, or a piece of an ear, so shall the people of Israel who dwell in Samaria
be rescued, with the corner of a couch and part of a bed." (3:12)

This ominous picture may have been what the prophet had in
mind when he said more in hope than in belief,

> "Behold, the eyes of the Lord God are upon
>   the sinful kingdom,
> and I will destroy it from the surface of
>   the ground;
> except that I will not utterly destroy the
>   house of Jacob," says Yahweh. (8:9)

Hosea

Hosea's prophecy belongs to the same general period as that of
Amos, though some few years later. His earliest preaching oc-

[83] Amos 4:6–11.

curred during the last days of Jeroboam II, but unlike that of Amos, Hosea's ministry continued into the hard days following the destruction of the Jehu dynasty and preceding the fall of Samaria. The collection of Hosea's oracles is badly preserved. The text can be restored in many places only with the help of the Septuagint and other versions and sometimes only by conjecture.[84] Matters of interpretation are as difficult as the text, for the book is filled with perplexing exegetical problems. Nevertheless, while detailed outlining is extremely difficult, the general structure of the book is plain.

Editorial Introduction. 1:1.
I. Hosea's domestic biography parallels Yahweh's experience with Israel. 1:2–3:1–5.
Hosea and Gomer. 1:2–9 and 3:1–5.
Yahweh and Israel. 1:10–2:23.
II. Yahweh's indictment of Israel. 4:1–9:9.
III. The lesson of history—Yahweh's grace and Israel's apostasy. 9:10–13:16.
IV. Israel's future hope. 14:1–9.

There is little doubt that the majority of this book came from Hosea. The only passages about which there is real question are those which refer to Judah.[85] These may have been natural additions made after the fall of the northern kingdom when Hosea's teachings circulated in the south. However, some of these references to Judah may have come from Hosea himself.[86]

The oracles in this book are the expressions of a compassionate man in love with his people, but aware of their sin. Like Amos he was sensitive to Yahweh's judgment, but through personal tragedy he had come to know God's heart and there he found _chesed_, covenant love. Therefore, he couched his message in tenderness which stands in dramatic contrast to the tone of Amos.

Hosea and Gomer: Yahweh and Israel. The book of Hosea opens with strange words from Yahweh to the prophet.

Go, take to yourself a wife of harlotry and have children of harlotry, for the land commits great harlotry by forsaking Yahweh. (1:2)

[84] The many footnotes in the Revised Standard Version give ample evidence of this fact.
[85] 1:10–2:1; 3:4 ff.; etc.
[86] Cf. John Mauchline, "The Book of Hosea," in _The Interpreter's Bible_, VI, 563 f.

This verse and those connected with it present one of the most difficult problems in Old Testament studies. To complicate the problem Hosea later records another similarly startling divine word.

Go again, love a woman who is beloved of a paramour and is an adulteress; even as Yahweh loves the people of Israel, though they turn to other gods and love cakes of raisins. (3:1)

Although there is some difference of opinion about the identity of these women, it is generally agreed that they are one and the same and that the latter verse is a reference to Hosea's later experience with the woman mentioned in chapter one. But even so, what does this mean? How are we to interpret the initial command for the prophet to marry a harlot? At least three alternatives are possible:

1. The whole account of the prophet's marriage relations is imaginary and symbolic—an allegory of Yahweh's experience with Israel, his bride.
2. Gomer, the woman involved, was chaste when Hosea married her. She may or may not have had tendencies toward harlotry before the marriage, but afterwards she was unfaithful. The words of chapter one, therefore, are judgments after the event as the prophet described her as a harlot from the beginning.
3. The literal interpretation says Hosea loved Gomer, even though she was a harlot, perhaps a Baal temple prostitute, and married her in obedience to what he conceived to be Yahweh's command. She remained after the marriage what she had always been, proving unfaithful to Hosea by going back to her former ways.

One cannot be dogmatic here, but the allegorical interpretation seems quite improbable. The decision between the other two alternatives is not as easy to make. This is not surprising, since Hosea's intention was not to give a detailed account of his domestic tragedy, but to tell only what was necessary to symbolize the story of Yahweh's relation to Israel.[87]

The prophet's experience may be reconstructed somewhat as follows. He loved and married Gomer, whatever her character might have been (we have to remember the power of love). She bore three children to whom the prophet gave names symbolic of

[87] For an able and thoroughly documented discussion of this entire problem, see H. H. Rowley, "The Marriage of Hosea," *Bulletin of the John Rylands Library,* XXXIX (1946), pp. 200–233.

Yahweh's word to Israel. The first he called "Jezreel," because at Jezreel Jehu had been established upon the throne by excessive bloodshed.[88] The name as borne by Hosea's child was a reminder of this bloodshed for which punishment must come and a prophecy of the place at which the judgment would fall. That historic battlefield was thought by Hosea to be the place where the whole fate and future would be decided. Hosea named the second child "not pitied," for Yahweh's pity was at an end and nothing could turn away divine judgment. "Not my people," the pathetic name given the third child, symbolized the rejection of the nation which had broken its covenant bond. For two hundred years Israel had been taught that she was Yahweh's people,[89] but now she had forfeited the privileges she had so flagrantly neglected and was in danger of rejection.

Evidently, after the birth of these children Gomer left her husband to pursue her lovers. She may even have become a prostitute of the streets. Nevertheless, love prevailed. Hosea bought the degraded woman, either paying her paramour for the loss of his mistress, or perhaps (if she had become a slave) her master for the loss of his slave. Then after a period of discipline he restored his beloved as his wife.

Clearly Hosea saw in Gomer's relationship to him an analogy of Israel's relationship to Yahweh. Like the other prophets, Hosea glamorized the wilderness period. At that time Israel, Yahweh's bride, had been faithful, but she like Gomer had become a wanton harlot, giving herself to the Canaanite baals. She said:

> I will go after my lovers,
> who give me my bread and my water,
> my wool and my flax, my oil and my drink. (2:5)

The nation had become insensitive to Yahweh's love and grace. Lewd and naked she had gone after lovers, utterly corrupted by the fertility cult of Canaan.

The transition from nomad to agriculturalist was completed when the nomads accepted the farmers' gods. Israel had not completely denied Yahweh; they had merely added gods associated with things of the soil, wine, grain, and oil. Such syncretism, how-

---

[88] See II Kings 10.
[89] See Exodus 3:7; 5:1; 7:16.

ever, was totally destructive to the true nature of Yahwism. Yahweh alone was God of both the nomad and the farmer.

> She did not know
> that it was I who gave her
> the grain, the wine, and the oil. (2:8)

For gods who were *no gods* and for worship of the basest sort, Israel had pushed Yahweh and his covenant demands into the background. Upon such a nation the divine judgment had to fall.

Sin, Sin, Sin. Like Amos before him, Hosea took seriously the social evils of the day, but he was more inclined to interpret these ills as a breach of Yahweh's covenant love (*chesed*) than as a breach of Mosaic law. Yahweh's controversy with his people was because there was "no knowledge of Yahweh in the land." [90] This lack of knowledge was not so much intellectual misunderstanding as it was a breakdown of the covenant relationship.[91] The "spirit of harlotry was within Israel." [92] Chapter four of Hosea shows the extent of her corruption and chapters 6–13:16 read like a catalogue of sin. The Decalogue, the basis of all Israel's law, had no meaning.

> There is swearing, lying, killing, stealing,
>   and committing adultery;
> they break all bounds and murder follows
>   murder. (4:2)

This collapse of law and order had created anarchy in which life was no longer safe.[93] Hosea doubtless had in mind the chaotic years following the death of Jeroboam II.

The heart had gone out of religious life and moral decay was complete. Religious leaders were in the vanguard of corruption. Priests fed on the sins of the people, speaking out against sin just enough to keep sacrifices and offerings flowing in. They wanted the people to be iniquitous since this would fill their larder. Little wonder that idolatry and baals were so important. Paganism's poison filled the vacuum of empty Yahwism.

---

[90] Hosea 4:1.

[91] The Hebrew word translated "knowledge" is used of the most intimate relationships.

[92] Hosea 5:4.

[93] Hosea 4:1–2; 7:1–7; 8:4.

> My people inquire of a thing of wood,
>> and their staff gives them oracles.
>
> . . . .
>
> They sacrifice on the tops of the mountains,
>> and make offerings upon the hills,
> under oak, poplar, and terebinth,
>> because their shade is good. (4:12–13a)

What little worship of Yahweh remained was meaningless, since it was devoid of real faith and mercy. Trouble, however, still brought the usual claim upon the traditional hope that Yahweh was bound to help his people.

> Come, let us return to Yahweh;
>> for he has torn, that he may heal us;
>> he has stricken, and he will bind us up.
> After two days he will revive us;
>> on the third day he will raise us up,
>> that we may live before him.
> Let us know, let us press on to know Yahweh;
>> his going forth is sure as the dawn;
> he will come to us as the showers,
>> as the spring rains that water the earth. (6:1–3)

But prayer without repentance is not prayer, and people who have transgressed the covenant cannot be redeemed by sacrifice.

> They love sacrifice;
>> they sacrifice flesh and eat it;
>> but Yahweh has no delight in them.
> Now he will remember their iniquity,
>> and punish their sins;
>> they shall return to Egypt. (8:13)

When help from Yahweh was not forthcoming, Israel turned to the nations, trimming "their foreign policy to every political wind that blew," [94] but they were always wrong.

> Ephraim is like a dove,
>> silly and without sense,
>> calling to Egypt, going to Assyria.
> As they go, I will spread over them my net;
> I will bring them down like birds of the air;
> I will chastise them for their wicked deeds.
> Woe to them, for they have strayed from me! (7:11–13a)

They, indeed, had strayed from Yahweh, who alone could help, and the nation was in ruin.

[94] John Bright, *The Kingdom of God,* p. 73.

To all of this the prophet voiced Yahweh's disheartened cry.

> What shall I do with you, O Ephraim?
> What shall I do with you, O Judah?
> Your love is like a morning cloud,
>   like the dew that goes early away.
> Therefore I have hewn them by the prophets,
>   I have slain them by the words of my mouth,
>   and my judgment goes forth as the light.
> For I desire steadfast love and not sacrifice,
>   the knowledge of God, rather than burnt
>   offerings. (6:4-6)

To this sinful people destruction would come and soon. Harlotry had to be punished and the judgment was about to fall.

> For behold, they are going to Assyria;
>   Egypt shall gather them,
>   Memphis shall bury them.
> Nettles shall possess their precious things
>   of silver;
>   thorns shall be in their tents.
> . . . .
> Ephraim's glory shall fly away like a bird—
>   no birth, no pregnancy, no conception!
> Even if they bring up children,
>   I will bereave them till none is left.
> Woe to them when I depart from them!
> . . . .
> Ephraim is stricken,
>   their root is dried up,
>   they shall bear no fruit.
> Even though they bring forth,
>   I will slay their beloved children.
> My God will cast them off,
>   because they have not hearkened to him;
>   they shall be wanderers among the nations. (9:6, 11–12, 16–17)

Yahweh and Israel Again. But Hosea, who as a man had so loved wayward Gomer, knew that Yahweh could not give Israel up. The sensitive prophet plaintively characterized Yahweh's desire.

> How can I give you up, O Ephraim!
> How can I hand you over, O Israel!
> . . . .
> My heart recoils within me,
>   my compassion grows warm and tender. (11:8)

He must punish, but he could not utterly destroy. Had he not called Israel as a child to be his son leading him from Egypt and teaching him to walk? Were they not his people whom he loved? Yahweh was God and not man, the Holy One in the midst of his people and his compassion was warm and tender. He would not utterly destroy. He could forgive. His divine love for Israel was greater than Hosea's human love for Gomer.

In the prophecy of Hosea we have an epochal combination of the wrath and the love of Yahweh. Hosea said to Israel that Yahweh had not forsaken the apostate nation and that the judgment of Yahweh upon her was a redemptive judgment. From the consequent wilderness of Yahweh's judgment, Israel could, even as in the days of the Exodus, respond to Yahweh's "overture of love." Then the "not-pitied" would obtain pity, "Not-my-people" would become "sons of the living God" and great would be the day of Jezreel.

The final chapter brings the book to a fitting conclusion as a chastened and repentant Israel brings Yahweh "words," not sacrifices, pleading that iniquity might be taken away. Unable to help herself and aware of the futility of seeking aid elsewhere, she could only appeal for help. Then help would come.

SUGGESTED READINGS

Background

OLMSTEAD, A. T., *History of Palestine and Syria* (Scribner's, 1931). Discusses the history of Palestine in the general context of Syrian history.

THIELE, E. R., *The Mysterious Numbers of the Hebrew Kings* (University of Chicago Press, 1951). Thorough study of the chronology of the monarchy.

The Book of Kings

GRAY, JOHN, *I & II Kings* (Westminster, 1963).

MATHENEY, M. PIERCE and HONEYCUTT, ROY L., "1–2 Kings" in *The Broadman Bible Commentary*, III.

MONTGOMERY, JAMES A., *A Critical and Exegetical Commentary on the Book of Kings* (Scribner's, 1951). The standard technical study on the books of Kings.

SNAITH, NORMAN H., "I and II Kings," in *Interpreter's Bible*, III.

Prophecy

ANDERSON, BERNHARD W., and HARRELSON, WALTER, eds. *Israel's Prophetic Heritage* (Harper & Row, 1962).

BUBER, MARTIN, *The Prophetic Faith* (Macmillan, 1949).

CLEMENTS, R. E., *Prophecy and Covenant* (S.C.M. Press, 1965).

GOTTWALD, NORMAN K., *All The Kingdoms of the Earth* (Harper & Row, 1965).

HESCHEL, ABRAHAM J., *The Prophets* (Harper & Row, 1963).

HYATT, J. P., *Prophetic Religion* (Abingdon-Cokesbury, 1947).

JOHNSON, A. R., *The Cultic Prophet in Ancient Israel* (University of Wales Press, 1944). The relation between the prophet and cult and the role of prophets in Israel's worship.

KNIGHT, HAROLD, *The Hebrew Prophetic Consciousness* (Lutterworth, 1947).

KUHL, CURT, *Prophets of Israel* (John Knox, 1961).

LINDBLOM, JOHANNES, *Prophecy in Ancient Israel* (Muhlenberg, 1963).

McKANE, WILLIAM, *Prophets and Wise Men* (Alex R. Allenson, 1965).

NOTH, MARTIN, "History and Word of God in the Old Testament," *The Laws in the Pentateuch and Other Studies*, tr. D. R. Ap-Thomas (Fortress Press, 1967).

PATERSON, JOHN, *The Goodly Fellowship of the Prophets* (Scribners, 1950).

ROBINSON, T. H., *Prophecy and Prophets in Ancient Israel* (2nd ed., Duckworth, 1953). Old but helpful.

ROWLEY, H. H., "The Nature of Prophecy in the Light of Recent Study," *The Servant of the Lord and Other Essays on the Old Testament* (Lutterworth, 1952).

SCOTT, R. B. Y., *The Relevance of the Prophets* (Macmillan, 1944). Best topical introduction to prophecy.

SMART, JAMES D., *Servants of the Word* (Westminster, 1960).

VON RAD, GERHARD, *Old Testament Theology*, II, tr. D. M. G. Stalker (Harper & Row, 1965).

WELCH, A. C., *Prophet and Priest in Old Israel* (S.C.M. Press, 1936).

WESTERMANN, CLAUS, *Basic Forms of Prophetic Speech* (Westminster, 1967).

Amos and Hosea

CRENSHAW, J. L., "Amos and the Theophanic Tradition," *Zeitschrift für die Alttestamentliche Wissenschaft*, LXXX (1968), 203–215.

———, "The Influence of the Wise upon Amos," *Zeitschrift für die Alttestamentliche Wissenschaft*, LXXIX (1967), 42–52.

HONEYCUTT, ROY L. JR., *Amos and His Message: An Expository Commentary*. (Broadman Press, 1963.)

KAPELRUD, A. S., "New Ideas in Amos," *Supplements to Vetus Testamentum*, XV (1965), 193–206.

MARSH, JOHN, *Amos and Micah*, Torch Bible Commentary (S.C.M. Press, 1959).

MAYS, JAMES LUTHER, *Amos* (Westminster, 1969).
————, *Hosea* (Westminster, 1969).
ROBINSON, H. WHEELER, *The Cross of Hosea* (Westminster, 1949).
————, *Two Hebrew Prophets* (Lutterworth, 1948). Discusses Hosea and Ezekiel.
SMITH, GEORGE ADAM, *The Book of the Twelve Prophets*, I and II (Harper & Row, 1928). An old and standard work.
SNAITH, NORMAN, *Amos, Hosea, and Micah* (Epworth).
————, *Mercy and Sacrifice* (S.C.M. Press, 1953). Studies in Hosea.
WARD, JAMES M., *Amos and Isaiah: Prophets of the Word of God* (Abingdon, 1969).
————, *Hosea: A Theological Commentary* (Harper & Row, 1966).
WATTS, JOHN D., *Vision and Prophecy in Amos* (Eerdmans, 1958).

8

The Divided Kingdom: Judah

TWO CENTURIES OF COEXISTENCE
(I KINGS 12:1–II KINGS 16:20) [1]

As far as the Deuteronomist was concerned, Israel's journey from 922 to 722/21 B.C. was primarily an experience of apostasy. The significant religious development of the covenant people was to be traced through the life of the southern kingdom, Judah.

When favored Judah is compared to her sister in the north during their two centuries of coexistence, however, a great deal is left to be desired. Ethically and religiously, neither north nor south could boast of much superiority. Apostasy permeated Judah as thoroughly as it did Israel. In an imaginary contest to do evil, Manasseh of Judah would have been judged second to Ahab only because of the latter's "assist" from Jezebel, and for blood-letting, Athaliah almost out-Jezebeled Jezebel. Certainly, the moral superiority of Judah could hardly have been the basis of the Deuteronomist's preference for that nation.

Militarily and politically Israel exceeded Judah. At some points, Judah was little more than a vassal to her much stronger sister. In the alliance of Jehoshaphat of Judah with Ahab of Israel, the northerner was clearly in control of affairs. Israel's moments of military resistance to both Syrian and Assyrian aggression had no counterparts in Judah.

Further, cultural and economic progress was much more pronounced in the north than in the south. The economic resources

---

[1] See also II Chronicles 10–28.

of Phoenicia, the cultural initiative of liberal attitudes, and the trade potential offered by the great plain of Esdraelon all belonged to Israel. Judah, on the other hand, was financially crippled by Shishak of Egypt during the reign of Rehoboam. Recovery came slowly and Judah remained conservative, much more reluctant to accommodate to Canaanite innovations. Moreover, isolated as she was, her recovery from the trauma of tribal revolution was much slower.

During the two centuries of coexistence Israel remained the stronger, more wealthy, and more progressive of the two kingdoms. However, there were two features of Judah's history which made her attractive to the biblical writer. First, Jerusalem remained the possession of the southern kingdom. Benjamin, on whose border lay the revered city of David, may have been more sympathetic to the north, but Rehoboam of the south was able to secure Judah's boundaries to include Benjamin. Consequently, the temple in Jerusalem remained the seat of religion for Judah and carried a religious significance far deeper in meaning than the shrines of Jeroboam. For the Deuteronomic historian worship of Yahweh at sacred centers other than Jerusalem endangered what was distinctive in Yahwism by mixture with the fertility cult of Baal. His narrative about Elijah presents the issue in unequivocable terms:

> How long will you limping with two different opinions.
> If Yahweh is God, follow him; but if Baal, then follow
> him. (I Kings 18:21)

Israel may on that occasion have chosen Yahweh. But that the issue was raised at all was for the Deuteronomist evidence of Israel's great error. She sought to keep covenant without the cultic context in which Yahweh came to his people and made his will known. Consequently, while she did not often openly choose Baal, she did regularly confuse Yahweh with that fertility deity. The concern was not primarily with sacredness of place, but with purity of faith. The Jerusalem cultus was for him the best protector of the Sinai covenant.

Second, the kings of Judah were of the line of David. In contrast to the nineteen kings of nine dynasties who ruled Israel for two hundred years, twenty kings of one dynasty [2] controlled Judah for more than three hundred and thirty years. This firm entrenchment of the single Davidic dynasty was providential for Judah. Whereas hopeful usurpers in Israel could advantage themselves of the custom of choosing rulers according to the charismatic motif, the populace of the south learned to depend upon the Davidic dynasty. In this context there was a degree of fulfillment of the prophetic word: "He shall build a house for my name, and I will establish the throne of his kingdom forever" (II Samuel 7:13).

These two features receive the endorsement of the biblical writers, the first primarily of the Deuteronomist and the second of the Chronicler. However, the importance of these features is more than the simple biases of the biblical historians. They are facts about Judah's life which not only provided a more consistent leadership, but also enlisted a stronger identification of the populace with their nation's destiny. The temple at Jerusalem and the house of David became foci around which developed a strong sense of unity. Without prominent centers of traditional loyalty comparable to these, Israel both yielded to native Canaanite and Phoenician influence while intact as a nation and also lost her identity when subjected to the dispersal and mixture policies of Assyria. In possession of centers of national consciousness, Judah, however, was able to endure a national disaster similar to that confronted by her sister without final loss of faith, tradition, and identity.

Futile Hostility

Rehoboam (922–915). The circumstances of the 922 revolt have already been reviewed.[3] With wiser action by Rehoboam, schism might not have been so pronounced, but after the Shechem meeting the division was definite. The immediate reaction of Rehoboam was to gather an army to attempt forcibly to bring the rebellious Jeroboam into subjection. Except for the inter-

---

[2] For the brief period 842–837 Judah's throne was controlled by Athaliah, who was non-Davidic.
[3] See above, pp. 264–272.

vention of the prophet Shemaiah, there might have occurred a bloody, civil war from which neither Israel nor Judah could have recovered. Such was averted, however, and Rehoboam recouped what loyalty remained after the revolt.[4]

Dramatically influential upon relations between Judah and Israel was the action of Shishak of Egypt, the same pharaoh who had protected Jeroboam when he fled the wrath of Solomon. This Libyan founder of the 22nd dynasty of Egypt moved as far north as Megiddo on a plundering expedition to demonstrate his prowess in Syria-Palestine.[5] In 918 B.C., Jerusalem was saved from the strong force of Lybians and Nubians by the payment of extensive tribute, including much of the wealth which Solomon had accumulated in his temple and palace.[6] Shishak undoubtedly was endeavoring to restore Egypt's empire, but his untimely death ended the effort. The damage in Judah, however, was lasting. Crippled economically, her suppliance to Israel became more pronounced. Shishak's invasion had robbed her of both wealth and military prowess, losses from which she would be exceedingly slow to recover. Judah's very best efforts would provide little more than survival under the shadow of a flowering Israel.

In spite of the low state of her military vitality following the Shishak invasion, Judah's hostility with Israel endured. After Rehoboam and Jeroboam I, tension between the two thrones continued. Border towns in the north and south were fortified. Gibeah, Saul's old capital, in Judah and Bethel in Israel were reinforced as defensive measures. The clearest evidence of rivalry is seen at a place seven miles north of Jerusalem, known today as Tel en-Nasbeh. Here excavators have uncovered the most formidable of Judah's fortifications.[7] The wall around this city was twenty feet thick. A heavy coat of plaster on the lower part of the wall made it almost impossible for an enemy to scale. The fortification of Tel en-Nasbeh was probably the doing of Asa (913–873)

---

[4] Cf. II Chronicles 11:5-17.

[5] An inscription on the temple at Karnak in upper Egypt depicts this as a campaign which brought a host of Palestinian towns into subjection.

[6] Pritchard, *Ancient Near Eastern Texts*, pp. 263–264, 242–243. Because of the exaggerated nature of the claims, the inscription cannot be taken as an accurate historical account of the campaign.

[7] See Wright, *Biblical Archaeology*, p. 150.

and remains "eloquent testimony to the ill-feeling and civil war between Judah and Israel." [8]

Surprisingly, these feelings erupted into open conflict only on rare occasions. Such fighting as did occur was sporadic and mostly concerned with the rectification of border lines between the two states. This seems to be the situation described in II Chronicles 13 where Abijah (915–913) is described as defeating rather convincingly the forces of Jeroboam I. At best such a victory could only have been temporary, for shortly thereafter the two states were warring over border fortifications. [9]

A more resounding success was Judah's resistance to "Zerah the Ethiopian." [10] Zerah may have been an ambitious garrison commander left by Shishak to protect Egyptian interests on Judah's southern border. Asa met and defeated him. Having thwarted the aggressive Egyptian effort, Judah was free to continue her border bickering with Israel.

Frustrated Alliance

Sectional friction continued throughout the first half century of coexistence. Even with the establishment of the Omri dynasty in the north, little progress in direct reconciliation was made. Yet with the passing of time, feelings of antipathy became less intense. Gradually formal enmity gave way to semblances of friendship culminating in alliance. The factor decisive to coalition was the common threat of Syria. [11] The molder of the alliance was Jehoshaphat (873–849), who "made peace with the king of Israel." [12]

In many ways Jehoshaphat was a political idealist. He dreamed of a day when Israel and Judah could be reunited under common rule and the glory of Yahweh's people could be reestablished. This explains his willingness to join ranks with Ahab of Israel, even though Judah's role would approximate that of a vassal state. Ahab's predominating concern was resistance to Benhadad of Syria, while Jehoshaphat additionally desired to

[8] *Ibid.*, p. 151.
[9] See above, p. 275.
[10] II Chronicles 14:9–14.
[11] See above, pp. 279–280.
[12] I Kings 22:44.

break down the divisive wall between the two Israelite kingdoms. Jehoshaphat's dream, however, was not realized. In battle with Syria at Ramoth-gilead, Ahab was killed and Jehoshaphat
narrowly escaped with his life.[13] In a later joint campaign against
Ammon and Moab,[14] the alliance of Israel and Judah may have
fared a little better, but it did not approach anything resembling
political reunion.

The Yahwistic enthusiasms of Jehoshaphat met with more success at home. Both Kings [15] and Chronicles [16] praise the king as
a champion of Yahwism who resisted encroachments of pagan
tendencies. Like his father, Asa, Jehoshaphat is remembered as
a defender of Yahweh against Baalism.

In addition, Jehoshaphat accomplished important judicial reform. The ideal of justice in the courts was reaffirmed and steps
were taken toward its greater implementation. Such judicial reforms undoubtedly conserved community feelings in Judah while
despotism was becoming the norm in the north.

The South's Upheaval

The days of Jehoshaphat were followed by a period of political
confusion contemporary with the Jehu purge in Israel. Both nations underwent revolution, but the one in Judah was much
milder. The Israel-Judah alliance had been secured with the
marriage of Jehoshaphat's son, Jehoram, to Athaliah, a relative
of Ahab and Jezebel,[17] who like Jezebel was an ardent worshipper of Baal. With the accession of Jehoram (849–842), Athaliah
became the real power behind the throne. Her personal antagonism to Yahwism became markedly evident in Judah's political
life during this period. Through her influence a purge aimed at
eliminating Davidic claimants to the throne was inaugurated.

"A disease of the bowels" soon removed the ineffectual Jehoram, who was followed to the throne by his son Ahaziah (842).
During his abbreviated reign, Athaliah remained his "counselor
in doing wickedly." [18] Ahaziah soon paid an untimely visit to his

[13] Cf. II Chronicles 18.
[14] Cf. II Kings 3.
[15] I Kings 22:41–46.
[16] II Chronicles 19:1–3.
[17] Cf. Chapter 7, footnote 21.
[18] II Chronicles 23:3.

relatives in Israel. His arrival in Samaria happened to coincide with Jehu's appearance with dripping sword swinging. By the hand of Jehu, Ahaziah died and Athaliah (842–837) seized the throne, freely putting to death any who opposed her.

Although Athaliah was able to maintain control of Judah for several years, the people did not support her. They had little sympathy with her Baal worship and less with her non-Davidic background. Consequently, when the priest Jehoiada set forth Joash, a son of Ahaziah who had been saved from execution and protected in the temple, the people immediately rallied to his side. Athaliah was executed and the house of David was restored.

Resurgence in Judah

Fortunately Athaliah's reign was both short in duration and temporary in influence. The days of the next two kings, Joash and Amaziah, provided an interlude after Athaliah's evil reign, thereby making possible the glory of the reign of Uzziah (also known as Azariah).

With reservations, both Kings and Chronicles praise the reigns of Joash (837–800) and Amaziah (800–783). Since Joash was a mere lad of seven when he became king, Jehoiada served as leader during the king's minority. Under the priest's influence the temple was purified from the abominations of Athaliah and partially repaired. As long as Jehoiada lived, Joash walked in the ways of godliness. When the priest died, however, Joash fell under the influence of more lax elements. Thus the final days of Joash were marred by a return of paganism.

The reign of Amaziah was not very remarkable. Although he is reported to have done "what was right in the eyes of Yahweh," [19] incidents supporting this judgment are missing from the records. He did reconquer Edom, but suffered a disgraceful defeat at the hands of Joash of Israel.[20] Amaziah, like Joash before him, was assassinated in a palace revolt and the resurgence of Judah was left to his son, Uzziah.

Uzziah (783–742) came to the throne when he was sixteen

[19] II Kings 14:3; II Chronicles 25:2.
[20] Cf. I Chronicles 25.

years of age, but under his long and able rule Judah reached a zenith of power comparable to that of Solomon. Both he and his contemporary in Israel, Jeroboam II, capitalized upon Assyrian weakness to strengthen the internal life of their kingdoms. Uzziah restored the fortifications of Jerusalem which had been destroyed during his father's day. He reorganized and reequipped the army, introducing siege engines of warfare. Edom's subjugation was continued and the Philistine and Negeb areas were secured. Further, the port of Ezion-geber, renamed Elath, was repaired and the nearby copper smelteries of Solomon were restored.[21]

Judah shared with her northern sister a prosperity unknown since the days of the united kingdom. "During this period Judah was the most stable state in Palestine and probably in all Syria." [22] The high regard with which the people held Uzziah is attested by the fact that he remained the real ruler even after he was stricken with leprosy and forced to yield the public exercise of his office to his coregent Jotham (750–735).

The inconsequential reign of Jotham was followed by the inglorious days of Ahaz (735–715), who was king of Judah at the time of Israel's fall to Assyria. With the revival of Assyria under Tiglath-pileser [23] the existence of Judah, like that of all other western states, was threatened. Pekah of Israel and Rezin of Damascus led in the formation of a coalition to resist Assyria. Naturally they invited Judah to join. Both Jotham and Ahaz preferred to remain neutral, however, and refused to become a part of the coalition. When Pekah and Rezin invaded Judah "to bring her into line" and when Edom took this as an occasion to revolt, Ahaz appealed to Tiglath-pileser for aid and accentuated his plea with an enormous gift.[24] Through such a policy of appeasement with Assyria he hoped for Judah's survival.

This foreign policy of Ahaz was vehemently opposed by the prophet Isaiah.[25] He chided Judah because her heart "shook as

---

[21] A seal of Jotham unearthed recently in this area probably belonged to Uzziah's son and coregent and attests the activity of the king in developing the Negeb regions. See D. Diringer, "The Seal of Jotham," in *Documents from Old Testament Times*, pp. 224–225.

[22] W. F. Albright, *The Biblical Period*, p. 40.

[23] See above, pp. 286.

[24] See II Kings 16:5–8.

[25] Cf. Isaiah 7.

the trees of the forest shake before the wind" when she heard
of the league between Syria and Ephraim. In his famous Immanuel sign the prophet pronounced the ultimate fate of Judah's
compromise with Assyria.

For before the child knows how to refuse the evil and choose the good,
the land before whose kings you are in dread will be deserted. Yahweh
will bring upon you and your people and upon your father's house such
days as have not come since the day that Ephraim departed from Judah—
the king of Assyria. (Isaiah 7:16–17)

In spite of the stern warning by Isaiah, however, this policy probably saved Judah from Israel's fate. Tiglath-pileser moved decisively to destroy the Syro-Ephraimitic coalition and Damascus
fell in 732. Ten years later Samaria met a similar fate and Judah
was left alone. Ahaz had made Judah a vassal of Assyria, but she
did survive.

THE ASSYRIAN AND BABYLONIAN SHADOW (II KINGS 18–25) [26]

The political decision of Ahaz to align Judah with Assyria
undoubtedly saved Judah from terrifying destruction. Although
the choice spared the nation's life, it transformed her into a vassal state, and even this came at great price. Tribute to Assyria
drained her of considerable wealth and the temple had to be
stripped to pay the bill.[27] The territory which had been lost to
the Pekah-Rezin coalition was not recovered, and the profitable
industries of Ezion-geber lost to Edom were not regained. Judah's economy remained in a sad state throughout the days of
Ahaz.

Further, the reign of Ahaz was marked by one of Judah's most
exaggerated movements toward idolatry. Political subservience
to Assyria was accompanied by recognition of her gods. Alongside the great altar in the temple Ahaz constructed a bronze
altar for nominal worship of Assyrian deities. Also, high places
to other gods were provided "in every city in Judah." Such apostasy led Isaiah to say,

[26] See also II Chronicles 29–35.
[27] II Kings 16:8, 17.

> Their land is filled with idols;
> they bow down to the work of their hands,
> to what their own fingers have made.   (Isaiah 2:8)

The apostasy was so complete that Ahaz, on an unidentified occasion, offered his son as a sacrifice to Moloch according to Syrian
custom.[28]

The two features of political subservience and rank paganism
characterized the reign of Ahaz and were inseparably intertwined.
Blatant paganism had entered a door set ajar by political acquies-
cence and the faithful man of the street met agony from two
directions. On the one hand, the heavy taxes paid to Assyria
evidenced political dependence. On the other hand, idols to
Assyrian gods symbolized religious contamination.

Both religious apostasy and political servitude met strong opposition within Judah. This is understandable since devotion to
Yahweh and national self-determination were deep-seated in the
traditions of the covenant people.[29] Although a blind and fool-
hearted reaction by secular standards, many began to support
certain religious and religio-political enthusiasts who defied the
policy of compromise to Assyria. Standouts among these leaders
of discontent were the son of Ahaz, Hezekiah, and the prophets,
Isaiah and Micah.

Reforms of Hezekiah (715–687 B.C.)

Hezekiah succeeded his father to the throne when times were
ripe for reform. The converging of religious devotion and political enthusiasm made "reform" almost equivalent to "revolt."
Should these be considered two motivations rather than one, a
question might be raised concerning the depth of Hezekiah's religious concern: Was he primarily concerned with purifying
Judah's religion or did he use religious reform simply as an instrument for expressing political resistance to Assyria? But such a
question would have been only academic for Judah, since neither
Hezekiah nor his associates would have made such categorical
distinctions between religious reform and political independence.
Identifying the two objectives, Hezekiah took advantage of the

---

28 II Kings 16:3.
29 Cf. John Bright, *A History of Israel*, pp. 261–263.

Near Eastern Power of Influence in Palestine		Judah	
Assyria		Ahaz	735–715
Tiglath-pileser	745–727	(734 Syro-Ephraimitic War)	
Shalmaneser V	727–722		
(724–22 Siege of Samaria)			
Sargon II	722–705	Hezekiah	715–687
(722–21 Fall of Samaria)		(714–711 Ashdod Rebellion)	
Sennacherib	705–681	Manasseh	687–642
(701 Siege of Jerusalem)			
Esarhaddon	681–669		
Asshurbanapal	669–633?		
Assuretililani	633–629?	Amon	642–640
Sinsharishkun	?629–612	Josiah	640–609
(612 Fall of Nineveh to Babylon)			
Egypt			
Necho	609–593	(609 Battle at Megiddo, Josiah killed)	
		Jehoahaz	609
Babylon			
Nabopolassar	626–605	Jehoiakim	609–598
Nebuchadnezzar	605–562		
(605 Battle of Carchemish)			
(597 First expedition to Exile)		Jehoiachin	598–597
(587 Fall of Jerusalem, second group to Exile)		Zedekiah	597–587
(582 Third expedition to Exile)			

Figure 8–1. Judah, 722–582 B.C.

international scene and launched an internal reform which a decade later erupted into open rebellion against Assyria.

Immediately after Samaria's fall in 722/21, Sargon was greeted with dissension elsewhere in his Assyrian empire. Merodach-baladan [30] of Babylon successfully rebelled and other vassal states were prompted to follow suit. With Sargon's attention diverted from Palestine, Hezekiah was free to proceed with internal innovations clearly *contra* Assyria.

The initial steps of Hezekiah's reforms were internal. Rather

---

[30] II Kings 20:12.

than seeking to throw off the Assyrian yoke immediately, he began to reemphasize the centralization of Yahweh worship in Jerusalem. Local shrines where pagan practices had prevailed were torn down. A bronze serpent, associated with Moses, was removed from the temple. Assyrian elements introduced by Ahaz were withdrawn. Although this was tantamount to repudiation of Assyria, Sargon was too preoccupied with Merodach-baladan and others to give much attention to Judah.

In his desire to enlist the support of all the people for the shrine at Jerusalem, Hezekiah sent couriers throughout the land, including regions of defunct Israel, urging the people to "come to the house of Yahweh at Jerusalem to keep the passover." [31] The Chronicler indicates that while some success was achieved in Galilee, the people in Ephraim were cold in their reception of Hezekiah's program. Although not universally accepted or permanently successful, the reforms prepared the way for the similar work of Josiah a century later.

Since the religious actions of Hezekiah reflected resistance toward Assyria and prepared the way for open rebellion, the astute king took steps to strengthen Jerusalem's military position. The clearest example was his step to secure the city's water supply. An unreliable water supply had been a major weakness in Jerusalem's defense since the time of David. Except for a perennial fountain called Gihon, a spring just outside Jerusalem, the city had to depend on rain-filled reservoirs. A successful siege of Jerusalem could easily cut off access to Gihon and thereby place the defenders of the city in dire circumstances.

Hezekiah undertook to bring water from Gihon into Jerusalem in such a way that concealed it from an enemy. In an amazing feat of engineering, the king's workmen cut an aqueduct, almost a third of a mile long, through the solid rock beneath Jerusalem. The diggers began at both ends and with only slight miscalculation joined the excavated channels, known now as the Siloam tunnel. The Gihon spring was so sealed and camouflaged that it could not be observed from the outside and all its water was conducted through the tunnel into the city [32] to form the "pool of Siloam." An inscription found near the Siloam end of the tunnel "has for many years been the most important monumental piece

[31] II Chronicles 30:1.
[32] Cf. II Kings 20:20.

of writing in Israelite Palestine, and other Hebrew inscriptions have been dated by comparing the shapes of the letters with it." [33]

Revolt Against Assyria. Although the internal policies of Judah implied discontent with Assyrian domination and Sargon continued to be harassed by Merodach-baladan, Hezekiah refrained from open revolt. Assyrian records suggest that Hezekiah was related to a rebellion by Ashdod of Philistia; [34] but if he actually joined the revolt, he was able to withdraw in time to avoid Assyrian reprisals against the western states. Jerusalem was untouched on this occasion and for a while Hezekiah seems to have been content to follow his father's policy of submission.

The death of Sargon in 705 B.C., however, evoked a dramatic change in Hezekiah's policy. As usual, the change in administration created a moment of instability throughout the Assyrian empire. Troublesome Merodach-baladan saw in the uneasy transition to the new king, Sennacherib, an opportunity for organizing resistance to Assyria. He immediately enlisted support for a general revolt, not only in the nearby areas of Mesopotamia, but also in the west. Judah had an important place in his plans. On pretext of congratulating Hezekiah upon his recovery from a serious illness, Merodach-baladan sent messengers to Palestine. Hezekiah received the embassy cordially, opened for their review the resources of Judah, and identified Judah with the conspiracy.[35] Because of its advantageous military position, Jerusalem as the capital of the strongest state in southern Palestine was made a primary center of the rebellion. The small western states joined the league of resistance.

The die was cast. Although the policy of Hezekiah was strongly criticized by Isaiah the prophet,[36] the long simmering discontent erupted into overt resistance from which there was no turning back. Sennacherib and Assyria now stood as enemy of Judah.

Sennacherib's reaction to the conspiracy is recounted in both Assyrian and Hebrew records [37] with vivid, though somewhat con-

[33] Wright, *Biblical Archaeology*, p. 169.

[34] Cf. the broken prism A published by Winckler and reproduced in Pritchard, *Ancient Near Eastern Texts*, p. 287.

[35] Cf. II Kings 20.

[36] Cf. Isaiah 39.

[37] The cylinder of Sennacherib, a hexagon prism containing an account of his westward expedition, augments the biblical description of Sennacherib's invasion of Palestine in 701 B.C.

Figure 8–2. The outlet of Hezekiah's tunnel bringing water from the spring of Gihon to the pool of Siloam. The tunnel was cut through more than 1700 feet of solid rock. (Source: Paul Popper, Ltd.)

fusing, details. After Merodach-baladan had been subdued in the east, Sennacherib moved freely against the rebellious western coalition. The Assyrian's arrival in the west heralded an early collapse of the coalition. Tyre fell, marking the end of her commercial preeminence on the Mediterranean. In rapid succession

Figure 8–3. Assyrian relief picturing Sennacherib's siege of Lachish during the 701 campaign through Judah. Siege engines move against the tower as men and women carry their goods from the town. Three captives are impaled on spikes. (Source: Trustees of the British Museum.)

king after king of the opposition gave in—rushing to Sennacherib with tribute in hand. Cities of the Philistine plain fell before the crushing power of Assyrian armies. Forty-six fortified cities of Judah, by Sennacherib's counting, were reduced to submission.[38]

---

[38] The swift Assyrian march through Judah is vividly portrayed in Micah 1.

Hezekiah soon was shut up "like a bird in a cage in the midst of Jerusalem." [39]

With the coalition destroyed, Hezekiah saw little hope in further resistance and yielded. Vast areas of Judah were stripped from Hezekiah's control. Tribute was increased to such an extent that Hezekiah was forced to deplete his royal treasury and remove adornments from the temple to meet the assessment. [40]

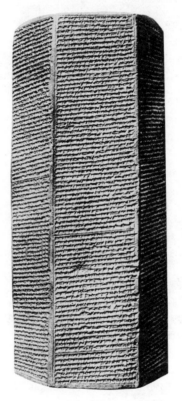

Figure 8–4. Hexagonal prism of Sennacherib recording details of eight campaigns, 705–681. The destruction of 46 cities and forts of Judah is recounted and Hezekiah is described as "a prisoner in Jerusalem, his royal residence like a bird in a cage." (Source: Courtesy of the Oriental Institute, University of Chicago.)

[39] Cf. the text of cylinder of Sennacherib, Pritchard, *Ancient Near Eastern Texts*, pp. 287 ff.

[40] II Kings 18:14–16.

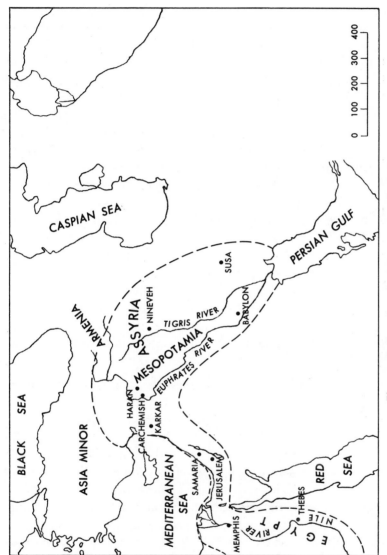

Figure 8–5. Assyrian Empire, c. 650 B.C.

Apparently Sennacherib soon left Palestine because of renewed trouble at home [41] only to return later to deal with another rebellion by Hezekiah.[42] About 691 B.C. Sennacherib, confronted by further revolt in Babylonia, suffered serious defeat. Conceivably this defeat encouraged Hezekiah to hazard a second revolt which recalled Sennacherib to Judah sometime during the closing days of the Judean king, 689–687 B.C. Jerusalem was spared by the intervention of an epidemic which crippled Sennacherib's army. Herodotus says that the Assyrian army was struck down by a plague of mice, possibly suggesting bubonic plague. Whatever the means, both the biblical historian and the prophet Isaiah saw Yahweh acting to redeem his people. Jerusalem was delivered, but Judah remained under the cloud of Assyrian control.

With strength derived from the prophetic support of Isaiah and Micah,[43] Hezekiah was able to resist idolatrous encroachments by his Assyrian overlord. The extent of his religious reforms is open to some question, and, as we shall see, they were not continuously effective. However, a reform party was established which, though early quiescent, would express unrest with the return of paganism and provide a milieu out of which a resurgent and thoroughgoing deuteronomic reform would explode during the day of king Josiah.

Manasseh (687–642). In spite of the immense struggle by Judah's religious leadership during the last half of the eighth century, Hezekiah's reforms were shortlived. Along with the passing of Hezekiah, Micah, and Isaiah went the gains of reform. With no outstanding prophetic voice to champion the cause of Yahwism, resistance to popular cults diminished; and when Manasseh followed his father to the throne in 687 B.C., a general retrogression from the high level of Isaianic faith set in which encountered no resistance from the new king.

Politically, Manasseh returned to the foreign policy of Ahaz. Throughout his long and infamous reign, the nation remained a voluntary vassal to Assyria. No other choice was left him since Assyria under Esarhaddon was at the zenith of her power, even controlling Egypt. Manasseh's submission, therefore, is under-

---

[41] II Kings 19:7.
[42] Cf. Bright, *A History of Israel,* pp. 282–287.
[43] See below, pp. 348–363.

standable, but not his enthusiasm for things Assyrian. Such an attitude of submission bore the same religious fruit under Manasseh as it had under Ahaz. Adoration of the gods of the suzerain became part of Judah's worship. Worship of Yahweh was not destroyed; he simply became one among many deities. This widespread downplay of Yahwism enabled old Canaanite fertility cults to be revived. Their local sanctuaries were rebuilt and their barbaric sacrifices of children as burnt offerings reappeared. All in all, the reforms of Hezekiah were, at least temporarily, swallowed up by broadening religious deterioration.

Such thoroughgoing idolatry was not without opposition. Quite likely it was ardent Yahwists whose blood "filled Jerusalem from one end to another." [44] Religious enthusiasts in the tradition of Isaiah could neither easily nor completely be silenced, and by the middle of the seventh century Judah once again needed and desired drastic and major religious reformation.

Josiah's Reforms

The half century following the death of Manasseh was undoubtedly the most tumultous time of Judah's life. Struggles between Assyria, Egypt, and Babylon for the control of the eastern world reached alarming proportions. As usual, the fate of Palestinian peoples was intimately entwined with these struggles. During these days Judah both soared to a zenith of glory on the tide of Josiah's deuteronomic reform and also prostrated herself in the dust of departed glory. So compact were the events of the period that one man, the prophet Jeremiah, could live to know a people who at one time sought "the fountain of living waters" and shortly thereafter "hewed out cisterns for themselves, broken cisterns, that can hold no water" (Jeremiah 2:13).

This is one of the better documented periods of Old Testament history. Although the Kings and Chronicles accounts devote most of their space to describing Josiah's reform, they are supplemented by the extensive prophetic writing of Zephaniah, Jeremiah, Ezekiel, Nahum, and Habakkuk. Additionally, Babylonian sources are exceedingly helpful in reconstructing the circumstances leading to the fall of Jerusalem. Especially informative

44 II Kings 21:16.

is the Babylonian Chronicle, a document giving detailed summary of Assyria's fall to Babylon. Altogether, these sources enable us to reconstruct in some detail the several decades prior to 587 B.C., the year of the destruction of the Judean state.

By the time of the accession of Josiah (640–609) the situation of world politics had developed to Judah's favor. During the closing decade of Manasseh's reign, Assyrian control over the eastern world had begun to waver. Although she was rivaled by no major world power, Assyria was torn by revolts within and continuing raids by barbarian tribes on her northern borders. Under Asshurbanapal (669–633?) she was barely able to maintain her integrity and equilibrium. By the time that Josiah had come to manhood, Asshurbanapal had passed from the scene and Assyria had lost effective control of her empire. Consequently, independence came to Judah in the 620's by default. Her severance of vassal ties with Assyria brought discredit to her former master's gods. Now political independence could merge with enthusiastic Yahwism to provide fertile ground for religious reforms.

Finding the Book. The early years of Josiah's reign are quite obscure. While he was still a child, the affairs of state were in other hands. Whether or not Yahwist enthusiasts were involved in the assassination of Amon, they certainly were in the role of advisors to the new young king. Also the prophet Zephaniah was probably active inside the palace during the early days of Josiah. His prophecy [45] describes circumstances before the reforms of the 620's, and it may be that he was among the young king's advisors.

Josiah's reform began around 626 when he came of age and began to assert himself as ruler of Judah. The initial event, which seems to have ignited the flames of religious reform by setting ablaze the tinder of growing independence and religious enthusiasm, was the finding of "the book (scroll) of the law" in the temple. This discovery came in 622 while the temple was undergoing repair. What was found was probably the major corpus of the book of Deuteronomy, a resume of Mosaic faith.[46] Hilkiah, the priest, took the work to Shaphan, secretary of the king, who in turn delivered it to Josiah. Josiah was immediately

[45] See below, pp. 364–365.
[46] See above, pp. 180–184.

and deeply moved by the radical contrast between the syncretism of contemporary religion in Judah and the lofty ideal of Mosaic faith.[47] The king's reaction enlarged the discovery of the law book into the most epochal of Judah's many religious reformations. What had been promoted for a long while behind the scenes by enthusiastic Yahwists had now found dynamic thrust and leadership.

The reforms of Josiah sought to establish religion of the character reflected in the book of Deuteronomy. Primary among the objectives was the centralization of worship in Jerusalem, entailing elimination of the adulterated cultic practices prevalent since the days of Manasseh. Calling a convocation of the people, Josiah read the newly discovered scroll in their hearing and decreed its prescriptions *the* law of the land.[48] This convocation took the form of a ceremony of covenant renewal, indicating that Josiah sought to incorporate certain amphictyonic ideals in the reform movement. The temple was cleansed of instruments for the worship of Canaanite and Assyrian gods. Astral worship, cult prostitution, child sacrifice to Moloch, mediums and wizardry were all "outlawed." High places and altars outside Jerusalem were destroyed. Included was that perpetual anathema in the deuteronomic tradition, the altar at Bethel. To the extent of Josiah's ability, worship was concentrated in Jerusalem.

The cultic reformation under Josiah had both political and religious implications. As had been the case with Hezekiah, purification of the cult was a graphic expression of Judah's independence from Assyria. And, since his reforms extended into the regions of the defunct northern kingdom,[49] it seems clear that Josiah's desire was to reestablish a united monarchy with a central religious shrine at Jerusalem. Further, the reclamation of the deuteronomic idea of centralized worship in Jerusalem tangibly expressed the unity of Judah's God. The following pointed words of Deuteronomy 6:4–5 [50] summarized the nation's understanding of her God.

---

[47] Cf. II Kings 22:11–20.

[48] II Chronicles 34:29–33.

[49] II Kings 23:19 speaks of the enforcement of his religious program in "all the cities of Samaria."

[50] These words open the *Shema,* the confession of faith which occupied a central place in the ritual of later Judaism.

Hear, O Israel: Yahweh our God is One Lord; and you shall love Yahweh your God with all your heart, and with all your soul, and with all your might.

The policies of Josiah affirmed this exclusiveness of Yahweh and undergirded the strong sense of nationalism which accompanied the rediscovery of Mosaic faith.

Externally, the Josianic reforms may be called successful. However, Judah's course was essentially unaltered. Outer change was accompanied by little inner commitment. The populace learned to trust the deceptive words, "the temple of Yahweh," without amending their ways and their doings.[51] Jeremiah, whose call came during the early days of the reform, reminded the people of Judah of the the fallacy of simple cultic reform without inward renewal.

Behold, you trust in deceptive words to no avail.
. . . .
Obey my voice, and I will be your God and you shall be my people; and walk in all the way that I commanded you, that it may be well with you. (7:8, 23)

Changing Political Scenery and Judah's Fall

The final decade of Josiah's reign witnessed a rapid and dramatic changing of the political scenery of the east. Assyria's mid-century heights of glory and strength faded with the passing of Asshurbanapal, but she succumbed only after great struggle. As late as 616 and 615 Nabopolassar of Babylon (626–605) failed in campaigns against her. In 614, however, the Medes joined forces with the Babylonians and the fate of Assyria became certain. Finally in 612 B.C. after an extended siege Nineveh, the proud capital of Assyria, fell to Medo-Babylonian power. Remnants of the Assyrian army led by a pretender king fled to Haran where they made a final furtive stand in 610 B.C.

The fall of Nineveh inflamed the growing anxiety of Egypt. Now only Palestine lay between her and the mounting force of the Babylonians and Medes. Consequently, Pharaoh Necho determined to take aggressive steps to halt the advance. Mustering his armies he began to march northward through Palestine to support the pretender Assyrian king in his attempt to repossess

[51] Jeremiah 7:3, 4.

Haran from the coalition of Babylonians and others. Josiah, long committed to an anti-Assyrian policy, elected to oppose Necho. If he could have stopped Necho, he would have been master of the west. Intercepting Necho on the famed battleground of Esdraelon at Megiddo, he challenged his right to pass. In the ensuing battle Josiah was tragically killed, or captured and executed, and his army fled the scene. This battle at Megiddo occurred in 609 and marked the end of Judah's most renowned king. Further, the death of Josiah terminated Judah's brief excursion in independence.

For a brief period after the battle at Megiddo, Judah fell to Egyptian control. A son of Josiah, Jehoahaz (609), was chosen by "the people of the land" to be the new king. But Jehoahaz, evidently not sympathetic enough with the conqueror, was deposed by Necho and taken to Egypt as prisoner. He was replaced by his brother, Jehoiakim (also known as Eliakim), who was more inclined to submit to Egypt.[52] A heavy tribute was laid on Judah insuring her vassalage to Necho.

Egyptian control of Palestine, however, was not of long duration. For several years the struggle between Egypt and Babylon was a standoff, but eventually the balance of world power shifted to Babylon. In 605 B.C. Necho was decisively defeated in battle at Carchemish by Babylonian forces led by Nebuchadnezzar (605–562). After this Egypt rapidly deteriorated as a power. Syria and Palestine were wrested from Necho's grasp and Judah stood naked before the onslaughts of surging Babylonian power.

Soon after his victory at Carchemish Nebuchadnezzar marched to the very edge of Egypt asserting his control over the Palestinian bridge of the Fertile Crescent. Jehoiakim (609–598), who owed his kingship to Necho's patronage, encountered no problem in switching allegiance to Nebuchadnezzar and Babylon. It was the same policy; only a new overlord. Judah became the vassal state of Babylon—an important factor in her ultimate downfall.

While Jehoiakim overtly paid homage to Babylon, he kept a watchful eye for opportunity to improve Judah's fortunes. In a further conflict between Egypt and Babylon in 601, Jehoiakim thought he saw Judah's hope. He rebelled and immediately

---

[52] By selecting the leader Necho asserted his full authority over Judah.

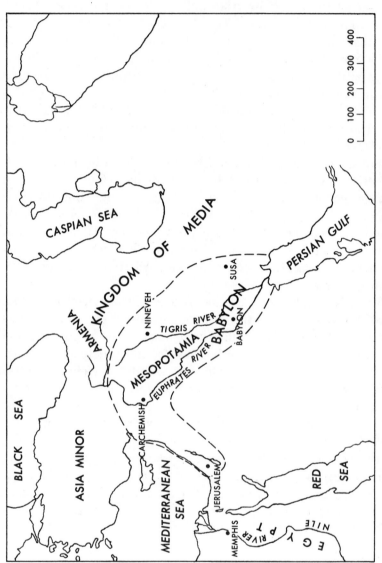

Figure 8–6. Babylonian Empire, 612–539 B.C.

Figure 8–7. Babylonian Chronicle for 605–594 B.C. After mentioning the battle of Carchemish and the accession of Nebuchadnezzar, the chronicle dates the capture of Jerusalem on March 16, 597 B.C. From this time of the first deportation, the final fall of Jerusalem in 587 can be accurately calculated. (Source: Trustees of the British Museum.)

found himself in difficulty with Nebuchadnezzar. By the time Nebuchadnezzar arrived in Palestine to crush the rebellion, Jehoiakim had died and been replaced by his son, Jehoiachin (598–3 months). The defense of Jerusalem was less than a full-scale operation and after only three months the city was open to the invader.

Nebuchadnezzar was surprisingly lenient with Judah on this occasion. A considerable number of captives [53] were taken to Babylon, although most of the populace remained around Jerusalem. Included among the deportees were the king, his royal family, and a major segment of Jerusalem's intelligentsia. The prophet Ezekiel and others of religious and political prominence were among the captives. Evidently, by diminishing Judah's

[53] Cf. II Kings 24:14, 16; Jeremiah 52:28.

leadership Nebuchadnezzar hoped to preclude further revolt. The Holy City itself was spared, but it suffered the loss of a heavy toll of booty. The deportation of 597 [54] marked an economic and political trauma from which Jerusalem and Judah never recovered.

Although in exile, Jehoiachin was still considered king of Judah by both the people at home and the Babylonians.[55] The practical affairs of state, however, were conducted in Jerusalem by his uncle Zedekiah (597–587), a weakling who could provide little of the much needed stability in the days of crisis. While Zedekiah must have sworn allegiance to Babylon to receive Nebuchadnezzar's support,[56] he was continually enamoured by ideas of rebellion. His limping between the two opinions of allegiance and rebellion brought him under the suspicions of Babylon [57] and incurred the opposition of Jeremiah.[58] As early as 594 Zedekiah began to toy with the idea of revolt. Conferences were held with ambassadors from the neighboring subject states of Edom, Moab, Tyre, and Sidon. Even some prophets encouraged the idea, actually predicting the return of the captives within two years. Jeremiah, however, supported submission and continually denounced the palace for every notion of rebellion. The yoke of Babylon was to be borne as the will of Yahweh.[59] Jeremiah went so far as to write the captives that they should make themselves at home in Babylon and plan for an extended stay.[60] This position of appeasement and apparent collaboration brought the hatred of the populace upon the prophet. The man in the street considered him a quisling who advocated selling out to the enemy.

For some reason Zedekiah's plan for revolt came to naught and he sent envoys to Babylon to make peace with Nebuchadnezzar. The tide of patriotism, however, was not held back for long. The "patriotic party" began to pressure Zedekiah to bid for Egyp-

---

[54] This date, long a subject of scholarly debate, was supplied in 1956 with the publication of a tablet of the Babylonian Chronicle in D. J. Wiseman, *Chronicles of Chaldean Kings: (626–566 B.C.) in the British Museum.*

[55] Cf. Wright, *Biblical Archaeology*, pp. 177–8. Also, Albright, "King Jehoiachin in Exile" in *The Biblical Archaeologist Reader*, pp. 106–112.

[56] Cf. Ezekiel 17:13 ff.

[57] Cf. Jeremiah 51:59.

[58] Cf. Jeremiah 21:3–7.

[59] Cf. Jeremiah 27–28.

[60] Jeremiah 29.

tian support and rebel. The king repeatedly consulted with Jeremiah, who resolutely advised submission to Babylon. Zedekiah, devoid of clear conviction himself and unable to control his nobles, finally yielded to the voices of revolution. Judah bolted in 589.

Nebuchadnezzar reacted with dispatch and ferocity. He marched into Palestine, overran outlying areas and laid siege to Jerusalem. The defense of the city was noble, but futile. Token help from Egypt brought only temporary relief.[61] Inside the city Jeremiah advised capitulation and almost lost his life.[62] Famine became a major problem. Morale sank to the bottom and pitiable Zedekiah ran continually to Jeremiah hoping for some word of optimism. Finally, in July of 587, after an eighteen months siege the city fell. The date of the fall may now be established with relative precision on the basis of calculation from the 597 date clarified by the Babylonian Chronicle.[63]

Zedekiah fled the city, but was captured and brought before Nebuchadnezzar at Riblah. After compelling Zedekiah to witness the execution of his sons, they put out his eyes and led him away in chains to Babylon. The captain of Nebuchadnezzar's guard was dispatched to Jerusalem to level her walls and burn the city to the ground. Many leading citizens were slain. The remainder of the inhabitants, save those who fled Jerusalem and some of the poorest vinedressers and plowmen, were carried captive to Babylon. This deportation left the political and economic life of Jerusalem at a standstill and Judah as a state gone forever. Jeremiah, given his choice of going to Babylon or remaining in Judah, chose to stay in the land with the peasantry.

The thankless task of trying to bring some semblance of order out of the chaos in and around Jerusalem fell to Gedaliah, a former palace official who was appointed governor by Nebuchadnezzar. Since Jerusalem was in ruins, the seat of government was transferred to Mizpah. Gedaliah began wooing the confidence of certain captains of the army who had escaped the Babylonian sword. Before any ordered structure could be achieved, however, the

---

[61] Jeremiah 37.

[62] Jeremiah 38.

[63] A summary discussion of this calculation may be found in David N. Freedman's article, "The Babylonian Chronicle," in *The Biblical Archaeologist Reader*, pp. 119–124. See above, Figure 8–7 and footnote 54.

new governor was assassinated by a group of overzealous patriots backed by the king of Ammon and led by Ishmael, a member of Judah's royal family. Captains of the army fearing further reprisals from Babylon fled with a following to Egypt, taking Jeremiah with them. Consequential to the assassination of Gedaliah, a third deportation to Babylon occurred, probably around 582 B.C.

THE PROPHETIC MOVEMENT IN JUDAH: EIGHTH CENTURY PROPHETS (ISAIAH: 1–39, MICAH)

During the chaotic period in the latter half of the eighth century B.C. when Israel to the north was moving through her final days toward destruction by the Assyrians in 722/21 B.C., two prophets were active in Judah. Isaiah of Jerusalem and Micah followed in the tradition established by Amos and Hosea in Israel. In fact, they were in some ways dependent on the religious concepts enunciated by their Israelite counterparts, although there is no recorded acknowledgement of their indebtedness.

Isaiah

The prophet Isaiah was called to his mission in 742 B.C., "the year that King Uzziah died," [64] and was still active during Sennacherib's siege of Jerusalem in 701 B.C. His wife was called a "prophetess," [65] and two sons bore names symbolic of important themes in his preaching. It is certain that he was city-bred, if not city-born. He knew Jerusalem well. Its streets, defenses (towers, wall, and water supply), and temple were all familiar places to him. He may have come from the Jerusalem aristocracy; at least he moved freely in circles of royalty and nobility. Whether he was an aristocrat or not, something aristocratic, if not regal, characterized his prophetic manner and his literary style.

Isaiah was "unofficially" court prophet to both Ahaz and Hezekiah, while not departing from the independent prophetic tradition begun by Amos and Hosea. He was no "hireling" of the court paid to predict good for kings upon whom he was depend-

[64] The date of Uzziah's death is debated between 746 and 742 B.C.
[65] Isaiah 8:3.

ent for support. Rather, he was Yahweh's representative before rulers and his counsel was heard, though not always heeded.

The Book of Isaiah. The message of the prophet is contained in the first part of our canonical book of Isaiah. Although Isaiah appears in the Bible as a single unit of sixty-six chapters, its material is neither the work of a single author, nor from the same historical period. Chapters 1–39 differ dramatically from chapters 40–66. For example: (1) the background of 1–39 is the Assyrian crisis; that of 40–66 is the exile and after; [66] (2) the former develops the idea of Yahweh's holiness, the latter gives emphasis to his infinity; (3) 1–39 is concerned with a messianic king, 40–66 proposes the idea of a "suffering servant"; (4) the atmosphere of the first part of the book, like that of Amos and Hosea, is one of rebuke, in 40–66 the writer's pronounced desire is to encourage and comfort Yahweh's people. These with many other reasons have led to the widely accepted conclusion that chapters 40–66 were written sometime after the fall of Jerusalem and are related to the captivity and return from exile. They are usually designated as Deutero-Isaiah.

The message of Isaiah of preexilic Jerusalem is confined, therefore, to chapters 1–39 of the book which bears his name. However, not all of these chapters are his. The oracles of the eighth century prophet are found primarily in chapters 1–12, 13–23, and 28–31. The remainder of the material comes from prophetic sources of other times. An annotated outline may clarify the complex structure of the prophetic anthology found in this first half of the book of Isaiah.

Editorial introduction. 1:1.
I. Early oracles against Israel and Judah. 1:2–Chapter 12.
These oracles are the core of Isaiah's message, containing words of doom and hope. Most of this material came from Isaiah of Jerusalem although there are a few minor additions throughout.
II. Oracles against foreign nations. 13–23.[67]
The oracles against Assyria, Philistia, the Syro-Ephraimitic coali-

---

[66] Jerusalem has been destroyed and the exile is a present fact (42:22; 49:14–21). Babylon is mentioned as place of exile (47:1–5; 48:14) and Babylon's conqueror Cyrus is even mentioned by name (44:28).

[67] This section is similar to collections of oracles on foreign nations found in Jeremiah and Ezekiel (Cf. Amos 1–2:8), indicating that the oracle of judgment upon Israel's enemies was a popular literary type among the prophetic group.

tion, and Arabia are from Isaiah. Those against Egypt and Tyre may be from him. The others all appear to be later additions.
III. The Little Apocalypse. 24–27.
   A picture of Yahweh's cosmic judgment, followed by full restoration. Similar to material from exilic and postexilic period. These chapters may be as late as the fifth century or even later, one cannot be sure. They contain the first clear references to the resurrection of the dead (25:8 and 26:19).
IV. Six woes. 28–32.
   Primarily from the time of the Sennacherib crisis, 705–701. Appeals for dependence upon Yahweh's power to save followed by the promise of a king who would rule in righteousness. Most of this material comes from Isaiah.
 V. A prophetic liturgy. Chapter 33.
   Probably comes from the Isaiah tradition, but not from Isaiah himself.
VI. Oracles of doom and salvation. 34–35.
   The situation presupposed here is that of the exile or later and the style is similar to that of chapters 40–66 with which the chapters should be associated.
VII. Historical narratives. 36–39.
   Almost identical with II Kings 18:13–20:19 from which it was taken.

How did it come about that all of these materials plus the prophecies in chapters 40–66 were gathered into one unit linked with the name of Isaiah of Jerusalem? The answer seems to be that Isaiah's words and deeds were remembered, recorded, and elaborated by a circle of disciples.[68] An Isaiah tradition developed based upon the teachings of the great prophet and was passed on and continued to influence Israelite life and faith. Gradually oracles consistent with Isaiah's teachings and originating among his followers were added to the original core of genuine Isaianic material. The majority of chapters 1–39 had thus been shaped by the time of the exile. During the exile, the Isaiah tradition influenced the great unknown (or unknowns) who produced the majestic materials of 40–66. When the exile was over, the two blocks of material were placed together as a great presentation of Isaianic prophetic faith. Isaiah of Jerusalem was, therefore, a man whose vision and spirit impressed those about him to the degree that his influence lived on long after his death.

[68] Isaiah 8:16 ff.

The Crises of Isaiah's Ministry. The oracles of Isaiah of Jerusalem can be gathered around three major crises in Judah's history.

1. The Syro-Ephraimitic War, 734 B.C. In general, chapters 1–12 belong to the period between the prophet's call in 742 and the Syro-Ephraimitic conflict which led to the preservation among his followers of the message so curtly rejected by King Ahaz.
2. The Ashdod Rebellion, 714–711 B.C. When Sargon II marched through Syria, Israel, and Judah to capture Ashdod, Isaiah warned Hezekiah that he should not take part in the Egyptian-inspired intrigue against Assyria. The prophet went naked for three years during the Assyrian threat as a reminder that those who depended upon Egypt rather than trusted in Yahweh would suffer similar fate as Assyrian prisoners of war. Apparently Isaiah's "prophetic symbolism" had the desired effect, because Hezekiah was not attacked by Assyria.
3. The Revolt of the Western Coalition and the Sennacherib Invasion, 705–701 B.C. Hezekiah participated in this rebellion bringing the Assyrian armies to Jerusalem. The prophetic faith of Isaiah inspiring both king and people saved the day.

A glimpse at oracles selected from these periods of Isaiah's ministry gives us some idea of the spiritual dimension and political insight characteristic of the man.

Called by the Holy One: Chapter 6. During the Syro-Ephraimitic crisis, Isaiah wrote an account of his call as he had come to understand it through the years. Even though written in retrospect, this is an authentic account of the determinative vocational moment in his life, the time when he became a prophet. The chapter describes the important psychological and spiritual experience through which Isaiah passed in the year king Uzziah died. The exact occasion is not mentioned, but in the background of the experience are the dramatic events connected with the death of one king and the coronation of another. The prophet was tragically disturbed because the long and prosperous reign of Uzziah had ended. The immediate situation was critical; the future ominous. The life of the people of Judah centered in their king,[69] and grief was great at the death of a good one. How could Judah face the increasing Assyrian menace under the leadership

---

[69] Johannes Pedersen, *Israel: Its Life and Culture,* p. 275.

of Uzziah's weak and ineffectual son Jotham? Out of disheartening sorrow of such an hour Isaiah became a prophet when he saw *The King* Yahweh, the real ruler of Israel, seated upon his throne. The prophet then realized that while kings on David's throne might come and go, Yahweh was Judah's everlasting king and upon him the security of the Davidic state depended.

The place of this inaugural vision was the Jerusalem temple and its form that of a cleansing ritual. The prophet stood in the temple where he may have served in some official capacity as a priest or, more likely, a temple prophet.[70] At a moment in the ritual in which the kingship of Yahweh was celebrated, he gained a new and deeper understanding of what it meant for Holy Yahweh to be king over Judah. He saw Yahweh seated in council with his heavenly court in judgment over the nation.

In the year that King Uzziah died I saw Yahweh sitting upon a throne, high and lifted up; and his train filled the temple. Above him stood the seraphim; each had six wings: with two he covered his face, and with two he covered his feet, and with two he flew. And one called to another and said:
"Holy, holy, holy is Yahweh of hosts; the whole earth is full of his glory." (6:1–4)

His response was a confession of sin and unworthiness.

Woe is me! For I am lost; for I am a man of unclean lips, and I dwell in the midst of a people of unclean lips; for my eyes have seen the King, Yahweh of hosts! (6:5)

After being symbolically cleansed the prophet responded to the divine call, "Whom shall I send and who will go for us?" with a positive affirmation of his dedication, "Here I am! Send me." He was then presented with a dreadful commission. He was to declare the will of Yahweh even though Judah's failure to respond would develop into stubborn opposition making response impossible. Isaiah protested: "How long, O Lord?" to be told,

Until cities lie waste without inhabitant, and houses without men, and the land is utterly desolate, and Yahweh removes men far away, and the forsaken places are many in the midst of the land. (6:11b–12)

But he was also given a glimmer of hope. Yahweh might build up a new Israel from the ruins of his faithless people.

[70] See R. B. Y. Scott, "Isaiah" in *The Interpreter's Bible*, V, 207–208.

And though a tenth remain in it, it will be burned again, like a terebinth or an oak, whose stump remained standing when it is felled. The holy seed is its stump. (6:13)

Isaiah developed this glimmer into a doctrine of a purged and purified remnant in whom the nation survived as the people of God.

Faith (Isaiah) and Expediency (King Ahaz): The Syro-Ephraimitic Crisis. When Ahaz was faced with war against Israel and Syria (Damascus), "his heart and the heart of his people shook as the trees of the forest shake before the wind" (7:2b). With confident faith Isaiah encouraged the king to trust Yahweh for deliverance. Israel and Syria were only smoking firebrands about to burn out and Yahweh would render them totally incapable of harming Judah.[71]

Ahaz refused to listen to Isaiah and out of expediency appealed for Assyrian help. To Isaiah this was unfaithfulness. Yahweh alone could deliver and alliance with Assyria was a covenant with death. To become debtor to that empire was to become its slave. Ahaz was opening the door of Judah's doom. When the king refused to heed the prophetic advice, Isaiah pronounced the famous sign of the royal child Immanuel.

Therefore the Lord himself will give you a sign. Behold, a young woman shall conceive and bear a son, and shall call his name Immanuel. (7:14)

The symbolic name given this child is intriguing because it may mean at once both judgment and promise. God's presence with his people can be the devastating divine presence acting in wrath against sin. Clearly Immanuel does have that significance. The child would see tragic days of Assyrian invasion of his land.

Therefore, behold, the Lord is bringing up against them the waters of the River, mighty and many, the king of Assyria and all his glory; and it will rise over all its channels and go over all its banks; and it will sweep on into Judah, it will overflow and pass on, reaching even to the neck; and its outspread wings will fill the breadth of your land, O Immanuel. (8:7-8)

But the name "God with us" also is intended to be a sign of promise. The child would live through the disaster as a reminder of Yahweh's presence to redeem a remnant through which the nation would be saved.

[71] Isaiah 7:3-9.

The Song of the Vineyard: The Summary of Isaiah's Early Ministry. When Ahaz refused to accept Isaiah's admonition to trust Yahweh, the prophet committed his teachings to his disciples for preservation until a time when they would be heeded.

Bind up the testimony, seal the teaching among my disciples. (8:16)

The testimony book must have included much of chapters 1–11, upbraiding the people for their sinful ways. Judah like Israel stood under Yahweh's judgment. More dumb than oxen and with less insight than asses they had been rebellious sons and now were utterly estranged (1:2–4). The prophet's thoughts on the sins of the people are climaxed by the minstral song of the vineyard in which Isaiah sings of a farmer who bestowed tender and loving care upon a vineyard on a fertile hill. He digged, cleared, and planted it with choice vines. He guarded its plants and made preparation to enjoy their wine. Then harvest came and the vines yielded wild, inedible grapes. In judgment he destroyed the vines and made the field a waste, forbidding the clouds to rain upon it. Then to climax the song and make his point quite clear, Isaiah explained:

For the vineyard of Yahweh of hosts is the house of Israel, and the men of Judah are his pleasant planting; and he looked for justice (*mishpat*), but behold, bloodshed (*mishpach*); for righteousness (*tsdakah*), but behold, a cry (*ts'akah*)! (5:7)

Emerging Messianic Expectations. Prominent among Isaiah's sermons are a number of oracles of messianic character. These proclamations deal with an ideal king from David's line who will come to establish the wholeness of life for which Israel's faithful people yearn. Beyond his judgment on the sinful nation Yahweh would reestablish the Davidic rule through a newborn child destined for the throne.

> For to us a child is born, to us a son is given;
> and the government will be upon his shoulder,
> and his name will be called
> "Wonderful Counselor, Mighty God, Everlasting Father, Prince
>   of Peace."
> Of the increase of his government and of peace there will be
>   no end,
> upon the throne of David, and over his kingdom,
> to establish it, and to uphold it with justice and with righteous-
>   ness from this time forth and for evermore. (9:6–7)

The destruction pictured by Isaiah was redemptive in its character. From the ruins of the Davidic dynasty a king would rise as Yahweh began again to establish for himself a covenant people. Also a remnant would emerge, purged of evil ways and anxious to be led by Yahweh's representative.   *Daniel Falba*

> There shall come forth a shoot from the stump of Jesse, and
>   a branch shall grow out of his roots.
> And the Spirit of Yahweh shall rest upon him, the spirit of wisdom and understanding, the spirit of counsel and might, the spirit of knowledge and the fear of Yahweh.
> And his delight shall be in the fear of Yahweh. (11:1–3)

With such a king to rule over them Judah would fare well and fulfill her place in Yahweh's plan for mankind.

Precisely who Isaiah had in mind in these messianic portraits cannot be determined, nor is it possible to discern how soon he expected them to be fulfilled. If they are related to the Immanuel sign of chapter 7 (and they may well be), the prophet felt that fulfillment was imminent. Likely they are coronation hymns for Hezekiah. At any rate, the prophet looked forward to a king from David's line who would embody what Yahweh intended kings to be, ruling his people with justice and equity and establishing for them "peace," which meant everything necessary for the good life. John Bright summed it up well when he said:

The messianic hope of Israel was thus tied firmly to the line of David, to Jerusalem and the temple, and given a form which it would never lose. A mighty faith was therewith created which nothing could shatter. Indeed, the darker the days, the brighter its flame. For Messiah does not come to a proud nation glorying in its strength, but to a beaten nation, a cut-down stump of a nation, a nation tried in the furnace of affliction. No humiliation could be so abject, no torment so brutally severe, but that faith might whisper: Who knows but that this suffering is the purge that is even now producing the pure Remnant; who knows but that tomorrow Messiah, the Prince of David's line, may come? [72]

There was in this prophetic hope, however, real danger. Israel did make the mistake of confusing the hope with this particular form of its expression, and dared to believe that Jerusalem and the Davidic state could never be destroyed. Later she even attached messianic expectations to unlikely pretenders from David's

---

[72] John Bright, *The Kingdom of God,* p. 93.

line and denied him who in Christian understanding was Messiah
because he was so unlike a king.

Quiet and Confident Faith: Isaiah and the Sennacherib Crisis.
When Sargon of Assyria died in 705 B.C., the western states raised
the signal for revolt, hoping that troubles at home would detain
the new Assyrian monarch from putting down the rebellions.
Encouraged by a promise of Egyptian and Babylonian help,
Judah's leaders made what Isaiah termed a "covenant with
death." [73] They joined the coalition against Assyria. Sargon's
successor, Sennacherib, quickly squelched the opposition to his
sovereignty in Assyria and moved to deal with the western rebels.

Isaiah proclaimed that only a covenant faith could annul the
covenant Judah had made with death. Alliance with Egypt, an
unreliable source of help, was useless.

> Egypt's help is worthless and empty,
> 　　therefore, I have called her
> 　　"Rahab (great dragon) who sits still."
> . . . .
> The Egyptians are men, and not God:
> 　　and their horses are flesh, and not spirit.[74]　(30:7, 31:3)

Then, in a word which sounded the ruling principle of his states-
manship, he told Judah of salvation's hope:

> In returning and rest you shall be saved;
> In quietness and in trust shall be your strength.　(30:15)

Repentance and faith in Yahweh, not political alliance and intrigue, was the solution to Judah's insecurity. Quiet faith, without anxiety or fear, and trust in sovereign Yahweh was Isaiah's
formula for deliverance.

For a while Judah would have none of this advice, trusting instead in military might and political alliances.[75] Soon, however,
she felt the fierce wrath of Assyrian might as Sennacherib swept
through the countryside leaving fields, towns, and walled cities
in ruins. From Jerusalem Isaiah looked out upon his land and
lamented:

> From the sole of the foot even to the head,
> 　　there is no soundness in it,

[73] Isaiah 28:18.
[74] Parentheses added.
[75] See Isaiah 30:2–5 and 16.

> but bruises and sores and bleeding wounds;
> they are not pressed out, or bound up,
>   or softened with oil.
> Your country lies desolate, your cities are
>   burned with fire;
> in your very presence aliens devour your
>   land; it is desolate, as overthrown by
>   aliens. (1:6–7)

Jerusalem alone was left to Judah, a "lodge in a cucumber field."

With the holy city itself threatened with destruction, Hezekiah and his "faithful remnant" repented in sackcloth and ashes. Then Isaiah declared that Jerusalem would not fall. Yahweh would protect the city of his habitation, the seat of David's line, from the anger of the haughty Assyrian who dared to question the power of Judah's God.[76]

Summary of Isaiah's Faith. Certain concepts emerge as determinative of Isaiah's message to his people. First, the idea of Yahweh's holiness was pivotal in his thinking. As a devoted Yahwist Isaiah denounced the efforts of the people to shun the ethical responsibilities consequent to their relationship to Yahweh. Yahweh was of a majesty that was austere. So vividly did Isaiah believe this that his sense of mission centered around it. His call to prophetic ministry, as recounted in Isaiah 6, was essentially his reaction to the presence of the holy Yahweh, who knows no comparison. In the presence of his Holy One the prophet immediately sensed his own sin. Amos prayed for the people, but Isaiah began with prayer for himself.

The holiness of Yahweh also brought national sin into focus. Yahweh of Hosts was the "Holy One of Israel." [77] In the same way that Amos had assailed the northern kingdom, Isaiah denounced the south for immoral conduct which violated the very character of Yahweh. Outward displays of religion without corresponding moral standards were a sacrilege to Yahweh. The decadent upper class meant that the nation was crumbling from within,[78] and the Day of Yahweh was to be a day of judgment. Against the background of the holy character of Yahweh the prophet painted his portrait of national catastrophe.

[76] See Isaiah 36–38.
[77] Isaiah 1:4.
[78] Cf. Isaiah 3.

A second determinative concern of Isaiah was what Martin Buber calls his "theo-politics." [79] That is, Isaiah believed that Judah as a nation should owe allegiance first, last, and only to a sovereign God. This concept directly determined the advice on foreign policy which Isaiah gave. He opposed all entangling alliances with foreign powers on the basis that such relationships violated complete dependence upon Yahweh. The real salvation of Judah rested in her confident trust in the rule of Yahweh.

This basic concept charted Isaiah's advice to the king (whether Ahaz or Hezekiah) on matters of foreign policy. He opposed joining the Syro-Ephraimitic coalition against Assyria; he also opposed appealing to Assyria for help.[80] Dependence upon Yahweh was the essence of deliverance. The same premise lies in the background of Isaiah's directive to Hezekiah. Redemption from the scourge of Assyria would come solely from the Holy One of Israel. Dependence upon "the shadow of Egypt" would only consummate in Judah's humiliation.[81] Isaiah would have agreed with the general of Sennacherib that dependence upon Egypt was like leaning on a broken staff.[82] However, Judah was not to submit quietly to Assyria's dominion. When siege was laid to Jerusalem by Sennacherib, Isaiah was confident that Yahweh would deliver his people.[83] Yahweh was Judah's sovereign and the destiny of his people was directly correlated to her reliance upon his promises. This Isaianic emphasis became the basis for an optimism in the religious thinking of Judah out of which would emerge the definite structure of hope expressed in Deutero-Isaiah.

Closely associated with this idea of "theo-politics" is Isaiah's emphasis upon the continuity of the Davidic monarchy. We have already seen how in Judah the "covenant with David" virtually replaced the Sinai covenant.[84] Isaiah's hope for a continued relationship between Yahweh and Israel was not based upon return to the principles of the covenant of Sinai, but upon the conviction that Yahweh would be faithful to his covenant with David and through his line establish peace and prosperity for the nation.

---

[79] See M. Buber, The Prophet Faith, pp. 135 ff.
[80] See Isaiah 7.
[81] Isaiah 30:1–5.
[82] Isaiah 36:6.
[83] Cf. Isaiah 37:5–7.
[84] See above, pp. 249–250.

Isaiah was from Jerusalem, David's city, "where the 'David idea' lived with tenacious power." [85] He naturally, therefore, associated Yahweh's redemptive activity with the promise made to Israel's greatest king. His faith in Yahweh was the basis of his hope, and his associations with Jerusalem and its kings prompted the expectations of the way that hope would be realized. When the ideal age dawned after the purging of the nation, the messianic king would come in Yahweh's redemptive activity. He would come from David's line,[86] a shoot from Jesse's stump to stand as an ensign to all people,[87] reigning over the redeemed faithful remnant of the people of God.

The final dominant concept is Isaiah's "doctrine of the remnant." Yahweh's purpose in history would be realized through the faithful few who remained loyal to him. Isaiah, therefore, distinguished between "Israel according to the flesh" and "Israel according to the spirit." Now with the northern state gone Yahweh would work out his salvation in Judah, never as guilty as her northern relative. But Isaiah was realist enough to know that such a distinction could not be so precisely drawn. Judah was not blameless; in fact, most of her people were as rebellious as their brethren to the north had been. Further, some from Israel now scattered among the nations had been faithful. The remnant, therefore, of which Isaiah had much to say was the remnant of Yahweh's faithful, whether from Israel or Judah (Isaiah perhaps believed more from Judah than Israel, which is understandable).

The judgment which had fallen upon Israel and would soon fall upon Judah was a purge out of which the remnant of God's people would emerge.

> I will turn my hand against you and will smelt away your dross as with lye and remove all your alloy.
>
> . . . .
>
> And he who is left in Zion and remains in Jerusalem will be called holy, everyone who has been recorded for life in Jerusalem. (1:25; 4:3)

The prophet named one of his sons Maher-shalal-hash-baz, "The spoil speeds, the prey hastens," symbolic of the fiery trial to befall

[85] John Bright, *The Kingdom of God*, p. 91.
[86] See Isaiah 9:7.
[87] Isaiah 11:1 and 10.

the nation, and the other Shear-jashub, "A remnant shall return," symbolic of the hope that from the purge would come forth the true people of God. The prophet left this idea with his disciples among whom it developed along the lines expressed by the Isaianic prophet of the exile in the portrait of the "Suffering Servant."

Micah

The prophet Micah was a contemporary of Isaiah and consequently preached to the same situation. Unlike Isaiah, Micah was a man "of the people." He was from a peasant background, a native of Moresheth in the Shephelah. But like Isaiah, he was not deceived by the pretentious facade of Judah's culture. He scathingly denounced the rich who exploit the small farmer (2:1-5), prophets who divine for money (3:11), and politicians who "tear the skin from off" the people (3:1-3). Micah knew first hand the sufferings of the poor and proclaimed his message in keeping with traditions common in the prophetic movement.

The superscription of his book relates his work to the kingship of Jotham (750-735), Ahaz (735-715), and Hezekiah (715-687), but the Micah oracles contained in the book belong generally to the time of Hezekiah. The activity of the prophet was primarily concerned with crises of the Ashdod rebellion of 714-711 and Sennacherib's invasion of Judah in 701. In both of these situations Micah saw the possibility of Jerusalem's destruction and may have been discredited when this did not come to pass. However, Jeremiah validates the work of Micah, indicating the effect which his preaching had on Hezekiah.

Did he (Hezekiah) not fear Yahweh and entreat the favor of Yahweh, and did not Yahweh repent of the evil which he had pronounced against them? (26:19)

The book which contains the preaching of Micah is a composite of doom and hope. Micah in its present form preserves the work of both the prophet and a circle of disciples and presents a balanced message of judgment and promise. The prophet himself may have given greater stress to disaster that was about to befall Judah and left largely to disciples the addition of oracles of hope. The final editor of the book has balanced the prophet's message by including both stern pronouncements of doom and oracles of comfort and consolation.

Generally chapters 1–3 come from the prophet himself. Of these materials only the oracle in 2:12–13 is seriously questioned as coming from Micah. Chapters 4–7 seem to be composed of two anthologies (4–5 and 6–7) at least interspersed with materials of later date, but certainly containing materials from the eighth century prophet. Chapter 4:1–5 is the same oracle preserved in Isaiah 2:2–4 and is probably included in Micah to bring hope to the grim despair portrayed in chapter 3. The final part of the book (7:8–20) is usually considered postexilic. In spite of diversity in origin, however, the book of Micah is unified by its message and may be outlined:

Superscription. 1:1
I. Oracles against Samaria and Jerusalem. 1:2–3:12
  A. Against Samaria. 1:2–7
  B. A lament over Jerusalem. 1:8–16
  C. Woe to Jerusalem. 2:1–11
  D. Interlude of hope. 2:12–13
  E. Appeal to Jerusalem leaders. 3:1–12
II. Oracles of hope and restoration. 4:1–5:15
  A. Visions of universal religion and peace. 4:1–8
  B. Visions of a restored kingdom. 4:9–5:15
III. Oracles of judgment and promise. 6:1–7:20

Micah shared with Amos an intense moral realism which issued in a stern message of rebuke upon social injustice. The first three chapters, interrupted only by 2:12–13, carry through this attitude:

> Woe to those who devise wickedness and work
>   evil upon their beds!
> When the morning dawns, they perform it,
>   because it is in the power of their hand.
> They covet fields, and seize them;
>   and houses, and take them away;
> They oppress a man and his house,
>   a man and his inheritance. (2:1–2)

These circumstances spelled disaster for the covenant people and would bring Yahweh's judgment upon them.

> Zion shall be plowed as a field;
> Jerusalem shall become a heap of ruins . . . (3:12)

Over against the plight of the people Micah saw Yahweh's basic requirements centering in social justice.

> With what shall I come before Yahweh,
>   and bow myself before God on high?
> ....
> He has showed you, O man, what is good;
>   and what does Yahweh require of you
> But to do justice, and to love kindness,
>   and to walk humbly with your God? (6:6, 8)

Some of Micah's oracles were directed toward Samaria, but most of his preaching was to Judah. His rural background sensitized the prophet to the problems that were immediately around him. He saw the failure of spiritual and political leaders in terms of internal moral decay more than entangling political alliances. He condemned priest and prophet for manipulating Yahweh's word for material gain and civil officials for profiteering off the poor. The Yahweh of social justice overshadowed the Yahweh of international sovereignty. The nation's base morality caused the prophet to repeatedly sound Judah's doom.

The book of Micah is not without its word of hope. For example, oracles in the second half of the book envision a day when the nation would attain a place of leadership and peoples will say,

> Come, let us go up to the mountain of the Lord,
>   to the house of the God of Jacob;
> that he may teach us his ways
>   and we may walk in his paths. (4:2)

This particular oracle belonged to the Jerusalem cultic tradition and was also used by Isaiah (2:2–5) to declare his hope for Yahweh's redemption even of the nations. Like Isaiah Micah emphasizes also the ideal ruler who would deliver Israel from injustice and oppression. He would be raised up like the judges of amphictyonic times to establish "peace," the full presence of all that means life and joy:

> But you, O Bethlehem Ephrathah,
>   who are little to be among the clans of Judah,
> from you shall come forth for me
>   one who is to be ruler in Israel,
> whose origin is from of old,
>   from ancient days.
> ....

> And he shall stand and feed his flock in the strength
>   of the Lord,
>   in the majesty of the name of the Lord his God.
> And they shall dwell secure, for now he shall be great
>   to the ends of the earth.
> And this (one) shall be peace.[88]   (5:2, 4–5a)

Oracles like these are often denied to Micah but they represent a genuine dimension of his thought. Judgment of the eighth century prophets was not without hope; it was rather the basis of hope. To deny positive oracles to men like Amos and Micah would be to question their belief in the redeeming sovereignty of God.

Generally, however, Micah emphasizes less hope for Judah than the high optimism for the nation's restoration expressed by Isaiah. Although they preached at the same time, their perspective on the situation differs. Neither prophet mentions the other, so the probability of their acquaintance with each other is remote. However, moving in different circles of Judah their messages must have complemented each other to give strength to the reforms of Hezekiah, an initial step in deuteronomic reformation coming to full fruition almost a century later.

THE PROPHETS OF JUDAH'S DECLINE

The last half of the seventh century B.C. produced four prophets whose preaching has been preserved in the Old Testament canon. Zephaniah, Habakkuk, and Nahum are generally associated with the period of Assyria's decline and Babylon's rise to a dominant role in the Near East, although details of their lives are lost to history and precise description of their prophetic ministry is impossible. Jeremiah lived and preached over the last several decades of the seventh century, continuing beyond the destruction of Jerusalem in 587. These men, chiefly Jeremiah, represent another era of spiritual verve in Israel's prophetic tradition. They were thoroughly involved in affairs which spelled disaster for Judah, witnessing the flow of international circumstances which culminated in the fall of Jerusalem. They were men of their own times, interpreting current events as Yahweh's judgment upon a way-

---

[88] Parentheses added.

ward people. Yet they were also men of the future, refusing to give in to despair and attempting to arouse a new religious awareness among God's covenant people. In a sense the seventh century prophets represent a powerful loyalty to Yahwism during a period when religion was largely decadent.

Zephaniah

In the superscription of his book Zephaniah is described as a descendant of Hezekiah and as prophet during Josiah's reign. The Hezekiah to whom reference is made could be the good king who ruled Judah, 715–687 B.C. If this were the intention of the designation, however, the superscription should have precisely called him king. Reliance upon this datum for interpreting Zephaniah's ministry would, therefore, be precarious.

Whether Zephaniah preached before or after Josiah's reforms cannot be decided with certainty. The book does portray the kind and depth of religious decline which immediately preceded Josianic reform. In an age which had lapsed into syncretism, Zephaniah attacked the adoption of foreign customs (1:4–9), including in his denunciation the Canaanite Baal, the Ammonite Milcom, and Assyrian astral worship. With vehemence he decried violence, fraud, idolatry, pride. Judah was thoroughly corrupt.

> Her officials within her are roaring lions;
> Her judges are evening wolves that leave nothing
> till the morning.
> Her prophets are wanton, faithless men;
> Her priests profane what is sacred, they do
> violence to the laws. (3:3–4)

Probably, therefore, the time is fairly early in the reign of Josiah before the reforms of 621.

The book containing Zephaniah's oracles includes the basic emphases found in other prophetic collections: judgment on Yahweh's people, judgment on the nations, and promise of restoration. This pattern of emphases clearly determinative in the collection and editing of the prophetic literature is evident in the literary arrangement of Zephaniah.

Superscription. 1:1
I. The Day of Yahweh against Judah. 1:2–2:3 and 3:1–7
II. Oracles against the Nations. 2:4–15

III. Proclamation of Salvation. 3:8–13
IV. Eschatological Hymn of Salvation. 3:14–20

Zephaniah saw the Day of Yahweh in which judgment would fall upon "those who do not seek the Lord or inquire of him" (1:6). Yahweh's "jealous wrath" would erupt against Judah in a day of distress and anguish, ruin and devastation, darkness and gloom, clouds and thick darkness (1:14–18). God's own people stand under the threat of a great cult day when they themselves will be the sacrifice (1:7)!

The nations too stand under the sovereign judgment of Yahweh, who will hold them responsible (2:4–15). The purpose of judgment, however, is not destruction of either Judah or the nations but redemption of both. Both Judah and the nations are to be judged so that Yahweh may gather a remnant of the "humble and lowly" who will "call on the name of Yahweh and serve him with one accord" (3:9). The oracles and hymn of salvation bear the mark of postexilic editing, but the vision of a redeemed and restored people is consistent with the prophetic hope that Yahweh's wrath fits his purpose to save.

Nahum

Nahum is quite unlike Zephaniah in his religious outlook, choosing to focus exclusively upon an outsider rather than Yahweh's people. Nothing is known about the prophet, except that he was a native of Elkosh, a village whose location is unknown. Probably he was from Judah.

The brief book which bears his name celebrates the destruction of Nineveh, capital city of the hated Assyrian empire. Some place the writing soon after the fall of the Egyptian city Thebes (663 B.C.) to which reference is made (3:8–10). Others see Nahum's words as description, not threat, and so date the work soon after 612 B.C., the date of Nineveh's fall. Probably the threatening element should be taken seriously and the book dated shortly before 612.[89]

The book portrays the destruction of proud Nineveh with brilliant metaphors and description. It consists of a brief and in-

---

[89] A full treatment of the dating problem appears in Walter A. Maier, *The Book of Nahum.*

complete acrostic [90] poem (1:1–10), whose authorship is the subject of much debate, and a longer poem (1:11–3:19) of superior
quality. A sketch outline suggests its basic theme:

> Title. 1:1
> I. Yahweh's vengeance upon his enemies. 1:2–11
> II. Judah's call to celebrate Nineveh's fall. 1:12–15
> III. An oracle on Nineveh's distress. 2:1–12
> IV. Nineveh cannot recover. 2:13–3:19

The intense hatred and vengeance which animates the book
denies the name of the prophet, which means "comfort," "consolation." To Nahum Yahweh intended Nineveh's destruction in
blood because of the city's gross immorality. The prophet spells
out the reason for Yahweh's judgment in unmistakable terms:
God is punishing a brutal and unscrupulous nation.

> The lion tore enough for his whelps
>   and strangled prey for his lionesses;
> He filled his cave with prey
>   and his den with torn flesh.
> Behold, I am against you, says Yahweh of hosts,
>   and I will burn your chariots in smoke . . . (2:12–13)

The brutality of Assyria is well attested in the literature and
art of the Near East and the prophet commendably understands
that God's control extends to the nations. But he has nothing to
say about Judah's also standing under divine judgment and thus
his work illustrates that unfortunate circumstance when religion
becomes too closely tied to a nationalistic outlook. The prophet
understands that Nineveh comes to her end tragically with none
to mourn her. But can God's people "clap their hands" with no
assuaging of hurt (3:19), even when destruction is deserved?

Habakkuk

The intriguing prophet Habakkuk also belongs to the period
encompassing the fall of Assyria and the rise of Babylon. Nothing
is known of the prophet's life or ministry. Bel and the Dragon, an
apocryphal addition to the book of Daniel, contains a tale of
Habakkuk carrying food to Daniel in the lion's den in Babylon,
but the story is legendary. Liturgical materials in the book sug-

---

[90] An acrostic is a poem in which successive verses begin with sets of letters
in order.

gest that the prophet was linked to the priesthood, probably in Judah.

The book of Habakkuk develops a central theme throughout its three chapters, but scholars have long debated whether such a diversity of materials as are found in the book could have come from a single hand. The commentary on Habakkuk found in the Dead Sea Scrolls, obviously a complete scroll, contains only the first two chapters, suggesting that chapter three may have been a later addition. Chapter three is a magnificent poem praising Yahweh's victory "for the salvation of thy people" (3:13). The poem was probably taken, by either Habakkuk or the later community, from an existing collection of hymns and used here because of its appropriateness for a prophetic liturgy.

Superscription. 1:1.
I. Dialogue of complaint and answer. 1:2–2:5.
II. Woes against various groups. 2:6–20.
III. Habakkuk's prayer. 3:1–19.

Habakkuk, like Nahum, interpreted international events toward the end of the seventh century [91] in the light of his understanding of Yahweh. Although the two viewed the same circumstances, their perspective was quite different. Nahum reveled in the pronouncement of disaster upon Judah's enemy, but Habakkuk saw the havoc wrought in the world by mighty nations as God's scourge. Moreover, Yahweh's scourge ought to be instruction to his people, who are called upon to

> Look among the nations, and see;
> wonder and be astonished.
> For I am doing a work in your days
> that you would not believe if told. (1:5)

Some believe that Habakkuk's reflection upon the international scene is "only a cloak for the prophet's real thought. He is indirectly attacking the cruel and merciless rule of Jehoiakim." [92] Certainly, unlike Nahum, he takes Assyrian oppression as the occasion to reflect upon Yahweh's relationship to his covenant people.

---

[91] Some relate the book specifically to the reign of Jehoiakim (609–598 B.C.). See Walter Harrelson, *Interpreting The Old Testament*, p. 375.
[92] *Ibid.*, p. 374.

The book of Habakkuk is a pioneer writing in Jewish speculation. It raises a profound question about the righteous character
of Yahweh. Like Jeremiah, Job, and an occasional Psalm, the
prophet engaged in an honest "struggle in depth" with God. In
light of the world situation belief in Yahweh's righteousness raised
two questions. "How can righteous Yahweh tolerate a covenant
people as unrighteous as Judah?" Yahweh's answer was that the
wickedness of Judah would cause her fall to Babylon, but this only
raised a second question. "Why would Yahweh select a nation
more evil than Judah as the instrument of her punishment?" How
can a just God remain "silent when the wicked swallows up the
man more righteous than he?" (1:13) To this question Habakkuk received no satisfying reply. With his human vision blurred,
the prophet could only continue his search for insight. His unwavering conviction that he should remain steadfastly faithful
to the righteous Yahweh who was in command and whose
righteousness would prevail is clarioned in his classic affirmation:

> Behold, he whose soul is not upright in him shall fail,
> but the righteous shall live by his faith. (2:4)

Jeremiah

The life of Jeremiah traversed Judah's changing fortunes during the last half of the seventh century. Born near the close
of the infamous reign of Manasseh, his public ministry extended
from his call in 626 past the fall of Jerusalem in 587 B.C. He witnessed the nation's most extensive revival of faith, yet pronounced
upon her some of the strongest of prophetic judgments. During
his lifetime, his nation came under the domain of Assyria, then
Egypt, then Babylon. To his own people, whom he dearly loved,
he was compelled to preach an unpopular and troublesome message.

Jeremiah was from Anathoth, a small village just north of
Jerusalem. His family was of the priestly line of Abiathar, who
had been removed from authority in Jerusalem by Solomon.[93]
The prophet himself may have been a practicing priest at the
Anathoth shrine. His destiny, however, was not to be fulfilled in
the simple rural atmosphere of the village of his birth. He was

---

[93] Cf. I Kings 1:28–2:26.

torn from this place while still a young man by a call to be Yah-weh's prophet to the nations. His early ministry was spent prior to the reforms of Josiah in both Anathoth and Jerusalem. After Josiah's reform Jeremiah worked in Jerusalem, but seems to have been relatively inactive during this period. Certainly, the most significant period of his work began with Josiah's death in 609 and continued until his deportation to Egypt around 582 B.C. During these catastrophic days for Judah, Jeremiah faithfully spoke his understanding of Yahweh's intention for the cove-nant people. Consistently he advised Judah to yield without rebellion to new Babylonian power which had wrested the east from Assyria. His advice, however, went unheeded, Judah felt the full and crushing weight of Babylon, and Jeremiah con-cluded his prophetic mission in exile in Egypt.

The Composition of the Book of Jeremiah. The record of Jere-miah's life and oracles is found in an anthology made up of three major types of material.

1. Prophetic oracles against Jerusalem and Judah, from Jeremiah him-self (most of chapters 1–25).
2. Biographical narratives about Jeremiah, presumably from Baruch, the prophet's scribe and friend (most of chapters 26–45).
3. Oracles against the foreign nations and certain biographical stories all in a style similar to that of the Deuteronomic historian. These materials probably came from a "school" of Jeremiah's followers (most of chapters 46–51).

The complex process by which these materials were organized into their present form is open to considerable conjecture and is a matter upon which no one should speak dogmatically. Obviously, Jeremiah, his scribe Baruch, and disciples who followed the great prophet all had a hand in bringing the book into its final structure. Any attempt to discover the various streams which gradually coalesce to give us the present book should begin with the scroll which the prophet dictated to Baruch in 604 B.C. This document contained a select group of oracles which Jeremiah remembered out of the first twenty-two years of his ministry. At the prophet's request Baruch delivered this summary of Jeremiah's thought to king Jehoiakim, who, finding the contents to his disliking, cut to pieces and burned the scroll as it was read to him. Having thus angered the king, Jeremiah went into hiding and redictated the scroll with many additions.[94] At this time historical or "biographical" sections and prayers (i.e., expressions of Jeremiah's inner feelings) were added, plus some strong words against Jehoiakim. Later Jeremiah himself made scattered additions to the roll.

To this expanded scroll, roughly equivalent to chapters 1–25 of the present book, were added the extensive biographical sections from the pen of Baruch (chapters 26–45) and Jeremiah's oracles against the nation (in 46–51). Later the Jeremiah "school" added other information about their prophetic master and additional oracles against the nations, bringing the book of Jeremiah to something quite like its present form. Finally, chapter 52 taken from II Kings 24:18–25:30 describing the fall of Jerusalem was appended as an historical conclusion.

A systematic outline of Jeremiah is impossible, but a survey of its contents indicating their general character is useful.

Editorial introduction and account of his call. Chapter 1.
I. The Scroll of 605. Judgments against Judah and Jerusalem. Chapters 2–25:14.
   A. Oracles from Josiah's time. Chapters 2–6.
   B. Oracles and biographical information from the time of Jehoiakim. Chapters 7–24.
   C. Summation. Chapters 25:1–14.
II. Oracles against foreign nations. 25:15–38 and chapters 46–51. A mixture of genuine oracles from Jeremiah and those of the Jeremiah "school."
III. Biographical materials from Baruch plus oracles of judgment and hope, the latter predominating. Chapters 26–35. Some of the oracles are from Jeremiah; others in the Deuteronomic style probably came from the Jeremiah "school."
IV. Jeremiah's passion. Biographical narratives from Baruch. Chapters 36–45. These chapters for the most part came from the period during and after the siege and destruction of Jerusalem.
V. Historical appendix. Chapter 52.

In reading the book of Jeremiah we meet an extremely sensitive spokesman of Yahweh's message to Judah. The prophet moved in the tragic circumstances of a lonely life, torn between love for his people and hatred of their sins. Glimpses of his inmost

---

[94] Jeremiah 36:32.

thoughts clarion the deep feeling of his mind and heart. His courage and strength induce admiration. If he were "the weeping prophet," as he has often been called, his tears were for his nation and her people whom he loved.

> O that my head were waters,
>   and my eyes a fountain of tears,
> that I might weep day and night
>   for the slain of the daughter of my people! (9:1)

His love for Judah and her people made Jeremiah's prophetic burden all the more difficult to bear, because his message was a forecast of their doom. How distasteful this condemnation was to the prophet is echoed in his empathetic words:

> My grief is beyond healing,
>   my heart is sick within me.
> Hark, the cry of the daughter of my people
>   from the length and breadth of the land:
> . . . .
> "The harvest is past, the summer is ended,
> and we are not saved." (8:18, 20)

When Jeremiah warned his people of their imminent doom, they turned in derision upon him because his oracles were not immediately fulfilled and denounced him because they disliked the tenor of his words.

> I hear many whispering.
>   Terror is on every side!
> "Denounce him! Let us denounce him!"
>   say all my familiar friends,
>   watching for my fall.
> "Perhaps he will be deceived,
>   then we can overcome him,
>   and take our revenge on him." (20:10)

They preferred the falsely optimistic words of the professional prophets who proclaimed peace, even when there was no peace (23:17). Therefore, Jeremiah's ministry seemed doomed to failure and to many, even to himself, it appeared that it did fail; but "some men's failures are eternities beyond other men's successes." [95] It was so with Jeremiah.

---

[95] George Macdonald as quoted by H. Wheeler Robinson, in *The Cross in the Old Testament*, p. 121.

Call and Inaugural Visions. The work of Jeremiah began in the thirteenth year of Josiah's reign (626 B.C.) with a call succinct and vivid to the prophet. The divine summons came in an ordinary way, not in temple splendor as had Isaiah's. The experience was an intimate confrontation between a young man and the God whom he already had come to know in deep personal faith. The call was the consummation of a life-long relationship with God rooted in the pieties of home and early training. A growing knowledge of God had ripened into the awareness of a special mission.

The call took the form of a dialogue between Yahweh and Jeremiah in which the divine commission and the prophet's answer stand over against one another, like challenge and response. The youth was told that he had been ordained to be a prophet even before his conception in the womb. Yahweh put Jeremiah on notice that the prophet had a role to play in the divine plan and purpose. In spite of evil filling the land during the reign of Manasseh, Yahweh had not forsaken his covenant intention and was preparing a spokesman to summon the nation back to worship and faithfulness. Jeremiah described his sense of urgency to prophesy as

> . . . a burning fire shut up in my bones,
> and I am weary with holding it in,
> and I cannot. (20:9)

His task was to be "prophet to the nations" in troubled days when national prophecy was no longer possible. Yahweh's purposes operative on the international level called for prophecy to the world situation.

Jeremiah's natural response was to cringe in a manner reminiscent of the ancient Moses.[96] His cry, "Ah, Lord God! Behold, I do not know how to speak, for I am only a youth," was swept aside by the promise that Yahweh would be present to give him the words to say. Yahweh would provide the oracles; the prophet would only speak Yahweh's word which would accomplish its purpose.[97] Then Yahweh told him the frightful nature of his task.

> See, I have set you this day over
> nations and over kingdoms,

[96] Cf. Exodus 3.
[97] Jeremiah 1:7–9.

> to pluck up and to break down,
> to destroy and to overthrow,
> to build and to plant.   (1:10)

Jeremiah sometimes concluded that destruction was to be his only message. His word was to be a fire to devour the people (5:14) or like a hammer smashing rock (23:29), so that once again Yahweh might build and plant a people unto himself to do his will. Upon the destruction of that which stands in his way Yahweh would construct a work of his own liking (18:1–11). Faithfulness to such a message would separate the prophet from family and friends—even public worship—but he would not be alone nor need he be discouraged. Jeremiah is in Yahweh's service and can be assured of his continuing presence (1:17–19).

Two "visions" [98] were directly associated with Jeremiah's call. The prophet looked out and saw in the shoots of an almond tree (shaqed) a reminder that Yahweh was watching (shoqed) over his word to perform it, a revelation that came by means of word association. Yahweh is "watching" over his word to bring it to pass (1:11). His judgment upon the people is certain and Jeremiah must sound the alarm. The prophet looked again and saw a boiling pot, perhaps the cooking pot in his home, tilted toward the south so that its contents were about to spill out from a northerly direction. As a complement to the "vision" of the shaqed, the boiling pot signified that an enemy was about to attack Judah from the north. Precise identity of this enemy is impossible. The Scythians in upper Mesopotamia were a real threat to Israel, but never wrought havoc to the extent envisioned by Jeremiah. If the Scythians provided the stimulus for Jeremiah's descriptions, the Babylonians later fulfilled his fears.[99] Quite clearly the prophet's main concern was not to identify the enemy, but to assert that Yahweh's judgment is about to come upon a people who have rejected covenant. Both visions underscore the depth of the nation's sin and the destiny of Jeremiah as Yahweh's spokesman.

[98] Visions here may not be the right word since it is probable that Jeremiah actually saw the objects concerned. Here and elsewhere in the prophetic books the ordinary sight becomes a means of revelation to the insighted prophet. Cf. Jeremiah 24:3; Amos 7:7–9; 8:1–2.

[99] See H. H. Rowley, "The Early Prophecies of Jeremiah in their Setting," *Bulletin of the John Rylands Library*, XLV (1962), 198–234.

Jeremiah and the Josianic Reformation. Apparently the prophet Jeremiah was less active during the period of Josianic reformation, from about 621 B.C. to 609, than after the death of Josiah. Perhaps reforms may have led the prophet to believe that Judah had heeded the warnings of his early preaching and would be spared. If Jeremiah had predicted a Scythian invasion which did not come to pass, he may have been discredited for a while. More likely the Josianic reforms made the prophet's preaching less necessary for a time and Jeremiah simply withdrew from public eye only to be summoned again by Yahweh when the good king came to his untimely death.

Jeremiah's earliest oracles, found in chapters 2–6, encouraged reformation and undoubtedly helped gain support for the attempts of Josiah. In these oracles the prophet dealt with the religious conditions which resulted from Manasseh's syncretistic policy. Using imagery like that of Hosea, Amos, and Isaiah, he pled for national repentance. Israel is likened to Yahweh's bride and entreated to remember his past favors and return to her youthful devotion and bridal love. Yahweh's people, however, did a strange thing, something that even the heathen would never do, something at which the heavens themselves would be shocked: they committed flagrant and inexcusable apostasy.

> My people have committed two evils:
>   they have forsaken me,
> the fountain of living waters,
>   and hewed out cisterns for themselves,
> broken cisterns,
>   that can hold no water. (2:13)

The robust and dynamic Yahweh faith had been replaced with the syncretistic faith of Manasseh. The true and living God had been rejected in favor of those who were not gods at all.

Judah may have protested that she had been led astray by the wickedness of the Manasseh administration, but in two vivid pictures Jeremiah reminded them of their wickedness and obstinacy. The guilt was theirs because they were like wild beasts unable to restrain their lust or like harlots of the streets with many lovers who were brazenly unashamed of their immoral actions (2:23–25). But even though these sins were grievous, forgiveness was possible if they would only repent.

> Return, faithless Israel,
>   says Yahweh.
> I will not look on you in anger,
> for I am merciful,
>   says Yahweh;
> I will not be angry for ever. (3:11b)

Then, as though this were too good to be true, Jeremiah sounded a note of doom in a series of oracles found in chapters 4–6.

> My anguish, my anguish! I writhe in pain!
>   Oh, the walls of my heart!
> My heart is beating wildly;
>   I cannot keep silent;
> for I hear the sound of the trumpet,
>   the alarm of war. (4:19)

These early oracles end with a vivid picture of judgment upon the sinful nation. The enemy is vividly described as if already in the land, raging, killing, ravaging, destroying. These oracles anticipating a coming destruction must have made an initial preparation for the cultic reform of 621.

Jeremiah supported the cause of reform with zeal because he was in general sympathy with its objectives. In fact, while the Josianic ceremony of covenant renewal was in progress, he openly advocated the acceptance of "the words of this covenant" (11:1–5). Such strong support created opposition to Jeremiah. Since the reform had as one of its tenets the unification of worship in Jerusalem, it did not attract enthusiastic promotion from many religious leaders in outlying areas. Jeremiah's friends and relatives at Anathoth even made an attempt on his life.

> But I was like a gentle lamb
>   led to the slaughter.
> I did not know it was against me
>   they devised schemes, saying,
> "Let us destroy the tree with its fruit,
>   let us cut him off from the land of the living,
>   that his name be remembered no more." (11:19)

Jeremiah, nevertheless, continued to support the reform and even went on a preaching tour of Judah to remind the people of the solemn responsibility placed upon them by covenant with Yahweh (11:6–8).

For a number of years, Jeremiah remained optimistic about the prospects of a people led by a model king who sought to purify

Judah's religion and re-establish the Davidic kingdom. During this optimistic period, there were no words of doom from Jeremiah, who perhaps thought that divine punishment was turned aside. Before long, however, the defects of the reform came into focus and Jeremiah saw how shallow and artificial it was. More than a cultic reform was needed to make Judah the people of Yahweh. In his famous "temple sermon" (7:1–8:3) Jeremiah decried dependence upon the presence of the temple as an assurance of God's presence. In an acid oracle delivered after Jeremiah had become disappointed by Josiah's reform, perhaps on the day of Jehoiakim's enthronement, the prophet denounced pride in the temple while sin swept through the land (7:8–9). Further he pronounced sacrifice as insignificant and irrelevant to the demands of true religion (7:21–24) and predicted the destruction of the temple (7:8–15).

Moreover, the prophet saw the impotence of the legal method of dealing with sin and spoke out against the new found law in blistering words.

> How can you say, "We are wise,
> and the law of Yahweh is with us?"
> But, behold, the false pen of the scribes
> has made it into a lie. (8:8)

His later emphasis upon rejuvenated religion embodied in a new covenant is likely a lesson drawn from the failure of the external effort under Josiah. The covenant could not be restored by external means, no matter how thorough their extent and sincere their intent.

The Crisis with Jehoiakim. Hope for better things through Josiah came to a bitter end at Megiddo when the good king was slain by Pharaoh Necho. Jeremiah mourned his sovereign and confessed real sympathy for Josiah's young successor, Jehoahaz, who was doomed to Egyptian exile.

> Weep not for him who is dead,
> nor bemoan him;
> but weep bitterly for him who goes away,
> for he shall return no more
> to see his native land. (22:10)

Then the prophet turned his attention to king Jehoiakim. At first Jeremiah pled with the new monarch to fulfill the expectation of both Yahweh and Judah, lest he be destroyed and his people with him.

Do justice and righteousness, and deliver from the hand of the oppressor him who has been robbed. And do no wrong or violence to the alien, the fatherless, and the widow, nor shed innocent blood in this place. (22:3)

When it became clear that Jehoiakim was to be a vain and pretentious king, Jeremiah unleashed the full force of his righteous wrath against him as one for whom he had lost all respect.

> Woe to him who builds his house by unrighteousness,
>   and his upper rooms by injustice;
> who makes his neighbor serve him for nothing,
>   and does not give him his wages;
> who says, "I will build myself a great house
>   with spacious upper rooms,"
> . . . .
> They shall not lament for him, saying,
>   "Ah, my brother!" or "Ah sister!"
> They shall not lament for him, saying,
>   "Ah lord!" or "Ah his majesty!"
> With the burial of an ass he shall be buried,
>   dragged and cast forth beyond the gates of
>   Jerusalem. (22:13–14; 18–19)

Such vigorous and open insult could not go unnoticed by the king and actually jeopardized the prophet's life. A multitude, led by priests and temple prophets, was about to put Jeremiah to death (26:7–11), but he was saved by the intervention of the princes and "elders" of the land, perhaps the conservative Judean landowners. Jeremiah was set free, but Jehoiakim seized another prophet who spoke against Jerusalem and had him executed.

Jeremiah further angered Jehoiakim and the temple officials by symbolically acting out the destruction of Jerusalem. He took a pottery flask and went to the Potsherd Gate of the city, most likely the gate to the refuse dump or valley of Topheth. There he broke the flask and said:

Thus says Yahweh of hosts: So will I break this people and this city, as one breaks a potter's vessel, so that it can never be mended. Men shall bury in Topheth because there will be no place else to bury. (19:11)

Then he went to the temple court and spoke to the same effect in the presence of the people gathered there. For the first time the prophet was called upon to suffer bodily in Yahweh's service.

Pashur, the priest, had him beaten and placed in stocks for a night. When he was released, he was forbidden admission to the temple area (36:5).

Rejected by his relatives and friends, exiled from the place of worship, and mocked because his words of doom went unfulfilled, Jeremiah gave bitter and unrestrained expression to the distress of his existence. In "confessions" or "prayers" [100] addressed to Yahweh, he angrily cried for vengeance upon his enemies. He lamented his prophetic calling and even cursed the day of his birth.[101] Certain that Yahweh had deceived him, he called him a "deceitful brook like waters that fail" (15:18). To these complaints the divine reply was encouraging and challenging:

> If you return, I will restore you,
> and you shall stand before me.
> If you utter what is precious, and not what
> is worthless,
> you shall be as my mouth.
>
> . . . .
> And I will make you to this people
> a fortified wall of bronze;
> they will fight against you,
> but they shall not prevail over you.
>
> . . . .
> I will deliver you out of the hand of the wicked,
> and redeem you from the grasp of the ruthless.
> (15:19-21)

But at the same time straightforward and realistic:

> If you have raced with men on foot,
> and they have wearied you,
> how will you compete with horses?
> And if in a safe land you fall down,
> how will you do in the jungle of the
> Jordan? (12:5)

Later in Jehoiakim's reign after the Babylonian victory at Carchemish in 605, Jeremiah was convinced that Judah's destiny was sealed. Babylon was clearly the foe from the north and Nebuchadnezzar was Yahweh's appointed sovereign of the Near

---

[100] Jeremiah 11:18–12:6; 15:10–21; 17:14–18; 18:18–23; 20:7–18. See studies of these in Gerhard von Rad, "Die Konfessionen Jeremias," *Evangelische Theologie,* III (1936), pp. 265–276, and J. Philip Hyatt, "Introduction and Exegesis to Jeremiah," *IB,* VI, pp. 777–793.

[101] Jeremiah 15:10 and 20:14 ff.

East.[102] Jerusalem was doomed to complete destruction.[103] The time was again right for the prophetic influence to be felt in the court. But Jeremiah was now under a ban and forbidden access to the temple. In order to fulfill his prophetic mission his message had to assume a new form. Whereas it had been oral, now it was written on a scroll to be read to the people by Baruch. It was not a new message, but a summary of what Jeremiah had been preaching for more than twenty years. This was the scroll frivolously destroyed by Jehoiakim and later reproduced with additions by Jeremiah and Baruch.[104]

Jeremiah and Judah's Last Days. Chapters 26–35 of the book of Jeremiah are primarily narrative materials concerning the prophet's ministry during the period following the 597 exile. The materials were apparently gathered and organized by Baruch and clarify Jeremiah's relationship to the successors of Jehoiakim. The prophetic message during these days is a mixture of doom and hope. Jeremiah desired to warn inhabitants remaining in Judah of the continued peril because of their sin and to encourage exiles in Babylon to prepare for an extended stay, taking seriously Yahweh's judgment upon their apostasy. But the prophet also was confident that God's message went beyond punishment and exile. Yahweh had a new day and a new covenant for his people. Both emphases were important for the full word of Yahweh to be known.

Zedekiah, Jehoiakim's successor, had genuine respect for Jeremiah, but lacked the necessary self-confidence to master the difficult situation which faced him. Unwisely goaded by those who hoped the Babylonian yoke could be cast aside, he again and again was tempted to rebel, in spite of continued counsel from the prophet to submit to Babylonian authority.[105]

An intended rebellion in 594 was forestalled by Jeremiah's drastic symbolic action. Wearing a wooden yoke on his shoulders he called for submission to Babylon's yoke. When the temple prophet Hananiah countered by breaking the yoke and predicting Babylon's doom, Jeremiah announced for him an imminent death

102 Jeremiah 25:1–14.
103 Jeremiah 16:1–17:8.
104 See above, p. 369.
105 Jeremiah 27–29.

and replaced the broken yoke with one of iron as if to say, "Break this if you can." Hananiah's death after a few weeks explains Judah's unwillingness to participate in the revolt.

For a few years Judah and Jeremiah enjoyed peace, but then came the fatal revolt of 589 and the final siege of Jerusalem. Throughout the siege Jeremiah counseled submission to Nebuchadnezzer, Yahweh's instrument for Judah's punishment. The city's destruction was inevitable, but strangely Jeremiah affirmed a hope for the future. He bought a field near Anathoth, signed the deed before witnesses, and placed it in a jar for safe keeping.[106] By this act Jeremiah revealed his faith in a restoration of Judah at some future date when fields in the war-torn countryside would again be of value.

All the while Judah's fortresses were being overrun and Jerusalem remained under siege. When only two of the fortresses, Lachish and Azekah,[107] were still offering resistance, Jeremiah determined to inform Zedekiah of the futility of continued opposition and to affirm surrender as the one option to save his life.[108] Whatever hope Jeremiah may have had for success in this advice was crushed when an Egyptian army attacked Nebuchadnezzar and temporarily freed Jerusalem from siege.[109] The war parties' hopes were high and they predicted an end to Jerusalem's woes. Jeremiah, however, stood firm to his previous conviction and informed Zedekiah that the enemy would soon return.

During the absence of the Babylonians, Jeremiah left Jerusalem to visit Anathoth to claim the field he had purchased earlier. His enemies thought he was deserting to the Babylonians, whose cause he had appeared to champion throughout the siege. Without inquiring of the king they had him beaten and imprisoned.[110] Again Jerusalem was besieged and Zedekiah secretly sent for the prophet to ask, "Is there any word from Yahweh?" Jeremiah's

106 The transaction described in 32:1–16 illustrates the application of the law stated in Leviticus 25:25 and the usual procedure for exercising the right of property redemption.
107 In the ruins of Lachish were found a number of military letters which vividly portray the rapid disintegration of the Judean opposition. Azekah fell, then Lachish, leaving the grim evidence of the thoroughness of the destruction in her ruins.
108 Jeremiah 34:1 ff.
109 Jeremiah 34:21; 37:5.
110 Jeremiah 37:11 ff.

reply was unchanged, "You shall be delivered into the hand of the king of Babylon" (37:17). Days of imprisonment, however, had taken their toll and the prophet pled not to be sent back to prison.[111] Zedekiah, out of concern for the prophet's safety, transferred him to the "court of the guard" in the palace area and commanded that he be given food as long as any was available in the city.

From this more public place of confinement Jeremiah continued to speak to all who came near, encouraging their submission.

Thus says Yahweh, He who stays in this city shall die by the sword, by famine, and by pestilence; but he who goes out to the Chaldeans shall live; he shall have his life as a prize of war, and live. Thus says Yahweh, This city shall surely be given into the hand of the army of the king of Babylon and be taken. (38:2–3)

The enraged princes called for his death and, with Zedekiah's toleration, Jeremiah was thrown into a muddy cistern from which he was soon rescued by the speedy action of a palace official.[112] He then remained in the "court of the guard" and until the capture of the city continued to advise the king to surrender. After the destruction of Jerusalem, Jeremiah was permitted to remain in Judah. He went to Mizpah and offered his services to Gedaliah, the Babylonian-appointed governor of the captured state.

The New Covenant. Jeremiah had long plucked up and broken down, destroyed and overthrown; now it was time for him to build and to plant. The few months he spent with Gedaliah at Mizpah were perhaps the happiest of his life. He and the governor were in complete accord in their attempt to create order and purpose out of 587's chaos. The destruction the prophet had predicted was past. Now he could devote himself to the constructive task of "strengthening the hands of a true patriot and servant of God in building up a new Israel on the ruins of the old."[113]

From this period came the promises of hope found in chapters 30 through 33, a section of the book commonly referred to as "The Book of Consolation." Although some of these materials may come from disciples of Jeremiah, the chapters depict the

[111] Jeremiah 37:20.
[112] Jeremiah 38:7–13.
[113] John Skinner, *Prophecy and Religion,* p. 279.

genuine optimism of a prophet who was able to see beyond Judah's immediate situation. The prophet believed that his nation had been punished to purge her of evil and call her to her senses. When the punishment had accomplished its purpose, however, Yahweh would restore his people.

> Thus says Yahweh:
> Behold, I will restore the fortunes of the tents
>   of Jacob, and have compassion on his dwellings;
> the city shall be rebuilt upon its mound,
>   and the palace shall stand where it used to be.
> . . . .
> Their children shall be as they were of old,
>   and their congregation shall be established
>   before me;
> and I will punish all who oppress them.
> . . . .
> And you shall be my people,
>   and I will be your God. (30:18, 20, 22)

At their head would be a prince submissive to Yahweh's will, the leader of a redeemed Israel.

> Their prince shall be one of themselves,
>   their ruler shall come forth from their midst;
> I will make him draw near, and he shall approach me,
>   for who would dare of himself to approach me?
>   says Yahweh. (30:21)

Both Judah and Israel would share in this bright future as Yahweh in redemptive love would make with them a new covenant, transcending in every way the old covenant of Sinai so often broken by the sinful people.

> But this is the covenant which I will make with the house of Israel after those days, says Yahweh: I will put my law within them, and I will write it upon their hearts; and I will be their God, and they shall be my people. And no longer shall each man teach his neighbor and each his brother, saying, "Know Yahweh," for they shall all know me, from the least of them to the greatest, says Yahweh; for I will forgive their iniquity, and I will remember their sin no more. (31:33–34)

Note the tenacity of Israel's religious heritage. Even the prophet who had seen covenant broken, covenant reform fail, and the nation go to ruin now foresaw a future reestablishment of that relationship between deity and people which covenant implies.

This new covenant would be made effective by the free grace of Yahweh which creates in the hearts of his people a knowledge of himself and his ways, making them obedient to his law. He will be their God and they will be his people in a fellowship unbroken by the sinful rebellions of the past. This hope of Jeremiah is the hope of Israelite faith and of the Christian faith as well, for Jesus had this passage in mind as he gathered for the last time with his disciples around the table to say:

This is my blood of the covenant, which is poured out for many.[114]

One wishes that Jeremiah's story could have ended in peace-producing hope, but it did not. The tragedy which stalked his life struck again. Gedaliah was murdered and the leaders who remained fearful of Babylonian reprisal fled to Egypt taking with them Baruch and Jeremiah. There they died.

One closing word should be said about Jeremiah, because it is often wondered how he could endure a life of unending misery. How could he condemn the people he loved and predict the destruction of his land and city? Baruch wondered too and in prayer found an answer in a word from Yahweh.

Behold, what *I* have built *I* am breaking down, and what *I* have planted *I* am plucking up—that is, the whole land.[115]

The land was Yahweh's land, the people his people. Thus, the burden of Jeremiah's heart was the burden of the heart of God.

SUGGESTED READINGS

Background

CONTENAU, GEORGES, *Everyday Life in Babylon and Assyria* (Edward Arnold, 1954). Emphasizes social and religious life.

OLMSTEAD, A. T., *History of Assyria* (Scribner's, 1923). Old, but still standard.

The Books of Kings

See listing in Chapter 7.

Isaiah

BLANK, SHELDON H., *Prophetic Faith in Isaiah* (Harper & Row, 1958).

CHILDS, BREVARD, *Isaiah and The Assyrian Crisis* (S.C.M. Press, 1967).

[114] Mark 14:24.
[115] Jeremiah 45:4b. Emphasis added.

KELLEY, PAGE H., "Isaiah" in *The Broadman Bible Commentary*, V.
KNIGHT, G. A. F., *Prophets of Israel (I)* (Abingdon, 1961).
LESLIE, ELMER A., *Isaiah* (Abingdon, 1963).
SCOTT, R. B. Y., "Isaiah" in *Interpreter's Bible*, V.
SKINNER, JOHN, *The Book of the Prophet Isaiah*, I and II (Cambridge University Press, 1915–17). Old standard work.
SMITH, GEORGE ADAM, *The Book of Isaiah* (Rev. ed., Harper & Row, 1928). Old, but worth reading.
VRIEZEN, TH. C., "Essentials of the Theology of Isaiah," in *Israels' Prophetic Heritage* (Harper & Row, 1962).
WARD, JAMES M., *Amos and Isaiah: Prophets of the Word of God* (Abingdon, 1969).

Jeremiah

BLANK, SHELDON H., *Jeremiah: Man and Prophet* (Hebrew Union College Press, 1961).
BRIGHT, JOHN, *Jeremiah*, Anchor Bible (Doubleday, 1965).
HYATT, J. PHILLIP, *Jeremiah: Prophet of Courage and Hope* (Abingdon, 1958).
LESLIE, ELMER A., *Jeremiah* (Abingdon, 1954).
ROBINSON, H. WHEELER, *The Cross in the Old Testament* (S.C.M. Press, 1955). The discussion of Jeremiah in this work is exceptionally good.
SKINNER, JOHN, *Prophecy and Religion* (Cambridge University Press, 1922). A fine standard interpretation.
SMITH, GEORGE ADAM, *Jeremiah* (Hodder and Stoughton, 1922).
WELCH, A. C., *Jeremiah: His Time and His Work* (Blackwell, 1951).

Micah

MARSH, JOHN, *Amos and Micah* (S.C.M. Press, 1959).
SNAITH, NORMAN, *Amos, Hosea, and Micah* (Epworth, 1956).

Both of the above are brief but valuable studies.
See also the works on prophecy listed in readings for chapter 7.

9

Covenant Community
Rediscovers Itself

The tragedy of 587 left the covenant community in shambles. Those who had seen Yahweh's faithfulness demonstrated in the "covenant with David" now had little basis for hope. The temple was rubble, the Davidic king had been taken away in disgrace, and the holy land had been desecrated by the heel of an invading enemy. Faith was in genuine crisis. Could one dare believe in Yahweh, whose concern for his people had been defined in Davidic terms? Reinterpretation of the meaning of covenant was necessary or faith in Yahweh would have to be surrendered altogether.

In spite of the crisis both Israel and her faith did survive. As when Abraham had no son and the Egyptian pharaoh "knew not Joseph," Yahweh's people were able to discover in exile new meaning of covenant and structures of religion. During the traumatic exile the nation maintained some semblance of identity and in the restoration the old covenant began to take new and enduring form. To be sure, the emerging faith would take on the character of the period; it would not be simply a continuation of the traditional national cult. Yahweh's action in behalf of his people would be reinterpreted in light of the particular historical situation and would take on a format which would persist through the centuries of the future. This was the time of Judah's testing by fire resulting in the production of refined Judaism, i.e., the religion of the Jews as it emerged and took form after the Babylonian exile.[1]

Information about this period is at best quite sketchy. Data come piecemeal from widespread and diverse sources. The Ezra-Nehemiah portion of the Chronicler's history is the only canonical history work relating to this period, although it deals primarily with the postexilic structure of Judaism. Considerable information is drawn by inference from the prophetic works of the exile and return. Ezekiel and Deutero-Isaiah are especially helpful. Babylonian and Persian royal archives provide some knowledge and archaeological finds give minor clarifications to life of the period. But all in all a great deal of cloudiness exists about many parts of the exile and restoration experiences. We are largely de-

Powers of Influence on Judah		Judah	
Babylonia			
Nebuchadnezzar	605–562	587–538	Judah in exile
Amel-marduk	562–560		in
Neriglissar	560–556		Babylonia
Nabonidus	556–539		
(539—Fall of Babylon to Persia)			
Persia			
Cyrus	539–530	538—Edict of Cyrus permitting the return of captives to Jerusalem	
Cambyses	530–522		
Darius I	522–486	520–516 Rebuilding of Jerusalem temple	
Xerxes I	486–465		
Artaxerxes I	465–424	445 Nehemiah became governor of Judah	
		428 Mission of Ezra	
Xerxes II	423		
Darius II	423–404		
Artaxerxes II	404–358		
Artaxerxes III	358–338		
Arses	338–336		
Darius III	336–331		
(333—Battle of Issus; Persia fell to Greece)			

Figure 9–1. Exilic and postexilic periods, 587–333 B.C.

[1] The term "Jew" is a contraction of "Judah." It is technically applicable to the covenant people only following the Babylonian exile when the majority of the returnees to Palestine were from this prominent tribe.

pendent upon the above-mentioned inferences from the prophetic writings and the more clearly delineated structure of Jewish life and faith during postexilic days.

THE EXILE (ISAIAH 40, 42, 44, 45, 49–55; EZEKIEL 1–4, 11, 18, 23, 37, 47)

Just how many Judeans were taken into exile is open to a great deal of question. II Kings 24:14–16 seems to indicate that from eight to ten thousand were taken in the major deportations of 597 and 587. However, a reference in Jeremiah 52, probably an extract from an official document of the Babylonian community, calculates the total number of deportees at less than five thousand. W. F. Albright [2] conjectures that the discrepancy may be partly due to the heavy mortality of hungry and diseased captives in their long desert trek to Babylon. Certainly the total number of exiles must have been considerably smaller than the number who remained in Judah.

Although in disorganized fashion, life continued in Judah. Clan groups from the Negeb probably used this period as an opportune time to move farther into Palestine away from marauding Arab tribes. A mixed population developed in the land. With Babylonia firmly in control, her gods would have been introduced with a consequential development of religious syncretism. Such a low ebb of religious, social, and political life in Palestine left this segment of Yahweh's covenant people in shadow in the future of Judah. The better classes, socially and religiously, belonged to the exile and with them rested the hope of the nation. This at least is the judgment of primary biblical sources.

Life in Judah

Politically the destruction of Jerusalem spelled at least temporarily the end of the Jewish state. Although deportations to Babylon did not completely depopulate Palestine, Jewish political life ceased in the land of David. The territory became a Babylonian province, although neither documents nor archaeological finds clarify the nature of its administration. Clearly Nebuchadnezzar did not intend to leave strong political leaders in Judah

---

[2] Albright, *The Biblical Period*, p. 47.

and even <u>Gedaliah</u> may have been more a fiscal officer than a provincial governor.[3] Politically Judah ceased to exist and, except for a brief period under the Maccabees, semblance of an independent and autonomous nation would not again appear until the twentieth century with the birth of the modern state of Israel.

Although disorganized, life did continue. Those displaced by Babylonian invasion but remaining in Palestine, took heart with the appointment of Gedaliah; and attempted to return to ordered life. Jeremiah reflects this effort: ". . . all the Jews returned from all the places to which they had been driven and came to the land of Judah, to Gedaliah at Mizpah; and they gathered wine and summer fruits in great abundance" (40:12). The Jewish settlement was concentrated in the vicinity of Jerusalem, and clan groups moved there from the Negeb. The Edomites used the instability of the day as an opportune time to move farther into Palestine away from marauding Arab tribes. A mixed population developed in the land.

Although the national cult must have disintegrated with the destruction of the temple, some worship undoubtedly continued around an improvised or temporary sanctuary. ". . . so sacred a site as that of the Jerusalem Temple could not have been thought to have lost its sanctity entirely . . ."[4] The site was probably cleared and re-used as a center of simplified worship. With Babylon firmly in control, her gods may have been syncretistically introduced into the religious practices of the old Jerusalem sanctuary. Overall social, political, and religious life in Jerusalem after 587 was at a low ebb. Study of this period has long ignored Judah on the assumption that nothing significant happened there during the exile of the elite in Babylon. Recent studies, however, have challenged this common conclusion by suggesting that the Judean community produced substantial and profound assessments of their experience and its meaning for a restatement of covenant theology. Most important of these was the Deuteronomic history work, that grand schematic interpretation of Israel's destiny found in Joshua-II Kings,[5] but also important were Obadiah, certain Psalms (44, 74, 79, 102) and Lamentations.[6]

---

[3] John Gray, *Archaeology and the Old Testament World*, p. 181.
[4] Peter Arkroyd, *Exile and Restoration*, p. 29.
[5] Cf. Martin Noth, *Überlieferungsgeschichte Studien I*, pp. 96 f., 107 ff.
[6] Cf. E. Janssen, *Juda in der Exilzeit*.

The Book of Lamentations. The despair that prevailed in Palestine following the destruction of Jerusalem is reflected in the book of Lamentations. The book was probably composed in Judah during this period, suggesting the presence of a creative stream in an area usually considered of no consequence in Israel's religious history. The work is a collection of five lamentation poems, and, since the poems correspond to the chapters, is quite easily outlined:

I. The agony of Jerusalem. Chapter 1.
II. Yahweh's judgment upon the city. Chapter 2.
III. A lament of personal distress and prayer. Chapter 3.
IV. Yahweh's wrath upon Jerusalem. Chapter 4.
V. A petition for Yahweh's mercy. Chapter 5.

The literary form and style varies from poem to poem, but the book is unified in religious outlook. Traditionally the poems were ascribed to Jeremiah, probably because of their common association with the fall of Jerusalem. Actually the poems are anonymous and were composed among those left in Jerusalem after the exile began. They almost certainly were brought together to provide liturgical materials for the annual remembrance of Jerusalem's fall.

The lamentations provide insight into the community's response to Nebuchadnezzar's siege, the fall of the city, and exile of the elite. Grief became the order of the day.

> She weeps bitterly in the night,
>   tears on her cheeks;
> among all her lovers
>   she has none to comfort her . . . (1:2)

Explanation for travail was found in the traditional deuteronomic doctrine: Yahweh has caused it as punishment for a sinful people!

> Yahweh gave full vent to his wrath,
>   he poured out his hot anger;
> and he kindled a fire in Zion,
>   which consumed its foundations. (4:11)

Obadiah. The book of Obadiah vents the frustrations of the poor people in Judah after the fall of Jerusalem by expressing intense animosity toward the Edomites. With vindictive hatred the brief book of twenty-one verses describes the unfair advantage which Edom took of Judah at the time of Jerusalem's fall

and predicts the punishment of Edom. The prophet, about which
nothing is known, anticipates the judgment of Yahweh upon the
enemy of his people.

> And your mighty men shall be dismayed, O Teman,
>> so that every man from Mount Esau will be
>> cut off by slaughter.
> For the violence done to your brother Jacob,
>> shame shall cover you,
>> and you shall be cut off for ever. (9–10)

The brief book concludes with an emphasis upon God's universal
moral judgment "upon all the nations" through history, but primarily it illustrates the understandable frustrations of the oppressed Jewish community fighting for its life in a leaderless and
desolated land.

Others in Judah were making some attempts to reinterpret
their tradition to account for the disaster which had fallen upon
them. Psalmists called to Yahweh:

> Rouse thyself! Why sleepest thou, O Lord?
>> Awake! Do not cast us off for ever!
> Why dost thou hide thy face?
>> Why dost thou forget our affliction and oppression?
> For our soul is bowed down to the dust;
>> our body cleaves to the ground.
> Rise up, come to our help!
>> Deliver us for the sake of thy steadfast love! (Psalm 44:23–26)

> Do not remember against us the iniquities of our forefathers;
>> let thy compassion come speedily to meet us,
>> for we are brought very low.
> Help us, O God of our salvation,
>> for the glory of thy name;
> deliver us, and forgive our sins,
>> for thy name's sake!
> Why should the nations say,
>> "Where is their God?"
> Let the avenging of the outpoured blood of thy servants
>> be known among the nations before our eyes!
> Let the groans of the prisoners come before thee;
>> according to thy great power preserve those doomed to die!
> Return sevenfold into the bosom of our neighbors
>> the taunts with which they have taunted thee, O Lord!
> Then we thy people, the flock of thy pasture,
>> will give thanks to thee for ever;
>> from generation to generation we will recount thy praise.
> (Psalm 79:8–13)

If this represents the cult of the Judeans, it is apparent that they genuinely desired the restoration of covenant. That they also asked for vengeance should not overshadow the deeply moving sense of need and expression of hope. These people had been driven to plead with Yahweh for help. There was nowhere else they could turn.

In another way the great Deuteronomic historian tried to see all of Israel's history in the light of the tragedy of the exile. He condemned Israel for not realizing the possibilities of the covenant and saw the exile as judgment upon a people who had been unfaithful to Yahweh. At the same time he promised salvation and hinted that even in the dark days of the exile redemption was possible because Yahweh would forgive.

Nevertheless, those who remained in Judah were largely consumed in despair with little time or interest in rethinking their religious commitments. Fortunately, Hebrew faith could also depend upon those who had to learn to sing the Lord's song in a strange land. In Babylon the cultural elite, political leaders and religious enthusiasts were giving serious thought to the future of the Israelite people as the community of Yahweh.

Life in Babylon

Identity Preserved. To think of the Jewish exiles in Babylon as "captives" in the sense of a people in bondage is misleading. Certainly their life was not easy. They had to endure the hardships and humiliation of a displaced people, but they were not slaves to Babylonian taskmasters. One historian has described them as ". . . recognized foreigners, affiliated to the plebeian class of citizens and naturally without the privileges of the Babylonian aristocracy, but distinctly higher in status than the slave-class." [7] The Babylonian experience was not a repetition of the Egyptian bondage of early days. Further, the lot of Judah was quite favorable when compared to that of her northern sister Israel. Whereas the dispersal of Israel by Assyria led to her loss of identity as a national group, the colonization of Judah in specific settlements around Babylon enabled her to preserve some

---

[7] H. Wheeler Robinson, *The History of Israel*, p. 134.

sense of unity. The relative freedom of the exiles in Babylon enabled the nation to retain some equilibrium in travail.

At first many anticipated an early deliverance from captivity. Later following the advice of a letter written to them by Jeremiah, the exiles soon settled down in the strange land and tried to establish a routine that would make their ordeal bearable. They continued to marry and have families. They maintained their own communal organizations, probably reaching back to the days of Samuel for the pattern. "Elders" of the captivity [8] occupied places of increased influence. Ezekiel seems to have presided over the elders in much the same way Samuel had done in the days of tribal organization.[9] "Communities" of the Jews existed near the river Chebar, at Tel-abib, and perhaps at other sites in Babylon with freedom of exchange between and among the groups.[10] Jehoiachin, the king of Judah deported in 597, was soon brought out of prison by his Babylonian captors and given status among them. He dined at the king's table and was given an allowance for his personal needs.[11] Such an atmosphere of honorable treatment enable the Jews to maintain their feelings of national and religious identity.

Influence of Babylonian Culture. Under these favorable circumstances Babylonian culture inevitably made inroads into the life of the Jews. They could not live in the most flourishing area of the east without being influenced by it. For one thing, the Aramaic language typical of official use in Babylon was only slightly different from the native Hebrew of the captives. Since the deported Jews were of the higher classes, many of them found little difficulty in using this tongue with facility. The relatively easy crossing of the language barrier enhanced the acceptance of Babylonian culture by the Jews. Many displaced people began to use Aramaic as their language of interchange with the Babylonians.[12] This ease of communication fostered cultural exchange.

The exile also brought opportunity for dramatic vocational

---

[8] Cf. Jeremiah 29:2.
[9] See Charles F. Whitley, *The Exilic Age*, pp. 78–79.
[10] Cf. Ezra 8:15–17.
[11] Jeremiah 52:31–34.
[12] After the return from exile, Aramaic gradually replaced Hebrew as the language of Palestine. In New Testament times "Palestinian Aramaic" was the language of Jesus and the Apostles.

changes in the life of a people whose way had been largely provincial. Earlier in Palestine traditional agriculture and pastoral callings had been preserved in "a land of grain and wine, a land of bread and vineyards, a land of olive trees and honey." [13] Now in Babylon these rural occupations were supplemented by more mercantile pursuits. Certainly many young Jewish men were caught up in the "city of merchants." Opportunities unknown to them in Palestine were now accessible. That they became involved in Babylonian trade and business is supported by the appearance of Jewish names in documents coming from later periods. Evidently some wealth developed. Many must have become enamored by the profitable life of the metropolis and lost their enthusiasm for return to the more strenuous agricultural life of Palestine. They were content to become absorbed in the world around them, especially since it yielded rich cultural and economic dividends. As a consequence, then, the exile widened the horizon of Jewish national experience.

Religious Life. While many became integrated with Babylonian life, at the same time a hard core of Jewish people endeavored to maintain their basic affiances through religious bonds. This nucleus was responsible for preserving the traditional faith. To them the movement toward amalgamation was offensive as a form of religious compromise. From them issued the prophetic hope of deliverance.

The faithful came to look upon the exile as an interim to end in an eventual return to their homeland. They felt themselves sojourners in a strange land. Longing for the succor of Mt. Zion, they dreamed of the day when proud Babylon would suffer the judgment of Yahweh and Israel would be reestablished in Palestine. When their dreams of an immediate return went unrealized, believers interpreted their prolonged estrangement as the consequence of sins and transgressions [14] and sought to revitalize their worship of Yahweh.

Of course, with the central Jerusalem sanctuary temporarily only a memory, the cultus had to undergo some transformation. The practice of sacrifice had to be discontinued, but the devout

---

[13] II Kings 18:32.
[14] Ezekiel 33:10.

Figure 9–2. A reconstruction of the impressive Ishtar Gate, entrance to the palace area through Babylon's double wall. In the right background are the famous "hanging gardens" above which can be seen the enormous ziggurat. (Source: Courtesy of the Oriental Institute, University of Chicago.)

could pray with faces toward Jerusalem. Other rituals not directly dependent upon the temple could be maintained and even given more emphasis.[15] Sabbath observance and circumcision continued to express the invincible faith of the people, even in a strange land. Probably to this period of absence from the temple is to be traced the rise of the synagogue. Just when, where, and how this new institution of Jewish religion came into existence is open to some question and a great deal of discussion. Its presence in postexilic Judaism implies its origin during the exile as a temporary "tabernacle" in a foreign land. The intense study of scriptures later so characteristic of the synagogue certainly was typical of the exilic period. In reassessing the meaning of their religion the faithful Jews turned with enthusiasm to the study and preservation of their religious literature.

At various worship centers the literature of Israel's faith was collected and edited. The reality of the exile validated the work of various preexilic prophets and consequently authenticity was given to their work. The authority given the prophetic oracles assured their preservation and hastened their inclusion in the canon. The Deuteronomist, from the setting of the exile, sought to apply the religious lessons of history to his people. From the circumstances of seeming disaster he endeavored to make plain the nation's sins and Yahweh's purposes in judgment. Since the people were separated from the revered temple in Jerusalem, their forms of cultus were cherished even more. Some of the cultic psalms and perhaps portions of the Priestly history work were collected. Thus, out of the disruption of ordinary patterns for practicing their religion came a concern for traditions which was expressed in literary achievement.

Perhaps the most dramatic alteration of Jewish religious life came in the area of the theology of national destiny. The fall of Jerusalem had created a theological trauma of gigantic proportions. Jerusalem's sanctuary had come to symbolize Yahweh's faithfulness in preserving both the nation and the Davidic dynasty. Now that the temple was gone, what could be said about Yahweh's faithfulness? Was Yahweh, with Jerusalem, gone forever? Confronted by such questions, the thinking Jew was com-

---

[15] Cf. Ezekiel 4:14; Ezra 8:21; Nehemiah 1:4.

pelled to reexamine his traditional expression of faith in Yahweh's active engagement in Israel's history. The direction which the answers to these questions took is suggested by the religious stalwarts of the exile, Ezekiel and Deutero-Isaiah, who undoubtedly had more to do with the formulation of the religious interpretations of the period than any other men. The canonical works of these men give us lucid insight into reformations within Jewish thinking as it righted itself after the catastrophes of 597 and 587.

Ezekiel

The prophet Ezekiel is a crucial figure in Israel's transition from preexilic to postexilic faith. His early oracles come prior to the destruction of Jerusalem and have led some interpreters to assume that he spent at least a part and possibly all of his ministry in Jerusalem. Certainly the holy city and its temple are the center of the prophet's early oracles, but the biblical tradition that Ezekiel spent his ministry in Babylon is as convincing as any reconstruction. The work of the prophet is so thoroughly grounded in the history of the exile that it is difficult to see how it may be dissociated from the actual historical situation.

Accordingly Ezekiel was a priest in Jerusalem, probably among those elite carried into Babylonian exile with Jehoiachin in 597. A few years after his deportation, his call to the prophetic office came through an ecstatic, awe-inspiring vision of Yahweh upon a throne borne by a chariot.[16] For the next two decades Ezekiel proclaimed Yahweh's message to the captives. Until the fall of Jerusalem the prophet's preaching was essentially an interpretation of the coming disaster. His message was delivered in Babylon, but addressed to the situation in Jerusalem. After 587 the prophet continued his preaching by addressing himself to the people within their exilic situation. This bilateral ministry indicates his actual involvement in the whole process of Judah's theological readjustment.

To say the least, Ezekiel was an unusual person. In any sophisticated culture he would be considered a religious eccentric of first magnitude. His personal religious experience was of ec-

---

[16] See Ezekiel 1–3.

static nature bordering on the abnormal. This unusual tempera-
ment enabled him to visualize Yahweh enthroned in a storm or
to feel himself bodily transported to Jerusalem to witness the
abominations practiced there. The same eccentricity enabled him
to couch his message in dramatic symbolic acts. By digging
through a wall, or carrying the baggage of a traveler, or dancing
menacingly with a sword he simulated the fate of exiles leaving
a beleaguered city. The famed valley of dry bones, a rusty caldron, or an eagle of multi-colored plumage provided rich imagery
for the graphic communication of his message. With brashness
he talked of Jerusalem and her sister Samaria as harlots abhorred.
The individuality of the prophet gives his message a picturesque-
ness seldom seen elsewhere in the Old Testament. Further, the
intensity with which Ezekiel proclaims the word of Yahweh
epitomizes what is happening to the covenant community. The
prophet, as the nation, experiences the reality of exile, not merely
theory about it. His involvement in catastrophic disaster and in
an awakening consciousness of God which followed it somewhat
parallel what is happening to Israel. The harshness, almost violence, of his language suggests the intensity with which the exile
demanded a rethinking of destiny by people of the covenant.

Ezekiel's message is a study in contrast. With Jeremiah he
shared the proclamation of unrelenting doom upon Jerusalem
prior to her fall. Before 587 he rebuked and condemned, declar-
ing that the inevitable razing of the city would be no less than
the accomplishment of the righteous judgment of Yahweh. Before holy Yahweh an apostate people could expect nothing other
than the vindication of his holiness. However, after the fall of
Jerusalem, Ezekiel's outlook became more optimistic. As if the
fall of Jerusalem had been salve to his wrath, he changed from
prophecies of woe to words of comfort and challenge. He sought
to instill in his discouraged contemporaries a new faith for their
trying times, a faith based on the hope of an eventual glorious
restoration of the Jewish nation. This restoration, like the destruction of Jerusalem, would be a miraculous act of Yahweh.
Only when his despondent generation repentantly accepted responsibility for their sin would Yahweh intervene to reclaim his
people. Then, like scattered sheep gathered by the shepherd,
the nation would be restored. Yahweh would be vindicated and

an utopian Palestinian community would be created. Such optimism doubtless brought great courage to a downcast people.

The Book of Ezekiel. The major source of the book of Ezekiel is the prophet himself although, like other prophetic materials, the book in its present form was shaped by a circle of disciples. Scholars are divided as to how much of the content comes from Ezekiel. Some poetic sections may predate the exile; other materials, notably chapters 38–39, seem to be later. The highly optimistic character of chapters 40–48 suggests a time closer to the return of the captives to Judah, but these probably originate with the sixth century prophet. Clearly, the book bears the mark of an editor's pen. Within the circle of Ezekiel's disciples original materials were compiled and additional oracles were added. Ezekiel himself may have begun the compilation which was finished subsequent to his death. The result is a book arranged according to a clear outline.

> Editorial introduction. 1:1–3.
> I. Account of Ezekiel's call. 1:4–Chapter 3.
> II. Oracles of doom against Judah and Jerusalem. Chapters 4–24. Delivered between 593 and the destruction of Jerusalem in 587.
> III. Oracles against foreign nations. Chapters 25–32. The lengthy poetic oracles against Tyre and Egypt came from Ezekiel. The shorter prose ones against Ammon, Moab, Edom, Philistia, and Sidon were added by Ezekiel's disciples to complete the collection.
> IV. Oracles predicting the restoration of Judah and Jerusalem. Chapters 33–39. Delivered after 587.
> V. Ideal sketch of the restored community. Chapters 40–48. Delivered after 587.

Many of these oracles are precisely dated and chronologically arranged. For the most part the chronological notices are in historical sequence (the major variation being due to the arrangement of the foreign oracles according to nations), but the materials in any one section do not necessarily belong to the date assigned to them. Evidently the editor wove together a group of oracles to which the prophet had affixed specific dates and a body of undated materials. The undated materials were placed here and there in the framework created by the dated oracles, producing some chronological confusion. The system of dating, however, faithfully represents the outline of a prophetic ministry divided between judgment and consolation and suggests a prophetic career lasting from 593–571 B.C.

The Vision of the Call. The character of Ezekiel is revealed by the visionary experience which culminated in his call to prophecy. Looking at an approaching storm, Ezekiel had a vision of Yahweh's throne chariot, splendid beyond description and filled with Yahweh's glory. The majestic chariot moved with the storm from the north bringing a sense of Yahweh's presence to the priest in Babylon. Before the awesome holiness of "the appearance of the likeness of the glory of Yahweh" Ezekiel fell on his face, conscious of the weakness and unworthiness of man in the presence of God. The voice of Yahweh summoned him to receive his prophetic commission and Ezekiel, like the prophets before him, became captive to the divine word. In the vision this word containing lamentation, mourning, and woe was extended to him in the form of a scroll, written on both sides. Ezekiel ate the scroll, symbolizing his willingness to speak Yahweh's word. Then the prophet was told to proclaim the message, even though his preaching would not be heeded. Overwhelmed and appalled by the task given him, Ezekiel sat seven days silent in the midst of his fellow exiles before beginning to speak.

Symbolic Actions, Visions, and Allegories. Ezekiel spent the first portion of his ministry impressing his fellow exiles that not only would their exile continue, but also that they would be joined by their fellows from Jerusalem, a city whose doom was certain. The nation had forfeited its right to exist and stood under unalterable judgment from Yahweh. Little else mattered to the prophet in face of his compulsive concern for the bittersweet word of Yahweh which was his to declare.[17] So impressed was he with his task and so unique was his personality that he went to extremes in the methods used to communicate the divine word.

Earlier Israelite prophets had characteristically spoken their oracles, occasionally illustrating them by performing certain symbolic deeds,[18] but Ezekiel made bizarre, symbolic action an integral part of his prophetic ministry. Such behavior had a major role in his proclamations about the fate of Jerusalem and the

---

[17] He neither wept nor mourned at the death of his wife. Cf. Ezekiel 24:15–27.
[18] Cf. Isaiah 20; Jeremiah 18, 19, 27, 28.

character of the exile. The prophet took a large, sun-dried brick incised with a picture of Jerusalem under siege and acted out a siege upon the city.[19] Then he lay upon his left side and then his right side, symbolizing the length of exile for both Israel and Judah.[20] With his face toward the brick portraying Jerusalem, he prophesied against the city. Daily for forty days he ate an odd mixture of three grains cooked over a dung fire,[21] suggesting the scarcity of food in the besieged city and the dire circumstances of its rebellious inhabitants. The fate of the people of Jerusalem was also graphically proclaimed. With a sword, war's own symbol, the eccentric prophet shaved his head and beard.[22] One third he burned on his model of Jerusalem, a third he cut to pieces with the sword, and a third he scattered to the wind. Thus Jerusalem's inhabitants would die in the besieged city, or be slain at its fall, or be scattered among the nations as exiles. However, a few of the hairs were bound in the skirt of the prophet's robe—not all of Yahweh's people would be lost. Finally, to represent Jerusalem's disastrous fall, Ezekiel dug through the wall of his house and carried his belongings through the hole.[23] In this way he pictured for those already in exile the fate of their brethren in Jerusalem.

These prophetic deeds were more than mere play-acting to the prophet. They were "signs for the house of Israel," depicting Yahweh's sovereign purpose against Jerusalem. It was as if the deed were already done. For Ezekiel the symbolic action precipitated divine activity against Jerusalem. Prophetic behavior, like prophetic word, was alive to accomplish its end. A mind as suggestive as Ezekiel's had little difficulty envisioning Yahweh's deeds.

When bizarre Ezekiel was not symbolically acting out a sermon, he was having a surrealist vision or composing an allegory. No prophet before him had used such peculiar media to convey his ideas. Nevertheless, whether it was genius or abnormality, his way certainly captured the attention and imagination of those who lived with him beside the river Chebar.

[19] Ezekiel 4:1–4.
[20] Ezekiel 4:4–8.
[21] Ezekiel 4:9–17.
[22] Ezekiel 5:1–17.
[23] Ezekiel 12:1–7.

In vision he was transported to Jerusalem to see strange and terrible portents of evil and destruction. In a mysterious inner chamber of the temple he saw

portrayed upon the wall around about . . . all kinds of creeping things, and loathsome beasts, and all the idols of the house of Israel. (8:10)

Standing before them were the elders of the house of Israel with censers in hand, and the smoke of incense filled the room. Then, as if the priestly prophet had recoiled in horror and disbelief, Yahweh said to him, "You will see still greater abominations which they commit." [24] In succession he was shown women weeping for Tammuz, a fertility deity,[25] and men worshipping the sun both within the sacred precincts of the temple. Forcefully Ezekiel proclaimed the judgment of Yahweh:

I will deal in wrath; my eye will not spare, nor will I have pity; and though they cry in my ears with a loud voice, I will not hear them. (8:18)

Visions of judgment followed as executioners descended upon the city to slaughter the inhabitants who remained after the righteous had been marked for deliverance. When the slaughter began, the prophet pled:

Ah Lord God! wilt thou destroy all that remains of Israel in the outpouring of thy wrath upon Jerusalem? (9:8)

Yahweh's reply was decisive:

The guilt of the house of Israel and Judah is exceedingly great; the land is full of blood, and the city full of injustice;
. . . .
My eye will not spare, nor will I have pity, but I will require their deeds upon their heads. (9:9, 10)

As if this were not sufficient to convince the exiles that the nation's doom was sealed, Ezekiel depicted her apostasy in vivid allegory.[26] Two of these (chapters 16 and 23) are reminiscent of

---

[24] Ezekiel 8:13.

[25] Ezekiel 8:14. This deity is known through the Gilgamish Epic as a Sumerian god of spring vegetation. The fertility powers of the god were celebrated in an annual Babylonian cult which had numerous parallels in other areas of the Ancient East. The Tammuz practice included women entreating the deity for their own impregnation.

[26] Ezekiel 15, the Wild Vine; 17:1–10, Two Eagles; 19:2–9, Lioness and her whelps; 19:10–14, the Uprooted Vine; 24:3–14, the Caldron of Judgment; and others.

Hosea's descriptions of Israel as a shameful harlot. The first allegory is the story of Jerusalem born in disgrace and abandoned.

Your origin and your birth are of the land of the Canaanites; your father was an Amorite, and your mother a Hittite.
. . . .
You were cast out on the open field, for you were abhorred, on the day that you were born. (16:3, 5)

Rescued and reared by Yahweh the ungrateful child grew to maidenhood and became a harlot. This was Jerusalem; this was Judah.

The second allegory describes the harlotries of twin sisters Oholah, Samaria, and Oholibah, Jerusalem. Lewd Oholah was given to Assyria for punishment, but Oholibah did not heed this warning, actually becoming more corrupt than her sister. Therefore, she too would go to captivity. To her Yahweh said:

> You shall drink your sister's cup
>   which is deep and large;
> you shall be laughed at and held in
>   derision,
>   for it contains much;
> you will be filled with drunkenness and sorrow. (23:32–33a)

The language of these allegories is bold, almost repulsive, and was intended to shock. Ezekiel obviously had no time for the observance of niceties, and in the face of his message, who among the exiles would not believe that Judah and Jerusalem were doomed?

The Hope and Plan for Restoration.   Once, however, Yahweh's judgment had fallen and Jerusalem was captured, Ezekiel ceased to be a prophet of disaster. His task then became constructive and visions of hope followed those of doom. The exiles were despondent because they felt caught by the inevitability of punishment. Their forefathers had sinned, and so had they. If the hitherto inflexible principle of sin and retribution were correct, they were without hope. To counter their pessimism Ezekiel challenged the older theology proverbially expressed; "The fathers have eaten sour grapes, and the children's teeth are set on edge." [27] He stressed that guilt is not fatalistically inherited, nor

27 Ezekiel 18:2.

is it irremediable. The man who sins bears the guilt,[28] but even so present righteousness may cancel past sin.[29] The exiles, therefore, had to act in righteous obedience to Yahweh. If they did so, they had hope.

In a vision of restoration Ezekiel saw "dry bones which would live again" by the life-giving spirit of Yahweh.[30] Exile was not the end for those of faith, for with them Yahweh would begin again.

Behold, I will open your graves (exile), and raise you from your graves, O my people; and I will bring you home into the land of Israel.
. . . .
And I will put my Spirit within you, and you shall live, and I will place you in your own land.[31]

First, however, he would replace their hearts of stone with hearts of flesh so that the covenant made with them might not be broken.[32]

Chapters 40–48 of Ezekiel contain a careful description of the restored community. These chapters may have circulated as a unit before the book was put into its present form; they certainly give evidence of the hand of an editor. In their present arrangement the materials bring the book to a fitting climax. A theocratic state centering in Jerusalem and its temple is envisioned. Around Jerusalem the restored tribes would live in orderly array occupying a territory which extended from the "entrance of Hamath" to the "River of Egypt" (the boundaries of the Davidic empire). The priests would rule in the new state assisted by a prince in the maintenance of peace and order. No apostate kings would destroy the peace of restored Israel.

Ezekiel placed great stress upon the importance of ritual and cult in the new state, almost making purity of ritual as important as purity of heart. One wonders if this concern for legalism was not a foreboding of weakness in later Judaism. Nevertheless, Ezekiel advocated obedience to covenant obligations and he dreamed of a state in covenant with the holy Yahweh, who would be its king and the source of life. The apocalyptic anticipation of this is not

[28] Ezekiel 18:10–13.
[29] Ezekiel 18:21–23.
[30] Ezekiel 37:1–14.
[31] Ezekiel 37:12, 14. Parentheses added.
[32] Ezekiel 36:26. See Jeremiah 31:33.

surpassed in the Old Testament. From beneath the temple altar welled an artesian river of life which flowed from Jerusalem toward the Arabah, where it brought to life the Dead Sea.[33] Along its banks grew fruitful trees in a delightful garden. All who lived in this Eden-like paradise would be blessed.

Hope proclaimed by Ezekiel was a significant ingredient in Israel's rebuilding her faith. In both destruction and reclamation he could see the hand of Yahweh. Before 587 he encouraged those in both Babylon and Palestine to move beyond resignation and despair to trust in Yahweh. The loss of all that Israel cherished—land, temple, king—spoke the name of Yahweh, who even in judgment could be known. Moreover, beyond judgment lay restoration. The holy city would be rebuilt and named, "Yahweh is there" (48:35). What better hope than that through judgment Yahweh's presence could be found!

Second Isaiah: The Exile's Great Unknown

The optimism injected into exilic theology by Ezekiel reached its crescendo in a prophet whose name is unknown. Since his work appears in the latter chapters [34] of the Isaiah scroll, he is designated as Second or Deutero-Isaiah. This superior prophet lived several decades after the time of Ezekiel and consequently nearer the actual time of the restoration. He witnessed the growing conflict between Judah's captors and the rising coalition of power in Media and Persia. In the light of the current imperial collisions Second Isaiah sought to interpret Yahweh's role in history. Consequently, his was a crucial voice in Israel's rediscovery of her role as Yahweh's people.

From Isaiah to Second Isaiah: Prophetic Tradition and Reinterpretation. Although he remains anonymous, there can be no doubt about the tradition in which the unknown prophet of the exile stood. He belonged to the disciples of Isaiah of Jerusalem, among whom that great prophet's ideas were preserved and passed on. In fact, he is the climax of the Isaianic heritage, since in many ways the disciple surpassed the teacher. Taking the determinative themes of the prophet of Jerusalem he interpreted

---

[33] Ezekiel 47.
[34] See above, pp. 349–350.

the work of his predecessor, blending with it the insight of Amos, Hosea, Jeremiah, and Ezekiel of whom he was also heir. With unequaled range of vision and passion of faith he cast the best of their thought into a form expressive of both poet and prophet at their best, bringing new vitality of meaning to the prophetic faith. Mastery of style and depth of theological perception give his oracles an exciting lilt and a profundity of meaning. His work is a symphony in words, with theme and counter theme blending into one vibrant and pleasing whole so theologically exhilarating that to read it is to rejoice at the wonder of God.

The work of Second Isaiah is found in chapters 40–55 of the book of Isaiah. To these oracles, which come from the end of the period of the exile (i.e., c. 540), were added the oracles in chapters 56–66, which presuppose the return from exile and the restoration of Jerusalem. The latter chapters perhaps include materials from Second Isaiah himself, but they are composed largely of oracles from disciples of the unknown prophet who desired to continue the Isaiah tradition into the postexile. Some scholars set 56–66 apart as a distinctive collection coming from Third or Trito-Isaiah. Rigid demarcation of units within the book, however, is somewhat arbitrary and may fail to recognize the complicated editorial work on each of these divisions over many years. Certainly Isaiah 1–66 is not simply the combination of three independent prophetic works. Scholarly opinion on the literary unit of either 40–55 or 56–66 varies widely. But the inclusion of all these materials in a single scroll testifies "that later followers continued to wrestle with the judgments and promises of Isaiah," giving "their minds and energies to the task of seeing that Israel did not lose sight of Yahweh's revelation through Isaiah." [35] From Isaiah of Jerusalem, through Deutero-Isaiah and associates in exile, to disciples of both in postexile the great emphases appear again and again. From time to time the message is set within diverse historical contexts, but both prophet and disciple regularly display Yahweh's continued working through his covenant people.

The collection of prophetic oracles in 40–66, the finest poems in the whole Old Testament, do not easily yield themselves to outline. The interplay of several themes ties them together, but

[35] Walter Harrelson, *Interpreting the Old Testament*, p. 228.

no logical progression of thought or development of ideas is evident. Nor can we reconstruct their sequence from the historical
situation of the prophet's life since he remains in every respect
(except in perceptive theological thought) the great unknown.
In a series of "ecstatic shouts" [36] he speaks of the imminence of
Yahweh's redemptive activity, the holiness of the incomparable
Yahweh, God of the nations, creator and redeemer; and of Israel
sinful, repentant, redeemed, and redeeming. "His thoughts are
poured out glowing and fluid, like molten metal before it has
hardened into definite shape." [37]

Yahweh, Lord of History.   A pivotal assertion of the prophet-
poet was that Yahweh is the one and only God—the sovereign
Lord of all nations and events.   He has by his own incomparable
power brought the world into existence and has absolute control
over all history.   All nations are under his domain.   The exile was
his judgment upon his people, but he thereby sacrificed none of
his dominion.   He would continue his action by redeeming the
repentant nation through the instrumentality of the foreign un-
believer, Cyrus of Persia.[38]
   Second Isaiah as the originator of a theology of world history
considered Yahweh a God beyond compare:

> Thus says Yahweh, the King of Israel and
>   his Redeemer, Yahweh of hosts:
> "I am the first and I am the last;
>   besides me there is no god.
> Who is like me?   Let him proclaim it,
>   let him declare and set it forth before me.
> Who has announced from of old the things to
>   come?
>   Let them tell us what is yet to be.
> Fear not, nor be afraid;
>   have I not told you from of old and
>   declared it?
>   And you are my witnesses!
> Is there a God besides me?
>   There is no Rock; I know not any." [39]

[36] Robert H. Pfeiffer, *Introduction to the Old Testament*, p. 465.
[37] *Ibid.*
[38] Cf. Isaiah 44:28–45:7.
[39] Isaiah 44:6–8. Cf. 40:18 ff., 25–26.

The exile's hope for redemption rested upon the sure foundation of Yahweh's sovereignty over creation and history.[40] The creative activity of the holy God set the stage for a history of redemption. Surely he who by a creative word brought the world from the darkness of primordial chaos to radiant order and purpose is more than able through an instrument of his choosing to rescue his people from exilic chaos to freedom's light.

> Thus says Yahweh, the Holy One of Israel,
>   and his Maker:
> "Will you question me about my children,
>   or command me concerning the work of my
>   hands?
> I made the earth,
>   and created man upon it;
> it was my hands that stretched out the heavens,
>   and I commanded all their host.
> I have aroused him in righteousness,
>   and I will make straight all his ways;
> he shall build my city
>   and set my exiles free,
> not for price or reward,"
>   says Yahweh of hosts.   (45:11–13)

The people of God, therefore, would be tragically mistaken to forsake Yahweh for Babylonian deities, profitless and man-made idols that they were.[41] Tragic and pathetic, indeed, was the experience of the one who trusted in Bel or Nebo, gods who were unable to redeem in time of crisis becoming burdens to their devotees, so that deity and worshipper entered captivity together. With scornful irony the prophet's perceptive lines ridiculed the worshipper of idols as one who from the same tree makes bench, fire and god.

It becomes fuel for a man; he takes a part of it and warms himself, he kindles a fire and bakes bread; also he makes a god and worships it, he makes it a graven image and falls down before it. Half of it he burns in the fire; over the half he eats flesh, he roasts meat and is satisfied; also he warms himself and says, "Aha, I am warm, I have seen the fire!" And the rest of it he makes into a god, his idol; and falls down to it and worships it; he prays to it and says, "Deliver me, for thou art my god!" (44:15–17)

[40] Cf. 43:1–21.
[41] Isaiah 44:9 ff.

Second Isaiah, thus, called his people away from the entice-
ments of Babylonian religion to Yahweh, whose activity of redemption was imminent.

> I bring near my deliverance, it is not far off,
>   and my salvation will not tarry;
> I will put salvation in Zion,
>   for Israel my glory. (46:13)

Proof of this was found in history. For he who created the world
ruled its affairs; nations and men were but instruments of the
divine purpose. Yahweh ruled the nations, but he had chosen
Israel to be his servant for the world's redemption. Hence if they
had faith, they had nothing to fear; Yahweh would strengthen,
help, and uphold them with his victorious right hand (41:10).
In fact, he was at that moment shaping events in preparation for
his servant's deliverance, choosing as the instrument of his purpose Cyrus of Persia, who was destined to conquer Babylon and
issue a decree permitting the exiles to return to Judah. Those
who waited in faith would, therefore, with strength renewed
"mount up with wings like eagles," "run and not be weary," "walk
and not faint" led by Yahweh in a new exodus.

A New and Greater Exodus. Once Yahweh had led his people
from Egyptian bondage across the sea, through the wilderness, to
the land of promise which they seized in a holy war of conquest.
What he did then he was about to do again as redeemer of his
people.

> Thus says Yahweh,
>   who makes a way in the sea,
>   a path in the mighty waters,
>
> . . . .
> "Remember not the former things,
>   nor consider the things of old.
> Behold, I am doing a new thing;
>   now it springs forth, do you not perceive it?
> I will make a way in the wilderness and
>   rivers in the desert. . . .
> for I give water in the wilderness,
>   rivers in the desert,
> to give drink to my chosen people,
>   the people whom I formed for myself
> that they might declare my praise." (43:16, 18–21)

He would ransom his people,[42] act in judgment upon their enemies,[43] lead them home to Palestine [44] where they would rebuild
Jerusalem [45] and restore the land.[46] Sovereigns would be so subject to *the* sovereign Yahweh that there would be no hardening
of rulers' hearts as in the time of Moses. Instead, Cyrus would
act in accord with Yahweh's will and purpose as an instrument in
the hand of the redeeming God.

> Who says of Cyrus, "He is my shepherd,
>   and he shall fulfil all my purpose";
> saying of Jerusalem, "She shall be built,"
>   and of the temple, "Your foundation
>   shall be laid." (44:28)

The opening oracle of Second Isaiah's work heralds this event
in words of consolation unequaled in the Old Testament:

> Comfort, comfort my people
>   says your God.
> Speak tenderly to Jerusalem,
>   and cry to her
> that her warfare is ended,
>   that her iniquity is pardoned,
> that she has received from Yahweh's hand
>   double for all her sins.
> A voice cried:
> "In the wilderness prepare the way of Yahweh,
>   make straight in the desert a highway for
>   our God.
> Every valley shall be lifted up,
>   and every mountain and hill be made low;
> the uneven ground shall become level,
>   and the rough places a plain.
> And the glory of Yahweh shall be revealed,
>   and all flesh shall see it together,
>   for the mouth of Yahweh has spoken." (40:1–5)

Across desert made to flower, on a highway prepared by Yahweh
himself, the holy God would lead his people home, to be welcomed
by those to whom his return had been exultantly announced.

> Get you up to a high mountain,
>   O Zion, herald of good tidings;

[42] Isaiah 43:3.
[43] Isaiah 41:11–13; 49:25–26.
[44] Isaiah 40:9–10; 55:12–13.
[45] Isaiah 49:16–17.
[46] Isaiah 44:26 and 49:8.

Lift up your voice with strength,
  O Jerusalem, herald of good tidings,
  lift it up, fear not;
say to the cities of Judah,
  "Behold your God!"
. . . .
He will feed his flock like a shepherd,
  he will gather the lambs in his arms,
he will carry them in his bosom,
  and gently lead those that are with young. (40:9, 11)

Redemption Through Suffering: The Servant of Yahweh. Scattered through the oracles of Second Isaiah are four poems about

Figure 9–3. A scroll of Isaiah opened to chapter 40. This manuscript was found in a cave above the Dead Sea and is the oldest extant copy of a complete book of the Old Testament. (Source: American Schools of Oriental Research.)

the "Servant of Yahweh." These "Servant Songs" [47] may have been the core around which the prophet or his disciples organized

---

[47] Isaiah 42:1–4; 49:1–6; 50:4–9; 52:13–53:12. This delineation represents the majority opinion. However, since the break between the "songs" and their context is not always clear, some scholars are reluctant to define the "Servant" sections of chapters 42 and 49 so precisely.

his other oracles.[48] In them the prophetic faith achieved a theological climax in its interpretation of the redemptive role of Yahweh's chosen people.

> Behold my servant, whom I uphold,
>   my chosen, in whom my soul delights;
> I have put my spirit upon him,
>   he will bring forth justice to the nations.
> He will not cry or lift up his voice,
>   or make it heard in the street;
> a bruised reed he will not break,
>   and a dimly burning wick he will not quench;
>   he will faithfully bring forth justice.
> He will not fail or be discouraged
>   till he has established justice in the earth;
>   and the coastlands wait for his law. (42:1–4)

In this quiet, unobtrusive way the servant would establish justice
and Torah in the power of Yahweh's own spirit. He would be a
"light to the nations" spreading salvation to the ends of the
earth.[49] The world's redemption, however, would be bought with
a price and the role of the servant would be hard.

> I gave my back to the smiters,
>   and my cheeks to those who pulled out the beard;
> I hid not my face
>   from shame and spitting. (50:6)

Nevertheless, strengthened by Yahweh he would see it through to
an end of bitter rejection, suffering, and death.

> He was despised and rejected by men;
>   a man of sorrows, and acquainted with grief;
> and as one from whom men hide their faces
>   he was despised, and we esteemed him not.
> Surely he has borne our griefs
>   and carried our sorrows;
> yet we esteemed him stricken,
>   smitten by God, and afflicted.

[48] Some scholars do not believe that these "Servant Songs" were written by
the same poet who composed the rest of 40–55. There are certain differences of
form, style, and content; nevertheless, the intimate relationship of the poems to
their context and the great similarity of ideas and formal characteristics between
the "Songs" and the oracles among which they are placed speaks for identity of
authorship.
[49] Isaiah 49:6.

> But he was wounded for our transgressions,
>   he was bruised for our iniquities;
> upon him was the chastisement that made us whole,
>   and with his stripes we are healed.
> All we like sheep have gone astray;
>   we have turned every one to his own way;
> and Yahweh has laid on him
>   the iniquity of us all. (53:3–6)

But the suffering of the servant is victorious as the work of Yahweh triumphs in one who in humility and lowliness was utterly faithful to the divine purpose.

Despite their clear portrayal of the servant's mission, the songs do not make the identity of their subject clear, raising a question which has been a matter of extensive debate in Old Testament scholarship.[50] "Who is the Servant of Yahweh?" At first glance the answer seems to be "Israel personified," since the second song actually makes that identification.[51] A closer reading of all the poems, however, indicates that this answer is inadequate. The servant has a mission to Israel [52] and does a work which the nation Israel had proven unfit to accomplish. Perhaps, then, the prophet had in mind the redeemed and redeeming remnant of Israel or an individual king or prophet [53] who would represent Yahweh in a redemptive role.

Did the prophet, however, have a precise identification in mind? Probably not. He spoke more of a principle of redemption than of its precise means. He perceptively portrayed the salvation from Yahweh as coming through a servant—nation of Israel, redeemed remnant, individual—who would be like the one here described. The thought of the prophet appears to be fluid, moving from Israel, Yahweh's chosen covenant people who failed to be faithful, to the remnant purged and made holy by Yahweh. Realism, however, tempered his idealism and he narrowed his ideal to an individual, an Israelite who through true faith and

---

[50] The sum and substance of this debate is well recorded in two works: H. H. Rowley, "The Servant of the Lord in the Light of Three Decades of Criticism," in *The Servant of the Lord and Other Essays on the Old Testament,* and C. R. North, *The Suffering Servant in Deutero-Isaiah.*

[51] Isaiah 49:3.

[52] Isaiah 49:6.

[53] Cyrus, Uzziah, Hezekiah, Josiah, and Zerubbabel have been suggested among royal figures; Moses, Isaiah of Jerusalem, Jeremiah, and Second Isaiah himself are among the prophetic suggestions.

dedication would represent all Israel by fulfilling the redemptive purpose for which Yahweh had chosen the nation. This one Israelite would, by becoming Suffering Servant, fulfill the destiny of all Israel.

Christian interpreters are unanimous that whoever the prophet had in mind in portraying the Suffering Servant, Jesus living, crucified and risen, alone is the adequate fulfillment. Further, those who through faith enter his church become heir to his Servant vocation as a new covenant people. Following Franz Delitzsch and C. R. North,[54] the idea may be diagrammed as below:

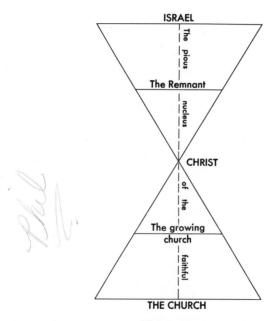

Figure 9–4.

In the two prophets Ezekiel and Deutero-Isaiah, then, we see the major expansion of Israel's faith that occurred during and after the exile. The old narrow provincialism which had expressed itself in the reverence for the Jerusalem sanctuary gave way to a

[54] Franz Delitzsch, *Biblical Commentary on the Prophecies of Isaiah* and C. R. North, *Isaiah 40–55*, p. 36.

broader and more sublime interpretation of Yahweh's concern. The restricted horizons of Israel's earlier theology were pushed back to include Yahweh's control of other nations. During the centuries that lay ahead, Jewish religion would sometimes violate this ideal. Leaders, political and religious, would often encourage a narrow nationalism which went contrary to the prophetic dream for the nation. But with the exilic prophets the appreciation of Israel's universal destiny was given clear expression. Henceforth, she began to become in fact "a light to the nations."

RESTORATION (HAGGAI; ZECHARIAH 1–8; EZRA 1–10; NEHEMIAH 1–13; MALACHI)

Politics for Restoration

Judah's years in exile coincided with the last days of the Babylonian empire. During the period, mastery over the east shifted to Persian hands. The supremacy of Babylon was primarily the work of Nebuchadnezzar, and during his tenure the empire was able to hold her own on the scene of world politics. The major threat to Babylonian dominance came from Media, who had been an ally in overpowering Assyria. During the long reign of Nebuchadnezzar, Media became a major power in the north, extending her control into the regions of Asia Minor. Nebuchadnezzar sought to maintain the balance of power by securing the Fertile Crescent territory. Probably the third deportation of the Jews in 582 B.C. was a part of this effort.

Decline of Babylon. As long as Nebuchadnezzar lived, the Babylonian empire was held intact. With his death in 562 B.C., however, internal instability became the order of the day in Babylon. Several weak kings followed and imperial power waned rapidly. While Babylon was declining, the forces of the East were being unified under the banner of Cyrus, the Persian. Revolting against Media, Cyrus seized the Median capital of Ecbatana and, blitzkrieging the empire, was soon the ruler of the north.

Nabonidus (556–539), now Babylonian king, originally had supported Cyrus, hoping thereby to hold in check the Median threat. Following the successful revolution, however, Cyrus was feared more than Media had been. As a safeguard Nabonidus entered a defensive alliance with Amasis of Egypt and Croesus of Lydia. Cyrus, in turn, marched against the alliance and, after overrunning Lydia, stood threateningly on the borders of Babylonia. In these circumstances Deutero-Isaiah could see the hand of Yahweh moving to redeem his people.

Edict of Cyrus. Preoccupation with eastern opponents delayed Cyrus' invasion of Babylon for several years, but, when he did march against it, he captured the city with remarkable ease. Babylonian records state that the capital fell without battle and the Cylinder of Cyrus reports that the "entire population. . . . bowed to him (Cyrus) and kissed his feet. They were glad that he was king. Their faces lighted up. The master by whose aid the mortally sick had been made alive, all had been preserved from ruin. . . . [For this] they praised him and honored his name." [55] Obviously the Persian records overstate the popularity of Cyrus' reception, but they probably are not without some basis in fact. Nabonidus had fallen into disfavor with his subjects

Figure 9–5. The Cylinder of Cyrus recording his capture of Babylon in 539. The inscription states his lenient policy of permitting captives to return to their own land where they would have freedom of worship. (Source: Trustees of the British Museum.)

[55] From Cyrus Cylinder as translated in W. Winston Thomas, ed., *Documents from Old Testament Times*, pp. 92–93.

because he displaced Marduk, the chief Babylonian deity, in favor of other gods. Consequently, the city had little heart for defending his cause. A decisive engagement at Opis on the Tigris River cast the battle in Cyrus' favor and in October of 539 Babylon fell with little resistance.

The fall of "proud Babylon" set in motion Israel's deliverance. The Cylinder announces an act of Cyrus' generosity toward captive peoples, allowing them not only to return to their homeland but also to restore their religious sanctuaries. This edict of 538 does not mention the liberation of the Jews specifically, but Ezra 1:2–4 applies the policy directly to the covenant community.[56]

Thus says Cyrus king of Persia: Yahweh, the God of heaven, has given me all the kingdoms of the earth, and he has charged me to build him a house at Jerusalem, which is in Judah. Whoever is among you of all his people, may his God be with him, and let him go up to Jerusalem, which is in Judah, and rebuild the house of Yahweh, the God of Israel—he is the God who is in Jerusalem; and let each survivor, in whatever place he sojourns, be assisted by the men of his place with silver and gold, with goods and with beasts, besides freewill offerings for the house of God which is in Jerusalem.

This order of Cyrus marked the conclusion of the exile and the beginning of the slow and sometimes tedious process of restoration.

The Return to Palestine: Sheshbazzar

Soon after the proclamation of the edict of Cyrus, a group of Jews, zealous in their desire to return to the homeland, set out for Palestine. The leader of the company was a "prince of Judah," Sheshbazzar, probably to be identified as Shenazzar, the fourth son of Jehoiachin.[57] Jews making up this expedition of return were probably the most devout religionists of the day. Less ardent ones had found life in Babylon to their liking. Older members of the community remembered Palestine only vaguely and had little desire and less enthusiasm to face another long trek across the desert. Younger Jews had never seen Palestine and would not abandon their "native" Babylonia easily. Only

[56] The attitude of Cyrus accounts for Deutero-Isaiah's high estimate of him as Yahweh's anointed deliverer. See Isaiah 44:24–45:13. The Chronicler also notes the edict in II Chronicles 36:22–23 and Ezra 6:3.

[57] See I Chronicles 3:18.

those who "had been fired by their spiritual leaders with a desire to have a part in the new day" [58] would have joined company with Sheshbazzar.

Exactly how many were in the first party of return is unknown. Probably the number was relatively small. The biblical account surprisingly gives little attention to the fortunes of this group and the Chronicler obviously telescopes the career of Sheshbazzar and that of his successor, Zerubbabel. Judging from the later works of Zerubbabel, the company of Sheshbazzar evidently concerned itself with laying the foundations for a reconstructed temple and reestablishing the cult in Jerusalem.[59] The religious ambitions of the returning exiles, however, soon were thwarted by the economic pressures which they faced.

The land to which the first returnees came offered little promise of productive economy. A half-century earlier the army of Nebuchadnezzar had left Judah in ashes. In both the Shephelah and central hill country practically every town of importance had been destroyed.[60] With the nation's leadership in exile little progress had been made during the interval in rebuilding the economy of the land. Also during the disordered years, the border regions in the Negeb, which had escaped the sword of Nebuchadnezzar, had become the possession of tribal groups who had moved in from the rim of the desert.

Further, the Jews who had inhabited Palestine through the exilic period did not welcome Sheshbazzar's company as long-lost brothers. Through the years they had arduously eked out a living from the land and this immigrant group, as any other would have been, was considered a further threat to their economy. The fact that these returnees considered themselves the true "Israel" and looked with scorn upon the "unclean" occupants of the land [61] could only have intensified feelings of antagonism and distrust between the two groups.

Against the harsh reality of circumstances as they found them in Palestine, the sharp religious enthusiasms of the returnees soon

[58] Bright, *A History of Israel*, p. 344.

[59] The possibility should not be overlooked that the author of Ezra may have mistakenly assigned the beginning of rebuilding from the second year of Darius (520 B.C.) to immediately after the edict of Cyrus (538).

[60] See Wright, *Biblical Archaeology*, pp. 175–176.

[61] Cf. Haggai 2:14.

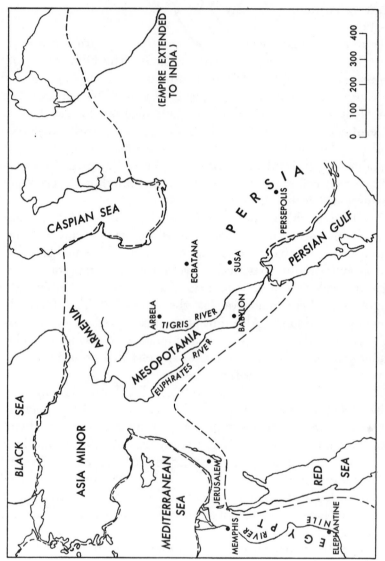

Figure 9–6. Persian Empire, c. 500 B.C.

became blunted. On the march they had been able to cherish the dream of Deutero-Isaiah about a new Exodus, but when faced with the sight of a desolate and harsh Palestine, the flowering hope of the desert began rapidly to wither and fade. Although almost no detailed information about the first two decades of the restoration are available, the words of Haggai looking back at the period must describe the situation accurately:

You have sown much, and harvested little; You eat, but you never have enough; you drink but you never have your fill; you clothe yourselves, but no one is warm; and he who earns wages earns wages to put them into a bag with holes. (1:6)

Before the cold reality of solving the economic problem of resettlement, the religious ideal of rebuilding the temple did not stand a chance. Those finding it almost impossible to build their own houses could generate little zeal for building the house of Yahweh. Opposition from the Samaritans served only to dishearten them the more. Also, when they began to compare what they were attempting to do with the magnificence of Solomon's temple, discouragement produced the conclusion that their ambition was futile. Small wonder that construction hardly begun was terminated! In 520, eighteen years after the reconstruction project had been launched, the temple structure still had not been raised above the foundations. In fact, work stopped altogether and it appeared that the grand vision of a restored and triumphant Israel, with Yahweh reigning in Zion, would never be realized. The first stage of return thus turned out to be an ineffective attempt at restoration, frustrated by economic pressure and a lack of cooperation between returning exiles and those who had remained in Palestine.[62]

Rebuilding the Temple: Zerubbabel

A second phase in Israel's restoration focuses upon Zerubbabel, Haggai, and Zechariah, three names mentioned in both the Chronicler's history and the prophetic books. Details of historical development are uncertain, but the general pattern of events is clear. At some time between 538 and 520 B.C. (probably nearer

---

[62] James Smart, *History and Theology in Second Isaiah*, pp. 281 f., interprets Isaiah 66 against this background.

538) Zerubbabel, a nephew of Sheshbazzar, arrived in Palestine as a Persian appointee to succeed Sheshbazzar as governor. The appointment of a new governor undoubtedly had political motivations for the Persians. A stronger government in Palestine might serve as a defense against Egypt. However, the biblical materials are more interested in Zerubbabel as a religious devotee. With him came another and perhaps larger contingent of Jews than those who had come with Sheshbazzar.

During the early days of Zerubbabel's governorship, the power of Persia was unabated. Cyrus and this successor Cambyses (530–522) held the empire intact. Judah remained a tiny and insignificant province with a population of barely twenty thousand [63] in a gargantuan and well-ordered empire. During these years, Israel by comparison seemed powerless and inconsequential. The "light to the nations" flickered feebly as a candle on the verge of being extinguished. With hope for a messianic era teetering on the brink of despair Judah needed more than the linear foundation of a temple around which to rally the faith of a nation.

At the time when Jews were too dispirited to return to temple building, events which revived their heart began to occur. Revolt rocked the Persian empire in 522. Although Darius I Hystaspis (522–486) managed to secure his accession to the throne, rebellion continued. Media, Egypt, Armenia, Babylon, Asia Minor— all were in turmoil. For fully two years the future of the Persian empire hung in the balance.

During these troubled days for Persia, two prophets stirred the embers of Jewish hope and fanned them into a flaming desire to complete the rebuilding of the temple. The prophets, Haggai and Zechariah, may have been among those returning with Zerubbabel or themselves may have led an additional group of returnees.[64] In either case their preaching came toward 520. Both saw in the continuous rebellion against Darius the opportunity for rekindling hope in Judah. Their immediate purpose in preaching was to spur the lethargic religious spirit of the people to rebuild the temple and restore cultic practice in Jerusalem.

The hopes of the exilic prophets had been grand and their

---

[63] Cf. Albright, *Biblical Period*, pp. 62–63.
[64] See Ackroyd, *Exile and Restoration*, pp. 148–149.

poetic description of these hopes exceptional. These hopes were not, however, realistic, or at least by 520 they were still unrealized. No one in early post-exilic Jerusalem imagined that the day of Yahweh's glory had dawned, that national life could be easily restored or that a new covenant community could face the future assured of Yahweh's presence. But Haggai and Zechariah (1–8) did hope for the future, speaking concretely and directly of the necessity to rebuild a sanctuary if the hopes of their more impressive predecessors were to be realized.

No one should say that Haggai and Zechariah were poorer prophets than the others, even though their themes do not compare favorably with those of the great prophets. They received a call like the others and were spokesmen for Yahweh to their contemporaries. As von Rad has suggested, the only proper criteria by which any prophet should be judged are whether he was a true minister to his day and whether he succeeded or failed in his task.

Haggai. The prophet Haggai is another of those prophets about whom personal details are lacking. He is mentioned only in the books of Haggai and Ezra and efforts to identify or characterize him move almost entirely on conjecture. The book which carries his name contains five oracles all dated in the second year of Darius I (520). These oracles were given on four worship occasions at the time of the Feast of Tabernacles. Each oracle is introduced with a chronological reference and the prophetic formula, "the word of Yahweh came by Haggai the prophet."

   I. Judgmental call to rebuild the temple. 1:1–6, 9–11, 12–14
  II. Prophetic promise in light of reconstruction. 1:15a and 2:15–19
 III. Promise of the second temple's greatness. 1:15b–2:9
 IV. Torah on what is clean and unclean. 2:10–14
  V. Eschatological hope and promise for Zerubbabel. 2:20–23

These oracles were compiled and edited by one of the prophet's friends or disciples who added the contextual elements which place the oracles in their historical setting. This short collection can hardly represent all that Haggai said on any of the four occasions he is reported to have spoken. They represent, rather, the disciple-collector's choice of oracles which most profoundly influenced the reconstruction of the temple.

The central concern of Haggai is the cultic problem posed by worship in a ruined sanctuary. For the prophet this indicated lack of any proper sense of orientation and meaning. Absence of an adequate cultic center was evidence that the people were unaware of commitment to any reality large enough to hold them together. And, being uncommitted, they were unable to perceive what life is all about. Therefore, they were lost in the present and were threatened with no future.

Haggai approached the problem by encouraging construction of the ruined sanctuary. Man cannot live without a center in which he finds life full of meaning and reality—where the powers that created him and sustain him can be encountered in their beneficial fullness. Therefore, the prophet promised the people of Jerusalem and their leaders, Zerubbabel and Joshua, the blessings of Yahweh's presence in the new temple. This would be the temple's glory and the community's hope. National, religious and cultic identity depended upon the reestablishment of the cultic center. The Jew could not know who he was apart from meaningful relationships with both God and the people of the covenant. These relationships should be proclaimed and accepted in the Jerusalem sanctuary. Haggai's concern went far beyond a building campaign. His interest was in a center of orientation that found the meaning of the past and the present and the hope of the future in the presence of God.

Haggai further anticipated that Yahweh's presence in the new sanctuary would have astonishing eschatological consequences. Cosmic upheavals would precede the elevation of Zion; treasures of the nations would come to Jerusalem and Zerubbabel would be messiah. In this he was incorrect, but his misidentification of Zerubbabel as messiah and the wrong anticipation of an immediate eschaton should not diminish appreciation of his significant sense of the value of orientation in which Yahweh is free to be present at any time and the corollary sense of divine presence which fills life with meaning.

Zechariah. The preaching of Zechariah overlapped and continued beyond the work of Haggai. More than likely this prophet was of priestly descent, but we have no information about the man himself. The book of Zechariah contains fourteen chapters, but it is almost universally accepted that only chapters 1–8 belong to the sixth century prophet. Chapters 9–14 come from a later historical setting.[65] These latter chapters contain two collections of prophecies each beginning with the phrase, "the burden of the word of Yahweh," found only here and at the opening of Malachi.

I. A plea for the people's repentance. 1:1–6
II. A series of eight dream visions. 1:7–6:8
III. The symbolic crowning of Zerubbabel.[66] 6:9–15
IV. Various prophecies on restoration. 7:1–8:23.

The major part of Zechariah's oracles utilize the dream vision with dialogue between God, prophet and interpreting angel. Here then the form and imagery of Jewish apocalyptic are given major development.

The prophet used apocalyptic visions to develop two major themes. Like Haggai he was concerned about the rebuilding of the temple which for him meant the reestablishment of Yahweh's rule.

Thus says Yahweh, I have returned to Jerusalem with compassion; my house shall be built in it, says Yahweh of hosts . . . My cities shall again overflow with prosperity, and Yahweh will again comfort Zion and again choose Jerusalem. (1:16–17)

The prophet saw Yahweh moving to establish his triumphant rule in Zion. Since the temple was the focus of Yahweh's reign, the people were to get on with its construction.

The presence of Yahweh in the restored sanctuary would inaugurate a new age over which Zerubbabel would rule as Yahweh's anointed. As a descendant of David he would be the "messiah" or "branch" through whom nationalistic hopes would find fulfillment. Alongside Zerubbabel Joshua would serve as high priest, also as Yahweh's "messiah." The climax of Zechariah is reached in the assertion that the new age of salvation is meant for the whole world.

Thus says Yahweh of hosts: Peoples shall yet come, even the inhabitants of many cities; the inhabitants of one city shall go to another, saying, "Let us go at once to entreat the favor of Yahweh, and to seek Yahweh of hosts; I am going." Many peoples and strong nations shall come to seek Yahweh

[65] See pp. 494–496.
[66] Most scholars agree that Zechariah 6:9–15 originally concerned Zerubbabel, not Joshua.

of hosts in Jerusalem, and to entreat the favor of Yahweh. Thus says Yahweh of hosts: In those days ten men from the nations of every tongue shall take hold of the robe of a Jew, saying, "Let us go with you for we have heard that God is with you." (8:20–23)

Stirred by the preaching of Haggai and Zechariah, the people under Zerubbabel's guidance returned to work on the temple. With messianic hope resurrected and centered in Zerubbabel they began to prepare for the new day. Late in 520 with mortar, stone, and resolve they returned to the temple foundations and by 516 the second temple had been completed.[67]

Joel.   Sometime after the restoration of the temple [67] and before the Hellenic mark of Alexander had been stamped upon the east, Joel made one of the infrequent breaks in post-exilic prophetic silence. The book cannot be precisely dated, but it resembles both prophetic and apocalyptic writings. It is in three parts:

I. Locust plague and drought as signs of the imminent Day of Yahweh. 1:1–2:27
II. The outpouring of Yahweh's spirit upon Judah. 2:28–32
III. The eschatological Day of Yahweh. Chapter 3

The first part of the work preserves themes akin to his predecessors who spoke the oracle of Yahweh. An ominous devastation of the area about his hometown Jerusalem by hordes of locusts provided the stimulus and setting for this division of Joel's prophecy. He visualized the destroyers as Yahweh's agents punishing priests and people for their sins. He summoned the residents of the land to penitence in anticipation of God's merciful forgiveness:

> "Yet even now," says Yahweh,
>   "return to me with all your heart,
> with fasting, with weeping, and with mourning;
> and rend your hearts and not your garments."
> Return to Yahweh, your God,
>   for he is gracious and merciful,
> slow to anger, and abounding in steadfast love,
>   and repents of evil. (2:12, 13)

Blended into the prophet's thought is a future Day of Yahweh which the present holocaust presages. Beyond an awful judgment would come an age of divine bliss and bounty.

[67] See Joel 1:14; 2:7–9, 17.

The apocalyptic portion of Joel is concerned with twin themes of a battle in which powers will be destroyed and a rapturous occasion of which Yahweh says,

> . . . I will pour out my spirit on all flesh;
> your sons and your daughters shall prophecy,
>   your old men shall dream dreams,
>   and your young men shall see visions. (2:28)

The dual emphasis portrays Yahweh's vindication of "Zion, my holy mountain" against her enemies and his protection of his own.

> And Yahweh roars from Zion,
>   and utters his voice from Jerusalem,
>   and the heavens and the earth shake.
> But Yahweh is a refuge to his people,
>   a stronghold to the people of Israel. (3:16)

Reaffirming the Faith: Nehemiah and Ezra

The third, and perhaps most crucial, phase of Israel's restoration came almost a century after the edict of Cyrus ended the exile. The two most significant leaders in this restoration were Nehemiah and Ezra, who lived and worked during the last half of the fifth century B.C. They attempted to restate and reaffirm Israel's faith to the restored community in such a way that traditional covenant concepts were conserved and made relevant in forms suitable for a new age.

The interval between the completion of the Zerubbabel temple in 516 B.C. and the work of Nehemiah and Ezra is obscure. Isolated and meager sources provide what little information is available. The prophet Malachi gives a glimpse of life during the times and the Chronicler in the books of Ezra and Nehemiah provides insight into religious and political conditions in Palestine. Certain archaeological finds, such as the Elephantine papyri and the Jehoiachin tablet,[68] assist in approximating some of the dates. Largely, however, we must move with caution in describing the history of Israel prior to the mid-fifth century B.C.

Persian control of Palestine during this time was unchallenged. Darius I Hystaspis (522–486), after establishing order in his empire, divided it into twenty satrapies (Palestine was included with Syria in the satrapy of Arabia). Over each of these areas was placed a governor (satrap) who was endowed solely with civil

---

[68] Wright, *Biblical Archaeology*, pp. 176–178, 206–208.

authority. Darius himself maintained direct control of the military and thereby assured the absolute authority of the emperor. For over three decades the strong and able hand of Darius guided the fortunes of Persia and under his leadership the empire reached its zenith. Building flourished. A network of roads was cut across the whole empire. A standardized system of coinage was instituted. All of this meant an energetic economy.

Darius' successors, however, were neither so able nor successful. Xerxes I (486–465) was initially successful in campaigns against the rising power of Greece, but came to Salamis and met tragic defeat. Further reverses ultimately caused Persia to withdraw from Greece. Xerxes was assassinated and succeeded by Artaxerxes I Longimanus (465–424). Throughout his reign the fortunes of Persia fared poorly. It became more and more evident that mighty Persia was declining in both power and prestige.

In Palestine during this period the impact of world affairs was felt very little. The revived messianic hope which encouraged the temple's reconstruction was short lived. Following the dedication of the new edifice, the hope soon faded into disillusion. Popular optimism generated by the preaching of Haggai and Zechariah had centered in Zerubbabel. In him the people had concentrated their hopes for the restoration of the Davidic line. Suddenly, and quite mysteriously, Zerubbabel disappeared from the scene. Suspicions concerning his disappearance logically center in the Persian king. To be sure, Darius Hystaspis had honored the edict of Cyrus by lending support to the temple's restoration, but his experience in dealing with opposition had taught him too much to tolerate a petty prince of Judah about whom royal claims were made. With the passing of Zerubbabel, natural or unnatural, went once again the high hopes of a restored nation. The role of leadership fell to a high priest named Joshua, son of Jahozadak,[69] and his successors.

Life in Palestine through the first half of the fifth century continued to be confused, indefinable, and unpredictable. Although they possessed a temple, Jews in Palestine were unable to assert dramatic leadership over Jewish communities in other parts of the world. They were an impoverished people, confined to an

---

[69] Haggai 1:1.

Figure 9–7. Gate of Xerxes, Persepolis, the major capital of the Persian Empire. (Source: Courtesy of the Oriental Institute, University of Chicago.)

area not much more than twenty miles square, still struggling for existence—let alone significance. They enjoyed religious liberty but remained politically dependent upon Persia. More compatible relationships between the returned exiles and the resident Jews must have developed, but animosities against non-Jewish groups became more strained.[70]

Religiously these decades were years of complaint and skepticism. Discouraged Jews seemingly made little progress in reviving the Davidic state. They were rather content with the amphictyonic-like union of groups bound loosely by social and national ties. In the narrow confines around Jerusalem they grubbed out a living relatively unconcerned about international movements. This low level of organizational and political concern fostered a syncretistic attitude on the part of many. Neigh-

[70] See below, pp. 466–471.

boring peoples were permitted to move in with freedom. Marriages between Jews and non-Jews became more common and more acceptable. Many lost their enthusiasm for the pure faith and thereby became susceptible to the infiltration of foreign worship practices. Casualness in the payment of tithes forced Levites to abandon their sacerdotal duties to earn a living. The Sabbath was neglected and social immorality prevailed. In short, the demoralized community of faith gave way to religious laxity. The rebuilt temple did not, as some had hoped, reestablish Yahweh to his central place in the people's life.

Malachi. The low ebb of the spiritual life of the nation is scored in the writing Malachi, the final book in the Old Testament canon. The identity of the author is unknown. The present title comes from the word translated "my messenger" which appears in 3:1.

> Behold, I send my messenger to prepare the way before me.

Whoever Malachi may have been, he stood in the tradition of the great prophets of Israel, denouncing the sin of both priest and people. However, in style of writing the author shows himself to be a precursor of later Judaism. The prophet drives home his message through the use of the dialectical question and answer. You say, "How have we despised thy name?" By offering polluted food upon my altar. And you say, "How have we polluted it?" By thinking that the Lord's table may be despised (1:6b–7). The spirit of this method is more that of the scribe than that of the prophet. Instruction by disputation takes the place of the fiery oracles of earlier prophets.[71] As one reads the book he senses that he is near the close of the prophetic age and stands at the threshold of the scholastic procedures of the later Jewish rabbis.

An outline of Malachi reveals how Judah's perversion of covenant relationship with Yahweh dominates the book:

Superscription. 1:1
I. Yahweh loves Israel, not Edom. 1:2–5.
II. Priests corrupt worship and mislead the people. 1:6–2:9.
III. People degrade marriage. 2:10–16.
IV. Yahweh's judgment is sure. 2:17–4:3.
Subscription. 4:4–6.

[71] Robert C. Dentan, "The Book of Malachi," *Interpreter's Bible*, VI, 1120.

The message of Malachi includes some exalted themes. He suggests that all true worship, even that of the heathen, is really offered to Yahweh (1:11); he denounces inhumane divorce as that which Yahweh hates (2:16); and he alludes to the brotherly unity of man (2:10). But the preaching of the prophet is mostly concerned with a form of organized religion to which people give only half-hearted devotion. Tithes were withheld and imperfect animals offered in sacrifice (1:7–14; 3:8–10). Social morality had degenerated (3:5) and religious leaders followed the rule of expedience (2:13–16). Such circumstances demanded repentance so that restoration might occur:

And they shall be mine, saith Yahweh of hosts (3:17),

. . . .

for you who fear my name the sun of righteousness shall rise, with healing in its wings. (4:2)

The religion of this period certainly reflects the disappointment of the Jews over the failure of their messianic dreams. The longed-for Davidic state seemed such a remote possibility that the time for a new—and perhaps different—step in religious development was at hand. Although the temple had been restored, the glory of Solomon had not returned. Although the returnees were entrenched in the land, the splendor of an anointed age was not apparent. Restoration was to be ground out in the hard experience of continuing history, and Ezra and Nehemiah worked as makers of a new day influencing Judaism for centuries.

Nehemiah. One of the most perplexing problems of Old Testament scholarship is the chronological order of the work of Nehemiah and Ezra. Ezra 7:7 seems to imply that Ezra preceded Nehemiah into Palestine. However, the reforms of Ezra seem to have been based on the achievements of Nehemiah.[72] To assume that Ezra's work came first implies that the work of Ezra was a failure, which does not seem to have been the case. Further, none of those who returned with Ezra [73] are mentioned as helping Nehemiah rebuild the walls of Jerusalem.[74] Reconstruction is made no easier by the fact that the Chronicler, the basic available

[72] Cf. Ezra 9:9.
[73] Ezra 8:1–14.
[74] Nehemiah 3.

source for the period, is more concerned with his theological emphases than with historical sequence.[75] Although the evidence is not conclusive and the problem continues to be debated, Nehemiah probably preceded Ezra in Palestine and commenced religious reforms later continued by Ezra.[76]

Nehemiah was a Jew of no little distinction. He prospered in Babylon as a prime example of the Jew who did well in the foreign land. When he appears on the scene in the biblical story, he is already a person of high rank, a cupbearer to King Artaxerxes I himself. Although ensconced in a position of honor in Persian affairs, Nehemiah remained truly devoted to the cause of Israel. Consequently, when in 445 he received news of unpleasant circumstances in Jerusalem, he was deeply distressed and took personal initiative to seek and secure the authority of the king to lead a deputation to Jerusalem for the primary purpose of rebuilding the walls of the city.

Artaxerxes, undoubtedly anxious to fortify himself against the ever restless Egypt, not only gave Nehemiah permission to rebuild the fortification of Jerusalem, but also provided materials for the enterprise. Additionally, Judah was made a separate province and Nehemiah was appointed its governor. By 440 the new governor had arrived in Palestine and was about the task of inspiring the Jerusalem leaders to join in his mission.

The mammoth project of building the walls was accomplished with signal rapidity. After a secret inspection of the ruins of the ancient walls, Nehemiah revealed his plans to the leaders. With their assistance a labor force was conscripted, organized, and set to work.[77] Within the brief span of fifty-two days the basic structure of the wall was completed. To this were added in the next two years the necessary reinforcements and fortifications to complete the master plan for the walls.[78]

Nehemiah was not without opposition in accomplishing his assignment. Instigator of the large part of his difficulty was Sanballat, the governor of Samaria, from whose district the new province of Judah had been separated. Sanballat was supported

[75] See P. R. Ackroyd, "History and Theology in the Writings of the Chronicler," *Concordia Theological Monthly*, XXXVIII (1967), 501–515.

[76] For a fuller discussion of the problem see Bright, *A History of Israel*, pp. 375–386.

[77] Cf. Nehemiah 3.

[78] Cf. Josephus, *Antiquities*, XI, v, 8.

in his resistance by the Arabs, Ammonites, and Philistines, who did not care to see Jerusalem fortified against their encroachments. Several raids were made on Jerusalem and a plot to murder Nehemiah was initiated. The opposition came to naught, however. Nehemiah was alert enough to avoid being lured into ambush and strong enough not to cower before threats upon his life. Wisely and fortuitously he armed his construction crews and work proceeded on schedule. When the walls were completed, they were dedicated in solemn convocation and a tenth of the Judean population was encouraged to move inside the refortified city. Zion was secure and "the joy of Jerusalem was heard afar off." [79]

Nehemiah's first tenure as governor lasted for twelve years. In accordance with the terms of his leave of absence from Artaxerxes, he returned to Babylon. Shortly, however, his leave of absence was renewed and he was back in Jerusalem. During this stint of duty, Nehemiah turned his attention to cultic reforms.[80] He was particularly disturbed because Eliashib, the high priest, had allowed Tobiah, an Ammonite, to take up residence in a room of the temple formerly used for cultic purposes. Tobiah and his household furnishings were "forcibly removed" and the temple room restored to its proper function. A series of executive orders designed to restore moral order to the land followed. Gates of the city were closed to Sabbath trading. The portions of the Levites were guaranteed. Mixed marriages with women of Ashdod, Ammon, and Moab were strictly banned. A grandson of Eliashib who had married the daughter of Sanballat was run out of the city.[81]

These, and perhaps other, efforts of the governor represent a sincere desire to give renewed meaning to Israel's faith. However, Nehemiah's approach was basically symptomatic. He sought to legislate against the evil of the day as he saw it, but such control of behavior by edict could be of little lasting influence. Any permanent cure of Israel's religious disease would need to be directed toward the cause more than the symptom.

---

[79] Nehemiah 12:43.

[80] Cf. Nehemiah 13.

[81] Josephus writes (*Antiquities,* XI, vii, 2 and viii, 2) that Sanballat compensated his son-in-law by building for him a temple on Mt. Gerizim to rival the one in Jerusalem as the divinely appointed place for worship. Josephus wrongly relates this to the time of Alexander the Great. By the time of Nehemiah the deep cleavage between Jew and Samaritan had been rather well established.

The coming of the priest Ezra gave occasion for such an approach. His point of attack was the basic religious commitment of the people.

Ezra.   Ezra was a priest who grew up and performed his early work among the Babylonian exiles. Like Nehemiah, he was of that group of exiles who never lost their sympathies with the homeland and followed closely the development of affairs in

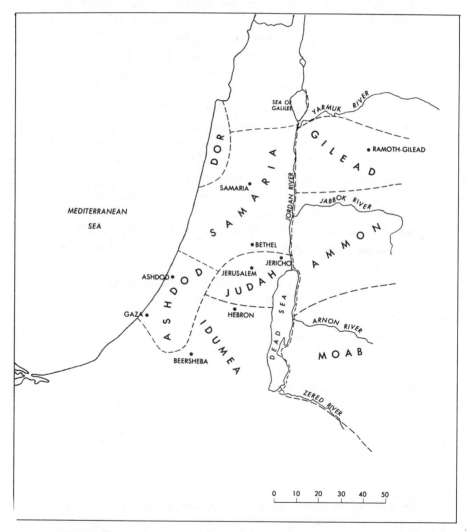

Figure 9–8.   Provinces of Palestine during days of Ezra-Nehemiah.

Jerusalem. Sometime during the late stages of Nehemiah's governorship, Ezra became intensely concerned about the reports of moral laxity among those who had the grand privilege of being in Palestine. Distressed, he sought and received, probably with the influence of Nehemiah, the permission of Artaxerxes I to head a company of devotees in an expedition to Palestine for the expressed purpose of regenerating the religious life of their people. Probably about 428 B.C. Ezra and his colleagues arrived in Palestine and set to the task of implementing the reforms already begun by Nehemiah.

The reformations of Ezra centered in "the law" which he brought with him from Babylon. The identification of this possession of Ezra is quite difficult, but it is rather certain that the Pentateuch was already considered as authoritative in the Jewish community. Whether "the law" brought by Ezra was the entire Pentateuch or only the Priestly portion, he certainly considered this law as his authority for reformation. To him this was Yahweh's injunction to Israel and, armed with this written "Thus saith Yahweh," he took significant strides to deepen the religious life of the people. His reform was according to the law of Yahweh, which was in his hand.[82]

Soon after his arrival in Palestine, Ezra led in an extended public reading of the law. The Hebrew text was translated and explained in the vernacular Aramaic so that all could understand. The hearers were moved to tears and there followed a prolonged period of study, confession, and recommitment. The leaders of Jerusalem were instructed in the requirements of the law. A persuasive program of education of the masses in the demands of the law was instituted. Participation by the people in the observance of the Feast of Tabernacles was begun.[83] The initial expression of rededication came within a few weeks when the people gathered in solemn convocation to renew their vows to Yahweh.[84] This, no doubt, was a kind of covenant renewal ceremony.

The ethical concerns of Ezra were essentially the same as those of Nehemiah. Singled out for special attention by him was the

[82] Ezra 7:14.
[83] The observance lasted an extra eighth day following the descriptions of the Priestly Code. This supports the inclusion of the Priestly Code within the Ezra law.
[84] See Nehemiah 9, 10.

matter of marriage to foreigners.[85] Men were persuaded to divorce foreign wives and covenanted to enter into no more marriages with foreigners.[86] Further, they obligated themselves to an annual temple tax, to the maintenance of the altar and to the giving of first fruits and the tithe.[87] In short, the people pledged themselves explicitly to the demands of the law. With this reorganization of the community of faith around the requirements of the law,[88] something of the ancient religio-political philosophy which had undergirded the amphictyony was restored in postexilic Judaism.[89]

As had been true of Nehemiah, Ezra's work was accomplished with rapidity. Probably within the span of a year or two the major portion of his labor in Palestine was over. What happened to him we do not know. Josephus reports that he died soon after his mission and was buried in Jerusalem.[90]

The impact of Ezra upon the future of Hebrew religion was enduring and many today refer to him as "the father of Judaism." His efforts to popularize the law started a trend which produced "the tradition of the elders." Inspired by the lead of Ezra, later teachers sought to interpret the law for the understanding of the people. In much the same way that the canonical scriptures came to be looked upon with authority, so the interpretation of revered leaders was accepted, organized, and preserved as authoritative tradition. Later sectarian groups within Judaism were often divided as to how much authority should be given to this oral tradition.

The work of Ezra may have contributed to a growing popularity of the synagogue in early Judaism. There is available no tangible evidence regarding the date of the origin of the synagogue.[91] Its beginnings are usually dated to the exile, when the

[85] Some scholars contend that the book of Ruth may have been written during this period as a polemic against the policy of Nehemiah and Ezra.

[86] Nehemiah 9:2; 10:28–31.

[87] Nehemiah 10:32–39.

[88] Cf. Bright, A History of Israel, pp. 372–374.

[89] "Judaism" refers to the religion of the Jews as it developed after the Exile.

[90] Antiquities, XI, v, 5.

[91] Synagogues are not mentioned in the Old Testament, but are most prominent in the New Testament. Archaeological information about synagogues prior to the first century A.D. is meager. See Floyd V. Filson, "Temple, Synagogue and Church" and Herbert G. May, "Synagogues in Palestine" in The Biblical Archaeologist Reader, pp. 185–200, 229–250.

Jews needed a center of worship to serve the purposes of fellowship and instruction formerly provided by the temple. Here, the exiles would meet for prayer and discussion of the Torah as they knew it. Ezra's practice of reading the law before the people may have been inspired by the synagogue practice of his day.[92] Whether this were the case or not, the emphasis by Ezra upon teaching the commandments of the law gave a vigorous impetus to the instructional aspects of Judaism. Since instruction focused in the synagogue in later Judaism, the work of Ezra certainly played a significant role in the growing status of the synagogue during the postexilic period. Even after the temple was restored, the synagogue continued to function, assuming a role of its own following the emphasis of Ezra. Whereas the temple was the special precinct of the priesthood and high sacrificial system, the synagogue served the common man by providing continued instruction in the Torah and common participation in worship. Synagogues dotted the eastern world wherever the Jews lived and through them the Ezra instructional tradition was continued.

The reaffirmation and preservation of Jewish faith in the post-exile period, then, was primarily the work of Nehemiah, the politician, and Ezra, the priest. Under the patronage of Persia they were able to lead in the establishment of a community identified primarily by its religious ideology. As Judaism faced her day of testing before the Hellenistic tide, her identification of religion and nationalism would be a major factor in survival. "Judaism might be stamped out by sheer force, but it was no longer in danger of absorption into other and lower forms of religion." [93]

The Chronicler.   For Israel the exile and restoration were both experience and idea.[94] The sixth century confronted the community of faith with historical realities from which they could not escape and in light of which they attempted to understand Yahweh. Beyond this, later reflection upon these realities developed attitudes and interpretations of the historic facts. Thus, exile and restoration continued to exert considerable influence upon the development of Israel's theology.

[92] Cf. R. H. Pfeiffer, *Introduction to the Old Testament*, p. 81.
[93] H. Wheeler Robinson, *The History of Israel*, p. 157.
[94] See Ackroyd, *Exile and Restoration*, pp. 232–256.

Soon after the days of Nehemiah and Ezra (probably early in the fourth century B.C.), the nation produced an historian usually referred to as the Chronicler, whose work illustrates one kind of interpretation which occurred. His writing appears in the Old Testament books—Ezra, Nehemiah, and I and II Chronicles. Using the framework available to him in Samuel and Kings, the Chronicler retold Israel's story from the perspective of the day in which he lived with the intention of reaffirming faith in Yahweh, who had always been at work in Israel's history. An outline of his work shows its historical scope: [95]

I. Judah's prehistory from Adam to Saul. I Chronicles 1–9.
II. David. I Chronicles 10–29.
III. Solomon. II Chronicles 1–9.
IV. From revolt of 722/21 to edict of Cyrus. II Chronicles 10–36.
V. Restoration under Zerubbabel. Ezra 1–6.
VI. Consolidation under Ezra and Nehemiah. Ezra 7–Nehemiah 13.

The Chronicler's method is pictorial and dramatic. He aims as much to communicate ideas as to describe events. Consequently, he is a poor technical historian as illustrated by his probable confusion of the order of Nehemiah and Ezra. But this does not detract from the author's genuine contribution to Israel's post-exile life and thought. Reflecting upon the experience in Babylon and restored Judah, the Chronicler intends to find a means by which divine will may be embodied in the nation's new life. He sees this possibility in Israel's cult. Jerusalem, temple, cult and prayer were channels for serving Yahweh in a restored community which had little else. In a continuous "history" the Chronicler writes to authenticate the place of Jerusalem and its sanctuary. Thus the story of the North is omitted and stress is laid on those who contribute directly to the development of Israel's ritual. His chief hero is David,[96] not as slayer of giants or warrior king, but as patron of Israel's cultic history. This intense concentration upon Israel's worship distinguishes his work from all other Old Testament traditions. The Chronicler, though, does have other concerns. Throughout he interprets history according to the doctrine of retribution. Events are presented to explain misfortunes

[95] Following Eissfeldt, *The Old Testament: An Introduction*, p. 531.
[96] See W. F. Stinespring, "Eschatology in Chronicles," *Journal of Biblical Literature*, LXXX (September, 1961), 209–219.

as punishment for sins, particularly abuse of priests or prophets. In addition, the Chronicler notably emphasizes Yahweh's control of history through miraculous intervention. Finally, there is the glorification of David, whose age is seen as the ideal for the restored nation in the future. Yahweh's covenant with David is referred to again and again. Here the Chronicler doubtless reflects the longing of his age for the restoration of the Davidic monarchy.

THE PSALTER IN THE POSTEXILE COMMUNITY (SELECTED PSALMS)

Love of the temple and its worship which dominates the Chronicler's history is the context in which the Psalter came to be cherished in Israel. Although individual psalms come from across the whole range of Israel's history, their final collection and arrangement belongs to the postexile. These were Israel's prayers and praises used for worship in the temple of Zerubbabel. Through these poems, known and loved by all in the Judeo-Christian tradition, Israel gave expression to every facet of her faith. In the study of the Psalter, therefore, one enters the worship life of Judaism at its best.

The Collection of the Psalter

The book of Psalms is an anthology of 150 poems which come from across the whole of Israel's history. In their present arrangement in the Old Testament these poems are divided into five sections. Each section, with the exception of the last, ends with a benediction, as in 41:13; 72:19; 89:52 and 106:48. These are not integral parts of the psalms with which they are placed, but each serves as a benediction for its section. The sections are: I, 1–41; II, 42–72; III, 73–89; IV, 90–106; and V, 107–150. Psalm 1 introduces the Psalter as a whole and Psalm 150 concludes the collection with a note of triumphant praise. Within each of these sections there is a variety of authorship, literary type, and subject matter; obviously the sections do not represent individual collections simply joined to form our present book. The five-fold division of the psalms was made in the postexilic period when Israel's religious poetry was again

being utilized for purposes of worship. Doubtless the divisions
were intended to correspond to the five divisions of the Torah.

Throughout the five sections of the Psalter several collections
can be distinguished. Evidently the book is a collection of collections upon which an arbitrary five-fold division has been imposed. (1) An Elohistic collection is characterized by the use of
the divine name Elohim instead of Yahweh. Even in such widely
used phrases as "O God, my God" and "O God, God of my salvation" where the personal name Yahweh would be expected, Elohim is used. Probably there was an independent collection in
which, for some unknown reason, the name Yahweh was changed
to Elohim.[97] Two collections based on subject matter are discernible. (2) The Hallelujah psalms [98] are hymns of great praise
and thanksgiving often used as special songs for the festivals of
Passover, Tabernacles, Weeks, and Dedication. (3) The Songs
of Ascent [99] may have derived the name from their use by pilgrims
who "ascended" Mount Zion at the time of the great festivals.[100]
Four collections are designated according to personal name. (4)
One of two groups prefaced by the title "Psalm of David" is almost identical with Book I in the postexilic division.[101] (5) The
second Davidic collection [102] is perhaps an anthology of prayers.
(6) Eleven psalms [103] are ascribed to "the sons of Korah," apparently a guild of temple singers mentioned in I Chronicles 9:19,
31 and 12:6. (7) A final collection [104] is ascribed to Asaph, either
the individual mentioned in I Chronicles 16:5 or a guild of singers
alluded to in II Chronicles 29:13.

Since these collections overlap at many points, obviously many
collections were available to the final compilers of the biblical

[97] This is borne out in two particular instances. Psalm 14 and 53 are identical
save that the Yahwehs of Psalm 14 are changed to Elohim. The same is true of
Psalm 40:14–17, which is repeated in Psalm 70 with the same kind of alteration.

[98] Psalm 111–114, 116–118, 135–136, and 146–150.

[99] Psalms 120–135.

[100] Some suggest that the "ascents" refer to the steps leading from the court
of the women to the court of the Israelites upon which the temple singers stood
while singing. Others say that it refers to the literary device of repeating in one
verse certain key words contained in the preceding verse. Kimchi, a Jewish rab-
binical interpreter, said that the "Ascent refers perhaps to the ascending of the
captives from Babylon." Quoted in W. O. E. Oesterley, *The Psalms*, p. 500.

[101] The exceptions are Psalms 1, 2, 10, and 33 (10 was originally part of 9).

[102] Psalms 51–65 and 68–70.

[103] Psalms 42–49, 84–88 (with the exception of 86).

[104] Psalms 50 and 73–83.

book. Further, all the Psalms found in the collections were not included in our Psalter. The Korah, Asaph, and Davidic collections were doubtless much more extensive. The appearance of many Psalms in the Old Testament outside the Psalter indicates that psalmody was widespread in Israel and that the Psalter collection is only a selective anthology.[105]

The Origin of the Psalms

The complicated process by which various collections of psalms were made and then used in the Psalter cannot be recovered. Walter Harrelson has suggested [106] a logical sequence: (1) An initial body of cultic materials was produced for use in the amphictyonic worship centers during and after the time of Joshua. (2) The establishment of Jerusalem as a worship center created a need for additional liturgical materials. David himself, by gift and inspiration, produced many hymns, laments, and confessions. (3) The division of the kingdom produced a rival temple in the North around which other psalms were written and collected. (4) Many of these found their way back to Jerusalem when the Northern Kingdom fell in 722/21. (5) During the Babylonian exile, the collection was put into writing and greatly expanded. (6) Finally, the postexile community elaborated and rearranged the collection, perhaps added superscriptions, and largely put the materials in their present order.

Whether or not this reconstruction is historically precise, it describes a process by which the Psalter likely came into being. ⟩ Obviously, the assumption that David was the author of the vast majority of the poems is an overstatement. The Psalter itself ascribes many of them to poets other than David and probably only a minority of the so-called Davidic psalms originated with Israel's greatest king. The preposition in the Psalter title "Psalm of David" may be translated as either "of," "by," "to," or "for."

---

[105] Psalms appear in the prophetic books: Jonah 2:2–9; Nahum 1:8; Habakkuk 3; Isaiah 1:2–31; Jeremiah 11:18–20. Poems contained in the Psalter are quoted at length in Old Testament prose works: II Samuel 22 equals Psalm 18; I Chronicles 16:8–36 is composed of Psalm 105:1–15, Psalm 96 and Psalm 106:1 and 47 f. Two psalms in prose books do not appear elsewhere: "The Song of Moses" in Deuteronomy 32:1–43 and "The Last Words of David" in II Samuel 23:1–7.

[106] *Interpreting the Old Testament,* pp. 407–408.

Thus, Psalms so titled may be considered to be "in David's style" or "dedicated to David." [107] By postexilic days David had become the patron saint of temple music. He reigned in memory as *the* poet and *the* musician. Further, the temple itself was traced to him and his son. Thus, as the tradition grew, a body of psalms gathered around his name and were attributed to the Davidic tradition.[108] David's major role, therefore, in the actual production of the Psalter was that of patron spirit and inspirational art-master.

Since the titles were not part of the original texts of the psalms, they cannot be taken too seriously as descriptive of authorship. At most they indicate the collection to which the particular psalm belonged. Actually, the author or the actual historical occasion can be determined only for a dozen or so of the psalms.[109] However, studies which seek to place the psalms in their proper cultic role and bring them to life in the worship experience of ancient Israel are more productive. The Psalms, like all great religious poetry, belong to both the individual and the group. Some were written by men who sought to express the experience of their inmost being and with no desire that their thoughts become public. Later readers found these works to be sublime statements of their own feelings. In time private psalms became precious possessions for public worship. They were recognized as expressing the feeling of all Israel. Other psalms were originally written for the cult by the temple singers or by cultic prophets. When these were used in worship, they took on special and personal meaning for individuals and thus became "favorites." No one psalm, therefore, is strictly personal or totally public. Authorship, then, is of secondary importance. The vital question is, "What place did a psalm play in the cult and what was its meaning in the experience of worship?"

---

[107] Psalm 30 is inscribed "A Psalm of David." Under no circumstances could he be its author since the title also describes it, "A Song at the Dedication of the Temple."

[108] The LXX shows a tendency to ascribe still more psalms to David.

[109] Whether a psalm came from the preexilic community or the community gathered around the second temple is often controversial. Opinion differs so widely that one scholar finds only one postexilic psalm while another finds only two which belong to the preexilic period. The truth doubtless lies somewhere between these two extremes with psalms coming from every period of Israel's history, more perhaps from the preexilic age.

The Use of Psalms in Worship

More recent studies of the Psalms have attempted to find their meaning in the cult rather than in specific historical events.[110] Hermann Gunkel,[111] whose studies have influenced all major works on the Psalter since his day, distinguished the following five major classes of psalms, all associated with the cult: (1) Hymns, (2) Communal Laments, (3) Royal Psalms, (4) Individual Laments, (5) Individual Songs of Thanksgiving. Careful examination of the Psalter in light of these classifications by literary types has led to a new understanding of Israel's worship. The Hymns were used to praise Yahweh at the sanctuary, the Laments to appeal for aid in time of some communal or individual calamity, the Songs of Thanksgiving to express gratitude for Yahweh's aid, and the Royal Songs to celebrate moments of significance in the life of Israel's king.[112]

Psalms were used in connection with almost every aspect of the temple ritual, and any adequate understanding of Israelite worship must imaginatively attempt to relate the Psalter to the book of Leviticus. Much of Leviticus is devoted to detailed descriptions of forms of worship. It served as a guide or handbook for those who presided at worship. The form of the ritual is presented without its liturgy and, therefore, stands stripped of its meaning.

Leviticus tells us what is to be done at this ceremony or that, and how it is to be done, but it does not tell us what was said, what ideas and emotions gathered around the rite, what it meant to those who participated in it.[113]

Since "it is the weakness of every cult-act that it is not self-explanatory, but may convey half a dozen meanings according to the mind of the worshipper who fulfills it," [114] the religious leaders

[110] The older tendency, found already in the titles of the Psalms themselves, to relate certain hymns to incidents in Israel's history is particularly characteristic of the commentaries of C. A. Briggs and A. F. Kirkpatrick.

[111] Hermann Gunkel, *Die Psalmen* and Hermann Gunkel and Joachim Begrich, *Einleitung in die Psalmen.*

[112] Sigmund Mowinckel goes a step farther and interprets a number of psalms in relation to a New Year's festival which he believes was celebrated in prexilic Israel.

[113] Nathaniel Micklem, "Leviticus" in *The Interpreter's Bible,* II, 5. See also A. C. Welch, *The Psalter in Life, Worship and History,* p. 70.

[114] A. C. Welch, *Prophet and Priest in Old Israel,* p. 110.

of Israel supplied rubrics which were repeated in connection with
the rites, either by the worshipper or by the officiating priests.
In general these rubrics contained an address to Yahweh, a statement as to his nature, and a description of his relation to the
worshipper or worshippers. They also stated the purpose of the
offering.

For the most part, the rubrics have been either lost or separated
from the description of the ritual with which they originally were
associated. Fortunately, however, two valuable and instructive
illustrations of combined liturgy and cultic form have been preserved. The confession which the worshipper was to recite when
he brought first fruits to the sanctuary is recorded in Deuteronomy
26, along with the prescription for performing the act. The
Israelite is commanded to bring first fruits in a basket and to
present them before the priest. The priest places the basket before the altar and the worshipper repeats the following liturgical
formula.

A wandering Aramean was my father; and he went down into Egypt and
sojourned there, few in number; and there he became a nation, great,
mighty, and populous. And the Egyptians treated us harshly, and afflicted
us, and laid upon us hard bondage. Then we cried to Yahweh the God of
our fathers, and Yahweh heard our voice, and saw our affliction, our toil,
and our oppression; and Yahweh brought us out of Egypt with a mighty
hand and an outstretched arm, with great terror, with signs and wonders;
and he brought us into this place and gave us this land, a land flowing with
milk and honey. And behold now I bring the first of the fruit of the ground,
which thou, O Yahweh, hast given me. (Deuteronomy 26:5b–10a)

Notice that what could be interpreted as a purely agricultural
rite has been transformed by the liturgy into a ceremony inseparably bound with the acts of God in history. The liturgical formula is more than a mere personal prayer of thanks; "it is a
confession or *credo*, which recapitulates the great saving acts
which brought the community into being." [115]

Deuteronomy 21:1–9 contains a similar combination of formal
instruction and liturgical utterance. A sacrifice was commanded
upon the discovery of a dead person in the open field. An un-
worked heifer was to be taken to a valley with running water and
there slain to make atonement for the blood of the victim. In the

[115] G. E. Wright, *The God Who Acts*, p. 71.

presence of the priests the elders of the city were to wash their hands over the body of the heifer while saying:

Our hands did not shed this blood, neither did our eyes see it shed. Forgive, O Yahweh, thy people Israel, whom thou hast redeemed, and set not the guilt of innocent blood in the midst of thy people Israel; but let the guilt of blood be forgiven them. (21:7–8)

Here there is both the sacrifice and the accompanying rubric with explains the ritual's intention and desired efficacy.

Leviticus presents us "with the bare bones of such ceremonies, and such an external description of these rites may be unintelligible or even misleading without an imaginative grasp of the words and thoughts that properly accompanied them." [116] For these it is necessary to turn to the Psalter, for the two books belong side by side and were likely so used in the worship of Israel.

If it were known to what ceremonies the singing or petition of certain psalms was attached, the rites presented in Leviticus could be better understood. For example, the ritual form for a thank offering is given in Leviticus as follows:

And this is the law of the sacrifice of peace offerings which one may offer to Yahweh. If he offers it for a thanksgiving, then he shall offer with the thank offering unleavened cakes mixed with oil, unleavened wafers spread with oil, and cakes of fine flour mixed with oil. With the sacrifice of his peace offerings for thanksgiving he shall bring his offering with cakes of leavened bread. And of such he shall offer one cake from each offering, as an offering to Yahweh; it shall belong to the priest who throws the blood of the peace offerings. And the flesh of the sacrifice of his peace offerings for thanksgiving shall be eaten on the day of his offering; he shall not leave any of it until morning. (7:11–15)

An imaginative combination of this matter of fact statement with Psalm 116 as the spoken part of the liturgical act produces a realistic picture of a man at worship.[117] The man wishing to give thanks to Yahweh presented himself at the temple to pay his vow. In the presence of others he stood near the altar and recited the psalm, beginning with a general ascription of praise to Yahweh.

> I love Yahweh because he has heard
> my voice and my supplications.
> Because he inclined his ear to me,
> therefore I will call on him as long as I live.

[116] Micklem, "Leviticus" in The Interpreter's Bible, II, 5.

[117] A similar comparison may be made between the account of the dedication of Solomon's temple in I Kings 8 and the rubric of Psalm 24.

Then he passed directly into the special reason for his gratitude.

> The snares of death encompassed me;
>> the pangs of Sheol laid hold on me;
>> I suffered distress and anguish.
> Then I called on the name of Yahweh:
>> "O Yahweh, I beseech thee, save my life!"
> Gracious is Yahweh, and righteous;
>> our God is merciful.
> Yahweh preserves the simple;
>> when I was brought low, he saved me.

Having expressed the reason for his happiness and the occasion for his sacrifice, he meticulously performed the ritual requirements for the payment of his vow. First there was the libation of the drink offering, often an accompaniment of animal sacrifice. Lifting his cup he poured out wine or water before the altar, at the same time reciting the proper liturgical formula:

> What shall I render to Yahweh
>> for all his bounty to me?
> I will lift up the cup of salvation
>> and call on the name of Yahweh,
> I pay [118] my vows to Yahweh
>> in the presence of all his people.
> Precious in the sight of Yahweh
>> is the death of his saints.
> O Yahweh, I am thy servant;
>> I am thy servant, the son of thy handmaid.
> Thou hast loosed my bonds.

Then he presented to the priest his kid or lamb or whatever he had brought in payment of his vow that it might be sacrificed upon the altar. As he handed the animal to the priest he said:

> I offer to thee the sacrifice of thanksgiving
>> and call on the name of Yahweh.
> I pay my vows to Yahweh
>> in the presence of all his people,
> in the courts of the house of Yahweh,
>> in your midst, O Jerusalem.

All now having been completed, the individual at the altar was joined by all who worshipped with him in a cry of praise,

Hallelujah!!

---

[118] The translation of the Hebrew imperfect by the English future as in the R.S.V. destroys something of the simultaneity of act and word.

Verses 1–2 and 12–19, exclusive of verse 15, may have formed the introduction and conclusion to a liturgical formula which accompanied the payment of other vows than that of deliverance from sickness. Between these passages the worshipper, perhaps with the help of the priest, would articulate his own peculiar cause for thanksgiving. This practice would have been at first informal and spontaneous, but later would have become more rigid and stylized as the cultic officials became possessors of well-phrased formulae appropriate for all occasions.

The Theology of the Psalter

The nature of the Psalter makes it difficult to speak of its theology. As has been seen, we are dealing with a collection of cultic materials brought together because of their use in worship. Thus the Psalter is not a "book" in the sense of developing an idea or ideas. The parts are not even unified by historical circumstances. Each psalm had its place in worship, each its emotion, and each its theology. Consequently we cannot speak of the theology of the Psalter in the same way that we refer to the theology of Isaiah or the Chronicler. Nevertheless, taken together these poems present a cross section of Israel's theological understanding. Sundry ideas from across an expanse of Israel's history are incorporated into the book because the ideas were expressed in the community's worship. The Psalter, therefore, gathers together the essence of Israel's thought and religion. The wide diversity of theological concepts preserved here is a chief factor in the popularity of the Psalter in both Jewish and Christian traditions.

Understandably the theology of the Psalter centers in the character and activity of Yahweh, because for Israel Yahweh was known by what he did. Throughout the Psalter Yahweh is seen as sovereign lord over nature. He is both its creator and sustainer. All creatures are objects of his concern and care and with love he pours out upon them all good things. The storm obeys his will and at his command the sun courses the sky. For Israel, however, Yahweh is always much more than a nature deity. History is also his realm of activity and the affairs of nations are under his control. Israel is his elect nation and the Exodus was his mighty act.

A large portion of the psalms, however, are not so sweeping in scope. In fact, they are almost or fully personal. In them Yahweh is God to be found in his sanctuary, a presence abiding on Mt. Zion as a resource and comfort to the weary pilgrims who wended their way to his sanctuary. Yahweh was in his holy temple and all the earth had to be silent before him. In many psalms the worshipper stands in Yahweh's presence in penitence, confession, petition, or praise. By doing so he acknowledged the Lord of nature and history as his God and the God of his people.

The personal quality of the Psalter gives this book a straightforward honesty in approaching life as it is. The dark and bitter side of experience comes in for its share of attention. The psalms praise, give thanks, reminisce, and reflect; they also lament and complain. They speak of the good which Yahweh has done [119] and question why he has not done more.[120] From the depths of despair they lift to God a daring cry which sometimes borders upon the blasphemous.[121] They curse their fate, their enemies and almost, but not quite, curse God himself. Such a realistic approach to life means that in the Psalter the integrity of Israel's faithful finds highest expression. They acknowledge life to be what it is, express their yearnings that it be different, and do both in the presence of the Holy God, whom they adore and who alone is their hope.

SUGGESTED READINGS

Background

ACKROYD, PETER R., *Exile and Restoration* (Westminster, 1968).

ANDERSON, HUGH, *Historians of Israel* (2) (Abingdon, 1962). A survey study of the work of the Chronicler.

OLMSTEAD, A. T., *History of the Persian Empire* (University of Chicago Press, 1948). The standard history of the Persian empire.

SNAITH, NORMAN, *The Jews from Cyrus to Herod* (Religious Education, 1949). Life and thought of Israel in the last four centuries B.C.

WELCH, A. C., *Post-Exilic Judaism* (Blackwood, 1935).

————, *The Work of the Chronicler* (British Academy, 1939).

WHITLEY, C. F., *The Exilic Age* (Longmans, 1957).

[119] Psalm 73:1.
[120] Psalm 73:3–14.
[121] Psalm 58:10.

Ezekiel

Bunn, John T., "Ezekiel" in *The Broadman Bible Commentary*, VI.
Eichrodt, Walter, *Ezekiel* (Westminster, 1970).
Matthews, I. G., *Ezekiel* (American Baptist Publication Society, 1939).
Robinson, H. Wheeler, *Two Hebrew Prophets* (Lutterworth, 1948). A study of Ezekiel and Hosea.

Second Isaiah

Anderson, Bernhard W., "Exodus Typology in Second Isaiah," in *Israel's Prophetic Heritage* (Harper & Row, 1962).
Knight, A. F., *Deutero-Isaiah: A Theological Commentary on Isaiah, 40–55* (Abingdon, 1965).
McKenzie, John L., *Second Isaiah*, Anchor Bible (Doubleday, 1968).
Muilenberg, James, "Isaiah 40–66" in *Interpreter's Bible*, V.
North, C. R., *Isaiah 40–55* (S.C.M. Press, 1952) and *The Suffering Servant in Deutero-Isaiah* (Rev. Ed., Oxford University Press, 1956). A brief readable commentary and a thorough technical study.
Scherer, Paul, *Event in Eternity* (Harper & Row, 1945).
Smart, James D., *History and Theology in Second Isaiah* (Westminster, 1965).
Westermann, Claus, *Isaiah 40–66* (Westminster, 1969).
Note also the listing on Isaiah in the suggested readings for chapter eight.

Psalms

Barth, Christopher, *Introduction to the Psalms* (Scribner's, 1966).
Dahood, Mitchell, "Psalms," I–III, Anchor Bible (Doubleday, 1966).
Durham, John I., "Psalms" in *The Broadman Bible Commentary*, IV.
Gunkel, Hermann, *The Psalms*, tr. T. M. Horner (Fortress, 1967).
Johnson, A. R., "The Psalms" in *The Old Testament and Modern Study* (Oxford University Press, 1951).
Leslie, E. A., *The Psalms* (Abingdon, 1949). Sets the psalms in liturgical context.
Mowinckel, Sigmund, *The Psalms in Israel's Worship* (Abingdon, 1962).
Oesterley, W. O. E., *The Psalms* (S.P.C.K., 1955).
Ringgren, Helmer, *The Faith of the Psalmists* (S.C.M. Press, 1963).
Terrien, Samuel, *The Psalms and Their Meaning for Today* (Bobbs-Merrill, 1952). Fine non-technical interpretation of the Psalter.
Weiser, Arthur, *The Psalms* (Westminster, 1962). Stresses place of many psalms in covenant-renewal festivals.
Westermann, Claus, *The Praise of God in the Psalms*, 2nd ed. (John Knox, 1961). Form critical study.

10

The Emergence of Judaism

The battle for religious purity and sincere loyalty to Yahweh was not completely won by the efforts of Nehemiah and Ezra. The struggle continued through the centuries between Ezra and the first century A.D.[1] During this time, Judaism as a structured religion was emerging and attaining an historical identity. Although the Judaism which is one of today's living religions has deep roots in preexilic heritage, its character and structure are traced to significant developments in thought and practice coming to the foreground after the Babylonian exile.

The period was marked by the appearance of the most monumental cultural crisis in the history of Israel—and perhaps in the history of the world. Under the leadership of aggressive Greek promoters, Hellenism, that culture represented by the ideals of the classical Greeks, enjoyed a rapid spread through the Near Eastern world. Jewish motifs, like all other thought patterns of the day, were brought into the clash of cultures. Pure Mosaic traditions were challenged and syncretism with Greek culture became a possibility for Israel's religion. The encounter occurred during the very period when Judaism was struggling to find itself and was therefore susceptible to the powerful attraction of Greek culture. The threat was doubly heightened by migration of Jews to all parts of the Mediterranean world and, in time, by the inforced imposition of Hellenism upon Palestine by Seleucid over-

[1] This period has sometimes been called the "inter-biblical" or "inter-testamental" period upon the erroneous assumption that no biblical writings came from these centuries.

448

lords. In dramatic fashion the meeting of peoples renewed the age-old struggle between faith and culture. Within this milieu of turmoil and crisis Judaism as a religious system, developing out of that for which Ezra stood, began to take semblance of ordered expression.

Surprisingly, sources about the religious and political developments of Israel's history during this period are quite scanty. The fortunes of Persia, Greece, and Rome are well documented, but the relevance of these events to the minor Palestinian province often remains obscure. Primary biblical histories are entirely absent. Both the Deuteronomist and the Chronicler conclude their work prior to this period and are of no help. No additional canonical history covers the post-Ezra era. The apocryphal I and II Maccabees illuminate the days of the Maccabean revolt, but this is only a small portion of the period of our concern. Flavius Josephus, a Jewish historian writing toward the close of the first century A.D., covers this period in his expansive *Antiquities of the Jews* and *History of the Jewish Wars*, but in evaluating his data allowance must be made for his glamorization of facts in the interest of making the Jews appear favorable to his Greco-Roman readers.

The most helpful source for understanding the rise of Judaism in the post-Ezra period is the non-historical biblical literature of the time. These writings reflect "theologies" of the day and from them can be inferred some of the evolving patterns of the era. They are supplemented by various non-canonical writings dating to the same general period (early apocryphal and pseudepigraphical works, for example) which reveal the outlook of the times. All in all, however, we must proceed with caution because of the meager documentation of period.

THE CHANGING POLITICAL SCENE

The Close of the Persian Period

Persia remained nominally in control of Palestine for most of the century following the labors of Ezra. Her dominance over Greece in the fifth century had not been auspicious (as witnessed by stinging defeats at Marathon Bay and Thermopylae) and the coming of the fourth century made realization of her cherished purpose to conquer Hellas more and more remote. The most dramatic feature of the fourth century was the gradual rise of Greece to dominate the Near East.

Figure 10–1. Impressive mound of Susa (biblical Shushan), the winter residence of Darius the Great and one of the three coexisting capitals of the Persian Empire. Excavations have uncovered levels of occupation from 4000 B.C. to A.D. 1200. (Source: Courtesy of the Oriental Institute, University of Chicago.)

For Persia the last quarter of the fifth century is largely the story of reign of Darius II Nothus (423–404). Darius was able to maintain Persian control of the eastern Mediterranean world primarily because the Peloponnesian Wars kept Greece in turmoil. Persian influence on the course of affairs in Palestine during this quarter century is undocumented outside some passing references in the Elephantine texts to a certain Bagoas, a Persian governor of Judah, and Johanan, the high priest. We know that during the reign of Darius II, the Jews in Babylon continued to live as prosperous tradesmen, agriculturalists, and officials of the government, but the circumstances of the restored community in Palestine remain clouded in mystery.

The Elephantine Jews. In contrast to the scarcity of information about Jews in Palestine, some data clarifying the state of the Jews in Egypt are available. A number of Aramaic papyri discovered at Elephantine in Egypt describe the life of a colony of Jews who lived there during the sixth and fifth centuries. Elephantine, located near the first cataract in southern Egypt, was the station for a frontier garrison composed of Jewish soldiers who enjoyed the patronage of Persia for serving as an outpost in her Egyptian defenses.

The papyri are mostly business and property documents, but two are especially helpful in understanding the religion of the colony. One contains the petition to Bagoas of Judah and Delaiah of Samaria begging their intervention to secure the permission of Persia for the restoration of the destroyed Elephantine temple. The other is the so-called "Passover" papyrus, which concerns the observance of a religious festival.[2]

The Jews of Elephantine felt a religious kinship with their Palestinian brethren, but they did not stand in the main stream of Israel's historic faith. Beings other than Yahweh were included in their allegiance and worship. Alterations in the traditional modes of animal sacrifice were made to avoid offending sensitive Egyptians. Festivals of earlier days were sometimes altered or even avoided.[3] Evidently the Elephantine cult yielded to the pressure of the local situation and became highly syncretistic.

At Elephantine a rather elaborate temple served as the center of this modified Yahwism. Both the temple and the colony survived most of the fifth century. However, in 410 B.C. Egyptian rebels attacked the colony as an act of protest against Persian domination in Egypt and the temple of the Jews was destroyed. This was the occasion for the above-mentioned appeal to Persia for permission to rebuild. Persian permission was granted and probably the temple was rebuilt soon after 408. However, the history of the colony suddenly comes to a close in 399 when this Persian garrison fell victim to a resurgence of Egyptian nationalism.

[2] A useful summary of the Elephantine finds may be read in Emil G. Kraeling's article, "New Light on the Elephantine Colony" in *The Biblical Archaeologist Reader*, I, 128–144.

[3] The "Passover" papyrus orders that a religious festival, probably the Passover-Feast of Unleavened Bread, be observed according to the Jewish law.

The Samaritans. Another group which stood near but outside the circle of emerging Judaism was the Samaritans, that people which had arisen in central Palestine following the fall of Samaria in 722/21. As early as the days of the divided monarchy, antagonism between Judah and the North had been pronounced and over subsequent centuries the communities drifted apart. The fall of Samaria and the consequent mixing of peoples widened the gap. Throughout the fifth century relationships between the Jews and Samaritans continued to worsen. The strict measures of Nehemiah and Ezra made little room for the Samaritans, whose ranks were probably swelled by many expelled from Jerusalem because of their noncomformity to the religious and political particularism of the reformers.[4] The appeals of the Elephantine colony to both Judah and Samaria reflect the division that existed between the two groups. Further, we know that Samaritans recognized only the Pentateuch as their scriptures, rejecting the Prophets, which were virtually canonical in Jerusalem by the third century. So, although the break cannot be dated precisely, it can be said with reasonable certainty that by the middle of the third century B.C. the breach with the Samaritans had become complete.

till 400 BC

At some time prior to the early second century, the Samaritans built a temple on Mt. Gerizim to rival the Jerusalem sanctuary. The Old Testament gives no account of this event and we are left almost entirely to conjecture as to when the building occurred.[5] The Mt. Gerizim temple illustrated the depth of contempt between the two groups and made the question of whether to worship Yahweh in Jerusalem or Gerizim a living issue.[6] In New Testament days a story about a "good" Samaritan [7] would be pure fancy to the Jew and a Jew whose "face was set toward Jerusalem" [8] would be unworthy of entertainment by Samaritan.

The Fourth Century. Jews both inside and outside Palestine spent much of the fourth century under the overshadowing in-

---

[4] Cf. Nehemiah 13:28. The priest's grandson was expelled because he was married to Sanballat's daughter.

[5] See above, p. 431, footnote 81. An excellent, although technical, discussion of this problem may be found in H. H. Rowley's article on "Sanballat and the Samaritan Temple" in *Bulletin of John Rylands Library,* XXXVIII (1965), 166–198.

[6] Cf. II Chronicles 25:7; John 4:20–24.

[7] Luke 10:25–37.

[8] Luke 9:53.

fluence of Persia, although this was a time of distress for the empire. Artaxerxes II Mnenon (404–358), the successor of Darius II, spent most of his long tenure trying to maintain order in the kingdom. At the turn of the century Egypt successfully rebelled and remained independent throughout the remainder of his reign. On the heels of the Egyptian revolt came a rebellion by a brother of the king named Cyrus the Younger, satrap of Asia Minor, who utilized Greek mercenaries in his army. Only with great effort (and the hiring of Greek troops himself) did Artaxerxes succeed in maintaining the upper hand in Asia Minor. The difficulty with Cyrus was followed by an unsuccessful revolt of western satraps, which failed more because of another uprising in Egypt than because of the power of Artaxerxes.

During the reign of Artaxerxes III Ochus (358–338), Persia appeared to mend. With an iron hand Ochus brought the empire under control, even to the reconquest of Egypt. His success, however, was only temporary. The king was poisoned and two years later his son and successor, Ares (338–336), was also assassinated. Darius III Codomannus (336–331) was left to face the growing surge of the Hellas, now united under Philip of Macedon and ready to move eastward under his illustrious son, Alexander.

Judah seems to have been little involved in these affairs of the first three quarters of the fourth century. She certainly acquiesced to Persian dominance and enjoyed extensive liberty in internal affairs. She struck her own coinage [9] and gradually began to use Aramaic, the official language of the Persian empire. Judaism continued to develop outside the entanglements of the complex struggles between Persia and the now-pulsating Greece. The religious cult grew around the Jerusalem center. In a nation of religious concern and without political designs, the high priest rose to a place of unequaled prominence. Development and consolidation accomplished during this period prepared Judaism for the battles which she was to face during the Greek period.

Greek Dominance

Alexander the Great. During the time that Artaxerxes III was struggling vigorously to recover the power of Persia, Philip

[9] See D. Winton Thomas, ed., *Documents from Old Testament Times*, pp. 232–234.

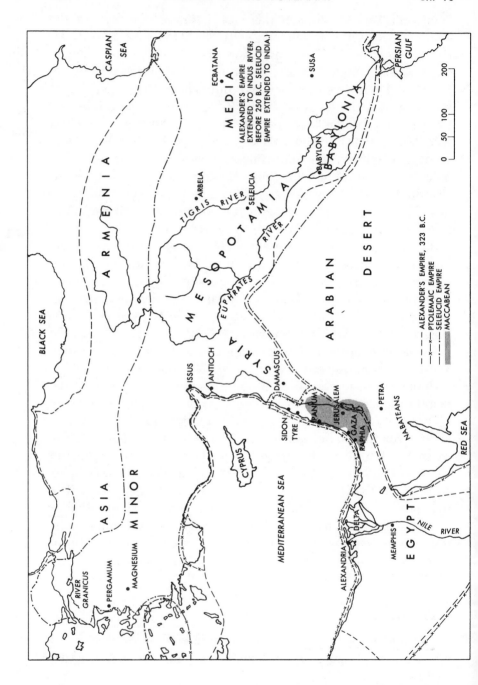

of Macedon (359–336) was rallying the support of the Greek states around himself. By 338 all Hellas was under his control. Upon his assassination, his youthful son Alexander succeeded in holding the Greek states together as a unit and assumed his father's role as leader. This event in 336 both spelled the end for the Persian empire and signalled an explosion of Greek culture on the Near East. In 334 Alexander crossed the Hellespont and routed a small Persian garrison at Granicus. Scarcely a year later, after moving in triumph across Asia Minor, he met the main Persian army at the pass of Issus and tore it to shreds. Darius III fled eastward for his life and gained a brief respite, but the days of the Persian empire were rapidly drawing to a close.

From Issus Alexander turned southward to secure his right flank and to make the eastern Mediterranean a Grecian sea before moving eastward in pursuit of Darius. Only the Phoenician city of Tyre met Alexander with strong resistance. After its fall in 332, the conqueror continued southward through Samaria and Judah, apparently receiving a warm welcome at every stop. The Egyptians welcomed Alexander with open arms as their liberator. When Alexander had completed his victorious march through Palestine and Egypt, he returned to the unfinished business of routing the Persians. Darius III made his final stand at Gaugamela near Arbela on the upper Tigris River, but his resistance was brief. In 331 Persia became the property of Alexander the Great. The conqueror continued his eastern march to the Indus River where, as legend has it, he wept because there were no more worlds to conquer. Probably, however, he turned back because his men lacked enthusiasm for additional conquest. A few years later his brief career came to a sudden end when the young master of the world fell sick and died at the age of thirty-three.

The impact of Alexander the Great upon the Near East is proverbially immeasurable. His conquests "signaled a revolution in the life of the ancient orient, and the beginning of a new era in its history." [10] After Alexander, old cultural and political boundaries became less and less significant. Rapidly the east

[10] John Bright, A *History of Israel*, p. 397.

Figure 10–3. Coins from the Hellenistic period showing the obverse and reverse sides. The top coin is from Alexander the Great and the other two are Ptolemaic. (Source: American Numismatic Society.)

became dotted with Hellenistic colonies. Alexandria in Egypt, Sebaste (Samaria) in Palestine, and Antioch in Syria exemplify those centers which were devoted to Alexander's aim of unification under the banner of Greek culture. Hellenistic gymnasiums and theaters sprang up in the major cities. The Greek language rapidly became the tongue of the world. Greek thought provided a motif for thinkers grappling with old ideas in new formats. Judah was not outside the sphere of Hellenistic influence. The career of Alexander gave impetus to a Greek influence which had slowly prevaded Palestine.[11] In the post-Alexandrian period the people of covenant again came to crisis. The coming of Hellenism created another of those times when the exclusiveness of Jewish faith was brought into question. This problem became acute in Palestine during the days of two groups of Macedonian rulers who fell heir to portions of Alexander's empire—the Ptolemies of Egypt and the Seleucids of Syria.

[11] W. F. Albright points out the pre-Alexander Greek influence in Palestine in *From the Stone Age to Christianity*, pp. 256–308.

The Ptolemies. Following Alexander's death the empire became booty for his generals. Two of these are especially relevant to Jewish history. Ptolemy gained control of Egypt, establishing

---

333–323 Control of Near East by Macedonian Empire under Alexander. Following his death, Ptolemies ruled Egypt and Seleucids ruled Syria

Egypt		Judah		Syria	
Ptolemy I	323–285	323–198	Judah under control of Ptolemies	Seleucus I	312–280
Ptolemy II (Philadelphus)	285–246			Antiochus I	280–261
				Antiochus II	261–246
Ptolemy III	246–221			Seleucus II	246–226
				Seleucus III	226–223
		198	Battle of Panium in which Seleucids gained control of Palestine	Antiochus III (the Great)	223–187
Ptolemy IV	221–203				
Ptolemy V	203–181			Seleucus IV	187–175
Ptolemy VI	181–146	167	Maccabean revolt	Antiochus IV (Epiphanes)	175–163
				Antiochus V	163–162
(Egypt controlled by Rome after 180 and became Roman province in 30 B.C.)		165	Religious emancipation of Jews		
		142–63	Jewish political independence until Pompey established Roman rule over Jerusalem		

Figure 10–4. The Hellenistic period, 333–63 B.C.

---

his capital at Alexandria and Seleucus won Babylonia, extending his rule to include Syria. Phoenicia and Palestine lay between these two and, predictably, became objects of a century and a half struggle for possession. During more than a century of the struggle (323–198), the prize belonged to Ptolemy and his successors. The rules of these Ptolemaic overlords need not concern us. Old administrative patterns were maintained.[12] The high priest continued to occupy a place of privilege and leadership.[13]

---

[12] The Zeno papyri dating to the time of Ptolemy II Philadelphus indicate that persons having authority from Persia were allowed to retain their positions.
[13] Called "that dignity" by Josephus, *Antiquities*, XII, iv, 1.

Tribute was paid to the Ptolemies and the Jews enjoyed comparative peace.

Under such congenial circumstances large numbers of Jews moved into Egypt, many seeking an economic advantage there. A large colony resided at Alexandria. Jewry in Egypt adopted Greek as their language and, thereby, provided the occasion for one of the most important events of the Ptolemaic era, the production of the Septuagint.[14] Over a period of years in the third century and perhaps under the partonage of the Ptolemies, the scriptures of the Jews (primarily the Torah) were translated into Greek to meet the needs of the times. This significant development furthered communication between Jew and Greek and enhanced their mutual influence. Thus, the Septuagint illustrates a tolerant attitude toward Hellenism during the Ptolemaic period, especially in those Jewish communities outside Palestine.

Seleucids. The encroachments of Hellenism, however, must have created a cleavage within Judaism. Many were enamored with the new ways of doing things and became avidly Greek. Extremists of this group may have thought of traditional Jewish laws and customs as nothing more than out-moded relics of by-gone days. To others, however, the evolving culture threatened the purity of their historic faith. To these no compromise was tolerable. Although the majority of Jews thought little about the problem and simply drifted with events, the breach between the extremes had become quite apparent by the time Palestine came under the domination of the Seleucid rulers of Syria.

The story of Seleucid influences in Palestine is largely the tale of two kings—Antiochus III the Great (223–187) and Antiochus IV Epiphanes (175–163). Ptolemaic control of Palestine for a century had been made possible by a series of provincial revolts which kept the Seleucid empire at bay. Gradually the power and territory of the Seleucids had decreased. But Antiochus the Great came to the throne determined to reverse the trend and gave his energies to the reexpansion of Seleucid borders. Included in his plans was the Palestinian province to his south. One successful campaign followed another until areas of Asia Minor, Mesopotamia, and Persia were restored to Seleucid con-

14 See above, pp. 34–35.

trol. Egypt, however, proved more difficult to overcome than any other area of his desired empire. At Raphia in 217 Antiochus the Great met defeat at the hands of Ptolemy IV. When the child Ptolemy V came to Egypt's throne, the Syrian was more successful. He won Palestine in 205, only to lose it again. Finally in 198 B.C. at the battle of Panium the back of Egyptian power in Palestine was broken and the territory of the Jews joined most of the eastern Mediterranean world under the banner of the Seleucids.

If Josephus can be believed,[15] the Jews received the Seleucids as a welcomed change from the Ptolemies, even taking up arms against the Egyptian garrison in Jerusalem. Their hopes were not in vain. Antiochus the Great treated the Jews with great generosity, allowing them to "live according to the laws of their own country." [16] He continued the rather lax policies of the Ptolemies. Priests and others connected with the cult were exempted of taxation, and the taxation of the general public was greatly reduced and for a time even discontinued. Antiochus gave support to the cult of the Jews, even supplying assistance for needed repairs to the temple. These benevolent actions undoubtedly won the hearts of many Jews and lessened the hostility of many religious leaders. Consequently, as in the early days for Ptolemaic control, the patronizing support of Antiochus the Great gave Hellenism a renewed attractiveness among the Jews.

The last decade of Antiochus' rule again brought decline to the Seleucid empire. From Asia Minor strongholds he marched into the face of the formidable force of Rome to meet inglorious defeat at Magnesium. Soon thereafter he was assassinated in disgrace while plundering a temple of Elam trying to raise Roman indemnities. Antiochus was followed to the throne by Seleucus IV (187–175) during whose twelve year reign Jewish affairs worsened. The former sweet savor of the Hellenism of Antiochus the Great rapidly became bitter gall when Hellenism began to become obligatory. A plot to confiscate the Jewish temple funds undoubtedly alienated many Jews who were already beginning to become zealous for the past.

Cleavage between ardent Jewry and their comparably ardent

---

[15] *Antiquities*, XII, iii, 3, 4.
[16] *Antiquities*, XII, iii, 3.

[handwritten margin note: Antiochus thought the was God]

Hellenistic overlords came to an open crisis during the days of Antiochus IV (175–163), called Epiphanes because of his claims to divinity (*theos epiphanes* equals "god manifest"). The policies of Antiochus Epiphanes were not new. From his predecessors he inherited an enthusiasm for unity under Hellenic culture and a claim to personal divinity. The distinctiveness of Epiphanes was the manner and degree of intensity with which he enforced adoption of the Greek way of life. His extreme measures interfered with Jewish religious affairs and precipitated an open crisis.

The feature which motivated Epiphanes to drastic action was the growing threat of Rome. He inherited from Seleucus IV a

Figure 10–5. Coins of Antiochus IV. Obverse shows the head of the Seleucid and the reverse shows Zeus seated on a throne. The inscription reads, "kingdom of Antiochus, god manifest" (Epiphanes). (Source: American Numismatic Society.)

disjointed empire in financial shackles to the power which was emerging as the dominant force of the New East. To withstand Rome the Seleucid provinces had to be united and all financial resources had to be tapped. The pressure of the situation caused Epiphanes to promote Hellenism with vigor and to bleed the empire of every possible source of revenue. Various temples, including that at Jerusalem, came in for his attention and plundering.

The strenuous policies of Antiochus naturally aroused opposition from those in Jerusalem who were already anti-Hellenic. His interference in selecting the influencial and prestigeous high priest provided an additional point around which opponents could rally. Aspirants sought to buy the office from Epiphanes at a time when the ruler was concerned with garnering all available support in Jerusalem. On one occasion Onias, the legitimate high priest, was outbid for the office by his brother Joshua, who used the Greek name Jason. The latter, in turn, was replaced by a certain Menelaus, whose priestly heritage may even be questioned. Both Jason and Menelaus were ardent Hellenizers and operated with the full sanction of Epiphanes. Such intervention by a Greek in the religious affairs of the Jews increased both the zeal and the strength of his opposition.

A swelling tide of resistance in Palestine merely inspired Epiphanes to more strenuous measure. By high hand and raw power he began to force his way upon the Jewish populace, property and customs. To replenish his treasury, Antiochus rifled the Jerusalem temple of its vessels and stripped the gold leaf from its facade. Angered by a Roman rebuff in Egypt he sent one of his generals, Appolonius, to Palestine to insure loyalty. Jerusalem was treated as an enemy city. Her fortifications were destroyed, the city looted, and many of her inhabitants slaughtered without cause. The temple was again ransacked and the regular cult was suspended. An altar to Zeus was erected in the temple and offerings of swine were made upon it.[17] Sacrifices to Olympian deities were made compulsory for the Jews. Completely reversing the policy of Antiochus the Great, Epiphanes outlawed the practice of Judaism under penalty of death. The offense of the infamous Seleucid had reached its maximum.

JEWISH INDEPENDENCE (I, II MACCABEES)

The awesome threat of the Hellenism of Antiochus Epiphanes was met squarely by a zealous priestly family dually remembered as the Hasmoneans[18] or the Maccabees.[19] Although some Jews

[17] The "abomination that makes desolate" of Daniel. See Daniel 11:29–35.
[18] The name of the great-grandfather of Mattathias.
[19] "Hammerer," apparently a nickname for Judas, the most prominent member of the family.

accommodated to Syrian demands and others acquiesced by simply relying on Yahweh for deliverance, the makers of a new age were led by this family of active rebels who attacked the policies of Epiphanes.

Maccabean Revolt (167–142 B.C.)

The spark which set off open rebellion against Seleucid oppression was struck in Modin, a remote mountain village which was the home of an aged priest Mattathias and his five sons.[20] When an official of Epiphanes came to Modin to enforce compulsory sacrifice, Mattathias slew both the visiting officer and a Jew who participated in the sacrifice. The event triggered revolt. Mattathias and his sons fled into the Judean hills for refuge and were soon joined by others willing to defend the worship of Yahweh with their weapons and their lives. An efficient guerilla band was formed and Judas, the most prominent of the Maccabee sons, became its leader.

At the outset the revolt was more for religious than political purposes. Strong support came from groups of the religiously devout. Chief among these were the Hasidim,[21] or Pious Ones, a conservative segment of the Jewish nation opposed to most forms of Hellenization. For them modification of Jewish religious tradition was tantamount to apostasy, repudiation of divine covenant, and league with the heathen.[22] Some of the Hasidim resisted independently and passively; others identified overtly with the organized Maccabean struggle. Both groups, as either compatriot in battle or supporter of anti-Seleucid sentiment, served the Maccabean objectives of religious freedom.

The rugged mountain existence proved too much for the aged Mattathias. Less than a year after the Modin incident, he died and was replaced as leader by Judas (166–161), his third but strongest son. This Maccabee was the maker of the revolution. His accomplishment bordered on the miraculous. With few weapons and limited manpower, he forged untrained soldiers

[20] Cf. I Maccabees 2:1–5.

[21] From the Hebrew word, *chesed*, the same word so frequently used in Hosea, translated there by R.S.V. as "steadfast love." This group, therefore, was characterized as steadfastly faithful to the covenant.

[22] Cf. I Maccabees 1:15.

into a fighting guerrilla unit seldom matched in the course of military history. Since Epiphanes had his major forces engaged in a campaign against the Parthians, he dispatched one of his generals, Lysias, to handle the Palestinian difficulty. The Seleucid opposition was still considerable and demanded of Judas ingenious military maneuver. The rebels both outthought and outfought their Seleucid opponents. Capitalizing on their knowledge of the Judean hills, they used surprise attack and hurried withdrawal to stack victory upon victory. Finally, in 165 B.C. Lysias was forced to negotiate the proscription of Epiphanes against the worship of Yahweh. Although political liberty remained a prize to be sought, religious emancipation of the Jews was achieved. Judas proceeded to Jerusalem and, with elaborate ceremony on the same day of its dedication to Zeus three years before, purged the temple and rededicated it to Yahweh.[23]

The achievement of religious freedom in 165 B.C. stirred Jewish hopes for political independence and furthered the spirit of resurging nationalism. When Epiphanes died, what had been a resistance movement against Hellenism flared into a full-scale war for political liberty. Many Hasidim considered their objective gained and severed their ties with the military machine, but Judas launched a new offensive. He broke into battle against the Idumeans, Ammonities, and Philistines; he penetrated Gilead to rescue harassed and mistreated Jews while his brother Simon relieved others in Galilee. The liberators tasted nothing but victory until Judas launched a misconceived attack upon the Acra, a fortified Syrian citadel at Jerusalem. Here he was forced to withdraw before the overpowering forces of Lysias and Antiochus V, Epiphanes' temporary successor. Only ill-advised behavior by the successful Seleucids returned the Jews to the support of Judas. Shortly thereafter Judas was killed in battle.

Jonathan (161–143), fifth son of Mattathias, succeeded Judas, but from the beginning his leadership was unpromising. The Hasidim gave him only limited support and Jewish Hellenizers were in control of Jerusalem. Jonathan, however, was gifted with political insight, as well as military prowess. To his good for-

---

[23] This religious emancipation is celebrated annually by the Jews in the Feast of Hanukkah (Rededication) on the 25th of Kislew. Josephus refers to the festival as the Feast of Lights. See *Antiquities*, XII, vii, 7.

tune, disputes and divisions developed within the upper echelons of the Syrian leadership and Jonathan played the confused situation to the advantage of the Jews. His gains did not go unappreciated and among the several rewards conferred by his people was appointment as high priest in 152 B.C. Matters were going well until Jonathan's diplomatic flair, with its consequential successes, led to overconfident and unguarded acts. Lured into a trap by a Seleucid general, Jonathan's devotion to Syria was questioned and he was imprisoned.

During Jonathan's tenure, the Maccabean battle forces were under the command of his brother Simon, whose successes along the coastal plain from Tyre to Egypt obtained for him the title "military governor" of the district. Simon attempted to ransom Jonathan, but his efforts were abortive and Jonathan was executed. Simon (143–135) assumed full command and continued to make impressive gains. The most significant of several strategic military victories came in 142 when he forced the capitulation of the Acra in Jerusalem. Thereby Seleucid control in Palestine was finally broken, amounting to political freedom for the Jews.

As with Jonathan before, Simon was rewarded for his military victories with the prize of the high priesthood. In addition, priestly authority was permanently conferred upon his house. This action is especially noteworthy since the Maccabees were not of the traditional priestly family. Simon was also declared the civil ruler and commander-in-chief of the military. Consequently, as in earlier days, the political leader was also the religious leader, reminiscent of the amphictyony. But more significantly, the cause of religion had been identified with the national life of the people—a fact which would influence the future development of Jewish religion.

Maccabean Decline and the Coming of Rome

The Maccabees established an independent rule in Palestine that lasted for the better part of a century. Marked pride in the military and political accomplishments of Mattathias and his sons continued through the second and into the first century, but the religious zeal with which the revolt began rapidly subsided. Concerns of state overshadowed religious matters. The period following the achievement of freedom was not a time of flourishing religion.

Leadership of the Maccabees beyond the first generation is hardly worth recounting. The decline of Seleucid power gave the Hasmoneans respite from that threat and created an impression of peace and prosperity for Palestine. Weak leadership within Palestine, however, and the developing strength of Rome spelled a pessimistic future for Jewish independence.

In 134 B.C. the last of Mattathias' sons was murdered and Jewish affairs fell to a second generation Maccabee named John Hyrcanus, who ruled for thirty turbulent years. His policies favored the temple priests and aroused opposition from the Pharisees. When Hyrcanus died, his successor was assassinated within a year and competent Alexander Janneus came to the throne. Janneus successfully secured Palestine for the Jews, but like Hyrcanus he was hated by the Pharisees. Alexandra, Janneus' widow, became queen at his death and ruled for nine years of relative peace, largely because she followed her husband's wise counsel that she cooperate with the Pharisees.

Maccabean rule, and the relative Jewish independence associated with it, came to an end through a series of events following Alexandra's death. Her two sons, Aristobulus II and Hyrcanus II desired the throne and neither would yield to the other. Lines of support from various Palestinean factions were rapidly drawn, but for a while Roman support went to neither aspirant. However, Aristobulus resorted to arms and thereby pushed Pompey to support Hyrcanus and his associates, including Antipater of Idumea. Roman troops were brought against Aristobulus, the Maccabean was defeated and imprisoned, and Pompey took charge of Jerusalem. For practical purposes, the year of Pompey's conquest (63 B.C.) ended rule by the Hasmonean house and provides a convenient date for the conclusion of the Old Testament period. — 63 B.C. Know

RELIGIOUS TRENDS IN EMERGING JUDAISM

The postexile years were crucial in the development of Israel's religion. The continued frustration of the period proved that cherished national and religious traditions had to be modified to meet the needs of rapidly and radically changing historical situations. The coming of Hellenism and Israel's intense reaction to it provided the setting out of which Judaism as a religious system began to emerge. Throughout the periods of Persian and Greek control of Palestine, the religious life of the Jewish community underwent extensive alteration. The trauma of unrealized national hope, somewhat caricatured in the Maccabees, further forced re-evaluation and reformulation of the historic tenets of Hebrew faith. Although no historical canonical works are available to describe these developments, late Old Testament and Apocrypha books suggest problems which the Jewish devotee confronted and the general lines along which he sought to preserve his faith.

Particularism

Ideally Israel had interpreted her true destiny as a peculiar people, elected by Yahweh to be a nation through whom divine blessings would be mediated to all nations. Her monotheistic faith carried as a corollary a redemptive mission to other people. Yahweh alone was God and Israel as his people was to work toward his universal rule. The nation as a kingdom of priests could meet her obligation by being Yahweh's chosen servant. The Babylonian exile kindled this missionary zeal among a small group of the faithful.

These ideals, however, were pushed into the background by the struggle for national identity during the postexile period. Shut up in a small area around Jerusalem and faced with threat to its very survival, the Jewish community turned in upon itself and created a sophisticated separatism. Although all Jews did not adopt a particularistic narrowness, important elements which included many religious and political leaders took this stance. Accordingly, the people of the covenant became in some measure a narrow and intolerant community, overly concerned with the preservation of the nation's purity. Association with Gentiles was frowned upon and intermarriage with them was strictly forbidden.[24] The returning exiles even refused to associate with kinsmen they found living in Palestine. They held that everyone

---

[24] Jubilees 30:7–10. Cf. also the policies of Nehemiah and Ezra on this matter.

who had not been in Babylon was a foreigner and a heathen who did not belong to the true people of God.

This disdain, even hatred, for the "non-Jew" created a spirit of bitterness and vengeance which became so extreme that some passionately desired that God's wrath consume all Israel's enemies. But worse, the particularistic attitude strengthened a growing feeling of pride in themselves. They were Yahweh's own people, governed by his Torah, chosen to be an elect nation. Forgetting that God had chosen them when they were no-people, and made of them a people for his service, they came to look upon themselves as a people elected for privilege. This pride may have bred responsibility and served to keep Israel's faith alive, but it also created a feeling "hardly conducive of much concern for the welfare of heathen and sinners." [25]

The conflict between the covenant ideal of a nation with missionary responsibility and ardent Jewish particularism is reflected in three canonical postexilic books. On the one hand, Esther illustrates the narrowness which too often characterized Israel's religious thinking during this period; on the other hand, Ruth and Jonah challenge exclusivism and remind Israel that the true people of covenant are obligated to be Yahweh's servant.

Esther. The book of Esther, against which Martin Luther directed scathing criticism,[26] is an historical romance written to explain the origin of the Jewish festival of Purim. Purim was an extremely popular festival which, however, had no specific authorization in the Torah. Purim as celebrated in post-exilic Judaism seems to have been the Jewish adaptation of a feast associated with the agricultural or natural year which in spring joyfully celebrated the overthrow of evil forces. Demonic powers were mocked as man celebrated the revival of the surging forces of life evident with the arrival of spring. Whatever Purim's origin, as with other cultic celebrations in Israel, this festival is associated more with Yahweh's historical guidance of his people than with natural cycles. For as we have already seen,[27] the understanding of reality by which Israel made sense of her existence was not grounded in mythological understanding of nature but

---

[25] John Bright, *A History of Israel*, p. 431.
[26] He expressed a wish that it had never been included in the Canon.
[27] See above, pp. 3–12, 72–74, 406–408, 465 f.

in the belief that Yahweh was active in history and that Israel could participate meaningfully in those actions. At best then Purim was celebration of Yahweh's sovereignty over historical events and nations. At the same time it was capable of a narrow and depreciating interpretation of Yahweh as the champion of Israel against the nations. As always the grandeur of Israel's noblest theological explanation of reality was subject to narrow and particular misinterpretation. The story of Esther is set during the reign of a Persian king Ahasuerus (Xerxes I, 486–465) and praises a Jewish girl who was chosen from among the most beautiful maidens in the kingdom to replace the deposed queen of Ahasuerus. The story is told in three parts.

I. Esther becomes queen. Chapters 1–2.
II. Conflict between Mordecai and Haman. Chapters 3–8.
III. Observance of Purim. Chapters 9–10.

Artistically the author demonstrates the futility of opposition to Jews. Esther's position as queen enabled her to forestall a plot to liquidate the Jewish people and turn it retributively against the enemies of the Jews. Haman, grand vizier of Persia, was offended by Mordecai, the Jewish cousin and guardian of Esther. Resentful against Mordecai and all his race, Haman persuaded the king to issue a decree calling for the massacre of all Jews on the 13th day of the month. Esther skillfully intervened and the tables were turned. Haman was given the death sentence intended for Mordecai, and the Jews were allowed to defend themselves against their enemies. They slaughtered 75,000 in the provinces on the 13th and 810 in Susa, the capital, on the 14th. These days of slaughter were days of rejoicing for the Jews and hereafter were observed with feasting and gladness as the festival of Purim (so called because Haman fixed the day of the disaster by lot, *pur*).

While the book may have been written toward the end of the Persian period,[28] more probably it comes from the Maccabean period when there was a strong spirit of Jewish nationalism and when proscriptions against the Jews were common. There must have been some persons who believed that the Jews should be disposed of. Throughout the Persian empire many would have

---

[28] See B. W. Anderson, "Esther" in *The Interpreter's Bible*, III, 825–828.

rejoiced at the destruction of the Jews. Haman represents this attitude and the day of Jewish vengeance represents a not too surprising counter attitude of the Jews. The natural tendency to be critical of the book's polemic against the Gentiles must, therefore, be tempered by sensitivity to the attitudes and actions which created for Judaism an atmosphere within which a vindictive spirit could develop. Thus, vindictive Jewish particularism while inexcusable is understandable. The book itself does not pretend to be actual history. While it reflects an accurate knowledge of many Persian customs, a number of obvious inconsistencies indicate that the book is a polemical short story.

Esther became one of five scrolls read on important Jewish festivals.[29] Although of little value, not even mentioning the name of God, it came to be regarded as the scroll *par excellence* and was given a place second only to the Torah.[30] Thus both the writing and use of the book of Esther point up the intense spirit of nationalistic particularism which characterized postexilic Judaism's attitude toward outsiders.

It is important to emphasize that this extremely negative attitude toward the Gentiles was not characteristic of all Jews. Accompanying the narrow exclusivism, and in tension with it, was a warm concern for the salvation of the nations. Israel never completely lost her sense of world mission. Some continued to hope that the nations would one day turn to the worship of Yahweh, even assigning Israel a role in bringing that day to reality. Two writers, the authors of Ruth and Jonah, made this point with telling wit and irony: Yahweh is concerned for all mankind and, therefore, Israel as his servant is obligated to be missionary.

Ruth. The book of Ruth is a charming short story written to encourage kindness and receptivity toward proselytes. The setting is the time of the amphictyony as the writer utilizes a story coming from the days of Israel's beginnings as the background of his book. The heroine Ruth is a Moabitess, the widow of an Israelite from Bethlehem. Through fidelity to Naomi, her mother-in-law, she becomes a proselyte to Yahwism and chooses to leave →

---

[29] Others were the book of Ruth (associated with Pentecost), Song of Solomon (Passover), Ecclesiastes (Tabernacles), and Lamentations (in remembering 587 B.C. destruction of Jerusalem).

[30] Cf. George Foot Moore, *Judaism*, I, 245.

her own people and return to Judah to share the destiny of God's people (chapter 1). She subsequently wins the love of Boaz, one of the great men of Bethlehem (2:1–4:12). The point of the story becomes clear in the last several verses (4:13–22) when the child of the marriage of Boaz and Ruth is shown to be a progenitor of David, Israel's most illustrious king. The point is tellingly made: the lineage of the great king David includes a Moabitess!

With real skill the author thus holds before his readers a proselyte worthy of receiving reward from Yahweh, under whose wings she had "come to take refuge." [31] Moreover, as an ancestress of David she was instrumental in mediating great blessing to Israel. In this light the particularism of the Jews is shown to be shallow and selfish and a stance that should be surrendered to a more hospitable attitude toward those Gentiles who desired to share blessings from Yahweh. Here is a reminder that the true people of God are always those who choose to serve him and, consequently, are not dependent upon purity of blood or correctness of genealogy.

Additionally, this short story illustrates Yahweh's beneficient providence by portraying events as falling along lines intended by God. Also prominent is the intention of the author to encourage fulfillment of traditional responsibilities when faced with the trials of life: Naomi seeks the good of her daughter-in-law rather than her own; Ruth respects Naomi above her own personal happiness; Boaz nobly meets his traditional responsibilities. These dimensions of the book's purpose are illustrated in a comment of Boaz to Ruth: "Yahweh recompense you for what you have done, and a full reward be given you by Yahweh, the God of Israel, under whose wings you have come to take refuge" (2:12).[32]

Jonah. Another critique of Israel's spirit of bitterness and vengeance toward non-Jews is the book of Jonah.[33] In a devas-

---

[31] Ruth 2:12.

[32] The substance of this paragraph comes from Georg Fohrer, *Introduction to the Old Testament*, p. 251.

[33] The book of Jonah is placed in the canon with the prophetic books because it is a narrative about a prophet. Unlike other prophetic books it contains no prophetic oracles and does not even claim to have been written by a prophet. As a matter of fact, its emphasis upon universalism is more characteristic of the wisdom than the prophetic tradition.

tating parable set in the eighth century a prophetic voice after the exile reminded Israel of her missionary role. Jonah is Israel; the book caricatures his attitude toward Nineveh, the capital of Assyria, to show the folly of Israel's rejection of foreigners.

I. Jonah is called to preach to a foreign people, but attempts to flee. 1:1–16.
II. Jonah is saved by a great fish. 1:17–2:10.
III. Reluctantly the prophet preaches and Nineveh repents. 3:1–10.
IV. Jonah pouts and is rebuked by Yahweh. 4:1–11.

All who heard or read the story of Jonah would have recognized the fugitive preacher as a personification of the narrow Jewish provincialism of the day. Commissioned by Yahweh to preach to the people of Nineveh, Jonah fled in the opposite direction, lest he be instrumental in the redemption of Israel's hated enemies. The Jews understood his plight. They could not conceive their role as Yahweh's servant to require them to be missionary to the Gentiles. Jonah, however, unable to escape Yahweh's call, was forced to preach in Nineveh. To his disgust the Assyrians repented and the doom he pronounced on the wicked city was averted. Disappointed, he sat down in the shade of a vine, only to have it die, leaving him exposed to the hot eastern sun. In anger he rebuked God for allowing all this to happen. Yahweh, however, with a devastating last word reminded the rebellious prophet of the divine concern for all creatures.

Small and recently restored Israel, suffering much from Gentile hands, had judged all non-Jews as unworthy of Yahweh's love and most certainly unworthy of Israelite time, patience, and concern. They needed to be reminded through the story of Jonah that Yahweh has pity even upon the Ninevehs of the world and that he had chosen Israel as an instrument through whom he might extend his mercy. This was a hard lesson for Israel to learn. Through the centuries of the postexile and on into the New Testament period the nation often became shut up in her own pride. Continually the voice of the devotee had to be added to that of Ruth and Jonah to remind the people of covenant that they were destined to be a kingdom of priests.

Wisdom and Life's Practical Problems

Another trend in the total religious picture of postexilic Judaism is represented in Israelite wisdom. Wisdom was concerned with the meaning of life. Some wise men approached life with practical intentions to provide counsel in proper standards of conduct. They understood their purpose in life to be that of teachers of wisdom and their vehicle for teaching was the wise and pithy saying, "derived from a critical evaluation of human experience." [34] Although "wisdom" meant many things to them (practical sagacity, cunning, skill, craftsmanship), its end was an "understanding of the highest ends of life and of the means of attaining them." [35] These wise men were concerned with the living of decent, comfortable, and happy lives with high moral standards. They were in essence teachers of religious ethics. Although their writings do not appeal to the covenant idea and their advice is framed on grounds of human experience and sagacity, the mainspring and motive of their wisdom was "the fear of Yahweh" [36] and its normative principle was the Torah. [37] Wisdom was the condition of well-being and happiness brought about by conformity to the revealed will of Yahweh.

Other wise men reflectively probed the question of the meaning of human existence with deep awareness of the anxieties and tensions of life. They had no ready advice or easy answers. In fact their wisdom often stands in judgment over the practically oriented methods of other wise men. They were frankly less optimistic about solutions to the human dilemma and often raised or bared real questions to which they offered no answer. Nevertheless their realistic confrontation of crucial and critical issues is more satisfying, if not as soothing, than the less perceptive efforts of practical wisdom. They have left us some of the most existentially challenging literature in all of the Old Testament.

The wise men did not speak with the authority of the prophet, nor with the piety of the priest, but with prophet and priest they molded the cultural and religious life of Israel. These earnest

---

[34] Walter Harrelson, *Interpreting the Old Testament*, p. 431.
[35] J. Coert Rylaarsdam, *Revelation in Jewish Wisdom Literature*, p. 11.
[36] Proverbs 1:7; 9:10; Psalm 111:10.
[37] Cf. Ecclesiasticus 24:33.

seekers of the good life aimed to teach their students what good life was. They directed their words to Israel's youth, teaching in public places [38] and in private schools. In preexilic days wisdom was taught at the city gate to all who would hear it, but in the community of the restoration schools of instruction were established and the youth of the upper classes, at least, were sent there to learn the maxims and principles which would guide them successfully through life.

l*The Wisdom Tradition.* Israel's wise men stood in an international wisdom tradition. Wisdom writings are among the most prolific literary works found in the Ancient Near East. Egyptian wisdom literature outnumbers all other documents from the civilization of the Nile. It appears as early as the end of the third and the beginning of the second millennium B.C., centering on instructions for young men living in the court.[39] Egypt's wisdom also contained reflective essays on the meaning and significance of life.[40] From Babylon comes wisdom literature of these same two kinds, but in less abundance.[41] Edom too had a tradition of wisdom, as the Old Testament itself attests. Israel recognized Edom's excellence in this area [42] and perhaps mentions by name some Edomite wise men, Herman, Calcol, and Darda, judged to be excelled by Solomon.[43]

Israel's Wisdom. Israel's wisdom literature is inseparably bound to this Ancient Near Eastern heritage. Hebrew wise men did not hesitate to borrow materials they found suitable for their

[38] Proverbs 1:20–21.

[39] Examples of these are "Instructions of Ptahhotep" (c. 2450 B.C.) the "Instruction of Prince Hordedof" (27th century B.C.), the "Satire on Trades" (2150–1750 B.C.), the "Instruction of Amenemhet" (c. 2000 B.C.), and the "Instructions for King Merikare" (end of 22nd century B.C.). Two later documents, Papyrus Lansing (c. 1100 B.C.) and the "Teaching of Amenemope" (1000–600 B.C.) are of the same general type.

[40] For example, "Dispute with His Soul of One Who Is Tired of Life," and the "Admonitions of Ipuwer," both from the last half of the third millennium B.C.

[41] Only one sample of instructional material is known, "The Babylonian Book of Proverbs." It employs the term, "My Son," characteristic of the O.T. book of Proverbs. Several reflective writings are extant: the "Bilingual Book of Proverbs," the "Babylonian Dialogue of Pessimism," the "Babylonian Job," and the "Wisdom of Ahikar." The last, while Babylonian in origin, was circulated widely and became part of the wisdom collections of many people.

[42] Obadiah 8; Jeremiah 49:7.

[43] I Kings 4:30–31.

purpose. Solomon exchanged riddles and proverbs with the Queen of Sheba and with Hiram of Tyre.[44] Agur and Lemuel, writers of some of the Proverbs,[45] were Arabs and the characters in the book of Job were from localities famed for wisdom. Israel's literary forms and subject matter were often that of the wisdom literature of Egypt and Babylon, and Proverbs 22:17–23:14 is based throughout on the Wisdom of Amenemope. The concept of wisdom found in Proverbs 8–9 is of Canaanite origin and many phrases and words throughout the book of Proverbs can be traced to Phoenician sources.[46] However, when Israel borrowed, she also "baptized" so that the wisdom of the world might be made Israelite. Whatever she adopted from other peoples was utilized in her tradition to illustrate the theme that "the fear of Yahweh is the beginning of wisdom."

Although most of her wisdom literature (in its present form) comes from the postexilic period, wisdom in Israel as elsewhere "belonged to the ages." Its origin is lost in the period of oral tradition. Indications are that a widespread wisdom movement among the Canaanites was carried over into Israel during the period of the amphictyony.[47] The Joseph stories in Genesis reflect certain motifs from Egyptian wisdom while Samson's riddles[48] and Jotham's fable[49] both are classic types of eastern wisdom. By the time of the monarchy a circle of wise men was present in the Israelite community[50] and by the time of Solomon, Israelite wisdom had begun to flourish.

Israelite wisdom gained its impetus from Solomon. Not only was he renowned as the wisest of kings and celebrated as a composer of proverbs by the thousands, he also "realized the delights and supremacy of things of the mind"[51] and sponsored literary activity of all kinds. With this dawning of Israel's cultural life wisdom became a staple part of the diet of Israel's

[44] I Kings 10:1.
[45] Cf. Proverbs 30:1 ff. and 31:1 ff.
[46] W. F. Albright, *From the Stone Age to Christianity,* pp. 367–368, and "Some Canaanite-Phoenician Sources of Hebrew Wisdom" in *Wisdom in Israel and in the Ancient Near East,* eds. M. Noth and D. Winton Thomas, pp. 1–6.
[47] *Ibid.*
[48] Judges 14:12–19.
[49] Judges 9:7–15.
[50] Cf. II Samuel 14:2 and 20:16–22.
[51] William A. Irwin, "The Wisdom Literature," *The Interpreter's Bible,* I, 215.

thinking men. Since Solomon became "patron saint of wisdom," later Israel ascribed to him the Old Testament books of Proverbs, Ecclesiastes, and Song of Songs, as well as the non-canonical writings of the Wisdom of Solomon, the Psalms of Solomon, and the Odes of Solomon. He was not, of course, the actual author of any of these in their present form, since they all belong to the postexilic period. The tradition attributing them to Solomon is based upon his proverbial fame as a wise man and springs from the custom of associating all literature of a type with some great man of old known to have contributed literature of a similar nature.[52]

Later during the period of the divided monarchy, there was a distinct class of wise men set alongside the priest and the prophet.[53] Each of the three made his own significant contribution to the intellectual and spiritual life of the community and they had an influence upon one another.[54] Once firmly established on Israel's religious scene, the wise man's approach to truth was not to be dislodged. His growing influence in the postexilic community produced the final collecting and editing of much of the wisdom writing which appears in Hebrew scriptures.

The wisdom tradition finds occasional expression throughout Hebrew literature, but its major expression in the Old Testament is in three books representing the two streams of wisdom.[55] A practical, didactic, optimistic tradition is illustrated in the book of Proverbs. The books of Job and Ecclesiastes represent a reflective and pessimistic trend in wisdom and may actually illustrate reaction against counsel of the sages who had become too facile or out of conformity with experience.

The Optimistic Tradition: The Book of Proverbs. The book of Proverbs contains sayings of Israel's sages intended to give prudential advice in how to live the good life. Sayings are heaped upon one another to distinguish the wise man from the fool, the good life from the bad. The book itself is organized into a collection of collections which may be divided as follows.

---

[52] Cf. Moses and Law, David and Psalms.
[53] Jeremiah 9:23 and 18:18; Isaiah 29:14.
[54] For a detailed study of one example see William McKane, *Prophets and Wise Men.*
[55] Walter Harrelson, *Interpreting The Old Testament,* pp. 431–433.

Each of these sections, except the last, contains material from various periods of Israel's history, as well as from the wider wisdom tradition of the Ancient Near East. The book of Proverbs, therefore, is a distillation of the teachings of Israel's wise men. It is exceedingly difficult to date the component parts from which the collections were made and there is considerable disagreement among scholars about the dates of the various collections themselves. The second collection is regarded as the oldest, but all of Solomonic collections I–IV probably represent the best pre-exilic Israelite wisdom.[56] Much of the remainder of the book is of foreign origin and these sections are generally considered to be postexilic, although there is no definite evidence to preclude a much earlier date for much of the materials.[57]

In Proverbs the teaching of the wise men is at its practical best. Whereas the Law called for obedience and the prophets for response to the word of Yahweh, Israel's sages appeal to scrupulous observation of prudence. Approaching the question from the human side, with little reference to Israel's historical faith and with almost no emphasis upon revelation,[58] they apply the principles learned by experience to the quest for a successful life. Their purpose was

> That men may know wisdom and instruction,
> understand words of insight,

[56] Cf. W. F. Albright, *From the Stone Age to Christianity*, pp. 367 ff., and "Some Canaanite-Phoenician Sources of Hebrew Wisdom," in *Wisdom in Israel and in the Ancient Near East*, pp. 1–15.

[57] Albright finds no postexilic materials anywhere in Proverbs. He holds that the materials are all 6th century or older and that the book was edited in the fifth (possibly fourth) century. Cf. "Some Canaanite-Phoenician Sources of Hebrew Wisdom," p. 5, fn. 1.

[58] The prophetic oracles are characterized by opening, "Thus says Yahweh"; the teachings of the wise-men appeal, "My Son, hear my words."

receive instruction in wise dealing,
    righteousness and equity;
that prudence may be given to the simple,
    knowledge and discretion to the youth—
the wise man also may hear and increase in
    learning,
    and the man of understanding acquire skill,
to understand a proverb and a figure,
    the words of the wise and their riddles.[59]

The counsel of the wise man took the form of practical and pithy sayings, the characteristic style of Proverbs:

Keep your heart with all vigilance;
    for from it flow the springs of life. (4:23)

· ·

When pride comes, then comes disgrace;
    but with the humble is wisdom. (11:2)

· ·

A good name is to be chosen rather than great riches,
And favor is better than silver or gold. (22:1)

The Pessimistic Tradition: Ecclesiastes and Job. Israel's wisdom tradition also includes an emphasis which is skeptical of the easy answer. Some wise men in Israel questioned the ease with which the Proverbialist assumed that the goodness of life could be achieved. Experience for them included evil, as well as good, and evil's very presence raised serious question about life's meaning. No mere human formula guaranteed success or happiness.

The harsh realities of life were brought home to Israel by the tragedy of the exile and compounded by the partial failure of all attempts to reconstruct the nation in the years that followed Cyrus' edict of emancipation. Israel had always been aware of evil as a fact as old as mankind,[60] and she had come to explain it as punishment for sin. But the collapse of nation and cult shattered to some extent this traditional explanation and forced thinking Israelites to seek more meaningful answers. The older idea of a causal relationship between sin and evil so typical of Proverbs [61] fell before the awareness that innocents do suffer and that in exile Israel had suffered extraordinarily for all her sin. Moreover, evil continued and even seemed to increase during the troubled postexilic days.

[59] Proverbs 1:2–6.
[60] Cf. Genesis 3 and 4.
[61] Found also in Chronicles and in the Deuteronomic history work.

Some sought to explain the problem by emphasizing the role played by Satan and demons, placing the blame upon them rather than upon Yahweh. Originally a semineutral prosecutor of sinful men, the figure Satan became in the postexilic period the tempter and the originator of evil. The Jews were uncertain of his origin, but they were increasingly sure that evil came from him. He ruled over a kingdom of darkness and was sovereign of a host of demons. He was evil personified, to be feared and yet respected for his cunning and power.

Other Jews were less interested in placing blame for evil than in explaining life in a world where evil is real. This attitude is typical of the Old Testament books, Ecclesiastes and Job. Both of these Wisdom books contradict the accepted belief that evil is the direct result of sin and that life's problems may be best resolved through the positive counsel of the sage.

(1) *Ecclesiastes.* Authorship of Ecclesiastes is attributed to Solomon, but this indicates its place in wisdom tradition rather than its origin. The language and thought of the book clearly suggest that Ecclesiastes belongs to the postexile period in Israel's history,[62] probably the fourth or third century B.C. Judaism came to associate the book with the observance of the feast of Tabernacles, "apparently in order to qualify the cheerfulness of that day with the thought that life and its joys are fleeting and that everything has its time.[63] Ecclesiastes is without formal structure and therefore difficult to outline. But the perspective and sustained arguments of the book are clear:

I. The author's philosophy of life. Chapters 1–4.
    A. Life is vanity. 1:1–2:26.
    B. God appoints a time for everything. 3:1–15.
    C. Good and evil men share a common fate. 3:16–4:16.
II. The author's advice in light of his philosophy. Chapters 5–11.
III. Concluding admonition and editorial footnotes. Chapter 12.

The book is permeated with an atmosphere of melancholy skepticism. The writer did not believe it possible to find answers to the questions raised by evil and suffering. He was cynical about

[62] Robert Gordis, *Koheleth, The Man and His World,* discusses this problem thoroughly.
[63] O. S. Rankin, "Ecclesiastes," *The Interpreter's Bible,* V, p. 4.

all tradition and authority, even the authority of God. Although he believed in God, he could not find the ways of God in human experience. He categorically denied those pious generalities of the past which directly associated sin and suffering, good and prosperity, but gave no alternative answer. He simply said, "Life has no meaning. It is like that, so live it as it comes."

> Vanity of vanities, says the Preacher
> vanity of vanities! All is vanity.
> What does man gain by all the toil at which
>   he toils under the sun?
> A generation goes, and a generation comes,
> but the earth remains for ever. (1:2–4)

Such pessimism provides no answer, but neither does it oversimplify the problem of evil.

The skepticism of an approach like that of Ecclesiastes may tear out inadequate foundations of an easy answer and thereby prepare the way for a deeper faith. First Ecclesiastes recognizes that God is not comprehended by easy formulas, whether theological or pietistic. The ways of God remain to a large extent a mystery beyond the ken of man. As far as the author of Ecclesiastes is concerned God remains the *unknown* and the *unknowable*. From the point of view of faith such a position is overly pessimistic about the possibility and reality of revelation, the self-disclosure of God. At the same time it is a caution against an alternative error of thinking that God completely gives himself away in revelation. Luther later reminded the church that God was both "*deus revelatus*" and "*deus absconditus*." Glib equations of areas of human activity and concern to the will of God, often follow the uncritical assumption that a religious community knows propositionally all that there is to be known about God. The preacher of Ecclesiastes apparently had had his fill of that kind of religious egotism. In reaction he claimed that God is not really known in theology or in history, and in Israel these two had been always closely related. History, he claimed, is no basis for formulation of satisfactory doctrines about deity. Nevertheless, just because God cannot be known it is not to be assumed that he does not exist. He is God, but his ways are inscrutable and his action in affairs of men indiscernable.

This meant that man is responsible for his own life. As man he must make the most of life in an alien and inhospitable environment. Above all he must be a realist. Pleasure and gain must not too quickly be taken as occasion for optimism, nor should sorrow and hard times occasion deep pessimistic despair. And even though man and his purpose end in the dust, God's purpose although unknown is fulfilled. This questioning faith of Ecclesiastes is one basis of the book's existential relevance. God is after all God, whether or not man is able to discern his action in history. As a kind of agnostic believer, therefore, man is called to live his life and discover meaning in even ordinary things.

This sense of the value of activities in and of themselves is one of Ecclesiastes most interesting concepts.

> For everything there is a season,
> and a time for every matter under
> heaven:
> > a time to be born, and a time to die;
> > a time to plant, and a time to pluck
> > up what is planted;
> > a time to kill, and a time to heal;
> > a time to break down, and a time to
> > build up;
> > a time to weep, and a time to laugh;
> > a time to mourn, and a time to dance;
> > a time to cast away stones, and a
> > time to gather stones together;
> > a time to embrace, and a time to
> > refrain from embracing;
> > a time to seek, and a time to lose;
> > a time to keep, and a time to cast
> > away;
> > a time to rend, and a time to sew;
> > a time to keep silence, and a time to
> > speak;
> > a time to love, and a time to hate;
> > a time for war, and a time for peace.
> > What gain has the worker from his
> > toil?

When life is lived under the sovereignty of God, nothing is trivial or merely routine. Everything and action has its place and purpose. This is in fact one of God's good gifts to man (3:10–15). At the same time the transitory nature of things and all human endeavor is a caution against the temptation to treat them as if they were eternal.

Therefore, by rejection of facile and insensitive answers to complex historical and theological problems the preacher of Ecclesiastes clears the air for honest and intelligent faith, offering a philosophy of life of significant value.

(2) *Job.* The great drama of Job also wrestles with the problem of evil and rejects the easy optimism of the Proverbialist. Here the issue is stated in terms of divine justice. Job, a man of exemplary character and unwavering devotion, is stricken with disaster and disease. How can a benevolent God permit such suffering of a righteous man? Arguments and attitudes growing out of this question are themes in the book. The traditional deuteronomic doctrine that the righteous prosper and the evil suffer is summarily rejected and new answers are sought.

The book of Job is not without its textual and literary problems.[64] It rivals Hosea in the number of vexing textual problems and issues of dating, authorship, and literary integrity are most difficult. Generally the book is best understood from a postexilic perspective in which both nation and individual Jew were confronted with the tragic predicament of suffering.

The book itself has been described as the "greatest poetic work produced by the Israelite community, in terms both of its poetic form and its intellectual honesty and perceptiveness."[65] Actually, the prologue and epilogue are in prose and furnish the context for extensive poetic dialogues. Minor incongruities and inconsistencies and some differences of perspective indicate that the prose materials were a part of Israel's cultural history prior to their use in Job. They apparently represent the Israelite version of an Ancient Near Eastern story of the trials and sufferings of a righteous man. The poetic section, however, is the heart of the book and exhibits a unity and "characteristic literary excellence which suggests the influence of a single personality."[66] The poet is steeped in the wisdom tradition, but with sensitive feeling and

[64] A useful treatment of these appears in introductory discussion by Marvin H. Pope, "Job," in *The Anchor Bible*, Vol. XV, xiii–lxxxii.

[65] Harrelson, *Interpreting The Old Testament*, p. 433.

[66] Marvin Pope, "Job," in *The Anchor Bible*, XV, xxxvii.

penetrating insight he conveys raw realism as boldly portrayed in the experience of his hero. The outline of the book shows his procedure.

The prologue sets the stage for argument about the problem. Job is an extremely wealthy man and deeply pious. According to the traditional deuteronomic understanding of retribution, Job's wealth came because of his devotion. That catastrophe would strike such a man would be least expected. Yahweh had obviously approved Job by giving him "seven sons and three daughters. . . . seven thousand sheep, three thousand camels, five hundred she-asses, and very many servants" (1:2–3). Yet before the heavenly court Satan [67] accuses Job of serving God for profit and is permitted to subject him to testing by affliction. Job loses his family, his possessions, and his health, but not his piety. In this circumstance he dares ask, "Why?" Could a man dare believe that God watched over him (29:2) when loathesome sores covered his body? Had he not been eyes to the blind, feet to the lame, and father to the poor (29:15–16)? How then could a just God take away even friendship as his consolation? The depth of Job's plight and the futility of traditional answers to his situation is shown in his wife's advice.

> Do you still hold fast your integrity? Curse
> God, and die. (2:9)

Yet, Job cannot resign himself to fate. His attempts to understand his own destitution and the God who does not fit the easy orthodoxy of reward and punishment form the heart of the book. In three cycles of debate the poet sets the advice of friends (Eli-

[67] The appearance of "the heavenly court" and "Satan" has regularly been cited in attempts to date the book by relating it to Persian and other Near Eastern influences.

phaz, Bildad, and Zophar) over against the response of Job. Over and over Job's comforters try to convince him that the suffering is punishment for some sin against God.

> Think now, who that was innocent
>   ever perished?
> Or where were the upright cut off?
> As I have seen, those who plow iniquity
>   and sow trouble reap the same.
> By the breath of God they perish,
>   and by the blast of his anger they are consumed. (4:7–9)

Additionally, a young man Elihu adds to the argument of the friends that Job must be guilty of sin.[68] Job continually protests that he has done nothing deserving such severe punishment, but confesses his sense of estrangement from God. Out of his distress he cries,

> I am blameless; I regard not myself;
>   I loathe my life.
> It is all one; therefore I say,
>   he destroys both the blameless and the wicked. (9:21–22)

> Oh, that I knew where I might find him,
>   that I might come even to his seat! (23:3)

From the torment of physical and mental pain the thoughts of Job "fly out like sparks struck from the iron as it lies between the hammer of God and the anvil of life." [69] Out of the void of the meaninglessness of his suffering and faced by death without assurance of life to come, he tries to find meaning.

The boldness with which Job questions God reveals the seriousness of the poet. He deals not simply with theological discussion, but with the possibility of faith. Is it possible to believe in God while facing life as it is? The book fails to explain why the innocent Job suffers, but it does speak to the reality of God in the midst of life. The discussion moves along several lines.

Clearly, the poet believes that Job is justified in defending his innocence; suffering is not a proof of sin. His appeal for an ex-

---

[68] These speeches are disruptive to the ordered plan of the book and represent a later addition either by the poet himself or by an editor. The issues they raise had already been presented by the three friends and adequately refuted by Job's replies.

[69] H. Wheeler Robinson, *The Cross in the Old Testament*, p. 19. Chapter 1 of this book is an excellent interpretation of Job.

planation is an act of faith and not defiance. Job's complaint is
neither a rejection of God who allowed his suffering, nor resignation to his fate. Rather, from an agonizing situation he seeks to
relate the moral God to his conviction of personal integrity. The
poet, unlike the friends, refuses an easy explanation for the suffering and repudiates any who would condemn Job for raising
the question, "Why?" God himself vindicates his servant in
words addressed to Eliphaz:

> My wrath is kindled against you and against
> your two friends; for you have not spoken
> of me what is right, as my servant Job has. (42:7)

Yet, the poet's "answer to Job" [70] is far more profound than
mere reassurance amid travail. His confidence, presented in the
Yahweh speeches (chapters 38–42:6), takes a different direction
than that posed by Job's question. No explanation for Job's suffering is offered; in fact Yahweh rejects presumptive questioning.
"The complete evasion of the issue as Job has posed it must be
the poet's oblique way of admitting that there is no satisfactory
answer available to man, apart from faith." [71] Job himself has
already acknowledged man's finitude and helplessness (Cf.
10:1–22) and now he must face the living God, whose character
is fearsome and mysterious. The hard facts of life cannot be
ignored and man is not denounced for daring to question. But
neither can Yahweh be summoned as a witness to testify against
himself. Job's ultimate answer cannot be formulated in rational
explanations, especially those of traditional deuteronomic outlook. Only a vision of God, who needs no more help in controlling the world than he did in creating it, brings consolation to
the inquirer. Such a vision comes only with struggle and agony,
a pilgrimage essential to the discovery of trust. Job's closing confession shows the depths of his faith.

> Then Job answered Yahweh:
> "I know that thou canst do all things, and
>   that no purpose of thine can be thwarted.
> 'Who is this that hides counsel without
> knowledge?'

---

[70] Carl G. Jung uses this phrase as title for a provocative book.
[71] Marvin Pope, "Job," *The Anchor Bible*, XV, lxxv.

> Therefore I have uttered what I did not
>   understand
>   things too wonderful for me, which I did
>   not know.
> 'Hear and I will speak;
>   I will question you, and you declare to me.'
> I had heard of thee by the hearing of the ear,
>   but now my eye sees thee;
> therefore I despise myself,
> and repent in dust and ashes." (42:1–6)

Job repents, not because his friends have been proven correct, but because this is what one must do when he confronts deity.

The prose epilogue seemingly reverts to the discredited doctrine of retribution. The vindicated hero is rewarded with the restoration of family and possessions to "twice as much as he had before" (42:10). Evidently this feature of the ancient material has been preserved by the author as a way of concluding the story without leaving the hero in utter despair. The deuteronomic conclusion, however, ought not detract from the main thrust of the book.

In the book of Job the Old Testament sets its stamp of approval on individual sincerity and religious pilgrimage. From his dung-heap Job ultimately defies the sufferings which almost rob him of his faith in a mysterious God. Moreover, the book is a prophetic word to the Israelite community whose circumstances gave it birth. From the exile where city and temple and king had been taken away, the covenant people could trust in Yahweh, who revealed himself in suffering and struggle as he had in the exodus and gift of the land. Further, the work speaks a universal word. Job is every man, reminding us that a deep and personal faith often comes by way of the long and sometimes dark corridor of sincere questions about the relevance of God for human existence. The book ultimately asserts that he who throws himself upon God, even though perplexed about life's evil, shall find him.[72]

The Community of the Torah

No change in postexilic Jewish religious life was more significant than the increasing importance given to the Torah. Gradually the Torah, brought to the foreground in the reforms of Ezra

Written Torah

[72] Robinson, *The Cross in the Old Testament*, pp. 32, 34, 43.

and Nehemiah, became a bond of cohesiveness for a people whose utopian dream of an early restoration of the "day of David" went unrealized. Unfulfilled political hopes caused the people to look more and more to the future. The perspective of the period thus became eschatological; that is, the hope of the nation was known not so much in immediate politics as in the theology of what she by Yahweh's activity might become. Ultimately Yahweh's purposes for Israel would be realized. But what was to happen during the interval preceding Yahweh's intervention to fulfill Israel's history? How was the covenant community to live in light of continuing political disappointments? Judaism's answer to these questions centered in the Torah. Obedience to the Law in the most thoroughgoing fashion became Israel's part in preparing for the new day when Yahweh's Prince of Peace would rule over a new community established upon an everlasting covenant.

The popularity of Torah was both possible and necessary because of the passing of traditional centers of Jewish loyalty. Long destroyed was the cult of the north with its shrines of Dan and Bethel. The Jerusalem-centered nationalistic cult of the south, with its Davidic associations, lived on only in the continually frustrated hope for the reestablishment of national entity. Jews were scattered throughout the known world,[73] many never to return to the land of the age-old covenant promise. For them the old bond of nationalistic cult no longer had meaning. Even the successful reconstruction of the Jerusalem sanctuary was not sufficient to hold the community together. Moreover, those who returned to Judah had been unable to restore the old institutions. The promised future with the re-establishment of the Davidic state had not come and all attempts to recapture the past proved tragically disappointing.

Even less possible was a return to the way of the covenant community of the old amphictyony. Israel was now far removed from the tribal way of life even though some of the amphictyonic ideals had remained alive through the turmoil of preceding centuries. The expectation of a new covenant, voiced by Jeremiah and echoed elsewhere in the later Old Testament literature,[74]

---

[73] Known technically as the Diaspora.
[74] Jeremiah 31:31–35; 34–40; Ezekiel 37:26.

had nationalistic, not amphictyonic, connotation and would never be literally fulfilled.

Therefore, with old formats frustrated the people of Yahweh turned in a new direction to establish her continued existence. The key to survival was found in an estimation of the Torah which established it as the basis of the community's life. This emphasis led to Israel's becoming a "people of a book." Amphictyonic structure, nationalistic institutions, and temple cult gave way to the cult of the Torah, and the people of the covenant became the people of the Torah.

The Role of the Torah. The distinguishing characteristic of postexilic Judaism was reverence for the Torah of Yahweh. Obedience to the law was not, of course, anything new in Israel. At the heart of the Sinai covenant had been the Decalogue, the amphictyony had centered in the divine law, and the national life of Israel was always regulated by covenant law. Even Israel's great prophets, far from being "legalists" in their role as reformers, viewed the law as Yahweh's ordained guide for national and personal life. Thus, the role assigned the Torah in the restored community was merely a heightening of one it had long held.

The Hebrew word *torah* means "instruction" or "direction" and its primary reference is to that direction which comes from Yahweh. The tribe of Levi was to teach "Jacob thy ordinances and Israel thy law (*torah*)." [75] Gradually, however, the word came to be used for a body of teaching, either prophetic or priestly. The code of Deuteronomy was called Torah and finally the word came to be applied to all of the "Law of Moses," the Old Testament books Genesis through Deuteronomy. This extensive collection of written law from all periods of Israel's history was largely brought together during the exile. When Ezra returned to Jerusalem about 428 B.C., he brought with him a form of the Torah and promulgated it as Yahweh's law by which the community of the restoration was to structure its way of life. Thus, the Torah, more than anything else, became determinative for Israel. He who assumed the burden of this law was the true Israelite.

[75] Deuteronomy 33:10.

After the exile Torah increasingly was considered the medium of revelation. The prophetic explanation of the exile as a judgment upon disobedience made it natural for Judaism's leaders to deem obedience to the law the basis of any reestablishment and continuation of the people of Yahweh. No other course was open to them. Therefore, when prophecy declined during the post-exilic period, the community turned to the Torah to find Yahweh's final word to man.

Gradually the law was accorded a growing place of importance until finally it was absolutized. Separated from the historical context out of which it had sprung, the law came to be viewed as unchanging, unalterable, and eternal.[76] It was portrayed as an eternal thing with absolute authority existing before Sinai and Israel.[77] The whole Torah was written upon heavenly tablets [78] and its prescriptions were obeyed in heaven itself.[79] By the time of the Christian era, the law had reached its ultimate exaltation, being extolled as the one possession left to Judaism apart from Yahweh himself.[80] All the blessings of the world to come were promised to "those who have been saved by their works, and to whom the law hath now been a hope, and understanding an expectation, and wisdom a confidence." [81]

The Religion of the Torah.   The place of the cult was elevated in the community which lived by the Torah,[82] since its precepts were taken with complete seriousness by devoted Jews. Some changes from the cult of preexilic days are noticeable but, in large, the cultic traditions of the earlier temple were carried forward. Sacrifices continued as before, except for an additional emphasis upon the sin offerings. The annual feasts and their historical significance were retained, and two nationalistic festivals were introduced: Purim, celebrating the events described in Esther, and Hanukkah, recalling the dedication of the temple in 165 in

---

[76] This is hinted at in canonical literature (Psalm 119:89, 160), but is made clear in apocryphal and pseudepigraphical writings.

[77] Cf. The Wisdom of ben Sirach, 16:26–17:24 and especially Jubilees 2:15–33; 3:8–14; 6:17 f.; 16:20–31; etc.

[78] Jubilees 3:10; 4:5; 5:13.

[79] Jubilees 2:18, 30, 33.

[80] Apocalypse of Baruch 85:3.

[81] Apocalypse of Baruch 1:27.

[82] See the helpful summary by N. H. Snaith, "The Priesthood and the Temple," in *A Companion To The Bible*, edited by T. W. Manson, pp. 418–443.

the midst of the Maccabean revolt. The Day of Atonement, the one fast day in Israel's liturgical calendar, gained in importance because of the accentuated sense of sin brought on by the catastrophic events of the exile.

Changes in keeping with interpretations of Torah are also discernible in the organization of cultic personnel. The high priestly office became hereditary and the position attained an eminence unheard of in preexilic days. The high priest was spiritual head of the community and often its secular ruler as well. The ordinary ranks of the priesthood were made up of those who were able to authenticate their Aaronic descent. The lower orders, all of whom had to claim descent from Levi, were for the most part descendants of the cultic leaders of the various Judean shrines outlawed during the Josianic reformation. These men were keepers of the temple, doorkeepers, servants. A large group of them, however, made up the temple choirs which played a vital role in the worship life of the community.

Cultic prophets associated with the temple played an increasingly important role in the liturgical services. Things which Yahweh had done and was doing for Israel were dramatically represented in the cult of proper worship. Yahweh's will had to be proclaimed, his answers to prayers communicated, and his great deeds for his people in past days recapitulated.

The Scribes. The elevation of Torah also raised its study to a place of paramount importance in postexilic Judaism and produced a class of men unrivaled in their devotion to the protection of the law's form and meaning. If Torah was to retain its rightful place, it had to become the possession of all Israel, and the will of Yahweh found within Torah had to be known without question.[83] Concern with these objectives produced a class of scribes devoted to the law's preservation, right interpretation, and application to life. These men stand in line with preexilic counterparts, but only in the days following Ezra did they really come into their own. Their tradition continued in the scholarly circles of the Sopherim and Masoretes.[84]

[83] See L. Rabinowitz, "The Scribes and The Law," in *A Companion to The Bible*, edited by T. W. Manson, pp. 444–452.
[84] *Ibid.*

The postexilic scribes established elaborate procedures for protecting the form of the law. They began to hedge Torah with *masora*, a mass of detailed information about the text. They preserved the various text forms from which the Masoretic texts ultimately arose. The fully developed masora and the elaborate "oral law" of the Pharisees both came later, but the work had its origin in the scribal group of postexilic Judaism.

The scribes also were concerned with proper interpretation of the Torah. Consequently, they established principles for its interpretation so that the law might be properly understood and applied. Scripture was explained in light of scripture and its commands were given detailed definition. Care was observed to explain every implication of the Torah lest the divine law inadvertently be broken. Under scribal influence Judaism was becoming a religion of precept and rule in danger of losing the true spirit of its faith.

Sectarian Interpretation of Torah. The high place given to Torah made it inconceivable that any problem could arise to which the law did not speak. Postexile Israel was determined to bring all of life under control of the Law. Yet mobile cultural conditions often made the discovery and application of this instruction quite difficult. New circumstances, specific problems, or changing needs obviously would not be directly covered in old legislation. At the beginning the divine word might be clear, but the passing of time demanded new enactments necessary to keep Torah relevant and up-to-date. Out of such circumstances oral law developed as a means to keep Torah viable and applicable. This oral tradition developed over several centuries and gradually came to include a wide range of customs and decrees considered to be clarifications of original Torah.

The growing status of oral law in postexilic Judaism produced a variety of reactions within the religious community. All agreed that Torah was holy and ought to be made the basis for living. But could oral law rival written law in significance? Three options seemed to be open: (1) the covenant community could bend with historical circumstances and interpret law to meet changing conditions, (2) it could pretend that change had not occurred and focus on maintaining established cult and Torah under the

Essenes

supervision of a constituted priesthood, or (3) it could withdraw from the world and its flux, attempting to create a static environment. Groups within Judaism exercised each of these alternatives and toward the end of the postexilic period these options were represented in Judaism: the Pharisees following the first alternative, the Sadducees the second, and the Essenes the third.

The most important party arising in Judaism was the Pharisees, who continued the tradition of the Hasidim of Maccabean days. They emerged as a distinct group sometime in the second century and were characterized by their zealous obedience to the Torah, which they adapted to meet the changing historical circumstances. They explained the meaning of the Torah so as to make it fit the new environs. While they traced to Moses the beginnings of this "tradition of the elders," as the oral law was called, the Pharisees obviously attempted to keep Israel's ancient law up to date and usable. This mass of oral tradition was eventually codified into the *Mishnah* (second law). The Mishnah in turn was explained and amplified to keep it up to date and relevant. The interpreted Mishnah (i.e., Mishnah plus its explanation, called *Gemara*) forms the Talmud. In addition to the Torah and the "oral law" the Pharisees also recognized as religious authorities the prophetic books and certain of the Writings. Consequently, they accepted doctrines not found in the Torah. They believed in the resurrection of the body, in angels, and looked for the coming of the apocalyptic kingdom. The Pharisees were never numerous, but they controlled the synagogues and their influence on the life and faith of Judaism was great. Pharisaism survived the fall of Jerusalem in A.D. 70 and thus had a lasting influence on Judaism.

① Pharisees

The Pharisees had no desire for political power itself and disapproved of revolutionary activity. They exerted political influence only in times of imperiled religious freedom. They felt that the Kingdom of God would come when his people kept the Law, written and oral, in its every detail.[85]

The Sadducees were the most conservative segment of the Jewish population, both politically and religiously. They belonged to the priestly aristocracy and the secular nobility of Jeru-

② Sadducees

[85] There was a radical left wing of Pharisaism which produced a group of brave men who, unwilling to wait for the rule of Torah to come, acted forcibly to establish God's dominion.

Zealots — obedient to Pharisaic law —

Jesus admitted one zealot.

salem. The Torah was their only source of divine authority, since they rejected the validity of the prophetic books and the oral law of the Pharisees. They likewise rejected theological innovations such as belief in resurrection, rewards, angels and demons, and most apocalyptic speculations. They were orthodox believers of the old school "holding fast to the spirit and the principles of genuine Yahwism as expressed in the Torah," [86] especially where it *centralized* religion in the temple and priesthood.

The Sadducees would go to any extreme to maintain the *status quo*, and generally followed a policy of collaboration and compromise with the powers which controlled the Jewish state during the later pre-Christian and early Christian eras. Hasmonean priest-kings, like Roman procurators of a later period, found support in Sadducee ranks. The political direction of the nation was

Figure 10–6. The ruins of the Essene settlement of Qumran near the Dead Sea. One of the large areas was a writing room where scholars worked to preserve manuscripts of Old Testament books. (Source: Jordan Tourist Information Center.)

[86] Ch. Guignebert, *The Jewish World in the Time of Jesus*, pp. 162–3.

Figure 10–7. Cave IV of the Qumran caves where the largest collection of Dead Sea Scrolls was found. The guide points to a hole where some of them were uncovered. (Source: Jordan Tourist Information Center.)

a secondary concern to the proper administration of the temple cult and its law.

In the face of continual pressure from outside Palestine one group of Jews withdrew from the world in an attempt to create an unchanging environment. These people, called Essenes, lived

Essenes

ascetic lives in community centers, some in towns, some in the countryside. They thought of themselves as the true Israel, that saving remnant through whom Yahweh's age-old promises might finally be realized. This self-styled community of the "new covenant" anxiously awaited the decisive inbreak of Yahweh. They felt that all prophecy was being fulfilled in their day and wrote commentaries on various biblical books to show that this was so, Semi-isolated from the world they held goods in common, frowned upon marriage, and enforced upon themselves a strict discipline of scholarship, work, and worship. New members came from a constant stream of seekers who were admitted to the full fellowship of the communities only after they had proved worthy. The most famous Essene center was the "monastery" at Qumran in the Judean wilderness, whose members produced the Dead Sea Scrolls, the subject of an appallingly voluminous amount of literature since their initial discovery in 1947.

Apocalyptic Interpretation of History

The Qumran experience suggests another theological trend in postexilic Judaism. Israel's undivided devotion to Torah enabled her to show faithfulness to Yahweh in the present, but she also must be able to meet the future as God's people. Some, as those at Qumran, attempted a disciplined withdrawal as an act of preparation for Yahweh's ultimate victory at the last day; others chose to draw sword against the enemy, as those who fought alongside the Maccabees. Both groups were motivated by their conviction that Yahweh joined forces with his faithful people to oppose all powers of darkness and evil.

Israel's hope in the ultimate triumph of God's cause was expressed in a novel type of Jewish literature which became popular in connection with the Maccabean revolt. This form is generally called "apocalypse," a name meaning "revelation" and suggesting that the authors intended to reveal truths which were surrounded by an aura of mystery. Fragmentary samples of apocalyptic writing appear in prophetic oracles, but the book of Daniel was the first full-fledged Jewish apocalypse. Response to the book's circulation won for the literary form a widespread prominence which lasted for almost three centuries. The writings, dating approximately between 200 B.C. and A.D. 100, are mysteriously difficult since they are intentionally esoteric.

Character of Apocalyptic Literature. Apocalyptic writing had great appeal to its readers. It captured the imagination with settings, creatures, and events frequently described in such cryptic language that their only reality existed in the mind of the author and the empathetic reader. Visions, exalted symbolism, ingenious manipulations of numbers, and fantastic descriptions (sometimes quite bizarre) served as vehicles to transport the responsive mind to the understanding intended by the writer. Although the writing of apocalypse required creative genius, the apocalyptist was not an originator of ideas. Appealing to the reader's accumulated experience, he built upon foundations laid by his prophetic predecessors and utilized literary imagery familiar to those to whom he wrote. The result was a powerful literary mode used with effectiveness in Judaism for several centuries.

Apocalyptic literature was written primarily during times of great distress and persecution. At historical moments which offered little or no hope, the apocalyptist lifted his sights to more distant horizons, willingly accepting defeat in the present, but remaining confident and optimistic about ultimate destiny. He expounded a deterministic view of history consistent with his belief in a transcendent deity who was in control of the terminus of human affairs. His eschatological hope was that Yahweh's sovereignty would be manifested at some end-time, that his indestructible will would finally prevail over forces here and beyond, and that on a day of judgment divine sovereignty would be fully asserted over Satan and evil. The eternal would be brought to bear upon the temporal; divine good would defeat wickedness and bring great rejoicing to the people of God. Even the dead would be resurrected to share in the glory. To the apocalyptist, a great new age was in the making. The future was Yahweh's, and he would bring it into being.

The apocalyptic writer placed his message before himself. He was not reluctant to put his oracles under the name of some illustrious person of an era long past. Since the age of prophecy was thought to be gone never to return, the apocalyptist could not claim prophetic authority himself. Ascribing the writing to a celebrated ancient enhanced the value of his message by making it read like a prediction of the present.

Apocalyptic literature was an offspring of the prophetic movement in Israel [87] and shared the burden of relating Yahweh's will to events in history. The apocalyptist, however, veered from the prophetic course in several ways. While the prophet was primarily a spokesman, the apocalyptist was a writer. The prophet was concerned with the problems of a particular generation and addressed Yahweh's word to the people in ways relevant to the time. The apocalyptist looked with a general vision and telescoped vast expanses of time into a single gaze, often encompassing a succession of empires in the range of his concern. The prophet directed his message to people he deemed disloyal to God; the apocalyptist spoke to the faithful under persecution which tried their faith. The prophet thought of a Kingdom of God in this world while his apocalyptic counterpart emphasized future and extramundane considerations.

The apocalyptic writer contributed significantly to the advancement of religious concepts. He supported the reality of life after death and kept alive the messianic hope. For him, Yahweh was in control of history; not an indifferent spectator impotent to take a hand in the course of affairs. He believed that Yahweh "had some purpose for the world He had made, and that His power was equal to its achievement." [88] The pious remnant of Israel, inseparably linked to Yahweh in their suffering, was engaged with Yahweh in a final struggle for the accomplishment of the eternal purpose and will of God. The best for them was yet to be and would surpass even the heightened imagination of man. Such a victory would originate and consummate in Yahweh and might involve the whole of eternity.

Daniel. The book of Daniel is the chief example of apocalyptic writing in the Old Testament. This work had its precursors in Isaiah 13, 14, 24–27; [89] Ezekiel 1, 28–39; Zechariah 9–14; and Joel 2, 3. Several non-canonical writings later than Daniel follow apocalyptic style. Enoch, the Testament of the Twelve

[87] H. H. Rowley, *The Relevance of the Apocalyptic*, p. 13.
[88] *Ibid.*, pp. 151 f.
[89] Isaiah 24–27 is sometimes called "The Little Apocalypse."

Patriarchs, the Assumption of Moses, Baruch, and the Book of Jubilees form a wake trailing from popular acceptance of the Book of Daniel.

Daniel is found in the Old Testament among the Writings, the last works to be given canonical status. Since the book is written in late Hebrew, contains several Persian and a few Greek words, and has a large section in western Aramaic,[90] a postexilic date is clearly in evidence. The Wisdom of ben Sirach (c. 180) does not list Daniel in its catalogue of Israel's "greats," [91] but the book is referred to soon after the middle of the second century B.C. in the Sibylline Oracles.[92] These factors suggest that the book was written during the strenuous early days of the Maccabean revolt, or about 168–165 B.C.

Daniel presents many historical problems. The combination of simple human interest stories with complicated apocalyptic visions, shifts from the first to the third person, and the combination of Aramaic and Hebrew suggest multiple authorship. The chronology of the author does not always coincide with what is known of the history of the period, as the misdating of the beginning of the Babylonian exile in the third year of Jehoiakim (1:1). In fact, the number of historical inaccuracies has led Walter Harrelson [93] to suspect the author to have misrepresented deliberately the historical events and notices in order to provide his readers with a subtle indication that he was actually writing in a much later period with a quite different historical enemy of God's people in mind. Whether or not the errors are intentional, they illustrate that the author writes later than the events and recasts materials in light of his own purpose to inspire men of faith to endure temptation and hardship.

The book of Daniel reflects important turns in Israel's religious development. The notion of angels, belief in resurrection of individuals from death, and the vicarious efficacy of martyr's death are all included in the book as if they are ideas accepted in the Israelite community. But more significantly, apocalyptic judgment has clearly become a part of the Judaism's view of his-

---

[90] Daniel 2:4b–7:28.
[91] Ecclesasticus 44:1–50:24.
[92] See 3:381–400.
[93] *Interpreting the Old Testament*, p. 458.

tory. Daniel affirms real confidence in an approaching rule of God upon earth and exhorts Israel to be prepared to meet that day with unwavering commitment. When the book was written, this meant for the faithful to draw swords and fight on Yahweh's side. The covenant community is solemnly responsible to share, by active participation, the rule of the sovereign Lord of all nations. Thus, although the book was written to a specific age with the distinctive purpose of reassuring Yahweh's people in a time of their distress, Daniel further intends to proclaim the sovereignty of Yahweh over history, a theological reality which stirs both confidence and commitment.

The theme of Daniel is that hope is best placed in Yahweh, who controls the final engagement with evil and who in his own time will usher in his kingdom. The author seems to have been one of the Hasidim who resisted the oppressive and blasphemous policies of Antiochus Epiphanes and intended by his writing to support the Maccabean revolt. Using well-known stories of the heroism of a certain Daniel who struggled faithfully and successfully against Babylonian tyranny,[94] he sought to encourage his kinsmen in their current distress. If Jews persecuted by Antiochus would as the earlier Daniel demonstrate perseverance in faith, display real courage and endure martyrdom, they would preserve the rich tradition of those who had kept alive faith in Yahweh's ultimate victory. Faithful commitment in the present difficulty was necessary to share in the glory of Yahweh's final triumph. Although the book did not promise immediate success for Maccabean resistance, opposition to Syrian tyranny must have been strengthened by its confidence in the future.

Daniel aims to (1) show how Yahweh aids faithful Jews to overcome their enemies and (2) interpret the future triumph that belongs to Yahweh and his followers.

I. Stories about Daniel and His Friends. Chapters 1–6.
    A. An introduction of Daniel and his four friends. 1:1–21.
    B. First story: Interpreting Nebuchadnezzar's dream. 2:1–49.
    C. Second story: Enduring the fiery furnace. 3:1–30.
    D. Third story: Nebuchadnezzar's madness. 4:1–37.
    E. Fourth story: Belshazzar's banquet. 5:1–31.
    F. Fifth story: Daniel in the lions' den. 6:1–28.

[94] H. H. Rowley, *The Relevance of Apocalyptic*, pp. 37 f.

II. Daniel's Apocalyptic Visions. Chapters 7–12.
    A. First Vision: the four beasts. 7:1–28.
    B. Second Vision: the ram and he-goat. 8:1–27.
    C. Third Vision: the seventy weeks. 9:1–27.
    D. Fourth Vision: the last days. 10:1–12:13.

Chapters 1–6 dramatically relate the adventures of four young Jewish men in the employ of the Babylonian government of the exile. Like Joseph in Egypt, these Israelite aliens in a foreign land impressively interpreted dreams for their captors:

> The king said to Daniel,
> "Truly, your God is God of gods and Lord of Kings,
>   and a revealer of mysteries,
> for you have been able to reveal this mystery." (2:47)

They remained true to their cultic teachings, keeping the letter of the law. Their faithfulness to Yahweh initially brought promotion in position, but later incurred the disfavor of their Babylonian sovereign. Even so, these Jewish devotees could not be separated from their steadfastness.

> If it be so, our God whom we serve is able to deliver
> us from the burning fiery furnace; and he will deliver us
> out of your hand, O king. But if not, be it known to you,
> O king, that we will not serve your gods or worship the
> golden image which you have set up. (3:17, 18)

Devotion of this character caused even the foreign rulers to acclaim Israel's God:

> For he is the living God,
>   enduring forever;
> his kingdom shall never be destroyed,
> and his dominion shall be to the end.
> He delivers and rescues,
>   he works signs and wonders
>   in heaven and on earth. . . . (6:26, 27)

Throughout the first part of the book, the lonely four stand as a minority against the crowds which capitulate to the will of tyrants. In due course the wisdom and power of Yahweh prevailed over Babylonian and Persian emperors. Masters of earthly empires are shown to come and go while Yahweh and his kingdom last forever. The kingdom moving on divine power prevails over those built on military strength. With "a stone cut out by no human hand" (2:34) God demolishes the temporal powers of this world.

The visions contained in chapters 7–12 parade four empires across the screen of Yahweh's vision. Babylonians, Medes, Persians, and Greeks are symbolized in varied and clear imagery, but attention is focused on the Greek age of the writer. These chapters make it clear that the contemporary agonies of devout Jews under the tyrannical pressures of Antiochus Epiphanes are analogous to the diverse trials of Daniel and his friends. The heroic behavior of the captives in exile is exalted as a pattern for Jewish conduct to be followed with greater fidelity in the presence of Epiphanes' "abomination of desolation."

In the first vision four awesome beasts emerge from the sea. The beasts represent the Babylonian, Mede, Persian and Greek imperial powers. The fourth beast had ten horns symbolizing the succession of Seleucid rulers. He was the most terrible beast of all and his little horn represented Antiochus Epiphanes, the reigning monster to the Jews. Yahweh ("the Ancient of Days") sentenced this beast to death and gave the eternal kingdom to "one like a son of man," [95] who was identified as the "saints of the Most High" (i.e., the faithful under oppression).[96] The writer is telling the struggling Jew that hope rests in the action of God, who is forever in control of the destiny of those who trust in him.

For the apocalyptist one powerful visionary statement of a theme would not suffice. Therefore, the idea of divine judgment upon Antiochus is repeated in additional fantasies. The second vision represents the victory of Greece (a he-goat) over Medo-Persia (a two-horned ram). The "great horn" of the he-goat was Alexander the Great, who was broken while strong and succeeded by four other horns, representing the divisions of his empire. From one of these horns emerged a "little horn," Antiochus Epiphanes, an arrogant, proud tyrant who would rage and plunder for three years (168–165 B.C.).

In the third vision Jeremiah's prediction of a seventy-year exile is restated as "seventy weeks of years." [97] Gabriel, the angel in-

---

[95] Daniel 7:13, 14. Jesus draws upon this imagery in describing himself as the "son of man."

[96] Daniel 7:18.

[97] Daniel 9:24. Jeremiah's prediction appears in Jeremiah 25:11, 12.

terpreter of the vision,[98] discloses that Babylonian, Persian, and Greek power had been broken by the dominion of Yahweh, who therefore would ultimately destroy Antiochus and his rule of oppression. Yahweh remained sovereign over history. The fourth vision continues this theme of Yahweh's ultimate victory. It covers the period from the third year of Cyrus, king of Persia, to an end "at the time appointed" (11:27, 29) beyond Antiochus Epiphanes. In apocalyptic imagery history is traced through Alexander, the Ptolemies, and the Seleucids to Antiochus Epiphanes. In due time the Seleucid oppressor "shall come to his end, with none to help him" (11:45).

The impact of the visions leaves Daniel impatiently asking a question quite typical to apocalyptic literature, "How long shall it be till the end of these wonders?" He receives the assurance and the admonition:

> Blessed is he who waits. . . .
> Go your way till the end; and you shall rest, and shall
> stand in your allotted place at the end of the days. (12:13)

The book of Daniel was written to a specific age with the distinctive purpose of reassuring Yahweh's people in a time of their distress. Its religious values, however, are abiding and apply to men of all ages. H. H. Rowley [99] has summarized these as follows.

1. Obedience to the will of God is the purpose of life, more important than life itself.
2. God is active in history. Only men of folly fail to take him into account.
3. Religion is not just "peace and poise of spirit," but life lived in fellowship with God and service of men.
4. Peace is God's gift to a world that does his will, not man's achievement.
5. To spread the spirit of loyalty to God is one's highest contribution to the well-being of the world.
6. Loyalty to God is loyalty to a person, not to an idea.
7. Life extends beyond death. In the Old Testament only the book of Daniel teaches a bodily resurrection.
8. An urgency of decision is known in the choice between loyalty or disloyalty to God.

[98] Angels appears in Daniel by name as mediators of God's will.
[99] H. H. Rowley, "The Meaning of Daniel for Today," *Interpretation*, XV (1961), 387–397.

Moreover, this latest book of the Old Testament serves both as an adequate climax to Israel's history and a fitting connection between the Old Testament and the New. The author of Daniel understands full well that Yahweh's authority is conferred upon the transformed and purified people of God, "saints of the Most High" through whose dedication all nations of the earth will be blessed.[100] Covenant is known when Yahweh rules over a devout people who live with the confidence of his sovereignty over history. Such an idea is the basis of Jesus' teaching about and the New Testament affirmation of a kingdom in which God reigns until the final day.

Epilogue of Hope. Maccabean rule, which proved a signal disappointment, fortunately was short-lived. Less than a century after the winning of independence in 142 Israel became subject to Rome, never again (in ancient times) to be free. Nationally she was dead. Her faith, however, was in Yahweh and her hope lived on. He who had chosen Abraham to father a great nation would still act to bless all men through Israel. Knowing that faith is hope, Israel looked for the coming of Yahweh's kingdom and the doing of his will. Nothing could stand in the way of its realization for its coming would be Yahweh's doing.

Thus, Israel's hope was the expectation of the work of sovereign Yahweh, whose ways are mysteriously beyond man's finding out. The shape of that hope had not crystallized by the close of the Old Testament period, nor would it ever do so. The hope was one, but its expressions were many. The prophets looked for the historical establishment of a kingdom ruled over by Yahweh's anointed ("messiah" from Hebrew *mashiach*) who would rule in righteousness, embodying the ideal of the Davidic monarchy. The apocalyptists yearned for the divine inbreak of an extramundane kingdom of glory which would be ushered in by the coming of "a son of man" bringing an end to the present evil age. Some saw the realization of Yahweh's purpose through the unselfish redemptive suffering of the Servant of Yahweh, whether Israel, the remnant, or some individual. In some sense all who had religious perception longed for the establishment of a new and ideal covenant between Yahweh and his people, a covenant

---

[100] Harrelson, *Interpreting the Old Testament*, p. 469.

which would never be broken and which would ultimately include both Israel and the nations.

For Judaism these hopes still wait for future fulfillment. However, for the church, which Paul called the new "Israel of God," [101] the expectations were realized in Jesus of Nazareth who, as both Davidic Messiah and Suffering Servant, brought to reality the Kingdom of God and established with men of faith a new covenant.

SUGGESTED READINGS

Judaism

ACKROYD, PETER R., *Exile and Restoration* (Westminster, 1968).

Box, G. H., *Judaism in the Greek Period* (Oxford University Press, 1932).

FOERSTER, WERNER, *From the Exile to Christ: A Historical Introduction to Palestinian Judaism* (Fortress, 1964).

MOORE, GEORGE F., *Judaism in the First Centuries of the Christian Era*, 3 vols. (Harvard University Press, 1927–30). The classic study on Judaism.

OESTERLEY, W. O. E., *The Jews and Judaism in the Greek Period* (S.P.C.K., 1941).

Wisdom

McKANE, WILLIAM, *Prophets and Wise Men* (S.C.M. Press, 1965).

MURPHY, ROLAND, *Seven Books of Wisdom* (Bruce, 1960).

NOTH, MARTIN, and THOMAS, D. WINTON, eds., *Wisdom in Israel and in the Near East* (Brill, 1955).

PATERSON, JOHN, *The Wisdom of Israel* (Abingdon, 1961). A readable introduction to Job and Proverbs.

RANKIN, O. S., *Israel's Wisdom Literature* (T. & T. Clark, 1936). Standard interpretation of wisdom literature.

RYLAARSDAM, J. C., *Revelation in Jewish Wisdom Literature* (University of Chicago Press, 1946).

Job

HANSON, ANTHONY and MIRIAM, *The Book of Job* (S.C.M. Press, 1953).

POPE, MARVIN H., *Job*, Anchor Bible (Doubleday, 1965).

ROBINSON, H. WHEELER, *The Cross in the Old Testament* (S.C.M. Press, 1955).

ROBINSON, T. H., *Job and His Friends* (S.C.M. Press, 1954).

WATTS, JOHN D. W., OWENS, J., and TATE, MARVIN E. JR., "Job" in *The Broadman Bible Commentary*, IV.

[101] Galatians 6:15; cf. Romans 9:6.

Proverbs and Ecclesiastes

GORDIS, ROBERT, *Koheleth, The Man and His World* (Jewish Theological Seminary of America, 1951).

McKANE, WILLIAM, *Proverbs, a New Approach* (Westminster, 1970).

SCOTT, R. B. Y., *Proverbs and Ecclesiastes*, Anchor Bible (Doubleday, 1965).

TATE, MARVIN E., JR., "Proverbs" in *The Broadman Bible Commentary*, V.

TOY, C. H., *A Critical and Exegetical Commentary on the Book of Proverbs* (Scribner's, 1904). Old and technical, but a standard work.

WHYBRAY, R. N., *Wisdom in Proverbs: The Concept of Wisdom in Proverbs* (S.C.M. Press, 1965).

Apocalyptic

FROST, STANLEY, *Old Testament Apocalyptic* (Epworth, 1952).

HEATON, E. W., *The Book of Daniel* (S.C.M. Press, 1956).

OWENS, JOHN J., "Daniel" in *The Broadman Bible Commentary*, VI.

PORTEOUS, NORMAN W., *Daniel* (Westminster, 1965).

ROWLEY, H. H., *The Relevance of Apocalyptic* (2nd ed., Lutterworth, 1947).

RUSSELL, D. S., *The Method and Message of Jewish Apocalyptic* (Westminster, 1964).

Messianism

KLAUSNER, JOSEPH, *The Messianic Idea in Israel* (Macmillan, 1955). Jewish interpretation of Messianism in the Old Testament. Apocrypha, Pseudepigrapha, and Talmud.

MOWINCKEL, SIGMUND, *He That Cometh* (Abingdon, 1954).

RINGGREN, HELMER, *The Messiah in the Old Testament* (S.C.M. Press, 1956).

Appendix

CHRONOLOGY CHART FOR THE OLD TESTAMENT PERIOD [1]

I. The Ancient World Before the Patriarchs

A. The Stone Age, beginning at least 100,000 years ago. This era is usually divided into the Old, Late, and Middle Stone Ages, which cannot be dated with precision. Culture appeared and began to take on refinements. Agriculture is in evidence in the Near East in the Middle Stone Age; villages and pottery appear in the 6th–5th millennium.

B. The Copper Stone Age, 4th millennium. Writing developed in Babylonia by 3500 B.C.

C. The Early Bronze Age, 3rd millennium. Great states of Egypt and Mesopotamia emerge.

II. Pre-monarchial Hebrew history, c. 2000–1020 B.C.

A. The Patriarchal Age, c. 2000–1500. Canaan was under Egyptian influence during this period. Abraham, probably 19th century.[2] Migrations into Canaan continued through the 14th century.

B. Backgrounds of National Formation, c. 1700–1020.

1. Sojourn in Egypt, c. 1700–1300
Israel's movement into Egypt began c. 1700.

Additional migrations throughout the period

Oppression of the Hebrews

2. Exodus from Egypt, c. 1280, Moses

Egypt

1710	Hyksos domination of Egypt
1570	18th Dynasty, Egyptian Resurgence
	Independence won by Ahmose I	1570–1546
	Egyptian strength reached peak
	Thutmose III	1490–1435
	Religious revolution, discontent,
	weakness in Amarna period	1370–1353
1310	19th Dynasty, Building and Strength
	Establishment of Delta capital
	Seti I	1308–1290
	Ramses II	1290–1224

3. Conquest of Canaan, c. 1250–1200, Joshua
4. Amphictyony, c. 1200–1020
   Struggle with Canaanites occurred c. 1100.
   Philistines dominated southern Canaan by
   time of Saul

1200	20th Dynasty
	Ramses III
1175–1174	Defeat of sea peoples resulting in settlement of Philistines in Canaan
1065	End of Egyptian empire

III. Period of Hebrew Kings, c. 1020–587 B.C.
   Near Eastern Power of Influence in Palestine

Palestine

1. United Monarchy, 1020–922 B.C.
   Saul, 1020–1000
   David, 1000–961
   Solomon, 961–922
2. Divided Monarchy, 922–587 B.C.

JUDAH		ISRAEL	
Rehoboam	922–915	922–901	Jeroboam I
Abijah	915–913		
Asa	913–873	901–900	Nadab
		900–877	Baasha
		877–876	Elah
		876	Zimri
Jehoshaphat	873–849		

EGYPT

918—Shishak invaded Judah

SYRIA

Benhadad I   c. 880–842

---

[1] Chronology for all periods is based on the revised edition of *The Westminster Historical Atlas to the Bible*, G. Ernest Wright and Floyd V. Filson, editors. This scheme largely follows a chronology developed by W. F. Albright (cf. *Bulletin of the American Schools of Oriental Research*, No. 100 [December, 1945], pp. 16–22).

[2] See Albright, "Abraham the Hebrew: A New Archaeological Interpretation," *Bulletin of the American Schools of Oriental Research*, No. 163 (October, 1961), pp. 36–54.

(853—Battle of Karkar)

Hazael   c. 842–806

Rezon   c. 740–732
(732—Fall of Damascus to Assyria)

ASSYRIA
Tiglath-pileser   745–727
Shalmaneser V   727–722
(724–2—Siege of Samaria)
Sargon II   722–705
(722/21—Fall of Samaria)
Sennacherib   705–681
(701—Siege of Jerusalem)
Esarhaddon   681–669
Asshurbanapal   699–633?
Assuretililani   633–629?
Sinsharishkun   ?629–612
(612—Fall of Nineveh to Babylonia)

EGYPT
Necho   609–593

Judah		Israel	
Jehoram or Joram	849–842	Tibni *	876–?
Ahaziah	842	Omri *	876–869
Athaliah	842–837	Ahab	869–850
Joash or Jehoash	837–800	Ahaziah	850–849
Amaziah	800–783	Jehoram	849–842
Uzziah *	783–742	Jehu	842–815
Jotham *	750–735	Jehoahaz	815–801
		Joash	801–786
		Jeroboam II	786–746
		Zechariah	746–745
		Shallum	745
		Menahem	745–736
		Pekahiah	736–735
Ahaz	735–715	Pekah	735–732
		Hoshea	732–722
Hezekiah	715–687		
Manasseh	687–642		
Amon	642–640		
Josiah	640–609		

* Note a period of co-regency.

(609—Battle at Megiddo; Josiah killed by Necho of Egypt)

BABYLON
Nabopolassar   626–605

Nebuchadnezzar   605–562   Jehoahaz   609
(605—Battle of Carchemish;   Jehoiakim   609–598
  defeat of Necho)
(597—First expedition of   Jehoiachin   598–597
  exile)
(587—Fall of Jerusalem to   Zedekiah   597–587
  Babylon)

IV. Exilic and Postexilic Periods, 587–333 B.C.

Powers of Influence   Judah
   on Judah

                                    587–538   Judah in exile in Babylon

BABYLON
Nebuchadnezzar   605–562
Amel-marduk   562–560
Neriglissar   560–556
Nabonidus   556–539
(539—Fall of Babylon to
  Persia)

PERSIA
Cyrus   539–530   538   Edict of Cyrus permitting the return of captives to Jeru-
Cambyses   530–522   salem
Darius I   522–486   520–516   Rebuilding of Jerusalem temple
Xerxes I   486–465
Artaxerxes I   465–424   445   Nehemiah became governor of Judah
Xerxes II   423   428   Mission of Ezra
Darius II   423–404

Artaxerxes II	404–358
Artaxerxes III	358–338
Arses	338–336
Darius III	336–331
(331–Battle of Issus; Persia fell to Greece)	

V. The Hellenistic Period, 333–63 B.C.

331–323 Control of East by Macedonian empire under Alexander. Following his death, Ptolemies controlled Egypt and Seleucids controlled Syria.

Egypt		Judah		Syria	
Ptolemy I	323–285	323–198	Judah under control of Ptolemies	Seleucus I	312–280
Ptolemy II (Philadelphus)	285–246			Antiochus I	280–261
				Antiochus II	261–246
Ptolemy III	246–221			Seleucus II	246–226
				Seleucus III	226–223
Ptolemy IV	221–203	198	Battle of Panium in which Seleucids gained control of Palestine	Antiochus III (the Great)	223–187
				Seleucus IV	187–175
Ptolemy V	203–181	167	Maccabean revolt	Antiochus IV (Epiphanes)	175–163
		165	Religious emancipation of Jews	Antiochus V	163–162
Ptolemy VI	181–146	142–63 B.C.	Jewish political independence until Pompey established Roman rule over Jerusalem		
(Egypt controlled by Rome after 180 and became Roman province in 30 B.C.)					

GENERAL RESOURCE WORKS

History of Israel

ALBRIGHT, W. F., *The Biblical Period* (Biblical Colloquium, 1950). An excellent resume of the entire Old Testament period.

BRIGHT, JOHN, *A History of Israel* (Westminster, 1959).

NOTH, MARTIN, *The History of Israel* (A. & C. Black, 1958). Represents a viewpoint quite different from Bright.

ROBINSON, H. WHEELER, *The History of Israel* (Duckworth, 1957).

Archaeology and Background

The Biblical Archaeologist Reader, I, eds. G. Ernest Wright and David N. Freedman (Doubleday, 1961).

The Biblical Archaeologist Reader, II and III, eds. David N. Freedman and E. F. Campbell, Jr. (Doubleday, 1964 and 1970).

GRAY, JOHN, *Archaeology and the Old Testament World* (Nelson, 1962).

GROLLENBERG, L. H., *Atlas of the Bible* (Nelson, 1957). Splendid pictorial coverage. Available in abridged edition as *Shorter Atlas of the Bible* (Nelson).

MAY, HERBERT G., ed., *Oxford Bible Atlas* (Oxford University Press, 1962).

NEGENMAN, JAN H., *New Atlas of the Bible*, ed. H. H. Rowley (Doubleday, 1969).

PRITCHARD, J. B., *Ancient Near Eastern Texts* (Princeton University Press, 1955). The basic collection of Near Eastern documents relating to the Old Testament.

WILLIAMS, WALTER G., *Archaeology in Biblical Research* (Abingdon, 1965).

WRIGHT, G. ERNEST, *Biblical Archaeology* (Westminster, 1957). The standard work on biblical archaeology. Available in paperback abridged edition without illustrations (Westminster).

WRIGHT, G. ERNEST, and FILSON, F. V., *The Westminster Historical Atlas to the Bible* (Rev. ed., Westminster, 1956). Excellent text and maps.

Introductions to the Old Testament

ANDERSON, BERNHARD, *Understanding the Old Testament*, 2nd ed. (Prentice-Hall, 1966).

ANDERSON, G. W., *A Critical Introduction to the Old Testament* (Duckworth, 1959).

BENTZEN, AAGE, *Introduction to the Old Testament*, I and II (2nd ed., Gad Copenhagen, 1952). Introduction for advanced student.

BUCK, HARRY M., *People of the Lord* (Macmillan, 1966).

EISSFELDT, OTTO, *Old Testament: An Introduction* (Harper & Row, 1965).

FOHRER, GEORG, *Introduction to the Old Testament* (Abingdon, 1965).

GOTTWALD, NORMAN K., *A Light to the Nations* (Harper & Row, 1959).

HARRELSON, WALTER, *Interpreting the Old Testament* (Holt, Rinehart and Winston, 1964).

ROWLEY, H. H., *The Growth of the Old Testament* (Hutchinson, 1950). Concise introductory handbook.

SANDMEL, SAMUEL, *The Hebrew Scriptures: An Introduction to their Literature and Religious Ideas* (Knopf, 1963).

WEISER, ARTUR, *The Old Testament: Its Formation and Development* (Association, 1961).

Religion and Theology

ALBRIGHT, W. F., *From the Stone Age to Christianity* (Doubleday Anchor Books, 1957).

———, *Yahweh and the Gods of Canaan* (Doubleday Anchor Books, 1969).

ANDERSON, BERNARD W., ed., *The Old Testament and the Christian Faith* (Harper & Row, 1963).

EICHRODT, WALTHER, *Theology of the Old Testament,* I and II (Westminster, 1961 and 1967).

JACOB, EDMUND, *Theology of the Old Testament* (Harper & Row, 1958).

MUILENBURG, JAMES, *The Way of Israel* (Harper & Row, 1961).

PEDERSEN, JOHANNES, *Israel: Its Life and Culture* (Branner Og Korch, 1940).

RINGGREN, HELMER, *Israelite Religion* (Fortress, 1966).

VON RAD, GERHARD, *Old Testament Theology,* I and II (Harper & Row, 1962 and 1965).

VRIEZEN, TH. C., *An Outline of Old Testament Theology* (Blackwell, 1958).

———, *The Religion of Ancient Israel* (Westminster, 1967).

Bible Dictionaries

MILLER, M. S. and J. L., *Harper's Bible Dictionary* (Harper & Row, 1952).

The Interpreter's Dictionary to the Bible, I–IV (Abingdon, 1962).

One-Volume Commentaries

Abingdon Bible Commentary, eds. F. C. Eiselen, Edwin Lewis and D. G. Downey (Abingdon-Cokesbury, 1929).

Interpreter's One-Volume Commentary on the Bible, ed. Charles M. Laymon (Abingdon, 1971).

Periodicals

Biblical Archaeology. Articles dealing with all aspects of biblical archaeology.

The Expository Times.

Interpretation. Superior exegetical, theological studies.

Journal of Biblical Literature. Technical studies of specific problems.

Vetus Testamentum. Multilingual technical journal of Old Testament studies.

ADDITIONAL BIBLIOGRAPHY

Works included in the suggested readings for each chapter and in the list of *General Resource Works* are not included here.

ACKROYD, P. R., "History and Theology in the Writings of the Chronicler," *Concordia Theological Monthly*, XXXVIII (1967), 501–515.

ALBRIGHT, W. F., *Archaeology and the Religion of Israel* (2nd ed., Johns Hopkins, 1946).

———, *The Archaeology of Palestine* (Penguin, 1949).

———, *Yahweh and The Gods of Canaan* (Doubleday, 1969).

———, "King Jehoiachin in Exile," *The Biblical Archaeologist Reader*, eds. G. E. Wright and D. N. Freedman (Doubleday, 1961).

———, "Abraham the Hebrew: A New Archaeological Interpretation," *Bulletin of the American Schools of Oriental Research*, no. 163 (October, 1961), 36–54.

———, *Journal of Palestine Oriental Society*, V (1955), 17–54.

ALT, ALBRECHT, *Essays on Old Testament History and Religion* (Doubleday Anchor Books, 1968).

BEEBE, H. KEITH, *The Old Testament: An Introduction to Its Literary Historical and Religious Traditions* (Dickenson, 1970).

BARNES, W. E., *The First Book of Kings*, Cambridge Bible (Cambridge University Press, 1911).

BEWER, J. A., G. DAHL, and L. B. PATON, "The Problem of Deuteronomy: a Symposium," *Journal of Biblical Literature*, XLVII (1928).

BLAIKIE, WILLIAM G., *A Manual of Bible History* (Rev. ed., Revised by Charles D. Matthews, Ronald, 1940).

BODENHEIMER, F. S., "The Manna of Sinai" in *The Biblical Archaeologist Reader*, eds., G. E. Wright and D. N. Freedman (Doubleday, 1961).

BONHOEFFER, DIETRICH, *Creation and Fall* (S.C.M. Press, 1959).

BOTTÉRO, JEAN, *Le Problème des Habiru A La 4ᵉ Rencontre Assyriologique Internationale* (Inprimerie Nationale, 1954).

BRIGHT, JOHN, *Early Israel in Recent History Writing* (S.C.M. Press, 1956).

———, "Has Archaeology Found Evidence of the Flood?" in *The Biblical Archaeologist Reader*, eds. G. E. Wright and D. N. Freedman (Doubleday, 1961).

The Broadman Bible Commentary II–VI, eds. Clifton J. Allen, John I. Durham, and Roy L. Honeycutt (Broadman Press, 1970–1971).

BUCK, HARRY M., *People of The Lord* (Macmillan, 1965).

BUDDE, KARL, *Religion of Israel to the Exile* (Putnam, 1899).

BURNEY, C. F., *The Book of Judges* (2nd ed., Rivingtons, 1930).

BURROWS, MILLAR, *The Dead Sea Scrolls* (Viking, 1955).

———, *More Light on the Dead Sea Scrolls* (Viking, 1958).

CALLAWAY, JOSEPH F., "New Evidence on the Conquest of Ai," *Journal of Biblical Literature*, LXXXVII (1968), 312–320.

CHAPMAN, A. T. and STREANE, A. W., *The Book of Leviticus*, Cambridge Bible (Cambridge University Press, 1914).

COOKE, G. A., *The Book of Joshua*, Cambridge Bible (Cambridge University Press, 1918).

CROSS, FRANK M., JR., *The Ancient Library of Qumran and Modern Biblical Studies* (Rev. ed., Doubleday, 1961).

———, "The Priestly Tabernacle," *The Biblical Archaeologist Reader,* eds. G. E. Wright and D. N. Freedman (Doubleday, 1961).

CUNLIFFE-JONES, H., *Deuteronomy: Introduction and Commentary* (S.C.M. Press, 1951).

DANELL, G. A., *Studies in the Name Israel in the Old Testament.* (Appelbergs boktrycheri, 1946).

DAVIDSON, A. B., *The Theology of the Old Testament* (Scribners, 1904).

DAVIDSON, ROBERT F., *The Old Testament* (Hodder and Stoughton, 1964).

DELITZSCH, FRANZ J., *Biblical Commentary on the Prophecies of Isaiah* (4th ed., T. & T. Clark, 1890).

———, *A New Commentary on Genesis* (T. & T. Clark, 1899).

DENTAN, R. C., *The Idea of History in the Ancient Near East* (Yale University Press, 1955).

DE VAUX, R., "Les patriarches Hébreux et les découvertes modernes," *Revue Biblique,* 53 (1946), 321–348; 55 (1948), 321–347; 56 (1949), 5–36.

DIRINGER, D., "The Seal of Jotham" in *Documents from Old Testament Times,* D. Winston Thomas, ed., Torchbook Series (Harper & Row, 1958).

DRIVER, S. R. *The Book of Exodus,* Cambridge Bible (Cambridge University Press, 1911).

———, *A Critical and Exegetical Commentary on Deuteronomy,* "International Critical Commentary" (Scribners, 1895).

———, *An Introduction to the Literature of the Old Testament* (4th ed., T. & T. Clark, 1892).

———, *Notes on the Hebrew Text and the Topography of the Books of Samuel* (Clarendon, 1913).

ELLIOTT–BINNS, L., *The Book of Numbers,* Westminster Commentary Series (Methuen, 1927).

———, *From Moses to Elisha,* Clarendon Bible Series (Clarendon, 1929).

EPSTEIN, I., ed., *The Babylonian Talmud* (Soncino, 1948).

FILSON, FLOYD V., "Temple, Synagogue and Church," *The Biblical Archaeologist Reader,* eds. G. E. Wright and D. N. Freedman (Doubleday, 1961).

FRANKFORT, HENRI, *Ancient Egyptian Religion* (Columbia University Press, 1948) Harper & Row Torchbook, 1961).

FRANKFORT, H. and H. A., JOHN A. WILSON, THORKILD JACOBSON and WILLIAM A. IRWIN, *The Intellectual Adventure of Ancient Man* (University of Chicago Press, 1946).

FREEDMAN, DAVID N., "The Babylonian Chronicle" in *The Biblical Archaeologist Reader,* eds. G. E. Wright and D. N. Freedman (Doubleday, 1961).

GARSTANG, J., *The Foundations of Bible History: Joshua, Judges* (Constable, 1931).

GLUECK, NELSON, "Explorations in Eastern Palestine" in *The Annual of American Schools of Oriental Research,* 1933–34, 1945–49 (University of Pennsylvania, 1934, and American Schools of Oriental Research, 1951).

———, *The Other Side of Jordan* (American Schools of Oriental Research, 1940).

GRAY, G. B., *A Critical and Exegetical Commentary on Numbers,* International Critical Commentary (Scribners, 1903).

———, *Sacrifice in the Old Testament* (Clarendon, 1925).

GREENBERG, MOSHE, *The Hab/piru* (American Oriental Society, 1955).

GUIGNEBERT, CH., *The Jewish World in the Time of Jesus* (Routledge and Kegan Paul, 1939).

GUNKEL, HERMAN, *Die Psalmen* (Vandenhoeck and Ruprecht, 1926).

——— and JOACHIM BEGRICH, *Einleitung in die Psalmen* (Vandenhoeck and Ruprecht, 1933).

HALDAR, ALFRED, *Associations of Cult Prophets Among the Ancient Semites* (Almquist and Wiksells Boktrycheri, 1945).

HARLAND, J. PENROSE, "Sodom and Gomorrah" in *The Biblical Archaeologist Reader,* eds. G. E. Wright and D. N. Freedman (Doubleday, 1961).

HAUPT, PAUL, ed., *The Sacred Books of the Old and New Testament* (Dodd, Mead, 1898).

HEATON, E. W., *Everyday Life in Old Testament Times* (B. T. Batsford, 1956).

HERBERT, A. G., *The Authority of the Old Testament* (Faber and Faber, 1947).

HITTI, P. K., History of Syria (Macmillan, 1951).

HOOKE, S. H., *In the Beginning,* Clarendon Bible Series (Clarendon, 1947).

The Holy Bible: Revised Standard Version (Nelson, 1946 and 1952).

HÖLSCHER, GUSTAV, *Die Propheten* (J. C. Heinrichs, 1914).

HYATT, J. PHILIP, ed., *The Bible in Modern Scholarship* (Abingdon, 1965).

The Interpreter's Bible, Vols. I–VI (Abingdon).

JANSEN, E. *Juda in der Exilszeit* (Forschungen zur Religion und Literatur des Alten und Neuen Testaments 69, 1956).

JENSEN, Joseph, *God's Word to Israel* (Allyn and Bacon, 1968).

The Jerusalem Bible, ed. Alexander Jones (Doubleday, 1966).

The Jewish People: Past and Present, I (Jewish Encyclopedic Handbooks, Central Yiddish Culture Organization, 1946).

JOHNSON, A. R., *The Vitality of the Individual in the Thought of Ancient Israel* (University of Wales Press, 1949).

———, *The One and the Many in the Israelite Conception of God* (University of Wales Press, 1942).

JOSEPHUS, FLAVIUS, *Complete Works of Josephus,* tr. William Whiston (Thompson and Thomas, 1901).

KAUFMANN, YEHEZKEL, *The Religion of Israel,* Trs. and abridged by Moshe Greenberg (Allen & Unwin, 1961).

KEIL, C. F. and F. DELITZSCH, *Biblical Commentary on the Old Testament* (T. & T. Clark, 1864).

KELLOGG, S. H., *The Book of Leviticus,* Expositor's Bible (A. C. Armstrong & Son, 1891).

KENNEDY, A. R. S., *Leviticus and Numbers,* Century Bible (T. C. & E. C. Jack, n.d.).

———, ed., *The Book of Samuel,* New Century Bible (Henry Fronde, n.d.).

KENYON, KATHLEEN, *Archaeology in the Holy Land,* 3rd ed. (Praeger, 1970).

KIERKEGAARD, SØREN, *Fear and Trembling* (Princeton University Press, 1941).

KÖHLER, LUDWIG, *Old Testament Theology* (Lutterworth, 1957).

KRAELING, EMIL, *Bible Atlas* (Rand McNally, 1956).

————, "New Light on the Elephantine Colony," *The Biblical Archaelogist Reader*, eds. G. E. Wright and D. N. Freedman (Doubleday, 1961).

KRAUS, HANS-JOACHIM, "Gilgal: Ein Beitrag zur Kultusgeschichte Israels," *Vetus Testamentum*, I (1951), 181–199.

LARUE, GERALD A., *Old Testament Life and Literature* (Allyn and Bacon, 1968).

MAIER, WALTER A., *The Book of Nahum* (Concordia, 1959).

MANSON, T. W., ed., *A Companion to the Bible* (Scribners, 1947).

MAY, HERBERT G., "Synagogues in Palestine," *The Biblical Archaeologist Reader*, eds. G. E. Wright and D. N. Freedman (Doubleday, 1961).

MCNEILE, A. H., *Deuteronomy, Its Place in Revelation* (Longmans, Green, 1912).

MEISSNER, B., *Babylonien und Assyrien*, II (Carl Winter Universitatsbuch-handlung).

MILIK, JÓSEF T., *Ten Years of Discovery in the Wilderness of Judaea* (A. R. Allenson, 1959).

MOORE, CAREY A., *Esther*, The Anchor Bible (Doubleday, 1971).

MOORE, G. F., *A Critical and Exegetical Commentary on Judges*, International Critical Commentary (Scribners, 1895).

MOULD, E. W. K., *Essentials of Bible History* (3rd ed. Revised by H. Niel Richardson and Robert F. Berkey, Ronald, 1966).

NAPIER, B. DAVIE, "On Creation-Faith in the Old Testament," *Interpretation*, XVI (January, 1962), 21–42.

NOTH, MARTIN, "Das Amt des 'Richters Israels,'" in *Festschrift für Alfred Bertholet* (J.C.B. Mohr, 1950).

————, "History and the Word of God in the Old Testament," *Bulletin of the John Rylands Library*, XXXII (March, 1950).

————, *Das System der Zwölf Stämme Israels* (W. Kohlhammer, 1950).

————, *The Laws in the Pentateuch and Other Essays* (McGraw-Hill, 1966).

————, *Uberlieferungsgeschichtliche Studien: I* (Schriften der Konigsberger Gelehrten-Gesellschaft, 1943).

O'CALLAGHAN, R. T., *Aram Naharaim* (Pontificium Institutium Biblicum, 1948).

OESTERLEY, W. O. E., and T. H. ROBINSON, *A History of Israel*, 2 vols. (Oxford University Press, 1932).

———— and T. H. ROBINSON, *An Introduction to the Books of the Old Testament* (S.P.C.K., 1934).

ORLINSKY, H. M., *Ancient Israel* (Cornell University Press, 1954).

ÖSTBORN, GUNNAR, *Cult and Canon: A Study in the Canonization of the Old Testament* (A. B. Lundequistska, 1951).

PEAKE, A. S., ed., *A Commentary on the Bible* (Thomas Nelson & Sons, n.d.).

PFEIFFER, R. H., *Introduction to the Old Testament* (Rev. ed., Harper & Row, 1948).

————, *Religion in the Old Testament* (Harper & Row, 1961).

PRITCHARD, J. B., *Archaeology and the Old Testament* (Princeton University Press, 1958).

————, *The Ancient Near East in Pictures Relating to the Old Testament* (Princeton University Press, 1954).

————, ed., *The Ancient Near East: An Anthology of Texts and Pictures* (Princeton University Press, 1965).

RINGGRAN, HELMER, *Israelite Religion* (Fortress, 1966.)

ROBINSON, H. WHEELER, *Deuteronomy and Joshua,* New Century Bible (Oxford University Press, 1908).

————, *The History of Israel* (Duckworth, 1938).

————, *Inspiration and Revelation in the Old Testament* (Oxford University Press, 1946).

————, *The Old Testament: Its Making and Meaning* (Hodder and Stoughton, 1937).

————, "The Religion of Israel" in *A Companion to the Bible,* ed. T. W. Manson (Scribner's, 1947).

————, *Religious Ideas of the Old Testament* (Duckworth, 1913).

ROBINSON, T. H., *The Decline and Fall of the Hebrew Kingdoms,* Clarendon Bible Series, Vol. III (Clarendon, 1926).

ROSS, JAMES F. and LAWRENCE E. TOOMBS, "Three Campaigns at Biblical Shechem," *Archaeology,* XIV (1961), 171–179.

ROWLEY, H. H., *The Book of Ezekiel in Modern Study* (Manchester University Press, 1953).

————, "The Early Prophecies of Jeremiah in Their Setting," *Bulletin of the John Rylands Library,* XLV (1962), 198–234.

————, "The Marriage of Hosea," *Bulletin of the John Rylands Library,* XXXIX (1956), 200–233.

————, "The Meaning of Daniel for Today," *Interpretation,* XV (1961), 387–397.

————, ed., *The Old Testament and Modern Study* (Oxford University Press, 1951).

————, *The Rediscovery of the Old Testament* (Westminster, 1946).

————, "Sanballat and the Samaritan Temple," *Bulletin of John Rylands Library,* XXXVIII (1955), 166–198.

————, *The Servant of the Lord and Other Essays on the Old Testament* (Lutterworth, 1952).

————, ed., *Studies in Old Testament Prophecy* (T. & T. Clark, 1950).

SANDMEL, SAMUEL, *The Hebrew Scriptures: An Introduction to Their Literature and Religious Ideas* (Alfred A. Knopf, 1963).

SIMPSON, C. A., *The Early Traditions of Israel* (Basil Blackwell, 1948).

SKINNER, JOHN, *Kings,* New Century Bible (Oxford University Press, 1904).

SMITH, G. A., *The Book of Deuteronomy,* Cambridge Bible (Cambridge University Press, 1918).

SNAITH, NORMAN H., *The Book of Job: Its Origins and Purpose* (Alex Allenson, 1968).

————, *The Distinctive Ideas of the Old Testament* (4th ed., Epworth, 1950).

————, *The Inspiration and Authority of the Bible* (Epworth, 1956).

STINESPRING, W. F., "Eschatology in Chronicles," *Journal of Biblical Literature,* LXXX (September, 1961), 209–219.

THATCHER, G. W., *Judges and Ruth,* New Century Bible (Oxford University Press, 1904).

THOMAS, D. WINTON, ed., *Documents from Old Testament Times* (Harper & Row Torchbooks, 1961).

————, *Archaeology and Old Testament Study* (Clarendon, 1967).

URIS, LEON, *Exodus* (Doubleday, 1958).

VON ALLMEN, J. J., *A Companion to the Bible* (Oxford University Press, 1958).

VON RAD, GERHARD, "Die Konfessionen Jeremias," *Evangelische Theologie,* III (1936), 265–276.

————, *Studies in Deuteronomy,* (Regnery, 1953).

————, *Old Testament Theology,* I–II, tr. D. M. G. Stalker (Harper & Row, 1962, 1965).

————, "Verheissenes Land und Jahwes Land im Hexateuch," *Zeitschrift des Deutschen Palästine-Vereins,* LXVI (1943), 191–204.

WELCH, A. G., *The Code of Deuteronomy* (James Clarke, 1924).

WEST, JAMES K., *Introduction to the Old Testament* (Macmillan, 1971).

WISEMAN, D. J., *Chronicles of Chaldean Kings: (626–566 B.C.) in the British Museum* (Trustees of the British Museum, 1956).

WRIGHT, G. ERNEST, "Cult and History," *Interpretation,* XVI (1962), 3–20.

————, *The Old Testament Against Its Environment* (S.C.M. Press, 1950).

————, "Shechem: The Archaeology of the City," *The Biblical Archaeologist,* XX (1957), 19–32.

GLOSSARY

Aetiology—See *Etiology.*

Amalekites—Desert tribe living south of Canaan in Negeb and Sinai peninsula. Biblical tradition traces them from Amalek, son of Esau. They were chronic enemies of Israel up to the time of the monarchy.

Ammonites—Amorite people of Transjordan. Lived along the Jabbok watershed. Although from the same racial stock, they were constant enemies of Israel. Biblical tradition traces them from Lot.

Amorites—Semitic people from northwest Mesopotamia. Flooded the Fertile Crescent after 2000 B.C. The migration of Israel's ancestors to Canaan was part of this movement. Name means "westerners" (Babylonian) or "highlanders" (Hebrew).

Amphictyony—A religious confederation centered in a sanctuary. Term derived from Greek word meaning "to gather around." Appropriate for Israel's religio-political organization between the conquest and monarchy, since their factor of unification was common worship at a central sanctuary. The amphictyonic center was first located at Shechem, then at Shiloh.

Anatolia—Ancient geographic name for Asia Minor.

Anthropomorphism—The ascription of human form, personality, or attributes to that which is not human, esp. deity.

Apocalyptic—Type of literature common in Judaism in the late centuries B.C. and early centuries A.D. Characterized by symbolic language and elaborate imagery. Best OT example is Daniel. Greek term meaning "to reveal." Book written in apocalyptic style is called Apocalypse.

Apocrypha—1. Generally non-canonical literature.
2. Specifically for Protestants, books included in the LXX and Vulgate, but not in the Hebrew OT.

Arabah—Arid desert plain between the Dead Sea and the Gulf of Aqabah. Rich in mineral deposits, especially copper and iron.

Aramaic—The language of the Arameans, spread by merchants throughout western Asia it became the *lingua franca* of the Ancient Near East. Became the common language of the Persian Empire after 500 B.C. and, in time, the language of postexilic Jews. Some portions of OT were written in Aramaic.

Arameans—Semitic people who entered the Fertile Crescent between 1500–1000 B.C. Established small kingdoms in Syria. Some of these people were among Israel's ancestors. Eventually Arameans became commercial middlemen of the Ancient Near East.

Archaeology—The scientific study by excavation, examination, and publication of the remains of ancient civilizations.

Ark—1. The box-like boat of the biblical story of the flood.
2. The portable throne of Yahweh symbolizing his presence among his people. First kept in the tabernacle; then in the inmost chamber of the temple.

Asherah—Female goddess of Canaan, Baal's consort. Fertility goddess of sex and war. In the OT Asherah is used loosely of the goddess herself, her wooden image, or the tree or pole used as her symbol.

Assyria—Empire on upper Tigris River. Its culture dates to the third millennium B.C. Assyrians dominated the Fertile Crescent between 1100 and 612 B.C. Nineveh was the capital of the empire during its period of dominance.

Aton—Egyptian solar (sun) diety. Championed by Akhnaton as *the one* diety.

Atonement, Day of—see *Fast Day.*

Baal—Name applied to various local Canaanite dieties, but also used as a substitute for Hadad, the chief Canaanite god of fertility in whom the other dieties were merged. Baal was the personification of natural forces which produce rain and vegetation.

Babylon—City on middle Euphrates, capital of Old Babylonian and Neo-Babylonian empire. The city gave its name to the surrounding territory and the empire which centered there.

Canaan—OT name for the land between the Jordan and the Mediterranean, from Egypt to Syria. The name probably means "land of the purple," so called because of purple dye made from the murex shellfish found along the coast. See *Palestine.*

Canon—A collection of authoritative sacred books.

Chaldeans—1. Mountain people who founded the Neo-Babylonian empire.
2. Astrologers of the postexilic period so called because of the proficiency of Babylonian priests in astronomy.

Charismatic—A leader endowed by Yahweh's spirit with extraordinary ability. Especially applicable to the military judges of Israel.

Cherem—The "ban" of the Holy War. The word means "to set apart" or "to dedicate."

Cherubim—Symbolic creatures of composite type. Half animal, half human. Cherubim were the guardians of Yahweh's earthly throne.

Chronicler, The—The historian who compiled and edited the OT books of Chronicles, Ezra, and Nehemiah, originally one continuous history.

Codex—Handwritten manuscripts in book form.

Covenant—1. Agreement between individuals or groups.

        2. Especially in the OT, an agreement between the sovereign Yahweh and Israel. Yahweh agrees to be Israel's God, if they in turn will bind themselves by his commandments and agree to be his people.

Cultus (Cult)—A system of worship.

Cuneiform—Wedge-shaped Semitic writing characteristic of Mesopotamia.

Dead Sea Scrolls—Numerous biblical and nonbiblical manuscripts and fragments found since 1947 in caves along the Dead Sea; they came from the library of the Essene community of Qumran. See also *Essenes.*

Decalogue—The "ten words." The Ten Commandments found in Exodus 20 and Deuteronomy 5.

Deutero-Isaiah—or Second Isaiah. The part of the book of Isaiah which was written during the exile by a prophet or prophets in the tradition of Isaiah of the eighth century. Includes chapters 40–55 and perhaps 56–66, although many scholars believe the latter to be the work of still another prophet (or prophets) whom they designate "Trito-Isaiah."

Diaspora—The Jews living outside of Palestine after the time of the exile.

Deuteronomic History—An extensive "history" of Israel written during or just after the Exile. It includes Deuteronomy, Joshua, Judges, Samuel, and Kings. Sometimes called "D." The author (or authors) of the history is known as the Deuteronomist.

Documentary Hypothesis—Theory of the authorship of the Pentateuch assuming four separate authors or groups of authors. See *Yahwistic History, Elohistic History, Deuteronomic History,* and *Priestly History.*

Edomites—A Semitic people who lived in the Arabah and Negeb, south of the Dead Sea. According to the OT, the descendants of Esau.

El—The Semitic root which expresses divinity. El was the name of the great "high" god of the Canaanite pantheon. In the OT El is applied indiscriminately to all gods, but also used as a proper name of a particular deity. When referring to Israel's god, El is most often followed by another word in apposition more specifically identifying the deity (El Bethel, El Roi, El 'Olam, El Shaddai, etc.). The OT prefers, however, the plural word Elohim.

Elohim—Plural for the common Semitic noun designating a god or goddess. Used in OT for Israel's God, perhaps to show that Yahweh was God in the highest sense of the word.

Elohistic History—A "history" of Israel's beginnings covering the period from creation to the conquest. Written sometimes around 900 B.C. in the kingdom of Israel from the perspective of the northern tribes. Sometimes called "E." Its author (or authors) is known as the Elohist.

Enuma Elish—The opening words of the Mesopotamian story of creation, commonly used as title of the work. Means "when on high."

Ephraim—1. Son of Joseph.

        2. Most important of the northern tribes.

        3. Poetic nickname for the kingdom of Israel.

Eponym—The person from whom a family, race, city, or nation is supposed to have taken its name.

Eschatology—The doctrine of last or final things, as death, the end of the age, etc.

Esdraelon—see *Jezreel.*

Essenes—Ascetic Jewish sect of late OT times. Lived in monastic type establishments, the most famous of which was at Qumran.

Etiology—the explanation of cause or reason.

Fast Day—The one regular fast day in the Israelite liturgical calendar was the Day of Atonement. Observed on the tenth day of Tishri, it was a most sacred day when atonement was made for the sins of all the people.

Feasts, The—There were three major festivals and two minor ones in the Israelite liturgical year:

Major festivals:

1. Passover—Unleavened Bread (Pesach-Mazzoth); great celebration of the Exodus deliverance. The first feast of the liturgical year.
2. Weeks (Shabhuoth) also called Pentecost in later Judaism. Agricultural festival at the end of the barley harvest. Fifty days after the Feast of Unleavened Bread.
3. Ingathering (Sukkoth) also called Tabernacle or Booths. Harvest festival of thanksgiving. Also commemorative of the deliverance from Egypt. Eventually this festival was celebrated in connection with New Year's and became the time of covenant renewal. Celebrated on the first of Nisan, the beginning of the calendar year.

Minor or Late Festivals:

1. Purim: Nationalistic celebration of events recorded in the book of Esther.
2. Dedication (Hanukkah): Also called Feast of Lights. Celebration of the rededication of the temple during the Maccabean revolt.

Fertile Crescent—A semicircular region of fertility between mountains and desert extending northwestward from the northern tip of the Persian Gulf through the Tigris-Euphrates valley to Haran and bending southwestward through Syria, Phoenicia and Palestine into the Nile River valley. The term was first used by James H. Breasted, a noted Egyptologist.

Fertility Cults—Systems of worship centered around the rhythmic cycle of nature, and rituals appropriate to deities primarily associated with the needs of primitive agricultural people. Orgiastic rites involving sex in some form largely characterized their religious practices.

Form Criticism—Analysis of the *forms* of the literature in the Old Testament.

Gemara—commentary on the Mishnah (Oral Law) and together with the Mishnah comprises the Talmud.

Gilead—Region east of Jordan, between Yarmuk and Arnon Rivers. Some areas well-watered and suited for grazing and grain production.

Gilgamesh Epic—An ancient Mesopotamian tale which deals with the quest for immortality and includes a flood story with features both similar and dissimilar to the Genesis account.

Habiru—A nondescript group of people of varied ethnic backgrounds who ranged across the Ancient Near East in the third and second millennia B.C. Although the term is cognate with Hebrew, it seems to have a wider application both temporally and geographically.

Hagiographa—see *Writings.*

Hanukkah—see *Feasts.*

Hasidim—The Pious Ones who resisted by both active and passive means the oppressive policies of Antiochus Epiphanes. Likely the precursors of the Pharisees.

Hasmoneans—see *Maccabees.*

Hebrew—1. A Semitic tongue learned by the Israelites from the Canaanites. The language of the OT—except for certain late sections in Aramaic, the tongue which replaced Hebrew in Jewish usage.

   2. An Aramean branch of Semites who traced themselves to Eber of Gen. 10:24. A term often used as a synonym for the pre-exilic Israelite.

Henotheism—Belief in a single deity without denying the existence of others.

Hexateuch—Term used for first six books of OT as a unit. Preferred to the traditional Pentateuch by some scholars in that (1) Joshua provides fulfillment to the promise of the Pentateuch and (2) the Priestly source runs from Genesis through Joshua.

Hittites—Non-Semites and probably Aryans, who formed a cultural tie between Europe and the Near East. Their formidable kingdom was centered in Asia Minor and Syria in the second millennium B.C.

Hieroglyphics—The picture writing of ancient Egypt. These "sacred carvings" likely originated with the priests.

Hyksos—Semitic people who overran Egypt and ruled there 1710–1570 B.C. with capital at Memphis.

Interpolation—The interruption of the biblical text by additions or comments.

Israel—1. The name given Jacob, second-born twin son of Isaac, after his religious experiences by the Jabbok ford.

   2. The people and their descendants bound together by religious and political ties formally established at Sinai.

   3. The Northern Kingdom, as opposed to Judah, following the division of the Israelite monarchy in 922 B.C.

   4. God's chosen people. The religious nation, rather than a political state.

Jamnia—The Palestinian town in which Jewish scholars assembled in A.D. 90–100 to set the OT canon. Their work led to an OT containing those books found within modern Protestant editions of the Bible.

Jebel Musa—Mountain in southern part of Sinai Peninsula. The traditional Mt. Sinai. The name means "mountain of Moses."

Jebusites—Early Canaanite residents of Jebus, the city which became Jerusalem.

Jehovah—see *Yahweh.*

Jews—common name for Israelites after the Exile. A contraction of Judah, the tribe of which most of returnees to Palestine were members.

Jezreel—1. A town on the edge of Mt. Gilboa overlooking the plain.

   2. A valley, also known as the Plain of Esdraelon, which extends from the north of Mt. Carmel on the west, to a pass to the Jordan on the east. Across the valley ran prominent highways. An important battlefield of Palestine.

Jordan Cleft—The geological fissure through which the Jordan River runs.

Josianic reformation—The most epochal of Judah's several religious revivals. Begun about 626 B.C. under the leadership of King Josiah, it was catapulted to great heights in 622 B.C. by the discovery of "a scroll of the law" (probably the core of our book of Deuteronomy). Centralization of worship in Jerusalem was a primary objective of the reforms.

Judah—1. The fourth son of Jacob and Leah.

2. The tribe named eponymously for (1).

3. The Southern Kingdom after the division of the Israelite monarchy in 922 B.C.

4. In postexilic days, the region around Jerusalem.

Judaism—1. The religion of the Jews as it developed after the exile.

2. Sometimes used for the religion of Israel beginning with Abraham or Moses.

Judea—A Greco-Roman term for the Judah of postexilic times. The extent of the area varied greatly until A.D. 70.

Judges—1. Tribal heroes of Israel in the era of the amphictyony. They became both civil and military leaders on the basis of their demonstration of charismatic sanction.

2. An OT book in the group known as the "Former Prophets."

Karkar—Scene of a battle in 853 B.C. between Shalmaneser III of Assyria and a coalition of kings of Syria-Palestine under Benhadad of Syria. Precise Assyrian dating of this battle makes it a pivotal event for OT chronology.

Kenites—Early Midianite metalsmiths living in the Arabah. Worshippers of God by the name of Yahweh.

Kenite Hypothesis—The belief held by many that the name Yahweh and certain religious practices came to Israel through Midian, possibly via Jethro, Moses' father-in-law.

Kethubim—See *Writings*.

Law—See *Torah*.

Levites—Those of the Israelite tribe named eponymously for Levi, the third son of Jacob and Leah. Priests whose entire function was cultic were supposed to come from this tribe. Its members who were not officiating priests performed menial cultic tasks.

LXX—See *Septuagint*.

Maccabees—The family which heroically commanded the successful Jewish war of independence against Seleucid oppression. Gained religion freedom in 165 B.C. and political freedom in 142 B.C. Remained in control until 63 B.C. Also called Hasmoneans, from Hasmon, the great grandfather of Mattathias, who launched the revolt.

Masora—Instructional and informational annotations placed in the margins of Hebrew manuscripts. Begun by the Sopherim and extended by the Masoretes ("Men of the Masora").

Masoretes—"Men of the Masora." Jewish scribes who copied manuscripts. They added vowel points to the consonantal text.

Megilloth—The canonical Hebrew scrolls read on festival occasions; Ruth, Esther, Ecclesiastes, Song of Songs, and Lamentations.

Mesopotamia—The area on either side and "between the rivers" Tigris and Euphrates. In general terms, the valley region between ancient Haran and the Persian Gulf.

Messiah—The looked-for "anointed" ruler of Davidic descent or deliverer of the Jewish people. In Greek, "the Christ."

Mishnah—1. A doctrinal decision of pre-third century A.D. rabbis.

2. Any collection of such tenets.

3. The mass of Jewish oral, legal traditions accumulated across several centuries. Reduced to written form by Rabbi Judah ha-Nasi (c. 135–220). The basic section of the Talmud.

Moabites—In Biblical tradition, the eponymous descendants of Moab, a son of Lot and one of his daughters. Residents of the land east of the Dead Sea and historic enemies of Israel.

Monotheism—The belief that there is only one God.

Myth—1. A story about God or divine-like beings.

2. A story which symbolically accounts for the origin of a belief, practice, or phenomenon.

3. The hypostatization or personification of an abstract idea.

Nab'i—See *Prophet*.

Negeb—The largely arid region south of Judea.

Omrids—Those of the dynasty of Omri, king of Israel. Ahab, Ahaziah, and Jehoram are of the house of Omri.

Ophel—The southernmost portion of the hill in Jerusalem upon which the temple rested.

Oracle—1. A divine declaration.

2. The medium of a divine disclosure. Used of the person, place, or thing.

3. Short prophetic sermon.

Oral Tradition—The preservation of sacred materials by word of mouth.

Ostraca—Ancient fragments of pottery or clay tablets used for records and correspondence.

Palestine—Called "Canaan" by the Patriarchs and "Palestine" by Herodotus. Name derived from early strong enemies of Israel, the Philistines. Generally, the land between the Jordan Valley and the Mediterranean Sea. See *Canaan*.

Parallelism—The most characteristic feature of Hebrew poetry: the couplet with intimate correspondence between the two lines.

Papyrus—An aquatic plant commonly used as writing material by superimposing a horizontal layer of thin wet strips upon a vertical layer and pressed to dry.

Parchment—Animal skin prepared as a writing material.

Passover—See *Feasts*.

Pentateuch—The first five books of the OT, Genesis through Deuteronomy. Also known as the Torah.

Pentecost—See *Feasts*.

Peshitta or Peshito—The standard Syriac version of the OT.

Pharisees—The post-Maccabean Jewish religious party which continued the tradition of the Hasidim. Devoted to the Law, written and oral.

Philistines—A group of non-Semitic people who settled along the southern end of the maritime plain of Palestine during the twelfth century b.c. They were a continual menace to the Israelites until the time of David.

Phoenicia—An ancient country lying between the Lebanon Mountain range and the Mediterranean Sea. Its chief cities were Tyre and Sidon, seaports of repute. In times of friendliness, Phoenicia gave Israel access to the ports of the Mediterranean world.

Polytheism—The belief in multiple gods.

Preexile—The period of OT history before the Babylonian exile.

Postexile—The period of OT history after the Babylonian exile. Used in the text to designate the period from 539 B.C. until the beginning of the Roman period about 63 B.C.

Priestly history—The exilic-postexilic "history" of Israel used in the writing of the OT, so-called because of its orientation toward Israelite cultic legislation. Sometimes designated "P."

Prophets, The—The second division of the Hebrew scriptures including the Former Prophets (Joshua, Judges, Samuel, and Kings) and the Latter Prophets (Isaiah, Jeremiah, Ezekiel, and The Book of the Twelve).

Pseudepigrapha—A group of non-canonical writings from the postexilic period, thus called because some were "falsely inscribed" with the name of some outstanding and revered person.

Ptolemies—Name given to the dynasty of Macedonian rulers of Egypt following the death of Alexander the Great. The dynasty took its name from Ptolemy I, surnamed Soter.

Purim—See *Feasts.*

Qumran—The monastic community of the Essenes in the foothills of the Judean wilderness near the Dead Sea. Members of this Essenes community produced the Dead Sea Scrolls.

Sadducees—A Jewish religious party arising during the late pre-Christian era. Conservative and aristocratic. Rejected the authority of oral tradition and theological beliefs in afterlife. Held fast to the Torah.

Samaria—1. The village enlarged and made capital of the Northern Kingdom by Omri.
2. Geographically the middle of three north-south divisions of Palestine. Extended between the Jordan and Mediterranean from the Plain of Esdraelon in the north to the territory of Benjamin in the south.

Samaritans—A mongrel group of people arising in the region of Samaria after the Assyrian conquest of 722/21 B.C. The import of foreigners by Assyrians resulted in this racially mixed people.

Scribe—A copyist charged with both the preservation and interpretation of the Jewish scriptures.

Seleucids—Name given to the dynasty of Macedonian rulers of Syria following the death of Alexander the Great. The dynasty took its name from Seleucus I.

Semites—"Shemites," supposed descendants of Shem. A group of nations from the Near East forming a linguistic, but not a racial unit. Babylonians, Assyrians, Phoenicians, Syrians, Israelites, Moabites, Ammonites, etc., were Semitic peoples.

Septuagint—The Greek translation of the Jewish scriptures dating to the third century B.C. Its name (from Latin "seventy") is derived from the doubtful tradition that 72 scholars did the work of translation in 72 days. Abbreviated as LXX.

Shema—The key confession of faith in Jewish liturgy. Opens with Deuteronomy 6:4–9 and focuses upon the phrase, "Hear, O Israel, the LORD our God is one LORD."

Sheol—The Hebrew equivalent of the Greek *Hades.* The place of the dead; a vague, shadowy, gloomy region beneath the earth to which all men go at death. No idea of reward or punishment.

Shephelah—The "lowlands" of Judah's western frontier. The region of low rolling hills between the Judean hill country and the Philistine plain.

Son of Man—A phrase in the OT typically meaning simply a human being. Ezekiel used the phrase as God's address to him and Daniel used the title to symbolize those who rule over the kingdom of God.

Sopherim—The "men of the book," a group of scholars charged with publishing and safeguarding the manuscripts of the Jewish scriptures. Began their work in fourth century B.C. and continued into the early Christian era. Responsible for dividing manuscripts into sentences and sections.

Stele—A stone pillar bearing an inscription, carving, or design usually set up to memorialize a person, deity, or event.

Succoth—Also Sukkoth. The Jewish feast of Tabernacles. See *Feasts.*

Suffering Servant—A figure of speech used by Second Isaiah to describe the obedient, self-sacrificing servant of God.

Synagogue—The local institution for Jewish religious instruction and worship. Not mentioned in OT, but prolific in the New Testament. Probably arose during or just after the exile.

Syria—The northern part of the land bridge between Asia and Egypt. Area included Phoenicia on the coast and the inland kingdom of Aram, whose capital was at Damascus.

Tabernacle—The portable tent sanctuary of the Israelites used during the exodus, wanderings period.

Tabernacles, Feast of—Also Sukkoth. See *Feasts.*

Talmud—The combination of Mishnah (the codified "tradition of the elders") and Gemara (the explanation of Mishnah). A Palestinian Talmud was completed about A.D. 275 and a Babylonian Talmud was completed about A.D. 500

Targum—An Aramaic paraphrase of the Jewish scriptures, coming from early in the Christian era when Aramaic replaced Hebrew as the common language of the Jews.

Temple, The—The sanctuary in Jerusalem, the center of Jewish religion after the time of Solomon. It served as the central Yahweh shrine throughout its history. The first temple in Jerusalem was built by Solomon; the second by Zerubbabel upon return from the Babylonian exile, and the third by Herod the Great just before the birth of Jesus. The history of the temple concludes with its destruction by the Romans in A.D. 70

Testament—A "will" or "covenant." The word itself is a Latin rendition of the Greek word for "covenant." It was first used in connection with the Bible by Tertullian and Origen in the early third century A.D. Also see *Covenant.*

Textual Criticism—The scholarly attempt to determine the original wording of a biblical text. Also called *lower criticism.*

Theophany—A manifestation of God to man through an appearance, such as an angel, or some natural phenomenon.

Torah—Hebrew "instruction" or "law." Sometimes used to refer generally to scriptures of Judaism, but specifically means the Pentateuch, the "law" of Moses.

Transjordan—The plateau region lying between the Jordan Cleft and the arid areas of the Arabian Desert. Extends from Bashan in the north to Edom in the south.

Twelve, The Book of the—The "Minor" Prophets, including Hosea, Joel, Amos, Obadiah, Jonah, Micah, Nahum, Habakkuk, Zephaniah, Haggai, Zechariah, and Malachi.

Urim and Thummin—Sacred lots in the care of the priests. Used in pre-exilic times to determine the will of God. Possibly marked stones cast as dice.

Vulgate—The Latin translation of the scriptures prepared by Jerome near the end of the fourth century A.D. The authorized version of the Roman Catholic Church.

Weeks, Feast of—Also called Pentecost. See *Feasts*.

Writings, The—The Third division of the OT scriptures, including Psalms, Proverbs, Job, Song of Solomon, Ruth, Lamentations, Ecclesiastes, Esther, Ezra, Nehemiah, and Chronicles. Also called Hagiographa or Kethubim.

Yahweh—The Israelite personal name for God. Since the name was regarded as too sacred to be pronounced, the Masoretes attached to the consonantal *Yhwh* vowel sounds indicating that it should be read either Adonai (Lord) or Elohim (God). The American Standard Version translates the name "Jehovah," a late medieval word resulting from a combination of the consonants *Yhwh* and the vowels from Adonai. The King James Version and the Revised Standard Version indicate the use of the word by LORD (or sometimes GOD).

Yahwistic history—The earliest of several "histories" of Israel used in the writing of the OT. It covers the period from creation to conquest. Its name is derived from its preference for the divine name *Yahweh*. Sometimes designated "J." Its author or authors is usually referred to as the Yahwist.

Ziggurat—An ancient Babylonian or Assyrian temple in the form of a step-pyramidal tower.

Zion—Literally the ridge of Ophel upon which early Jerusalem was located. Used poetically to refer to the city itself.

Index